THE OXFORD HISTORY
OF ENGLAND

Edited by SIR GEORGE CLARK

THE OXFORD HISTORY OF ENGLAND

Edited by SIR GEORGE CLARK

ENGLISH HISTORY

1914–1945

A. J. P. TAYLOR

OXFORD UNIVERSITY PRESS

NEW YORK

© Oxford University Press 1965

First published in 1965 by the Clarendon Press, Oxford
First issued as an Oxford University Press paperback, with corrections, 1970
Reissued in paperback, 1985, by Oxford University Press, Inc.,
200 Madison Avenue, New York, NY 10016

Library of Congress Cataloging-in-Publication Data
Taylor, A. J. P. (Alan John Percivale), 1906-
English history, 1914-1945.
Bibliography: p.
Includes index.
1. Great Britain—History—20th century.
I. Title.
DA566.T38   1985   942.082   85-15496
ISBN 0-19-500304-7 (pbk.)

Printing (last digit): 9 8 7 6 5 4 3 2 1

Printed in the United States of America

PREFACE

WHEN the Oxford History of England was launched a generation ago, 'England' was still an all-embracing word. It meant indiscriminately England and Wales; Great Britain; the United Kingdom; and even the British Empire. Foreigners used it as the name of a Great Power and indeed continue to do so. Bonar Law, a Scotch Canadian, was not ashamed to describe himself as 'Prime Minister of England', as Disraeli, a Jew by birth, had done before him. One volume in this history treats Scotch universities under the head of English education; others treat the internal affairs of the colonies as part of English history. Now terms have become more rigorous. The use of 'England' except for a geographic area brings protests, especially from the Scotch.[1] They seek to impose 'Britain'—the name of a Roman province which perished in the fifth century and which included none of Scotland nor, indeed, all of England. I never use this incorrect term, though it is sometimes slipped past me by sub-editors. 'Great Britain' is correct and has been since 1707. It is not, however, synonymous with the United Kingdom, as the Scotch, forgetting the Irish (or, since 1922, the Northern Irish), seem to think. Again, the United Kingdom does not cover the Commonwealth, the colonial empire, or India. Whatever word we use lands us in a tangle.

I have tried to stick to my assignment, which is English history. Where the Welsh, the Scotch, the Irish, or the British overseas have the same history as the English, my book includes them also; where they have a different history, it does not. For instance, Wales is an integral part of the English administrative and legal system, but it has (since 1919) no established church. Scotland has a different established church, a different legal and administrative system, and a largely autonomous administration. Northern Ireland since 1922 is more autonomous still. None of these things is my concern. On the other

---

[1] Some inhabitants of Scotland now call themselves 'Scots' and their affairs 'Scottish'. They are entitled to do so. The English word for both is 'Scotch', just as we call les français the French, and Deutschland Germany. Being English, I use it.

hand, it would be impossible to discover a specifically English foreign policy, and foolish, though not impossible, to discover the specifically English contribution to British budgets or to British overseas trade. It is, however, reasonable, I think, to talk about English feelings or English patterns of life. At any rate, this book is about thirty years in the history of the English people, and others come in only if they made a stir in English politics or aroused English interest in other ways. Thus, I discuss the impact of events in India on English politics and do not attempt to narrate India's political history. Similarly, I have passed over developments in Africa which were significant for Africa, but not, at the time, for England.

My book begins precisely on the day, 4 August 1914, almost at the hour, 11 p.m., when the volume by Sir Robert Ensor in this history ends. Its own ending is more ragged. There was much unfinished business: the reordering of Europe, the American loan, the establishment of the welfare state and of Indian independence. The new patterns were much clearer in 1951 than in 1945. However, I had to stop somewhere. I have written in the form of a continuous narrative, though with occasional pauses for refreshment. Most themes chose themselves. For ten of the thirty-one years which this volume covers the English people were involved in great wars; for nineteen they lived in the shadow of mass unemployment. When I had dealt with these subjects, and with the politics which sprang from them, there was not much room left. Some omissions are excused only by ignorance. There were, for instance, advances in science of the greatest importance: beneficent as with vitamins, potentially catastrophic as with nuclear explosions. I do not understand the internal-combustion engine, let alone the atomic bomb, and any discussion of scientific topics was beyond me. Nor could I have made much sense of modern philosophy. At any rate, I chose the subjects which seemed most urgent, most interesting, and with which I was most competent to deal.

I have followed Sir Robert Ensor's example and have treated all those mentioned in this book, living or dead, as historical figures—I hope without offence. The biographical notes are designed only for the period covered by the book, though they occasionally stray beyond it. I have received information and ideas from many people and taken them from many books.

The bibliography especially could not have been compiled without assistance from individual historians and the authorities of various institutions. I am deeply grateful for all this help, so generously given, and hope that those who gave it will feel free to criticize the results.

My colleague, Kenneth Tite, Fellow of Magdalen College, read my entire manuscript twice. He saved me from many mistakes, questioned many of my judgements, and tempered the dogmatism of my style. He must take part of the blame if the word 'probably' occurs too often. Sir George Clark, the general editor, honoured me by his invitation to write this book and sustained me when I was slighted in my profession. He has read my manuscript with critical care and reinforced it at many points. One other historian gave me inspiration and guidance. I had hoped to place this book in his hands. Now I set down in bereavement the name of Max Aitken, Lord Beaverbrook, my beloved friend.

A. J. P. T.

PREFACE TO PAPERBACK EDITION

When this book was completed, the fifty-year rule of secrecy was still in operation, and I hoped to be well out of the way before a thorough revision would be needed in 1995. Now, with the thirty-year rule, the official records will become available in 1975, and I foresee a laborious task with which to occupy my declining years. Meanwhile for this edition I have corrected mistakes of detail which careful readers detected and have added a few new points, together with a list of the more important books which have appeared during the last five years.

A. J. P. T.

CONTENTS

III. A NATION AT WAR, 1916–18

CONTENTS

CONTENTS xi

IV. POSTWAR, 1918–22

CONTENTS xi

IV. POSTWAR, 1918–22

V. NORMAL TIMES: 1922

VI. THREE-PARTY POLITICS, 1922-5

VII. THE YEARS OF GOLD, 1925-9

VIII. UNEXPECTED CRISIS, 1929–31

IX. HALF TIME

X. THE NATION SAVED: ECONOMIC AFFAIRS,
1931-3

XI. THE NATION NOT SAVED: FOREIGN AFFAIRS, 1931–6

XII. APPEASEMENT, 1936–9

XIII. RELUCTANTLY TO WAR, 1939-40

CONTENTS xvii

XIV. FINEST HOUR, 1940–1

XV. THE GRAND ALLIANCE, 1942–4

XVI. ENDING, 1944–5

BIBLIOGRAPHY

GRAPHS

MAPS

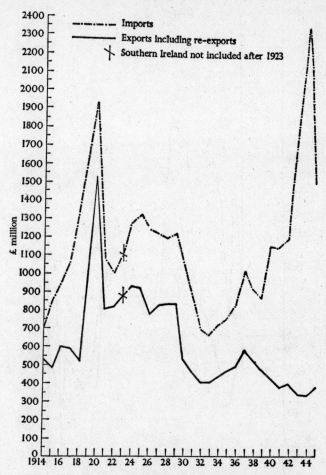

FIG. 1. U.K. Imports and Exports by value, 1914–45. Based on figures from Mitchell and Deane

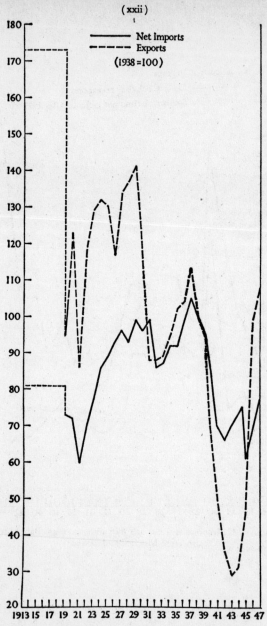

FIG. 2. U.K. Imports and exports by volume, 1919–47.

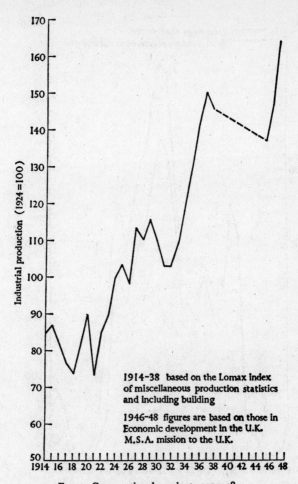

Fig. 3. Gross national product, 1914–48.

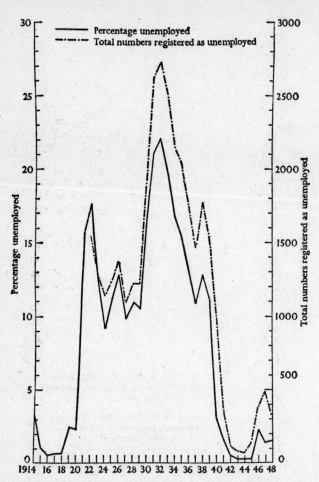

FIG. 4. Unemployment in Great Britain, 1914–48. Based on figures from Mitchell and Deane and E.C.A. Mission

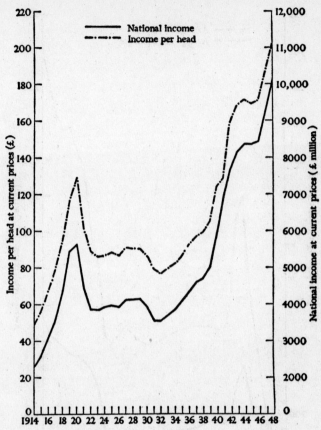

FIG. 5. National income, 1914–48. Based on E.C.A. Mission figures

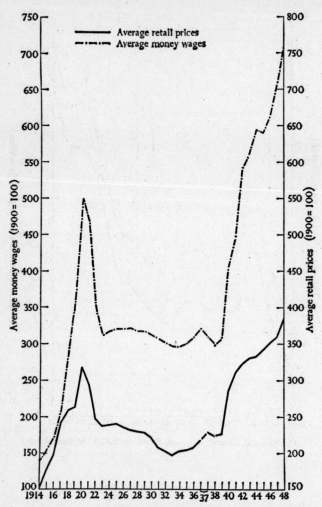

Fig. 6. Prices and wages, 1914–48. Based on figures from Mitchell and Deane and E.C.A. Mission

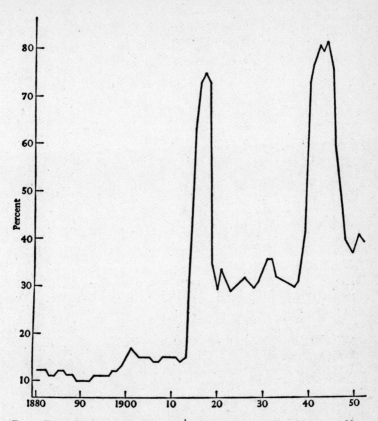

FIG. 7. Expenditure of public authorities as percentage of national income, 1880–1950. Based on figures in Hicks

ENGLISH HISTORY
1914-1945

I

THE GREAT WAR: OLD STYLE, 1914–15

UNTIL August 1914 a sensible, law-abiding Englishman could pass through life and hardly notice the existence of the state, beyond the post office and the policeman. He could live where he liked and as he liked. He had no official number or identity card. He could travel abroad or leave his country for ever without a passport or any sort of official permission. He could exchange his money for any other currency without restriction or limit. He could buy goods from any country in the world on the same terms as he bought goods at home. For that matter, a foreigner could spend his life in this country without permit and without informing the police. Unlike the countries of the European continent, the state did not require its citizens to perform military service. An Englishman could enlist, if he chose, in the regular army, the navy, or the territorials. He could also ignore, if he chose, the demands of national defence. Substantial householders were occasionally called on for jury service. Otherwise, only those helped the state who wished to do so. The Englishman paid taxes on a modest scale: nearly £200 million in 1913–14, or rather less than 8 per cent. of the national income. The state intervened to prevent the citizen from eating adulterated food or contracting certain infectious diseases. It imposed safety rules in factories, and prevented women, and adult males in some industries, from working excessive hours. The state saw to it that children received education up to the age of 13. Since 1 January 1909, it provided a meagre pension for the needy over the age of 70. Since 1911, it helped to insure certain classes of workers against sickness and unemployment. This tendency towards more state action was increasing. Expenditure on the social services had roughly doubled since the Liberals took office in 1905. Still, broadly speaking, the state acted only to help those who could not help themselves. It left the adult citizen alone.

All this was changed by the impact of the Great War.[1] The mass of the people became, for the first time, active citizens. Their lives were shaped by orders from above; they were required to serve the state instead of pursuing exclusively their own affairs. Five million men entered the armed forces, many of them (though a minority) under compulsion. The Englishman's food was limited, and its quality changed, by government order. His freedom of movement was restricted; his conditions of work prescribed. Some industries were reduced or closed, others artificially fostered. The publication of news was fettered. Street lights were dimmed. The sacred freedom of drinking was tampered with: licensed hours were cut down, and the beer watered by order. The very time on the clocks was changed. From 1916 onwards, every Englishman got up an hour earlier in summer than he would otherwise have done, thanks to an act of parliament. The state established a hold over its citizens which, though relaxed in peacetime, was never to be removed and which the second World war was again to increase. The history of the English state and of the English people merged for the first time.

Formally speaking, the war came as though King George V[2] still possessed undiminished the prerogatives of Henry VIII. At 10.30 p.m. on 4 August 1914 the king held a privy council at Buckingham Palace, which was attended only by one minister[3] and two court officials. This council sanctioned the proclamation of a state of war with Germany from 11 p.m.[4] That was all.[5] The cabinet played no part once it had resolved to defend

[1] In contemporary parlance, the war of 1914-18 was always, not surprisingly, the Great War. It did not need the war of 1939-45 to change it into the first World war. Repington devised the phrase at the time of the armistice, 'to prevent the millenian folk from forgetting that the history of the world is the history of war'. Repington, *The First World War*, ii. 291.

[2] George V (1865-1936), second son of Edward VII: married Princess Mary of Teck, 1893; king, 1910-36; changed name of royal family from Saxe-Coburg to Windsor, 1917; his trousers were creased at the sides, not front and back.

[3] Lord Beauchamp, first commissioner of works, who succeeded Morley as lord president of the council on the following day.

[4] Why 11 p.m.? It is impossible to say. The ultimatum to Germany demanded an answer *here* (i.e. London) by midnight. After its dispatch someone unknown recollected that German time was an hour in advance of Greenwich mean time, and it was decided that the ultimatum should expire according to the time in Berlin. Why? Perhaps for fear that the German government might give a favourable, or equivocal, answer; perhaps to get things settled and to be able to go to bed; probably for no reason at all.

[5] War was declared against Austria-Hungary on 10 Aug.

the neutrality of Belgium. It did not consider the ultimatum to Germany, which Sir Edward Grey, the foreign secretary,[1] sent after consulting only the prime minister, Asquith,[2] and perhaps not even him. Nor did the cabinet authorize the declaration of war. The parliament of the United Kingdom, though informed of events, did not give formal approval to the government's acts until it voted a credit of £100 million, without a division,[3] on 6 August.

The governments and parliaments of the Dominions were not consulted. The Canadian parliament alone subsequently expressed its approval. Apart from this, each governor general issued the royal proclamation on his own authority, as did the viceroy of India. The white populations of the Empire rallied eagerly to the mother country. Some 50 million Africans and 250 million Indians were involved, without consultation, in a war of which they understood nothing against an enemy who was also unknown to them. Use of the prerogative went further. The administrative measures, consequent on the outbreak of war, had long been laid down in the War Book, which Maurice Hankey, secretary of the committee of imperial defence,[4] elaborated. These measures were now brought into force by proclamation. Military areas were closed to aliens; trade with the enemy was forbidden; merchant ships were requisitioned (some 250 at once, and later over a thousand) for the transport of the armed forces.

[1] Edward Grey (1862–1933): educ. Winchester and Oxford; foreign secretary, 1905–16; cr. Viscount, 1916; special mission to United States, 1919; chancellor of Oxford University, 1928–33; a devoted bird-watcher until he lost his sight; the first foreign secretary to publish a full account of his work in office.

[2] Herbert Henry Asquith (1852–1928): educ. City of London school and Oxford; prime minister of Liberal government, 1908–15; of Coalition government, 1915–16; secretary for war, Mar.–Aug. 1914; defeated at East Fife, 1918; returned for Paisley, 1920; defeated (by Labour), 1924; cr. Earl of Oxford and Asquith, 1925; rejected as chancellor of Oxford University in favour of Cave, a man otherwise unknown, 1925; resigned leadership of Liberal party, 1926; generally regarded as 'the greatest parliamentarian'. In cabinet, Asquith wrote letters to Venetia Stanley (later Mrs. Edwin Montagu).

[3] Ramsay MacDonald and some Radicals spoke against the declaration of war.

[4] Maurice Hankey (1877–1963), an officer of marines; secretary to the committee of imperial defence, 1912–38; of war cabinet, 1916–19; of cabinet, 1919–38; clerk to the privy council, 1923–38; cr. Baron, 1938; minister without portfolio and member of war cabinet, 1939–40; chancellor of the duchy of Lancaster, 1940–1; paymaster-general, 1941–2. Balfour said: 'Without Hankey we should have lost the [first World] war.'

This reliance on the prerogative was in part a quaint, and
convenient, survival; a reminder that Great Britain had advanced towards democracy, and the Empire towards Commonwealth, without any open break in the traditional constitution.
It also reflected the general view that war was an act of state,
if not of prerogative, with which ordinary citizens had little to
do. Even the ministers most responsible assumed that Great
Britain would wage the war with the armed forces which she
possessed at the outset. The British navy would fight a great
engagement with the German high seas fleet in the North Sea,
while the armies of the continental Allies defeated Germany on
land. All would be over in a few months, if not in a few weeks.
The ordinary citizen would be little affected. As Grey said in
the house of commons on 3 August: 'if we are engaged in war,
we shall suffer but little more than we shall suffer if we stand
aside.' No preparations had been made for changing civilian
life—no register of manpower or survey of industrial resources, no accumulation of raw materials nor even consideration of what raw materials would be needed. The duty of
the civilian was to carry on normally; in Churchill's[1] phrase,
'Business as usual',[2] the notice which a shopkeeper stuck up after
a fire.

There were some breaches of this rule. Financial panic was
widely expected to follow the outbreak of war. The government
proclaimed a standstill, or moratorium, and took over responsibility for bills on neutral and enemy countries. The alarm seems
to have been overdone, and panic rather the other way—
foreigners striving desperately to meet their obligations. Pounds
grew scarce on the international market. The American exchange reached $7 to the pound (as against the normal rate

[1] Winston Spencer Churchill (1874-1965), grandson of duke of Marlborough
and of American tycoon, Jerome: educ. Harrow and Sandhurst; first lord of the
admiralty, 1911-15; chancellor of the duchy of Lancaster, 1915; commanded a
battalion in France, 1915-16; minister of munitions, 1917-19; secretary for war
(and air), 1918-21; for colonies, 1921-2; supported Lloyd George on break up of
Coalition and defeated at Dundee, 1922; Conservative M.P. for Woodford, 1924-
64; chancellor of the exchequer, 1924-9; left Conservative shadow cabinet and
opposed concessions to India, 1931; supported Edward VIII at time of abdication,
1936; first lord of the admiralty and member of war cabinet, 1939-40; prime
minister of National government and minister of defence, 1940-5; leader of
Conservative party, 1940-55; Conservative prime minister, 1945, 1951-5; K.G.,
1953; the saviour of his country.

[2] And pleasure as usual also. County cricket matches continued to be played
until the end of August.

of $4.86). The government also took over the insurance of war
risks on shipping—an arrangement which showed a profit at
the end of the war. It was feared, too, that people might take
to hoarding gold sovereigns, then the general currency, and
the treasury was empowered to issue paper notes for £1 and
10s.[1] Here, too, the alarm seems to have been unnecessary.
These improvisations were the first wartime act of Lloyd George,
chancellor of the exchequer.[2] He had opposed entry into the
war until the last moment, and now handled the financial
problems without, as yet, committing himself further.[3]

The president of the board of trade was also busy. The railways were taken over by the government, and guaranteed their
1913 dividends—another arrangement which finally showed a
profit.[4] In practice, the take-over made little difference. A
committee of railway managers ran the railways for the board
of trade. The companies were not coordinated; and, as late as
Easter 1916, leave trains from France were stopped for five
days so as not to interfere with holiday traffic. There was one
foreshadowing of future developments. War cut off British
supplies of sugar, two-thirds of which had come from Germany
and Austria-Hungary. On 20 August a royal commission was
set up to buy and sell sugar, and to regulate its distribution—
a first exercise in state trading which remained autonomous
throughout the war. All these arrangements were made primarily for the benefit of the traders concerned—bankers and
billbrokers, railway managers and sugar refiners. Otherwise

[1] This was not an abandonment of the gold standard. The notes could be
changed into gold at the old fixed rate. Nor did paper money contribute much to
inflation. Though the note circulation went up from £34 million prewar to £299
million by 1918, much of this was covered by the return of gold coins to the Bank
of England. Legal tender money (i.e. gold plus notes) increased only from £200
million in June 1914 to £383 million in July 1918.

[2] David Lloyd George (1863–1945); educ. Church school; Liberal M.P., 1890–
1945; chancellor of the exchequer, 1908–15; minister of munitions, 1915–16;
secretary for war, 1916; prime minister, 1916–22; leader of the Liberal party,
1926–31; cr. Earl Lloyd-George, 1945. A master of improvised speech and of
improvised policies. Though he was dangerous to most women, he gave his heart
to few. After leaving office, he farmed ambitiously, though unprofitably, and
propagated the 'Lloyd George' raspberry. He disliked his correct surname, 'George',
and imposed 'Lloyd George' on contemporaries and on posterity.

[3] In a shortlived anticipation of coalition, Austen Chamberlain, former Unionist
chancellor of the exchequer, presided at the treasury board during the emergency,
when Lloyd George had to be absent on other business.

[4] The government paid £95 million to the railways during the war. Their
traffic would have cost £100 million at prewar rates.

the state stood aside. Parliament dispersed on 10 August. Men waited, aloof, for the great shock of arms.

Naval plans had long been settled by the admiralty. The Grand Fleet was already fully mobilized on the outbreak of war,[1] and at its battle stations in the North Sea, twenty British battleships facing thirteen German, tense for the Armageddon which Fisher had prophesied for September 1914.[2] On 3 August the cabinet authorized the mobilization of the regular army— an expeditionary force of six infantry divisions and a cavalry division. Mobilization began on the afternoon of 4 August.[3] No decision on the use of the army had been taken before the war. The plans which Sir Henry Wilson, director of military operations,[4] had elaborated with French staff officers carried no commitment. On the afternoon of 5 August, Asquith, as secretary for war, held a council of war—really an enlarged meeting of the Army Council.[5] Sixteen men, 'mostly entirely ignorant of their subject',[6] speculated in the void. They agreed that the fourteen Territorial divisions could protect the country from invasion. The B.E.F. was free to go abroad. Where to? Antwerp? Amiens? merely to Le Havre and then ramble across the country? Or stay at home and train a mass army? Wilson cut in. He explained that railway time-tables, unlike horses, could not be changed. There could be no question of

[1] In Mar. 1914 it was decided, for reasons of economy, to hold a trial mobilization in July instead of the usual summer manœuvres. On 26 July the fleet was instructed not to disperse; on 28 July it was ordered to war-stations. Churchill, first lord of the admiralty, decreed full mobilization on the night of 1–2 Aug. This was approved by the cabinet on the following day.

[2] John Arbuthnot Fisher (1841–1920): first sea lord, 1904–10, 1914–15; cr. Baron, 1909; devised Dreadnought type of battleship.

[3] Not on 3 Aug., as subsequently stated by Haldane, and, following him, in vol. xiv of this History.

[4] Henry Hughes Wilson (1864–1922): director of military operations, 1910–14; served in France, 1914–16; Eastern command, 1917; chief of imperial general staff, 1918–22; cr. baronet and voted £10,000 by parliament, 1919; Conservative M.P., 1922; assassinated by members of Irish Republican Army, 1922.

[5] Strictly the meeting was summoned by Haldane, who was deputizing for Asquith at the war office. There attended Asquith, Churchill, Grey, and Haldane; the first sea lord (Prince Louis of Battenberg); the four military members of the Army Council; Sir John French who was to command the B.E.F.; Archibald Murray, his chief-of-staff; Haig and Grierson, his two corps commanders; Sir Ian Hamilton; and the two senior soldiers of the Empire, Roberts, who was over 80, and Kitchener, who had been out of England for forty years. Haldane's list of those to be summoned, with Hankey's ticks for attendance, is in the Imperial War Museum.

[6] Wilson's phrase. Callwell, *Wilson's Life and Diaries*, i. 159.

helping the Belgians, though this was why Great Britain had gone to war. The B.E.F. had no choice: it must go to Maubeuge on the French left, as he had long planned. The great men found no answer. They agreed: all seven divisions to Maubeuge.

On the following day the cabinet insisted that two divisions must stay at home. Meanwhile, Lord Kitchener[1] had reluctantly agreed to become secretary for war. His prestige propped up the Liberal government. He became at once the symbol of patriotic enthusiasm. In India and Egypt he had run military affairs like an oriental despot; now he did not change his ways. He had no expert advice—the imperial general staff were all off to France with the expeditionary force. Nor did he consult the civilian ministers, whom he distrusted and despised. He ran strategy by occasional flashes of genius. Kitchener foresaw the great German advance through Belgium. Maubeuge seemed to him too dangerous and exposed. On his prompting, the cabinet changed the destination of the B.E.F. to Amiens.

Kitchener soon wavered. On 12 August French staff officers, coached by Sir Henry Wilson, tackled him. They argued that the British forces would be useless if they tried to act independently of the French army. The real French motive was political, not military. They attached little value to the British army and wished only to ensure that Great Britain should be firmly embedded as an ally, instead of remaining—on the later American model—an Associated Power. Kitchener was ashamed at the smallness of the British contribution. 'Did they consider when they went headlong into a war like this, that they were without an army, and without any preparation to equip one?'[2] He acquiesced in the French prompting, on condition Asquith agreed, as, of course, he did. Sir John French[3] was instructed to go to Maubeuge. On 19 August Kitchener sent the fifth division to France; on 1 September, when French lost his nerve, Kitchener promised to send the sixth also. These random, and no doubt inescapable, decisions had lasting consequences. The

[1] Horatio Herbert Kitchener (1850–1916): conquered Sudan, 1898; commander-in-chief in South Africa, 1900–2; in India, 1902–9; British representative in Egypt, 1911–14; cr. Baron, 1898, Viscount, 1902, Earl, 1914; secretary for war, 1914–16; drowned on way to Russia, 1916; promised posthumous glory after the war; received none.

[2] Arthur, *Kitchener*, iii. 265.

[3] John Denton Pinkstone French (1852–1925); commander-in-chief, B.E.F., 1914–15; cr. Viscount, 1916; commander-in-chief, home forces, 1916–18; lord-lieutenant of Ireland, 1918–21; cr. Earl of Ypres, 1922.

entire regular army, as it existed on the outbreak of war, was sent to France, and it seemed obvious from this moment that further forces should go to France as they accumulated. Moreover, by going to Maubeuge, the B.E.F. ceased to be an independent force; it became an auxiliary to the French army, though as time went on an increasingly powerful one. In previous wars Great Britain had followed an independent strategy, based on sea power. In the first World war she lost this independence by accident, almost before fighting had started.

The British Expeditionary Force was, in the words of the official history,[1] 'incomparably the best trained, best organised and best equipped British army which ever went forth to war'. It was, however, according to the same authority, 'wholly deficient' in materials for siege or trench warfare—hand grenades, howitzers, entrenching tools; an unfortunate deficiency, since siege or trench warfare was soon to be its lot. The B.E.F. was well adapted for war on the veldt: khaki uniforms, unique skill with the rifle. The Royal Flying Corps, with a strength of sixty-three machines, added a new dimension to observation.[2] Otherwise, modern ingenuity passed the army by. Each division had only twenty-four machine guns, or two per battalion. On the outbreak of war the British army had a total stock of eighty motor vehicles. Guns and supplies were drawn by horses: each infantry division had 5,600 horses to its 18,000 men. Messages were carried from one unit to another, or to and from headquarters, by officers on horseback. There were at first no field telephones or wireless equipment—unlike the navy, where the commander-in-chief was bedevilled by a stream of wireless messages from the admiralty. Such was the force which carried British arms to the continent, and carried also to immortality a music-hall song, *It's a Long Way to Tipperary*.

Sir John French, the commander-in-chief, was a cavalry officer, like many British generals of the first World war: red-faced, 62 years old, exuberant at one moment, easily depressed the next. His instructions, drafted by Kitchener, were 'to support and cooperate with the French army'. But 'your command is an entirely independent one, and you will in no case

---

[1] *Military Operations: France and Belgium, 1914*, i. 10.
[2] On 23 Aug. the R.F.C. observed the German move to outflank the B.E.F. at Mons. On 3 Sept. a British aeroplane reported Kluck's swerve south east towards the Marne, which exposed the German flank to attack from Paris.

come in any sense under the orders of any Allied General . . .
greatest care must be exercised towards a minimum of losses
and wastage'.[1] On 20 August the B.E.F. completed its concentration before Maubeuge. French plunged cheerfully into the
unknown. Two days later the first shots were fired near Mons.
As the British pushed northwards from Maubeuge, they ran,
without prevision, into the German 1st army under Kluck,
which was swinging south-west through Belgium in order to pass
by and then to encircle the French. On 23 August two British
divisions faced six German at Mons and, by rapid rifle-fire
(which the Germans mistook for machine guns), beat them off.
Mons was a small engagement by later standards: the 1,600
casualties were often exceeded in the Boer war. It achieved
legendary importance, if only because it was the one occasion
when Heavenly Powers intervened in the war. The Angels of
Mons, varying in number from two to a platoon, fought on the
British side.[2] French, encouraged perhaps by this assistance,
meant to stand on the same line the next day. During the night,
he learnt that the French 5th army on his right had ordered
a general retreat and that large German forces were advancing
on his empty left. He, too, ordered the retreat. Three days
later, the IInd Corps could march no further. It stood against
the Germans at Le Cateau on 26 August, anniversary of the
battle of Crecy.[3] The German pursuit was halted, though
mainly because the Germans were more eager to resume their
march south-west than to destroy the British army. After Le
Cateau the B.E.F. could continue its retreat undisturbed.

The retreat from Mons was an impressive physical performance. The B.E.F. marched 200 miles in 13 days, often with
only four hours' sleep a night. Strategically, it had grave results.
Once French had, as it were, stretched out his hand to the
French 5th army on his right, he could not relinquish his grasp.
He found himself being pulled due south instead of south west,
the direction from which he had come. In one way this was
fortunate: it pulled him out of the path of the advancing Germans. But it also pulled him away from his lines of supply and
from St. Nazaire on the Atlantic coast, his ultimate point of

[1] *Military Operations: France and Belgium, 1914*, i, appendix viii.
[2] A more prosaic version has it that Arthur Machen, writer of short stories,
invented the Angels of Mons in 1915 during the campaign for raising war loan.
[3] The numbers engaged on the British side, and the casualties, were almost
exactly the same as at Waterloo: 30,000 and 8,000.

retreat. Anxious to preserve his army and staggered by what seemed to him crippling losses, he determined to withdraw from the line altogether and 'refit'.[1] The news of this decision raised alarm when it reached the government in London. Kitchener held a midnight conference with Asquith and such other ministers as could be hastily assembled. He then crossed to Paris and met French at the British embassy on 1 September. There was a stormy scene, Kitchener assuming the airs of a supreme commander. French was overawed, though resentful. He agreed to keep his place in the line, 'conforming to the movements of the French army'. Kitchener wrote: 'please consider it as an instruction.'[2] Thus Joffre, the French commander-in-chief, came to command the British army in practice, though not in theory.

On 5 September Joffre decided to strike back at the pursuing Germans. French duly conformed. With tears in his eyes, he said to the interpreter: 'tell him we will do all that men can do'. In fact, the B.E.F. did little. The new order went out too late to stop further retreat beyond the Marne on 5 September. The next day, the B.E.F. started two marches behind the French. As it moved forward it found no Germans, but an empty hole. Kluck, commanding the German 1st army, having first swung south east to encircle the Allies, had again swung west to hold off attack from Paris. Bulow, commanding the German 2nd army, was pinned by the French offensive further east. Thirty miles separated the two armies. The B.E.F. advanced slowly into this gap—the men tired, the officers made cautious by their previous engagements with the Germans. Even so, the British cavalry were sometimes forty miles behind the German lines. On 9 September the Germans began a general retreat, before the B.E.F. had made effective contact with the enemy. There were virtually no British casualties on the Marne. It was a manœuvre, not a battle, so far as the British were concerned. Leisurely pursuit followed until 14 September. British staff officers speculated whether they would be on the Rhine in three weeks or six. Then the weary Germans, unable to march

---

[1] Poor French has been universally condemned for this loss of nerve which, if persisted in, might have forfeited victory on the Marne. On 30 Aug. French could only see that the defeated French armies were heading straight for encirclement, and he wished to break out in time. Gort saved the British army in 1940 by taking much the decision which French has been blamed for wanting to take in 1914.

[2] *Military Operations: France and Belgium, 1914*, i. 264.

further, stopped on the Aisne. Unwittingly, they stumbled on
the discovery which shaped the first World war: men in trenches,
with machine guns, could beat off all but the most formidable
attacks. The Allied advance ground to a halt. On 16 September
French issued his first instructions for trench warfare.[1]

Both combatant lines hung in the air. Some 200 miles of
open country separated the German and French armies from
the sea. Each side tried to repeat the original German strategy
of turning the enemy line. This was not so much a 'race to the
sea', its usual name, as a race to outflank the other side before
the sea was reached. Both sides failed. The Allies seemed to
have a splendid opportunity. The Channel ports—Calais,
Dunkirk, Ostend, and Zeebrugge—were available to the British.
The Belgian army was still intact, far away in the German
rear at Antwerp. Nothing was made of this. Joffre wrote the
Belgians off. Kitchener refused to send any of the eleven
Territorial divisions which were now mobilized. He hesitated
over the one remaining regular division, and sent it too late.

Churchill, first lord of the admiralty, plunged into land warfare, regardless of protocol. He sent an ill-equipped naval
brigade to Antwerp; then on 3 October arrived himself to
inspire the Belgians. In the excitement of the firing line, he
proposed to relinquish the admiralty and take 'formal military
charge' of the British forces in Antwerp—a proposal which the
cabinet received with 'ill-concealed merriment'. This token of
British assistance was too slight to stiffen the failing Belgian
resolve. Antwerp fell on 10 October. The Belgian army withdrew down the coast, where it managed to hold a fragment of
national territory throughout the war. The British marines
were sacrificed, most of them being interned in Holland. The
affair brought Churchill much discredit. He had operated a
bold strategy with inadequate means, and thus laid a first stone
in the reputation for impulsive irresponsibility which was to
dog him for many years. Yet maybe the delay before Antwerp,
due rather to the Belgian defence than to Churchill and his
marines, prevented the Germans from winning the 'race to
the sea'.

The B.E.F. was by now no longer on the Aisne. It had been
awkwardly wedged there between two French armies. Joffre
agreed that it should move further north. It arrived in Flanders

[1] See Note A, p. 32.

with the intention of outflanking the Germans, just when more powerful German forces, released by the fall of Antwerp, arrived in Flanders with the intention of outflanking the Allies.[1] The head-on collision from 12 October to 11 November, though known as the first battle of Ypres, was no battle in the old style, where movement in the open field produced decision within a single day. It was the first spluttering attempt at trench warfare, new forces fed in each day on a narrow front until mutual exhaustion followed. At first French thought he was winning in the old way. On 22 October he wrote: 'the enemy are vigorously playing their last card'.[2] Two days later he had to report that the B.E.F. had run through their supplies and would soon be fighting without artillery.[3] He even proposed the construction of an entrenched camp at Boulogne 'to take the whole Expeditionary Force'. On 31 October the Germans broke through the British line; then, as happened so often later, could make nothing of their opportunity—French troops sealed the breach before German reserves could start moving. Ypres was saved from the Germans. The British were saddled with a sharply exposed salient and, what was worse, with the constant temptation of a Flanders offensive, a temptation to which they bloodily succumbed in 1917. The first battle of Ypres marked the end of the old British army. The B.E.F. fought the Germans to a standstill, and itself out of existence. More than half of those who crossed to France in August were now casualties; one in ten had been killed (three quarters of them at Ypres). The high command and the staff officers survived. The old army was gone past recall.

By November 1914 the almost universal expectation of a short war had proved false. Instead of decision, there was deadlock. In France a continuous line of trenches ran from the Swiss frontier to the sea—a thin line by later standards but solid enough to prevent a war of movement. On the eastern front, too, there had been victories, but no decisions. The Russians rolled into east Prussia, only to be routed at Tannenberg (26-29 August). They defeated the Austrians in Galicia and were again halted by German intervention. The front was less solid in the east than in the west: movement was still possible

---

[1] The Germans had twenty divisions at Ypres, against fourteen Allied.
[2] *Military Operations: France and Belgium, 1914*, ii. 520.
[3] In reply, he was 'requested to see that economy was exercised'. Ibid. 203.

on a great scale, but, until 1917, no final victory. The greatest disappointment for the British public was that there was no great battle at sea. The German high seas fleet remained obstinately in harbour. The directors of British naval strategy had made stupendous preparations for the wrong sort of war: everything for an immediate engagement, little or nothing for a prolonged period of waiting. They had not foreseen the danger either from submarines or from mines.

Three British armoured cruisers[1] were sunk by a single U-boat on 22 September; the battleship *Audacious* was sunk by a mine on 27 October. The admiralty were so perturbed by the latter loss that they kept it secret until the end of the war.[2] Scapa Flow, the base of the Grand Fleet, was not secured from submarines. At the (false) alarm of an enemy periscope, Sir John Jellicoe[3] led his fleet in precipitate flight, first west of Scotland, then to the west coast of Ireland. The British fleet did not return to Scapa Flow until well on in 1915 and then remained mostly in harbour. The North Sea became a no-man's sea, occasionally raided by each side. The Germans never ventured to attack British communications with France, still less to attempt an invasion of the British Isles. Perhaps they, too, were deterred by mines and submarines, perhaps by Nelson's long shadow. Their utmost enterprise was to bombard the British coast twice. They killed a number of people at Bridlington and West Hartlepool; broke the windows of boarding houses at Scarborough; and damaged the ruins of Whitby Abbey. On a third attempt, they were caught by British battlecruisers and badly knocked about. After this, the German navy did not come out again for a long time.

British sea power struck harder on the outer oceans. The Germans, equally obsessed with battleships, had few cruisers for raiding commerce. One of them, the *Emden*, ravaged British shipping in the Indian Ocean. Seventy-eight British ships hunted her. She was caught and destroyed at Cocos Island by the Australian cruiser *Sydney* on 9 November. At the outbreak of

[1] *Aboukir, Hogue*, and *Cressy*.

[2] The loss was generally known long before. Liners passed the wreck on their way to America, and an illustrated paper published a photograph of it, entitled 'an Audacious Picture'.

[3] John Rushworth Jellicoe (1859–1935); commander-in-chief Grand Fleet, 1914–16; first sea lord, 1916–17: governor of New Zealand, 1920–5; cr. Viscount, 1918, Earl, 1925; received grant of £50,000 from parliament, 1919.

war a German squadron under Admiral von Spee was in Chinese waters. It crossed the Pacific and on 3 November destroyed a weaker British force under Sir Christopher Cradock off Coronel in Chile. Churchill and Lord Fisher, restored as first sea lord when anti-German prejudice drove Prince Louis of Battenberg from office, at once sent two battlecruisers under Sturdee[1] to the South Atlantic. On 8 December von Spee was tempted to destroy the British wireless station on the Falkland Islands, where, unknown to him, Sturdee happened to be coaling. It was now the turn of the Germans to be outgunned. Four out of their five ships were sunk. The fifth escaped, and was sunk in the following March. In both engagements, the stronger force annihilated its opponent virtually without loss.[2] Danger from surface raiders was virtually ended. Britannia ruled the waves. Supplies poured into Great Britain from all the world. The British drew an invisible noose of distant blockade around Germany. German ships were arrested. Neutral ships were brought into British ports, and their cargoes checked. Later, British consuls in far-away countries issued neutrals with a clean bill, if they conformed to the rules. All this was in flagrant contradiction with the Declaration of London, which the British government had accepted in 1909 and the house of lords had then thrown out. The British blockade caused much difficulty with the United States. It was to prove, nevertheless, a potent weapon of victory.

What was to happen now that the illusion of a quick victory had been dispelled? This riddle was posed to the rulers of the British Empire. They were not equipped to answer it. The Liberal cabinet was a government of departments. Churchill ran the naval war, Kitchener the war on land; Grey looked after what remained of foreign policy. The cabinet stood aside. Asquith, the prime minister, was a strong character, unshakeable as a rock and, like a rock, incapable of movement. His initiative, if he ever had any, was sapped by years of good living in high

[1] Frederick Charles Doveton Sturdee (1859–1925): admiral of the fleet; chief of war staff, admiralty, 1914; commander-in-chief, South Atlantic and South Pacific, 1914; commanded fourth battle squadron, 1915–18; commander-in-chief, Nore, 1918–21; cr. Baronet, 1916; received thanks of parliament and £10,000, 1919.

[2] At Coronel von Spee sank two British cruisers; two German sailors were wounded. At the Falkland Islands, Sturdee sank four German cruisers. There were thirty British casualties.

society.[1] He claimed rightly that he and Grey were the two men most responsible for bringing Great Britain into the war. With this, he supposed, his task was exhausted. Statesmen, in his view, should keep out of the way, while free enterprise provided the arms with which generals won the battles. Most of the cabinet ministers were Free Traders, hostile to government initiative. Runciman, president of the board of trade,[2] told the house of commons: 'No government action could overcome economic laws and any interference with those laws must end in disaster.'

The situation in the house of commons reinforced the government's unwillingness to act. Since the general election of December 1910, the two main parties—Liberal and Unionist—almost balanced.[3] Asquith had a stable and substantial majority with the eighty Irish and forty Labour men. He assumed that their tame acquiescence would continue, apart, of course, from the half-dozen Labour men who actually opposed the war. It did not occur to him that their support would now have to be earned. Bonar Law, the Unionist leader,[4] had no wish to detach them; it was inconceivable that he could head a Unionist government,[5] sustained by Irish Nationalist votes. Though 'meekly ambitious', in Asquith's phrase, Law always bided his time, and this made him the most formidable giant-

---

[1] Asquith was the first prime minister since the younger Pitt who is said to have been manifestly the worse for drink when on the Treasury Bench. George Robey was uncomfortably near the truth when he sang:

Mr. Asquith says in a manner sweet and calm:
Another little drink won't do us any harm.

[2] Walter Runciman (1870–1949): educ. S. Shields H.S. and Cambridge; son of a shipowner; Liberal M.P., 1899–1900, 1902–18, 1924–31; Lib. National, 1931–7; succeeded his father as Baron and created Viscount, 1937; president of board of trade, 1914–16, 1931–7; lord president of the council, 1938–9; mission to Czechoslovakia, 1938.

[3] At the general election they exactly balanced: 272 members each. Since then the Conservatives had gained 15 seats from the Liberals and 2 from Labour. The Liberals had gained 1 from the Conservatives and 2 from Labour. Thus, in August 1914 the totals were 260 Liberals and 288 Conservatives.

[4] Andrew Bonar Law (1858–1923), educ. Canada and Glasgow; b. in New Brunswick; an iron-merchant in Glasgow; leader of Unionist party, 1911–21, 1922–3; colonial secretary, 1915–16; chancellor of the exchequer and member of war cabinet, 1916–18; lord privy seal, 1919–21; Conservative prime minister, 1922–3. His ashes were interred in Westminster Abbey. Asquith said: 'It is fitting that we should have buried the Unknown Prime Minister by the side of the Unknown Soldier.'

[5] The Conservatives had adopted the name Unionist, in order to embrace the Liberal Unionists who broke with Gladstone over Home Rule. The name ceased to have much relevance after the creation of the Irish Free State, and the older name came back into common use.

killer of the century. Balfour, Asquith, and Lloyd George all
fell beneath his reluctant axe. At the moment, Law wanted to
keep the Liberals tied to the war. He believed, perhaps correctly, that the Unionists could conquer power and even win
a general election if they forced the patriotic note. The price
would be too high: the Liberals might then turn against the
war which they had so tardily supported. National unity would
be shattered.

Even so, this unity was not easy to maintain. It was threatened
almost immediately when parliament resumed (from 25 to
31 August and again from 9 to 17 September), in order to
complete business left unfinished on the outbreak of war.
Welsh Disestablishment and Irish Home Rule, having passed
three times through the house of commons, were ripe to become
law under the provisions of the Parliament Act. Both were
placed on the statute book, together with acts suspending their
operation until six months after the end of the war. Welsh
Disestablishment created little stir, except among Welsh members and Lord Robert Cecil[1]—the Welsh holding that they
should have disestablishment at once, Cecil that they should not
have it at all.[2]

Home Rule was a different matter. The parties had been
locked in dispute over the exclusion of Ulster; no agreement
had been reached. The Unionists wanted exclusion of Ulster
tacked on to the original bill. Asquith at first acquiesced; then,
faced with a revolt of the Irish Nationalists, insisted that Home
Rule must go on the statute book undiluted. The Unionists
were indignant at what they regarded as a breach of faith.
On 15 September they protested by leaving the house of commons in a body, led by Law. Asquith described them as 'a lot
of prosaic and for the most part middle-aged gentlemen, trying
to look like early French revolutionists in the Tennis Court'.[3]
The controversy was mighty irrelevant in present circumstances.
Home Rule, suspended for the duration, brought no change in
Ireland: the viceroy, the chief secretary, and Dublin Castle still
ruled. The Irish question was deeply changed all the same.

[1] Robert Cecil (1864-1958): educ. Eton and Oxford; third son of third marquis
of Salisbury; minister of blockade, 1916-18; lord privy seal, 1923; cr. Viscount,
1923; chancellor of the duchy of Lancaster, 1924-7; High Churchman and Free
Trader; after the war, became an enthusiast for the League of Nations.
[2] Welsh Disestablishment duly came into force after the war, much to the benefit
of the disestablished Church.   [3] Asquith, *Memories and Reflections*, ii. 33.

When it came to be discussed again, Home Rule would be the starting point, not the goal: the Union of 1801 had been given notice to quit. There was another change, less noticed at the time. During the final wrangle, Asquith gave an assurance which he had never given before: 'employment of force, any kind of force' for the coercion of Ulster was 'unthinkable', 'a thing we could never countenance or consent to'. Thus, the unity of Ireland, too, was implicitly ended.

The row left deep marks. Unionists refused to appear with Liberal speakers on patriotic platforms. There was much more dividing them under the surface. The Unionists, by and large, regarded Germany as a dangerous rival, and rejoiced at the chance to destroy her. They meant to fight a hard-headed war by ruthless methods; they condemned Liberal 'softness' before the war and now. The Liberals insisted on remaining high-minded. Many of them had come to support the war only when the Germans invaded Belgium; even the less Radical among them were relieved to escape from a 'realist' position. Entering the war for idealistic motives, the Liberals wished to fight it by noble means and found it harder to abandon their principles than to endure defeat in the field. In particular, the Liberals were determined to maintain the system of Free Trade which they had successfully defended before the war. Many Unionists hoped that the war would kill Free Trade along with other Liberal illusions. There would have been raging conflict between the parties if these differences had been brought into the open. Asquith and Law combined to keep them under cover. Throughout the remaining life of the Liberal government, that is, until May 1915, the house of commons did not once discuss the war.

There were other reasons for this silence. Surprise was supposed to be a vital ingredient of war, and the Great War produced an excessive enthusiasm for secrecy, or 'security' as it came to be called. Military grounds perhaps justified this at first. The B.E.F. took the Germans unawares at Mons, and apprehension that the British might land at the Channel ports in their rear, though this never happened, embarrassed them still more. Soon, security operated more against the British public than against the enemy. The authorities, military and civil, had no idea how to win the war and therefore maintained silence until, by some miracle as yet unforeseen, the war should

be won. No war correspondents followed the army to France.[1]
In May 1915 six correspondents were invited to headquarters
'for a limited period'; they remained in this temporary, and
somewhat privileged, position throughout the war. A press
bureau distributed statements from G.H.Q. and from government departments; it advised, on request, about the publication of other news. The war office, relying on the Defence of
the Realm Act,[2] censored all cables and foreign correspondence
—a censorship which was avowed only in April 1916. Any
newspaper publishing unauthorized news, or still worse specu-
lating about future strategy, ran the risk of a prosecution under
D.O.R.A., and most newspapers walked warily. Reports of
parliamentary proceedings were not censored. In practice,
indiscreet questions were rejected by the Speaker, on the private
instruction of some government department, and members were
struck dumb by their own freedom. Curiously, the Lords were
more outspoken than the Commons. In November 1915 Lord
Milner[3] brazenly referred to the coming evacuation from Gallipoli—a defiance which the bewildered Germans wrote off as
deception. The one leakage in the house of commons was
trivial. On 27 January 1916 a junior minister revealed that
museums were being used to house government departments
and were thus a legitimate object for attacks from the air.[4]
Enemy information about conditions in England hardly existed.
The public were still more in the dark.

The English people could not be ignored so easily. War produced a great surge of patriotic enthusiasm; all lesser passions
were laid aside. H. G. Wells expressed this in his Mr. Britling,
who discarded his mistress in order to make plans for a better
world. Mr. Britling was typical, too, in his restless bicycling
to the nearest village in quest of news. He found little. Instead
rumour flourished. The Angels of Mons were one such rumour,

[1] The prospective correspondents were instructed to provide themselves with
horses. These were taken over by the war office six weeks later.
[2] First enacted Aug. 1914, and repeatedly strengthened thereafter. 'Dora', an
elderly lady, became the symbol of restriction.
[3] Alfred Milner (1854–1925): educ. Germany, London, and Oxford; cr. Viscount, 1902; member of war cabinet, 1916–18; secretary for war, 1918; for colonies,
1919–21; admired by 'the Milner kindergarten' of young men who had worked
under him in South Africa after the Boer war.
[4] An attempt to take over the British Museum was defeated by Sir Frederic
Kenyon, the Director. He suggested instead the Bethlehem Hospital, 'commonly
known as Bedlam'.

universally believed. Even more famous were the Russian troops —'little short of a million', according to a *Times* reporter[1]— who landed at Aberdeen early in September 1914 and passed through England on their way to the western front. Nearly everyone knew someone who had seen them, though the snow on their boots, which gave the last touch of authenticity, was probably a later, light-hearted gloss.

With rumour came hysteria. Harmless old men, who had forgotten to take out naturalization papers during their forty years in England, found their sons in the army and themselves interned in the Isle of Man. Shops of bakers with German-sounding names were sacked. Hard tennis courts[2] were suspect as gun emplacements, prepared for the invading German army. Flickering lights, particularly near the coast, were denounced as signals to the enemy. The arrival of some hundred thousand Belgian refugees increased the hysteria. They brought stories of German atrocities—some true, most of them inflated by the heat of war: the violated nuns and the babies with their hands cut off were never found.[3] The Belgians were given at first an emotional welcome. Lord Curzon[4] entertained the king and queen at his country house; Lord Lonsdale provided for their horses as 'a further contribution to the national cause'. This sympathy did not last. Most of the refugees were ordinary working-class people, aggrieved at having been driven from their homes and resentful that Great Britain had not defended the neutrality of Belgium more adequately. Their competition was feared on the labour market.[5] Before the war ended, the Belgians were far from popular.

[1] Macdonagh, *In London during the World War*, 21. The story was denied by the Press Bureau on 15 Sept.

[2] Tennis courts were replacing the billiards room at the homes of richer people —a victory somehow for morality and perhaps for equality of the sexes. (Few women played billiards; many played tennis.)

[3] In the first World war nearly everyone believed the stories of German atrocities, though relatively few were true. In the second World war nearly everyone refused to believe the stories, though they were true, and German crimes the most atrocious ever committed by a civilized nation.

[4] George Nathaniel Curzon (1859–1925): educ. Eton and Oxford; viceroy of India, 1898–1905; cr. Earl 1911, Marquis, 1921; lord privy seal, 1915–16; lord president of the council and member of war cabinet, 1916–19; foreign secretary, 1919–24; lord president, 1924–5. At time of armistice, hoped that there would be 'no be-ano'. Seeing soldiers bathing, was surprised that the lower classes had such white skins. Many of the best stories against Curzon were made up by Curzon himself.

[5] The Local Government Board handled, in all, 119,000 Belgian refugees. As

The war was in fact coming home to people's lives despite the silence in high places. Kitchener, the least public-minded of ministers, was responsible for this. He startled his colleagues at the first cabinet meeting which he attended by announcing that the war would last three years, not three months, and that Great Britain would have to put an army of millions into the field.[1] Regarding the Territorial army (which he mistook for the French 'territoriaux' of 1870) with undeserved contempt, he proposed to raise a New Army of seventy divisions[2] and, when Asquith ruled out compulsion as politically impossible, agreed to do so by voluntary recruiting. Soon Kitchener's finger pointed balefully from every hoarding: 'Your Country needs YOU.' Rupert Brooke gave the almost unanimous answer: 'Now God be thanked who has matched us with His hour.' Kitchener asked for an initial one hundred thousand—175,000 men volunteered in the single week ending 5 September; 750,000 had enlisted by the end of September. Thereafter the average ran at 125,000 men a month until June 1915 when it slackened off. In all over two and a half million men enlisted[3] before voluntary recruitment came to an end in March 1916.

The achievement was staggering; the method clumsy. After the first flood of volunteers, enthusiasm had to be kept constantly astir. Supposedly eligible young men were presented with white feathers. Recruiting meetings built up an exaggerated hatred of the Germans, and equally exaggerated hopes of the better world which would follow victory. On these platforms staid politicians, with their old-time style, were eclipsed by demagogues. Horatio Bottomley, in particular, rose to new

well, 'better-class refugees' were dealt with by a committee which Lady Lugard had originally organized to receive women and children fleeing from the expected civil war in Ulster. Later, a munitions area was created at Birtley, Durham, where Belgian policemen, Belgian law, and even Belgian beer created the illusion of a Belgian town.

[1] Kitchener expected the French army to be defeated in the field. He did not foresee trench warfare and, when it came, said: 'I don't know what is to be done; this isn't war.'

[2] This was a rule-of-thumb figure. On the German analogy, the British, allowing for the difference in population, should have raised 105 divisions. Kitchener arbitrarily knocked off a third for the needs of the navy, the merchant service, and industry. The answer was 70. Thus, Great Britain's military effort was determined by a crude calculation of available manpower, not by considering strategical requirements.

[3] One and three quarter million in the regular army; three quarters of a million in the Territorials. As well 329,000 volunteered for the navy and, later, about 60,000 for the air force. N. B. Dearle, *Labour Cost of the Great War*, 8.

fame: an undischarged bankrupt at the beginning of the war, acknowledged tribune of the people at the end.[1] Sane thinking about how to run the war, or why it was being fought, was difficult in these conditions. Moreover, enthusiasm brought in more recruits than the existing military machine could handle. There were not enough barracks, often not even rifles for them. Recruits spent the winter months in tents and trained with sticks. There were few qualified men to train them. Kitchener formed the remaining regular troops into divisions and sent them to France, instead of using them to shape the New Army.[2] The young enthusiasts were handled by elderly officers and sergeant-majors, who had completed their service before the death of Queen Victoria. It was the beginning of disenchantment.

Kitchener's authority had another unfortunate result. At the beginning of the war there were two private armies in Ireland: the Ulster Volunteers, who had been formed to resist Home Rule, and the Irish Volunteers, who had been formed to defend it. Both were now anxious to be embodied in the British army. Kitchener, who had been born and partly brought up in Ireland though not an Irishman, shared the outlook of the Protestant garrison. He accepted the Ulster organization; he rejected the Home Rulers. The Red Hand of Ulster was acknowledged; the Irish Harp was not. Recruits from Ulster had their own officers; those from the south of Ireland were placed under Protestants. Redmond, the Irish leader, had believed that Ireland would win her freedom by fighting for the freedom of Belgium and other small nations. Thanks to Kitchener, the surge of Irish loyalty was dissipated. A minority of the Irish Volunteers, under John MacNeill, swung round to an anti-British attitude; many of the rest slipped into sullen indifference.

Nevertheless, the New Army was Kitchener's triumph: the greatest volunteer force ever raised in any country. His prestige brought in recruits, and the recruits added to his prestige. He

[1] Horatio Bottomley (1860–1933), editor of *John Bull*; independent M.P., 1918–22; convicted of fraudulent conversion, 1922; died a pauper. At recruiting meetings, the strength of his peroration was determined by the size of the 'take', and he took, in all, £78,000. He used to recite a poem with the line: 'This is more than a war, mate—it's a call to the human race.' Bottomley murmured the words with a more personal meaning as he slapped the £5 notes into his pocket at the end of the meeting.

[2] 'Of the many mistakes made in the war, . . . probably the most expensive.' *Military Operations: France and Belgium, 1915*, ii. viii.

was England's Hindenburg, like him a wooden titan. As virtual war dictator, Kitchener was responsible also for supply[1] and for strategy. These proved his undoing. The war office was equipped only to supply a small army. At the outbreak of war there were twenty clerks in the Army Contracts department. Kitchener clung to the cheese-paring economy with which he had once run the campaign in the Sudan. He neglected the finance for expansion which Lloyd George offered him. A Shells committee of the cabinet, which sat between 1 October 1914 and 1 January 1915, failed to move him. The war office refused to extend its list of authorized firms and deluged these firms with orders which they could not fulfil. It insisted that only experienced firms knew how to produce munitions of satisfactory quality, and this was confirmed when the first shells, ordered from a wider list by the ministry of munitions, brought the word 'dud' into common use. Nevertheless, whatever the excuse, there was a shortage of shells. The blame fell on the war office and so on Kitchener.

Strategy was his greatest failure, though no one in the first World war did any better. Kitchener insisted on determining strategy all alone; he was at a loss what to determine. The British army was in France and was being steadily reinforced. Joffre had a single aim, to which he insisted the British ought to conform: liberation of the national territory. Kitchener had no faith in this strategy. The German lines, he believed, had become 'a fortress which cannot be taken by assault'. On the other hand, he 'anticipated a call' to become Supreme Allied Commander some day when the British armies reached full strength, and therefore felt that he must defer to the French now in the hope that they would defer to him later. Hence he became more than usually incoherent when the cabinet looked to him for strategical advice. Civilian ministers were provoked into devising strategy themselves—some of them not at all reluctantly. The key thought for these amateur strategists, Churchill and Lloyd George in particular, was sea power. Surely, they argued, this gigantic power could somehow be used to turn the German flank without the sacrifice of millions

[1] The admiralty always kept supply for the navy in its own hands and enforced the doctrine of 'absolute priority' for naval needs. Even in 1918 it was taking men from working on merchant ships and tanks to build battleships which were never used.

of men. They wanted a dodge in a double sense: a clever trick which would evade the deadlock of the western front. They sought a field of action where the Germans could not get at them, and forgot that then they would not be able to get at the Germans.[1] If this field of action were outside Europe, so much the better: it would bring territorial gains for the British empire.

In November 1914 the cabinet acknowledged that its expectation of a short war had proved false. The committee of imperial defence, which had hitherto been restricted to organizing the conquest of the German colonies,[2] was transformed into a war council. Rival projects were aired. Lloyd George favoured an expedition to Salonika or the Dalmatian coast. Hankey, secretary of the council, suggested an attack on Turkey, who had entered the war against the Allies in October. This idea attracted Kitchener, with his long service in the East. He favoured it still more when an urgent appeal for help against the Turks reached him from Grand Duke Nicholas, Russian commander-in-chief, at the end of the year. Churchill and Fisher (the first sea lord) both wanted some great 'amphibious' operation, though Fisher pointed to Sleswig and Churchill to the Dardanelles. All these schemes were debated without staff advice or consideration of detailed maps. There was no inquiry whether shipping was available, nor whether there were troops to spare—Kitchener ineffectually observing that there were none. The war council cheerfully assumed that great armadas could waft non-existent armies to the ends of the earth in the twinkling of an eye.

The man of most persistence won. Churchill pressed for the Dardanelles. Fisher believed that he ought not to oppose his political chief at the war council.[3] Also he agreed with Kitchener's judgement that 150,000 men would be needed to take

[1] The 'easterners', as they were called, were misled by the analogy of Wellington's campaign in Spain. They overlooked (a) that it involved a very large army by the standards of the time; (b) that it made only a marginal contribution to the defeat of Napoleon's Grand Army.

[2] Togoland was occupied in Aug. The New Zealanders took Samoa (Aug.), the Australians New Guinea (Sept.), the South Africans South-west Africa (Dec.). The Cameroons were conquered in 1917; German East Africa not until the end of 1917 (at a cost of £75 million). Von Lettow, the German commander there, retreated into Portuguese East Africa and did not surrender until after the armistice.

[3] This constitutional rectitude had not prevented his briefing the Unionist editor, Garvin, against the naval plans of the Liberal government in 1909, nor was it long to prevent his briefing Law against Churchill.

the Dardanelles, and therefore expected the army to be drawn in after all. Kitchener was won over by an opinion, extracted with some difficulty from the British admiral in the Mediterranean, that the navy could force the Dardanelles alone. Sir John French hurried over to assert the unique importance of the western front. The bewildered war council grasped at an apparent way out: a naval attack at the Dardanelles which would break the deadlock of trench warfare without diverting troops from France. On 13 January 1915 the war council unanimously resolved that the Admiralty 'should prepare for a naval expedition to bombard and take the Gallipoli Peninsula, with Constantinople as its objective'. On 28 January the naval plan was approved by the war council, after Fisher (who was technically responsible for it) had been persuaded not to protest against it by Kitchener (who had technically nothing to do with it).

As the great ships massed in the eastern Mediterranean, Kitchener had second thoughts. If the naval action succeeded, troops would be needed to occupy the Peninsula; if it failed, they would be needed to restore British prestige in the East. Somehow, he hoped to trickle forces to the Dardanelles without Joffre or French noticing that they had gone. On 16 February he agreed that the 29th division, composed of regulars from India, could be sent to the eastern Mediterranean.[1] On 20 February he refused to release it. On 24 February he told the war council: 'if the Fleet cannot get through the Straits unaided, the Army will have to see the business through'. On 10 March he finally decided that the 29th division should go. Two days later he sent for his favourite general, Sir Ian Hamilton,[2] and said to him: 'We are sending a military force to support the Fleet now at the Dardanelles, and you are to have command.' Hamilton received one inaccurate map, no information about the Turkish army and little about the fortifications of the Dardanelles, no firm guidance as to the forces which he could expect. He left without a staff, Kitchener saying to him: 'If the

---

[1] To cajole the French, Kitchener suggested that the division might go to Salonika, the one 'side show' which they favoured. Lloyd George, who also favoured Salonika, was the only member of the war council to argue that troops should not be sent to the Dardanelles if the naval attack failed.

[2] Ian Standish Monteith Hamilton (1853-1947): chief of staff to Kitchener in South Africa; defended voluntary system of recruitment against Roberts, 1910; commanded Central Force for home defence, 1914; commanded at Gallipoli, 1915; after this, not employed again; wrote agreeable volumes of reminiscences.

Fleet gets through, Constantinople will fall of its own accord, and you will have won not a battle, but the war.'[1]

The bottom soon fell out of these hopes. On 18 March the British fleet and some French ships entered the Straits. The waters, it was supposed, had been swept clear of mines. The Turkish forts were bombarded. It is now known that their ammunition was exhausted by the end of the day, and that no more was available. One line of mines had been missed: it had been laid parallel to the Asiatic shore, not across the Straits. On the way back the fleet ran into it. Two British battleships and a French ship were sunk; one British ship and one French ship were severely damaged. The ships were old and due for scrap. All the same Sir John de Robeck,[2] the admiral in command, was dismayed at their loss. On 22 March he held a first conference with Hamilton. According to Hamilton, de Robeck said: 'he was now clear that he could not get through without the help of all my troops'. According to de Robeck, Hamilton took the initiative in offering to clear the Straits with the army. At any rate, the naval attack was called off and never renewed. Hamilton discovered that the transports had been sent out in such confusion that no immediate action was possible. He decided to take his army back to Alexandria and to organize it there for a landing in about three weeks' time. During these three weeks, which grew into a month, the Turks increased their forces at Gallipoli from two divisions to six—one more than Hamilton commanded.

Thus, when the campaigning season of 1915 opened, Great Britain was committed to offensive action in France which would absorb more than all her available resources, and to an improvised offensive in Gallipoli. Military failure followed. On 25 April British and Australian troops attacked at Galli-

---

[1] It is a mystery why most people, then and since, assumed that the fall of Constantinople would lead to the defeat of Germany. The only immediate gain would be to open a line of supply to Russia, and this gain was purely theoretical since neither Great Britain nor France had, at this time, supplies to send. Turkey might have been knocked out of the war, but this would have lessened the burden on Germany. An army would have had no light task to march from Constantinople to Central Europe and, in any case, there was no army to spare. Later, the Allies sent large forces to Salonika, a better port, without achieving any result until the end of the war, when the German army was already defeated.

[2] John Michael de Robeck (1862–1928): commanded naval forces at the Dardanelles, 1915–16; commanded second battle squadron, 1916–19; commander-in-chief of Mediterranean fleet, 1919–22; of Atlantic fleet, 1922–4; received thanks of parliament, grant of £10,000, and baronetcy, 1919.

poli. They had no landing craft and were not trained for the difficult operation of landing on a hostile coast. They got safely ashore only by landing at the extreme end of the peninsula, where their presence could do the Turks little harm. Their generals lacked drive, and Hamilton failed to provide it. He was too polite to be a successful commander. He drifted helplessly up and down the coast on a warship, refusing to interfere with his subordinates. The Turks recovered from their surprise and pinned Hamilton's men to the shore. Instead of a war of movement, a new line of trenches was drawn on the Peninsula, more intractable than that on the western front.

In France Sir John French staged an assault, independently of the French, known as the battle of Neuve Chapelle (10-13 March). This attack pierced the German line; the Germans closed the gap before reserves could arrive. The Germans, on their side, first used gas in an attack on the Ypres salient—the 'second battle' of Ypres (22 April-25 May); this, too, miscarried after heavy British losses. Henceforth soldiers had to add gas-masks to their other burdens. Finally, there was an assault, in cooperation with the French, known variously as the battle of Festubert or of Aubers ridge (9-25 May). All three engagements demonstrated the futility of narrow attacks against a fortified line. French cloaked his failure by complaining about the shortage of shells. These complaints reached the ear of Northcliffe,[1] greatest of the press lords. He resolved to launch an outcry against the 'shells scandal', which would drive Kitchener, and maybe the Liberal government, from office.

The press reached perhaps its highest point of influence during the first World war. Radio was in the future. Newspapers were the only source of news, and their circulation rose still more when the casualty lists began to appear. With the politicians almost silent, the newspapers provided opinions as well. Lloyd George said in 1916: 'The Press has performed the function which should have been performed by Parliament, and which the French Parliament has performed.'[2] Great editors, thundering out their convictions, were by no means new. Delane

---

[1] Alfred Harmsworth (1865–1922): cr. Baron Northcliffe, 1905; Viscount, 1917; head of British mission to the United States, 1917; director of enemy propaganda, 1918; founder of modern journalism; created and inspired the *Daily Mail*; owned *The Times* which he transformed from a derelict property into a profitable undertaking.

[2] Riddell, *War Diary*, 151.

of *The Times* had been their finest example long before. Such editors were now in profusion—Scott of the *Manchester Guardian*, Garvin of the *Observer*, Massingham of the (weekly) *Nation*: men placed in authority by the proprietor[1] and expressing, in their own terms, policy in the widest sense. Though they were all individuals with pronounced character, they were associated with some broad political circle, Liberal, Unionist, or Radical. Northcliffe was different: hence the hostility which he provoked. He was proprietor of the *Daily Mail*, the daily newspaper with the largest circulation, and of *The Times*, which claimed to be, in a particular way, the national voice. He was also, or at any rate regarded himself as being, 'Chief Editor'. He determined policy; the editors were his instruments. Unlike other editors, he did not express the opinions of a party or political group. He was, in Beaverbrook's words, 'the greatest figure who ever strode down Fleet St.',[2] and he expected men to follow his lead merely because he was the great Northcliffe. This was his mistake. Editors succeeded by voicing or by stimulating opinions, not by dictating them. Though men bought Northcliffe's papers for their news, they were no more impressed by his political sense than by that of any other successful businessman. They did not obey his orders. Men did not wear the *Daily Mail* hat; they did not eat the *Daily Mail* loaf. Nor did they accept the *Daily Mail* 'Chief'. Northcliffe could destroy when he used the news properly. He could not step into the vacant place. He aspired to power instead of influence, and as a result forfeited both.

Northcliffe was not alone in planning a political offensive. The Unionist backbenchers resented the silence to which Law had committed them. They, too, wished to force a discussion of the shells scandal, though their target was the Liberal Free Trade ministers, not Kitchener. The Liberal auxiliaries were also preparing to desert. The Irish Nationalists had no reason to support Asquith once Home Rule was laid aside, and much reason to attack Kitchener after his contemptuous handling of the Irish Volunteers. Labour was moving towards independence. The Labour party had opposed the war till the last

[1] In the discussions of the freedom of the press, it is often overlooked that the political character of a paper was determined, in every case, by its proprietor. Scott was unique in being, after 1905, owner as well as editor.
[2] Beaverbrook, *Politicians and the War*, i. 93.

moment. On 5 August it swung round. Ramsay MacDonald[1] resigned as leader of the parliamentary party. Arthur Henderson[2] took his place. On 24 August the trade unions declared an industrial truce for the duration of the war. Labour leaders spoke on recruiting platforms; they pressed for an energetic conduct of the war. They dreaded industrial conscription; this is why they had opposed war earlier. To avert this the unions had to abandon their traditional attitude of leaving decision to the bosses; they had to become partners, if only junior partners, in the conduct of affairs.

The hand of cooperation which they held out was grasped from within the government by Lloyd George. He had already established himself as 'the man of the people'—product of an elementary school, pioneer of social welfare. He cared nothing for the conventional rules—neither the rules of personal behaviour nor those economic rules of free enterprise to which his Liberal colleagues attached so much importance. Lloyd George lived in the moment, a master of improvization. He had few friends in political circles. He followed opinion, and sometimes shaped it, by his intimate contact with editors and proprietors of newspapers.[3] Before the war he was the chief industrial conciliator of the government. Then he had been the complement to Asquith, not his rival; the two worked together and ran in harmony. On 19 September 1914 the situation changed. Lloyd George spoke publicly in all-out support for the war. From that moment, he challenged Asquith. He might declare that he would dig potatoes if Asquith ceased to be prime minister. Unconsciously, perhaps even unwillingly, he was offering himself as the man who could run the war better. In his own sphere as chancellor of the exchequer, Lloyd George contributed little. His first war budget of November 1914, which doubled the

[1] James Ramsay MacDonald (1866–1937): leader of Labour party, 1911–14, 1922–31; prime minister and foreign secretary, 1924; prime minister of Labour government, 1929–31; of National government, 1931–5; lord president of the council, 1935–7; died at sea.

[2] Arthur Henderson (1863–1935): president of board of education, 1915–16; member of war cabinet, 1916–17; home secretary, 1924; foreign secretary, 1929–31; president of world disarmament conference, 1932–5; known in the Labour movement as 'Uncle Arthur'.

[3] Lloyd George numbered among his close friends and advisers Scott, owner and editor of the *Manchester Guardian*; Riddell, chairman of the *News of the World*; Dalziel, owner of *Reynolds' News*; and Robertson Nicholl, editor of the *British Weekly*, the most influential nonconformist organ. Robert Donald, editor of the *Daily Chronicle*, was another devoted supporter, at any rate until 1918.

income tax,[1] merely added £1 million a week to the revenue when expenditure had already increased by £1 million a day and was going steadily up. His second war budget of May 1915 added no new taxes at all. Lloyd George was no longer interested in balanced budgets, if he ever had been. He was intent only on unlimited supply.

His opportunity soon came. The most urgent problem in the munitions factories was 'dilution'. Unskilled workers and women had to be brought in if the engineering shops were to expand. The skilled workers refused to relax their traditional standards. The government had some compulsory powers under D.O.R.A. and could no doubt get more. The price would be the renewal of industrial strife. The union leaders took a decisive initiative: they would accept 'dilution' if it were carried through voluntarily and under their direction. Lloyd George responded. He met the union leaders at the treasury from 17 to 19 March; other unions, especially the Amalgamated Society of Engineers, were drawn in. The resulting Treasury Agreement revolutionized the position of trade unions: where formerly they had opposed, they now participated. They were to accept and to operate 'dilution'. They received in return three promises. Traditional practices were to be restored at the end of the war; this promise was kept, to everyone's surprise. Profits were to be restricted, in exchange for the sacrifice of union rights; this promise, too, was kept, though less effectively than the unions expected. Finally, the unions were to share in the direction of industry through local joint committees; this promise was not kept—the committees were used only to organize dilution. Nevertheless, Lloyd George was right when he called the treasury agreement 'the great charter for labour'. It was his great charter too: it established his claim to be the man who could enlist 'the people' for the war effort.

The net was closing round Kitchener. On 12 April Lloyd George got a new cabinet committee on munitions, with himself in the chair, and Kitchener excluded. In Fleet Street, Northcliffe was preparing his outcry against the shells scandal. In parliament, Unionist backbenchers, Irish nationalists, and Labour were uniting in a common discontent. On 13 May the Unionist Business Committee put down a motion on the shell

[1] Basic rate went up from 1s. 3d. to 2s. 6d. in the pound, though the many exceptions made this crude figure misleading.

shortage. This was a direct attack on the Liberal government. It cut clean across Law's strategy: he meant to hold the Liberals to support of the war, not to overthrow them. With great difficulty he persuaded the rebellious Unionists to hold their hand. Suddenly a mine exploded in a different quarter. The failure of 25 April meant that more ships and more men must be sent to Gallipoli. The war council so resolved on 14 May—its first meeting since 6 April. Fisher feared for the strength of the Grand Fleet. He could stand the drain of ships no longer. On 15 May he resigned as first sea lord. This was a stroke of luck for Law: a crisis which he could initiate, instead of having it forced on him by his backbenchers. Moreover, the outcry could be directed solely against Churchill, who was supposedly responsible for the Dardanelles campaign. The Unionists hated him both as a deserter from their ranks and as the man who had planned forcible action—a pogrom, as it was called—against Ulster.

On 17 May Law told Lloyd George that, if Fisher went and Churchill remained, there would be an outcry in the house of commons which he could not restrain, even if he would. Lloyd George replied: 'Of course we must have a Coalition, for the alternative is impossible.' The two men then saw Asquith. He had no belief in the administrative capacity of the Unionists. On the other hand, here was a fine chance to saddle them with the responsibility for 'side-tracking Kitchener': they, not he, would bear the brunt of 'the horrible Harmsworth campaign'.[1] Coalition was made, and the last Liberal government in British history killed, within a quarter of an hour.[2]

Asquith's calculations did not altogether work out. The Unionists, instead of throwing Kitchener out, insisted on keeping him. However, this had the advantage in Asquith's eyes of closing the war office against a Unionist. Besides, Kitchener's powers were shorn. Northcliffe's campaign against the shells scandal exploded too late to affect the Liberal government, which was already dead; but it gave the final push to Lloyd George's demand for an independent ministry controlling

---

[1] Addison, Four and a Half Years, i. 79.
[2] The making of the first Coalition is one of the few political episodes in the first World war on which solid evidence is lacking. I am not sure that Lloyd George played so passive a part. Perhaps he pushed Law forward. In any case, this was a foretaste of the future: Law and Lloyd George dictating action to Asquith.

supply. Who should head it except Lloyd George himself? He became minister of munitions.[1] This apparently exposed the exchequer to a Unionist. Asquith was a match for this problem also: Lloyd George's move was announced to be temporary. Obviously a Tariff Reformer could not keep the place warm for him. McKenna,[2] supposedly a sound Free Trader, was willing to oblige. Grey, of course, remained at the foreign office. The Unionists received only the crumbs. Law, their leader, was fobbed off with the colonial office.

Churchill was the one great casualty,[3] as Law had intended. He was pushed aside to the duchy of Lancaster, a setback from which he did not recover for many years. Balfour,[4] Asquith's only friend among the Unionists, took Churchill's place at the admiralty. There were other gestures of national unity. Arthur Henderson joined the cabinet, ostensibly in charge of education, actually the voice of 'Labour'. This was a portent: the industrial working class took a share of power, however slight, for the first time. Carson,[5] the former Ulster rebel, became attorney general. Redmond, the Irish Nationalist leader, would also have joined the government if he had been given an Irish post. But this would have recognized his claim to lead Ireland. He was offered an English office, and refused. Thus Redmond, the projected Irish Botha, remained out, just when Botha himself was conquering new territories for the British empire. Otherwise national unity seemed complete. The

[1] Strictly the first 'Minister' in British history. Previously there had been secretaries of state, presidents of boards, &c., but no ministers. The new phrase was an echo of French practice. 'Minister without portfolio' (instead of with a sinecure) was another, introduced at the same time (for Lansdowne).

[2] Reginald McKenna (1863–1943): educ. K.C.S. and Cambridge; home secretary, 1911–15; chancellor of the exchequer, 1915–16; offered the exchequer by Baldwin in 1923; failed to find a constituency and remained chairman of a bank.

[3] The Unionists also insisted on excluding Haldane, the lord chancellor, because of his alleged pro-German sympathies. His two close friends, Grey and Asquith, made no effective protest. Asquith perhaps meant to send a message of explanation, but, write his biographers, 'the moment passed and Haldane went in silence'. Spender and Asquith, Asquith, ii. 167.

[4] Arthur James Balfour (1848–1930): educ. Eton and Cambridge; Unionist prime minister, 1902–5; former Unionist leader (resigned 1911); first lord of the admiralty, 1915–16; foreign secretary, 1916–19; lord president of the council, 1919–22, 1925–9; cr. Earl, 1922. Clemenceau called him 'cette vieille fille'.

[5] Edward Henry Carson (1854–1935): educ. Portarlington and Dublin; uncrowned 'king of Ulster'; attorney general, 1915; first lord of the admiralty, 1916–17; member of war cabinet, 1917–18; cr. Lord of Appeal, 1921. Dangerous in opposition, he was ineffective in office.

Opposition vanished.[1] A truce between the parties prevented contests at by-elections—at any rate until the appearance of unofficial candidates. The backbenchers on both sides were exasperated by this coalition between their leaders—a coalition indeed of the front benches against the back. The Liberals saw their government spirited out of existence without a word of explanation;[2] the Unionists were deprived of their expected victory. This was a perfect government, if the object of politics be to silence criticism. Could it be equally successful against the enemy?

NOTES

NOTE A. *The battle of the Marne.* The German strategy, devised by a deceased chief-of-staff, Schlieffen, aimed at turning the flank of the French by going through Belgium, and then encircling them. Moltke, the German chief-of-staff, carried out Schlieffen's plan, actually providing a stronger force than Schlieffen had postulated—fifty-five divisions instead of fifty-three. The plan worked. The Germans got beyond the end of the Allied line, and swung south. What were they to do as they approached Paris? They could not sit down and besiege the city, for this would destroy the momentum of their advance. If their 1st and 2nd armies divided, one going west of Paris and the other east, they could be attacked in detail by the Paris garrison; if they kept together and swung east of Paris, they offered an exposed flank to the Paris garrison. Schlieffen had foreseen this problem and failed to solve it. Hence he concluded that his plan was 'an undertaking for which we are too weak'. So it proved. Kluck's 1st army wavered to and fro like the tentacles of an octopus, as it approached Paris. First Kluck intended to go west of Paris. Then he hoped to encircle the French army before the Paris garrison noticed and so swung south-east. Finally, he swung west again to ward off the new French 6th army, which was threatening his flank from Paris. This created the gap into which the B.E.F. so cautiously advanced.

Who deserved the credit for the French counter-attack—Joffre, the commander-in-chief, or Galliéni, the commander in Paris? The answer seems to be: both, though with conflicting strategical ideas. Joffre planned to meet the German advance head on. Galliéni hoped to break through the German rear. In other words, Galliéni was trying to close the neck of the sack behind the Germans, while Joffre was actually hitting the bottom of the sack and so driving them out of Galliéni's trap. Joffre's forces were the stronger. Galliéni did not receive the reinforcements needed to carry out his

[1] The front Opposition bench was occupied by Henry Chaplin, as the senior ex-cabinet minister, but he did not lead an Opposition.

[2] Subsequently Asquith appeased his followers in twenty minutes of emotional oratory at the National Liberal Club. 'Some of the members were moved even to tears as was the Prime Minister himself.' Addison, *Four and a Half Years*, i. 80.

manœuvre. The Germans were able to hold their flank, indeed to force Galliéni back, and then to retreat in time. They were not defeated in battle. They retreated because they imagined themselves to be in a dangerous strategical position, as they were by peacetime standards. The battle of the Marne was a last manœuvre of the prewar type, not mutual slaughter on the first World war pattern. Hence its effect ran to nothing when the Germans dug trenches on the Aisne. Did the intervention of the B.E.F. make any difference? Not much. The Germans would have fallen back in any case when they saw the gap between their 1st and 2nd armies.

II

THE PRESSURES OF WAR, 1915–16

THE Coalition government, which Asquith announced on 26 May 1915, claimed to demonstrate national unity and to promote a more efficient conduct of the war. Only appearances were changed. The Liberals still cherished free enterprise and Free Trade; the Unionists still kicked against them. There was little unity even within the cabinet. McKenna soon turned against Lloyd George, for whom he was supposed to be deputizing. Lloyd George's impatience, he complained, was 'wrecking before capture'. McKenna himself was content with wrecking. Runciman, at the board of trade, opposed every creative suggestion. Some Unionist ministers, Curzon in particular, wrote off loyalty to Law, their leader. Asquith behaved like a referee in the boxing ring, supervising the combats of others, not as a reconciler of differences, still less as a national leader asserting authority over his subordinates. Each minister still ran his department in isolation and occasionally sniped at his colleagues. Though the national effort grew steadily, this was imposed from outside, by the enemy and by popular pressure, not by any coordinated direction. It was a last experiment in running a great war on the principles of *laissez faire*.

Lloyd George at the ministry of munitions provided the great exception. His year of office there transformed British economy, and his own national standing also. Though he told the workers of Clydeside: 'Boys, I'm as keen a Socialist as any of you', his acts sprang from no doctrine of policy; they were the response of genius to the challenge of events. When Lloyd George entered the requisitioned hotel which was to house the new ministry, he found no tables, no staff, and too many mirrors. By the end of the war the ministry was employing a staff of 65,000, and had over three million workers under its direction. The cabinet set up a committee to control the new ministry. The committee met once and then dispersed, never to meet again. The ordnance board of the war office was suspended in

December 1915. Lloyd George ruled alone and provided munitions far exceeding the demands of the war office. By 1918, though not before, the ministry of munitions actually caught up with the army's appetite for shells. Haig[1] reported that 'two machine guns per battalion were more than sufficient'. Kitchener thought that four per battalion might be useful, and anything more a luxury. Lloyd George said: 'Take Kitchener's figure. Square it. Multiply by two. Then double again for good luck.' The army began the war with 1,330 machine guns. During the war 240,506 were manufactured—thanks to Lloyd George. The war office turned down the Stokes light mortar, one of the best weapons of the war. Lloyd George got an Indian maharajah to finance its manufacture out of his own pocket. The admiralty, under Churchill's impulse, were already experimenting with armoured tractors or 'tanks', though Kitchener dismissed them as 'a pretty mechanical toy'. The ministry of munitions took them over, and made them a practical instrument of war.

The ministry was, as Lloyd George wrote, 'from first to last a business man organisation'. Staffed by businessmen, it naturally handled other businessmen gently. In theory, the government had power to requisition, based on an obscure clause in the Army Act, and more doubtfully on the prerogative.[2] In March 1915 two army officers demonstrated the efficacy of this power by requisitioning a million and a half sandbags in Liverpool one Saturday afternoon.[3] Thereafter the government could control an industry by requisitioning its raw material. The ministry of munitions did this with steel; the war office (which still clothed and fed the troops) with leather and later with wool. Manufacturers were therefore glad to accept the system of 'costing', which gave them the costs of production plus 'a reasonable profit'; a system legalized

---

[1] Douglas Haig (1861–1928): commanded 1st Army Corps, 1914, First Army, 1915; commander-in-chief in France, 1915–19; of Home Forces, 1919–21; cr. Earl and given £100,000 by parliament, 1919; given Bemersyde Mansion by public subscription, 1920; president of British Legion, 1921–8.

[2] In 1920 this latter power was successfully challenged in the courts on the ground that the government could not do by prerogative anything which they had power to do by statute. An Indemnity Act was hastily passed to protect the government from the bill of £700 million which they would otherwise have had to pay. Here, as elsewhere, men were reluctant to restrain the government until the war was over, and 'war socialism' rested to some extent on consent.

[3] They paid 2d. a sack, where the merchants were asking 6d.

in 1916 by a clause in D.O.R.A., though the house of commons did not realize what it was doing. The system worked satisfactorily where the government were dealing with a few large firms, all roughly on the same level of efficiency, and the ministry of munitions had some check on the costs of production in the 218 national factories which it set up. Usually, however, costs had to be those of the least efficient firm. This was particularly true in the munitions industry itself, where 20,000 small factories were hurriedly built or converted to catch the £2,000 million which the ministry of munitions dispersed. It was a great achievement to provide for an army of four million men within a couple of years. The price was a crop of profiteers, men who shot up from nothing to great fortunes (and often later down again). These men subsequently sustained Lloyd George, to mutual advantage.

Labour, on the other hand, was handled from outside. No union official was employed in the ministry of munitions, and Henderson had to be called in from the board of education whenever there was a crisis. Nor was any existing government department competent to deal with labour questions. The hand-to-mouth growth of welfare had produced a chaos of authorities. The local government board ran the Poor Law; the home office administered the factory acts; the board of trade ran the labour exchanges created in 1909; autonomous commissions directed National Insurance. During the early months of the war the two service departments distributed 'badges' to their respective munitions workers: the admiralty, always lavish, gave out 400,000, the war office only 80,000. These perhaps protected workers from white feathers. They could not keep men fixed at their jobs nor prevent their joining the army. By June 1915 one fifth of the male workers in engineering had enlisted, at a time when the army could not equip the men it already had. The ministry of munitions extended the system of 'badges' and resisted further recruitment. In July 1915 an act of parliament laid down that a munitions worker could not be taken on by another firm within six weeks of leaving his last job, unless he had a leaving certificate from his previous employer. This was intended to prevent 'poaching'. In practice, it tied the worker to his existing wage and to a bad employer. Labour hated the leaving certificate as an instrument of industrial conscription. Strikes and 'go slow' made it more trouble than it was worth, and it was abandoned in July 1917. Henceforth a worker could be kept in munitions only by the threat of call-up if he left the industry.

Before the war there was no mass army, and no idea that one would ever come into existence. Shortage of munitions was therefore inevitable. Men looked, however, for easier explanations. They blamed slackness. Of course workers, who were receiving high wages for the first time in their lives, did not always turn up regularly. The optimism of government statements weakened any sense of urgency. One union leader complained: 'We have made sufficient progress now to have crossed the earth if what the papers say is true.'[1] The workers were also alleged to be spending their money on heavy drinking. In the last days of the Liberal government, Lloyd George proposed state purchase of the 'liquor traffic', a scheme which he hoped would also please his somewhat estranged Radical admirers. The 'trade' reluctantly acquiesced. The temperance advocates, however, revolted, and the scheme was dropped. Restriction took its place. Hours of drinking were cut down; in particular, the afternoon gap (still with us) was imposed—a lasting memorial of the Great War. An experiment in state ownership (also still with us) was tried at Carlisle, in the neighbourhood of a large munitions centre at Gretna. Beer was reduced in strength, and its price increased. Though these measures halved the consumption of beer by 1918, they were unpopular with the working classes and gave an easy handle to demagogues like Bottomley, who combined denunciation of liquor control with demands for a more energetic conduct of the war. Exhortation was also tried. George V was persuaded to take the King's Pledge of total abstention for the duration of the war. No one followed his example except Kitchener—certainly not Lloyd George, still less Asquith. The ruling class of the time continued to consume champagne.

Improvement of working conditions did more to reduce absenteeism. Lloyd George called in, among other businessmen, the cocoa magnate, Seebohm Rowntree, advocate of industrial welfare. Factory canteens could be written off against wartime taxation and now first became a general feature of British industry. The ministry of munitions itself promoted 867 of them. All this did little to touch the real problem: the shortage of

[1] Q. Huwtz, *State Intervention*, 118.

labour. The appeal of higher wages helped; so, too, did the desire to avoid military service and, to a lesser extent, the return of wounded men from the army. The gap remained.[1] Women did something to fill it. In July 1915 Christabel Pankhurst, the militant suffragette, staged her last demonstration. Thirty thousand women marched down Whitehall with the slogan: 'We demand the right to serve.'

The demand was soon granted. Nearly 200,000 women entered government departments. Half a million took over the clerical work in private offices. Women acted as conductors on trams and buses. A quarter of a million worked on the land.[2] The greatest increase of women workers was in the engineering shops: here almost 800,000 were recruited, mostly in the first year after July 1915. Against this there was one striking decline: domestic servants were fewer by 400,000. Of course, not all this work survived the war, emphatically not in the engineering trades. Much did. The male clerk with his quill pen and copperplate handwriting had gone for good. The female shorthand-typist took his place. It was a decisive moment in women's emancipation. Women became more independent and more enterprising. The woman worker in munitions paid for her round of drinks at the public house. Practical needs revolutionized fashion. Never again did skirts sweep the ground. The petticoat disappeared, though not for good. Women's hats became neater. A few women cut their hair, though the 'bob' and its successors were not really established until after the war.

The arrival of women caused turmoil in the engineering shops. Few women were in unions. None cared about established craft practices. They cared about 'equal pay', which Lloyd George had promised for piece work only, and which the men opposed. The union officials, though pledged to dilution by the treasury agreement, had to proceed warily, negotiating

[1] Some 4·9 million industrial workers joined the armed forces. Set off 650,000 for the natural increase of population, and 290,000 for the postponement of retirement, &c. Women provided 1·6 million; Belgians 60,000; 700,000 wounded men returned from the army. Dearle, *The Labour Cost of the Great War*, 259, calculates the average net loss of labour during the war as 1·6 million men or, allowing for the inferior capacity of women, 2 million.

[2] In addition, nearly 100,000 women joined the auxiliary services of the three armed forces, now first instituted (except for F.A.N.Y.). Rather more than 100,000 became nurses (mostly V.A.D.); 30,000 worked in the Y.M.C.A. These figures do not include the unpaid voluntary workers, mostly middle class, in canteens and other welfare services.

for each craft on a geographical basis. Against them, and against the government, the shop stewards acted for all workers in the shop, whatever their craft and whether members of a union or not. The shop stewards were often revolutionary socialists, particularly on Clydeside; some of them were opposed to the war. Essentially they represented a working-class interest wider than trade union conservatism, and Lloyd George was often tempted to work with them against the established union leaders. It was Henderson's job, as conciliator, to keep him in line. Women were not the only cause of industrial unrest. Resentment against high profits counted even more. The most militant workers were often also the most patriotic—South Wales and Clydeside, the two centres of industrial discontent, also provided the highest proportion in the country of recruits for the army. But the workers were unwilling to sacrifice their rights, or to work overtime, if this brought increased profits to their employers, as it inevitably did. The government dared not act effectively against the bosses; therefore, however unwilling, they had to conciliate the workers also.

The government had great powers on paper. In July 1915 the treasury agreement was given the force of law. Henceforth strikes or resistance to dilution in the munitions industry could be punished in the courts. Lloyd George would not use this bludgeon. He appreciated instinctively that any threat of industrial conscription would provoke working-class resistance. He preferred conciliation. In July 1915 the miners of South Wales struck in order to enforce the closed shop. Runciman, at the board of trade, wished to use the powers of the law against them. Lloyd George settled the strike by conceding the demands of the miners behind Runciman's back. His intervention on Clydeside was less successful. On Christmas Day 1915 Lloyd George, supported by Henderson, addressed a rowdy meeting of 3,000 shop stewards in Glasgow. His oratory miscarried. Coercion was then attempted. The socialist paper, *Forward*, was suppressed for publishing an accurate account of Lloyd George's attempt to speak. David Kirkwood, the chief shop steward, was deported to Edinburgh.

Soon there was a return to conciliation. As time went on, the ministry of munitions worked hand in hand with the revolutionary shop stewards, despite growls of protest from the union officials. In 1917 Churchill, then minister of munitions, asked

Kirkwood to return to Glasgow as shop steward at Beardmore's, the greatest works on Clydeside. Munitions were produced throughout the war without any direct compulsion of labour, and there were no serious strikes, despite the talk of labour unrest or later of 'Bolshevik' shop stewards. Working days lost in strikes during the war years averaged a quarter of those lost before the war and only a tenth of those lost immediately after it.[1] No doubt simple patriotism was the main reason for this industrial peace. Lloyd George was the only man high in government who contributed to it, and this ability to handle labour was a great asset for him when he entered the decisive struggle for power in December 1916.

Lloyd George's success at the ministry of munitions did not stand quite alone. In September 1915 McKenna introduced an effective war budget, with some attempt to promote taxes against the swelling expenditure. Since every increase of indirect taxation increased the cost of living (and hence labour discontent), most of McKenna's new money came from direct taxes. Income tax went up to 3s. 6d. in the pound, and the exemption limit was lowered. There were two innovations of principle. To meet the outcry against war profits, McKenna imposed an excess-profits duty of 50 per cent. (raised to 80 per cent. in 1917) on any increase in prewar profits. This somewhat clumsy instrument did not prevent 'profiteering', but it provided in all a quarter of the total tax revenue in the war period. McKenna also imposed duties at 33⅓ per cent. on a number of supposedly luxury articles such as motor cars, clocks, and watches. These duties were intended to reduce 'luxury' imports rather than for any Protectionist purpose. All the same, they were a sin against Free Trade. Lloyd George threw a note across the cabinet table to Walter Long,[2] an extreme Protectionist: 'So the old system *goes* destroyed by its own advocates';[3] and the McKenna duties, as they were called, dismayed rank-and-file Liberals. They seemed to be the first price of Coalition.

---

[1] Days lost in strikes (yearly average) 1915–18: 4·2 million. In 1910–14: 17·9 million. In 1919–21: 49·1 million.

[2] Walter Long (1854–1924): educ. Harrow and Oxford; M.P., 1882–1921; president of local government board, 1915–16; colonial secretary, 1916–19; first lord of the admiralty, 1919–21; cr. Viscount, 1921. Chesterton wrote (incorrectly):
   Walter, beware! scorn not the gathering throng . . .
   It suffers, but it cannot suffer Long.

[3] Hewins, *Apologia of an Imperialist*, ii. 52.

The increased taxes did not go far to meet the increasing expenditure, though they did a little better when income tax was pushed up first to 5s. in the pound (1916), and ultimately to 6s. (1918), and when taxable incomes themselves increased. In 1915–16 only a fifth of the national expenditure was being met from taxation; the later improvement only raised this to 30 per cent. Even treasury officials were not much disturbed by this. The budget was artificially divided into a normal peacetime budget, which was balanced in the ordinary way, and wartime expenses, which were left to look after themselves. McKenna even laid down the doctrine that there need be no limit on government borrowing so long as taxation was enough to cover interest and sinking fund on the National Debt. With his blessing this rose, during the war, from £625 million to £7,809 million. War loan provoked a patriotic campaign second only to that for recruiting. Men supposed that they were somehow shifting the cost of the war on to the shoulders of future generations. Actually, in physical terms, the war had to be paid for while it was on, and war loans—unlike increased direct taxes— were merely a promise that any sacrifice made by the wealthier classes would be temporary.[1] In any case, much of this sacrifice never took place. The rate of interest on war loan, usually 5 per cent., was kept unnecessarily high in the belief that otherwise foreign money would leave the country. Moreover, the money, subscribed to war loan, often came from bank credits and even more often from the government, who were thus paying interest on money which they had themselves manufactured. The rich had actually more money to spend than before as the result of their patriotic lending. Yet there were fewer goods. Prices therefore rose, until by 1919 the pound bought only a third of what it had done in 1914. Wages lagged behind until late in 1917.[2] The burden of increased prices fell on the poor, who thus paid for the war without getting the credit.

Inflationary finance was not the only cause of the rise in prices. War pushed up the price of manufactured goods at home. The price of imports rose still more. Great Britain had, however, no difficulty in paying for her imports during the first World

---

[1] This did not apply to the smaller sums raised later from the poorer classes by National Savings.

[2] Or rather wage rates lagged. Increased overtime did something to redress the balance.

war. Exports, though much reduced in volume, brought in as much sterling as before the war, thanks to the rise in their price. British services, such as shipping, also brought higher profits. Great Britain's international balance of payments, as a result, actually remained favourable until the last year of the war.[1] There was a more limited exchange problem. The war increased the British need for supplies from the United States, without increasing British exports to them. There was therefore a dollar shortage, which was met partly by loans on the American market, partly by sales (some voluntary, some, from 1917 on, compulsory) of American securities held by British citizens. At the end of the war, men noted sadly this loss of some £207 million invested in the United States. They failed to notice that British foreign investments elsewhere had gone up during the war by £250 million. Even so, the pound sterling held its own on the international exchange by its own strength. There was no exchange control during the first World war, no check on the export of capital, theoretically not even an embargo on the export of gold.[2] Indeed, if Great Britain had been fighting the war alone, she would have come out with her international financial position slightly stronger than when she had gone in.

This rosy picture was changed by the lavish loans which Great Britain distributed to her allies—oddly, without any parliamentary sanction. The British government imagined that they could not only conduct war on a continental scale such as they had never attempted before, but could also finance their allies as they had done during earlier wars. Russia received £586 million, France £434 million, Italy £412 million; a total, including lesser countries and the Dominions, of £1,825 million. This could not be covered from British resources. It was met largely by American loans (something over £1,000 million in all), particularly after the United States entered the war in 1917. The problem was ignored during the war. When mentioned, it was obscured by the assumption, held even by McKenna, that the loans to the allies were solid assets which would be repaid in full when the war was over.

[1] There was a favourable balance of £200 million in 1915; of £101 million in 1916; an equal balance in 1917; and an unfavourable balance of £107 million in 1918.

[2] In practice, the export of gold was prevented at first by penal rates of insurance and, later, by the refusal of export licences.

The wartime problem was not shortage of money with which to buy goods abroad. It was shortage of ships with which to carry them. Requisitioning for naval and military purposes took nearly a quarter of British shipping out of ordinary service in the course of 1915. The shipyards could not fill the gap. Their claims on men and materials were eclipsed by those of the admiralty and the ministry of munitions; their output sank to a third of the prewar figure. In 1915 the Germans added to British difficulties. They answered the British blockade by using submarines to sink merchant ships. The submarines, or U-boats, had to sink without warning if they were to achieve any effective results, and this brought a moral condemnation on the Germans which the almost invisible British blockade escaped.

The greatest German stroke was to sink the *Lusitania*, a ship carrying passengers (including some American citizens) and also munitions, in May 1915. This act, barbarous by the standards of the time, produced anti-German riots in England. At Liverpool, troops had to be called in after three days of general destruction. The German knights of the Garter were solemnly struck off the roll, and their banners removed from the chapel at Windsor. More seriously, the sinking of the *Lusitania* provoked strong protest from President Wilson of the United States. The Germans, who were in any case short of submarines, offered to end the sinkings if the British would allow food through the blockade. Grey favoured the offer. The admiralty turned it down. Somewhat later the Germans, after sinking more passenger ships and provoking more protests from Wilson, imposed restrictions on their submarines all the same. There was no sinking at sight during most of 1916, and the more limited submarine attacks, though still a nuisance, were kept under control. This was, of course, gain for the British. It was also loss. The comparative ease with which they had overcome this first threat led them to neglect precautions against a more powerful campaign later.

In another way, also then regarded as barbarous, the British people had their first direct experience of war. The first Zeppelin appeared over the British coast on 29 December 1914. London was bombarded from the air in April 1915; and when the lighter-than-air ships proved vulnerable, aeroplanes followed them. The raids provided much drama, with British 'aces' shooting the clumsy German machines down from the sky. The effects were trivial by the standards of the second World war—1,117 civilians and 296 combatants lost their lives as a result of bombing from the air. The raids, however, caused much dislocation and outcry. Lighting restrictions were imposed throughout the country, and factories stopped work when a single raider was sighted far away. The U-boats and the Zeppelins heightened popular hysteria. Leading ministers were denounced as weaklings, if not traitors. There was a demand for reprisals against German submarine crews, taken prisoner: a demand to which the admiralty disgracefully yielded, despite a protest from George V,[1] until the Germans retaliated in kind. Pemberton Billing, the first man to challenge the party truce successfully (at East Hertfordshire in March 1916), owed his success mainly to being the 'member for air'. He can claim the credit for initiating the modern doctrine that war should be directed indiscriminately against civilians, not against the armed forces of the enemy. The Royal Air Force was created before the war ended, specifically to practise what Pemberton Billing preached.

These were still side-issues. The war meant predominantly the war on land. Here the Coalition government did not improve on their predecessors. The war council was dissolved with the government which had created it. Only in June 1915, after almost a month's delay, was the Dardanelles committee set up to replace it.[2] It had ten members, chosen to satisfy the balance of parties, not for their competence, and every recommendation was fought over again in cabinet a second time. Kitchener gave little guidance. He trembled at the blow to British prestige in the Orient if the attack at Gallipoli failed; he trembled still more at Joffre's indignation if men and supplies were diverted from the western front. Churchill again took the initiative, despite his humble position. In mid-June the Dardanelles committee resolved to reinforce Hamilton. Kitchener could only give five raw divisions, thus raising Hamilton's force to twelve— the Turks had by now fifteen in Gallipoli. What was worse, Kitchener refused to move any experienced general from the western front and, insisting on 'Army List seniority', sent out the elderly Stopford, who had never commanded in war.

[1] Nicolson, *George V*, 272.
[2] The western front was still expected to run itself.

On 6 August Hamilton again achieved surprise in a landing
at Suvla bay. Again nothing was made of it. Stopford remained
on board ship and slept throughout the afternoon. Even personal
promptings from Hamilton did not shake him. The men settled
down to bathe on the peaceful beach, while the surrounding
hills were empty of the enemy. The Turks had time to take up
position. By 10 August a new line of trenches had been formed,
as unbreakable as the others. Asquith wrote: 'The generals and
staffs engaged in the Suvla part of the business ought to be
court-martialled and dismissed from the Army.'[1] Stopford
was sent home, at his own request. The British forces clung
to the barren coast, like a climber stranded halfway up a rock
face.

The British government thought that they had decided
against any fresh offensive on the western front until Kitchener's
armies could take the field in 1916. French and his senior army
commander, Haig, agreed with this policy of waiting. On 6
July 1915 leading British ministers met their French colleagues
at Calais: the first inter-allied conference ever held and the
precursor of many such meetings in both World wars. Kitchener,
with his fluent French, dominated the proceedings, and the
British view was apparently accepted, to everyone's surprise.
The offensive was indefinitely postponed. This was a deception. Kitchener went for a walk with Joffre and promised not to
oppose an offensive in the autumn if Hamilton's further attack
at Gallipoli were allowed to take place first. A little later he
accepted from Joffre, a new instruction to French: 'Initiative
in combined action of the British and French forces devolves
on the French Commander-in-Chief, notably as regards effec-
tives, objectives, dates.'[2] Kitchener sent this instruction to
French without informing the cabinet or the Dardanelles
committee.

After Hamilton's failure, Joffre presented his bill, and Kitchener honoured it. He told the Dardanelles committee: 'We
have to make war as we must and not as we should like to.'[3]
The French ministers, who had no faith in an offensive, agreed
to it in order to please Kitchener; the British ministers agreed
in order to please the French. Joffre insisted that the British

[1] Magnus, *Kitchener*, 347.
[2] *Military Operations: France and Belgium, 1915*, ii. 125.
[3] Churchill, *World Crisis*, ii. 465.

should attack at Loos (25 September–13 October), in a district of mining villages. The German line was shaken. British reserves arrived too late to take advantage of this. The British suffered 50,000 casualties against 20,000 German. French had kept his reserves too far in the rear and made matters worse, from his own point of view, by blaming Haig for this in his official report.

Loos brought doom to Sir John French. Kitchener had long lacked faith in him, or perhaps never had any, and was in correspondence with Haig behind his back. Haig had other means of influence. He and his wife were highly regarded by the royal family—they were the first couple not of royal blood to be married in the private chapel at Buckingham Palace, and he wrote to the king constantly on military affairs, no doubt from patriotic motives. George V said to Kitchener, with his usual common sense: 'If anyone acted like that, and told tales out of school, he would at school be called a sneak.' Kitchener replied: 'We are beyond the schoolboys' age.'[1] French was not the only one endangered. Most ministers had lost faith in Kitchener; some of the more resolute were determined to have done with the Dardanelles. Kitchener wavered despairingly. On 11 October he proposed to reinforce Hamilton. Three days later Hamilton was superseded, and Sir Charles Monro sent from France to take his place. Monro recommended evacuation within twenty-four hours of arriving at Gallipoli. Kitchener could not stomach this and appealed to Monro's subordinates against it. The Dardanelles committee was at sixes and sevens: Churchill and Curzon still for going on, Lloyd George and Law eager for coming out. The French, usually against distractions, increased the confusion by urging an expedition to Salonika, in belated aid for Serbia.

Asquith produced an adroit solution, in his usual spirit of 'wait and see': Kitchener should be sent out to write Monro's report all over again. Meanwhile, Asquith himself would take over the war office and carry through sweeping changes. He explained to Lloyd George: 'We avoid by this method of procedure the immediate supersession of K. as war Minister, while attaining the same result.'[2] The plan miscarried. Kitchener duly went. But on 6 November the *Globe* reported that he was about

---

[1] Haig, *Private Papers*, 98.
[2] Asquith to Lloyd George, 3 Nov. 1915. Lloyd George, *War Memoirs*, i. 520.

to resign. Kitchener was still a popular figure. Public opinion was disturbed. The *Globe* was suppressed for a fortnight, and when it reappeared had to state that there were 'no grounds of dissension between Kitchener and his colleagues such as to affect their future ministerial co-operation'. After this it was impossible to get rid of Kitchener, and he obstinately refused to stay in the Near East.

When he returned he found that things had changed. The Dardanelles committee had gone, and Churchill with it.[1] In its place was a war committee with fewer members[2] and supposedly wider powers. Sir John French had gone,[3] and Sir Douglas Haig became commander-in-chief in France. Kitchener, too, had virtually gone. Sir William Robertson[4] had become chief of the imperial general staff and wrote his own terms of appointment. Henceforth the C.I.G.S. alone, not the secretary of state for war, was to determine strategy. He alone was to advise the government. He alone was to issue orders to the commanders in the field. Kitchener's functions, in his own words, were 'curtailed to the feeding and clothing of the army'. He wished to resign, but was persuaded that it was his duty to remain. In any case, he told Robertson: 'I need leisure to think. I have no fear as to our final victory, but many fears as to our making a good peace.'[5] Actually he did no thinking. He remained only as a patriotic symbol—'the great poster' of Margot Asquith's wounding phrase—still worshipped by the public, disregarded and even despised by his colleagues.

Haig and Robertson between them set their stamp on British experience in the first World war. They were the supreme 'Brass Hats'. Haig was certainly a stabler character than Sir John French: resolute in command, loyal to subordinates, unruffled by defeat. He was as able a staff officer as any in the British army, unrivalled in his mastery of railway timetables. He was

---

[1] For the next eighteen months Churchill commanded a battalion in France.

[2] Initially Asquith, Balfour, Kitchener, Grey, and Lloyd George. Law was forced in by the Unionists ten days later; and McKenna was added also to balance him.

[3] Asquith told him he was needed at home to advise against Kitchener.

[4] Sir William Robertson (1860–1933): first field-marshal to start in the ranks; chief of staff in France, 1915; C.I.G.S., 1915–18; Eastern Command, 1918; commander-in-chief, Home Forces, 1918, of Army on the Rhine, 1919–20; cr. Baronet and voted £10,000 by parliament, 1919. The dropping of aspirates, attributed to him in many delightful stories, is probably mythical.

[5] Arthur, *Kitchener*, iii. 299.

confident that he could win the war, though he did not know how. Like most British generals of the time, he disliked politicians, especially Liberals, and got on badly with them. All the same, he was more adroit and supple than he seemed, and this hidden skill enabled him to out-manœuvre even Lloyd George, though only just.

Robertson was more direct and more obstinate. He claimed greater power than any British general before or since: virtually that of supreme command over all British armies.[1] His main concern was to deny civilian ministers any say in the conduct of the war.[2] Far from acting as chief adviser to the government on strategy, he refused to supply them with strategical information. He met all civilian criticism or suggestion with the reply: 'I've 'eard different.' His own mind was clear. The Germans, he believed, could be beaten only by beating their main army in France. He reiterated that the British armies were in France because this was the principal theatre of war and that everything else must be sacrificed to it.

Robertson's firm hand was shown at once over Gallipoli. Kitchener refused to recommend evacuation, though admitting that it must take place. Admiral Wemyss,[3] who was acting temporarily for de Robeck, believed that the navy could force the Straits. The war committee proposed to abandon two beaches and to hang on at one. Robertson stamped on all these suggestions and insisted on ending the entire enterprise. Suvla and Anzac beaches were evacuated on 18 and 19 December, Helles beach on 8 January 1916—all three without loss, the successful end to a sad adventure. The Gallipoli campaign was to cause interminable controversy later. Twice it seemed to have come near to success; twice it had failed allegedly from lack of men and supplies. On a wider view, it failed rather from lack of room. Gallipoli, far from being an easy backdoor into Germany, was a narrow, tight crack, and stronger forces would not have made the crack wider. They would only have increased

---

[1] The Duke of Marlborough, who had something approaching the same power, was also a politician.

[2] According to the talk at G.H.Q., Robertson's original intention was to have a war committee of the C.I.G.S., the First Sea Lord, and no civilian minister. Bourget, *Gouvernement et Commandement*, 117.

[3] Rosslyn Erskine Wemyss (1864–1933), second in command at Dardanelles, 1915–16; first sea lord, 1917–19; did not receive thanks of parliament or money grant, 1919; cr. Baron Wester Wemyss, 1919.

the congestion on the peninsula. The campaign could have succeeded only if it had been fought somewhere else. No doubt it helped to wear down Turkish strength and made some demand on German supplies. Otherwise nothing redeemed the blow to British prestige.

Failure at Gallipoli had a lasting consequence. Rightly or wrongly, there was never again a serious attempt to break into Germany from behind, until the very end of the war when her armies were already defeated. The westerners won, despite a continuing argument. Not that withdrawal from Gallipoli freed men for the western front. A quarter of a million men were kept in Egypt to guard the Suez canal from an imagined Turkish attack. Next the British forces crossed the desert of Sinai in order to make the canal yet more secure and then advanced progressively further for no particular purpose. Some of the Arab tribes were induced to revolt against Turkish rule, and a young Oxford archaeologist, T. E. Lawrence, acquired legendary fame as their leader. His adventures, aided by his considerable literary gifts, made him the only old-style hero of the first World war. At the end of 1917 the British armies captured Jerusalem—Lloyd George's Christmas present to the British people. A year later, when the war ended, the armies, now swelled to half a million men, were still plodding forward along the Syrian coast. This was a romantic campaign, redolent of history, where a cavalry engagement could be dignified with the name Armageddon. But little harm was done to the Germans.

In Mesopotamia the Indian government had already embarked on a campaign of their own to protect the Persian oil wells, which supplied the British navy. There was a medley of authorities: the commander in Mesopotamia; the commander-in-chief in India; the viceroy; the India office in London. Between them, they propelled the British forces towards Baghdad. Early in 1916 the advance was speeded up to atone for the failure at Gallipoli. It ran into failure. In April 1916 Townshend surrendered at Kut with 10,000 men. Fresh forces were sent to redeem the disaster: 300,000 troops were finally committed. As well, the French insisted on keeping an army at Salonika, though Serbia, which it had been intended to relieve, had been overrun. The British government tried to refuse, then agreed that the Allied army should remain there 'on a temporary

basis'. It remained throughout the war: 600,000 Allied troops—
200,000 of them British—more or less interned at Salonika by
a Bulgarian army[1] which would otherwise have played no part
in the war. Thus, despite Robertson's disapproval of 'side
shows', over a million men, and sometimes nearer two million,
were diverted from the Western front.

The continental Allies, and particularly the French, suspected that the British were picking up the spoils of empire,
while the French and Russians were bleeding to death in Europe.
The British tried to remove this suspicion by a series of partition treaties. On 12 March 1915, as a preliminary to the
attack on Gallipoli, they agreed with the Russian government
that Constantinople and the Straits should go to Russia, 'subject
to the war . . . being brought to a successful conclusion'. They
received in exchange Russian consent to their absorbing the
neutral zone in Persia and a free hand (or so they thought) in
settling Asiatic Turkey. Subsequently they negotiated with the
French a partition of Turkey-in-Asia, an agreement never
properly concluded, though the British secured Mesopotamia
and Palestine partly by its means.[2] As well, the Allies bribed
Italy into the war by the treaty of London (26 April 1915),
which promised her Tyrol, Istria, and north Dalmatia without
Fiume (Rijeka). These 'secret treaties' caused much outcry
when they were revealed by the Bolsheviks. Even before then
the British government were accused of fighting in order to
give Constantinople to Russia and Alsace-Lorraine to France,
or to add Asiatic Turkey to the British Empire. This was not so.
The British government did not underwrite the French claim
to Alsace and Lorraine until October 1917, and the secret
treaties (except for the treaty of London, which promised
unconditionally what Italy 'will receive') were attempts to
avoid conflict between the allies after victory, not definitions
of the objects for which the war was being fought. They evaded
the real problem: what to do about Germany. No answer
was found to this problem while the war was on, nor after it
ended.

The British people were clear why they had gone to war: it
was for the sake of Belgium. Liberation of Belgium, and full
reparation, remained always their primary aim, and the Ger-

---

[1] Bulgaria entered the war against the Allies in Nov. 1915.
[2] See Note A, p. 70.

mans would have caused great turmoil in British opinion if they had offered it—which, fortunately for national unity, they never did. But this was not enough. The British could not be content with righting the wrong done to Belgium; they wanted a guarantee that it would never happen again. How was this to be done? The obvious answer was the defeat of Germany, and from this it followed that there need be no war aim except victory.

Many people did not like this barren conclusion and dreamt of some organization which would make future war impossible. Though the actual phrase, a League of Nations, was invented by Lowes Dickinson, an opponent of the war, it was taken up by many who were also fervent for the defeat of Germany: by H. G. Wells, by most Liberal newspapers, by Grey himself. There was deep confusion in this proposal. Some supposed that it could be achieved only after victory over Germany; others that it made victory unnecessary. Those who were sceptical of idealistic solutions also split into two: a majority hoped for a crushing military victory, others favoured a 'realistic' peace of compromise with a return to the conditions of 1914. In general, British people thought themselves engaged in 'a war to end war', and expected victory to provide this of itself.

A small minority was dissatisfied with this negative attitude. In September 1914 the scattered remnants of those who had opposed entry into the war set up the Union of Democratic Control, in order to ensure that the diplomatic errors or crimes which had, in their opinion, caused the war should never be made again. Ramsay MacDonald was the outstanding politician of the group. E. D. Morel, the secretary, supplied the attacks on secret diplomacy, and also the plans for a better way. The outlook of the U.D.C. won some support from middle-class intellectuals. It was also shared by the Independent Labour Party, which—though affiliated to the Labour party—became increasingly critical of the war. The two U.D.C. demands for ending the war by negotiation and for open or democratic diplomacy afterwards, were theoretically distinct. No one troubled to distinguish them in the hysteria of the time. The supporters of the U.D.C. tended to think of themselves as 'pacifists' (a word used now for the first time), and so, still more, did others. Meetings of the U.D.C. were broken up by soldiers on leave. Morel himself was imprisoned, and Bertrand Russell, a prominent supporter, fined, on trumped-up charges.[1] Passion drowned any cool discussion of war aims. All the same, like Charles James Fox in an earlier period of patriotic frenzy, though E. D. Morel lost the present, he won the future. There was no peace by negotiation, but in the end the ghost of E. D. Morel determined British foreign policy.[2]

Public opinion, as voiced by the *Daily Mail* and by the demagogues of the recruiting platforms, was impatient with all such discussions. Victory was its sole concern. The war still seemed a long way off: something 'over there', as symbolized by the leave trains departing each night from Victoria Station. At home, life rolled on almost unaffected. There was plenty of food, and, indeed, of everything else. Statesmen still appeared in top hats. Businessmen rarely lapsed into bowlers. Some standards were slightly relaxed. Short black jackets took the place of tail coats for evening dress. Some men wore unstarched collars at the weekend. Maidservants, instead of footmen, handed round the sandwiches at afternoon tea and were to be seen even in west end clubs. War brought some minor benefits. The zip-fastener escaped from the ban which the makers of buttons had long imposed upon it. Life in the trenches popularized safety razors and toothpaste (instead of powder). Entertainment became more entertaining: no more plays by Galsworthy or Bernard Shaw. Instead, George Robey and Violet Lorraine appeared in the *Bing Boys* and sang: 'If you were the only girl in the world.' A comparatively worthless musical play, *Chu Chin Chow*, established what was for many years a record-breaking run.[3] The spirit of 1915 was best expressed by Ian Hay, a writer of light fiction, in *The First Hundred Thousand* —a book which treated soldiering as a joke, reviving 'the best days of our lives' at some imaginary public school.

Popular feeling wanted some dramatic action. The agitation crystallized around the demand for compulsory military service. This was a political gesture, not a response to practical need.

---

[1] Morel was imprisoned for sending printed matter to a neutral country (though he had supposed the recipient to be in France). Russell was fined for a pamphlet which was alleged to discourage recruiting. Russell was also deprived of his lectureship at Trinity College, Cambridge, despite the protests of Fellows who were on active service. In 1944 Russell was elected a Fellow of Trinity.

[2] See below, 199.

[3] The record was broken in the nineteen-fifties by Agatha Christie's detective play, *The Mousetrap*, which threatened to run for ever.

The army had more men than it could equip, and voluntary recruitment would more than fill the gap, at any rate until the end of 1916. Auckland Geddes,[1] who was in the best position to know, later pronounced this verdict: 'The imposition of military conscription added little if anything to the effective sum of our war efforts.'[2] However, there was a general belief that thousands of 'slackers'—650,000 was the figure usually given—were somehow evading their country's call. In the autumn of 1915 the question of conscription broke into a blaze. Some Unionist ministers threatened to resign unless it were adopted. They were seconded by Lloyd George, who was looking for new worlds to conquer now that the ministry of munitions was running at full spate. Asquith produced an ingenious evasion. Lord Derby,[3] though an advocate of conscription, was set to organize a scheme by which men of military age 'attested' their willingness to serve when called upon. The Liberals were told that this would avoid conscription, the Unionists that it was the preliminary to it. The Labour leaders were especially strong for a scheme which would, they believed, save the voluntary system. Two and a half million men attested, thanks largely to Labour advocacy.

Asquith sold the pass, perhaps without meaning to do so. He promised that no attested married men should be called up until all unmarried men had been taken. Did this mean only attested unmarried men or all unmarried men whether attested or not? Asquith did not explain. The answer of public opinion was clear: the married men would have felt outrageously cheated if they had been called up while a single unmarried man walked the streets. Compulsory service was now inevitable. In January 1916 Asquith took the plunge. The first Military Service act ended voluntary recruitment and imposed compulsion on unmarried men between the ages of 18 and 41.[4] The

---

[1] Auckland Geddes (1879–1954): educ. George Watson's College and Edinburgh; professor of anatomy at McGill University; director of national service, 1917–19; president of board of trade, 1919–20; ambassador to United States, 1920–4; cr. Baron, 1942. [2] Simon, *Retrospect*, 100.

[3] Edward Stanley, 17th Earl of Derby (1865–1948): educ. Wellington; uncrowned (Conservative) 'king of Lancashire'; secretary for war, 1916–18, 1922–4; ambassador to France, 1918–20; close friend of George V. Haig said of him: 'like the feather pillow he bears the mark of the last person who sat on him'.

[4] There was a promise that no one should be called up until he was 18½, and a further promise (withdrawn in 1918) that no one would be sent abroad until he was 19.

political consequences were less serious than Asquith had feared. Labour protested, and acquiesced. Some fifty Liberals voted against the bill. Sir John Simon[1] resigned as home secretary, thus drawing on a stock of moral inflexibility not much replenished later. That was all. Runciman and McKenna had opposed conscription in the belief that the seventy divisions which it envisaged were beyond the economic resources of the country. Instead of resigning, they decided to stay in office and to defend *laissez faire*, which they did to some purpose.

One gesture of conciliation was made towards Liberal principle: men with a conscientious objection to military service were allowed to state their case before a local tribunal, which could grant them absolute or conditional exemption. This provision, almost without parallel in other countries, worked clumsily. The tribunals were composed of the elderly and retired, unsympathetic to all young men and especially unsympathetic to conscientious objectors. Many of the claims, muddled no doubt and incoherently expressed, were rejected. Some 7,000 objectors agreed to perform non-combatant service, usually in ambulance work; another 3,000 were put in rather useless labour camps, run by the home office. Later, the tribunals learnt to evade the question of conscience by deeming an objector's present work to be of 'national importance' and hence qualifying him for exemption on other than conscientious grounds. There remained 1,500 'absolutists'—men who refused all compulsory service—some from religious conviction, some as believers in liberty, a few as Marxists who would take no part in a capitalist war. These men were drafted into military units, and sentenced to imprisonment by court-martial when they refused to obey the order of an officer. Forty-one of them were transferred to France, where being on active service, they could be sentenced to death for disobedience, and they lived under this shadow for a month until personal intervention by Asquith had them brought back to England. Lloyd George, once a pro-Boer, took the lead in harrying the conscientious objectors: 'I will make their path as hard as I can.' The question seemed trivial at the time; it had great effect later. The

---

[1] John Simon (1873-1954): educ. Fettes and Oxford; attorney general, 1913-15; home secretary, 1915-16; foreign secretary, 1931-5; home secretary, 1935-7; chancellor of exchequer, 1937-40; lord chancellor, 1940-5. Lloyd George said: 'Simon has sat on the fence so long that the iron has entered into his soul.'

1,500 'absolutists' drove the first nail in the coffin of Lloyd George's Radical reputation.

Compulsory service did not achieve its alleged purpose of providing more men for the army. On the contrary, it kept them out. Munition workers and coal miners could not be prevented from succumbing to patriotic emotion when enlistment was voluntary. The military authorities had to reject them once conscription went through. Instead of unearthing 650,000 slackers, compulsion produced 748,587 new claims to exemption, most of them valid, on top of the million and a half already 'starred' by the ministry of munitions. In the first six months of conscription the average monthly enlistment was not much above 40,000—less than half the rate under the voluntary system.[1] Of course it was more sensible to keep men in essential occupations than to let them join the army, but this was not how it appeared to generals or fire-eating Unionists, who thought that war was won at the front, not in the factories. The agitation for compulsion started all over again: this time for married men as well. Lloyd George once more threatened to resign unless compulsion were made general. Runciman, McKenna, Grey threatened to resign if it were. Asquith despaired, and expected the government to break up. He devised another elaborate compromise which pleased nobody, and on 26 April presented it to the house of commons in the first secret session of the war. The secrecy was imposed to conceal the party rifts from the public, not to deny knowledge to the enemy.

Asquith had a stroke of luck—his last. 26 April was the Tuesday after Easter. On the previous day there was a rebellion in Dublin. The house of commons was stirred to patriotism. It demanded a final, comprehensive measure, and this demand grew stronger three days later, when news arrived of Townshend's surrender to the Turks at Kut. Asquith gave a sigh of relief. He withdrew his compromise, carried universal military service to the age of 41, and yet preserved the outward unity of his government. This affair, though tactically successful, was disastrous for Asquith's prestige. Everyone knew that the solution had been imposed upon him. The house had intervened

[1] Compulsion was not the only cause of the decline. Enlistment was bound to become less after the first surge of patriotism. But compulsion did not arrest this decline.

directly for the only time in the war. It had dictated to the government instead of being led. Moreover, Asquith had escaped trouble over conscription only by raising the darker shadow of Ireland. This had now to be faced.

The Military Service Acts did not apply to Ireland—another unconscious repudiation of the Union. Even so, the Irish question could not be ignored 'for the duration'. The discontented minority of Irish Volunteers continued to drill and talked openly of rebellion. Birrell, the Irish secretary, felt that it would be unfair to disarm them, when the Ulster Volunteers, who had also talked of rebellion, were not disarmed before the war. The Irish extremists sought German assistance, as the Ulster rebels had done before them. In Germany Sir Roger Casement, formerly a British consul, attempted, unsuccessfully, to recruit an Irish legion from among prisoners of war. A rising, with German backing, was planned for Easter Sunday, 1916. The plans miscarried. The Germans had never meant their promises seriously; and when Casement landed from a German submarine on Good Friday, it was with a warning to call off the rising, not with German arms or German soldiers. In any case, he was captured within a few hours of landing. In Dublin, John MacNeill, Volunteer chief-of-staff, first resigned and then cancelled the plans for mobilization. On Easter Sunday the Volunteers stayed at home. On Monday a group in Dublin, unsupported in the rest of the country, seized the General Post Office and proclaimed the Irish Republic. Five days of fighting followed. A hundred British soldiers, and 450 Irish, were killed. The G.P.O. was destroyed. On the Friday after Easter, the first Provisional Government of the Irish Republic surrendered.

This was the only national rebellion in any European country during the first World war[1]—an ironical comment on the British claim to be fighting for freedom. The rising was repudiated by Irish public opinion. Here was the chance for a new start. The British government made little of it. General Maxwell, the military commander, was left in sole charge for a fortnight. The seven men who had signed the proclamation of independence were shot. So, too, were all the Volunteer commandants involved except one—Eamonn de Valera, who, having been born in the United States of a Spanish father and

[1] Outside Europe the Arab rising against the Ottoman Empire can perhaps be dignified as national.

an Irish mother, was technically stateless and escaped with imprisonment for life.[1] Asquith went to Dublin. He found the atmosphere changing: the blood of the martyrs now stood in his way. He believed that all could be redeemed, if Home Rule were instituted at once. Then, as usual, he shrank from the creative effort which a solution of the Irish question demanded. Lloyd George seized the opening: if he settled Ireland, he would win back his Radical supporters and eclipse Asquith as well. Lloyd George negotiated with Carson and Redmond. He secured agreement between them, by means however equivocal: Home Rule at once for twenty-six counties; six counties of Ulster to remain part of the United Kingdom until after the war, when an imperial conference would review the question afresh. The unity and confidence of the Liberal party were restored; the Unionists were in confusion. Law cared much for Ulster, little for the rest of Ireland. He accepted Lloyd George's proposals; so also did Balfour and F. E. Smith.[2] Opposition came only from the 'magnates', once Whig, now Unionist. It was enough for Asquith. The backing of Law—'a very good ironmaster who had come into politics late'[3]—meant nothing to him. He started back in alarm at the protests of Lord Lansdowne.[4]

The Heads of Agreement were progressively weakened at Lansdowne's dictation. When Redmond refused to compromise further, they were scrapped.[5] Dublin Castle continued to rule Ireland. This failure gave the deathblow to the Irish constitutional party. Force seemed the only remedy in Ireland, and the extremists, who had been discredited by the Easter rebellion,

[1] The American ambassador is said to have intervened on de Valera's behalf. One hundred and sixty others were sentenced to prison; 1,862 men and 5 women were interned in England without trial. Casement was tried for high treason at the Old Bailey. F. E. Smith—Carson's 'galloper' in 1914—led for the prosecution. Casement was convicted. On 3 Aug. he was hanged. To discredit any campaign for reprieve, British agents circulated diaries, allegedly Casement's and probably genuine, containing homosexual passages.

[2] Frederick Edwin Smith (1874–1930): educ. Birkenhead and Oxford; solicitor general, 1915; attorney general, 1915–19; lord chancellor, 1919–22; secretary for India, 1924–8; cr. Baron Birkenhead, 1919, Viscount, 1921, Earl, 1922. Beaverbrook rated him 'the cleverest man in the kingdom'.

[3] H. A. Taylor, *Robert Donald*, 121.

[4] Henry Petty-Fitzmaurice, fifth Marquess of Lansdowne (1845–1927): educ. Eton and Oxford; formerly governor general of Canada, viceroy of India, foreign secretary; minister without portfolio, 1915–16; published letter in *Daily Telegraph* advocating a compromise peace, 29 Nov. 1917.

[5] See Note B, p. 71.

soon began to triumph at by-elections. The Irish Nationalists lost interest in parliament, and virtually seceded—eighty
supporters lost to Asquith. This was not his only loss. He
attempted to appease the house by agreeing, on 20 July, to a
select committee of inquiry into the Mesopotamia campaign,
and threw in, for good measure, an inquiry into the Dardanelles as well—an inquiry which, it was hoped, would hit
only Churchill. Few were distracted by these red herrings.
The Liberals had seen their cherished causes abandoned one
by one: peace; Free Trade; voluntary recruiting; now Home
Rule. What held them behind Asquith any longer? Only a
determination (which he shared) to win the war. It was increasingly difficult to believe that he was the man to win it.

Lloyd George once more claimed the vacant place. He was
lucky to be on offer. Ireland saved Lloyd George's life. He and
Kitchener had projected a visit to Russia, in order to inspirit
their flagging ally. At the last minute, Lloyd George called off,
because of the negotiations over Ireland. Kitchener went alone.
On 5 June the *Hampshire*, with Kitchener on board, struck a
mine within two hours of leaving Scapa Flow. Kitchener and
most of the crew were drowned. So perished the only British
military idol of the first World war. The next morning Northcliffe burst into his sister's drawing-room with the words:
'Providence is on the side of the British Empire after all.' This
reflected a common view that the secretary for war still held
the key to victory and that Kitchener had been incapable of
turning it. Few men appreciated how his powers had been
diminished, first by the encroachments of Lloyd George, then
by those of Robertson. Haig and Robertson understood it well
enough. They wished to ensure that Kitchener's successor,
too, should be a figurehead, and therefore proposed Lord Derby,
who would do whatever the C.I.G.S. told him to.

Asquith was ready to accept the generals' nominee. Law and
Lloyd George were not. Though personally still on cool terms,
they agreed that the new secretary must be a strong man,
in other words, Lloyd George. Asquith reluctantly bowed to their
order—dramatic indication that his authority as prime minister
was crumbling.[1] Lloyd George became secretary for war, glad

---

[1] This was the occasion when Law, pursuing Asquith into the country, allegedly
found him playing bridge with three ladies on a Monday morning and was outraged at this frivolity during a great war. Since it was Whit Monday when all the

no doubt to escape from the coming breakdown over Ireland. He was in a hurry. He took his new office on 4 July. The battle of the Somme had started on 1 July. Lloyd George believed that Haig was about to win the war, and wished to be at the war office so as to claim the credit for this achievement. In his hurry, he failed to insist on a change in the system of supreme command and so was as much under Robertson's dictation as Kitchener had been.

The Somme was the first great action by a British army of continental size. The army in France had grown steadily as the men who had responded to Kitchener's call completed their rudimentary training. At the beginning of 1916 it numbered thirty-eight divisions; nineteen more had come over by the middle of the year.[1] The army had an incomparable spirit: it was by far the greatest volunteer force ever to go into battle. But it was a clumsy instrument. The senior officers were elderly, unimaginative professionals from the old peacetime army, who refused to contemplate the problems of trench warfare. In the words of the official history, 'the failures of the past were put down to reasons other than the stout use of the machine-gun by the enemy and his scientifically planned defences.'[2] The junior officers were, for the most part, former public schoolboys. They were expected to set an example to their men, as indeed they did;[3] tactical leadership was held to be beyond them. The men had been trained to man a trench, and to advance in a regular line, bayonets glinting in the sun.

Haig believed that previous attacks had failed from lack of weight. This time a battering ram was to be driven into the enemy lines by a prolonged 'barrage'. The infantry would merely clear up the wreckage. Then, in Haig's vision, would come the 'breakthrough', with cavalry operating in open country. Many hundred thousand horses were kept in France throughout the war, waiting for the opportunity which never came, and using, for their forage, more shipping space than was lost to German submarines. In the rear, motor transport was now fairly

government offices were closed, it is difficult to see how Asquith could have been better employed—quite apart from his belief that ministers should keep out of the way while the generals won the war.
[1] This compares with 95 French and 117 German divisions on the western front.
[2] *Military Operations: France and Belgium, 1916,* i. 34.
[3] The ratio of casualties between officers and men was 3 to 1. A special decoration, the Military Cross, was instituted in 1915 for acts of bravery by junior officers.

common;[1] near the front line, great dumps of shells bore witness to the work of the ministry of munitions. There was a network of dugouts and communicating trenches. A fantastic complication of flares and rockets carried messages back to the gunners or to the aeroplanes 'spotting' overhead. Despite this, the battle of the Somme was fought as though infantrymen, armed with flintlock muskets, were the last word in military science.

Haig had favoured an offensive in the north. Here British communications were best, and a breakthrough would create an open flank. The entire German line could then be 'rolled up'—a version in reverse, in fact, of the original Schlieffen plan, to which Ludendorff also conformed when he took the offensive in 1918. But Haig had been instructed to follow Joffre's strategic direction. Joffre wanted a combined Anglo-French operation, in order to ensure that the British did their share of the fighting, or rather more. The Somme happened to be the place where the two armies joined hands. Strategically, there was nothing to be gained on the Somme. Victory there would merely free the Germans from an awkward salient or, if extremely successful, saddle the Allies with one of their own. Moreover, the combined offensive did not work out. In February the Germans attacked Verdun, and this absorbed the bulk of French resources. By July, when the British were ready, the Somme had become predominantly a British enterprise—hence with even less purpose than before. However, Haig did not hesitate. He had now become convinced that a powerful offensive, even on the Somme, would win the war. He wrote on the eve of battle: 'I feel that every step in my plan has been taken with the Divine help.'[2] Others did not share his confidence. Rawlinson, the army commander on the Somme, expected at best limited gains; Joffre merely 'attrition'—the killing of Germans.

On 1 July thirteen British divisions went 'over the top' in regular waves. The attack was a total failure. The barrage did not obliterate the Germans. Their machine guns knocked the British over in rows: 19,000 killed, 57,000 casualties sustained—

---

[1] A traffic-census at Fricourt on 21-22 July 1916 (the only one ever taken) shows the mixture of old and new. In 24 hours there passed 26,000 troops; 568 motor cars; 95 motor buses; 617 motor cycles; 813 motor lorries; 3,800 horse wagons and carts; 5,400 riding horses; 8 machine guns. *Military Operations: France and Belgium, 1916*, i. 283.

[2] Duff Cooper, *Haig*, i. 327.

the greatest loss in a single day ever suffered by a British army and the greatest suffered by any army in the first World war. Haig had talked beforehand of breaking off the offensive if it were not at once successful. Now he set his teeth and kept doggedly on—or rather, the men kept on for him. The generals, though without hope, flattered their chief's obstinacy. 'Captures of prisoners, but not the heavy casualties, were regularly reported.' The slaughter was prolonged for weeks, then for months. It tailed off in November when it foundered in the mud. No strategical gain had been made. Three British soldiers were lost for every two German.[1] 'The troops were tried almost to the limit of their endurance.'[2]

Kitchener's army found its graveyard on the Somme. Not only men perished. There perished also the zest and idealism with which nearly three million Englishmen had marched forth to war. C. E. Montague, a writer on the *Manchester Guardian* who dyed his grey hair in order to volunteer, has recorded this process of *Disenchantment*. The change was shown also in the war poets. The early poets, Rupert Brooke and Julian Grenfell, wrote with a lyrical innocence which they had carried over from peacetime. After the Somme came a new school, poets who saw in war only horror and suffering, tempered by the comradeship of the trenches. Edmund Blunden expressed this spirit sensitively, Siegfried Sassoon and Robert Graves more savagely. Most of them remained war poets, not—as later readers inclined to regard them—anti-war poets. Sassoon, indeed, turned against the war altogether, after winning the Military Cross, and claimed to be a conscientious objector. The others still wanted to destroy 'Prussia', though they saw this 'Prussia' in their own commanders as well as on the other side.[3] In any case, these poets spoke only for a minority. All except Isaac Rosenberg were officers—and Rosenberg was by no means a representative 'other rank'. Even Wilfred Owen, incomparably the greatest poet of either war, saw his 'men' from outside.

[1] British losses: 420,000. French: 194,000. German (against the British): 280,000; (against both armies): 465,000. The official history revised these figures and claimed the true German losses as 680,000, thus implying—against all experience—that the attackers lost less than the defenders.

[2] *Military Operations: France and Belgium, 1916*, ii. 538.

[3] Wilfred Owen wrote in the unfinished preface to his poems:
If I thought the letter of this book would last,
I might have used proper names; but if the spirit of it
survives Prussia,—my ambition and those names will be content.

With astonishing virtuosity, the British army grew from 200,000 to five million and kept its antiquated class-structure inviolate. The colonels and adjutants, though incompetent for modern war, knew how to preserve social standards and turned the young officers into temporary gentlemen, who wore riding boots and passed the port in mess.

The 'Tommies' have left few memorials. One or two, such as Frank Richards and David Jones, became writers and published reminiscences many years later. Otherwise the Tommies speak in the songs which they composed on the march or to beguile the tedium of the trenches—songs which survive mainly in oral tradition. The tunes were usually adapted from contemporary music-hall 'hits'. The words were self-depreciatory and often obscene.[1] No other army has ever gone to war, proclaiming its own incompetence and reluctance to fight, and no army has fought better. The humble Englishman found his voice, and these songs preserve him for posterity. In more literary compositions, the Tommies were presented with affectionate contempt. 'Ol' Bill' was their symbol, created by Bruce Bairnsfather (himself an officer of course)—a hoarse-voiced walrus of a man with a crude wit that was almost human. Old Bill had no ideas, no ambitions, no resentment against his blundering superiors. With mud and water up to his waist, he made only the philosophic remark: 'If you know a better 'ole, go to it.' This was the epitaph of the men who died on the Somme.

While fighting raged on the Somme, Lloyd George had been numbered with the enthusiasts. He said on 22 August: 'We are pressing the enemy back. . . . We are pushing the enemy on the Somme. . . . He has lost his tide.' A month later he championed 'the knock-out blow'. He made out afterwards that he did this in order to silence in advance President Wilson's proposal for a negotiated peace. In fact, he committed himself to the knock-out blow in the belief that, as secretary for war, he was about to deliver it. All the more fiercely therefore did he turn against Haig and Robertson when he discovered that they had misled him. In November he said to Hankey: 'We are going

---

[1] During the first World war use of the four-letter word, as it is now called, became universal, or more probably its universal use was first observed by the literate classes. Between the wars the word was presented by writers in a modified form—mucking or flicking—or with its initial only—f - - - ing. Its use in full—fuck—now seems to be approaching literary, though not conversational, respectability.

to lose this war.'[1] Failure on the Somme was only one of many
troubles. A Russian offensive miscarried on the eastern front
after initial success. Rumania tardily joined the Allies in August,
only to be overrun by the Germans—Lloyd George attempting
in vain to stir up Allied assistance by an advance from Salonika.
Events at sea were still graver.

In the spring of 1916 the Germans called off unrestricted
submarine warfare. As a sort of psychological compensation,
their battlefleet began provocative sweeps on the North Sea.
The British Grand Fleet responded to the challenge. On 31 May
Beatty,[2] commanding the British battlecruisers, encountered his
German opposites. A running engagement drew him under the
guns of the German High Seas fleet. Beatty swung away and
drew the Germans, in their turn, on to the British Grand Fleet,
under Jellicoe, which was at sea some fifty miles northwards.
At about 6 p.m. there took place the only battle between two
great modern fleets ever fought in European waters.[3] It lasted
little more than five minutes. The German admiral turned
away, discharging torpedoes as he did so. Jellicoe turned away
also to avoid the deadly stream. Half an hour later the German
fleet reappeared. More shots were exchanged. Then the Germans vanished again, and this time for good. The battle of Jutland was over. The inconclusive result was a great disappointment for British opinion, educated in the legend of Nelson and
Trafalgar. The German fleet had not been destroyed. British
losses were greater than German; the British ships had proved
inferior in armour and guns.[4] But appearances were deceptive.
The Germans had turned tail on sight of the British monsters.
Their High Seas fleet only left harbour again three times in the
course of the war, and then to no purpose.

The Germans came within sight of victory after Jutland, not
because they won the battle, but because they recognized that
there was nothing to gain by repeating it. Henceforth they

---

[1] T. Jones, *Lloyd George*, 78.
[2] David Beatty (1871–1936): commanded battlecruisers, 1913–16, Grand Fleet,
1916–19; first sea lord, 1919–27; cr. Earl and given £100,000 by parliament, 1919.
[3] 250 ships were present at Jutland, and 25 admirals.
[4] The British lost 3 battlecruisers, 3 armoured cruisers, and 8 destroyers; the
Germans 1 battleship, 1 battlecruiser, 4 light cruisers, and 5 destroyers. British
designers had not allowed for the fact that, in battles fought at long range, shells
would fall from above. They had armoured the sides of the vessels, not the decks.
They had also failed to guard against sparks in mid-air, which would flash down the
hoists and explode the ammunition.

neglected their battlefleet and increased the submarine attacks on shipping. Here was the jugular vein of the British empire. Ships and all they brought began to run short. Requisitioning of ships was no solution. This worked only where the government had a monopoly of the article moved, as with the armed forces, sugar, and—from October 1916—wheat.[1] Otherwise it merely pushed up the freight on ships not requisitioned. The shipowners, though making fantastic profits, were also patriotic men. They wanted government direction and control; in practical terms, the licensing of imports. Much more followed though the shipowners did not say so. Licensing of imports meant in its turn rationing more or less directly: the controlled distribution of raw materials to industry and of food to individual consumers. This again implied control of home production, particularly of agriculture, that most obstinately anarchic of industries. On top of this, all British economic life had to be transformed in order to provide more men and more capital for the making of munitions. Here was a terrifying prospect: an economic revolution to be carried out helter-skelter in the midst of war, with little accurate information, no previous experience, and no trained administrators. The political implications were also alarming. Controlled economy challenged the Liberal system of free enterprise which had made England prosper ever since the repeal of the Corn Laws.

This challenge had already been dimly on the horizon when the Coalition government was formed in May 1915. To meet it, Asquith had left all the key positions in Liberal hands. The Liberal champions did not fail. Runciman, himself a great shipowner, remained adamant in helplessness. In November 1916 he submitted to the government a report which Addison[2] called 'the most invertebrate and hopeless of any memoranda presented to the Government during the war by a responsible head of a department on a great issue'.[3] According to Runciman, shipping losses must inevitably bring Great Britain to

---

[1] Wheat, like sugar, was bought by an autonomous Royal Commission.

[2] Christopher Addison (1869–1951): educ. Harrogate and London; minister of munitions, 1916–17; minister of reconstruction, 1917–19; president of local government board and first minister of health, 1919–21; minister of agriculture, 1930–1; commonwealth secretary, 1945–7; lord privy seal, 1947–51; the only doctor of medicine since the second duke of Montagu (d. 1759) to receive the Garter; cr. Baron, 1937, Viscount, 1945.

[3] Addison, *Politics from Within*, ii. 10.

collapse by the summer of 1917. He drew no conclusion from this, nor could he do so. His economic principles ruled out licensing or control. Yet he, like most Liberals, was tied to the war by the fact that the Liberals had been in power when it started, and the closer Liberals were to Asquith, the more they were tied. Law might fear that the Liberals would turn against the war, if driven from office, and other Conservatives might hope it. Asquith remained resolute for war, though for nothing else— a contradiction which threatened either him or the country with ruin.

The logical alternative to a controlled economy was peace by negotiation. Hardly anyone stated this clearly or even realized it. Churchill was almost alone when he preached 'war socialism' from the backbenches.[1] On the other side, the small group associated with the U.D.C. advocated a negotiated peace for its own sake, and their views reached a wider audience through the I.L.P. The I.L.P. sympathized with the efforts being made in Switzerland to revive the Socialist International, and its delegates would have attended the meetings at Zimmerwald and Kienthal, if the government had not refused them passports.[2] The Labour party, however, remained resolute for the war; yet, regarding war socialism as synonymous with industrial conscription, imagined that it was on Asquith's side—Henderson, its leader, describing him as 'the indispensable man'. The strongest support for a negotiated peace came from within the government, though few people knew this at the time. In November 1916 Lansdowne circulated a paper to the cabinet, in which he argued that the war would destroy civilization and that therefore peace should be made on the basis of the *status quo ante bellum*. This proposal, which would in any case have been rudely rejected by the Germans,[3] received rough treatment from other Unionists—Balfour and Robert Cecil. The

---

[1] In the house of commons on 22 Aug. 1916.

[2] Among European countries, only Russia and Turkey required passports for entry before 1914. The requirement then became general and was not got rid of afterwards.

[3] It is now known that the minimum German terms, favoured even by Bethmann Hollweg the Chancellor, included German acquisition of the Longwy–Briey basin from France; military and economic control over Belgium, including a German garrison at Antwerp; acquisition of part, or all, of the Belgian Congo; a kingdom of Poland dependent on Germany; dependent states on the east coast of the Baltic; and a share of Persia for Germany. Fritz Fischer, *Griff nach der Weltmacht* (1961).

military leaders were also contemptuous of it. Haig said that
the prospects for 1917 were 'excellent'. Robertson, when asked
whether the war could be won, replied: 'Quite frankly, and at the
same time quite respectfully, I can only say I am surprised that
the question should be asked. The idea had not before entered
my head that any member of His Majesty's Government had
a doubt on the matter'[1]—fine bulldog stuff, though hardly the
strategical guidance which Robertson was supposed to provide.

War socialism or a negotiated peace were the stark alternatives over which men would have disputed if they had been
conscious of what they were doing. They were not. To judge
from the press,[2] the attitude of backbenchers, and by-elections[3]
—and we have little other guide—English people were almost
unanimous in wanting to win the war, and they wanted it run
better, though they did not know how. Lloyd George had an
answer: he could win the war. He had shown that he could
produce munitions. He alone could manage Labour. Now he
claimed the supreme direction. He proposed a war council of
three, with himself in the chair, which should run the war free
from control by the cabinet. His original target was Robertson,
under whom he groaned at the war office. His target changed
as the crisis developed. He came to demand that Asquith should
be put on the shelf, more or less politely. By a curious twist, this
demand was favoured even by Robertson, who did not yet
appreciate the troubles in store for him from Lloyd George.
Here was a dramatic conflict. On the one side, Lloyd George,
man of the people, supported by almost the entire nation; on
the other, Asquith, supported by every Cabinet minister, and
mighty, as he believed, in the force of the two party machines.

Lloyd George could not launch the rebellion. It had to come
from outside. Many backbench Unionists had long been restless
against Asquith's Liberal negations. They were marshalled by
Carson, always happiest in rebellion.[4] On 8 November Carson
almost captured a majority of the Unionists from Law over

---

[1] Duff Cooper, *Haig*, ii. 9.
[2] When the crisis exploded, Lloyd George had on his side every leading newspaper except the *Daily News*—the respectable *Times*, *Manchester Guardian*, and
Observer, as much as the popular *Daily Mail*, *Daily Express*, and *Daily Chronicle*.
[3] Kennedy Jones, rogue candidate in the spring with the cry 'Do It Now', was
returned unopposed as an official Unionist in December.
[4] Carson had resigned from the government in November 1915 as a protest
against the failure to aid Serbia.

an apparently trivial question.[1] Law took alarm. He was determined to maintain his leadership of the Unionist party and appreciated now that he could do this only if he produced a more energetic conduct of the war. His adviser, Max Aitken,[2] drew him steadily towards Lloyd George, and events drew him still more strongly. Law, like Lloyd George, did not spring from the charmed circle of traditional politics; in the last resort he, too, went with the people. Still, it seemed a terrifying prospect: two men of humble origin challenging the massed ranks of the established order.

But Asquith had feet of clay. His supremacy rested on the artificial silence which the whips imposed on the house of commons. Now, not only the backbench Unionists were turning against him. The Irish Nationalists had no interest in Asquith, and little in British politics, since the failure over Home Rule. Labour, though it supported Asquith, would equally support any other prime minister who could win the war. Above all, Christopher Addison, Lloyd George's only intimate who was in the house of commons, brought the sensational news that forty-nine Liberal members of parliament supported Lloyd George unconditionally and that another eighty would support him if he formed a government. This division in the Liberal party had been long a-growing. The Liberal leaders associated with Asquith, were men of excessive refinement—almost too fastidious for politics in peacetime, let alone at the turning point of a great war. Lloyd George's supporters were rougher in origin and in temperament: mostly Radical nonconformists, and self-made men in wool or engineering who were doing well out of the war. None was a banker, merchant, or financial magnate; none, a Londoner. Theirs was a long-delayed revolt of the provinces against London's political and cultural dominance: a revolt on behalf of the factories and workshops where the war was being won.

[1] The issue was the disposal of enemy property in Nigeria. Carson wished to limit the sale to British subjects; the government, true to Liberal principles, insisted on a free market. Seventy-three Unionists voted with the government; 65 against. Law, though carrying the free market, saw to it that only British subjects bought the property.

[2] William Maxwell Aitken (1879–1964); Scotch-Canadian by birth and son of a Presbyterian minister; self-made millionaire; cr. Baron Beaverbrook 1917, to his subsequent regret; minister of information, 1918; minister of aircraft production, 1940–1; member of war cabinet, 1940–2; minister of supply, 1941–2; lord privy seal, 1943–5. Owner of *Daily Express*, *Sunday Express*, and *Evening Standard*; the greatest newspaperman since Northcliffe and also a considerable historian.

On 1 December Lloyd George formally proposed to Asquith a war council of three with himself in the chair. Asquith insisted that he himself must preside over the council and that it must be subordinated to the cabinet. Lloyd George wrote to Law: 'The life of the country depends on resolute action by you now.' On 3 December Law met his principal Unionist colleagues, led by the 'three C's'—Robert Cecil, Austen Chamberlain,[1] and Curzon.[2] He told them that he intended to support Lloyd George. The Unionist leaders were angry at the little trouble-maker. They determined to resign, not in order to support Lloyd George, but rather to force an end to the conflict one way or the other. The same afternoon Law gave the Unionists' decision to Asquith. Perhaps he did not make its meaning clear. Perhaps Asquith failed to grasp it.[3] More probably Asquith was alarmed at the prospect of wholesale resignations. At any rate, he took the easy way out. He wrote to Lloyd George, accepting the war council as Lloyd George had proposed it. The crisis seemed over. To clinch things, Edwin Montagu,[4] a Liberal who straddled between Asquith and Lloyd George, persuaded Asquith to inform the press that the government was about to be reconstructed. This was an announcement that Lloyd George had won and that Asquith would become a figurehead.

On 4 December the Liberal ministers, who had hitherto been kept in the dark, came to Asquith in high indignation. They demanded a fight. The 'three C's' also indicated that they were on Asquith's side. Curzon declared that no Unionist except Law would join a Lloyd George government. As to himself, 'I would

[1] Austen Chamberlain (1863-1937): educ. Rugby and Cambridge; secretary for India, 1915-17; member of war cabinet, 1918; chancellor of exchequer, 1919-21; lord privy seal, 1921-2; foreign secretary, 1924-9; first lord of admiralty, 1931. Birkenhead said: 'Austen always played the game and always lost it.'

[2] Balfour, the other prominent Unionist, was in bed ill.

[3] It was later made a serious charge against Law that he had failed to give Asquith the exact words of the Unionists' decision. If he had, it is claimed, Asquith would have grasped that they were against Lloyd George and on his side. Aitken certainly interpreted the decision in this sense and strongly urged Law not to reveal it. It is difficult to believe that Law ignored Aitken's advice. On the other hand, Law told Donald: 'Asquith did not like our proposals [i.e. of resignation] and asked me to consider that the paper had not been delivered. I, therefore, did not deliver it'. H. A. Taylor, *Robert Donald*, 131.

[4] Edwin Montagu (1879-1924): educ. City of London and Cambridge; chancellor of duchy of Lancaster, 1916; minister of munitions, 1916; secretary for India, 1917-22; Asquith called him 'the Assyrian'; opposed Balfour declaration, though a Jew.

rather die than serve under Lloyd George'.[1] Asquith repented
of his weakness the evening before. He withdrew his agreement
to Lloyd George's war council.[2] On 5 December Lloyd George
resigned. Asquith answered by resigning himself, thus bringing
his government to an end. He defied Law or Lloyd George to
form a government: 'then they will have to come in on *my*
terms'.[3] Asquith was not manœuvred out of office. He deliberately resigned office as a manœuvre to rout his critics. His
complaints, when this manœuvre failed, were those of an ageing
heavyweight, who has been knocked out by a younger, more
agile opponent.

The king, in accordance with constitutional practice, sent
for Law, leader of the second great party. Law would form a
government only if Asquith joined. Asquith refused. Even a
conference at Buckingham Palace, proposed by Arthur Henderson and summoned by the king, did not move him. Law, Lloyd
George, Balfour—he would serve under none of them. 'What is
the proposal? That I who have held first place for eight years
should be asked to take a subordinate position.' Law returned
his commission and advised the king to send for Lloyd George.
The king did so. The next morning, 7 December, Lloyd George
met the Labour M.P.s and the national executive of the Labour
party. He said to them:

Politicians make one fundamental mistake when they have been
in office. They think that the people who are in office, or who have
been in office, are absolutely essential to the Government of the
country, and that no one else is in the least able to carry on affairs.
Well, we are a nation of 45 millions, and, really, if we cannot produce at least two or three alternative Cabinets, we must really be
what Carlyle once called us —'a nation of fools'.[4]

Thus Lloyd George appealed from the ruling classes to 'the

Young, *Balfour*, 371.
[2] Asquith used the excuse of a leader in *The Times* that morning, which supported Lloyd George. Asquith alleged, and probably believed, that Lloyd George
had inspired the article through Northcliffe. Actually Dawson, the editor, wrote
it independently after a talk with Carson. Northcliffe had indeed visited Lloyd
George on 3 Dec., but with quite a different object: to offer Lloyd George a lucra-
tive contract as a columnist if he left office. Later both men concealed this. Lloyd
George was ashamed at his lack of confidence in thus guarding his financial future;
Northcliffe was annoyed at not landing his fish. Both therefore shammed guilt,
where they were in fact innocent.
[3] H. A. Taylor, *Robert Donald*, 121.
[4] Beaverbrook, *Politicians and the War*, ii. 309.

people'. Labour, speaking for 'the people', answered his call.[1]
In wartime the people mattered; and Lloyd George was home,
once Labour backed him. Law delivered the backbench Unionists; Addison had gathered the backbench Liberals. Yet this
government of the people was not composed of backbenchers
after all. The Unionist leaders heard their country's call, or
the call of office, once they saw that Lloyd George had succeeded. Balfour joined first, won by a promise of the foreign
office. He declared: 'you put a pistol at my head'. The 'three
C's', including Curzon, yielded later in the day, on condition
that neither Churchill nor Northcliffe was given office and that
Haig remained commander-in-chief. On the other hand, all
the prominent Liberals followed Asquith's lead, and stayed out.[2]
Asquith in fact, not Lloyd George, pursued a personal vendetta.
He split the Liberal party and riveted on his adherents,
however unwillingly, the appearance of opposing a government that was fighting the war. On the evening of 7 December
Lloyd George returned to Buckingham Palace, and kissed hands
as prime minister. He was the first son of the people to reach
supreme power, or, as he put it himself, the first except Disraeli
'who had not passed through the Staff College of the old Universities'.[3]

NOTES

Note A. *The partition of Turkey in Asia.* Mark Sykes and Georges Picot,
the British and French negotiators, reached a preliminary agreement in
January 1916. Broadly, this gave Syria to France, and Mesopotamia to
Great Britain; the British sphere was to have an outlet on the Mediterranean
at Haifa. The Anglo-French agreement was conditional on the agreement of
Russia. This was obtained in May 1916 at the price of allotting Turkish
Armenia to Russia. (It is this agreement which is usually, though wrongly,
known as the Sykes-Picot agreement.) There was also a pledge in the treaty
of London to satisfy Italy. The Italians proved obstinate. Agreement with
them (wrongly called the agreement of St. Jean de Maurienne—the place
of an inter-allied meeting in April 1917) was reached only on 18 August
1917. It marked part of Asia Minor as the Italian sphere. This agreement
began with the words: 'under reserve of Russian assent'. No reply came from

---

[1] The Labour M.P.s were almost solid for Lloyd George. The executive supported him only by 14 votes to 11.

[2] Lloyd George invited Herbert Samuel and Montagu to join his government.
Both refused, Samuel saying that he saw in it 'no element of endurance'. Montagu
became secretary for India when Austen Chamberlain resigned later in 1917.

[3] Lloyd George, *War Memories*, iii. 1041. Lloyd George was wrong: he forgot
Wellington. In the forty years since Lloyd George's time, the score of the old
Universities *v.* the rest was 4 all.

Russia before the Bolshevik revolution put an end to allied relations. The British and French therefore asserted that the agreement with Italy had lapsed. Was it the only casualty? Was the agreement of May 1916 still valid, even though one of the signatories, Russia, had fallen out? Alternatively, could the original agreement of January 1916 be resurrected, although it postulated Russian approval? The British and French tended to argue that one or other agreement was valid—they could not decide which—where it benefited themselves, but not where it benefited the other signatory or a third party.

There were further complications. In January 1916 a British agent, Sir Henry McMahon, vaguely promised the Arab lands of Turkey to Hussein, Sherif of Mecca, though without indicating what these lands were. Zionist representatives put in a claim for Palestine as 'a national home' or 'the national home' (the distinction is important), or even as 'a national state' for the Jews. Sir Herbert Samuel supported this claim in the Asquith cabinet. Grey did so also, less decisively. The British government did not at all welcome the prospect of the French as neighbours next door to the Suez Canal. Zionism was a way of keeping them out. Palestine was chipped out of Syria. It became first an international, then a British trust. On 2 November 1917 the Balfour declaration promised 'a national home' in Palestine for the Jews. The French who had expressed vague sympathy with Jewish aspirations, discovered that their promised share of the spoils had been reduced by half.

NOTE B. *The proposed Irish settlement, 1916.* The Irish Nationalists were reluctant to surrender any part of their (apparently) favourable position, with Home Rule for all Ireland on the statute book, though suspended for the duration of the war, and any special treatment of Ulster still therefore to be negotiated. They made two conditions with Lloyd George: (i) the Irish members should remain at Westminster in undiminished numbers; (ii) the arrangements should be temporary, strictly for the duration of the war. Lloyd George agreed, and added this guarantee: 'he had placed his life upon the table, and would stand or fall by the agreement come to'. Thus assured, Redmond and his supporters acquiesced in what they supposed to be temporary partition, i.e. Home Rule for twenty-six counties alone. To Carson on the other hand, Lloyd George wrote: 'We must make it quite clear that at the end of the provisional period Ulster does not, whether she wills it or not, merge in the rest of Ireland.' This promise of permanent partition led Carson to renounce three (Roman Catholic) counties of Ulster, and he persuaded the Ulster Unionists to renounce them also. These somewhat contradictory promises would no doubt have caused trouble after the war, if the Heads of Agreement had been accepted; nevertheless, they were not the cause of breakdown at the time—despite Carson's statement to the contrary in 1924.

The objection of Lansdowne, and some other Unionists, was over southern Ireland, not over Ulster. Lansdowne wrote to Asquith on 28 June: 'With a Nationalist executive, would it be possible to deal effectively and promptly with domestic disorder?' He therefore demanded assurances that

[1] Lloyd George, *War Memoirs*, ii. 705.

the Defence of the Realm Act should be continued under Home Rule, and that there should be no amnesty for the Easter rebels. It was impossible to give these assurances without making Home Rule meaningless. Asquith, therefore, tried to weaken Unionist opposition by reducing concession elsewhere. Redmond was told (i) that the exclusion of Ulster from Home Rule must be permanent, failing new legislation at Westminster; (ii) that Irish representation at Westminster must be reduced to forty-three. Redmond refused these conditions. The government offer was then withdrawn. Lloyd George did not fulfil his promise to resign, pleading that this would merely jeopardize the energetic conduct of the war (he had just become secretary for war), without helping Home Rule. All the same, he deservedly got credit for having nearly succeeded, and Asquith deservedly got the blame for failure. Addison, a Liberal who later played a decisive part in making Lloyd George prime minister, wrote: 'His [Asquith's] conduct of this business had more to do with determining the attitude of many Liberals, including myself, than any other circumstance.'[1]

[1] Addison, *Politics from Within*, i. 260.

III

A NATION AT WAR, 1916-18

Lloyd George's accession to power in December 1916 was more than a change of government. It was a revolution, British-style. The party magnates and the whips had been defied. The backbenchers and the newspapers combined in a sort of unconscious plebiscite and made Lloyd George dictator for the duration of the war. Balfour said: 'If he wants to be a dictator, let him be. If he thinks that he can win the war, I'm all for his having a try.'[1] Lloyd George was the nearest thing England has known to a Napoleon, a supreme ruler maintaining himself by individual achievement. A detached observer wrote at the end of the war: 'The effects of the change in direction two years ago may be compared to the substitution of dynamite for a damp squib.'[2] The dynamite exploded. There were new departments of state; new men; new methods of control and regulation; and a new form of cabinet government. The explosions were sporadic. Lloyd George was not a man of plan and system. When faced with a difficulty, he listened to the ideas of others and saw, in a flash, the solution. He liked to air his problems in company over the breakfast-table,[3] feeling his way with both men and ideas. There was in him a strange mixture of resolution and timidity. His shirt, as he came to make a speech, was always wet through from nervous anxiety. Though Lloyd George often provided leadership of great moral courage, he trembled before he acted.[4]

At any sign of opposition, he saw a 'great crisis' and anticipated that his government might fall. He feared that the forces which had carried him to power might as easily turn against him. Public opinion might revolt against heavy casualties. The Unionist backbenchers, he knew, wanted more power for

[1] Dugdale, *Balfour*, ii. 170.
[2] Sir Almeric Fitzroy, clerk to the privy council, *Memoirs*, ii. 191.
[3] These breakfasts increased Robertson's dislike of Lloyd George. Lloyd George sat long. The habits of a lifetime made Robertson wish to withdraw at once. Hankey, *The Supreme Command*, ii. 775.
[4] Lloyd George lacked physical courage. The air raids of the first war, and still more those of the second, terrified him, and he rarely spent a night in London.

the generals, whereas he planned to cut them down. His enemies ranged, or so he supposed, from Northcliffe to the king.[1]
Lloyd George stood alone against the best-entrenched governing
class in Europe. He did not lead a party. Though Coalition
Liberal whips were appointed, they were never clear who their
whip should go to.[2] He had no friends and did not deserve any.
He repaid loyalty with disloyalty, as Churchill and Addison
experienced.[3] He was surrounded by dependants and syco-
phants, whom he rewarded lavishly and threw aside when they
had served their turn. His rule was dynamic and sordid at the
same time. Its spirit was expressed in the popular catch:

> Lloyd George knew my father.
> My father knew Lloyd George.

He himself gave hostages to fortune (never in fact impounded)
by the irregularity of his private life. He was the first prime
minister since Walpole to leave office flagrantly richer than he
entered it, the first since the Duke of Grafton to live openly
with his mistress. Essentially his devious methods sprang from
his nature. He could do things no other way. He defined these
methods in a classic sentence: 'I never believed in costly
frontal attacks either in war or politics, if there were a way
round.'[4] Though Lloyd George became 'the Big Beast of the
Forest', he remained also 'the Goat'.

On the issue which had brought Asquith down, Lloyd
George did not hesitate. War committee and historic cabinet
alike were swept away. Lloyd George's war cabinet was a
committee of public safety, exercising supreme command under
his direction. It had only five members,[5] chosen—in theory at
any rate—for their executive ability, not because of the offices

[1] On New Year's Day 1917 the king made Haig a field marshal, as a gesture
against Lloyd George.

[2] Ninety-eight Liberals revealed themselves as against Lloyd George in the vote
after the Maurice debate. It by no means followed that the remaining 170 were
for him. In Nov. 1918 the Coalition Liberal whips claimed to have 150 followers.
See below, 126.

[3] Churchill stood unflinchingly by Lloyd George in 1913 at the time of the
Marconi scandal. Lloyd George allowed Churchill to be saddled with all the blame
for Gallipoli and said (quite untruly): 'Churchill is the man who brought Turkey
into the war against us.'

Addison helped to make Lloyd George prime minister. After the war Lloyd
George offered him as scapegoat when there was an outcry against 'homes for
heroes'.

[4] Lloyd George, War Memoirs, iv. 2274.

[5] Later six and, for a few months, seven.

they held or to satisfy the balance of parties. Only Law had departmental duties, as chancellor of the exchequer. Henderson spoke for 'Labour'. Curzon and Milner[1] did the steady routine work. There was little division of functions. Any one of the five—though Law, because of his commitments in the house of commons, less than the others—would explore a topic from labour unrest to the future of the air force, and bring it to the war cabinet for decision. Other ministers were summoned to attend individually when questions affecting their department were discussed. Balfour, the foreign secretary, perhaps spoke with some independent authority on foreign affairs. The holders of the other great historic offices merely received their marching orders. Where the old cabinet had met once a week or so, and had kept no record of its proceedings, the war cabinet met practically every day—300 times in 1917—and Hankey, brought over from the committee of imperial defence and its successors, organized an efficient secretariat. He prepared agenda; kept minutes; and ensured afterwards that the decisions were operated by the department concerned. Hankey was also tempted to exceed his functions, and to initiate proposals, particularly on strategy, instead of merely recording decisions.

He had some excuse. The war cabinet lacked a staff. This was its great defect. Essentially it was an instrument for enforcing the will of the prime minister, and he had been without a department or expert advisers of his own, since his office became virtually divorced from the treasury in the course of the nineteenth century. Lloyd George attempted to remedy this by creating a private staff, housed in huts in St. James's Park and known as 'the Garden Suburb'. He thus came to resemble a president of the United States, who often relies more on

[1] Milner received his summons to attend the war cabinet only one hour before its first meeting on 9 Dec. His appointment, though apparently an afterthought, was characteristic of Lloyd George. Carson, the third member of the rebel group, had the obvious claim, but, as Lloyd George put it, 'whether in or out of office . . . he was always "agin the Government" for the time being'. Milner, to quote Lloyd George again, 'carried great weight with the Tory intelligentsia and Diehards (not by any means identical groups)'; he was the favourite of the generals and, at this time, of Northcliffe. He was eager to exert his abilities after years of exclusion and, once appointed, gratitude made him loyal. Indeed, he soon became Lloyd George's most stalwart supporter against the generals and shouldered without hesitation the most dangerous tasks.

The juxtaposition of Curzon and Milner in the war cabinet had its piquant side. Curzon was the lover of Elinor Glyn, the romantic novelist. Milner was her devoted admirer and improved her prose.

unofficial advisers than on members of his cabinet. The Garden
Suburb stirred the jealousy of established departments, as it
encroached increasingly on their functions, and it was, in the
end, a principal count against Lloyd George. In any case, it
took some time to get going.

Meanwhile, Lloyd George had to fall back on inspiration and
guile. He had intended to establish his mastery over the service departments. The result of his revolution was the exact
opposite. The service ministers, being no longer in the cabinet,
became more independent and defiant than before. Carson,
having been denied the war cabinet, went to the admiralty,
where he fiercely championed his professional advisers. The
war office was even worse. Derby had been the loyal second of
Lloyd George when under-secretary—the only Unionist to
back him from the first. He became the equally loyal second of
Robertson, when elevated to the post of secretary for war.
Robertson regarded the war cabinet as 'the enemy'. Lloyd
George, in particular, was 'a real bad un'. Robertson and, to a
lesser extent, Jellicoe (who became first sea lord in December
1916), compelled the war cabinet to fight the war blindfold.

Resistance was more easily overcome on the civilian side.
The generals were supported by backbench Unionists; the
laissez faire officials at the treasury and the board of trade only
by frontbench Liberals. The problems which had baffled the
Asquith Coalition were faced at last. Five new departments of
state were set up almost overnight—four of them 'ministries':
shipping, labour, food, national service, and food production.[1]
These improvizations created a curious pattern, with unforeseen results. The new departments evolved a system of war
socialism. The peacetime departments continued to discharge
their old functions, or even had new functions, which they had
accumulated, taken away from them. War and peace ran side
by side. Hence, at the end of the war, the temporary 'socialist'
departments could be disbanded, and the old departments
emerged in their prewar innocence. The only new creation
intended to be permanent was the ministry of labour, which

[1] Labour, shipping, and food became ministries at once; national service in
Mar. 1917. There was also a ministry of pensions. One new ministry had been
created in Asquith's time after the ministry of munitions: the ministry of blockade
(Feb. 1916), a more or less autonomous offshoot from the foreign office under Lord
Robert Cecil, which also took over some functions from the board of trade. Cecil
also continued to act as deputy foreign secretary.

took over labour relations from the board of trade and unemployment insurance from the autonomous commission. Even here wartime functions were kept separate in the ministry of national service. So, too, with agriculture: the old board continued unchanged, and the new department, directing food production, could be disbanded, as it was, at a moment's notice.

The new ministries—and one old one, the board of trade[1]—were headed by new men, mostly businessmen with no political background, certainly of no political importance. They were there to do vital jobs, not to carry on parliamentary government. One of the most successful, Maclay, the shipping controller, refused to enter parliament at all. The new ministers had no theory of 'planning' or of anything else. Like the country at large, they entered war socialism backwards, and were surprised at what they had done. Though they had almost unlimited powers by statute, they preferred to enlist the cooperation of producers and owners, who thus largely ran war socialism themselves for patriotic motives. Maclay first requisitioned all British merchant ships and then employed the owners as managers, a system which they continued to operate even when the courts ruled that one part of the requisitioning was *ultra vires*.[2] Similarly, the county committees which directed agriculture were composed of local landowners who rarely attempted to coerce their neighbours. 'A strike of farmers would have brought down the whole machinery of food control.'[3] Even the rationing of food, when it came, was really a voluntary system, operated by the retailers.[4] The ration books were little more than symbols with which to impress the public, and the

[1] Albert Stanley, later Lord Ashfield, became its president. Aitken had hoped to receive this office as reward for his services in bringing Law and Lloyd George together. Instead he was compelled to become Baron Beaverbrook so that Stanley could have his seat at Ashton-under-Lyne.

[2] Maclay concluded 'Heads of Arrangement' with the owners of liners, by which they ran liners for the government. This, being a requisitioning of services not of ships, was held by the courts to be *ultra vires*. The victor was the firm of old Liverpool radicals, Alfred Holt & Son.

[3] Lloyd, *Experiments in State Control*, 288.

[4] The ministry of food had intended to ration individuals on the basis of a central register. This register was far from complete when social discontent made rationing imperative early in 1918. The ministry then used the shopkeepers for want of anything better. Thus 'the Ministry made its own and much of Lord Rhondda's reputation by putting accidentally into practice one system of rationing while it was formally engaged in devising a different system'. Beveridge, *British Food Control*, 229.

mountains of 'coupons' were rarely checked before being consigned to the bonfire. The most powerful instrument, operated by all these ministries, was control of prices. This virtually stabilized the cost of living until after the war. Like all their other instruments, it depended on cooperation. Prices were fixed on the basis of 'cost plus', and industrialists usually accepted this as a fair arrangement.

There were many odd features, which caused trouble or set precedents later. Control of rents, for instance, had been introduced haphazard in Glasgow in 1915, at a time of labour discontent. It was made general without any thought of the problems which this would create in the future. Again, coal miners—perhaps the most essential element in the community—resented the owners' profits, even on the basis of 'cost plus'. The mines were therefore nationalized for the duration, though without any attempt to reorganize the industry or to modernize the pits. Cotton, that other old staple, saw a paradoxical control to lessen production (and hence the import of American cotton) at 60 per cent. of the prewar level. Those sections of the industry which remained in work[1] paid a levy to compensate those who did not. Hence men and women were tempted to remain as unemployed cotton operatives instead of moving to more useful war work elsewhere. Cotton thus devised, by accident, the model for planned reduction in the nineteen-thirties. Wheat provided a precedent for an even later period. The war cabinet early decided that there should be no rationing or limitation imposed on 'the staff of life', and they stuck to this even when cheap flour was diverted to the making of cakes. People could always buy as much bread as they wished, though with some deterioration in quality,[2] and the price of bread was kept stable by subsidy when the cost of wheat imports rose. The subsidy cost £60 million. From it sprang all the subsidies which kept the cost of living stable during the second World war.

The 'war socialists' ran into plenty of difficulties, and did not always overcome them. Devonport, though a great grocer, was

[1] The 'Egyptian' section remained prosperous, as it did in the nineteen-thirties, though for a different reason. Plenty of Egyptian cotton could be brought back in the ships, which supplied the army in Palestine. Later, the section prospered because it produced the finer counts.

[2] The extraction rate was raised, which probably improved the nutritive value. Maize, oats, barley, and potatoes were not, however, agreeable adulterants. The bread caused a psychological 'war-indigestion'—imaginary, but no less painful for that.

a failure at the ministry of food, appealing to the public instead of telling them what to do. Rhondda, the next minister of food, remedied this, and issued 500 orders during his time in office—one for each working day. Neville Chamberlain[1] fell into hopeless confusion over national service; as Lloyd George said, 'not one of my successful selections'. Chamberlain tried to work out rules varying for each individual case. Auckland Geddes, his successor, developed a schedule of protected occupations and applied a 'clean cut' in it—the block release of men according to age—when this became necessary. Even Maclay had his troubles. Though he did wonders with the existing stock of ships, he could build few new ones because of the admiralty's insistence on priority. In May 1917 he adroitly turned the flank of this obstacle by saddling the admiralty with responsibility for all shipbuilding, mercantile and naval.

These improvements were arrived at hit-and-miss. The war cabinet gave little direction. It was almost as distracted as its predecessor by being theoretically responsible for everything, and came to the rescue of a minister only when he knew how to appeal to it, as Neville Chamberlain, for example, did not. Lloyd George, not content with being dictator at home, aspired also to coordinate the policy of the Allies. His first task, forced on him from outside, was to define war aims. It was easy to brush off the negotiations proposed by Bethmann Hollweg, the German chancellor. For Bethmann demanded a peace based on German victories, and Lloyd George was pledged to reverse them. It was less easy to brush off the mediation offered by President Wilson, however much the Allies resented being put on a level with the Germans. Terms had to be devised which would rule out mediation without estranging Wilson. To please him, the Allies championed 'self-determination', which meant, in practice, the end of the Ottoman empire and 'the liberation of the Italians, as also of the Slavs, Roumanians, and Czechoslovaks from foreign domination'.[2] In this casual way, the

---

[1] Neville Chamberlain (1869–1940): half-brother of Austen; educ. Rugby and Birmingham; director of national service, 1917; postmaster general, 1922–3; paymaster general, 1923; minister of health, 1923, 1924–9, 1931; chancellor of exchequer, 1923–4, 1931–7; prime minister, 1937–40; lord president of council, 1940. His failure over national service gave him an enduring hostility towards Lloyd George, who returned the feeling and called him a 'pinhead'.

[2] The British and French intended to specify 'South Slavs'. The Italians coveted territory inhabited by South Slavs, and objected. 'Czechoslovaks' were therefore

British people were committed to redrawing the map in both
east-central Europe and western Asia—objects infinitely remote
from those with which they had entered the war, but inescapable
once they needed some great cause. Few knew anything of
these distant races, and still fewer cared. But they regarded the
war as a crusade, or so those who spoke for them supposed, and
a crusade inevitably turned against the Turk and the Habsburg.

These were still distant problems. The immediate need was
victory, and this could be achieved, Lloyd George thought, only
if the Allies acted as one. Early in 1917 he attended at Rome the
first general conference of the Allies. Lloyd George wanted a
combined offensive on the Italian front—principally no doubt
in order to take the conduct of the war away from British
generals. Cadorna, the Italian commander-in-chief, refused the
doubtful honour. The Rome conference produced only empty
talk. Another opening soon presented itself. In December
1916 Joffre had been dismissed as French generalissimo.
Nivelle, his successor on the western front, had a fine presence;
a reputation inflated by some minor successes at Verdun; and
spoke good English. He claimed to have discovered the secret
of victory: a dramatic surprise, followed by 'the rupture of the
front'. It would all be over in 48 hours; decisive victory and no
great casualties. Lloyd George, though impressed, hesitated.
Nivelle came to London. Haig and Robertson acquiesced in
his plan, less from belief in it, than because at least it ensured the
primacy of the western front. The war cabinet agreed. Lloyd
George, once committed, went in without reserve. He always
had a curious faith in French generals, though none in British.
On 26 February, by means even more conspiratorial than usual,
Lloyd George placed Nivelle in supreme command over the
British armies in France.[1] This was an odd outcome for the

stuck in to make the list look more concrete, and without any realization that it
involved the destruction of the Habsburg monarchy.

[1] On 19 Feb. Lloyd George asked Nivelle, through a French military attaché
in London, to devise a directive, subordinating Haig to himself. On 24 Feb. the
war cabinet approved this directive, Robertson having been told that he need not
attend as nothing important was to be discussed. On 26 Feb. an Anglo-French conference was held at Calais, ostensibly to discuss railway transport in north France.
Nivelle produced the directive. Lloyd George pretended to be surprised, and
accepted it. Robertson threatened to resign. Haig appealed to the king. The
directive was limited to the coming offensive, and Haig was given the right of appeal
to his government—a right which he exercised. *Military Operations: France and Belgium, 1917,* i. 536-8.

upheaval of December 1916. Lloyd George, the 'easterner', had swallowed Nivelle's strategical direction more credulously than Kitchener ever accepted Joffre's and was now forcing an offensive in France on his reluctant generals.

Nivelle's offensive, if there were any sense in it, depended on swift action. Instead there were wrangles and delays. The Germans observed the elaborate preparations and forestalled attack by withdrawing to a shorter, heavily fortified 'Hindenburg line', on which they had been working throughout the winter. The British generals turned against Nivelle's operation, once they realized that it interfered with their own plans. All the French generals were against it except Nivelle himself. The French ministers lost what faith in him they originally had. Nivelle could hardly have got his way without Lloyd George's relentless backing. The preliminary British offensive, known as the battle of Arras (9–14 April), had one success to show: the taking of Vimy ridge by the Canadians. British casualties were nearly twice those of the Germans,[1] and the great problem remained unsolved: new defensive positions were improvised faster than the attackers could plod forward on their two feet. Nor were the Germans diverted by any threat at Arras from their precautions against Nivelle. His offensive on the Aisne, delayed until mid-April, was almost as great a failure as Joffre's offensives had been. The Germans were unshaken. No strategical gain was made. The French armies were brought to the verge of mutiny, and in many cases over it. Nivelle was dismissed in May.[2] The cautious Pétain took his place. Nivelle left two grievous legacies. The French armies were incapable of any further offensive in 1917; Haig and Robertson were vindicated in their opposition to Lloyd George's project of a supreme command.

He, meanwhile, was projecting a supreme command in other ways. The Canadians at Vimy ridge were evidence of the manifold contributions which the Dominions were making to the war. There was a Canadian army corps in France; New Zealanders and Australians in the Near East and in France. The South Africans conducted most of the campaign against the Germans in East Africa. The hopes of English imperialists

[1] British: 142,000. German: 85,000.
[2] Nivelle was one of the few generals who did not write his memoirs after the first World war. He died in 1924.

revived. Imperial unity was being demonstrated on the battle-fields; Milner, its apostle, was in the war cabinet; the McKenna duties had breached Free Trade. Hard-headed Unionists, who disliked a war for remote ideals, embraced the economic imperialism of which Marxists had long accused them. They wanted to prolong the war into peacetime and to turn the 'undeveloped estate' of the Empire into a closed economic system, with Great Britain monopolizing its supplies of raw materials. Lloyd George took the lead, though principally with the hope of using imperial sentiment against the generals. In March 1917 the prime ministers of the Dominions[1] gathered for a meeting of the Imperial War Cabinet in London. Lloyd George, the old pro-Boer, thus fulfilled the dreams of Joseph Chamberlain, or so it appeared.

The reality was different. Lloyd George had intended the imperial war cabinet to be an executive for the Empire. The prime ministers of the Dominions insisted that they were responsible exclusively to their own governments. In their eyes, the British empire was already an association of sovereign states, and the imperial war cabinet was no more than a diplomatic conference of intimates. The one tribute to unity was that prime ministers were invited, when available, to each other's cabinets; and this was more honorary than effective. It is unlikely that Borden of Canada contributed much to British deliberations, or Hughes of Australia to Canadian. Smuts[2] was the one exception. Lloyd George seized on a general who was also, as a Boer, presumably a good Radical, and persuaded Smuts to remain in England as a member of the war cabinet. Smuts was a unique case: the only full cabinet minister of modern times to have no connexion with either house of parliament. As a weapon against the generals, Smuts did not come up to expectations. Professional loyalty worked even with a former rebel, and Smuts became the champion of British generals whom he had once beaten in the field.

The imperial war cabinet had another significance, pregnant

---

[1] Hughes of Australia was delayed until April. Botha of South Africa was represented by Smuts, his minister of defence.

[2] Jan Christian Smuts (1870–1950): Boer general, British field marshal; South African minister of defence, 1910–19; prime minister of South Africa, 1919–29, 1939–48; member of war cabinet, 1917–19; chancellor of Cambridge university, 1948–50. Smuts had a high opinion of his military gifts and, in 1918, wished Lloyd George to propose him as commander-in-chief of the American armies in France.

for the future. The Dominions had excluded India from previous imperial conferences, as a mere dependency of the crown. Indeed, the Indian empire, directed by the secretary for India, had been entirely distinct from the British empire, which was in the care of the colonial secretary. Now half a million Indians were fighting on the British side, and more men were killed from India than from any Dominion. A pretence, at any rate, had to be made that India had a say in affairs. India was therefore represented at the imperial war cabinet, though only by the secretary of state and three assessors—one a representative of the native princes. Still, this was a grudging admission that India was outgrowing the trammels of British autocracy, and that she, too, must become a Dominion, autonomous or even, if she wished, independent. The line ran, after long delays, from the imperial war cabinet of 1917 to the British withdrawal from India thirty years later.

Lloyd George also returned to the problem of Ireland which he had so nearly settled the year before, though his aim now was more to satisfy American and Dominions opinion than to find a solution. He offered Redmond the previous bargain: immediate Home Rule for twenty-six counties, and a final settlement after the war. Redmond refused to tread this worn path again. The republican party of Sinn Fein was now winning every by-election in southern Ireland, and Redmond dared not compromise. Smuts, in his first contribution to British politics, proposed a convention on the South African model, at which the Irish should settle things for themselves. Lloyd George and Redmond agreed. The men interned or imprisoned after the Easter rebellion were released. For nearly a year there was peace in Ireland. The convention duly deliberated in Dublin, though Sinn Fein refused to attend. The more distant prospect was still misty, and Lloyd George did not help to clear it. Though he promised to back the proposals of the convention if there were 'substantial agreement', he privately assured Carson that nothing would be done without Ulster's consent; and Ulster, strong in this assurance, rejected any solution in advance. The convention bought time; it could not bring settlement.

Lloyd George had reason to tread warily with Carson over Ireland, for naval affairs had already brought them to odds. On 1 February 1917 the Germans renewed unrestricted submarine warfare, with more submarines. This time more was heard from Washington than the rattle of President Wilson's typewriter. In February Wilson broke off relations with Germany. In April the United States declared war on Germany and entered the war as an 'Associated Power'.[1] The Germans were confident that they could bring Great Britain to collapse before American action became effective, if it ever did. They nearly succeeded. The number of ships sunk by U-boats rose catastrophically. In April 1917 one ship out of four leaving British ports never returned. That month nearly a million tons of shipping were sunk, two thirds of it British. New building could replace only one ton in ten. Neutral ships refused cargoes for British ports. The British reserve of wheat dwindled to six weeks' supply. Even more menacing was the almost complete interruption in the supply of pit props from Norway, with the inevitable consequence that the coal industry itself must soon stop.[2]

There seemed no effective measure of defence. Jellicoe was helpless: 'there is absolutely no solution that we can see'. Carson was resolutely helpless along with him. Lloyd George thrashed around for other advice. A junior officer, Commander Kenworthy,[3] was smuggled into 10 Downing Street by Northcliffe late at night through the garden door, Lloyd George asking: 'Now tell me who are the good men. I want to use any men with brains.'[4] The men with brains, Hankey among them, urged convoy. Coal convoys were already working successfully to the ports of western France. The Grand Fleet never moved without convoy. Yet the admiralty remained adamant. Merchant captains, they argued, could not keep station,[5] the convoys would only offer a larger target to U-boats; 2,500 vessels entered and left British ports each week—an impossible number to convoy.

On 26 April Lloyd George secured the backing of the war cabinet for 'peremptory action'. On 30 April he went to the

[1] The last push was given by a German offer to Mexico of an offensive alliance against the United States. The British intelligence service had broken the German code, and passed 'the Zimmermann telegram' to the Americans.

[2] The timber shortage led to the creation of a Forestry Commission, which was to ensure supplies of homegrown timber for the future.

[3] Later a Radical, and then a Labour, member of parliament.

[4] Kenworthy, *Soldiers, Statesmen—and Others*, 70.

[5] The admiralty even arranged a meeting of merchant captains to declare their incapacity.

admiralty, escorted by Curzon,[1] and took command—the only occasion in British history when a prime minister has directed a great department of state in the teeth of the minister responsible for it. The board of admiralty acknowledged defeat, and produced a scheme for convoy, which they claimed to have prepared on 27 April. This was a face-saving device. Convoys were due to Lloyd George alone, his most decisive achievement of the war. The first convoy left Gibraltar on 10 May. Soon convoys, at different speeds, were organized from Canadian and American ports. By the end of the war 80 per cent. of shipping to British ports came in convoy. The official naval history states frankly: 'the chief objections urged against the system before it was tried had one and all proved to be unfounded'.[2]

The merchant captains kept station without difficulty. A convoy of a hundred ships offered a single, strongly defended target in place of a hundred defenceless targets when ships were sailing unescorted. The number of ships requiring convoy turned out to be 140 each week, not 2,500.[3] Less than 1 per cent. of the ships convoyed were lost from all causes.[4] By the end of 1917 British and American yards were almost replacing ships lost; by the middle of 1918 they were building more ships than were being sunk. The strain was still great. Many ships not in convoy were still sunk, particularly in the Mediterranean —a high price for the imperial side shows. Still, convoy enabled Great Britain to survive and to win the war. Yet men of high professional competence and integrity had faced disaster rather than try something new and, as it turned out, successful—a parable illustrating the obstinacy of Great Britain's traditional rulers in many spheres.

Lloyd George still shrank from dislodging Carson, despite this great stroke. Carson was not moved from the admiralty until July, and then only by the subterfuge of elevating him to the war cabinet, where he proved useless. Though Eric Geddes[5]—

---

[1] Law, already apprehensive of conflict with Carson over Home Rule, declined the dangerous post of honour.

[2] *Naval Operations*, v. 141.

[3] The admiralty had included coastal shipping, and even the Solent ferries, in their original figure.

[4] 154 ships out of 16,657 convoyed to or from this country; 456 out of 88,000 convoyed overall (including the Mediterranean and American shipping to France). 25 per cent. were lost before convoys started.

[5] Eric Campbell Geddes (1875–1937): educ. Merchiston and Edinburgh;

Lloyd George's best find in the business world—became first lord, he was saddled with Jellicoe until the end of the year, when Jellicoe's dismissal brought Carson's final resignation along with it. In these circumstances, Lloyd George dared not risk a conflict with the generals as well, particularly as Haig— a master at unloading embarrassing friends—supported Lloyd George against Jellicoe. Yet conflict or agreement with the generals was imperative. The failure of Nivelle's offensive left Haig free to determine his own strategy regardless of the French,[1] and he was eager to take up the project which he had cherished since he became commander-in-chief: a great offensive in Flanders. Here, he believed, he could win the war— with the added attraction of doing so before the Americans arrived. The British forces would break out of the salient at Ypres, reach the Belgian coast, and then roll up the entire German front. The official history suggests that Haig's plan 'may seem super-optimistic and too far-reaching, even fantastic'.[2] It was no doubt impressive as grand strategy, and looked fine on the map. In fact everything was right about Haig's plan except the first step. He had devised no solution for the initial 'break out' and, as well, had chosen a field of operations where the preliminary bombardment churned the Flanders plain into impassable mud. None of Haig's subordinates expected decisive success. Nor did Robertson. But he could think of nothing better and was anxious to prevent the diversion of British resources from the western front. At any rate, the offensive would kill Germans.

Lloyd George was determined not to be responsible for another Somme. The war cabinet examined Haig closely. He

general manager designate of North Eastern Railway; made a major general when he directed railway transport in France, and a vice-admiral when he organized naval supply; first lord of admiralty, 1917–19; in war cabinet, 1919; minister of transport, 1919–22; subsequently chairman of Dunlop Rubber Co.

[1] Many years later Haig and his apologists invented the story that Pétain had appealed for a British offensive in order to distract the Germans from the mutinous French army. The story has no contemporary foundation. The French mutinies occurred in May. Discipline had been restored long before the British offensive started. During the autumn the French, though anxious to wait for the Americans before resuming large-scale attacks, actually made more substantial gains than the British. There is no evidence that the Germans projected an offensive on the western front in 1917, and much that they did not. At the time Haig was lured on by promises of French support—promises which Pétain did not fulfil. John Terraine, *Douglas Haig*, 363.

[2] *Military Operations: France and Belgium, 1917,* 101.

radiated confidence. Robertson concealed his own doubts from the cabinet, thus failing in his duty as chief adviser on strategy. Smuts supported Haig, and Curzon, as usual, went irresolutely with what appeared to be the stronger side. Law reported that the house of commons would not tolerate interference with the military leaders. Only Milner, once the darling of the generals, stood by Lloyd George. Men who had promised to win the war found it hard to resist a general who insisted that he could win it. Besides, the war cabinet had many other things to do. They could not go on arguing with Haig day after day. He wore them down. They implored him to think again, and, when he refused, gave in. On 25 July they sent him their wholehearted support.

On 31 July Haig launched what is officially called the third battle of Ypres; popularly, from its final episode, Passchendaele; and, most truly, by Lloyd George, the battle of the mud. Everything went wrong. The drainage system of Flanders broke down, as had been foretold. To make matters worse, it was the rainiest August for many years. Men struggled forward up to their waists in mud. The guns sank in the mud. The tanks could not be used. Haig had declared his intention to stop the offensive if the first attack failed. He did not do so. The futile struggle went on for three months. The British advanced, in all, four miles. This made their salient more precarious than before, and they evacuated it without fighting when the Germans took the offensive in March 1918. Three British soldiers were killed for every two German. The loss of officers was still worse —more than three to one.[1] No doubt the morale of the German army was shaken by Passchendaele. It is unlikely that the morale of the British army was much improved.

[1] The official British statistics, published in 1922, gave British casualties in the Flanders offensive as 324,000. The comparable German figure was given in the British return as 202,000. This was slightly better than on the Somme, where, according to the same source, the British lost 420,000 against 280,000 Germans. The volume of the official history, published in 1948, revised the figures drastically. British losses now appeared as 244,897. The German figures were recalculated, and shown to be 'about 400,000'. Captain Falls, who worked with General Edmonds on the official history, does not accept this revision altogether and puts the German losses at 240,000 (*First World War*, 285). The 'revision' is more easily understood if it is remembered that Lloyd George had meanwhile attacked Haig in his *War Memoirs*. A polemic against the greatest prime minister of the century was thus conducted in an official history, published under the authority of the cabinet office. Yet 'unofficial' historians are denied access to cabinet papers, for fear that they would turn their information to improper use.

The campaign in France was not quite over. The new Tank Corps had been useless in the mud of Flanders. Belatedly, Haig allowed it a chance to show what it could do elsewhere. The tank commanders chose a section of the front further south on high, hard ground. On 20 November 381 massed tanks broke through the German defences in front of Cambrai and reached open country. Bells to celebrate victory were rung in London for the only time during the first World war. The rejoicing was premature. No preparations had been made to exploit the success. There were no infantry reserves with which to consolidate the opening. Ten days later the Germans recovered all the ground they had lost and a bit more into the bargain. Smuts made an inquiry into the failure for the war cabinet. He reported that 'no one down to and including the corps commanders was to blame'. The fault lay entirely with 'the junior officers and N.C.O.s and men'.[1] These complacent conclusions were wisely kept from the public. They would have done little to allay the rising discontent.

Nineteen-seventeen was for civilians the worst year of the war. *Laissez faire* had broken down. The new controls were only beginning to work. Food and fuel were running short; trains were slow and crowded; the queue became a characteristic British institution, despite its foreign name. Some ministers wished to silence the discontent by industrial conscription. Lloyd George, more wisely, set up eight regional commissions of inquiry, and these reported that the discontent had solid economic causes. There followed a general increase of wages in all government work, while prices remained rigorously controlled. As a result, wages, which had lagged behind the cost of living in the first two years of the war, now rose beyond it, and the prewar level of real wages was almost reached before the war ended. The poor, in fact, were no longer carrying the burden of the war alone. At the same time, with markedly less to buy, genuine savings increased, and government borrowing came from these savings instead of coming, as it did earlier, from new money created by the banks. National Savings were invented to attract the humble man, and the Savings campaign gave demagogues something to do just when they lost their old occupation on the recruiting platform. National Savings were the only new element in public finance introduced by Law,

---

[1] *Military Operations: France and Belgium, 1917*, iii. 296.

while chancellor of the exchequer—unless we count his abolition of the penny post in 1918. Law considered what the house of commons would stand, not what financial needs demanded, and it was no thanks to him that British finances were not worse after the war.

Economic discontent slipped easily into political protest. Shop stewards, agitating over wages or dilution, also endorsed the criticisms of foreign policy made by the Union of Democratic Control. In March 1917 the Russian revolution added to the political stir. The tsar was overthrown, and Russia became, in theory at any rate, a democratic republic. Though all the Russian parties except the extreme socialists or 'Bolsheviks' were ready to continue the war against Germany, they would fight only for an idealistic cause, and proposed a peace with 'no annexations and no indemnities'. This seemed to imply that others, including the British and French governments, were seeking annexations and indemnities—as indeed they were. It was easy to allege that the war was dragging on for the sake of Alsace and Lorraine or the spoils of Turkey-in-Asia. In England opponents of the war found a new vigour, and divided the house of commons three times during the year in favour of peace by negotiation.[1] The Independent Labour party and the British Socialist party, which was avowedly Marxist, set up a United Socialist Council—first taste of the Popular Front, though by no means the last, and in June this body summoned a convention at Leeds to inaugurate the British revolution. Eleven hundred delegates attended, among them men usually moderate such as MacDonald and Snowden.[2] The convention endorsed the Russian peace programme, and instructed the British government to do likewise. It also called for the setting up of workers' and soldiers' councils, or, to give them their Russian name, soviets. It was the first breath in England of the Bolshevik wind.

The Leeds convention assembled only those already critical of the war. The effects of the Russian revolution soon cut deeper into the Labour movement. In May Henderson went to

[1] The support was not impressive. Thirty-two M.P.s voted in favour of the Russian peace programme on 16 May; 19 in favour of the (German) Reichstag peace resolution on 26 July; 18 in support of the Stockholm conference on 16 Aug.

[2] Philip Snowden (1864–1937); educ. elem. school; prominent member of I.L.P.; chancellor of exchequer, 1924, 1929–31; lord privy seal, 1931–2; cr. Viscount, 1932.

Russia on behalf of the war cabinet. He came home convinced that, in order to keep the Russian people in the war, the British Labour party, too, should accept the Russian peace programme and should send delegates to a conference of all socialist parties —allied, neutral, and enemy—which was being promoted at Stockholm. The war cabinet did not like this proposal. Lloyd George first agreed; then, to please the French government,[1] retracted. Henderson remained unshaken. He carried the Labour party conference in favour of sending delegates to Stockholm, though none actually went—the seamen refused to carry them. Henderson had to resign from the war cabinet, after being kept 'on the mat' while his colleagues discussed, and condemned, his behaviour. George Barnes,[2] a former leader of the party, took Henderson's place in the war cabinet; the other Labour ministers remained in office.

Lloyd George attached little importance to the incident. He imagined that Barnes, by entering the war cabinet, had automatically been made Labour leader, much as the king made a politician leader of his party by appointing him prime minister. Nothing of the kind. Henderson remained the Labour leader, and he had learnt his lesson. Never again, he declared, would he join a government in which Labour did not predominate. From this moment, 'Lib–Lab' was dead. Under Henderson's guidance, Labour set out to be a national party instead of an interest group, aiming at an independent majority and running candidates nearly everywhere in the country. Constituency organizations needed individual members of the party where trade unions were weak, and it now became possible to join the Labour party directly for the first time. This, in turn, demanded a clear party programme. It was drafted by Sidney Webb, the Fabian,[3] and appealed to 'the producers by hand and by brain'. Inevitably, the programme had a socialist ring, demanding 'common ownership of the means of

[1] The French government feared an uncontrollable movement in France against the war, if French and German socialists were allowed to meet.

[2] George Nicoll Barnes (1859–1940): educ. elem. school; sometime general secretary of Amalgamated Society of Engineers; leader of Labour party, 1910–11; member of war cabinet, 1917–19; minister without portfolio, 1919–20; resigned from Labour party, 1918; left public life after conclusion of the peace treaties.

[3] Sidney Webb (1859–1947): educ. City of London College, president of board of trade, 1924; colonial secretary, 1929–31; cr. Baron Passfield, 1929; his wife insisted on remaining Mrs. Beatrice Webb; the ashes of both were interred in Westminster Abbey.

production'.[1] A national party needed also its own foreign policy, and where could it turn for ideas? Only to the Union of Democratic Control which had been preaching an alternative foreign policy ever since the outbreak of war. In practical terms, this meant the return of MacDonald as Henderson's partner, or even as unacknowledged leader.

The new Labour party, with its national organization and socialist programme, threatened both Liberals and extremists. On the one hand, Labour offered a new party of the Left, not associated with past failures and free from the Liberal trammels with the privileged classes. Labour found new causes for 'the people', just when the traditional Liberal issues of Home Rule, Free Trade, and non-sectarian education no longer made hearts beat faster. In particular, Radical critics of conventional foreign policy, such as Charles Trevelyan, swarmed into the Labour party, without reflecting on the socialism to which they were also being committed. At the same time, the Labour party—being still financed by the trade unions and largely controlled by them[2]—was a barrier against extremism, just when this extremism was receiving new stimulus from the Russian revolution.

It is not surprising that Lenin saw in MacDonald and Henderson the rocks on which European Communism foundered. Nor was it only the Communist party, yet unborn, which was thwarted by Henderson's new model. Ultimately the I.L.P., too, was ruined. Socialists could now join the Labour party as individual members. They no longer needed the I.L.P. as intermediary, and it became a diminishing sect. Labour, with its loose federal organization, had room for all sorts and sizes from cautious trade unionists without a creed to revolutionary shop stewards or middle-class idealists—on condition that they observed certain broad limits of 'loyalty'. Many were tempted to break away. They were restrained, or their revolt was rendered futile, by the fact that only the Labour party

[1] It is often said that Webb wrote Fabianism into the Labour programme, *Labour and the New Social Order*. This is not so. He merely pieced together resolutions from previous annual conferences of the party.

[2] The unions still had a majority on the national executive of the party, though the constituency organizations were now represented as well as the affiliated societies (I.L.P., Fabians, and B.S.P.). Curiously, the one disqualification for membership of the Labour national executive was (and still is) to be a member of the T.U.C. General Council.

could tap the flow of funds from the 'political levy'. This, in the last resort, sustained the Labour party as decisively as subscriptions from the dukes had once sustained the Whigs.[1]

The threat from Labour lay in the future. At the moment, Lloyd George feared only the 'Squiffites'[2]—the followers of Asquith, now seated on the Opposition benches. Asquith claimed to be giving the government independent support, as Law had done for the Liberals in the first nine months of the war. There was a difference. Law had sustained the Liberal government against his own backbenchers; Asquith hoped to turn the Lloyd George government out, so far as he hoped for anything. Yet Asquith, as leader of the Opposition, proved a godsend to Lloyd George. It only needed the question—Asquith or Lloyd George as prime minister?—and the most discontented Unionists cowered into silence. Asquith could not even reunite the Liberals. After all, what could he reunite them on except his divine right to be prime minister for ever? The old dispute between *laissez faire* and controlled economy had been settled by events. Even Runciman no longer denounced convoys or food rationing. An Opposition to a war government might have been expected to urge peace by negotiation, but decisive victory was the one point on which Asquith never wavered. Indeed, he and his followers, in their anxiety not to be tarred with 'peace by negotiation', failed even to formulate war aims, leaving this task first to Labour and then to Lloyd George. On the other side, Lloyd George was deterred from following up the openings for a negotiated peace which presented themselves in 1917 partly by the fear that Asquith would buckle on the armour of the knock-out blow if he himself laid it off.[3]

Asquith, in view of his previous record, could hardly claim to run the war better than the existing government. But others could make the claim. On 10 May 1917 Lloyd George held a secret session, apparently to prepare the ground for direction of labour and food rationing. Though he spoke well, he was eclipsed by Churchill. Lloyd George did not waste a moment. He caught Churchill behind the Speaker's chair, and, says Churchill, 'from that day . . . I became his colleague'.[4] Two

[1] See Note A, p. 114.
[2] The nickname is said to be derived from Asquith's convivial habits. Was it not simply a shortening of his surname?
[3] See Note B, p. 115.
[4] Churchill, *World Crisis 1916-1918*, i. 255.

months later, Churchill was made minister of munitions.
The Unionists protested in vain: Lloyd George could not allow
Churchill to rage untamed. The appointment was cloaked by
a general reshuffle of ministers who had not come up to expectations. Lloyd George's most skilful stroke was to send
Northcliffe on a special mission to America, where he proved surprisingly successful. There was another important consequence.
Addison, dislodged by Churchill from munitions, was made
minister of reconstruction. Under his direction, committees
surveyed practically every aspect of British life. Much of this
was windowdressing, to allay labour discontent. Many of the
plans were never executed. Nevertheless, it was a startling recognition of the obligations which the state owed to its citizens
and a first attempt to bring public affairs into some kind of
rational order.

Reconstruction brought also the end of an auld sang which
had haunted politics for more than a hundred years: it virtually
completed parliamentary, or strictly franchise, reform. The
existing householder or occupancy franchise dating from 1885,
though often called democratic, gave the vote only to three
adult males out of five, and of course women did not have the
vote. Radicals were also aggrieved that there was no limit to
the number of votes an owner of property could cast so long
as he cast them in different constituencies. The prewar register
was flagrantly out of date. A new one, on the same basis, could
not include the millions of men in the services. Yet it would be
monstrously unjust to leave them out. And if men serving their
country were to be enfranchised, why not women in the services
also? The problem came to a head in 1916 when there was
talk of a general election. Asquith, in his usual fashion, ran
away from it. He first asked the house of commons to decide.
When it refused, he remitted the problem to a conference,
presided over by the Speaker. This conference reported soon
after Lloyd George became prime minister. It unanimously
recommended a six months' residence qualification, instead of
occupancy, and one plural vote only. A majority also recommended votes for women on the old occupancy basis, at a
higher age than for men.

The war cabinet backed the report, even though over a
hundred Unionists, led by Carson (himself a member of the
government), protested against it. Only women's suffrage was

left to a free vote of the house, and even here opposition was small. Most members agreed with Asquith, previously an opponent of votes for women, when he said: 'Some years ago I ventured to use the expression. "Let the women work out their own salvation." Well, Sir, they have worked it out during this war.' The bill passed the house of commons in December 1917. It was held up by a dispute with the house of lords over the rival merits of proportional representation and the alternative vote, neither of which was in the end adopted at all seriously. The act, which became law in June 1918, marked the victory of the Radical principle 'one man, one vote', except for the University seats and a second vote for business premises, both of which survived until 1948. The act added more voters to the register than all its predecessors put together. It settled in principle the question of votes for women, which had caused so much turmoil before the war. Yet it went through almost without fuss. War smoothed the way for democracy—one of the few things to be said in its favour.[1]

Franchise reform and 'reconstruction' had little appeal in the autumn of 1917. The war was going badly, except at sea. There had been military failure on the western front. In October the Germans, stiffening the Austro-Hungarian army, broke through the Italian lines at Caporetto and almost reached Venice. In November the Bolsheviks seized power in Russia and at once signed an armistice with the Germans. They proposed negotiations for a general peace. When the Allies refused to join them, they negotiated alone with the Central Powers. Russia was clearly out of the war; the eastern front had ceased to exist. Lansdowne took the opportunity to refurbish his proposal of a year before for a compromise peace and published it in the Daily Telegraph.[2] He had supporters even within the government. The British entente or alliance with Russia had always been an uneasy affair, imposed only by the greater threat from Germany. Now it had gone. Why not swing back to the support of Germany so far as eastern Europe was concerned? Milner, the protagonist of Empire, strongly urged this view. If the Germans would renounce their lost colonies; abandon their useless navy; and respect the independence of Great Britain's continental outposts, Belgium and France, then they could retain their eastern spoils, including the rich

[1] See Note C, p. 115.   [2] It had earlier been refused by The Times.

Ukraine. Thus Germany would be satisfied, and eastern Europe preserved from Bolshevism.[1] Here was a sketch for the programme which Hitler was to lay down later in *Mein Kampf* and which he was allegedly to apply when he came to power. It is not surprising that the members of Milner's kindergarten were, in the nineteen-thirties, apostles of appeasement. At the time, the policy did not bite. On the one side, the rulers of Imperial Germany—more ambitious than Hitler—sought to dominate the west as well as the east. On the other, the British people, as distinct from sophisticated statesmen like Milner, were obstinately set on the defeat of Germany. On 2 November Ben Tillett, the only rogue candidate to repeat Pemberton Billing's success, defeated a 'Squiffite' with the old cry of 'a more energetic conduct of the war'.

Public opinion had little idea how this could be done. Indeed, its restlessness took some odd forms. For instance, sudden panic swept the country about the distribution of food—a panic as unreasoning as 'the great fear' which had accompanied the French revolution. The food position was in fact better than it had been earlier in the year. The wheat harvest of 1917 was the best of the century. Supplies of meat and fat were coming in faster. Yet, without warning, people everywhere took alarm and bought food irrationally. There were disappointed queues at every butcher's and grocer's shop. The ministry of food had to introduce rationing helter-skelter early in 1918, not at all because food was scarce, but simply to allay this strange disturbance. There was no intention of reducing the consumption of food. The ration book was a promise that all demands would be met, as indeed they were, and, since people took up their full ration, consumption slightly increased. This was war psychology at its most mysterious.

There was another outbreak with more sinister consequences. The cry for reprisals against German air attacks was common to all demagogues. The experts, such as they were, opposed this

[1] On 3 Nov. 1917 Milner told an American diplomatist that the Allies 'ought to listen to every peace whisper'. He continued to advocate a compromise peace at Russia's expense until the conclusion of the armistice. On 1 Mar. 1918 Beatrice Webb noted (*Diaries 1912–1924*, 111–16): 'The P.M. and Milner are thinking of a peace at the expense of Russia. . . . I gather that Haldane is also looking forward to a reconciliation between the Junkers of Germany and those of England over an agreed extension of both Empires. With Russia to cut up, the map of the world is capable of all sorts of rearrangements. . . .' The fullest discussion of this obscure subject is in chapter xx of Gollin, *Proconsul in Politics*, 522–77.

demand. They held that aeroplanes were best used in cooperation with the army at the front: to act as observers for the
artillery; to fight the enemy fighters; and to carry out tactical
bombing. This did not suit public opinion at home. Smuts
stepped into the breach, his first assignment as a member of
the war cabinet. His report, completed in October 1917, was
an epoch-making document. There stem from it all the great
achievements of our contemporary civilization: the indiscriminate destruction of cities in the second World war; the
nuclear bombs dropped on Hiroshima and Nagasaki; and the
present preparations for destroying mankind. Smuts laid down
that, given enough aeroplanes, the enemy could be brought to
his knees without fighting on land at all. This did not merely
endorse the popular demand for reprisals. It was another
version of the Gallipoli dream—a way of achieving decisive
victory without mass casualties. Lloyd George naturally
snatched at it. An independent air ministry was set up under
Rothermere.[1] Trenchard, head of the Royal Flying Corps,
was made chief of staff to the Royal Air Force; and, when he
quarrelled with Rothermere, given command of an Independent Air force in France, with the task of bombing Germany
into submission. Trenchard never got the 100 squadrons which
he demanded—his highest effective force was nine. His independent force achieved nothing. Nevertheless, he insisted that
victory by air power alone was theoretically possible, and he
riveted this doctrine on the R.A.F. after the war. This was
probably the most permanent, certainly the most disastrous,
legacy of the first World war.

The air offensive had no relevance at the time except as a
demagogic gesture. Lloyd George sought other means of holding 'the people' to his side. They had to be told more clearly
what they were fighting for, particularly when the unmannerly
Bolsheviks discredited Allied war aims by publishing the secret
treaties. Besides, Labour took up the running. In December
1917 the Labour party and the T.U.C. agreed on a joint statement of war aims, which had been drafted mainly by Mac-
Donald. This was almost indistinguishable from the programme

[1] Harold Sidney Harmsworth (1868–1940): younger brother of Northcliffe;
cr. Baron Rothermere, 1914, Viscount, 1919. Director of army clothing department,
1916–17; secretary for air, 1917–18; director of propaganda to neutral countries,
1918; took over the *Daily Mail* on Northcliffe's death.

which the U.D.C. had been preaching since the beginning of the war. There was the same repudiation of secret diplomacy, the same refusal to discriminate between enemies and allies, the same emphasis on reconciliation with Germany—an outlook far removed from that of most supporters of the government in the house of commons. Nevertheless, Lloyd George endorsed the programme unreservedly when he spoke to a conference of trade union leaders on 5 January 1918. 'We are not fighting a war of aggression against the German people. . . . Nor are we fighting to destroy Austria-Hungary or to deprive Turkey of its capital, or of the rich and renowned lands of Asia Minor and Thrace.' There must be reparation and independence for Belgium. 'We mean to stand by the French democracy to the death in the demand they make for a reconsideration of the great wrong of 1871.' There should be an independent Poland, and the nationalities of Austria-Hungary should receive 'genuine self-government on true democratic principles'. Above all, 'a great attempt must be made to establish by some international organisation an alternative to war as a means of settling international disputes'.[1]

This was the fullest statement of British war aims made in the course of the war. It had been formally approved beforehand by the king, by the governments of the Dominions, and by Asquith and Grey on behalf of the Opposition. Yet it was made to a trade union conference, not to the house of commons —a striking illustration of Lloyd George's offhand attitude towards traditional institutions. His appeal to great moral principles carried the day with the trade unionists. Moreover, he received a practical reward. The unions, after some embarrassing questions about the conscription of wealth, agreed to a more rigorous comb-out in the factories. Manpower was indeed now the most pressing problem. Haig demanded 600,000 men in order to maintain Kitchener's arbitrary target of seventy divisions.[2] A committee of the war cabinet attempted to define priorities. They put the navy[3] and air force first; next, the merchant navy, shipbuilding, and coalmining, and, after these,

[1] See Note D, p. 116.
[2] Haig inflated his demands by treating men in the tank corps, the machine-gun corps, the R.A.F., and maintaining communications as 'lost' to the army.
[3] Churchill, who after all knew a great deal about the navy, thought the figure fixed for it much too high; but, of course, he wanted more men for munitions, again on no precise basis—simply, 'the sky's the limit'.

the manufacture of tanks and aeroplanes; finally, the production of food and timber. The army could then have what was
left over. The war cabinet, guessing blindly, thought this would
be 150,000 men. It turned out to be less than 60,000.

Haig and Robertson cast envious eyes on the two million men
in the Near and Middle East. Lloyd George resisted them. The
fighting here had produced great victories which, in popular
opinion at any rate, did something to atone for the failures in
France. The army of Mesopotamia was in Baghdad. The army
of Palestine took Jerusalem in December 1917. The oil of the
Middle East was falling into British hands, while the conquest
of Palestine enabled the British government to win the favour
of Jews in the United States—and perhaps in central Europe
also—by promising that there should be a national home in
Palestine for the Jews.[1] Lloyd George was unshakeably convinced that these victorious armies could somehow defeat even
Germany if they swept on far enough. Robertson waved Lloyd
George's proposals aside, asserting the unique importance of
the western front as dogmatically as Lloyd George rejected it.
Yet Robertson, too, contributed his bit towards limiting the
flow of men to France. On his authority, the reserve of 120,000
men, destined for France, was held in England—partly for the
quaint reason that it was economically better that they should
spend their pay at home.[2]

Lloyd George wished to grasp the supreme direction for
himself. His immediate target was Robertson, though he would
have been glad to get rid of Haig as well. Lloyd George trembled
before acting. The king supported his generals. The Unionist
backbenchers had unquestioning faith in them. Asquith was
ready to take up their cause for want of anything better.

[1] This was the Balfour declaration (2 Nov. 1917). Palestine was at this time
inhabited predominantly by Arabs, a fact which the British government brushed
lightly aside. Apparently it was assumed that the Arabs would gladly abandon
Palestine to the Jews in gratitude for receiving some sort of national existence in
the other Ottoman territories. Or maybe Lloyd George and Balfour merely took
their knowledge of Palestine from the Bible, which in this respect happened to be
out of date. Of course, one purpose of the Balfour declaration was to put a barrier
between the French in Syria and the Suez Canal. This was an aspect not aired in
public.

[2] The war office also asserted that the reserve could be more easily concealed
from the Germans in England than in France, and that public opinion, shocked
by the heavy casualties, would be calmed if the reserve remained in England.
Lloyd George added: 'I don't trust Haig with men.' All the same, the decision was
made by the war office, not by Lloyd George.

Lloyd George made out, and perhaps believed, that there was a cabal to 'enthrone a Government which would be practically the nominee and menial of the military party'.[1] He sought a way round. He played again the card of Allied cooperation, as he had done earlier with Nivelle. In November 1917, at his prompting, a Supreme War Council, composed of the Allied prime ministers and specially appointed military advisers, was set up at Versailles. The council was supposed to provide a coordinated direction of the war, and so, to some extent, it did. Its subordinate bodies pulled together Allied resources, particularly in finance and shipping.[2] In the military field it proved ineffective. Robertson refused to work with the Versailles council. He alarmed the Liberal Opposition. There was a stir of isolationist complaint in the house of commons. Lloyd George ran away. The supreme council, he explained, had no powers; it could only discuss and advise. As to an Allied generalissimo, 'personally, I am utterly opposed to that suggestion'.

In February 1918 Lloyd George tried again. The supreme council resolved to set up a general reserve of British and French divisions, under the control of its own military advisers. If this scheme operated, grand strategy would be determined in Versailles, not by the C.I.G.S. in London. Once more Robertson resisted. He refused either to go to Versailles himself or to remain C.I.G.S. with reduced powers. The king and Asquith rallied to his support. Derby, Lord Robert Cecil, and Walter Long threatened to resign. Curzon from within the war cabinet hinted that he would join them—playing with both sides as he had done in December 1916. Only Milner and Law stood by Lloyd George. This time he resolved to fight. He challenged the Commons to turn the government out. He told the king's secretary: 'If His Majesty insisted upon Robertson's remaining in office . . . the King would have to find other Ministers.'[3] Opposition crumbled before this threat. The Commons did not divide; the king explained that he had been misunderstood.

---

[1] Lloyd George, *War Memoirs*, v. 2786.

[2] An Anglo-French buying commission coordinated orders in the United States. The Allied Maritime Transport Council, composed of ministers from each country, agreed on shipping requirements and transmitted their decisions to an Allied Maritime Transport Executive, which ran all shipping, Allied and American, until the end of the war.

[3] Memorandum by Stamfordham, 16 Feb. 1918. Beaverbrook, *Men and Power*, 412.

On 18 February Robertson read in the morning papers that he had resigned. He was given the command in eastern England—a good joke at the expense of an uncompromising 'westerner'.[1]

Sir Henry Wilson, the new C.I.G.S., was as much a 'westerner' as Robertson, or even more so: his prewar plans had caused the British army to join the French front in the first place. But, unlike most generals, he knew how to cajole civilians in high places—'frocks' though he called them. Henceforth the war cabinet had an articulate military adviser, who listened to Lloyd George's ideas and occasionally carried them out. There was a flaw in Lloyd George's victory. At the last moment Haig adroitly abandoned Robertson and declared that 'he was prepared to accept whatever was decided by the Cabinet'. Smuts, after touring the western front, reported that there was no one better to take Haig's place. Perhaps he did not look very far;[2] perhaps Lloyd George shrank from tackling the king's favourite. At any rate, Haig survived. The upheaval, in any case, came too late. Lloyd George lost freedom of strategic decision just when he thought he had won it. In previous years the Allies were on the offensive and could debate whether to fight in France or somewhere else. In 1918 the Germans decided to strike in France before the Americans arrived in overwhelming numbers, and therewith the Allies had their strategy settled for them—they had to fight on the western front, whether they would or no.

Ludendorff, who directed German strategy, had exactly the same aim as Haig, though, of course, in the reverse direction. He, too, planned to break through in Flanders and then to swing round behind the line of fortified trenches. He had devised a new and, as he hoped, a more successful method. Far from attacking in Flanders, he would begin his offensive on the Somme, further south, and would strike at the vital point only when the British forces had been drawn away from it. Nor

[1] The affair of the Versailles council was shown to be a manœuvre against Robertson. The general reserve was never formed. Rawlinson, the military representative at Versailles, was put under the orders of the C.I.G.S., just as Robertson had demanded, and no one turned a hair.

[2] Allenby and Plumer have been put forward as superior to Haig. The Australian, Sir John Monash, has also been praised. But he was, by profession, a civil engineer; he was a Jew; and he commanded an army corps only for six months. Lloyd George alleges that he did not learn about Monash until after the war. *War Memoirs*, iv. 2267.

did Ludendorff propose to repeat Haig's heavy casualties. He had made tactical improvements also: no warning bombardment beforehand; attack by surprise; and advance against the weak spots, leaving the pockets of resistance to be dealt with later. The German preparations, though made in great secrecy, did not pass unobserved. British intelligence officers warned Haig. He refused to move troops from Flanders—perhaps for sound defensive reasons, perhaps still dreaming of a renewed offensive there. Nor did he ensure that the forces actually on the Somme were in strong positions. He was confident that the German offensive would be halted, as his own had been.

On 21 March the Germans attacked on the Somme, exactly at the join between the British and French armies. Heavy fog completed the surprise. The British line was blown wide open. Within a few days, the Germans advanced forty miles. The British army was composed now of wartime soldiers, trained only for the trenches. They were unprepared for a war of movement and fell back in disarray once they were driven out of their fortified positions. Haig faced defeat in the field. Only Lloyd George rose undismayed to the height of the crisis. On 23 March he took over direction of the war office from the helpless Derby. He found, to his surprise, that 88,000 men were home on leave. With Maclay's assistance, transports were stepped up from 8,000 to 30,000 men a day. Beforehand, Haig had said that he could hold the Germans without the reserve for eighteen days. Lloyd George got it over to him in a week. On 28 March Lloyd George acted independently at the foreign office also. Without consulting Balfour, he telegraphed to President Wilson, appealing for the immediate use of American troops on the battlefield. Wilson responded: he overruled his own commander, Pershing, as Lloyd George had wished to overrule his own generals.

The Allies were not only retreating. They were falling apart. Haig proposed to cover the Channel ports. Pétain prepared to cover Paris. Combined strategy had ceased to exist. Haig, once its opponent, was now ready for it, if it brought him French assistance. On 26 March Milner crossed to France, on behalf of the war cabinet.[1] A conference with the French was held at Doullens. Pétain prophesied capitulation first for Haig, then for

---

[1] Lloyd George claimed that he was too busy to leave England. No doubt he was glad to leave Milner with the decisive battle against Haig.

himself. Foch insisted that the Germans would stop, if resisted
hard enough. On Milner's initiative, Foch was empowered
'to co-ordinate the action of the Allied armies'. On 3 April
a further conference at Beauvais, attended this time by Lloyd
George, gave Foch 'the strategic direction of military operations'. On 14 April the British war cabinet named Foch
'commander-in-chief of the Allied armies'. This impressive
title, though acknowledged also by the Americans, gave Foch
little real power. There was no inter-allied staff, nor did the
Allied commanders ever confer together.[1] Foch shaped the battle
to some extent by his control of the reserves, so long as the Allies
were on the defensive. When their turn came to attack, Foch
did little more than accept the pet schemes of the national
commanders and hope for the best. In his own words, he was
merely a conductor who beat time well.

The Germans still beat the time in the spring of 1918. Their
first offensive against the British from 21 to 28 March carried
them forward across the old battlefields of the Somme. Their
second blow from 9 to 25 April, also against the British, brought
them less gain, though it provoked Haig's despairing cry:
'With our backs to the wall and believing in the justice of our
cause each one of us must fight to the end.' In England this
sentence was ranked with Nelson's last message. At the front,
the prospect of staff officers fighting with their backs to the
walls of their luxurious chateaux had less effect. After a month's
pause, the Germans struck against the French and advanced
across the Marne to within forty miles of Paris. On each
occasion, Ludendorff was lured by success into prolonging his
attack without purpose. Each offensive ended with the Allied
line unbroken and the Germans in an awkward bulge or salient,
the sides of which threatened to close in behind them. 'Hagen',
the decisive stroke in Flanders, was still delayed. Meanwhile, the
Allied armies grew stronger. Half a million men were added
to the British forces in France—some from Palestine, most of
them from England. The Americans had twenty-seven divisions
in France by the end of July, thirty-four by the end of the war.
Most of them had been brought over in British ships. Their
equipment of guns, tanks, and aeroplanes came almost entirely
from British and French factories.

[1] Haig, Pétain, and Pershing were only once, all three, in the same room with
Foch.

The war against the U-boats continued with full intensity. During 1918 the British and Americans laid a line of mines from Norway to the north coast of Scotland. Young naval officers favoured a more aggressive policy. On 23 April Sir Roger Keyes, now in command of the Dover Patrol, attacked the U-boats in their wasps' nests at Ostend and Zeebrugge. The attempt at Ostend was a failure. Three blockships were sunk at Zeebrugge, though the channel was not completely closed. In any case, Ostend and Zeebrugge were less used by U-boats than the British imagined. Still, this was a romantic venture, and brought a gleam of light during the days of gloom.

The dark hour before the dawn produced a fresh stir of discontent in England. The war cabinet solemnly consulted Bottomley, 'the soldiers' friend', about popular feeling and perhaps even offered him a place in the government. Pemberton Billing, the other leading demagogue, was the triumphant hero in a libel action, brought against him by the dancer Maud Allan, when he made great play with a Black Book, allegedly in German hands, and which was supposed to contain the names of 47,000 British perverts in high places. Among the names were those of Mr. and Mrs. Asquith (as also of Darling, the judge who conducted, or misconducted, the case); not, however, that of Lloyd George. The case, though no doubt trivial, was a striking illustration of the disrepute into which the governing class had fallen. The most powerful outcry was still against 'slackers'. Lloyd George responded by raising the age of compulsory military service to 50. This was no more than a dramatic gesture: none of the men now conscripted served on the battle front.

A more unfortunate gesture went with it. Backbenchers complained against the new drafts while Ireland remained free from compulsion. Informed opinion, including even Carson, was against extending compulsion to Ireland: it would merely provoke resistance and would need more British soldiers to enforce it than it brought in. Lloyd George thought he saw yet another way round. Just at this moment, the convention, which had been trying to find a solution of the Irish question, announced that it had failed: Ulster had been unyielding. The problem was back on the government's desk. Something had to be done, if only to conciliate Irish opinion in the United States. Lloyd George therefore extended compulsion to Ireland, with an assurance that it would be applied only when she received Home Rule. In this way, he hoped, the Unionists would swallow Home Rule, and the Irish would swallow compulsion. The manœuvre did not work. The Irish were not won over by the distant promise of Home Rule. The Irish Nationalist M.P.s left the house in a body, most of them never to return, and joined hands with the Sinn Feiners. De Valera became the acknowledged leader of the Irish people. The Roman Catholic hierarchy, which had hitherto kept aloof from politics, denounced conscription as 'an oppressive and inhuman law which the Irish have a right to resist by every means that are consonant with the laws of God'. The congregations at Mass the following Sunday pledged themselves to resist conscription. On 23 April a general strike closed all Ireland, including the bars, for twenty-four hours, except in Belfast. The British government hastily invented a 'German plot'. The Sinn Fein leaders were arrested and sent to prison again in England; French was made Viceroy, to rule by military force; the talk of Home Rule was dropped—in Lloyd George's evasive phrase, 'it passed for the time'.[1] Conscription disappeared also: it was never applied in Ireland. The withdrawal came too late. This was the decisive moment at which Ireland seceded from the Union. Ludendorff, though he lost the war for Germany by his great offensive, also caused the British empire to lose Ireland.

Lloyd George faced more immediate dangers at home. Under cover of the crisis in France, he got rid of Derby in April and sent Milner to the war office[2]—civilian control asserted there at last. Robertson's satellite, Sir Frederick Maurice, who relinquished at this moment his post as director of military operations, feared that a new intrigue was brewing against Haig. He resolved to thwart it. Disregarding the rule against public criticism of official superiors, he wrote to *The Times* on 7 May and accused Lloyd George of lying to the house of commons about the strength of the British army in France

[1] Lloyd George, *War Memoirs*, v. 2670.
[2] Lloyd George was in such a hurry that he informed the king by telephone only when the appointment had been made. Derby became ambassador in Paris. Milner left the war cabinet, with a promise that he would be called in whenever military matters were discussed. The promise was not kept. Austen Chamberlain took Milner's place in the war cabinet. This was a political appointment to appease the Unionists, and the first open abandonment of the war cabinet's aloofness from party considerations.

at the beginning of 1918. This was really a dead issue. There was no sense in quarrelling over the past, but in these uneasy days nerves were on edge, and few men judged sanely. The Squiffites thought that their chance had come. They pushed Asquith into demanding a select committee to inquire into the truth of Maurice's allegations. Lloyd George and Law at first lost courage. They offered an inquiry by two judges. Asquith refused the offer. Lloyd George had to face battle. He had the great asset that the attack came from Asquith. Carson, himself a virulent critic, attended a meeting of Unionist backbenchers, and reported sadly: 'their hate of Asquith overrides all other considerations, and they will not back him to-morrow'.[1]

Lloyd George developed an unexpectedly good case. With miraculous sleight of hand, he showed that the figures of man-power which Maurice impugned, had been supplied from the war office by Maurice's department.[2] Asquith, supinely obstinate to the last, did not withdraw his motion. One hundred Liberals voted for it, and one Unionist—even Carson voted with the government.[3] The attack had been bungled, as were most things which Asquith, or for that matter Maurice, had a hand in. The conspirators, if such they were, forgot the advice of F. E. Smith: 'The man who enters into real and fierce controversy with Mr. Lloyd George must think clearly, think deeply, and think ahead. Otherwise he will think too late.'[4] The 'Maurice debate', though irrelevant to the war, was of historic importance. The official Opposition had divided the house against the government for the only time in the war. The Liberal party was split in two, a split which was never healed. On 9 May 1918 the historic Liberal party committed suicide. Maybe liberalism was dying in any case. It was a strange fate that the final sacrifice should be made on behalf of generals and against the authority of civilian government.

Lloyd George triumphed in parliament. The Maurice debate marked the beginning of his personal dictatorship. Yet, just at this time, his power was being sapped elsewhere. Lloyd George

[1] Repington, *First World War*, ii. 398.
[3] Six anti-war Labour, 1 Unionist, and 1 Irish Nationalist voted for Asquith's motion; 293 M.P.s voted against it. The victory of Lloyd George would have looked less impressive if the other 75 Irish Nationalists had been present to vote for the motion, instead of agitating in Ireland against conscription.
[4] Tom Jones, *Lloyd George*, 152.

was a demagogue. He owed his power to 'the people', not to party; he was a great individual, not a party leader. The people to whom he appealed were unorganized, like himself. But there was now also an organized 'people', the workers in the factories. Where once the typical man of the people had been a shopkeeper (preferably a cobbler), he was now a shop steward. With him Lloyd George's magic failed to work. In the summer of 1918 there was a new wave of strikes, concerned less with wages than with questions of status: a strike by munition workers in Coventry against further 'dilution'; a strike by the London police for recognition of their union; strikes by the cotton workers against their humiliating dependence on their 'rota'. Churchill, though previously generous with increased wages,[1] wanted firm action, and indeed broke the strike at Coventry by threatening to draft the strikers into the army. Lloyd George met the strikers with soft words, and some concessions. The strikes were not only alarming in themselves—particularly the unparalleled display of working-class feeling by the guardians of public order—unlike the strikes of previous years, they were led by the union leaders, themselves driven on by pressure from the shop stewards. The political Labour party, too, was breaking away. In May Labour actually ran a candidate in a by-election at Wansbeck against the official Coalition nominee—and nearly won. Though England was still far from the conditions which had produced revolution in Russia, patriotic unity was fading. The working classes resented the great profits of 'the bosses'. Class conflict was waiting round the corner while the great battles were still being fought.

To counter this feeling, an attempt was made to formulate more clearly the great ideals of the British cause. The attempt happened more or less by accident. Hitherto opinion had been left much at the mercy of the press, from pacifists and socialists on one side to Bottomley on the other. The Press Bureau had only a negative function, to prevent the publication of news which might be of use to the enemy. A few papers were prosecuted for breaches of security, none for expressing unwelcome opinions.[2] In February 1918 a ministry of information (the

---

[1] In July 1917 Churchill granted a bonus of 12½ per cent. to munition workers on time rates, to compensate them for the great increase in piece rates. When there was an outcry, he gave a bonus of 7½ per cent. to pieceworkers as well.

[2] In July 1917 a short-lived ban was placed on the foreign circulation of the *Nation*, because of its advocacy of peace by negotiation.

last new ministry created during the war) was set up under Beaverbrook.[1] Theoretically this had no concern with opinion at home. One department, under Rudyard Kipling, aimed at American and Allied opinion; a second, under Rothermere, at the neutrals. The most important conducted enemy propaganda—an innovation as remarkable in its way as the tank or the aeroplane and, like them, still in an experimental stage when the war ended. Since the press was, at this time, the only means, apart from speeches, of influencing opinion at home, it was supposed that newspapermen were the ones to employ also against the enemy. Beaverbrook, himself a beginner in this field,[2] therefore called in Northcliffe, who suspended his attacks on the government in order to turn his talents against 'the Huns'.

His political grasp was small. He understood how to spread ideas, not how to manufacture them. He brought to his new post a delight in ingenious methods. Balloons deluged Germany with news of Allied successes, and the German lines with certificates promising good treatment for those who surrendered. Northcliffe had nothing to contribute when it came to policy. He turned to the enthusiasts for a better world: men convinced that the war was being fought for great ideals, and almost convinced that these ideals would win the war of themselves. H. G. Wells and Wickham Steed, for instance, rejoiced that they could now define British policy without waiting for directives from the government, least of all when expressed in the icy tones of the foreign office. Crewe House, Northcliffe's headquarters, probably did not do much to shake enemy morale—certainly less than enemy writers later alleged. But it committed Great Britain firmly to the League of Nations and to the cause of national self-determination. The government trailed behind Northcliffe for want of anything better. In June they committed themselves to 'a united and independent Poland with free access to the sea'. In August they recognized a national council, headed by Masaryk, as 'the present trustee

[1] Beaverbrook combined this post with that of chancellor of the duchy of Lancaster. The king objected that the chancellor had some ecclesiastical preferment and that Beaverbrook was a Presbyterian. This was an inappropriate objection to make to a prime minister who was a Baptist and who yet nominated the bishops of the Church of England.

[2] The *Daily Express*, in which Beaverbrook held a controlling interest, had a small circulation. He developed it as a mass organ only after the war.

of the future Czechoslovak government'. They would have endorsed Yugoslav ambitions also, had it not been for Italian objections. These acts did not destroy the Habsburg Monarchy. It was destroyed by defeat in war, and then abandoned by its peoples. But, thanks to Crewe House, national liberation, when it came, was—or seemed to be—a victory for the British cause.

Lloyd George and Balfour welcomed this outcome. Lloyd George's Welsh heart responded eagerly to the call of small peoples, and it gave him material for a peroration. Balfour, once the hardest opponent of the national principle in Ireland, was now the most resolute for destroying German hegemony. Others were more hesitant. None of the military leaders believed that the war could be won in 1918. Sir Henry Wilson reported on 25 July that the decisive battle might be fought in July 1919.[1] Smuts told the war cabinet on 14 August that the war would probably last until 1920, and asked: 'was that worth while?'[2] He and Milner still pressed for a compromise peace, which would allow Germany to keep her gains in eastern Europe on condition that she withdrew in the west. In July 1918 Allied forces began to intervene in Russia: ostensibly to revive an eastern front against the Germans, but with a hope also that the Bolsheviks would somehow be accidentally overthrown in the process. Hostility against the Germans merged easily into anti-bolshevism, particularly with those who saw Bolshevism in every movement of industrial unrest at home.

The advocacy of Smuts and Milner for a compromise peace, though not their anti-bolshevism, was overtaken by events. On 15 July the Germans staged their last offensive against the French. It miscarried within three days. Ludendorff was already in Flanders, waiting to give orders for the decisive blow there, when news arrived of the failure further south. On 20 July 'Hagen' was called off. The German attempt at victory was over. Initiative was passing to the Allies. There was little new in their strategy. Foch had been saying, 'attack! attack!' on every occasion since the battle of the Marne in 1914. Haig had been prophesying an early German collapse ever since the battle of the Somme. Now the facts caught up with their preconceived theories.

On 8 August the British attacked in front of Amiens, in order to protect the railway junction there. Four hundred and fifty-

---

[1] Lloyd George, *War Memoirs*, vi. 3116.   [2] Ibid. 3123.

six tanks were used in massed formation. The success was almost as great as that of Cambrai, though, once again, the means were lacking with which to widen the break in the German lines. Haig had, however, learnt a lesson from his previous failures, and Ludendorff's. He stopped the attack short after a couple of days, instead of creating an unwieldy salient, and started a second attack at another point, where the Germans had depleted their reserves in order to stem the first advance. These sharp jabs compelled the Germans to fall back in one place after another, and then to withdraw their whole line. In September Foch adopted the same method, without acknowledgement, along the entire Allied front. All the armies were now on the move for the first time since the battle of the Marne. Previous battles had been fought with limited forces: only twenty-two British divisions, for example, were engaged at the height of the fighting on the Somme. By September 1918 more than ninety divisions were often in action on each side on the same day.

Even now the German line was never broken for more than a few hours. The tanks were clumsy instruments, as likely to break down from mechanical failures as to be destroyed by enemy gunfire. They, and still more the supporting infantry, soon outran their supplies. Though a good deal of motor transport was now used—more for munitions than to move men—the British army, like those of its allies, was still basically dependent first on railways, and, nearer the front, on carts drawn by horses. Petrol for the tanks and motor vehicles had to come in two-gallon cans from the depots at Calais and Rouen,[1] and this limited the supply drastically. Manpower, too, was not inexhaustible. Though the Allies could count on an American army of five million men in 1919, they had to make do until then with what they had in hand, and, as always happened, Allied casualties again exceeded the German once they went over to the offensive. Strategy, too, did not work out. Foch wanted a great encircling movement, attacking the Germans on the two extreme wings—the British in Flanders, and the Americans towards Metz. The American offensive, conducted in the old battering-ram fashion, broke off short. The main British strength was too far south. The French armies,

---

[1] Even these depots had been set up only in 1916. Before then all petrol had been brought over in cans from England.

which also attacked, were in the centre. Hence, Allied successes
pushed back the German centre instead of turning the flanks,
and so, by compelling the Germans to shorten their line,
actually improved their position.

Soon, it seemed, the Allied drive would slow down, and the
Germans would then stand in a strong defensive position.
Final victory still appeared remote. Northcliffe said in Sept-
ember: 'None of us will live to see the end of the war.'[1]
Ludendorff was still confident that his armies would survive
the Allied onslaught and that Germany would then get favourable terms in a peace of general exhaustion. But now the rear
of the Central Powers began to crumble. On 19 September
Allenby destroyed the last Turkish army at the battle of
Megiddo. A few weeks later he entered Damascus. In mid-
September also, the armies which had mouldered at Salonika
so long, at last moved northwards. The Bulgarians, who had
done no fighting since 1915, decided that it was now too late
to begin and signed an armistice on 29 September. The way
was open for the Allies to break into central Europe. Ludendorff
had no forces to send against them. On 29 September he told
the German government that they must seek an armistice at
once, so that he could snatch a breathing space and consolidate
his defensive line. The German government did not like this
proposal. They wished to secure a statement of peace terms
from the Allies before seeking an armistice. Ludendorff, however, was insistent, and German military authority prevailed
over civilian for the last time. On 4 October the German
government appealed to President Wilson for an immediate
armistice and for the opening of peace negotiations.

The German approach to Wilson only, and not to the other
belligerents, was deliberate. They believed that they could get
softer terms from the idealistic President. They believed, too,
that, by professing a similar idealism, they could drive a wedge
between the United States and the Allies. Wilson responded to
this approach. He had little faith in the high principles of the
Allies, and reverted eagerly to his old position as an impartial
mediator. In this way he hoped first to tie the Germans to the
Fourteen Points, and then to force these Points on the Allies
with German assistance.[2] For nearly three weeks Wilson and
the Germans negotiated alone. Some of the Allies took alarm.

---

[1] E. Wrench, *Struggle*, 334.   [2] See Note F, p. 118.

The French, and still more the Italians, wished to formulate their own peace terms, in defiance of the Fourteen Points. Some British ministers also wished to protest. Lloyd George damped down the discontent. He knew that the Allies could not risk a real breach with the United States. Also, as a magician with words himself, he was confident that the Fourteen Points could be made to mean everything or nothing according to the ingenuity of their interpreter.

The Germans accepted the Fourteen Points on 23 October. The supreme war council considered them only on 4 November. House, Wilson's personal representative, threatened that America might make a separate peace if the Allies hesitated. Lloyd George held out firmly against 'the freedom of the seas'. He said: 'The English people will not look at it. On this point the nation is absolutely solid.' House was satisfied with an assurance that the Point should be discussed, though without prior commitment, at the peace conference. The French also managed to insert a claim to compensation from Germany 'for all damage done to the civilian population of the Allies and to their property by the aggression of Germany by land, by sea, and from the air'. The Italians tried to make reservations about their territorial claims under the treaty of London. They were told that these had nothing to do with terms for Germany and were browbeaten into silence. The supreme war council then accepted the Fourteen Points with the British and French reservations. In this roundabout way, the British and the Allies generally, having failed to lay down precisely their war aims against Germany, had their terms defined for them by the American President, a commitment which some of them later regretted.

The armistice terms were also arrived at in a roundabout way. Wilson referred the Germans to the commanders in the field for an armistice, as soon as they accepted the Fourteen Points. There were hasty and confused discussions among the Allies. Haig believed that the Germans had still plenty of fight in them, and the Allies, apart from the British, not much. He would therefore have been content with a German withdrawal from Belgium and northern France. Pershing, on the other hand, in defiance of his President, did not want an armistice at all: he proposed to fight on until the Germans agreed to 'unconditional surrender'. Foch rejected this: there was, he insisted, no case for continuing the war if the terms 'give us the desired results'. Privately he meant to smuggle into the terms of armistice the gains which he hoped to see in the future treaty of peace. He wished to take the Rhineland for France and therefore made out that German evacuation of the left bank of the Rhine and Allied bridgeheads on the right bank were essential as security against any renewal of the war. The British cabinet did not like Foch's condition, but they had their own anticipation of the final settlement: they wished to ensure that the German navy should at once cease to exist—a condition which Foch, in his turn, did not like. The outcome was a horse trade. Foch agreed to demand the surrender, or internment, of the entire German battlefleet; the British agreed to the Allied occupation of the Rhineland. Both British and French tried to anticipate the future and grabbed at the first measures which came into their heads.

These negotiations were conducted in a hugger-mugger of haste and confusion. The Fourteen Points were being wrangled over at one moment; armistice terms were being drafted the next. Present apprehensions of German strength clashed with future apprehensions that Bolshevism would sweep across a weakened Europe. In intervals snatched from debating the future of the world, Lloyd George and Law debated political tactics. They decided to maintain the Coalition and to hold a general election as soon as fighting stopped. On 5 November George V agreed reluctantly that parliament should be dissolved. Henry Wilson, meanwhile, concluded every war survey by urging, yet again, that conscription be applied to Ireland. All the time, fighting went on. Men were being killed till the last moment, though now Allied casualties were eclipsed by the flood of Germans who surrendered. Real fever heightened the temperature. An epidemic of influenza spread across the world. Starting apparently in the Near East, it reached central Europe in August, and England in October. Something like three quarters of the population were struck down. Lloyd George himself was confined to bed for ten days shortly after the armistice—in Manchester Town Hall of all places. All told, some 150,000 English people died of influenza in the winter of 1918–19. The death roll was even more severe elsewhere. Sixteen million Indians died from influenza—a greater number than the total war deaths in all countries. No one can say whether the epidemic was peculiarly virulent or whether it found easy victims among peoples worn down by the hardships of war. In either case, it increased the tension during the autumn of 1918, just as its terrible predecessor of 1847 sharpened tempers before the revolutions of 1848.

The end came abruptly. On 30 October the Ottoman government signed an armistice of surrender with a British admiral.[1] On 3 November the Austro-Hungarian high command concluded a similar armistice with the Italians. By then both Ottoman empire and Habsburg empire had ceased to exist. In Germany news of the negotiations with President Wilson produced a general desire to have done with the war. The fleet mutinied when the naval high command prepared for a futile 'death ride' against the British. Only the best units of the army showed any will to continue the fight. On 7 November a German armistice delegation passed through the lines. They were received in a railway carriage at Rethondes by Foch and by Admiral Wemyss, chairman of the Allied Naval Command. They asked for an armistice. The agreed terms were handed to them. The German army was to withdraw behind the Rhine; large quantities of arms and railway equipment, all submarines and most battleships were to be interned; the treaty of Brest Litovsk was to be annulled, and all German troops in eastern Europe withdrawn from beyond the German frontier of 1914. The Germans were in little condition to bargain. The Hohenzollern Reich, too, though not Germany itself, was collapsing. On 9 November William II fled to Holland where he abdicated. A republic was proclaimed in Berlin. At 5 a.m. on 11 November the German delegation signed the armistice. It came into force at 11 a.m. At that moment, German troops were still everywhere on foreign soil, except for the tiny corner of upper Alsace which the French had conquered in August 1914. Canadian forces entered Mons about an hour before the armistice and thus, appropriately, ended the war where the 'old contemptibles' had begun it.

In the fighting-lines there was bewildered relief when the guns ceased to fire. There was no fraternization and little rejoicing. In England people were less restrained. Work ceased in shops and offices, as news of the armistice spread. Crowds surged through the streets, often led by airmen and Dominion

---

[1] Clemenceau was angry that a French admiral had not signed also.

troops on leave. Omnibuses were seized, and people in strange garments caroused on the open upper deck. A bonfire heaped against the plinth of Nelson's column in Trafalgar Square has left its mark to this day. Total strangers copulated in doorways and on the pavements. They were asserting the triumph of life over death. The celebrations ran on with increasing wildness for three days, when the police finally intervened and restored order.

The house of commons met on the afternoon of 11 November. Lloyd George read the armistice terms, and concluded: 'I hope we may say that thus, this fateful morning, came to an end all wars.' The house adjourned and gave thanks at St. Margaret's 'for the deliverance of the world from its great peril'. The procession was led by the Speaker. Immediately following him, Lloyd George and Asquith walked side by side. They conversed about the progress of their respective daughters.

NOTES

NOTE A. *The Political levy.* Trade unions at first paid for political activities (salaries of M.P.s, subscription to the Labour party, &c.) from their general fund. In 1909 the Osborne judgement held these payments to be illegal— incidentally on most doubtful grounds. In 1911 payment of M.P.s was instituted from public money: one call on union funds thus removed, though some unions supplemented the salaries of their M.P.s, when free to do so later. In 1913 the Trade Union Amendment Act authorized unions to raise money for political purposes by a separate 'political levy', from which their members could contract out. This was intended to hamper their political activity: the general funds could not be used for it. Instead it proved an advantage. The political fund could not be used for anything else. In the old days a union felt generous when it subscribed £100 to the Labour party. Now it thought nothing of handing over £5,000, if the money were lying idle in the political fund. Not all the political fund was paid to the national Labour party. Some went to union M.P.s; some to assist local associations and to pay the local expenses of elections. All the same, the income of the Labour party multiplied by ten overnight, and it shot up further when unions increased their membership during the war. Thus the act of 1913, designed to cripple the Labour party, accidentally gave it a watertight guarantee of a regular and fairly substantial income, though not of course as substantial as that received by the two older parties (particularly the Unionists) from the secret subscriptions of rich men. The income of the Labour party was all a matter of public knowledge, audited twice over—once in the union accounts, and again in those of the party. The Labour party did not need to rely on the sale of honours or other shady devices, which the other two parties had to use, and it alone could publish (as it still does) honest accounts with little to conceal. Of course it had 'paymasters', but at least everyone knew who they were.

NOTE B. *Peace negotiations in 1917.* These provided a fruitful ground for many a wistful 'If only . . .' in later years. The most solid approach came from Charles, who had succeeded as Emperor of Austria in November 1916. He would have been glad enough to get out of the war on the basis of the *status quo ante*, or maybe with a new Habsburg kingdom of Poland, and was ready to express a pious wish that Alsace-Lorraine should return to France. These negotiations broke down on two grounds: (i) Austria-Hungary was incapable of breaking away from Germany even if her ruler wished to do so; still less could she actually turn against Germany, which is what the Allies really hoped for; (ii) the only Ally fighting against Austria-Hungary (now that Russia was virtually out of the war) was Italy, and the Italian statesmen refused to contemplate anything less than the full terms of the treaty of London. Even then they wanted to defeat Austria-Hungary as well. Direct negotiations with Charles failed in May. They were renewed later in the year between Smuts and the former Austro-Hungarian envoy in London, Mensdorff, but these, too, always met the barrier that Austria-Hungary could not become independent of Germany until after the war.

In the summer of 1917 Kühlmann, the German secretary of state, attempted to initiate peace negotiations, first through the Vatican, later through Madrid. This attempt, too, was futile. The minimum Allied terms were always the complete restoration of Belgium and north-east France and, less avowedly, the return of Alsace-Lorraine to France. Kühlmann demanded the retention of the French iron-fields by Germany and restrictions on Belgium's sovereignty in Germany's favour; all he offered in exchange was the cession of a tiny corner of Alsace. The negotiations, far from bringing the warring powers nearer together, drove them apart. Kühlmann's 'No, no, never' in regard to Alsace-Lorraine provoked in return a British declaration, for the first time, that the return of Alsace-Lorraine to France was a British war aim. Belgium was the decisive stumbling-block. This was the reason why Great Britain went to war, and no British statesman—not even the advocates of peace by negotiation—would accept anything less than complete independence and reparation, to which Germany would never agree except after total defeat. The true 'if only . . .' must therefore be 'if only Germany had not invaded Belgium . . .', a singularly barren speculation.

NOTE C. *The Representation of the People Act (1918).* This passed its second reading in the commons by 329 votes to 40; third reading by 214 to 7. Women's suffrage passed in committee by 385 to 55. The voting qualification for men over 21 was six months' residence (this excluded, as it still does, about 5 per cent. of the adult population—the one lapse from full universal suffrage); for women over 30 occupancy, which could be derived from the husband. It was feared that, without this inequality, women would outnumber men. No one was sure of the figures. There were expected to be 10 million male voters, and 6 or 7 million female. The actual figures, after demobilization in 1919, were 13 million men and 8·5 million women—

altogether over 20 million against 7 million before the war. One second vote could be cast either in a university constituency or for business premises. The City of London and a few other business constituencies such as central Manchester, thus survived.

The house of commons, favouring single-member constituencies, wanted the alternative vote. The house of lords wanted proportional representation, which involved the grouping of constituencies. In the end, the university constituencies got a form of alternative vote which changed the result on one occasion (A. P. Herbert, Independent, elected for Oxford in 1935). Provision was also made for an experimental run of proportional representation in 100 constituencies of large towns, which returned three or more members. This experiment was never tried.

All voting at a general election was to take place on the same day instead of being spread over several weeks, as it had been previously. The expenses of the returning officer (which might amount to several hundred pounds) were to be paid from public funds instead of by the candidates. As an alternative precaution against 'freaks', every candidate had to deposit £150, which he forfeited if he polled less than one-eighth of the total votes cast in his constituency.

The act also included a redistribution of seats, aimed at creating uniform constituencies, each of about 70,000 inhabitants and each returning one member. Twelve two-member boroughs, which did not merit increase to more than two or reduction to one, were allowed to remain as anomalous survivals of a system which had once been universal. Only four were 'historic', i.e. went back to the beginning (Derby, Norwich, City of London, Southampton). Otherwise the distinction between boroughs and counties vanished, except that boroughs, being more compact, usually held their count the same evening, and counties the following day. The representation of nineteenth-century industrial England reached its highest point, just before its predominance began to wane.

Conscientious objectors were disfranchised for five years after the war— a sad product of wartime bitterness. This clause was carried only by 209 to 171. The high Tory, Lord Hugh Cecil, was a teller for the minority.

NOTE D. *Lloyd George's war aims.* Lloyd George's speech was not so unreservedly idealistic as it appeared on the surface. The German colonies were to be disposed of on 'the general principle of self-determination'— in other words, they would not be returned to Germany. Again, though 'national' Turkey was respected, the Straits were to be 'internationalised and neutralised', and 'Arabia, Armenia, Syria and Palestine are in our judgment entitled to a recognition of their separate national conditions'— meaning that they were to be largely partitioned between England and France. The recognition of Austria-Hungary was largely tactical, due to the fact that Smuts was still negotiating with Mensdorff in Switzerland for a compromise peace.

Lloyd George had, of course, other aims beyond satisfying Labour. His speech was in part an answer to Lansdowne's appeal for peace by negotiation; in part an answer to the Bolshevik programme of no annexations and no indemnities. It was also designed to forestall President Wilson's enunciation of the Fourteen Points which followed a few days later. Lloyd George then claimed that his programme and Wilson's were 'substantially the same'.

NOTE E. *The accusations made by General Maurice.* Maurice challenged three government statements made in the house of commons. (i) On 23 April Bonar Law denied that the extension of the British line in France (which took place shortly before the German attack) had been imposed on Haig by the supreme war council; (ii) on 9 April Lloyd George asserted that the British army in France was stronger on 1 January 1918 than on 1 January 1917; (iii) on the same occasion Lloyd George said that there were only four white divisions in the Middle East. Maurice alleged that all three statements were lies. Maurice was undoubtedly wrong regarding the first statement. The only extension of the British line which actually took place was arranged privately between Haig and Pétain before the supreme war council came into existence, though Haig very likely carried it out for fear of something worse. Maurice had not been present at the supreme war council when the question was discussed; he had been in the corridor at Versailles and evidently read more into Robertson's hot-tempered comments than he should have done.

There was not much in the third charge. The vital question was as to the number of troops in France on 1 January 1918. Lloyd George, in his speech on 9 May, quoted a statement from the department of military operations—Maurice's own department—that the combatant British troops in France were greater on 1 January 1918 than on 1 January 1917. This proved decisive. Maurice was overwhelmed. He came to the surface only in 1922 when he claimed that the department had made a mistake in its figures. He further claimed that the mistake had been detected and a correction sent to Lloyd George. Lloyd George, still prime minister in 1922, brushed aside Maurice's request for a further inquiry. However, there remained a suspicion—particularly among those who always believed the worst of Lloyd George—that he had bewitched the house of commons on 9 May 1918 with figures which he knew to be wrong.

A slightly different version appeared in 1956. Beaverbrook then published a passage from the diary of Frances Stevenson, who was in 1918 one of Lloyd George's secretaries and who became many years later his second wife.[1] The passage was written in October 1934. It records that, shortly after Lloyd George's statement of 9 April, J. T. Davies—his principal private secretary—found the correction in a box which had accidentally not been opened. Davies put the correction in the fire, saying: 'Only you and I, Frances, know of the existence of this paper.' Was Davies deceiving his master or covering up for him? Either way it was a sensational story.

The truth is less sensational as often happens. The figures which Lloyd George gave on 9 April 1918 were correct: there were more British troops in France on 1 January 1918 than on 1 January 1917. But the 1918 figure included some 300,000 troops working in labour battalions, transport, and other non-combatant services. A Unionist M.P. noticed this flaw and set down a question asking for the comparative figures of combatant troops. Macpherson, parliamentary undersecretary at the war office, asked the

---

[1] Beaverbrook, *Men and Power*, 262–3.

department of military operations for an answer. Maurice, though still technically director, was away in France, seeking the command of a division from Haig. A subordinate officer sent the figures to Macpherson: more combatant British troops in France on 1 January 1918 than on 1 January 1917. Macpherson gave this answer in the house of commons on 18 April. The officer in the D.M.O. then noticed that he had made a mistake by including 113,000 troops in Italy. He sent a correction to Macpherson and also to Philip Kerr, another of Lloyd George's private secretaries. The correction came too late. The question had been asked and answered. Maurice, returning from France, cleared out his desk and handed over to his successor. He knew nothing of the figures supplied to Macpherson. Apparently he did not even read *The Times* for the days when he had been away.

When the storm blew, Lloyd George told Hankey to assemble the material for his speech. Hankey looked through *Hansard* and came upon the devastating figures given by Macpherson on 18 April. Neither Hankey nor Lloyd George could know that these figures had been corrected afterwards. On the other hand, neither Macpherson nor Kerr could know that Lloyd George was going to use these figures in his defence. Clearly Lloyd George acted in good faith.

On 13 May 1918 Milner, now secretary for war, told Lloyd George during the interval of a committee meeting that there had been a mistake in the figures supplied by the war office. Lloyd George replied: 'He could not be held responsible for mistakes originating in General Maurice's own department'. This remark was justified. The only person to blame in the affair was Maurice himself when he set the match to a political explosion without doing his homework.

The Maurice affair affected Lloyd George in another, more remote way. No disciplinary action was taken against Maurice—the government deciding, wisely from their point of view, not to make him a martyr. Robert Donald, editor of the *Daily Chronicle*, made him military correspondent of the paper, which had hitherto given Radical backing to Lloyd George. The latter was angry at this change of front and, shortly before the armistice, got his friend Dalziel—a press magnate whom he subsequently made a peer—to buy the *Daily Chronicle*. Donald was sacked overnight. The money to buy it came, either at once or a little later, from the fund which Lloyd George accumulated from the sale of honours. This purchase turned out a good speculation. The fund put in £1 million. In 1926 it sold out for £3 million to a syndicate, headed by Yule, Catto, and Reading. (This syndicate, in its turn, sold the paper to Henry Harrison, a maker of newsprint, who ran into financial difficulties and amalgamated it with the *Daily News* at a moment's notice in 1930.) The fund is generally held to have been a decisive element in discrediting Lloyd George. If this be so, Maurice—by provoking Lloyd George to a step which greatly increased the fund—helped him, in the end, on the road to political ruin.

NOTE F. *Wilson's fourteen points* (8 January 1918):

1. Open covenants of peace, openly arrived at. . . .

2. Absolute freedom of navigation upon the seas . . . alike in peace and in war. . . .

3. The removal, so far as possible of all economic barriers and the establishment of an equality of trade conditions. . . .

4. Adequate guarantees given and taken that national armaments will be reduced to the lowest point consistent with domestic safety.

5. A free, open-minded, and absolutely impartial adjustment of all colonial claims . . . the interests of the populations concerned must have equal weight with the equitable claims of the government whose title is to be determined.

6. The evacuation of all Russian territory and such a settlement of all questions affecting Russia as will secure the best and freest co-operation of the other nations of the world. . . .

7. Belgium . . . must be evacuated and restored, without any attempt to limit the sovereignty which she enjoys in common with all other free nations. . . .

8. All French territory should be freed and the invaded portions restored, and the wrong done to France by Prussia in 1871 in the matter of Alsace-Lorraine . . . should be righted.

9. A readjustment of the frontiers of Italy should be effected along clearly recognizable lines of nationality.

10. The peoples of Austria-Hungary . . . should be accorded the freest opportunity of autonomous development.

11. Rumania, Serbia, and Montenegro should be evacuated; occupied territory restored; Serbia accorded free and secure access to the sea; . . .

12. The Turkish portions of the present Ottoman Empire should be assured a secure sovereignty, but the other nationalities which are now under Turkish rule should be assured an undoubted security of life and an absolutely unmolested opportunity of autonomous development, and the Dardanelles should be permanently opened . . . under international guarantee.

13. An independent Polish state should be erected, . . . which should be assured a free and secure access to the sea, . . .

14. A general association of nations must be formed under specific covenants for the purpose of affording mutual guarantees of political independence and territorial integrity to great and small states alike.

IV

POSTWAR, 1918-22

THREE quarters of a million men from the United
Kingdom were killed during the first World war. The
Empire lost another 200,000—nearly a third of them
Indians; in all, a death roll approaching one million. The price
of victory, though high, was less than that paid by other countries. France, for instance, with a smaller population than the
United Kingdom, had a death roll nearly twice as great, and
felt the effects for many years afterwards. Moreover—perhaps
a cynical consolation—the slaughter of war was less than the
loss by emigration, mostly of able-bodied young men, which in
the years immediately before the war had been running at
nearly 300,000 per annum. Though the majority of these went
to the Dominions, principally to Canada, many went to the
United States, and the net result of the war was to make the
loss of men less than it would have been if emigration had continued at its old rate. This was particularly true in Ireland,
which contributed only 6 per cent. of its adult male population
to the armed forces, as against 24 per cent. in Great Britain.[1]
The mass killing of young men slightly increased the proportion of women in the population.[2] As a further scar, the war left
one million and a half men who were permanently weakened
by wounds or the effects of gas. Moreover, war selected its
victims in a peculiarly harsh way. Casualties were about three
times heavier in proportion among junior officers than with
common soldiers. This struck at the highest in the land. Asquith lost his eldest son; Law lost two sons. The roll of honour in
every school and college bore witness to the talents which had
perished—the men of promise born during the eighteen-nineties
whose promise was not fufilled. Though the death roll was not
large enough to create statistically a 'lost generation',[3] there

---

[1] Irish emigration continued until May 1915, when riots in Liverpool stopped
the departure of the emigrant ships.

[2] 1,068 females to 1,000 males in 1911; 1,096 in 1921.

[3] The 'lost generation' later provided three prime ministers (Attlee, Eden, Macmillan).

may have been an exaggerated sense of loss among those who survived. Or maybe the true misfortune of the war was that the older men remained obstinately alive.

Most of the deaths were directly due to battle. The armies in Salonika and Mesopotamia were ravaged by malaria. Medical science protected the forces in France from typhoid and other fevers, which in the Boer war had killed five men for every one killed in battle. Shell shock was the new malady of the first World war: a psychological collapse due more to the despair and futility of trench warfare than to mere battering. In the more mobile campaigns outside Europe it rarely occurred. The worst remaining scourge was venereal disease, which affected something like one man in five. The military authorities had no previous experience in dealing with a mass army and tried to pretend for some time that their men were only a little lower than the angels. French cooperation in organizing brothels, with some rudimentary medical control, was not enlisted until 1916; protective sheaths were not issued until 1917. In the end the problem was faced. Free treatment of venereal disease was the sole innovation in 'welfare' directly attributable to the first World war.

The civilian population suffered little physically, unless the deaths from influenza in the winter of 1918 to 1919 can be ascribed to the war. Less than 1,500 civilians were killed by enemy action from sea or air. There was some food shortage, due to bad distribution, before rationing was introduced in February 1918. Thereafter, rationing served to guarantee supplies, not to reduce consumption, and did so at moderate price.[1] The intake of calories—the only measure then known—almost kept up to the pre-war level. In other ways, of course, the civilian had a drab time. The diversion of labour to the army and to work on munitions had much the same effect as though three and a half million men had been unemployed throughout the war years.[2] Clothing, shoes, furniture were scarce and often of poor quality; trains were fewer and slower; coal sometimes ran short; there was, in many areas, no street

[1] Even so, the ministry of food showed a final profit of £6 million when it was wound up. The autonomous wheat and sugar commissions showed heavy losses, each incurred because of the decline in world prices after the war.

[2] Dearle, *The Labour Cost of the Great War to Great Britain*, 259–60. The net loss to the armed forces was 2 million, after setting off the recruitment of women; the diversion to munitions 1½ million.

lighting.[1] Against this, there was no unemployment. Welfare services greatly increased: canteens and sometimes medical attention in the factories; hostels for war workers; care for soldiers' wives and families. Wages had lagged behind the cost of living until the summer of 1917. Then they almost caught up, though they slipped behind once more when prices ran away in the post-war boom. Unskilled labour benefited most: the gap between its wage rates and those of skilled labour was permanently narrowed by the war.

Material loss was also slight, the gravest being the sinking of about 40 per cent. of the merchant fleet. Much of this was replaced during the last year of the war, and all soon afterwards. It was not long before the owners were complaining that they had too many ships. The cessation of many peacetime activities had a more damaging effect. Building of private houses stopped before the end of 1914, and the housing shortage became acute. By 1919, 610,000 new houses were needed.[2] The railways had been overworked, and much of their equipment was worn out. In the coal mines, the richest seams had been impatiently exploited. There had been no reorganization or regrouping, despite government control.

Elsewhere, there had been much capital investment, often in ways harmful for the future. Shipbuilding resources, for instance, greatly exceeded normal needs. New steel works had been created on the old sites near the ports (South Wales, Cumberland, Sheffield), instead of on the more economical sites, such as Lincolnshire, near the ore fields. The steel industry between the wars had too much capital in the wrong places and too little in the right ones. Again, the Cotton Control Board had preserved intact the pattern of an industry which was both over-capitalized and capitalized wrongly—too much equipment for Indian, and not enough for Egyptian, cotton. Yet immediately after the war new capital was poured into the old pattern. Most of it was sheer loss.[3] On the other side, the army never went over thoroughly to mechanized transport and so failed to encourage the mass manufacture of automobiles.[4]

---

[1] The 'black out' was not universal as it became in the second World war.

[2] The arrest in building was not, of course, the sole cause of the shortage. Increase of population, especially of young married couples, and the decline of older houses into slums contributed even more.

[3] In Oldham alone many fine mills completed in 1920 never operated.

[4] Army vehicles in Nov. 1918: 56,000 lorries; 23,000 motor cars; 34,000 motor

The war, in short, promoted further expansion in industries of which Great Britain had already too much, and did little to promote industries which would be valuable for the future.

The serious damage of the war was financial, not material. Before the war foreigners ran up large short-term debts in London; during the war Great Britain ran up short-term debts with foreign or Dominion countries, and the old-style creditor position was never restored. Privately owned investments abroad had been sold on government order, mainly to sustain the exchange value of the pound in the United States. Contemporary estimates put these sales at £850 million or even £1,000 million, i.e. nearly a quarter of the prewar total. Later investigation reduced the figure to £550 million, and discovered as well £250 million of new investment.[1] The net loss was therefore only about £300 million—not two years' investment on the prewar average, and in fact more than replaced by 1928. Greater losses came afterwards from causes not directly due to paying for the war—the revolution in Russia and repudiation by South American states. These causes were often lumped together with the war in the popular mind.

Debts between governments were larger. Great Britain lent about £1,825 million to her allies and borrowed £1,340 million.[2] These figures include transactions with the Dominions. More narrowly, the British government owed about £850 million to the United States and were themselves owed more than twice this sum by Allied governments, principally by Russia. The British would have done a good day's work for themselves and everyone else if they had proposed the general writing-off of inter-allied debts, while the Americans were still in the flush of wartime enthusiasm. But it was hard for the financiers in London to grasp that most European countries were no longer 'good' debtors, and that the central pillar of international finance, sanctity of contract, had fallen. By the time common sense broke in, the great opportunity had been lost. Inter-allied debts haunted international relations for many years, as figures on

bicycles. In Aug. 1914 the B.E.F. had 827 motor cars (all except 80 requisitioned) and 15 motor bicycles.

[1] Morgan, *Studies in British Finance*, 323–42. There was no exchange control during the first World war, and evidently many rich people sought profit abroad instead of investing patriotically in war loan.

[2] The gap was filled by the sale of securities. Great Britain paid her own costs of the war from current account.

paper. Their practical effect was small. Great Britain paid
slightly more to the United States than she received from others,
but not much. The war caused astonishingly little damage to her
financial position in the world. The injury came later with the
crumbling of the conditions—free exchanges and unimpeded,
though not free, trade—on which that position rested.

The internal debt was a more formidable matter. The war
cost the British exchequer £9,000 million, or £12,000 million
if the extraordinary expenditure of the two nominally postwar
years be included. Only 28 per cent. of this had been met
from taxes, or 44 per cent. counting in 1919-21. Such increase
of revenue as there was came mainly from direct taxation—
increased income tax and surtax, and excess profits duty[1]—
which contributed 80 per cent. of the total at the end of the war,
as against 54 per cent. before it. Direct taxes were the easiest to
increase, as Gladstone had warned long ago. Reliance on them
was also a matter of social policy: it appeased the working
classes by 'soaking the rich' and did not push up the cost of
living, as increase of indirect taxation did. This aim was, however, largely nullified by the even greater reliance on borrowing.
More money chasing fewer goods meant higher prices, as everyone knows nowadays, with demands for higher wages limping
after them. Few understood it then, and the wickedness of the
working classes in seeking higher wages was a favourite theme
of the postwar years. The National Debt stood at a terrific
figure, fourteen times greater than prewar. Its service took
nearly half the yield from taxation, against 14 per cent. before
the war. The National Debt had the effect of a snake on a
rabbit: it deprived even the most educated of sense.

In itself, the Debt did not diminish the wealth of the community at all, just as an individual does not impoverish himself
by transferring some of his money to a No. 2 account. The war
had been paid for while it was being waged, and the Debt was
a book-keeping transaction, its only real cost to the community
being the salaries of the clerks who handled it. Its significance
was purely social. The obligation to holders of War Loan, most
of it raised in depreciated pounds, ranked before the claims of

---

[1] The duty was prolonged until 1921 as a patriotic gesture. By then, many firms
were incurring losses and could set these off against their previous profits. The
final yield of E.P.D. was therefore less than it would have been if it had been taken
off in 1919.

the poor or of ex-servicemen, and nothing did more to restrict
social policy. Immediately after the war, the Labour party proposed to eliminate the Debt by a capital levy. The proposal was
taken up by men far from socialist, such as Beaverbrook and
Churchill. It was applied privately by Stanley Baldwin, then
a junior minister,[1] who devoted one fifth of his fortune to buying
War Loan and handing it over to the exchequer for cancellation.[2] Few followed his example. Law, at the exchequer, rejected a capital levy, for fear that it might be turned later to
more radical purposes than paying for the war. The National
Debt therefore remained in full, its service soon dictating economy
in every sphere of public expenditure. Few men foresaw this
when they campaigned during the general election of November 1918 with promises of a new and better country for the
returning heroes.

The case for a general election was overwhelming. The existing parliament had outlived its statutory term by three years;
the electorate had been more than doubled by the extension of
the franchise to all males and many women; the government
needed popular endorsement before they negotiated a peace
settlement. Lloyd George was naturally eager to preserve
national unity, of course under his own leadership. He urged
Labour to remain in the Coalition. He offered to make Asquith
lord chancellor and to include at least two other Liberal
ministers. Both invitations were refused. Labour was resolved
to become the second party in the state, with a clear socialist
programme. Bernard Shaw achieved his one historic moment,
at a special Labour conference on 14 November, with the words:
'Go back to Lloyd George and say: Nothing doing.' Most
Labour ministers resigned. The few who remained—including
George Barnes in the war cabinet—ceased to be members of
the Labour party. Labour fought the election uncomplainingly
as an avowed Opposition.

The position of the Liberals was more equivocal. The

[1] Stanley Baldwin (1867–1947): educ. Harrow and Cambridge; launched on
his official career by Law who made him financial secretary to the treasury in June
1917, in order to do the treasury entertaining which Law disliked; president of
board of trade, 1921–2; chancellor of exchequer, 1922–3; prime minister, 1923,
1924–9, 1935–7; lord president of council, 1931–5; lord privy seal, 1932–4; cr.
Earl, 1937.

[2] Baldwin announced his project in a letter to *The Times* signed F. S. T. (i.e.
Financial secretary to the treasury, Baldwin's office). At the time no one guessed
who F. S. T. was. Later the secret became known. Who can have divulged it?

Squiffites had in fact harassed Lloyd George and had done their best to overthrow him. Yet they were aggrieved to be treated as an Opposition and seem to have thought that the wartime electoral truce should still be continued for their benefit. This was impossible. With the country in a violent, anti-German mood, the Unionists were rightly confident of crushing victory and, whatever Lloyd George might say, would insist on fighting, and defeating, every Liberal, unless somehow restrained from doing so. Lloyd George's Liberal whips struck a bargain with the Unionists that 150 Liberals should be spared, i.e. that Unionist candidates should not be run against them.[1] These favoured Liberals—'100 of whom are our Old Guard'— gave a pledge in return that they would support the Coalition. Asquith alleged that the 'coupon' as he called it[2]—the endorse- ment by Lloyd George and Law of Coalition candidates—was a device for slaughtering the independent Liberals and, in particular, that the test of shibboleth was the vote after the Maurice debate. Both accusations, though accepted almost universally by historians, were untrue. The coupon was Lloyd George's device to save as many Liberals as he could. Without it the Unionists would have swept the country. As it was, 'more Liberals were elected in 1918 than ever after'.

Nor was the distribution of the coupon determined by the Maurice debate. Two hundred and twenty-nine Liberals did not receive the coupon, yet only 100 Liberals had voted against Lloyd George; 25 of these 100 were not candidates and 12 more were not Liberal candidates. Eleven of the Liberals who voted against Lloyd George, and one Unionist, actually received the coupon. Asquith himself had no coupon issued against him.[3] Of the 159 Liberal candidates who received the coupon, only 54 had voted for Lloyd George after the Maurice debate, and 4 of these had the coupon issued against them.[4] In a wider way, too, the parties had a fair field. The Unionists ran only 410 candidates, against 425 Liberals (Asquithian and Coalition)

[1] Lloyd George's whips did better than they expected: they received in fact 159 coupons. The National Democratic party (a pro-Coalition breakaway from the B.S.P.) received 18.

[2] An echo of the coupons in the ration books.

[3] He was defeated by a Unionist who refused to withdraw. Law and the Unionist whips failed to secure the withdrawal of rebel Unionists in many constituencies.

[4] Full details in T. Wilson, 'The Coupon and the British General Election of 1918', *Journal of Modern History*, xxxvi.

and 447 Labour.[1] But most of the Unionist candidates were
returned. This was the work of the electors, not of Lloyd George
or of the party managers.

Another myth soon grew up that the two Opposition parties
advocated a peace of reconciliation, and the Coalition a peace
of revenge. The few Radicals and Labour men who had stead-
fastly opposed the war certainly preached a moderate peace,
and most of them lost their seats as the result. Otherwise there
was little to choose between the parties. Most Labour and
Asquithian Liberal candidates demanded 'reparations' and were
eager to try the Kaiser.[2] Lloyd George, as an experienced
solicitor, had grave doubts about trying the Kaiser—a project
which was forced on him by Curzon and Birkenhead. Both
Lloyd George and Law grasped the economic impossibility of
extracting the full costs of the war from Germany. Lloyd George
at first tried to make this clear in his public speeches. As the
national temper mounted, he temporized and announced that
he would claim the full costs from Germany, adding only in an
undertone that the claim was unlikely to be met.[3] He allowed
popular frenzy to rage and hoped to behave more sensibly
when the storm had abated. Still, there are no grounds for supposing that the house of commons would have been more moderate if the victory of the Coalition had been less complete. Nor
did rigour towards Germany rule out an idealistic peace in
other ways. Northcliffe, for instance, than whom no man could
be more anti-German, published in The Times peace terms,
drafted by Wickham Steed, which embraced the principle of
national self-determination.

The peace settlement was not the dividing issue. The election
was fought around Lloyd George—his past record and his
promises for the future. Lloyd George had won the war. Those

[1] Only 363 were endorsed by the Labour national executive. Ten of the others
were Cooperative candidates; 36 were Coalition Labour; the rest were independent,
mostly Left wing.
[2] Asquith and Grey had been the first to demand reparations for Belgium and
France. Barnes, who had only just ceased to be a member of the Labour party, was
the first to announce that he was for hanging (not even for trying) the Kaiser.
When the projected trial of the Kaiser was abandoned, the strongest protests in
the house of commons came from Lord Robert Cecil, a Unionist who had refused
the coupon, and from Sir Donald Maclean, leader of the Asquithian remnant.
[3] Few remarked at this time that, since the Allies had accepted the Fourteen
Points only with the reservation that Germany should pay for damage done to the
civil populations, they were not entitled to claim the whole costs of the war.

who had supported him now received the popular vote, even when, as happened with some pro-war Radicals and with Labour men who had been Coalition ministers, they did not receive the coupon. When Lloyd George talked of making 'a fit country for heroes to live in', his record in social legislation seemed to justify this promise. Probably many of the new electors cared as little for party as did Lloyd George himself. They voted mainly for Unionists, simply because there were more Unionists pledged to support Lloyd George. The result was a sweeping triumph for the Coalition, though less sweeping in votes than in seats won.[1] Three hundred and thirty-nine Coalition Unionists and 134 Coalition Liberals were returned.[2] The independent Liberals were annihilated. Every one of their former ministers lost his seat; only 26 Liberals were returned.[3] Labour also lost its 'pacifists'—MacDonald, Snowden, even Henderson. Otherwise it did better than the Liberals, increasing its members from 39 to 59, all but one of whom had been put forward by a trade union.[4]

There were two striking groups of absentees. No woman appeared in the house of commons, though women were now entitled to do so.[5] The Irish benches were almost empty. Sinn Fein won in Ireland as decisively as the Coalition won in Great Britain. Seventy-three Sinn Feiners were returned, capturing every seat outside Ulster, except Dublin university and two others. They refused to come to Westminster and instead set themselves up as the Dail, or parliament, of the Irish republic. Thus the Union was repudiated still more formally, and Irish unity was threatened along with it.

The new parliament has come in for much abuse. Baldwin

[1] The supporters of the Coalition received 6 million votes and 533 seats; its opponents (excluding Sinn Fein) received 4 million votes and 101 seats.

[2] There were also 4 so-called Labour supporters of the Coalition, all of whom soon disappeared from political life, 9 members of the National Democratic party, and 48 Unionists who had not accepted the coupon.

[3] Other counts give 29 independent Liberals. Many Liberals were of doubtful allegiance, and Coalition Liberals continued to frequent the National Liberal Club.

[4] The one exception was William Graham, a Labour journalist and a graduate of Edinburgh university. Forty-nine of the union nominees had been union officials.

[5] The one woman elected, Countess Markiewicz (Constance Gore-Booth), was a Sinn Feiner and so did not take her seat. The first woman to appear in the house of commons was a Unionist, Lady Astor, returned at Plymouth in 1919 in succession to her husband, when he went to the house of lords.

called its members 'hard-faced men who looked as if they had done well out of the war'. Austen Chamberlain described them as 'a selfish, swollen lot'. There were 260 new members,[1] and the average age was higher than before the war. Since the young men were mostly away fighting and not available for adoption as candidates, this was not surprising. There were more business-men than usual—some 260 against a normal 200 between the wars, and, of course, more trades union officials. Lloyd George, on the treasury bench, felt that he had the Trade Union Congress in front of him and the Association of Chambers of Commerce at his back. These were the men who had run the war on the home front, and they provided the only alternative when established political figures were rejected. In practice, the new house soon settled down into traditional behaviour. Some of the defeated leaders returned at by-elections, and in any case there were more than enough experienced members to keep things near to the old pattern. The hard-faced men were often blamed un-justly. The outcry against conciliating Germany, for instance, came from old-timers and from impeccable members of the traditional governing class, such as Sir Samuel Hoare[2] and Edward Wood, later Lord Halifax,[3] as much as from the inarticulate representatives of the Lloyd George revolution.

The war had brought something like a revolution in the organization of government also. This revolution was not main-tained. A ministry of health, combining the duties of the local government board and the health insurance commissions, was the only attempt at regrouping. The ministry of labour sur-vived: it ran the employment exchanges and unemployment insurance. There was also a new ministry of transport, to which the control of electricity was curiously tacked on, in the

[1] Namier found a normal turnover in the eighteenth century, unaffected by party, of about 150. Allowing for the defeat of sitting Liberals, the turnover in 1918 must have been much the same.

[2] Samuel John Gurney Hoare (1880–1959): educ. Harrow and Oxford; suc-ceeded to baronetcy, 1915; secretary for air, 1922–4, 1924–9, 1940; secretary for India, 1931–5; foreign secretary, 1935; first lord of admiralty, 1936–7; home secre-tary, 1937–9; lord privy seal and member of war cabinet, 1939–40; ambassador to Spain, 1940–4; cr. Viscount Templewood, 1944.

[3] Edward Frederick Lindley Wood (1881–1959): educ. Eton and Oxford; presi-dent of board of education, 1922–4, 1932–5; minister of agriculture, 1924–5; viceroy of India, 1926–31; cr. Baron Irwin, 1925; succeeded father as Viscount Halifax, 1934; secretary for war, 1935; lord privy seal, 1935–7; lord president of council, 1937–8; foreign secretary, 1938–40; member of war cabinet, 1939–45; ambassador to United States, 1941–6; cr. Earl, 1944.

mistaken belief that the railways would soon be electrified.[1] Otherwise the new administration, which Lloyd George announced on 10 January 1919 was little changed from the old one. Most of the wartime ministries were marked down to disappear, and their business chiefs along with them.[2] Churchill moved to the war office,[3] though he would have liked the admiralty; the air ministry was added unto him as a consolation. F. E. Smith became lord chancellor under the name of Birkenhead, an appointment not to the taste of George V. Law gave up the exchequer, though remaining leader of the house of commons and virtually deputy prime minister. Austen Chamberlain succeeded Law as chancellor of the exchequer.

Chamberlain found, to his indignation, that he was not to be included in the cabinet—to say nothing of being also kept out of No. 11 Downing Street, the chancellor's official residence, where Law proposed to remain. Lloyd George argued that, as he, Law, and Barnes (nominally the leaders of the three Coalition parties), and Balfour, the foreign secretary, would all be away in Paris negotiating peace, a cabinet could not be assembled.[4] He therefore proposed to do without one. Chamberlain rebelled, and Lloyd George agreed to continue the existing war cabinet, of which Chamberlain was already a member.[5] In practice, the war cabinet hardly functioned with most of its members absent—Chamberlain and Curzon were often the only ones in England. Plans were aired for reducing or rearranging the cabinet. Those whom it was intended to leave out protested, and in October 1919 Lloyd George casually restored the old peacetime cabinet of some twenty members, though keeping Hankey as secretary with his businesslike innovations.[6]

The restoration of cabinet government was far from com-

[1] This was the result of a deal between the Geddes brothers. Auckland Geddes, president of the board of trade, offered to surrender either shipping or electricity, but not both. Eric Geddes, minister of transport, chose electricity.

[2] The ministries slaughtered were information (Nov. 1918); national service (Mar. 1919); blockade (May 1919); reconstruction (June 1919); munitions (Apr. 1921); food (Apr. 1921); shipping (Apr. 1921).

[3] Milner, being now estranged from Lloyd George, was diverted to the colonial office.

[4] He could have added that, with Hankey, secretary to the cabinet, also in Paris, the conduct of cabinet business would be impossible. Hankey was called in as secretary to the Council of Four and brought its affairs to order.

[5] Chamberlain did not, however, get No. 11 Downing Street.

[6] Hankey's importance was enhanced when he became secretary to the revived committee of imperial defence and, in 1923, clerk to the privy council also.

plete. Lloyd George was now a renowned world statesman and slipped easily into dictatorial ways. He treated his most distinguished colleagues, except Law, as subordinates, disregarded the cabinet, and settled affairs with a few cronies or by means of the 'Garden Suburb'.[1] Arrogant self-confidence was not the only reason for this. His situation condemned him to success. His wartime government had been a true Coalition. Though the Unionists provided the most substantial support, Lloyd George and his Liberals were also essential. A government based on reunited Liberals and Labour was always a possible, if a remote, alternative. After December 1918 there was no such alternative. The Unionists had an independent majority and could set up a government of their own if Lloyd George broke with them. The ruin of the Squiffites was a disaster also for Lloyd George.

He tried to overcome it by invoking the social peril. He welcomed postwar discontent and looked forward to the day when there would be 200 Labour members of parliament. Then surely all moderate men would be scared into accepting his leadership. His calculation did not work out. The Unionists certainly wanted a single anti-Labour party, but claimed that they were themselves capable of providing it. The Coalition Liberals also held out against 'fusion'. They did not want to be eaten up, as the Liberal Unionists had been in the previous generation. Besides, they had convictions of their own, especially over Free Trade, which divided them from the Unionists. Hence Lloyd George had to rely on his personal achievements. His own instincts were all for conciliation: of Germany, of Soviet Russia, of Ireland, of the unions. These policies were repugnant to his Unionist supporters, and Lloyd George had to follow devious ways. David Low, the cartoonist, later attributed to Baldwin the words: 'If I hadn't told you I wouldn't bring you here, you wouldn't have come.' This was exactly Lloyd George's attitude to the Unionists. He beguiled them with unexpected and, for the most part, unwelcome successes, until, in the end, they preferred less ambitious, but also more consistent, policies without him.

Lloyd George, on the hunt for success, had to handle every problem himself: peace abroad, reconstruction at home, Ireland, the Empire. He darted from one problem to another,

[1] Until 1922 the Garden Suburb, not the foreign office, handled League of Nations affairs.

rarely finding enough time to work one of them through to the end. Immediately after the general election he was eager to be off to the peace conference. Virtually the whole foreign office was transferred to Paris,[1] and a good deal of the treasury and war office along with it. Ostensibly there was a British peace delegation of five.[2] In practice, Lloyd George handled every big question himself, using his colleagues as reinforcement in disputed issues, and otherwise delegating them to less important topics. This was particularly true after the first few weeks, when the leaders of the Great Powers disregarded the formal machinery of the peace conference and set themselves up as the 'Big Four'—President Wilson, Clemenceau, Orlando of Italy, and Lloyd George, with a Japanese representative hovering in the wings. Unlike earlier British negotiators of peace—Castlereagh, for example—Lloyd George did not even write his own instructions, let alone get them approved by the cabinet. He had no instructions and relied solely on his gift for improvization.

Peace was waiting to be made with all the former enemies— Austria and Hungary (now two separate states), Bulgaria, Turkey, as well as Germany, to say nothing of peace or restored relations with Soviet Russia. In practice, most of these questions were pushed into the background by the peace treaty with Germany. The Habsburg monarchy had already disintegrated, and the only problem was to draw the frontiers of her succession states—a task left mainly to the experts of the various foreign offices. The future of Fiume provoked a long and barren wrangle between President Wilson and the Italian government, much to the embarrassment of the British and French.[3] This was a tiresome distraction, never settled by the peace conference. The Ottoman empire had also disintegrated. Anglo-French forces were in occupation of Constantinople. The other Turkish

---

[1] Curzon, who was destined to succeed Balfour as foreign secretary after the peace conference, ran what remained of the foreign office in London. As a result of this odd arrangement, Balfour, who was not a member of the war cabinet (still theoretically in existence), exercised more power and influence than Curzon, who was.

[2] Four British ministers (Lloyd George, Law, Barnes, Balfour) and one Dominion prime minister (not always the same). The Dominions also secured independent representation after some wrangling with President Wilson (two each for Australia, Canada, India, and South Africa, and one for New Zealand). The total British Empire delegation was thus fourteen. Law rarely attended. When he did, he came to Paris by air—the first British statesman to use this new means of transport.

[3] See Note A, p. 161.

territories were in turmoil. The British and French, though disputing over the secret treaties, did not want to bring their dispute into the open, and Wilson, who disapproved of the secret treaties, had little claim to intervene, since the United States had never declared war on Turkey. In any case, settlement with Germany was obviously the most pressing topic for the future of Europe. The victors could no longer escape the question which had baffled them during the war: the German problem.

The British came to the problem with a great advantage: most of their worries had already been removed. The German navy had been handed over and was interned under British control at Scapa Flow. Germany had thus ceased to be a naval power even before the Germans scuttled their fleet at the time of the peace treaty. The fate of the German colonies had also been settled, mainly on the insistence of the British Dominions. South Africa and Australia refused to surrender the territories which they had conquered—German South-West Africa and New Guinea. Lloyd George derived malicious amusement from the way in which the spokesmen of these two democratic countries, supposedly unspotted with European wickedness, defied Wilson on old-fashioned imperialist lines. 'Mandates' were hastily invented to save appearances, and the British themselves took German East Africa, and some miscellaneous territory in West Africa, as their share. Now the British could approach the German problem as impartial mediators, not as combatants grasping the prizes of victory.

Wilson, too, saw himself as a mediator above the battle. The United States had no demands on Germany once she had been defeated. Wilson's obsession was the League of Nations, and he believed, quite wrongly, that the European Allies would oppose it violently. On the contrary, the British foreign office had prepared a draft scheme, under the inspiration of Robert Cecil and Smuts, while the Americans talked generalities, and this draft mainly provided the Covenant of the League. Clemenceau, too, had no objection, though little faith. The League was duly settled and written into the treaty of Versailles, before agreement was reached on anything else. Underneath, to be sure, there was profound divergence. The 'Anglo-Saxons' envisaged the League as an instrument of conciliation, softening all international antagonisms. The French wanted merely an additional

machine of security against Germany, perpetuating the wartime alliances. This divergence was to cause much trouble in
the future. What mattered in 1919 was that Wilson, like the
British, had got his way. Both he and Lloyd George were free
to moderate the French projects against Germany. Of the two,
Lloyd George was the more active and the more successful.

The French could not be freed so easily from the German
problem. In their eyes, Germany, though defeated, was still
dangerous. They would have liked to see Germany break up,
and, since this failed to happen, wanted elaborate precautions
against her for the future. Lloyd George held that, since Germany existed, she must be conciliated. Once more, he talked
'hard' with the intention of acting 'soft' when men, including
himself, came to their senses. He tolerated such gestures of
victory as the proposal to try the Kaiser and other 'war criminals'.[1] Otherwise he tried to keep the door of future conciliation
open. It was fortunate for him that Clemenceau was more concerned than perhaps any other French statesman to retain the
friendship of the Anglo-Saxon powers, and gave way when
pressed by Wilson and Lloyd George. The Rhineland remained
part of Germany, instead of being fabricated into an independent state. France received some temporary securities: de-
militarization of the Rhineland; its occupation by Allied forces
for fifteen years; and control of the Saar, with its coal mines, for
fifteen years, after which its future was to be determined by a
plebiscite. Clemenceau was also lured into concession by the
promise of an Anglo-American guarantee against any new
German aggression. Subsequently, the American Senate refused
to ratify this guarantee, and the British government then walked
out also. On Germany's eastern frontier, Lloyd George stood
alone against Clemenceau and Wilson. Thanks to him, Danzig
became a Free City, instead of being annexed to Poland, and
a plebiscite was held in Silesia. The territorial clauses of the
treaty of Versailles were 'fair' from the ethnic point of view.
This was mainly Lloyd George's doing.

Reparations caused greater bitterness. Wild claims had been
made against the Germans immediately after the armistice, and
even wilder estimates, some by British financial experts, of their

[1] Little came of this. William II had taken refuge in Holland, and the Dutch
refused to hand him over. A few minor war criminals were tried by German courts.
They received derisory sentences, and the Allies then dropped further proceedings.

capacity to pay. Lloyd George recognized that any precise figure, fixed in the disturbed atmosphere of 1919, would be punitively and unrealistically high. He therefore urged that the treaty should merely state the principle of Germany's liability and that the sum should be fixed later after a cool examination of her financial resources. Once more he got his way. His moderation was not apparent at the time. Not only had he to stress the obligation of the Germans to pay as much as they could. He also pushed up the British share of any reparations received, and snatched at a guileful suggestion from Smuts that war pensions were a legitimate civil damage. Though this was a move against France, not against Germany, few appreciated it at the time, and Lloyd George, too, appeared as the advocate of a harsh peace. On one thing the Big Four were agreed: Germany was not to be allowed equality of armaments. She was deprived of most heavy weapons, forbidden to manufacture them, and her army was restricted to 100,000 men. As window-dressing, bodeful for the future, the Allies threw in a pious declaration that this was a preliminary to general disarmament. This was later interpreted wrongly as a binding pledge.

These great topics were discussed amid a tangle of other issues. The Big Four were also the supreme war council. At one moment they were drafting peace terms with Germany; at another wrangling over Fiume, or considering what to do with Bela Kun, the Bolshevik dictator of Hungary. Then they would turn aside to debate how to end the civil war in Russia, whether to conciliate the Bolsheviks there or to intervene against them. All Europe was clamouring for food and economic assistance. The great men were also exposed to shots from the rear—Clemenceau literally with an attempted assassination. In April over 200 Unionist M.P.s[1] sent a telegram to Lloyd George, expostulating against his weakness towards Germany. On 16 April he returned to Westminster, and routed his critics by lumping them with Northcliffe, whom nearly all M.P.s disliked. After the signature of the peace treaty with Germany on 28 June, Lloyd George came back to London in triumph. The house of commons accepted the treaty almost without a murmur. Even Liberal and Labour members agreed that the Fourteen Points had been broadly applied. Only four members

[1] Two hundred and thirty-three M.P.s signed the telegram before it was sent. Forty-six more added their signatures later.

voted against the treaty; of these only one was an Englishman[1] —the other three were Home Rulers, protesting against the failure to apply self-determination to Ireland. This was a delusive victory. Progressive opinion outside the house swung against the peace treaty, and Lloyd George, the man who had tried to moderate the treaty, was soon saddled with the blame for its supposed faults.

There had always, of course, been a minority who favoured reconciliation with Germany even during the war. Their opinions had been largely disregarded while the war was on. They came into their own afterwards. MacDonald, for instance, was shaping the outlook of the Labour party with Henderson's support, and this outlook was identical with that of E. D. Morel and the Union of Democratic Control. Labour condemned the entire treaty when the first draft was published in May: condemned in particular reparations, the occupation of the Rhineland, and the transfer of German territory to Poland. Many people—Liberals, Radicals, as well as Labour—had regarded the war as a crusade for great ideals, not as a mere struggle of force against Germany. They now denounced anything which discriminated between Germany and her former antagonists. As in home affairs, 'reconstruction' looked both back and forward: forward to the League of Nations, but also back to the happy days before 1914, when Germany was treated as an equal and friendly power.

This attitude was strengthened later in 1919, when a former treasury official, J. M. Keynes,[2] fired a broadside against reparations in his famous book, *The Economic Consequences of the Peace*. Keynes argued that Europe could prosper only when Germany was restored to her old economic strength, and he blamed the peacemakers for all the sufferings which the Germans had brought on themselves, and on Europe, not only by being defeated but from having waged war at all. Ironically, much of the outcry against the peace treaty had been engineered by Lloyd George himself. During the peace conference, he tried to

[1] Lt.-Commander J. M. Kenworthy, later 10th Baron Strabolgi, who had just won a by-election at Hull as a Radical.

[2] John Maynard Keynes (1883-1946): educ. Eton and Cambridge; economist; member of Bloomsbury set; treasury official, 1915-19; principal treasury adviser, 1940-6; cr. Baron, 1942; opposed return to gold standard, 1925; advocated virtual return to gold standard, 1946; denounced Lloyd George, 1919; devised Lloyd George's election programme, 1929; invented most of modern economics.

strengthen his hand by stirring up a campaign for conciliation among Liberal journalists and Labour leaders. Smuts prompted Keynes to attack the settlement, probably with Lloyd George's approval.[1] The campaign was intended to hit the French and the men of violence at home. So it did. France was soon regarded as the new militaristic power, pursuing Napoleonic dreams of empire. But the campaign hit Lloyd George also. After all, he had signed the treaty. In his anxiety to diddle the Right, he overreached himself and failed to diddle the Left. In no time at all, Lloyd George, the adroit conciliator, was identified with Bottomley, Northcliffe, and other haters of the Huns.

The settlement with Germany was not the only cause of estrangement between Lloyd George and his former admirers on the Left. He was blamed for the failure of the peace conference to restore immediate prosperity in war-ravaged Europe. He was particularly blamed for 'creating' the new national states, Poland, Czechoslovakia, and Yugoslavia, though these states had in reality created themselves, and Lloyd George had little sympathy with them. Allied intervention against the Bolsheviks was another running sore. Here, too, Lloyd George secretly agreed with his critics. He exasperated Clemenceau by arguing that the French were repeating in Russia the mistake which the younger Pitt had made when he launched a crusade against the French Jacobins in 1793. But he shrank from defying the French or his anti-Bolshevik supporters at home. In March 1919, while Lloyd George was temporarily in London, Churchill slipped over to Paris, fervently denouncing 'the baboonery of Bolshevism', and persuaded the supreme council to try intervention on a large scale.

Surplus British tanks and other munitions of war, to the tune of £100 million, were provided for the Russian 'Whites'. British volunteers served with Kolchak, self-styled supreme ruler of all the Russias, in Siberia. A few served with Denikin in

[1] Smuts, the general who spent his weekends with Quakers, urged a conciliatory peace with Germany once South Africa had carried off German South West Africa, and signed the treaty, as a delegate for South Africa, only with reluctance. He encouraged Keynes to attack the treaty; then repented and advised Keynes not to publish his book. As a further irony, Keynes, when a treasury official, was responsible for a higher estimate of Germany's capacity to pay than Lloyd George would accept. Even in *The Economic Consequences of the Peace*, Keynes thought £2,000 million a practical figure for reparations. Germany paid in all £1,000 million, and this only with money borrowed from the United States.

southern Russia. There were substantial British forces at Archangel and Murmansk—originally sent to guard the Allied
munition dumps there against the Germans and now propping
up anti-Bolshevik governments. A British force occupied Baku,
and another ranged along the frontier which divided Russia
from Afghanistan. In England Labour campaigned against
intervention and won increasing support, probably more from
war-weariness than from any feeling of solidarity with the supposedly working-class government in Russia. By the autumn of
1919, most of the British troops had been withdrawn, and the
supply of munitions to the Whites gradually petered out as
their scattered forces were destroyed by the Red Army. These
futile interventions deepened the suspicion which the Bolshevik
rulers of Russia had assumed, from the start, against the 'capitalist' West. They also had a profound effect at home. Though most
Labour men disliked the Bolshevik terror and dictatorship, they
could not escape the feeling that, since they and the Bolsheviks
were fighting the same enemy, Lloyd George, they were somehow on the same side. Sympathy with Soviet Russia, 'the
workers' state', added a new, though no doubt a minor, element
    Everyone had expected trouble to follow the war. Men, it was
said, would not go back to the old conditions. Bolshevism was
supposed to be sweeping Europe. Demobilization threatened
to provoke violent disturbance. The ministry of labour had
devised an elaborate scheme for releasing first the key men most
required by industry. These were, of course, usually the last to
have been called up. Men who had served longer were indignant. There were mutinies in the camps at Calais and Folke-
stone, where Bottomley—now discharged from bankruptcy and
a bouncingly Independent M.P.—was called in as the soldiers'
friend. Three thousand men marched from Victoria station and
occupied the Horse Guards Parade. Sir Henry Wilson doubted
whether any troops could be relied upon to disperse them.
Churchill settled the trouble at a stroke by scrapping the existing scheme and substituting the simple principle 'first in, first
out'. With this, discontent died away, except among the Canadians, whose return home was delayed by shortage of shipping.
A mutiny in their camp at Rhyl was put down in March only
after a number of men had been killed. By the summer of 1919
four out of five men serving in the British army had been

discharged. Though they received free insurance against un-employment, they were nearly all absorbed into industry with surprising ease.

Economic demobilization also proved easier than had been expected. In Glasgow a general strike was called to secure the forty-hour week. The red flag was hoisted on the town hall. Troops were sent, though the police managed to restore order without them. Gallacher, a future Communist; Shinwell, a future minister of defence; and Kirkwood, a future peer, were imprisoned. Then the danger died away. There was a runaway boom in the confident hope that the world was crying out for British goods. The new hands who had come in during the war now withdrew. Women and the unskilled recruits to munitions left the industry,[1] and the old restrictive practices were restored, much to the harm of British engineering in the long run. There was still a fund of goodwill left over from the war. In February 1919 a national industrial conference met, to promote better relations between employers and employed. Arthur Henderson led the labour delegates, despite his distrust of Lloyd George.

What was lacking was not so much goodwill as understand-ing. Nearly everyone, Labour and Conservative alike, regarded the wartime controls and direction as evils which should be got rid of as soon as possible. Union officials wanted to get back to their old defensive tasks; employers wanted their old freedom of enterprise. No Labour man sat on any of the committees for reconstruction, and none wanted to do so. Reconstruction of capitalism was a job for the bosses, not for Labour. There was equivocation in the policy of reconstruction itself: the aim was to return to 1914 and to build a better country at the same time. Lloyd George naturally shared this outlook, as did even Addison, the minister for reconstruction. Great Britain, it was held, had been a wealthy country before 1914. The war had shown that there was virtually no limit to national resources. Therefore Great Britain could afford extensive social reform without any fundamental change in her economic system. Wealth would again flow of itself, once the controls of wartime were removed.

Freedom burst out overnight. Price controls, control of raw materials and of foreign trade, direction of industry, were swept away. Since the export of gold could no longer be checked by

[1] By 1921 the proportion of women in paid employment was smaller than before the war.

refusing licences, the bank of England was relieved of its duty to sell gold at a fixed price,[1] and the government no longer supported the pound in New York. The pound fell from par to $3.50. The step was meant, from the first, to be temporary. 'Going off gold' was intended as a preliminary to restoring the working of the gold standard in the old free way. The bank of England soon restricted credits in order to push up the exchange value of the pound. This had little immediate effect. With the new freedom from controls, prices rose twice as fast during 1919 as they had done during the worst years of the war.[2] Wages soared after them, and the employers, flush with money, did not resist wage increases. The government, in alarm, continued food rationing (until 1921) after meaning to abandon it. Otherwise public policy seemed helpless to stem inflation.

The government were directly drawn in by the two great industries still under their control, the mines and the railways. In February 1919 the miners, the railwaymen, and the transport workers resurrected the prewar 'triple alliance', which had been preparing something like a general strike for the autumn of 1914. The miners (and the mine owners) were the toughest, most intractable element. The miners were bought off by a royal commission under Sankey, a high court judge. The commission was unique. It was created by act of parliament; it represented fairly both owners and men.[3] The inevitable result was disagreement. In June 1919 the Sankey commission came up with four reports, which ranged from complete nationalization on the part of the workers' representatives to restoration of undiluted private ownership on that of the owners'.[4] On 18 August Lloyd George used the excuse of this disagreement to reject nationalization. He offered a measure of reorganization. When the miners rejected this palliative, it also was dropped. The miners kept their existing wages; the seven-hour day was imposed by act of parliament; government control was prolonged. A strike was

---

[1] The £5 note was still exchangeable for 5 gold sovereigns, but, of course, there were not many of these notes in circulation.

[2] Taking 1914 as 100, wholesale prices were over 200 early in 1919 and over 300 early in 1920.

[3] Three miners, three owners, three businessmen, and three economists favourable to the miners—Tawney, Webb, Chiozza Money (hero later of the Savidge case, below, p. 261)— with Sankey as chairman.

[4] Sankey recommended a modified nationalization; Duckham, one of the businessmen, reorganization under private ownership.

impractical for the hypothetical cause of nationalization in some undefined future. The miners were forced back on a political campaign, 'The Mines for the Nation', which created little stir even among themselves.

The railwaymen did not wait for their supposed partners. In September 1919 they struck against a threatened reduction of wages. Lloyd George allowed Auckland Geddes, president of the board of trade,[1] to provoke the strike by his intransigence; then stepped in and settled it on the railwaymen's terms. This was a great stroke for the National Union of Railwaymen and for their accomplished leader, J. H. Thomas.[2] It was also a great stroke for Lloyd George. The railwaymen had got what they wanted without calling on the triple alliance. Their wages showed a greater improvement on prewar than in any other industry.[3] They had no further interest in a general strike except on grounds of working-class solidarity. Something of the same kind happened with the transport workers. The dockers, the strongest element among them, were given a commission of inquiry early in 1920, before which Ernest Bevin[4] first made his name and which gave them greatly improved conditions. Bevin and Thomas, with all their differences, were outstanding union leaders of a new type. Though aggressively working class in character, they were no longer concerned merely to resist. Nor would they put off improvement till the distant dawn of socialism. They bargained with the employers as equals, displaying equal or greater skill, and never forgot that compromise was their ultimate aim, whether with a strike or preferably without.

The leaders of the miners had a different outlook. They fought class war, and the employers responded with zest. Birkenhead remarked after a meeting with the miners' representatives: 'I should call them the stupidest men in England if I had not

---

[1] The new ministry of transport had not yet taken over the railways.

[2] James Henry Thomas (1874–1949): educ. elementary school; engine driver on G.W.R.; general secretary N.U.R., 1917–31; colonial secretary, 1924, 1935–6; lord privy seal, 1929–30; dominions secretary, 1930–5; left public life after being found guilty of revealing budget secrets; depicted by Low as Rt. Hon. Dress Shirt; devised a supposed working-class accent of his own; when asked who would be first Labour prime minister, replied (incorrectly): 'Me or 'Enderson.'

[3] In 1920 their real wages stood at 117 (1914 = 100).

[4] Ernest Bevin (1881–1951): educ. elementary school; leader of Dockers' Union, 1910–21; creator and general secretary of Transport and General Workers' Union, 1921–40; minister of labour and national service and member of war cabinet, 1940–5; foreign secretary, 1945–51.

previously had to deal with the owners.' The affairs of the coal industry dragged the whole nation into turmoil. In 1920 Great Britain was still booming, and the Labour movement was in high confidence. Labour candidates were steadily successful at by-elections.[1] Henderson and other leaders found their way back to the house of commons. Trade union membership reached a peak of over eight million. The Trade Union Congress replaced its ineffective parliamentary committee by a general council, which was presented, somewhat optimistically, as a 'general staff' for industrial action. A National Council of Labour, re-presenting the general council of the T.U.C., the national executive of the Labour party, and the parliamentary party, claimed to speak for 'Labour' throughout the country.

Labour also found its voice in a more literal sense. A socialist daily newspaper appeared, the *Daily Herald*.[2] It was edited by George Lansbury, revered leader of the emotional Left,[3] and written for the most part by young middle-class intellectuals. Some of them, such as William Mellor and G. D. H. Cole, had already been socialists before the war. Others—Siegfried Sassoon, Osbert Sitwell, W. J. Turner—had become radicals as the result of their wartime experiences. All contributed a gay, self-confident contempt for the doings of the governing class. The *Daily Herald* had a hard struggle against the organs of the 'capitalist' press. It never made ends meet in Lansbury's time, when it was still, of course, despite its socialist principles, a private venture. But it broke the old monopoly of established opinion and bore witness that the people of England were not all thinking as their rulers thought they should.

On the extreme Left, things were astir. The example of Soviet Russia was infectious. In July 1920 various revolutionary fac-tions—principally the British Socialist party, with some support from the Socialist Labour Party of Glasgow, and shop stewards from Glasgow and Sheffield—set up the Communist Party of Great Britain in the inappropriate surroundings of the Cannon

[1] Between 1918 and 1922 Labour increased its representation in the house from 63 to 76.

[2] Founded as a more or less syndicalist daily in 1912, the *Herald* relapsed into a weekly during the war.

[3] George Lansbury (1859–1940): educ. elementary school; edited *Daily Herald*, 1919–22; later founded and edited *Lansbury's Labour Weekly*; first commissioner of works, 1929–31; leader of Labour party, 1931–5; the most lovable figure in modern politics.

Street Hotel. The intention was to repeat Lenin's success, and to establish the dictatorship of the proletariat in Great Britain. The new party had few members, and these few did not understand what they had committed themselves to. It was eyed askance even by the I.L.P., the majority of whom refused after a long period of debate to put themselves under the orders of Moscow. The Labour party, which had formerly taken in all and sundry from Hyndman's Marxists to the Lib.-Lab. Richard Bell, refused the affiliation which the Communists asked for on Lenin's instruction.[1] The Labour party had now a defined outlook of its own and was taking sides in the world-wide cleavage between democratic socialism and revolutionary Communism. Nevertheless, the Communists had great influence in a watered-down way. Many, if not most, socialists shared their belief that capitalism was about to collapse and, like the Communists, blamed capitalism for 'imperialist wars'. Most socialists talked class war, though without any serious intention of using more violent weapons than the strike and the ballot box.

Plans for a general strike flourished in this atmosphere, and the idea received a shot in the arm from a demonstration of its practical effectiveness, a demonstration, moreover, of a directly political kind. In the summer of 1920 the threat of a general strike was used to stop a war. Though intervention against the Bolsheviks was virtually at an end, Poland and Russia were still at war. Early in 1920 the Poles set out to conquer the Ukraine, their old empire. Poland was disliked by moderate socialists, who sympathized with Germany; Soviet Russia was admired by the more extreme; all of them distrusted the British government. On 10 May London dockers refused to load munitions for Poland on to the *Jolly George*. Labour men applauded, and the government acquiesced in the ban while the Poles were winning. In July, however, the Poles were routed; the Red Army was in full march on Warsaw. The French were eager to intervene on the Polish side; Lloyd George, pushed on by Churchill and others, seemed ready to go along with them.

Labour acted in solid resistance. Councils of Action were set up in many towns. The National Council of Labour took control. Plans were made for an immediate general strike. Even the

[1] Lenin wrote: 'We will support Henderson as a rope supports a man who is hanged.' It is curious how Communists used outrageous phrases publicly and were indignant when these phrases were turned against them.

most cautious Labour leaders, such as Clynes and Thomas, were prepared to challenge 'the whole Constitution of the country'. On 10 August Bevin presented Labour's ultimatum. Lloyd George was delighted to turn the storm against his unruly colleagues. Labour, he said, was knocking at an open door so far as he was concerned; he even urged Bevin to act as negotiator between Russia and the British government. The danger of war vanished overnight, partly no doubt because the Poles managed to save themselves without British assistance. Nevertheless, it had been a glorious victory. Despite Lloyd George's subsequent denials, it is difficult to believe that there would have been no British aid to the Poles, if the threat of a general strike had not been made—and made with such unanimity. The door may have been open; a strong push was needed to send Lloyd George through it. Yet the victory had its misleading side. For once, that amorphous creature, public opinion, was on the side of unconstitutional action. Even the sanctity of parliamentary government has its limit. That limit was drawn by the war-weariness of the British people. 'Hands off Soviet Russia' counted for something; 'No More War' was irresistible.

It was different when the old dispute over the coal mines returned to the centre of the stage. Here the Labour movement was on its own, and less united into the bargain. In October 1920, with the mines still under government control, the miners went on strike for an increase of wages. The triple alliance grudgingly prepared to support them. Lloyd George played things both ways. By the Emergency Powers Act he made permanent the dictatorial powers which the government had possessed in wartime under the Defence of the Realm Acts— as big a blow against the traditional constitution as any ever levelled. At the same time, he temporarily settled the strike on the miners' terms. This was only preparation for the decisive struggle, and one fought in conditions unfavourable to the miners. The postwar boom broke abruptly in the winter of 1920-1. Everything combined to bring disaster. Government spending had been slashed fiercely—from £2,696 million in 1917-18 to little over £1,000 million in 1920-1. At the same time taxation had gone up, to a peak of £1,426 million in 1920-1. The budget that year showed a surplus of £230 million against a deficit of £326 million in the previous year, and one of nearly £2,000 million at the height of the war. British manufacturers had assumed that there would be an insatiable demand for the goods which they had been unable to export during the war. They had pushed up their prices, invested wildly in new capital.

This world market turned out to be a phantom. Europe was in political turmoil, and its exchanges in chaos. Even worse was the catastrophe which overcame the overseas producers of food and raw materials. These primary producers had flourished before the war, and their increasing prosperity then was the main cause for the rise in British exports. They had been encouraged during the war to produce still more at any price they liked to charge. Now their productive powers exceeded the demand in European industrial countries, even when these countries could afford to buy. Over-production of primary products dominated the interwar years, and the impoverishment of these producers brought something near ruin to the old British industries. There was a glut of shipping throughout the world. Exports of coal and cotton ran down to almost nothing. British prices tumbled faster than they had risen, and employment tumbled with them. Unemployment more than doubled between December 1920 and March 1921. In June 1921 it passed two million and, though it then fell again, never went under a million between the wars. In the coal, engineering, and cotton towns often more than half the insured population were out of work. *The Economist* called 1921 'one of the worst years of depression since the industrial revolution'. This was no moment for a general strike.

The British government jettisoned their economic responsibilities helter-skelter. They abandoned the plans for reconstructing and electrifying the railways, and handed these back to the private companies, now regrouped into four regions. They resolved also to hand the coal mines back to the owners on 31 March 1921. The owners were incapable of reorganizing the industry. The only economy they understood was a reduction of wages. The new agreement they offered not only cut wages; it also returned to the old system of district rates, which gave miners at inferior pits less than those working on richer seams. The miners demanded a 'national pool' to equalize wages. The owners refused and on 1 April began a lockout. Once more the triple alliance was called on, and in an embarrassing way. Previously, when the mines were under government control, a sympathetic strike could be used to get better terms. Now the railwaymen and transport workers could not coerce the mine owners. They could only threaten the government, and the government could only offer to mediate. Lloyd George was as eager as Thomas and Bevin for new negotiations. The refusal came from the miners. They wanted a fight to a finish, at whatever cost to themselves and everyone else.[1]

Herbert Smith, the miners' president, replied to appeals for a flexible approach: 'Get on ta t'field. That's t'place.' Frank Hodges, the miners' secretary, who was more moderate, accepted the offer of a standstill on wages while negotiations went on for a national pool. The miners' executive turned down the offer by a majority of one. At this, the railway and transport unions called off their strike a few hours before it was due to begin—on Friday, 15 April 1921. 'Black Friday' became a date of shame in the Labour movement, the day when the miners were betrayed by timid allies. This was a romantic view. Black Friday marked rather a clash between two conceptions of union policy—the old outlook of class war, to be fought with the bull-headed obstinacy of the trenches, and a new unionism, aiming at compromise or even partnership. Herbert Smith spoke for the past; Thomas and Bevin for the future. This was poor consolation to the miners. They held on alone until 1 July. Then the lockout ended on worse terms than the miners could have secured by negotiating at the beginning. The only remnant of government concern was a subsidy of £10 million, not all of which was drawn on before September, when it lapsed. To the general rejoicing of the educated, prosperous classes, the miners worked once more on terms which now seem to us, less than half a century afterwards, as remote and barbaric as serfdom.

The defeat of the miners set a general pattern. Wages fell heavily in every industry during 1921, sometimes after a strike, sometimes without one. The promises of 'a fit country for heroes to live in' seemed a mockery. Lloyd George lost his last shadow of hold over the working class. He had become for them a fraud, a sham. Yet he had solid achievements to show, though they

[1] This obstinacy rested mainly on the sound human belief that men performing an essential service ought to receive a decent wage. The rational arguments for it were contradictory. One held that British capitalism, being highly prosperous, could afford to pay high wages. The other regarded British capitalism as being near ruin and hoped to push it over the edge by demands for wages which it could not meet.

passed almost unregarded at the time, achievements which left
a powerful legacy of good for the future. Housing was the most
substantial. Homes for heroes had been a universal promise
during the general election of 1918. Everyone agreed that more
and better houses should be provided. Christopher Addison,
now minister of health, brought to housing the zest which he
and Lloyd George had once shown at the ministry of munitions.
He lacked the means which had then brought success. He had
no control over prices or over raw materials, no power to direct
capital or to influence the supply of labour. He had to bid
against competing claims in the open market—the very method
which he and Lloyd George had denounced when advocated by
laissez faire Liberals in regard to munitions. Addison was in a
hurry. He did not mind how much money he spent or how he
spent it. Nor did he create his own agencies. The ministry of
health, as successor to the local government board, was used to
acting through the local authorities. These already had limited
powers for inspecting slums, and so some staff trained in
housing. Addison merely ordered the local authorities to build
unlimited houses and to let them at the equivalent of controlled
rents, which were fixed at the 1914 level. The government automatically met, by subsidy, any cost over a 1d. local rate.

'Expense no object' proved an expensive way of building
houses. Early in 1921, Addison was paying £910 for houses
which a year or so later could be built at a cost of £385 each.
There was an outcry against this waste of public money. In
March 1921 Addison left the ministry of health. For a few
months he was minister without portfolio and was then driven
from office altogether, Lloyd George apologizing to the house
of commons that misplaced personal loyalty—not usually one
of his characteristics—had made him cling to an incompetent
minister. In July 1921 the grants for new houses were sharply
limited. In 1922 they were stopped—the last houses under the
programme were completed in 1923. Perversely, by then,
building costs had fallen, and the building of houses would have
alleviated unemployment. The shortage of houses (estimated at
822,000 in 1923) was worse than in 1919, thanks to the increasing number of young married people. The breach with Addison
snapped another link between Lloyd George and his old
radicalism. The 'Housing Scandal' discredited both of them.
Yet much had been done. Addison built 213,000 houses, many

for people who could not afford to pay for them. He, more than any other man, established the principle that housing was a social service, and later governments had to take up his task, though they tried to avoid his mistakes. His work had another lasting effect. The local authorities had become the instruments for the housing policy of the state and found themselves spending vast sums of money, most of which they did not provide. Thus they acquired new functions in social service, just when their share of financial contribution to these services was decreasing.

Lloyd George had something even greater to his credit. He extended insurance against unemployment to virtually the entire working class and so transformed British economic life. This was done without foresight or calculation. The original Insurance scheme of 1911 had been carefully limited to three trades in which employment was expected to fluctuate more or less regularly (building, engineering, and shipbuilding). It covered some three million workers. Another million were brought in when insurance was extended to munitions during the war. After the war ex-servicemen were given non-contributory security against unemployment for a limited period as they left the armed forces; on the precedent of service allowances, there was provision for their wives and families also. When this scheme ran out, something more permanent was needed to take its place. There seemed little risk or difficulty in 1920 when men still found jobs easily during the postwar boom. At a stroke, unemployment insurance was extended to cover, in all, twelve million workers—virtually all earning less than £5 a week, except domestic servants, agricultural labourers, and civil servants. The sole object was to provide insurance against casual short-term unemployment. It was to be financed from contributions by employers and employed, which were held in an independent fund.

The scheme assumed an unemployment rate of 4 per cent. No one foresaw unemployment by the million, lasting for years. When this came, it was expected at first to be temporary, and it seemed impossible to refuse benefits merely because they were not actuarially sound. In March 1921 those in the scheme were allowed 'uncovenanted benefit'—that is, a period of insurance which they had not paid for. In November 1921 the benefit was extended to provide allowances, on the service model, for wives and families. The deficit was covered by so-called loans, really subsidies, from the exchequer. There was another odd feature. The incidence of unemployment was extremely uneven between different industries and different parts of the country. Hence those more or less regularly in work helped to provide for those who were more or less regularly unemployed.[1]

A strange new system thus grew up haphazard. Unemployment insurance, administered through the labour exchanges, cut across the Poor Law, which was in local hands. The foundations of *laissez faire* were shaken. 'Insurance', though largely fictitious, was not felt to be humiliating as reliance on the Poor Law had been. Men were no longer driven to work at lower wages, and in harsher conditions, by the lash of hunger. If they could not find employment at their usual jobs, they drew prolonged benefit at the expense of the taxpayer and the employed. Unemployment insurance retarded the shift of workers from declining to rising industries. On the other hand, it took the edge off discontent. Even when the unemployed rioted, this was to get higher rates of 'benefit', not to bring down a system which had made them unemployed. Once Labour had demanded 'the Right to Work'. Now it demanded 'Work or Maintenance', and the emphasis was on maintenance. Thanks to Lloyd George, barricades were not set up in English streets.

At the time, he did not appreciate what he had done. He wanted to get rid of unemployment, not to make it bearable. He believed, like nearly everyone else, that all would be well if the happy days before 1914 could be restored. He learnt from Keynes and other economists that the decisive contribution would be to restore the prosperity of Germany and, in particular, to get reparations settled. International conferences were held throughout 1920 and 1921, with Lloyd George for ever trying to find a mean between what the French demanded and what the Germans could, or would, pay. He failed, and the failure did him much harm. Some Englishmen were angered at his supposed desertion of the French; more complained that he had not reconciled the Germans. Lloyd George claimed to be a world statesman, sole survivor of the great men who had conducted the war. When he failed, the claim was counted against him.

[1] In 1926 it was found that 48 per cent. of insured workers had not drawn any benefit for the preceding five years.

Lloyd George was ready to try 'Tory', as well as 'Liberal', methods. He had no deep reverence for Free Trade and was tied to it only by his Liberal supporters, who gave him some semblance of being a national leader above the parties. He niggled against Free Trade as far as he dared. The duties originally put on certain 'luxuries' by McKenna to save shipping were retained after the war for Protectionist reasons. In 1921 key industries, supposedly essential in wartime, were 'safeguarded' (another euphemism for Protection) against foreign dumping. Lloyd George also edged ineffectively towards Empire Free Trade. The Dominions wanted British capital; some of them wanted British men. They were not prepared to surrender any of their sovereign independence. They would only pass resolutions that the mother country should make greater efforts. Schemes for imperial investment and migration rested solely on British initiative. The Dominions could have been won only by British taxes—'stomach taxes'—on foreign food. These were too dangerous an issue for Lloyd George to handle. In 1921 he tried his favourite device of a great conference. The Dominion prime ministers met in London. They were not cajoled. They asserted the exclusive authority of their own parliaments. The imperial cabinet of wartime, itself never a working executive, was not renewed. The elaborate plans for exploiting the colonial Empire also crumbled. Their basis had been the wartime economy of siege. It had been assumed that for years after the war Great Britain would gain from monopolizing the raw materials of her colonies. They were an undeveloped estate, a precious heritage. It was now discovered that they were already developed too much for present needs, and the British government, far from monopolizing their raw materials, anxiously ransacked the world for outlets of colonial goods abroad.

In one way, the Dominions influenced British policy decisively and with lasting effect. Immediately after the war Lloyd George talked, in his arrogant way, of a naval race with the United States. Great Britain, he asserted, would never relinquish her rule of the waves. He inclined also to go with Japan against the United States in the Far East. The Dominions objected. Canada would not be hostile to the United States. Australia and New Zealand distrusted Japan. The Dominions got their way. A conference on naval and Far Eastern affairs was held at Washington from November 1921 to February 1922.

Balfour led the British delegation. He agreed to parity in battleships with the Americans. The Japanese accepted inferiority
(5 American and 5 British battleships to 3 Japanese). There
was not much deliberate policy in this—certainly no conscious
recognition of Anglo-American partnership. The Dominions
pushed. The British yielded, and the desire to save money
during the economic depression did the rest. All the same, this
was the only effective international agreement on limitation of
armaments ever concluded. The British, again spurred by the
Dominions, also relinquished their alliance with Japan. As an
alternative security for Japan, the British and the Americans
promised not to develop their naval bases at Hong Kong and in
the Philippines. Japan thus received a local supremacy which
she later used with results disastrous for the Far East, for British
interests, and ultimately for herself. Still, Balfour earned the
Garter which awaited him on his return.

The shape of the British empire was changing in other ways.
The war underlined the difference between the Dominions and
the colonies. The Dominions, now often known collectively as
the British Commonwealth of Nations, were next door to independent sovereign states, represented separately at the Paris
peace conference and thereafter at the League of Nations, soon
maintaining their own representatives abroad. They were bound
to Great Britain predominantly by sentiment—a common past,
similar institutions, and, to a large extent, the same language.[1]
They had some economic interests in common. All produced
raw materials—wheat, wool, gold, copper, timber—which Great
Britain consumed. All aspired also to develop their own industries, to Great Britain's regret. The colonies, strictly so-called,
were still administered autocratically from Whitehall. The
West Indies were not much more than a relic from a vanished
past. The colonies in tropical Africa had been regarded as great
prizes in the days of late-Victorian imperialism. Their development proved disappointing. They turned out to be liabilities, not
assets. Kenya was perhaps an exception, when it was discovered
that white men could live in the highlands. Englishmen escaped
democracy and high taxation by establishing themselves in
Kenya as territorial aristocrats on the old model.

[1] The Boers, speaking Afrikaans, were more numerous than the British in South
Africa; the French were a sizeable minority in Canada, where there were other
minorities also.

The rise of a new British empire in the Middle East was more important. For a little while, in 1919, it seemed that this empire would stretch from the Mediterranean to the confines of India. With Russia out of the way, Curzon established a protectorate over Persia, and a British army occupied Afghanistan. This did not last. The British withdrew from Afghanistan; French and American protests compelled them to abandon Persia. Still, much remained. Mesopotamia, now called Irak, became a British mandate, bringing with it the rich plum of the Mosul oilfields. Palestine, too, was a British mandate under the convenient guise of a national home for the Jews, the troubles which this provoked with the Arabs still in the future. Egypt, which had been made a British protectorate early in the war, was recognized as a nominally independent kingdom in 1922. The British insisted on maintaining their military occupation in order to protect the Suez Canal and, failing a treaty with Egypt allowing them to do this, stayed in Egypt without one. The motive for their presence there had changed. Previously the British had been in Egypt solely because the Suez Canal was the route to India. Now the Middle East, with its oil and potential markets, was precious in itself, and India began to fall into the second place.

India was indeed becoming a liability. Gone were the days when the Indian market kept the cotton mills of Lancashire busy. Instead, India was manufacturing her own cotton goods and buying them from Japan. In 1917 India had been promised 'responsible government . . . as an integral part of the British Empire'. Now constitutions were devised for the provinces: fancy names, many elections, but no transfer of power, mere pictures of still life offered to a hungry man. The viceroy still ruled as a despot; the India office in London still wielded final authority. Yet the British were digging their own graves. They gave Indians a European education, and with this education came the demand for national independence. The Indian National Congress had long advocated this in a modest way. It now found an inspired leader in Gandhi, barrister of the Middle Temple, saint, and wily politician. He soon strode into action. The hardships of war, and the influenza epidemic at its end, provoked widespread discontent. At Amritsar, in April 1919, General Dyer opened fire on an unarmed crowd and killed 379 of them. This was the worst bloodshed since the

Mutiny, and the decisive moment when Indians were alienated from British rule. Gandhi answered with a new weapon of political warfare: civil disobedience. The British Raj, once so highminded, came to depend on *lathis*—the sticks which beat down unresisting Indians. Congress leaders were imprisoned. The first wave of disobedience died away. British administrators resumed their unchecked sway, so happily compounded of high purpose and high salaries.

But the heart had gone from the Raj. Gandhi held the moral lead. The British had only power. The Indian empire was kept going largely from habit. The British sensed the notice to quit. The difference between them and Congress was only over timing, not over the principle of 'Dominion status'. In the nineteenth century the British had shown a considerable gift of timing when they granted responsible government to their colonies. In India they got their timing wrong. They delayed and drifted, postponing their abdication to some future generation. Gandhi pressed them remorselessly. Perhaps the British found it more difficult to treat peoples of alien culture and different coloured skins as equals; perhaps the traditions of autocratic power were too strong; perhaps the British politicians were too weary and too burdened by problems elsewhere. At any rate, they did not produce a Lord Durham for their Indian empire. The Congress leaders were treated as enemies and rebels, instead of being welcomed as the brown Britons which their education had made them.

India was not the only nationalist challenge to British statesmanship, nor even, immediately after the war, the gravest. The Irish problem reached its most acute phase. The problem had harassed British politics for more than a century. Earlier, men had been able to claim, with some justification, that the real problem was religious or economic—Roman Catholic disabilities, or the exploitation of the peasants by their landlords. These grievances had been remedied. The Roman Catholics had been emancipated; the Protestant church had been disestablished; the landlords had been bought out. Ireland remained discontented, on the single issue of national independence. Formally, nothing was changed. Ireland was still part of the United Kingdom, and authorities, appointed by the British, still ruled from Dublin castle. The reality was different. An independent Irish parliament, or Dail, was set up by the Sinn

Fein victors in the general election of 1918.[1] The Republic,
proclaimed at Easter 1916, was solemnly renewed. The British
government, with curious indifference, actually completed
attendance at the Dail by releasing all Irish prisoners from
British jails in April 1919 (apparently because they feared that
some might cast discredit on their jailers by dying from influenza). The Dail behaved as though the republic were in full
being and the British no longer existed. De Valera, sole survivor of the 1916 leaders, was elected president of the Dail.
A republican government was formed and extended its administration throughout the country. Taxes were levied. Justice was
conducted by republican courts—so much so that the British
courts were deserted. The local authorities took their orders
from the republican minister, or had their letters readdressed
to him by the post office, if they wrote by mistake to Dublin
castle.

The original Sinn Fein plan was non-violent. They intended
simply to disregard the British authorities and put them on the
shelf, as the Hungarians, according to Arthur Griffith, had
done with the Imperial Austrian agents between 1861 and 1865.[2]
The old secret society, the Irish Republican Brotherhood,
decided otherwise. At its direction, the Irish Volunteers,
organized before the war, were reconstituted in January 1919
as the Irish Republican Army under the command of Michael
Collins, a former post-office clerk who had fought in the Easter
rising—a command somewhat disputed by another fierce
republican, Cathal Brugha.[3] The I.R.A. plunged into war
against the British without waiting for authority from the Dail,
or indeed ever receiving it. Money was lavishly supplied by
...erican sympathizers. Arms and explosives were easily come
by in t e confused state of Europe after the war, and as easily
smuggled past complacent customs officers. It was a perpetual
handicap to the official government that the administration,
though technically British, was almost entirely in the hands of

---

[1] Though Sinn Fein won 73 Irish seats out of 103, the actual voting was less
decisive. Sixty per cent. of the electors voted (a slightly higher percentage than in
Great Britain); of these only 47 per cent. voted for Sinn Fein.

[2] Griffith described *The Resurrection of Hungary* in 1904. Hungarian historians,
when asked what happened in Hungary in 1861–5, reply only by quoting Griffith's
book.

[3] He was the only prominent Irish leader to Gaelicize his name. In English it
had the prosaic form: Charles Burgess.

Irishmen, and no one could be sure where their loyalty lay. Collins had his agents at the highest posts in Dublin castle and received information from at least one British staff officer. He knew every British move before it was made; hence, in large part, his miraculous escapes from arrest.

The 'troubles', as they were called, had a topsy-turvy character. The I.R.A., though stigmatized as rebels, fought in the name of an existing republic against the British 'invaders'. The British, though claiming to maintain order, were fighting to recover an authority which they had already lost. The conflict was, of course, on a small scale. The total strength of the I.R.A. has been variously estimated from 15,000 to 120,000. In any case, it never had more than 5,000 men on active service at a time, and usually only 3,000. Its men wore no uniform except a trench-coat. A unit assembled to attack a police station or to ambush a convoy of arms, and then dispersed into civilian life. The British had an army in Ireland of about 50,000 men and an armed police force of about 10,000, the Royal Irish Constabulary. Neither was suited to guerrilla war. The army was a garrison on peacetime training. The police were scattered throughout the country for ordinary duties. They had to be withdrawn from most of their isolated posts as the struggle went on—another victory for the republic.

In 1920 the British government brought in less scrupulous forces: first the Black and Tans, who were theoretically recruits to the R.I.C., then the 'Auxis', or Auxiliary Division, men with a taste for fighting and brutality,[1] who became an autonomous terror squad. Terror answered terror. About 750 Irishmen are thought to have been killed, many of them not even members of the I.R.A.; on the British side, about 500 police, and something under 200 soldiers. Order was not restored. Arthur Henderson said after visiting Ireland: 'A state of affairs prevails which is a disgrace to the human race.' Asquith spoke even more strongly: 'Things are being done in Ireland which would disgrace the blackest annals of the lowest despotism in Europe.'

The British government were conducting this policy of murder and terrorism from sheer obstinacy. Home Rule was already on the statute book, its operation deferred only until the legal end of the war. Lloyd George had little sympathy with the

---

[1] One of the most brutal became a commander in the International Brigade during the Spanish civil war and was killed fighting for the Spanish Republic.

Irish, since the distant days when the Roman Catholics refused
to cooperate with the Free Churches against Balfour's Education
act, and opposition always provoked his fighting spirit. But he
recognized that negations were not enough. He devised an
arrangement of fantastic complexity, the Government of Ireland
Act (1920): the United Kingdom, united Ireland, a separate
Ulster, all mixed together. There were to be two Home Rule
parliaments, one for most of Ireland at Dublin, the other for
six counties of Ulster at Belfast; both parts of Ireland were to
retain a reduced representation at Westminster; and a Council
of Ireland, drawn from the two Irish parliaments, would preserve or restore Irish unity. Most of this ingenuity was dead
from the start. Sinn Fein refused to recognize the southern parliament and used it merely as a device to elect a second Dail.
Only the four members for Dublin university turned up for the
opening.[1] Equally Ulster refused to recognize the Council of
Ireland. On the other hand, the Ulster Unionists appreciated
that the act secured them from Dublin rule and therefore
grudgingly accepted their own parliament—and with it, their
own government. In this paradoxical way, Ulster, which had
once prepared to fight a civil war for a united Ireland under the
British crown, authorized partition and was the only part of
Ireland to receive Home Rule.

Indirectly, the Government of Ireland Act ended the troubles.
George V resolved to open the first North of Ireland parliament
personally in June 1921, despite the risk of assassination. He
had disliked the British campaign of terrorism and wanted to
speak more than conventional phrases. He consulted Smuts,
who had always urged the Irish to accept the Dominion status
which had satisfied the Boers—or at any rate some of them—
and who now happened to be in England for the imperial conference. Smuts drafted a warm plea for civil peace and pressed
it on Lloyd George. He, on his side, was looking for a way out.
He had just been warned by Sir Henry Wilson, the C.I.G.S.,
that Ireland could be reconquered only by a full-scale war: an
army of 100,000 men, specially recruited; martial law; block-
houses; and the banning of all civil traffic except under licence.
Some members of the cabinet, led by Churchill, refused to
endorse this policy until a great effort of conciliation had been

---

[1] The Irish university constituencies, like most of those in Great Britain, could
be relied on to return reactionary members.

made. Lloyd George therefore accepted Smuts's proposal, and soon made it his own. George V deserves some of the credit. His initiative was perhaps the greatest service performed by a British monarch in modern times.

The response was immediate. De Valera, now president of the Irish republic, had been secretly in touch with British representatives since early in the year. The I.R.A. was perhaps at the end of its tether. Collins told Hamar Greenwood, the chief secretary, afterwards: 'You had us dead beat. We could not have lasted another three weeks.'[1] At any rate, De Valera agreed to negotiate. A truce was signed on 8 July, and fighting ended three days later. Months of bargaining followed. Sinn Fein wanted an independent republic for all Ireland. They were offered Dominion status on the Canadian model for twenty-six counties, that is, excluding six counties of Ulster. The wrangling over Dominion status seems in retrospect strangely theoretical. If the Irish remained disloyal, they would not be restrained by such symbols as the oath of allegiance; hence it was futile for the British government to insist on them. Equally, since the symbols had no practical force, Dominion status gave Ireland the reality of independence, and it was pedantic for Sinn Fein to kick against them.

Men could not cut down to common sense after years of impassioned debate. The republic was an emotive symbol for one side, the Empire for the other. Besides, the full implications of Dominion status were not then clear as they became shortly afterwards. In 1921 it was still possible to believe that the Dominions were, in some way, subordinate to Whitehall. De Valera was much abused at the time for his impractical romanticism when he took his stand against the British terms. Yet, in view of the conflicting sentiments, he was the only realist of the lot. His plan of external association preserved the republic and yet gave to the British all the practical securities which they needed. This plan brought reconciliation later, and the reconciliation might have been warmer if it had come at once. Lloyd George would not look at the idea. He was determined to preserve 'the Empire'. Perhaps, as a Welshman, he grudged to the Irish what was not granted to the Welsh. He saw a different way out—a masterpiece, as usual, of strategical ingenuity at everyone's expense except his own. The Irish were

[1] Amery, *My political Life*, ii. 230.

to be tempted into the Empire by the offer that Northern Ireland should be put under Dublin instead of under London for a limited period, six months or a year. During this time, the Ulster Unionists would learn the delights of paying lower taxes and would remain with the rest of Ireland for good.[1]

The Sinn Fein representatives jumped at this bargain, though it would probably have transferred civil war from the south to the north. It was abruptly forbidden by Law. He had left office and active politics in March 1921 on grounds of ill health.[2] He now threatened to return and to lead Unionist opposition unless Ulster were left alone. The threat was formidable. The Unionists were increasingly restless against Lloyd George and eager to bolt. Austen Chamberlain, their new leader, had no authority. Lloyd George retreated. The proposal to force Northern Ireland under Dublin was abandoned. Instead Sinn Fein was threatened with renewed war. The Irish negotiators were shaken. As well, Lloyd George had a last trick up his sleeve. He hinted privately to the Irish that the commission, which was to draw the boundary between Northern Ireland and the rest, would so whittle down Ulster as to make her unworkable and anxious therefore to join the Irish Free State. In this roundabout way the unity of Ireland would be saved after all. It is impossible to determine whether the hint was seriously meant or whether it was fraudulent from the start.[3] What mattered was that it worked. The Irish grasped at the excuse, however thin, for avoiding war. In the early hours of 6 December, they and the British negotiators signed 'Articles of Agreement for a Treaty between Great Britain and Ireland'. This was a curious document. It implicitly recognized the right of the Dail, or its representatives, to speak for a republic of united Ireland and, in the next breath, ordered this republic out of existence.

Many tangles and conflicts followed. The British parliament approved the treaty on 16 December 1921. In Ireland De Valera

[1] In retrospect partition seems the inevitable and obvious solution of the Irish question. At the time, it seemed inconceivable that an ancient kingdom should be dismembered. Sinn Fein went on hoping to the end that they would somehow save Irish unity, just as the Ulster Unionists believed that they were preserving the United Kingdom by refusing to be placed under Dublin.

[2] The ill health was no doubt genuine. But it had psychological causes as well. Law sensed Lloyd George's coming doom. He knew that he alone could plant the dagger in Lloyd George's back. He knew that he must do it and hoped by withdrawal to escape the hateful duty.

[3] See Note B, p. 162.

led a fierce opposition. The Dail approved the treaty on 7 January 1922 by only 64 votes to 57.[1] De Valera resigned as president. A new provisional government was set up under Arthur Griffith,[2] and in March the British parliament transferred power to them. In June a general election was held in southern Ireland. Though the two Sinn Fein factions (for the treaty and against it) made an electoral pact, the intrusion of other parties gave a 72 per cent. majority for the treaty. Despite this, a considerable section of the I.R.A. stuck to the republic and fought a civil war which lasted until April 1923. The war was more terrible and more destructive than the previous 'troubles' had been. Many Irish leaders, including Michael Collins, were killed. Somehow the Irish Free State came through. The Dail devised a constitution for the new State, which was approved, after some amendment, by the British parliament on 5 December 1922. The Irish Free State came formally into existence precisely one year after the signing of the treaty. Northern Ireland cut itself off from the Free State, with equal formality, on the following day. Tim Healy, former Nationalist M.P., became the first governor general. The last British troops left Ireland on 17 December 1922.

However, for all practical purpose, the Union ended on 6 December 1921, and the unity of Ireland with it. A terrible chapter in British history was closed. Ireland received in twenty-six counties a greater measure of independence than had been dreamt of by O'Connell, Parnell, or Redmond. She had her own government: complete autonomy in finance, justice, administration, and education. The southern Irish members disappeared from the parliament at Westminster. The southern Unionists, whose security had once been treated as a vital British concern, were abandoned without protection, though, as things turned out, they became a prized and cosseted minority—a contrast indeed to the condition of the Roman Catholics in Northern Ireland. The British government held three 'treaty ports' for the use of the navy (Queenstown, Berehaven, and Lough Swilly—also Belfast Lough in Ulster). The

---

[1] The British insisted that the treaty be also approved by the parliament of Southern Ireland, set up by the act of 1920. This parliament, attended only by the pro-treaty members, held its only meeting for this sole purpose on 14 Jan. 1922.

[2] Strictly there were two provisional governments: one, under Griffith, elected by the Dail; the other, under Collins, elected by the southern parliament. The new Dail re-elected Griffith, and the other government disappeared.

members of the Dail had to take an oath, acknowledging 'the
common citizenship of Ireland with Great Britain and her
adherence to and membership of the group of nations forming
the British Commonwealth of Nations'. The governor general
was appointed by the king. Otherwise nothing remained of the
Union, over which so many generations had contended. Moreover, Ireland received Dominion status on the Canadian model.
As Canada's rights grew, hers grew with them, until the Irish
discovered that they could legally repudiate the treaty from
which the Free State derived its existence.

The Irish had won. Yet they were not reconciled or friendly.
Their victory had come after terror and troubles, not as a work
of conciliatory statesmanship. They had nothing to be grateful
for. Moreover, the grievance of the boundary between Northern
Ireland and the Free State hardened with the years. The still-
born Council of Ireland, last remnant of unity, was formally
abolished in 1925. Northern Ireland drew increasingly on the
British treasury, and every British subsidy cut it off more from
the Free State.[1] The government of Northern Ireland rigged
the constituencies, exercised special police power, and so maintained a Protestant monopoly, despite one third of the population's being Roman Catholic. Continuation of a separate
Northern Ireland was not only a British obligation,[2] it brought
for the Conservatives political advantage. The religious divisions there impeded the growth of a Labour party. Hence
Northern Ireland representation at Westminster, apart from an
occasional Nationalist, gave a built-in bias of ten members on
the Conservative side[3]—a dramatic change from the days when

---

[1] In the nineteenth century the three lesser members of the Union (Scotland,
Wales, Ireland) paid more to the British treasury than they drew from it. In the
twentieth century the position was reversed. Scotland, Ulster, and Wales would
have had inferior social services (as southern Ireland had and has) if they had been
independent.

The victory of the Irish was, in one sense, a misfortune for the Scotch and the
Welsh—perhaps even for the English. During the controversies over Home Rule,
there was often talk of devolution or Home Rule all round—four separate parliaments for home affairs. The talk grew stronger in the last years before the first
World war. With the establishment of the Irish Free State it died away, and the
single parliament at Westminster survived, with only Northern Ireland to show
how men had once envisaged Home Rule.

[2] The obligation was formally acknowledged only in 1949, strangely by a Labour
government.

[3] The university constituencies in Great Britain gave a further Conservative
bias of nine or ten.

Irish M.P.s brought a reinforcement of eighty or so to British radicalism.

Still, the settlement with Ireland was a great achievement, despite its faults. The Irish question had baffled and ruined the greatest statesmen. Lloyd George conjured it out of existence with a solution which was accepted by all except rigorous extremists in the I.R.A. Of course times favoured him. Men were bored with the Irish question. Most Unionists recognized that the Union must go, though they resented the manner of its going. Most Irish nationalists recognized that they must lose Northern Ireland, though they resented that also. Perhaps the bloodshed of the Great War made men turn against bloodshed in Ireland.[1] Religious animosities were waning, except for the artificial survival of militant protestantism in Northern Ireland. Common sense broke in. Griffith, defending the treaty, said: 'I was told, "No, this generation might go down, but the next generation might do something or other." Is there to be no living Irish nation?' Lloyd George, the supreme opportunist, was for once justified in his opportunism. Yet his triumph did him no good. Liberals and Labour never forgot the Black and Tans. The Conservatives, as they may now again be called, were angry that they had been made to face reality. Ireland ruined Lloyd George, as it had ruined Peel and Gladstone before him. But at least he was ruined by success, they by failure.

NOTES

NOTE A. *Fiume.* This question, though of little direct moment to British policy, distracted the peace conference and helped to estrange Italy from her wartime allies. By the treaty of London in 1915 Italy was promised south Tyrol, Istria (including Trieste), and the northern part of Dalmatia. Fiume was not included. It was assumed that Hungary would continue undiminished, with Fiume as its outlet to the sea. At the end of the war Hungary was disrupted by national upheavals. Croatia, hitherto a subordinate kingdom under Hungary, broke away and joined with Serbia (and with the Slovenes) to constitute Yugoslavia, the kingdom of the South Slavs. The new state claimed Fiume, which was now cut off from Hungary. The Italians regarded Yugoslavia with none of the affection which they had had for great Hungary; on the contrary, she seemed to them a dangerous rival in the Adriatic. They therefore demanded Fiume on top of their other gains. This demand was predominantly strategical; it had also some national justification. Fiume, narrowly considered, had an Italian majority, artificially promoted by the Hungarians; the South Slavs, however, predominated if the suburb and surrounding countryside were included. Meanwhile,

[1] Perhaps also the dismemberment of historic states, especially Hungary, by the peace settlement made the idea of partition more acceptable.

Fiume remained under joint Allied control; its future had to be determined by the peace conference.

President Wilson felt strongly. He was not a party to the treaty of London and acknowledged only such Italian claims as were justified on national grounds (though he did not extend this principle to south Tyrol, the northern part of which was predominantly German). He accepted the Italian claim to Istria, though even this was nationalistically doubtful; he rejected the claim to Fiume and, of course, to northern Dalmatia. Clemenceau and Lloyd George recognized that they were bound by the treaty of London. If the Italians took their stand on the treaty, Great Britain and France would back their claim to Dalmatia; but in that case they could not have Fiume. If they claimed Fiume, this would be an abandonment of the treaty of London, and all their claims must be considered on grounds of national principle. The Italians tried to have things both ways round. In vain. Orlando withdrew in protest from the peace conference, though an Italian representative hastily returned in time to sign the treaty with Germany. Wilson appealed to the Italians over the head of their government. This move was also unsuccessful. The peace conference never settled the question of Fiume.

In September 1919 the romantic Italian poet d'Annunzio seized Fiume and turned it into an independent state. In November 1920 Italy and Yugoslavia reached agreement in the treaty of Rapallo. Italy received Istria and renounced Dalmatia, except for four islands and the town of Zara; Fiume was made a Free City. In September 1923 Italy annexed Fiume, and Yugoslavia acknowledged this annexation in January 1924. After the second World war, Yugoslavia acquired Zara and the Dalmatian islands, Fiume (now called Rijeka), and most of Istria, except for Trieste and Gorizia.

NOTE B. *The Irish Boundary.* The hint was conveyed to Michael Collins on 5 December by Tom Jones, assistant secretary to the cabinet and a Welshman after Lloyd George's own heart. On 13 December 1921 Lloyd George said that no doubt the majority of Tyrone and Fermanagh would prefer being with their southern neighbours. Other British signatories of the agreement said much the same: Austen Chamberlain on 16 December, Churchill on 16 February 1922. By 1924, when the Boundary Commission was set up, all had changed. Austen Chamberlain, Birkenhead (another signatory of the agreement), and finally Lloyd George himself said that only minor rectifications of the existing boundary had been intended. Probably no conscious swindle was designed. In 1921 the British looked forward to friendly relations with the Free State and were willing to sacrifice Ulster. Soon they were estranged by the civil war in Ireland. As well, by 1924 there was a Conservative government in Great Britain: Lloyd George was out of office; the others were laboriously working their way back into the Conservative party which they had deeply offended by their 'surrender' to Ireland. The Irish discovered that the commission would give them only trivial gains in Tyrone and Fermanagh, and would demand concessions from them elsewhere. They therefore abandoned the commission, and the boundary of the six counties remained unchanged, after ten years of dispute.

V

NORMAL TIMES: 1922

NINETEEN-TWENTY-TWO was the first orderly year which Great Britain had known since the outbreak of war. Though her troubles were by no means over, there began a new stability which set the pattern for most of the interwar years. Industrial strife diminished sharply. Eighty-five million working days had been lost by strikes in 1921. Only 19 million were lost in 1922, and 10 million in 1923. Budget estimates fell below £1,000 million. Income tax was reduced, by 1s., to 5s. in the pound. Prices and wage rates both fell from the inflated levels of 1920–1, settling down for some years at about one third above the prewar figure. Practically all the wartime regulations disappeared during 1921. Registration of individuals came to an end with the last scraps of food rationing. Foreign travel was again unrestricted, though the traveller was now burdened with a passport.[1] Sterling could be freely exchanged into foreign currencies, at about 10 per cent. below prewar parity ($4.40–$4.50 to the pound).

The war left few permanent marks on British life. Ex-servicemen never became a separate, let alone a violent, political group as they did in some countries. Their organization, the British Legion, over which Lord Haig presided, brought all ranks together on a more or less democratic basis. It voiced their grievances when the need arose and sometimes exerted discreet pressure on parliamentary candidates. Its usual activities were benevolent and social. The war was, of course, not forgotten. There were war memorials in every town and village;[2] the grave of the Unknown Soldier in Westminster Abbey; and the Cenotaph, to which passers-by doffed their hats, in Whitehall. Armistice Day (11 November) was observed by a nation-wide silence for two minutes at 11 a.m. Theatres and cinemas continued the patriotic demonstration, which they had begun

---

[1] The passport was, of course, required by foreign governments. British citizens do not need a passport to leave this country in peacetime nor to return to it, though the authorities try to conceal this.

[2] The second World war had few memorials of its own. The names of the new dead were simply added to an existing memorial.

during the war, of playing the national anthem at the end of every performance.[1] Summer Time was kept on, despite protests from farmers on behalf of their cows.[2] F. W. Hirst, the Radical individualist, remarked of it: 'Of useful inventions perhaps . . . the best that we can connect with the war period.'[3] Two less useful inventions also survived. The opening hours of public houses continued to be tightly limited, especially with the afternoon gap and on Sundays. The entry and employment of aliens were severely controlled, almost to the point of exclusion. A mistaken fear for jobs reinforced xenophobia, a legacy of war.

The first World war, more conveniently than the second, did not interfere with the holding of the decennial census at its appointed time. In 1921 there were 37,887,000 people in England and Wales; 42,769,000 in Great Britain. The population was still increasing, though more slowly than in the nineteenth century. Since 1911 there had been only a net increase of 0·49 per cent. each year, against a previous annual average of over 1 per cent. The decline in the death rate was just keeping ahead of the decline in the birth rate. There is no mystery about the decline in the death rate. It was caused by improved medical services, improved housing, and improved hygiene. Infant mortality had been more than halved since 1900. Fewer people died in early adult life. In particular, the old scourge of tuberculosis was being mastered. The new killers were cancer and weak hearts, diseases which usually attack people at a more advanced age. As a result, though more people survived to be old, the old—contrary to common belief—did not live longer. The expectation of life for a man of 65 was little greater than it had been a century before.[4] The general effect was to make the working population a considerably larger proportion of the whole, and the average age of the workers was higher—hence perhaps their adherence to old industries and old practices.

---

[1] Of these customs, the raising of the hat to the Cenotaph declined during the thirties, as men took to going without hats, and then lapsed altogether. Armistice Day was not observed during the second World war. After it, both wars were commemorated on the Sunday nearest to 11 Nov. The playing of the national anthem has continued to the present day and is now becoming less universal.

[2] It was renewed annually until 1925, and then made permanent. It also then lost its earlier name of daylight saving.

[3] F. W. Hirst, *The Consequences of the War to Great Britain*, xvi.

[4] The expectation of life for women at 65 was about three years longer than a hundred years before, presumably because they had borne fewer children and were therefore less worn out.

The birth rate fell to below 20 per thousand in 1923 and never rose again above 20 in this period. The number of children under 15 was much the same in 1921 as it had been in 1891, though the population was ten million greater, and thirteen years later there were fewer children under 5 than in 1871, though the population was twenty million greater.[1] We do not know how this came about. People were not marrying later, rather the contrary. Nor is there any reason to suppose that natural fertility had lessened. Abortion, though illegal, had always been common, though there is no means of knowing how common. There is no reason to suppose that it increased. Conception must therefore have been deliberately restricted by some means or other.[2] There is some indication that in the eighteen-eighties, when the decline in the birth rate appears statistically, the middle classes, who were the first to limit their families, simply abstained from sexual intercourse. Artificial impediments to conception were frowned on, and their advocates were still being sent to prison shortly before the first World war. That war introduced millions of men to an effective male contraceptive, the sheath. A satisfactory diaphragm for women was invented in 1919.[3] Soon afterwards Dr. Marie Stopes made contraceptive devices respectable in a somewhat gushing book, *Married Love*. For this she deserves to be remembered among the great benefactors of the age.

The change of attitude did not go far. No medical school gave its students instruction in contraceptives until after the second World war, and professional advice was difficult to obtain except later at a few clinics or, for the rich, from a specialist. Usually the devices had still to be bought surreptitiously, and birth control became more erratic with each step down the social scale. Figures of manufacture, and other inadequate sources, suggest that between the wars one man in ten used a sheath regularly, and that the diaphragm, which alone gave satisfactory intercourse, was used by only a few enlightened women

[1] Children receiving compulsory education (i.e. to the age of 13) reached their highest number (over six million) in 1915.

[2] 'Birth control', the explanation usually given, is a tautology. It only means that conception was being restricted and does not explain how.

[3] Actually by a Dutchman. The phrase 'Dutch cap' is therefore correct, whereas 'French letter' (*capote anglaise* in French) for the sheath is not. The diaphragm became a more reliable obstacle in 1932, when an Oxford scientist devised a contraceptive jelly to go with it.

in the higher classes. Interrupted intercourse was apparently the normal pattern in at least 70 per cent. of marriages.[1] Women, not surprisingly, got little joy from their marital relations and complained to health workers that their husbands 'used' them so many times a week. The historian should bear in mind that between about 1880, when limitation started, and 1940 or so, when the use of the sheath at any rate became more general in all classes, he has on his hands a frustrated people. The restraint exercised in their private lives may well have contributed to their lack of enterprise elsewhere.

The census of 1921 also tells us that the preponderance of women over men, which had long existed, was then at its height. Though the excess had been exaggerated by the death of three quarters of a million men in the war, the cause was mainly natural: more male babies were born, but still more died in infancy. The excess of women—a million and three quarters in all—may have provided a practical incentive towards their 'emancipation', though it was rarely used as an argument. After 1918 they achieved an almost absolute equality in theory. They had the vote, though not on equal terms with men until 1928. The Sex Disqualification Removal Act removed many legal barriers. Most professions were open to them. The Church and the stock exchange provided two quaint exceptions. Higher education was available for them on a fairly generous scale. They received equal treatment at the universities, except at Oxford and Cambridge, where the historic endowments continued to benefit only men.[2] In practice, most women remained dependants, particularly in the working class. Wives were lucky to be given a housekeeping allowance. Very few knew what their husbands were earning. In almost every occupation women were paid less than men for doing the same work. This was less true

[1] The principal English manufacturer produced about two million sheathes a year during the nineteen-thirties and over 100 million (not including those for export), twenty years later. However, that is not the whole story: before the second World war most sheathes were imported from Germany. The sociological information rests on inquiries made of married people in the nineteen-fifties about their practice twenty or thirty years earlier. Rowntree and Pierce, 'Birth Control in Britain', *Population Studies*, xv, and John Peel, 'The Manufacture and Retailing of Contraceptives in England', ibid. xvii.

[2] Oxford also applied against women the *numerus clausus*, reserved in other countries for Jews. Fellows of colleges argued that colleges, having been founded when only men received a university education, must remain true to the wishes of their founders. They were themselves disregarding these wishes by marrying and by not taking a religious test.

in the professions, except for the scandalous cases of the civil service and teaching. It was hard for a woman to rise to the top. There were never more than twenty women M.P.s. There were no women directors of large companies; no women judges; virtually no women professors at universities.

The people of England were physically much of a piece. There were Chinese settlements in Liverpool, Swansea, and the eastend of London. Otherwise all English people were pink or, as it was absurdly called, 'white' in colour. Every county had in it some inhabitants who had been born in every other county. Though regional accents persisted to a declining extent, full dialect disappeared except as a literary exercise. The stories by T. Thompson, in Lancashire dialect, were published in the sophisticated columns of the *Manchester Guardian*.[1] There was a fairly clear line between north and south, a distinction roughly defined by the river Trent. Though nearly half the people of England lived north of this line, one would hardly guess it from most works of literature or political history.

Another clear division was between the England of industrial towns and the rural England of traditional imagining. Twenty per cent. of the population took up 33 million acres. Eighty per cent. had to make do on the remaining 5 million acres—49 per cent. in towns with more than 50,000 inhabitants. This division was becoming less sharp than it had been. Fewer families now lived in the centres of towns, and many were moving into the adjacent country. Between the census of 1911 and that of 1951, the county of London (i.e. the inner built-up area) was the only county in the country which showed an actual decline in population. At the same time Middlesex doubled its population; Kent, Essex, and Surrey almost did so.[2] Extremes in town fortunes show the same trend. The towns which declined in numbers between 1911 and 1951 were Blackburn, Bolton, Gateshead, Halifax, Manchester, Oldham, Salford, South Shields, and Wigan. The towns which doubled their populations were Blackpool, Bournemouth, Cambridge, Coventry, Luton, and Southend-on-Sea. Watering places flourished. Industrial towns decayed. All England became suburban

---

[1] There was a sizeable number of Welsh-speakers, most of them bilingual, in North Wales. Lloyd George was one of them.

[2] The entire population of England and Wales increased from 36 to 43 million.

except for the slums at one extreme and the Pennine moors at the other.

Religion, or rather sectarianism, had drawn sharp lines between English people ever since the sixteenth century. The English, though almost exclusively Christian in background,[1] fell into three warring groups: the Established Church of England; the Roman Catholics; and the Free Churches (first called Dissenters and after that Nonconformists). By no means all English people kept up active religious devotions. There were at this time roughly two and three quarter million practising Anglicans (Church of England); two and a half million Roman Catholics; and nearly two million members of the Free Churches.[2] Only the Roman Catholics made difficulties about intermarriage, the mark of real difference in religion as in colour. Otherwise the zest had gone from religious quarrels. There was no longer a political test of Protestantism except for the monarch and, more doubtfully, the lord chancellor. In education the act of 1902 had done its work.

More broadly, religious faith was losing its strength. Not only did church-going universally decline.[3] The dogmas of revealed religion—the Incarnation and the Resurrection—were fully accepted only by a small minority. Our Lord Jesus Christ became, even for many avowed Christians, merely the supreme example of a good man. This was as great a happening as any in English history since the conversion of the Anglo-Saxons to Christianity. It had many causes: the old rationalism of the eighteenth century; the new rationalism of science, particularly of biology; the higher criticism which discredited the verbal inspiration of the Bible—a hard knock especially against Protestantism. More prosaically, the advance in material comforts made men less concerned with pie in the sky, and the sight

[1] There were also some 250,000 Jews, though it is not known how many were practising; 25,000 Unitarians; and perhaps some 50,000 avowed unbelievers (rationalists, atheists, or agnostics).

[2] Carr-Saunders and Jones, *Social Structure* (1927), 84. The figures are not really comparable. The Anglicans (England and Wales) are Easter communicants. If instead those confirmed were counted, the figure would be over 8 million; if those baptized, it would be 28 million. The Roman Catholics (Great Britain) are 'population', which presumably means all those baptized or perhaps all those born to Roman Catholic parents. The Free Churches (some England and Wales, some Great Britain, some United Kingdom) are enrolled members—again much less than those baptized.

[3] Sunday newspapers became respectable for the first time—another indication of the decline in Sabbatarianism.

of priests and bishops blessing guns or tanks during the Great War was not a good advertisement for the gospel of the Prince of Peace.

The Roman Catholics held up best. They had a hard core of believers. They were reinforced by Irish immigrants and made a number of intellectual converts, roughly balancing the old Catholics who lapsed. The Church of England reaped the advantages of Establishment. Three English people out of four were baptized, four out of five were married, in an Anglican Church. Army recruits, with no avowed allegiance, were entered as 'C. of E.'. Most civilians, if asked, would have given the same reply. The old grammar schools were all Anglican, and the new secondary schools tended to follow their example. The Anglican church retained a monopoly of college chapels at Oxford and Cambridge. Anglican dignitaries played their part at every official occasion from City dinners to the coronation. Twenty-six Anglican bishops sat in the house of lords.[1] The opinions of leading Anglicans and their peccadilloes secured top-billing in the newspapers. The Free Churches were hardest hit. They had rested on belief and preaching. Their influence faded as belief declined. None of their ministers repeated the fashionable success of Sylvester Horne. The nonconformist conscience ceased to count in politics, as Lloyd George discovered when he tried to mobilize it.

The weakening of Christian dogma had little immediate result other than the decline in church attendance, despite a widespread belief to the contrary. England remained Christian in morality, though not in faith. There was a vast appetite for unrevealed religion and for a vague religiosity, supplied by ingenious astronomers such as Sir Arthur Eddington and Sir James Jeans. Standards of honesty and public duty were astonishingly high. The commercial and financial system rested securely on sanctity of contract. England was one of the few countries where those liable to income tax could be relied upon to reveal their correct incomes, as near as made no difference. There were still unacknowledged exclusions against Jews and, to a lesser extent, against Roman Catholics. The gravest handicap, however, was avowed atheism, and few ventured to avow it.

Sexual morality was alleged to have become laxer. There is

[1] Free Church ministers were eligible for membership of the house of commons; Roman Catholic priests were not.

little serious evidence for this, and some against it. Divorce remained a serious barrier in public life and, in Court circles, an
insuperable one. Riddell, a newspaper proprietor, was the first
'guilty' party in a divorce suit to be made a peer, after ineffective
protests from George V; Josiah Wedgwood, the first to sit in a
cabinet (the Labour government of 1924). These were isolated
cases, and the Conservative party maintained a ban on divorce
until after the second World war.[1] In one way, morality became
stricter. The prudish Victorians had published full reports of
the most scandalous divorce cases—even to Sir Charles Dilke
and his 'three in a bed'. Their supposedly lax descendants had
less respect for the publicity of justice and the freedom of the
press. In 1926 a particularly remarkable divorce case[2]—the best
reading since Pemberton Billing and the Black Book—provoked
an act of parliament which forbade the publication of any proceedings in the divorce courts other than the judge's summing
up. It is still on the statute book.[3]

Since creeds had ceased to divide, class stood out the more
sharply. England had always been class conscious, perhaps more
than most European communities. English was the only European language where accent was determined more by class than
by region. The English were the only European people who
sorted themselves out by class at mealtimes: the masses took
their principal meal at midday, their betters in the evening.[4]
Even the drinkers of beer divided automatically between the
saloon and public bars. Education, usually a solvent, produced
in England a further hardening of class lines. Education for All
was an obvious democratic slogan, and in one sense a successful
one. After 1918 all children received full-time education to the
age of 14. An increasing, though still small, proportion continued their education in adolescence, and an increasing, though

---

[1] Divorce, though frowned on, was at any rate legal. Homosexuality, however,
remained a criminal offence. Most assizes had a long list of charges. Under its
shadow, one former cabinet minister in this period committed suicide, and one
went into permanent exile.

[2] The wife had borne a child. The husband gave evidence that the marriage had
not been properly consummated, and adduced the child as proof of adultery. The
wife answered by describing his 'Hunnish practices'.

[3] The act also restricted the publication of physiological details in other cases.
To judge from results, this was not much observed in reports of murder trials.
In any case, a judge with an appetite for headlines could be generous in his sum-
ming up.

[4] The division was less sharp in the north of England where even the wealthy
often had high tea not dinner, in the evening.

very small, proportion went to universities. This was, however, not achieved by opening the existing educational doors wider and wider until they admitted everyone. It was done by developing a different, and mainly inferior, education for those who had previously received none. Thus class differences were not only maintained. They were made clearer and more effective than before.

The children of the masses went to free day schools until the age of 14; the children of the privileged went to expensive boarding schools until 13. The dividing line here was as hard as that between Hindu castes. No child ever crossed it. At the secondary level, the division was almost as complete. Nearly all the children of the privileged proceeded to expensive private schools —public schools as they were perversely called. A minority of children from the other classes went to modern day schools, maintained from public funds. The grammar schools straddled in between, mainly and appropriately for the middle class, and with a few poor boys as well. At the highest level, the modern universities in large towns were socially inferior to Oxford and Cambridge, which remained in spirit, and largely in numbers,[1] preserves of the privileged classes. The two systems of education catered for different classes and provided education, different in quality and content, for rulers and ruled.

There was still an unmistakable upper class, despite the bleat about increasing economic equality. One per cent. of the population owned two thirds of the national wealth; 0·1 per cent. owned one third. Three quarters of the population owned less than £100.[2] Territorial magnates, their wealth reinforced by mining royalties and urban rents, kept up great town and country houses with staffs of thirty or forty servants. The political governing class was largely drawn from a few hereditary families. Most of its members were educated at Eton, and some others at Harrow. Nearly all went to Oxford or Cambridge. They moved with little effort to high posts in government,[3] though rarely to

[1] Though about a third of the students at Oxford and Cambridge now came from grammar schools, only one in a hundred came from a working-class family. Carr-Saunders and Jones, *Social Structure* (1927), 127–8.

[2] Even this was an improvement on prewar when 88 per cent. owned nothing. Put differently, 2½ per cent. of occupied persons over 20 owned two thirds of the national wealth, and 0·25 per cent. owned one third. Ibid. 114.

[3] Only the second Labour government was without at least one peer of the second generation in the cabinet.

the very top.[1] A rich field of sinecures lay open to them, especially overseas. 'Go out and govern New South Wales' was their abiding consolation. The war was expected to threaten both their power and their incomes. The threat proved less than expected. But the war brought some change. The rich, though still rich, became less idle. Many men who had been officers during the war did not slip back into a life of leisure. They earned their livings, principally in finance and industry. They retained their sense of class and their aristocratic ways. But they were no longer shocked at the idea of 'business', and in return businessmen accepted them as leaders. Oliver Lyttelton provides a good example: member of a traditional political family, who preferred the delights of business until pulled into politics by the second World war.[2] The old cleavage between landowners and capitalists almost disappeared—hence in part the decline of the Liberal party. The Conservatives were more homogeneous than they had been. They caught up with the modern world, and their leaders added wider experience to their traditional toughness.

At the opposite extreme, the masses were also easy to identify. The working man was one who received a weekly wage, and the state now singled him out further by issuing him with insurance cards for health and unemployment. Theoretically England was a democracy, attenuated only by the monarchy and by the restricted powers of the house of lords. In practice, most of the population showed little interest in public affairs, even when mismanagement of these affairs threw them out of work or carried them off to fight in foreign fields. Only slightly over half the households in the country took a daily newspaper even in 1939, and no newspaper voiced the outlook of the masses until the second World war,[3] when the *Daily Mirror* won the circulation race by doing so. Only a minority voted in local elections, though about 75 per cent. voted in general elections. Only one trade unionist in ten attended his branch meetings.

[1] No prime minister came from the aristocracy between 1905, when Balfour resigned, and 1940, when Churchill was appointed, and Churchill was half American.

[2] Oliver Lyttelton (1893–   ): educ. Eton and Cambridge; minister of state in Middle East, 1941–2; minister of production, 1942–5; member of war cabinet, 1941–5; president of board of trade, 1945; cr. Viscount Chandos, 1954.

[3] The *Daily Herald*, being at first socialist and then Labour, appealed only to the politically conscious minority of the working class. The *News of the World* had a mass readership on Sundays, not, however, for its political content.

Nevertheless, the history of modern England was not an uninterrupted story of class war. England always had a powerful middle class, and this class encroached both on those above and on those below it. Engels complained long ago that in England even the proletariat was bourgeois, and the aristocracy was becoming bourgeois as well. Many habits were flattening out. Dress provides a striking example. It became more uniform, or rather, by becoming universal, ceased to be the uniform of different classes. It varied now according to the time of day or of activity, not by rank. The frock coat disappeared almost entirely.[1] The upper-class uniform of top hat and tail coat was worn only on ceremonial occasions, such as weddings and race-meetings. It was unmistakably fancy dress. The richest men went to work in what had previously been known as 'lounge suits'. Working men wore similar suits except when dressed in overalls.

Women's clothes were even more of a piece. The well-dressed woman of the nineteen-twenties followed a fashion set by workers in munitions during the war, though it was not until after the second World war that all women enjoyed the luxury of fresh underclothes every day. The ideal of the boyish figure, not always achieved, is less easy to explain. Perhaps women thought that, as men were not much use to them, they had better turn themselves into men as nearly as they could. The war produced another curious equality in social habits. Previously the rich smoked Havana cigars; the poor smoked pipes; only the elegant smoked cigarettes. Now high taxation made cigars expensive. Soldiers had learnt to smoke cigarettes in the trenches; so, to a lesser extent, had women on war work. The cigarette (made of Virginian, no longer Egyptian or Turkish, tobacco) became almost universal.[2] No doubt it provided some redress against the many strains of life. Smoking also ceased to be a private indulgence. It was permitted in cinemas and on the upper decks of buses. Lloyd George lifted the ban against smoking at cabinet meetings, and it was never reimposed.[3]

The middle classes set the standards of the community. They

---

[1] Churchill wore one on great occasions during the second World war.

[2] A pipe-smoking minority persisted among both rich and poor. The pipe was respectable without being ostentatious. Its use was, however, frowned upon in public places and fashionable restaurants.

[3] Another informality was the increasing use of Christian names among politicians and business associates. Baldwin was the first prime minister who always did this with his cabinet colleagues, even when he did not know them well.

were its conscience and did its routine work. Their number increased dramatically. Salaried workers in private employment went up from one million to two and three quarters between 1911 and 1921. Civil servants, as employees of the state were called, had more than doubled since 1914—from 60,000 to 130,000.[1] Those in local government rose rather more. The power of these administrators is generally supposed to have grown at the expense of the politicians, as public affairs became more complex and technical. In 1919 the permanent under-secretary to the treasury was given the title 'Head of the Civil Service', equivalent almost to the military Chief of the Imperial General Staff, and a little later the government appointed a civil servant as Chief Economic Adviser. Here was certainly power without responsibility, power behind the scenes. However, it is hard to believe that Sir Warren Fisher or Sir Horace Wilson, powerful as they were, counted for more than Sir Charles Trevelyan or Sir Robert Morant had done before them, and an efficient politician such as Neville Chamberlain still set his individual mark on the public record. Similarly in local government, the permanent officials, though influential, were dependent on their elected town councils, and a Lansbury or an Ernest Simon counted for more than the town clerk, the borough treasurer, or the medical officer of health.

The most influential figures in public life were indeed voluntary workers. Even the members of the house of commons received little more than a subsistence wage and shrank from admitting that they did a full-time job. Their conditions of work were those of amateurs—no desks, no secretaries, no research assistants. Those who administered justice in the courts of first instance all worked for nothing except the few stipendiary magistrates in large towns. The members of county and town councils were also unpaid. The new responsibilities in housing, education, and roads were all in the hands of these local authorities, despite the fact that much of the money for them came from the central government. The police were directed by local watch committees except in London.[2] The poor law was administered by local boards of guardians. Even more was done purely on an individual basis. Secondary education was largely,

---

[1] This is the total of non-industrial state employees, excluding the post office.

[2] In the counties the police were controlled by Standing Joint Committees—half of the members appointed by the county council, and half by the magistrates.

university education entirely, provided by private associations. More than half the hospitals were privately run. So were most charities. Voluntary societies, old and new, protected animals and children; defended ancient monuments and rural amenities; gave advice on birth control; asserted the rights of Englishmen, or encroached upon them. The public life of England was sustained by a great army of busybodies, and anyone could enlist in this army who felt inclined to. Though most of its members came from the middle class, they were joined in this period by trade union officials and even by self-educated manual workers. These were the active people of England and provided the ground swell of her history.

Though this army served without financial inducement, it received rewards of another kind. Honours were a mainspring of public life. The Order of the British Empire was created specially for these humble political workers, just as the Military Cross had been created for junior officers during the war.[1] Its holders went over the top for the governing class, just as the officers had done for the generals. It had at least the distinction that it was rarely obtained by contributing to party funds. Patronage played as great a part as it had done in the eighteenth century, though it now bestowed honour, not cash. Religion, learning, and law danced to the prime minister's tune. He appointed the bishops and many professors. He even appointed the poet laureate, though no longer for political reasons. The law was more closely tied to politics. The justices of the peace were mainly nominated by the local agents of the political parties.[2] Many of the high court judges won their position by assiduous labours on the backbenches of the house of commons. The Lord Chief Justice was always a political reward in this period with one exception,[3] though, unlike the lord chancellor, he did not remain politically active. The system of patronage was a cheap way of getting public work done—even judges earned less than successful lawyers. It was also conservative, though not entirely in a party sense. Rewards went, on the whole, to the conformists, those who saw nothing but good in the British way of life.

[1] The Order ranged from Knights Grand Cross (G.B.E.) for a select few to Members (M.B.E.) for stationmasters who whistled off the royal train.

[2] Advisory committees, composed of senior magistrates, scrutinized these nominations and occasionally added others.

[3] Lord Trevethin, the exception, proves the rule. He was appointed in 1921 on condition he resigned as soon as Hewart, the political nominee, wanted the job.

The men in public life were not, however, merely the most dutiful members of the community. They were usually also the most conscientious. Nearly all of them wanted to leave their country a better place than they found it. There was also a practical consideration. The modern community could not work without some cooperation from the masses, and the war in particular had made their active cooperation essential in factories as in the trenches. The Germans did more than John Stuart Mill could to justify the ways of democracy to Englishmen. There was also no doubt apprehension of popular discontent. But probably conscience came first, and fear second. At any rate, concern for the conditions of the masses became the dominant theme of domestic politics. The state now provided some security against sickness, unemployment, and old age. It fussed over housing, education, and health.

There was at least some tiny fulfilment of the old Radical dream, by which taxation was to redistribute wealth from rich to poor. The high rates of income tax, surtax, and death duties, introduced during the war, were little reduced afterwards. A rich man paid 8 per cent. of his income in tax before the war, one third of it after. Direct taxes now provided 49 per cent. of the state's revenue, where before they had provided one third. Before the war the masses paid to the state a good deal more than they received from it in social services. The rich, considering their gross disproportion in public employment, were net profiteers. After the war the poor did not quite pay even for their social services. The wealthy had to make up the balance and to carry defence and the national debt as well. It is thought that between the wars taxation transferred something like 5 per cent. of the national income from rich to poor, or perhaps rather less.[1]

Economic inequality was not lessened only by state action. The war accelerated the process which was already giving manual workers an increasing share in the national income. Here again, fear and conscience were mixed. The strength of the trade unions and apprehension of strikes counted for much. As well, intelligent employers discovered that higher wages brought also higher profits, even though traditional economists were telling them that they ought to bring wages down. In 1924,

[1] Pollard, *Development of the British Economy*, 207. Unemployment relief was the greatest redistributor. If the workers had been less unemployed (i.e. better off), there would have been less redistribution.

when industrial production had only just reached again the prewar level, if that,[1] real wages for those in employment were 11 per cent. above prewar, or 5 per cent. if unemployment be allowed for. Wages, even in the most unorganized trades, were above the level of primary poverty, as defined by Seebohm Rowntree in 1899.[2] Manual workers, particularly unskilled manual workers, received more of the national cake, mainly at the expense of those who lived by investments.

There was a general change of economic outlook. Previously the idle rich had been proud of being idle. Now they were ashamed of it, and idleness was more difficult. Domestic servants, for instance, were hard to come by. Their number had been halved during the war and did not recover even during times of economic depression. Households which had kept five servants dropped to two; those formerly with two to one; and the rest of the middle class made do with a daily woman. All this was far from a social revolution, but it took the edge off the class war. The majority of manual workers never voted Labour. Even the majority of trade union members rarely did so. National loyalty transcended class consciousness except for a small minority, and it is possible in this period to write the history of the English people rather than the history of the exploiting classes.

This was hardly recognized at the time. On the contrary, men thought that they were living in a disintegrating society. The Special Irish Branch at Scotland Yard (London police headquarters) found fresh fields to conquer. It dropped the 'Irish' and operated now against Communists—tapped telephones, opened letters, quite in the Metternich style. The alarm was misplaced. The Communist party only once managed to raise 10,000 members during the nineteen-twenties (immediately after the general strike of 1926). Usually it was hard pressed to claim 5,000. Still, conventional ideas were shaken. In literature the war seemed to have produced an unbridgeable chasm between the generations. The established writers, who had once been rebels, now had an old-fashioned air in outlook and still more in technique. John Galsworthy was an extreme case.

[1] Estimates of industrial production in 1924 range from 10 per cent. above prewar to 10 per cent. lower. The latter figure is generally thought to be wrong. Pollard, *Development of the British Economy*, 96.

[2] This does not mean that primary poverty had disappeared, though it had been about halved. It now hit mainly those who had never settled to a trade.

When he started on the Forsyte family before the war, it was to pillory Soames Forsyte as *The Man of Property*, who claimed to own his wife. By the time Galsworthy finished the Forsyte saga, dear old Soames had become the incarnation of traditional virtues. Even the writers who tried to remain subversive became unwillingly respectable. Bernard Shaw, though still discharging paradoxes, could think of no better advice than that men should live for 300 years; achieved his greatest postwar success by a schoolgirl 'crush' on Joan of Arc; and had a festival devoted to him at Malvern—just like Shakespeare at Stratford. H. G. Wells turned from novels to write the most acceptable of universal histories, and then preached the World State, to be provided by the benevolence of rich men who travelled on the Blue Train. The only writer of undiminished stature was Thomas Hardy: as much at home with the new poets as he had been with the old ones, or perhaps more so; the first writer to be buried in Westminster Abbey since George Meredith, and with Kipling as his only successor to date.[1]

The new writers and artists breathed an air of cultural and moral disintegration. Like the changing economic circumstances of England, this, though blamed on the war, was only accelerated by it. Movements against the traditional patterns were well under weigh before the war started. Picasso, Stravinsky, and the Futurists had all asserted themselves in the prewar world. They had little impact on most forms of English art. Architecture continued to follow a decaying Imperial style. Nash's Regent Street was destroyed. A nondescript blatancy took its place. Giles Gilbert Scott outdid the worst achievements of the Victorians in his New Bodleian building at Oxford. All that redeemed the period were some Underground stations by Charles Holden and the *Daily Express* building in Fleet Street.

Music also clung to conventional standards. A little earlier Sir Edward Elgar had been the first English composer of European stature since Henry Purcell. None of his successors rose as high. Delius was a provincial Debussy. Gustave Holst and Vaughan Williams had solid achievements to show—Vaughan Williams rated the more warmly at the time with his production of symphonies, Holst now showing greater powers of endurance. William Walton stood out among the younger men, with a certain gift for spritely tunes. These English composers learnt from

[1] Unless Sidney and Beatrice Webb count as writers.

Ravel—hardly an example of startling modernity. None gave the slightest indication that he was the contemporary of Stravinsky and Webern. Sculpture and painting were more affected by the new styles, enough at any rate to create an occasional stir at exhibitions. Henry Moore, the sculptor, was without a peer and a figure of unique eminence in English art. Of the painters, only Ben Nicholson ranked with the continental masters and justified the visit of an art-lover to English soil.

Literature was a different matter, with giants towering above any continental rivals. T. S. Eliot in poetry, James Joyce in prose, disintegrated the traditions of English literature, much as the wartime barrage disintegrated the French landscape. They had gone right through literature and come out on the other side. With these writers, English literature became more difficult and esoteric just when there were more potential readers than ever before. Writers with a new technique had encountered initial hostility from Wordsworth onwards. This was the first time that acknowledged masters were, and remained, unintelligible not only, say, to a coal miner, but to a secondary schoolmaster or a doctor. The fashion held only in part. Eliot determined the main shape of English poetry for a generation. Joyce was an isolated figure. Poetry perhaps did not need to make sense. Prose cried out for meaning, and Joyce ran into a blind alley where, in his last work, *Finnegan's Wake*, even the words were gibberish.

The writers with a meaning conveyed a doleful lesson. Nearly all turned against their age and repudiated it as far as they could. They were expatriates in spirit and usually in place as well—Eliot perversely to London (from Missouri). Joyce lived in Trieste and Paris, though he remembered only Dublin. He commented on life: 'Je suis bien triste.' D. H. Lawrence, the greatest English novelist of the twentieth century, ran around the world after strange gods, including physical passion, and did not reach again the prewar height of *Sons and Lovers*. His last written words were: 'This place no good.' T. E. Lawrence (no relation), whose writings provided the upper classes with a substitute for literature, tried to escape his fame by becoming an aircraftsman under an assumed name—though he was angry when people failed to recognize him.[1] Aldous Huxley, if anyone,

[1] Estrangement of writers from society was shown in an even more practical way. For the first time works by writers of the first rank had to circulate

might have been expected to go with the times. Combining literary sophistication and scientific descent of the greatest distinction, he was a walking reconciliation between art and science. Somehow the reconciliation failed to work, or Huxley failed to provide it. He turned against both and withdrew to a life of contemplation in California. The two men who came to the front as novelists towards the end of the interwar period, Graham Greene and Evelyn Waugh, were both converts to Roman catholicism, though this only served to increase their woe.

These interwar writers present a puzzle to the historian. Literature, according to historical convention, reflects contemporary life and reveals its spirit. To judge from all leading writers, the barbarians were breaking in. The decline and fall of the Roman empire were being repeated. Civilized men could only lament and withdraw, as the writers did to their considerable profit. The writers were almost alone in feeling like this, and it is not easy to understand why they thus cut themselves off. By any more prosaic standard, this was the best time mankind, or at any rate Englishmen, had known: more considerate, with more welfare for the mass of people packed into a few years than into the whole of previous history. It is hardly surprising that ordinary people found the great contemporary works of literature beyond them.

The masses had their own form of cultural satisfaction. High-grade literature was beyond them. Low-grade literature—the novels of Nat Gould[1] or Edgar Wallace—hardly improved on its nineteenth-century predecessors. The serious theatre, which had been full of life before the war, did not recover from the strains, partly emotional, partly financial, of the war years. Even the music hall began to decline after producing its first knight in Sir Harry Lauder.[2] The radio, which began to operate in 1922, remained for some time a technical curiosity, listeners receiving distant voices through headphones in awed amazement. The great new medium was the cinema, before the war also a technical curiosity, now a fully fledged form of art. During the nineteen-twenties it was still 'silent', and perhaps

surreptitiously—*Ulysses* by James Joyce, *The Rainbow* and *Lady Chatterley's Lover* by D. H. Lawrence, *The Mint* by T. E. Lawrence.

[1] Though Nat Gould died in 1919, his novels flowed on until 1926.
[2] Technically Lauder was knighted for his service to war savings. The only music-hall artist to repeat Lauder's elevation was George Robey, in extreme old age.

the more consciously artistic as a result. The English film-making industry had been ruined by the war. Hollywood dominated. But the greatest artist produced by the screen was an English cockney, Charlie Chaplin, who never gave up British nationality and who retained the innocent utopian socialism of his early years. He was England's gift to the world in this age, likely to be remembered when her writers, statesmen, and scientists are forgotten, as timeless as Shakespeare and as great. The cinema changed the pattern of English life, particularly for the lower middle class. It took people from their homes; eclipsed both church and public house; spread romantic, but by no means trivial, values. Women joined their husbands in enjoyment, as they had never done at football matches or other public pleasures. The cinema was the greatest educative force of the early twentieth century. Yet highly educated people saw in it only vulgarity and the end of old England.

The contradiction was equally clear, and even more unfortunate, when men considered economic and social affairs. Technical achievements were being made at an unparalleled rate: industrial revolutions, for instance in transport and power, advancing every day. Men were producing more while working shorter hours. Wealth or at any rate welfare for all was becoming a practical reality. Yet the most articulate members of the community deplored what was happening, and looked back regretfully to an imaginary prewar society. Few economists had changed their doctrines since the days of Adam Smith. Where once they had been missionaries of progress, they could not now imagine any improvement on the old order, or lack of it, which had made Great Britain economically supreme a century before. This was partly unconscious resentment on the part of the middle classes that, while their standard of life was still rising fast, the gap between it and the standard of the working classes was narrowing. But even working-class radicals did not escape this outlook. English socialism, whether Fabian or Marxist, had started in an age of advancing capitalism. Socialists, too, assumed prosperity and merely sought to distribute its rewards differently. They expected the laws of *laissez faire* economics to continue in operation, with the slight change that profits would go to the community instead of to individuals.[1] They were at a

---

[1] English Socialists were not alone in this. German Socialists were embarrassed by the economic collapse of their country and refused to take over a derelict

loss when faced with the decline of Great Britain's traditional exports and the collapse of stable exchanges. They felt that capitalism must be put back on its feet before it was got rid of, and could only answer with emotional protest those who demanded public economy and the end of social reform. English people, both Left and Right, blamed everything on the war and believed that all would be well if its effects were somehow undone. This was a hopeless ambition. As things turned out, England got change and reform, whether men wanted them or not.

The war, and its consequences, were of course partly to blame. It had impoverished some of Great Britain's former customers, though not all; it had helped her competitors, particularly Japan; it had shattered the system of international finance. Against this, it actually improved the position of Great Britain in one peculiar way. With increased production, the prices of food and raw materials fell; the prices of manufactured goods did not. The terms of trade turned strikingly in Great Britain's favour. Taking 1938 as 100, 142 units of exports were needed before the war to buy 100 units of imports; in the twenties only 115 units of exports. Great Britain could, as it were, afford both higher unemployment and a higher standard of living at the same time.

This was small consolation to the depressed export industries. British economic life relied to a dangerous extent on a few industries, themselves often antiquated, the share of which was declining on the world market, and which catered mainly for the primary producing countries—themselves impoverished. In 1911–13 textiles provided 39 per cent. and coal 9 per cent. of British exports. Eighty-nine per cent. of cotton piece-goods and a quarter of British coal production went abroad. These were the very things which other people could produce more cheaply or for which there was, at best, a static demand. Textiles were being made by Asiatic nations in the first stage of industrial awakening. Coal was threatened by increased efficiency in fuel consumption, by oil, and by electricity. These old industries all declined between the wars. Cotton in 1924 had still the third place among British industries for value of net output; by 1935 it had fallen to eleventh. In the same period, the workers in coal mining were halved, though they were still more than

order. Even Lenin supposed in 1918 that the laws of capitalism would go on working, once the capitalists had been expropriated.

in any other single industry.[1] The decline in these industries was not uniform. Each of the old staples had some modern and prosperous sections: coal mines in Nottingham and South Yorkshire, steel in Lincolnshire, mills working Egyptian cotton. Much confusion was caused by seeking remedies for the industry as a whole, thus often benefiting those who were already making high profits.

Still, the effective way of escape was by developing new industries, catering for a more sophisticated world. Motor cars and electrical equipment were obvious examples. They developed against great handicaps. They needed a prosperous home market as a foundation, and this was hard to find when the bulk of the working population was still in the old industries. To put the problem crudely, England could prosper only when men moved from the old industries, with low wages, to the new industries with high ones; but these new industries could flourish only when men had already moved. This was a vicious circle, which public policy often reinforced. Again, the new industries needed to get on a mass-basis of uniform production. But they had all started on a small scale and with great variety. In 1913 there were 198 different models of motor cars being produced, all by hand one at a time. In 1922 there were still ninety-six different makers. Electricity was in equal chaos. Voltage varied widely, even in the same town, and there were twenty-three different types of plug for an electric fire. This was a situation to baffle contemporaries. Should they promote new industries or seek to revive the old ones? Should they increase British exports or should they make Great Britain less dependent on imports? They tried to go back and, to their bewilderment, were pushed forward. Here, as elsewhere, men lamented the new world which became their salvation.

In 1922, when the postwar boom burst, men grasped at the old remedy of public economy. Heavy taxation was regarded as the root of all evil. The anti-waste campaign against squandermania and against the two mythical civil servants, Dilly and Dally, swept all before it. Sir Eric Geddes, whose schemes for modernizing the railways had been an early victim of economy, presided over a committee on government expenditure. It reported in February 1922. Geddes, himself embittered, swung his axe indiscriminately. Apart from cuts in the army and

---

[1] Ashworth, *Economic History of England*, 332.

navy, the committee recommended economies in education and
public health; reductions in teachers' salaries; and the abolition
of five government departments, including the ministry of
transport and the ministry of labour. Much of this was knocking
at an open door. The temporary civil servants who came in
during the war had now mostly been eased out. The Washington
treaty led to considerable reductions in the navy, despite public
protest from the admiralty. The army was on a peacetime footing of voluntary regulars, solely for the defence of overseas
interests, and with no thought that it would ever again be needed
in a European war. The Geddes axe was most devastating in
education. When H. A. L. Fisher, a recruit brought in by Lloyd
George from academic life, promoted his Education Act in
1918, he introduced two new principles. He raised the school-
leaving age, without exception, to 14. This survived, though the
classes remained grotesquely large.[1] Fisher also proposed to institute part-time education in 'continuation schools' up to 16.
The Geddes axe slaughtered these schools. None was ever set
up on a compulsory basis except, for some unknown reason, at
Rugby. Perhaps the massacre was all to the good. The continuation schools would have provided a strictly proletarian
education and so have made the class cleavage in education
worse than ever.

The act of 1918 had not been Fisher's only contribution to
education, perhaps not even his most important. Teachers'
salaries were made uniform throughout the country, the rates
determined by a joint committee under Lord Burnham. As well,
teachers were brought into a national scheme for pensions. Free
places were provided at secondary schools for the abler pupils.
By 1922 they already covered 34 per cent. of the pupils in
publicly maintained schools. The local education authorities,
themselves committees of the local councils, administered
education. Half the cost and all the policy came from the state.
Fisher does not seem to have appreciated what was involved.
He told his colleagues in 1918 that the extra cost would be
£3 million a year. It turned out to be ten times this figure, and
soon more. Not only was a sum of this magnitude an easy target
for the advocates of public economy, the fact that the expendi-

[1] In 1922 a quarter of the classes had more than sixty pupils. The highest
ambition of educational policy between the wars was to reduce the classes to under
fifty. Even this was not achieved.

ture was incurred at national direction meant that it could also be challenged on a national basis.

The Geddes axe made this challenge clear. Teachers' salaries, which had previously been debated by local authorities, were now scrutinized, and reduced, by parliament. The same happened with school buildings and with free places. The economies were soon undone. The arguments which accompanied them left a permanent mark. The old controversy over education, a bitter one, had been sectarian: what form of religious teaching should be given in primary schools, and by whom? Now, just when this controversy was dying, a new one took its place: how much should the community spend on education? and how far should secondary education become a free social service instead of a charge on parents? Finance was the great educational issue between the wars, and a reforming president of the board of education thought he had done well if he managed to spend more money.

No one between the wars commented on the social consequences of providing a second-rate education solely for the children of those who could not afford to buy something better.[1] Above all, politicians never raised the great question of what should be taught, except in the now exhausted field of religious instruction. This was a stroke of unplanned good fortune. Though the state increasingly paid the piper, it did not call the tune. Teachers, headmasters, examining boards, wrestled with the problem behind the scenes and came up with contradictory answers. This is a subject which has still to be explored. We know roughly how many children were educated, and what it cost to educate them. We know little of what they were taught and virtually nothing of its underlying character. What did they learn about religion or about public affairs? Were they taught to respect their betters or to criticize them? Which came first— the British empire or the League of Nations? At a guess, teachers inclined to the Right in the twenties, and to the Left in the thirties. But it is pure guesswork. The educators were left to decide things for themselves. Anarchy prevailed, a last great bastion of English freedom.

At the end of the war the state broke into a sphere of education from which it had hitherto been excluded: the universities.

[1] The enlightened contracted out of the problem by sending their children to 'progressive' schools at high fees.

Previously the state had merely called new universities into being by royal charter or, with Oxford and Cambridge, imposed reforms by a commission. The universities derived their income solely from fees and endowments, except for a small grant made by the board of education to the new universities from 1911 onwards. Now the state began to subsidize the universities more lavishly. The board of education was accustomed to act through the local authorities. The universities, being national institutions—particularly Oxford and Cambridge—could not be handled in this way. An annual grant was therefore made directly by the treasury, and distributed by a committee of academics. The minister in charge of education had thus no say in education at the highest level. The University Grants Committee had no policy except to some extent the levelling of salaries between 'Oxbridge' and the rest. The universities retained their traditional autonomy, indeed increased it. The new universities had always been free from clerical control. Oxford and Cambridge were shaking it off. As a result, teachers in English universities enjoyed a freedom with few parallels elsewhere in the world. If they made comparatively little use of it, this was due to their class affiliations, or more vaguely to the spirit of the times, not to external pressures.

Men no longer wanted miracles, particularly when the miracles failed to work. They wanted a quiet life. By an appropriate chance, two great figures of irregular achievement disappeared at this time. Horatio Bottomley, after a last blaze of glory as an independent M.P., came a cropper over one of his ingenious swindles and in May 1922 was sent to prison for fraudulent conversion.[1] *John Bull*, though it survived in other hands, lost its power and found no successor: the last degenerate representative of the popular journals which had started with Cobbett and his *Political Register*.

In August 1922 Northcliffe died. Though then insane, he remained a great newspaperman. His last coherent message was that his death should be treated in *The Times* 'by the best man available on the night'.[2] He deserved this tribute. Northcliffe

---

[1] Bottomley invited small subscriptions which would be clubbed together for the purchase of £5 Victory Bonds, and the interest on these distributed as prizes. Most of the subscriptions were never invested, but spent by Bottomley or used to buy off the few complainers. Bottomley was engagingly frank. An acquaintance, finding him stitching mail bags in prison, said: 'Ah, Bottomley, sewing?' Bottomley replied: 'No, reaping.'   [2] Pound, *Northcliffe*, 881.

created the modern newspaper. Until his time, papers gave their readers slabs of solid information. Northcliffe gave news, presented in an interesting way. He saw no purpose in a paper which was not read and, unlike his predecessors, put the reader first. Many journalists and editors deplored his influence. All, in time, followed his example. The long reports of political speeches, for instance, which occupied many columns before 1914, disappeared. Reports of sporting events took their place, to the reader's joy. Newspapers followed Northcliffe in another way. His papers made a profit. Hence they were free from government influence or party control. Other papers realized that they, too, must pay in order to remain independent.[1] Northcliffe gave England the rare gift of a free press. Journalists also reaped the benefit. Northcliffe made their position more secure and their incomes greater.

Northcliffe's popular papers passed at his death to his brother Rothermere. Who would be the new owner of *The Times*? The question excited as much interest as the other question which was now pushing forward: who would be the next prime minister? Lloyd George thought of running the two questions together: a group of his rich friends should buy *The Times* and set him up as editor. This was a remarkable proposal. The editor of *The Times* has often thought himself more important than the prime minister. Lloyd George was the only prime minister who apparently shared the belief. Nothing came of the idea. Perhaps the rich friends were no longer there, perhaps no longer forthcoming.

Lloyd George was in difficulties. He, too, was ruined by the end of the inflationary era. Whatever his gifts, he was obviously not cut out to be the statesman of retrenchment and economy. Yet he could find no way of escape. The rise of the Labour party made it increasingly difficult for him to pose as the man of the people. The end of the boom sapped the spirit of his remaining Radical supporters. Some went back to business life; some, like Eric Geddes, turned traitor; many were themselves in financial

---

[1] The *Daily Herald* did not show a profit and depended on the Labour party and the T.U.C. It would be hard to say which was cause and which effect. Northcliffe was supposed to have acquired *The Times* in order to exercise political influence and even power. This was not so. Northcliffe regarded *The Times* as a national monument and acquired it in order to put it back on its feet financially, just as he subscribed handsomely to the restoration of Westminster Abbey. As a newspaper, it always took second place in his mind to the *Daily Mail*.

difficulties. The Coalition Liberals were on the way out. The Independent Liberals, or Squiffites, were not tempted to accept Lloyd George as their leader. He was dependent on the Conservatives, who had no longer much use for him. They suspected that he would destroy their party as he had previously disrupted the Liberals. Some of them harassed him over the sale of honours. Lloyd George pleaded, rightly, that every government did it, and, indeed, his distribution of honours, wartime leaders apart, had been no greater than that of Asquith, his predecessor. Still, some of his recommendations had been unusually improper. There was besides a difference between raising money for party funds and peddling honours for his own account, as Lloyd George—the man without a party—seemed to be doing.[1] He virtuously promised reform, and a committee of elder statesmen was set up to scrutinize future recommendations—probably to little serious effect. It was more to the point that the days of easy money were over. Those who had bought honours now wished to enhance their position by ensuring that no one could follow their example; those still unhonoured wished to save their money.

Lloyd George's appeal had turned sour. Reconstruction and homes for heroes were a faded mockery. Events in Ireland brought further embarrassment. The treaty, which was still being debated, had been expected to end the Irish troubles and so to reconcile even its sternest critics. Instead, the republicans agitated. The I.R.A. split, and a section of it rose in arms against the Free State. Conservatives felt cheated, and their indignation became unmanageable when Sir Henry Wilson, now M.P. for a Northern Ireland constituency, was killed by two members of the I.R.A. on the doorstep of his London house.[2] The British government were driven to threaten that their troops would be used in Dublin against the republicans unless the Free State acted. The Irish civil war was thus begun on British orders. All Irishmen resented this, even when they were fighting against each other.

[1] The purpose of the Lloyd George fund, derived from these sales, was (and is) 'to promote any political purpose approved by the Rt. Hon. David Lloyd George'. In the moral outcry, it was often forgotten that the Conservative party took an equal cut: something like £3 million went to each partner in the Coalition.

[2] The indignation would have been greater still if it had been known that the assassination was ordered by Michael Collins, now leader of the pro-treaty party. Perhaps the order was given before the treaty, and Collins had forgotten to countermand it; perhaps it was given in the belief that Wilson was organizing Unionist forces in Northern Ireland to resist Sinn Fein.

Manœuvre was Lloyd George's last resource: some master-piece of political tactics which would scatter his enemies. At one moment he offered to resign the premiership in favour of Austen Chamberlain. Chamberlain refused, perhaps from his accustomed loyalty, perhaps from a shrewd guess that Lloyd George was withdrawing only to come back with renewed impact later. Lloyd George talked, too, of an appeal to the country in a general election. This was a barren idea. His opponents were the rank and file among his nominal Conservative supporters: back-bench M.P.s and party-workers in the constituencies. These were the very people who would have had to fight an election in his favour. Sir George Younger, chairman of the Conservative party organization, publicly denounced the proposal to hold a general election on a Coalition ticket. Birkenhead might jeer that 'the cabin boy' was trying to run the ship. A revolt of the cabin boys had made Lloyd George prime minister. He was, in fact, repeating Asquith's mistake. Despite his troubles he, too, regarded himself as 'the indispensable man' and imagined that he was safe so long as the Talents, such as Churchill, Balfour, and Birkenhead, were on his side. It worried him little that by-elections went steadily against the government.[1] Somewhere, somehow, he would find a dramatic rallying cry and sweep back to renewed power.

International affairs offered the sphere for this miracle. Lloyd George was the last of the great war leaders, survivor of twenty-three full-scale conferences since the war. He inspired a twenty-fourth: the conference at Genoa in April 1922, which was to put every great problem to rights. German reparations were to be settled. Soviet Russia was to be brought back into the comity of nations, and her markets reopened to international trade. The United States were to write off the war debts of the Allies. The conference was a failure. The Americans refused to attend. The French attended only to insist on their full claims to reparations. Germany and Soviet Russia feared that they were to be played off against each other, which was indeed true,[2] and made a pact of mutual friendship at Rapallo, to ensure that this should not happen. Lloyd George returned from his last foreign excursion

[1] Between 1918 and 1922 Labour won 14 by-elections and lost 1; independent Liberals made a net gain of 7.

[2] In Lloyd George's calculation, Soviet Russia was to be encouraged to demand reparations from Germany, and Germany was to promise not to trade with the Russians unless they paid their debts.

empty-handed. Reparations remained unsettled; Soviet Russia remained unrecognized and an outcast. The British government tried to rush the United States over war debts. In August the Balfour Note[1] formally proposed the cancellation of inter-allied debts, and announced that Great Britain would collect from her former Allies only enough to pay her own debt to the United States. This was no doubt a wise initiative, even though it involved a loss on paper of £500 million or more. The United States, however, remained unmoved.

Then unexpectedly a great storm blew. Lloyd George, the daring pilot in extremities, could mount to the bridge once more. The world was again in turmoil, Lloyd George again the man to win a war or to save the peace. In 1920 the treaty of Sèvres had theoretically made peace with Turkey. There was a shadow sultan at Constantinople. The Straits were neutralized and held by Allied garrisons. France, Italy, and Greece were given great chunks of Asia Minor. The treaty was a dead letter from the start. The Turks, freed from their empire, developed a new national spirit under the leadership of Kemal Pasha, hero of Gallipoli. A national state sprang up in the interior of Turkey in Asia. Both France and Italy abandoned their respective spheres in the course of 1921 and made their peace with Kemal. Soviet Russia made an alliance with him. Only the Greeks hung on at Smyrna. They were out of favour even with the British government since the return of King Constantine in 1920.[2] Churchill, Birkenhead, Curzon all wished to reach agreement with Kemal. Lloyd George procrastinated: secretly he still planned to back the Greeks. In March 1922 Edwin Montagu, secretary for India, resigned in protest against Lloyd George's pro-Greek attitude. Even the Greeks began to despair. They proposed to seize Constantinople. The Allies forbade this. In August 1922 Kemal struck against the Greeks and routed them. Smyrna fell to the Turks amid scenes of massacre. The victorious Turkish army advanced to the Straits and reached Chanak, an outpost of the neutral zone, held by a small British force.

Lloyd George took up the challenge. Birkenhead and

[1] Balfour was in temporary charge of the foreign office while Curzon was away sick—the effect of his rough treatment at the hands of Lloyd George.

[2] He had been turned off the throne in 1917 by the Allies and was succeeded by his son Alexander. In 1920 Alexander was bitten by a pet monkey and died. Constantine was restored. His first act was to dismiss prime minister Venizelos, the Allies' favourite.

Churchill were roused by the trumpets of war and responded to the call, despite their previous hostility to the Greeks. Harington, the British general, was instructed to stand firm. France and Italy were invoked as allies, though Lloyd George had shown little loyalty to them elsewhere. On 15 September Lloyd George and Churchill appealed to the Dominions for military assistance. The replies were cold. France and Italy were eager to keep on good terms with Kemal. The Dominions were indignant at the attempt to commit them without previous consultation.[1] Only Newfoundland and New Zealand promised support. Mackenzie King returned from Canada a firm refusal. Dominion status was openly displayed for the first time as Dominion independence. Tense weeks followed. On 29 September Harington was instructed to deliver an ultimatum to the Turks, ordering them to withdraw. He wisely failed to do so. The Turks, with equal wisdom, did not attack the British forces. On 11 October, by the pact of Mudania, they agreed to respect the neutral zone until the conclusion of peace. The Chanak crisis was over. It has been called 'the last occasion on which Great Britain stood up to a potential aggressor before the outbreak of the second World War'.[2] This is a melodramatic verdict. Kemal was only reclaiming Turkish territory and, knowing he would get this at a peace conference, had no intention of going to war with the British empire. Lloyd George merely ensured that the new Turkey would not be friendly to Great Britain. The British government had little backing at home. The British people felt that they were being recklessly hurried into an unnecessary war.

Lloyd George and his associates misunderstood the situation. Excited themselves, they thought that they could use the excitement to sweep the country. On 10 October the cabinet decided to fight a general election at once on a Coalition ticket. Dissent came only from Baldwin, president of the board of trade, obscure and almost silent. Chamberlain undertook to break resistance within the Conservative party at a meeting of M.P.s, which he

[1] Their indignation was increased by a muddle of Churchill's. 15 Sept. was a Friday, and the Dominion prime ministers decoded the appeal from the British government only on the Monday morning. On 16 Sept. Churchill gave the news to the press. He released it too late for the English Sunday newspapers, but forgot the difference of time in the Dominions; and the prime ministers of Australia and Canada read the message in their newspapers on Sunday morning.

[2] Boothby, *I Fight to Live*, 28.

summoned for 19 October.[1] He assumed that the rank and file
would find no leaders: 'they would be in a d—d fix'. The rank
and file felt much the same. Many of them, including Baldwin,
expected to be defeated and to be driven from public life. The
mistake of Asquith in December 1916 was being repeated: the
failure to realize that backbenchers could make their will
triumph, if they were resolute enough. In any case, they found
a leader as they had done then.

Law once more saved the unity of the Conservative party.
He had long disliked Lloyd George's adventures. He opposed
the Chanak policy and on 6 October wrote to *The Times*: 'We
cannot alone act as the policemen of the world.' Even so, he
hesitated to go back into politics. He was urged on by the
younger Conservatives, by Wickham Steed, editor of *The Times*,
finally and decisively by Beaverbrook, who thus helped to bring
down the Coalition as he had helped to raise it up.[2] At the last
minute, Law agreed to attend the meeting at the Carlton Club.
There Baldwin attacked Lloyd George as 'a great dynamic force.
. . . a very terrible thing'—words which announced the spirit
of his own future conduct. Law spoke in favour of ending the
Coalition. By 187 votes to 87 the Conservatives resolved to fight
the election as an independent party.

Lloyd George resigned the same afternoon, never to hold
office again. He was the first prime minister since Lord North
to resign because of a decision taken at a private meeting of
M.P.s, and not as the result of an adverse vote in parliament or
at a general election.[3] Thus he maintained to the end his disregard for the established constitutional machinery. He was
the most inspired and creative British statesman of the twentieth
century. But he had fatal flaws. He was devious and unscrupulous in his methods. He aroused every feeling except

---

[1] Usually a party meeting of Conservatives was composed of M.P.s, peers, and
parliamentary candidates. Chamberlain knew that the peers and the candidates
were mostly hostile to the Coalition, whereas he thought that he could threaten
the M.P.s with the loss of their seats. Hence the limitation of the meeting to M.P.s.

[2] Though Beaverbrook was Law's faithful adherent, he had also a public
motive. His one political aim was Empire Free Trade, and he believed that a
Conservative government, led by Law, would promote this.

[3] Even Asquith's fall was touched off by the vote after the Nigerian debate. In any
case Asquith was not driven from office. He resigned in the calculation (mistaken
as it turned out) that he would strengthen his position by doing so. Of course prime
ministers have also resigned because of sickness, old age, or (in earlier times) loss
of royal favour.

trust. In all his greatest acts, there was an element of self-seeking. Above all, he lacked stability. He tied himself to no men, to no party, to no single cause. Baldwin was right to fear that Lloyd George would destroy the Conservative party, as he had destroyed the Liberal party. With his fall, the sheet-anchors of party came back. The Conservative party repudiated him. The rise of the Labour party prevented his becoming the leader of the Left. This was Arthur Henderson's delayed revenge for being kept on the mat in 1917—not that so nice a man ever thought consciously of revenge.

Law remained true to his principles. With unique democratic punctilio, he refused to accept office as prime minister until a Conservative meeting[1] elected him leader of the party on 23 October. On the same day, *The Times* returned to the control of John Walter, its traditional proprietor, now in alliance with John Astor, 'a New College man' and, more important, an American millionaire.[2] This was an appropriate coincidence. The dynamic years were over: Lloyd George out, Northcliffe dead. Law, a Canadian, promised 'tranquillity'; Astor, an American, made *The Times* once more respectable—and 'stodgy'. The New World had been called in to redress the morality of the Old.

NOTE

NOTE A. *The sale of* The Times. Northcliffe owned *The Times* absolutely at the time of his death, having recently acquired the remaining shares of John Walter, the former proprietor. Northcliffe's executor, Rothermere, prepared to sell the paper as part of the estate. Walter had an option to buy the paper back at its market value, but no money with which to buy it. Astor, younger son of the first Viscount Astor, agreed to back him with £3 million. At the last moment a friend of Walter's overheard a telephone conversation, in which Rothermere said that he intended to bid £3,250,000 himself. Astor, who had been sent off to hide in the country, raised his bid to this figure, and won the day. It is usually held that Rothermere was outwitted. However, according to a more reliable account, he had no desire to acquire *The Times*, and the telephone conversation was a plant to squeeze more money out of Astor. Astor took 90 per cent. ownership, Walter 10 per cent. A trust deed was drawn up to prevent transfer of shares outside the two families except with the consent of a strange collection of dignitaries such as the Lord Chief Justice and the Warden of All Souls College, Oxford. Thus, though *The Times* claimed to be a national

[1] This time of M.P.s, peers, and parliamentary candidates.
[2] See Note A below.

institution, the only guarantee of its character was the perpetual integrity of two families, one of which drew its wealth from the United States. This reliance on family tradition was by no means unique in the newspaper world: the Radicalism of the *Manchester Guardian*, for instance, depended in a similar way on the continuing radicalism of the Scott family.

The new proprietors at once exercised their power. Wickham Steed, Northcliffe's editor (though dismissed by Northcliffe in his last insane weeks), was turned out overnight; Geoffrey Dawson, the former editor who had been dismissed by Northcliffe in 1919, was restored. He wrote his own terms and secured complete freedom—a freedom which, it is often held, he did not turn to good purpose.

John Astor's elder brother, the second Viscount Astor, also counted in the newspaper world. He inherited the *Observer* and J. L. Garvin, its prolix editor (whom he dismissed in 1942), along with it. The Astors' wealth derived from property in New York and increased with every advance in American prosperity.

VI

THREE-PARTY POLITICS, 1922-5

POLITICS after the fall of Lloyd George seemed far from the tranquillity which Law had promised. There were three general elections in less than two years (15 November 1922; 6 December 1923; 29 October 1924), and the terrible portent of a Labour government. The turmoil was largely technical. Though Labour had emerged as the predominant party of the Left, the Liberal party refused to die; and the British electoral system, mainly of one-member constituencies, was ill adapted to cope with three parties. The general election of 1931 was the only one in which a single party (the Conservatives) received a majority of the votes cast.[1] Otherwise a parliamentary majority was achieved more or less by accident, if at all. However, there was no profound cleavage between the parties, despite much synthetic bitterness. They offered old policies which had been their stock-in-trade before the war. Labour offered social reform; the Conservatives offered Protection. The victors in the twenties were the Liberals, in policy though not in votes. The old Liberal cause of Free Trade had its last years of triumph. If Sir William Harcourt had still been alive, he could have said: 'We are all Liberals nowadays.' By 1925 England was back, for a brief period, in the happy days of Gladstone.

The government which Law formed was strikingly Conservative, even obscurantist, in composition. There had been nothing like it since Derby's 'Who? Who?' ministry of 1852. The great figures of the party—Austen Chamberlain, Balfour, Birkenhead—sulkily repudiated the decision at the Carlton Club: 'The meeting today rejected our advice. Other men who have given other counsels must inherit our burdens.' The only minister of established reputation, apart from Law himself, was Curzon, who deserted Lloyd George as successfully as he had deserted Asquith and, considering the humiliating way in which Lloyd George treated him, with more justification;[2] he remained

---

[1] None has done so since the second World war. Butler and Freeman, *British Political Facts 1900–1967*, 143, manage to give the Conservatives an overall majority in 1935 by including the National Labour and Liberal National vote in the Conservative total.

[2] During the second World war, Lloyd George was condemning the way in which Churchill rode roughshod over his colleagues. He said 'I never treated the

foreign secretary. Law tried to enlist McKenna as chancellor of the exchequer—an odd choice for a Protectionist prime minister to make, but at least McKenna, though a Free Trader, hated Lloyd George. McKenna doubted whether the government would last and refused to leave the comfortable security of the Midland Bank. Law then pushed Baldwin into the vacant place, not without misgiving. Otherwise he had to make do with junior ministers from Lloyd George's government and with holders of historic names. His cabinet was the most aristocratic of the period,[1] and the only one to contain a duke (the duke of Devonshire). Churchill called it 'a government of the second eleven'; Birkenhead, more contemptuously, of second-class intellects.

The general election of 1918 had been a plebiscite in favour of Lloyd George. The general election of 1922 was a plebiscite against him. Law's election manifesto sturdily promised negations. 'The nation's first need', it declared, 'is, in every walk of life, to get on with its own work, with the minimum of interference at home and of disturbance abroad.' There would be drastic economies and a foreign policy of non-interference. The prime minister would no longer meddle in the affairs of other ministers. Law returned the conduct of foreign affairs to Curzon. He refused to meet a deputation of the unemployed—that was a job for the ministry of labour. In the first flush of reaction, Law announced his intention of undoing all Lloyd George's innovations in government, including the cabinet secretariat. He soon thought better of this, and, though he dismantled Lloyd George's body of private advisers, 'the garden suburb', he kept Hankey and the secretariat. The cabinet continued to perform its work in a businesslike way with prepared agenda, a record of its decisions, and some control on how they were carried out.

This preservation of the cabinet secretariat was Law's contribution as prime minister to British history. The contribution was important, though how important cannot be gauged until the cabinet records are opened. The cabinet became a more formal, perhaps a more efficient body. Maybe also there was an increasing tendency for a few senior ministers to settle things

members of my War Cabinet like this.' Then, as an afterthought: 'Oh, yes, there was one—Curzon.'
[1] Law's cabinet had 6 peers, not counting the lord chancellor. Lloyd George's had had 2. No later cabinet has had more than 5; 3 has been usual, 2 not uncommon. Moreover, 3 of Law's peers were from the great territorial families (no other government has had more than 1); 5 held inherited, not created, peerages.

between themselves and then to present the cabinet with a virtual *fait accompli*, as MacDonald did with J. H. Thomas and
Snowden or Neville Chamberlain with Halifax, Hoare, and
Simon. But this practice had always existed. A cabinet of equals,
discussing every question fully, was a legend from some imaginary Golden Age. On the other hand, the power and authority
of the prime minister certainly increased in this period, and no
doubt his control of the cabinet secretariat was one of the causes
for this. It was not the only one. Every prime minister after
Lloyd George controlled a mighty party machine.[1] The prime
minister alone determined the dissolution of parliament after
1931,[2] and the circumstances of 1931 were peculiar. Above all,
the loaves and fishes of office, which the prime minister distributed, had a greater lure than in an aristocratic age when
many of the men in politics already possessed great wealth and
titles. At any rate, Law, willingly or not, helped to put the
prime minister above his colleagues.

Gloomy as ever, Law doubted whether the Conservatives
would win the election and even thought he might lose his own
seat at Glasgow. When pressed by Free Trade Conservatives
such as Lord Derby, he repudiated Protection, much to Beaverbrook's dismay, and gave a pledge that there would be no fundamental change in the fiscal system without a second general
election. The other parties were equally negative. Labour had
a specific proposal, the capital levy, as well as its general programme of 1918; but, deciding half-way through the campaign
that the capital levy was an embarrassment, dropped it, just as
Law had dropped Protection. The independent Liberals, led
by Asquith, merely claimed, with truth, that they had never
supported Lloyd George. The Coalition, now called National
Liberals, hoped to scrape back with Conservative votes. Beaverbrook spoilt their game by promoting, and in some cases financing, Conservative candidates against them; fifty-four, out of the
fifty-six National Liberals thus challenged, were defeated. The
voting was as negative as the parties. Five and a half million voted
Conservative; just over 4 million voted Liberal (Asquithians
2·5 million, National 1·6 million); 4·2 million voted Labour.
The result was, however, decisive, owing to the odd working of

---

[1] Except Churchill between May and Oct. 1940.
[2] In theory the decision rested with the king, but on every occasion he accepted
the advice of the prime minister.

three- or often four-cornered contests. The Conservatives held almost precisely their numbers at the dissolution: with 345 seats they had a majority of 77 over the other parties combined. Labour won 142 seats; the Liberals, with almost exactly the same vote (but about 70 more candidates), only 117.[1] All the National Liberal leaders were defeated except Lloyd George in his pocket borough at Caernarvon. Churchill, who had just lost his appendix, also lost his seat at Dundee, a two-member constituency, to a Prohibitionist[2] and to E. D. Morel, secretary of the Union of Democratic Control. This was a striking reversal of fortunes.

The Conservatives and Liberals were much the same people as before, with a drop of twenty or so in the number of company directors—mainly due no doubt to the reduction of National Liberals by half. Labour was so changed as to be almost a different party. In the previous parliament the Labour members had all been union nominees, as near as makes no odds (all but one in 1918, all but three at the dissolution); all were of working-class origin. Now the trade unionists were little more than half (80 out of 142), and middle-class, even upper-class, men sat on the Labour benches for the first time.[3] In composition Labour was thus more of a national party than before and less an interest group. In outlook it was less national, or at any rate more hostile to the existing order in economics and in nearly everything else. The old Labour M.P.s had not much to distinguish them except their class, as they showed during the war by their support for Lloyd George. The new men repudiated both capitalism and traditional foreign policy.

There were combative working-class socialists of the I.L.P., particularly from Glasgow. These Clydesiders, as they were called, won twenty-one out of twenty-eight seats in their region. They imagined that they were about to launch the social revolution. One of them, David Kirkwood, a shop steward who ended in the house of lords, shouted to the crowd who saw him

---

[1] It is difficult to sort these out between independent and National. One version gives 60 for Asquith, 57 for Lloyd George; another 54 for Asquith, 62 for Lloyd George.

[2] The only one ever returned specifically as such.

[3] C. P. Trevelyan, later Sir Charles Trevelyan, Bart., was a large landowner in Northumberland and great-nephew of Macaulay's. Arthur Ponsonby was the son of Victoria's private secretary, and had been one of the queen's pages of honour. Both were former Liberal M.P.s, and both were founder-members of the U.D.C.

off: 'When we come back, this station, this railway, will belong to the people!' The men from the middle and upper classes had usually joined the Labour party because of their opposition to the foreign policy which, in their opinion, had caused and prolonged the war. Often, going further than the U.D.C. and its condemnation of secret diplomacy, they believed that wars were caused by the capitalist system. Clement Attlee,[1] who entered parliament at this election, defined their attitude when he said: 'So long as they had capitalist governments they could not trust them with armaments.'[2]

The cleavage between old Labour and new was not absolute. Not all the trade unionists were moderate men, and the moderates had turned against Lloyd George after the war, even to the extent of promoting a general strike to prevent intervention against Russia. All of them, thanks to Henderson, had accepted a foreign policy which was almost indistinguishable from that of the U.D.C.[3] On the other hand, not all the I.L.P. members were extremists: both MacDonald and Snowden, for example, were still I.L.P. nominees. The new men understood the need for trade union money and appreciated that they had been returned mainly by working-class votes. For, while Labour had now some middle-class adherents at the top, it had few middle-class voters; almost any middle-class man who joined the Labour party found himself a parliamentary candidate in no time. Moreover, even the most assertive socialists had little in the way of a coherent socialist policy. They tended to think that social reform, if pushed hard enough, would turn into socialism of itself, and therefore differed from the moderates only in pushing harder. Most Labour M.P.s had considerable experience as shop stewards or in local government, and they had changed things there simply by administering the existing machine in a different spirit. The Red Flag flew on the Clyde, in Poplar, in South

[1] Clement Richard Attlee (1883–1967); educ. Haileybury and Oxford; lecturer in social science, L.S.E., 1913–23; mayor of Stepney, 1919, 1920; member of Simon commission, 1927; chancellor of duchy of Lancaster, 1930–1; postmaster general, 1931; leader of Labour party, 1935–55; lord privy seal, 1940–2; deputy prime minister, 1942–5; prime minister, 1945–51; cr. Earl, 1955. Attlee was one of the few middle-class Labour men who became a socialist for domestic reasons (before 1914), and came over to the U.D.C. only after fighting in the war.

[2] Labour party annual conference, June 1923.

[3] Almost, but not quite. The trade unionists, like Henderson himself, were not pacifists, as many of the U.D.C. were. Hence they had no difficulty later in supporting collective security, even if this meant armaments or even war.

Wales. Socialists expected that all would be well when it flew also at Westminster.

Nevertheless, the advance of Labour and its new spirit raised an alarm of 'Bolshevism' particularly when two Communists now appeared in parliament—both elected with the assistance of Labour votes.[1] The alarm was unfounded. The two M.P.s represented the peak of Communist achievement. The Labour party repeatedly refused the application of the Communist party for affiliation and gradually excluded individual Communists by a system more elaborate than anything known since the repeal of the Test Acts.[2] Certainly there was throughout the Labour movement much interest in Soviet Russia, and even some admiration. Russia was 'the workers' state'; she was building socialism. The terror and dictatorship, though almost universally condemned, were excused as having been forced on Russia by the Allied intervention and the civil war. English socialists drew the consoling moral that such ruthlessness would be unnecessary in a democratic country.

Democracy—the belief that the will of the majority should prevail—was in their blood. They were confident that the majority would soon be on their side. Evolution was now the universal pattern of thought: the idea that things were on the move, and always upwards. Men assumed that the curve of a graph could be projected indefinitely in the same direction: that national wealth, for example, would go on increasing automatically or that the birth rate, having fallen from 30 per thousand to 17 in thirty years, would in the next thirty fall to 7 or even 0. Similarly, since the Labour vote had gone up steadily,

---

[1] Saklatvala, a wealthy Parsee, was returned at Battersea North (more or less John Burns's old seat) as official Labour candidate. Walton Newbold, a former Quaker and a pupil of Professor Tout's, was returned at Motherwell without Labour opposition. Newbold made some sensation with his dissection of capitalist interests, on the lines of his prewar pamphlet, *How Europe Armed for War*. He lost his seat in 1923, and left the Communist party soon afterwards. Saklatvala lost his seat in 1923, regained it in 1924, and sat until 1929. He never made much mark.

[2] 1924: Communists not eligible for endorsement as Labour candidates; Communists barred as individual members of the Labour party (reaffirmed 1925). 1928: Communists barred as trade union delegates to the annual party conference. Like the Test acts, the system depended on the honesty of those against whom it was directed, though by definition they were dishonest. The only basis for exclusion was an admission of membership of the Communist party. Yet the system worked— as the Test acts had done. The T.U.C. did not encroach on the autonomy of the unions, and Communists could therefore appear as delegates at the annual Congress, unless the union concerned made a rule against them.

it would continue to rise at the same rate. In 1923 Sidney Webb solemnly told the Labour annual conference that 'from the rising curve of Labour votes it might be computed that the party would obtain a clear majority . . . somewhere about 1926'.[1] Hence Labour had only to wait, and the revolution would come of itself. Such, again according to Webb, was 'the inevitability of gradualness'.

When parliament met, the Labour M.P.s elected Ramsay MacDonald as their leader. The election was a close-run thing: a majority of five, according to Clynes, the defeated candidate; of two, according to the later, perhaps jaundiced, account by Philip Snowden. The Clydesiders voted solid for MacDonald to their subsequent regret. The narrow majority was misleading: it reflected mainly the jealousy of those who had sat in the previous parliament against the newcomers. MacDonald was indeed the predestined leader of Labour. He had largely created the party in its first years; he had already led the party before the war; and Arthur Henderson had been assiduously preparing his restoration.[2] He had, in some undefined way, the national stature which other Labour men lacked. He was maybe vain, moody, solitary; yet, as Shinwell has said, in presence a prince among men. He was the last beautiful speaker of the Gladstone school, with a ravishing voice and turn of phrase. His rhetoric, though it defied analysis, exactly reflected the emotions of the Labour movement, and he dominated that movement as long as he led it.

There were practical gifts behind the cloud of phrases. He was a first-rate chairman of the cabinet, a skilful and successful negotiator, and he had a unique grasp of foreign affairs, as Lord Eustace Percy, by no means a sympathetic judge, recognized as late as 1935.[3] With all his faults, he was the greatest leader Labour has had, and his name would stand high if he had not outlived his abilities. MacDonald's election in 1922 was a portent in another way. The Labour M.P.s were no longer electing merely their chairman for the coming session. They were electing the leader of a national party and, implicitly therefore, a future

---

[1] Labour has never obtained a clear, overall majority of votes at any general election.

[2] Even to the extent of inviting him to attend the meetings of the parliamentary party in 1921 and 1922 as adviser and unofficial leader, even though he was not a member of parliament.

[3] Eustace Percy, *Some Memories*, 169.

prime minister. The party never changed its leader again from session to session as it had done even between 1918 and 1922. Henceforth the leader was re-elected each year until old age or a major upheaval over policy ended his tenure.

Ramsay MacDonald set his stamp on the inter-war years. He did not have to wait long to be joined by the man who set a stamp along with him: Stanley Baldwin. Law doubted his own physical capacity when he took office and did not intend to remain more than a few months. It seemed obvious at first who would succeed him: Marquis Curzon,[1] foreign secretary, former viceroy of India, and sole survivor in office (apart from Law) of the great war cabinet. Moreover, in the brief period of Law's premiership, Curzon enhanced his reputation. Baldwin, the only possible rival, injured what reputation he had. Curzon went off to make peace with the Turks at the conference of Lausanne. He fought a lone battle, almost without resources and quite without backing from home, in the style of Castlereagh; and he carried the day.[2] Though the Turks recovered Constantinople and eastern Thrace, the zone of the Straits remained neutralized, and the Straits were to be open to warships in time of peace—a reversal of traditional British policy and an implied threat to Soviet Russia, though one never operated. Moreover, the Turks were bewitched by Curzon's seeming moderation and laid aside the resentment which Lloyd George had provoked. More important still, Curzon carried off the rich oil wells of Mosul, to the great profit of British oil companies and of Mr. Calouste Gulbenkian, who drew therefrom his fabulous 5 per cent.[3]

Baldwin, also in search of tranquillity, went off to Washington to settle Great Britain's debt to the United States. Law held firmly to the principle of the Balfour note that Great Britain should pay her debt only to the extent that she received what

[1] Curzon had hoped to be made a duke in Lloyd George's resignation honours. He was disappointed.

[2] Curzon attended only the first session of the conference which was held from 19 Nov. 1922 to 4 Feb. 1923. Though he then broke off, he had in fact got his way, and the second session of the conference from 24 Apr. to 24 July, which he did not attend, merely formalized his victory.

[3] Technically Mosul was disputed between Turkey and Great Britain's protégé, Irak. It was agreed to refer the dispute to the League of Nations; and the League, suitably influenced by Great Britain, duly allotted Mosul to Irak in 1926. Gulbenkian received his 5 per cent. as compensation for a somewhat dubious concession which he had acquired from the Ottoman Government before the war.

was owed to her by others. Anything else, he believed, 'would reduce the standard of living in this country for a generation'.[1] Baldwin was instructed to settle only on this basis. In Washington he lost his nerve, perhaps pushed into surrender by his companion, Montagu Norman, governor of the bank of England, who had an incurable zest for financial orthodoxy. Without securing the permission of the cabinet, Baldwin agreed to an unconditional settlement on harsh terms[2] and, to make matters worse, announced the terms publicly on his return. Law wished to reject the settlement: 'I should be the most cursed Prime Minister that ever held office in England if I accepted those terms.'[3] His opposition was sustained by the two independent experts whom he consulted, McKenna and Keynes. The cabinet, however, was for acceptance. Law found himself alone. He wished to resign and was persuaded to stay on by the pleas of his colleagues. He satisfied his conscience by publishing an anonymous attack on the policy of his own government in the columns of *The Times*.[4]

As things worked out, Great Britain was not ruined by the settlement of the American debt, though it was no doubt irksome that France and Italy later settled their debt on easier terms. Throughout the twenties the British collected a balancing amount from their own debtors and in reparations. The real harm lay elsewhere. While the settlement perhaps improved relations with the United States, it compelled the British to collect their own debts and therefore to insist on the payment of reparations by Germany both to others and to themselves. This was already clear in 1923. Poincaré, now French premier, attempted to enforce the payment of reparations by occupying the Ruhr. The Germans took up passive resistance, the mark tumbled to nothing, the finances of central Europe were again in chaos. The British government protested and acquiesced. French troops were allowed to pass through the British zone of occupation in the Rhineland. While the British condemned

[1] Blake, *The Unknown Prime Minister*, 491.
[2] The full liability was £46 million a year, as interest at 5 per cent. Baldwin settled at 3 per cent. for 10 years, and 3½ per cent. for 52 years, with a sinking fund of 1 per cent., making £34 million for 10 years, and £40 million thereafter. Law is reputed to have been prepared to offer 2½ per cent. (£25 million a year).
[3] Blake, *The Unknown Prime Minister*, 494.
[4] Under the signature of *A Colonial Correspondent*. Evelyn Wrench, *Geoffrey Dawson and his Times*, 215.

Poincaré's method, they could no longer dispute his aim: they were tied to the French claim at the same time as they opposed it.

The debt settlement might have been expected to turn Law against Baldwin. There were powerful factors on the other side. Law knew that Curzon was unpopular in the Conservative party—disliked both for his pompous arrogance and his weakness. Curzon lacked resolution, despite his rigid appearance. He was one of nature's rats. He ran away over the Parliament bill; he succumbed to women's suffrage. He promised to stand by Asquith and then abandoned him. He did the same with Lloyd George. Beaverbrook has called him 'a political jumping jack'. Law regarded the impending choice between Curzon and Baldwin with more than his usual gloom. He tried to escape from it by inviting Austen Chamberlain to join the government with the prospect of being his successor in the autumn. Chamberlain appreciated that his standing in the Conservative party had been for ever shaken by the vote at the Carlton club, and refused.[1]

The end came abruptly. In May Law was found to have incurable cancer of the throat. He resigned at once. Consoled by the misleading precedent of what happened when Gladstone resigned in 1894, he made no recommendation as to his successor.[2] He expected this to be Curzon, and was glad that it would be none of his doing. However, the king was led to believe, whether correctly or not, that Law favoured Baldwin, and he duly followed what he supposed to be the advice of his retiring prime minister as the monarch has done on all other occasions since 1894.[3] Law lingered on until 30 October. He was buried in Westminster Abbey—the first prime minister to follow Gladstone there and with Neville Chamberlain, so far, as his only successor.[4] The reason for this distinction is obscure. Was it

[1] Thus Austen Chamberlain twice refused the succession to the premiership—from Lloyd George in Feb. 1922, from Law in Apr. 1923. This is a record surpassed only by Hartington who refused both to be Liberal prime minister (in 1880) and Unionist prime minister (in 1886).

[2] Gladstone was prepared to recommend a successor (a bad one); Victoria deliberately did not consult him. Law was unwilling to make a recommendation even if consulted.

[3] See Note A, p. 224.

[4] Neither of the men so honoured was a Christian, let alone an Anglican. Law, Presbyterian by birth, was a sceptic. Chamberlain was a Unitarian, i.e. not a believer in the Trinity.

because he had reunited the Conservative party? or because he had overthrown Lloyd George?[1]

Baldwin did not follow Law's example of waiting to accept office until he had been elected leader of the Conservative party. He became prime minister on 21 May, was elected leader on 28 May. Curzon proposed the election with phrases adequately fulsome. Privately he is reputed to have called Baldwin 'a person of the utmost insignificance'. This was Baldwin's strength. He seemed, though he was not, an ordinary man. He presented himself as a simple country gentleman, interested only in pigs. He was in fact a wealthy ironmaster, with distinguished literary connexions.[2] His simple exterior concealed a skilful political operator. Lloyd George, after bitter experience, called him 'the most formidable antagonist whom I ever encountered'—no mean tribute. Baldwin played politics by ear. He read few official documents, the newspapers not at all. He sat on the treasury bench day after day, sniffing the order-paper, cracking his fingers, and studying the house of commons in its every mood. He had in his mind a picture, no doubt imaginary, of the patriarchal relations between masters and men at his father's steel works, and aspired to establish these relations with Labour on a national scale. This spirit met a response from the other side. MacDonald said of him as early as 1923: 'In all essentials, his outlook is very close to ours.' It is hard to decide whether Baldwin or MacDonald did more to fit Labour into constitutional life.

Baldwin did not set the Conservative pattern alone. He acquired, almost by accident, an associate from whom he was never parted: Neville Chamberlain.[3] The two were yoke-fellows rather than partners, bound together by dislike of Lloyd George and by little else. Chamberlain was harsher than Baldwin,

[1] Other prime ministers have been offered burial in Westminster Abbey, and their families have declined.

[2] Rudyard Kipling was his first cousin. His own speeches were widely admired for their literary quality. They were, however, largely written for him by Tom Jones, assistant secretary to the cabinet.

[3] Law made Neville Chamberlain postmaster general, in the hope of using him as a bridge to his brother Austen. Griffith-Boscawen, minister of health, lost his seat at the general election, and failed again at a by-election in Feb. 1923, thanks to the unpopularity of his Rent Bill. Neville Chamberlain then took over as minister of health. In Aug. 1923 McKenna agreed to become chancellor of the exchequer. He failed, however, to find a seat, and once more Neville Chamberlain was promoted to fill the empty place.

more impatient with criticism and with events. He antagonized where Baldwin conciliated. He was also more practical and eager to get things done. He had a zest for administrative reform. Nearly all the domestic achievements of Conservative governments between the wars stand to his credit, and most of the troubles also. Active Conservatives often strove to get rid of Baldwin and to put Chamberlain in his place. They did not succeed. Chamberlain sinned against Napoleon's rule: he was a man of No Luck. The cards always ran against him. He was humiliated by Lloyd George at the beginning of his political career, and cheated by Hitler at the end. Baldwin kept him in the second place, almost without trying.

Chamberlain's Housing Act (introduced in April, enacted in July) was the one solid work of this dull government. It was provoked by the complete stop in house building when Addison's programme ended. Chamberlain believed, like most people, that Addison's unlimited subsidies were the main cause of high building costs. He was also anxious, as a good Conservative, to show that private enterprise could do better than local authorities. His limited subsidy (£6 a year for twenty years) went to private and public builders alike, with a preference for the former; and they built houses only for sale. Mean houses ('non-parlour type' was the technical phrase) were built for those who could afford nothing better. Predominantly, the Chamberlain act benefited the lower middle class, not the industrial workers. This financial discrimination caused much bitterness. Chamberlain was marked as the enemy of the poor, and his housing act lost the Conservatives more votes than it gained.

Still, there seemed no reason why the government should not jog on. Its majority was solid; economic conditions were not markedly deteriorating. Without warning, Baldwin raised the ghost which Law had exorcized in 1922. On 25 October he announced that he could fight unemployment only if he had a free hand to introduce Protection. His motives for this sudden decision remain obscure. Protection had been for many years at once the inspiration and the bane of the Conservative party. There would hardly have been a lively mind or a creative personality on the Conservative benches without it. On the other hand, it had repeatedly brought party disunion and electoral defeat. Hence Balfour had sworn off it in 1910, and Law in 1922. There seemed little reason to revive this terrible controversy now. An imperial conference was indeed in session, principally to ensure that no British government would ever take such an initiative as Chanak again. The conference expressed the usual pious wish for Imperial Preference. This meant in practice British tariffs on foreign food, while foodstuffs from the Dominions came in free. There would be Dominion preferences for British manufactures only in the sense that Dominion tariffs, which were already prohibitively high, would go up further against the foreigner. This was not an attractive proposition to put before the British electorate, and Baldwin did not attempt it. He pledged himself against 'stomach taxes'. There would be 'no tax on wheat or meat'. Imperial Preference was thus ruled out.

Later, when Protection had brought defeat for the Conservatives, Baldwin excused himself on grounds of political tactics. Lloyd George, he alleged, was returning from a triumphal tour of North America with a grandiose programme of empire development. Baldwin 'had to get in quick'. His championing of Protection 'dished the Goat' [Lloyd George].[1] Austen Chamberlain and other Conservatives who had adhered to Lloyd George swung back on to Baldwin's side. This story seems to have been devised after the event. Chamberlain and the rest were already swinging back; there was no serious sign that Lloyd George was inclining towards Protection. Perhaps Baldwin, a man still little known, wished to establish his reputation with the Conservative rank and file. Perhaps he wished to show that he, not Beaverbrook, was Law's heir. The simplest explanation is probably the true one. Baldwin, like most manufacturers of steel, thought only of the home market. He did not grasp the problem of exports and hoped merely that there would be more sale for British steel if foreign supplies were reduced. For once, he took the initiative and learnt from his failure not to take it again.

Protection involved a general election in order to shake off Law's pledge of a year before. The cry of Protection certainly brought the former associates of Lloyd George back to Baldwin. This was more than offset by the resentment of Free Trade

---

[1] On the other hand, Baldwin also said that his move had been 'long calculated'. There is a more sophisticated, and even more doubtful story, that Baldwin deliberately provoked electoral defeat, in order to bounce back more strongly when others had made a mess of things.

Conservatives, particularly in Lancashire. Defence of Free Trade at last reunited the Liberal party, much to Lloyd George's discomfiture—though this was hardly Baldwin's doing. With Free Trade the dominant issue, Lloyd George was shackled to the orthodox Asquithian remnant. Asquith was once more undisputed leader; Lloyd George, the man who won the war, merely his unwilling lieutenant. It was small consolation that the Asquithians had their expenses paid by the Lloyd George Fund.[1]

The election of December 1923 was as negative as its predecessor. This time negation went against Protection,[2] and doing nothing favoured the once-radical cause of Free Trade. Though the overall vote remained much the same— the Conservatives received about 100,000 less,[3] the Liberals 200,000, and Labour 100,000 more—the results were startlingly different. The Conservatives lost over ninety seats, the Liberals gained forty, and Labour fifty.[4] The dominant groups of 1918 were further depleted, relatively in one case, absolutely in the other. The trade unionists, once all-powerful, were now a bare majority in the Labour party (98 out of 191). The National (Lloyd George) Liberals, already halved in 1922, were now halved again, despite the Liberal gains. There were only twenty-six of them. Their former seats nearly all went to Labour, evidence that they had formed the Liberal Left wing. The outcome was a tangle: no single party with a majority, yet the Liberals barred from coalition by their dislike of Protection on the one side, of socialism on the other.

It was obvious that the government would be defeated when parliament met. Then, according to constitutional precedent, the king would send for the leader of the next largest party, Ramsay MacDonald. Harebrained schemes were aired for averting this terrible outcome. Balfour, or Austen Chamberlain,

---

[1] The Lloyd George fund contributed £100,000 or, according to another account, £160,000 to Liberal party expenses. Labour raised £23,565 mainly from the trade unions.

[2] This was the only election in British history, fought solely and specifically on Protection.

[3] Their loss was held at this small figure only because they ran seventy more candidates. Their share of the vote in contested seats declined from 48·6 to 42·6 per cent.

[4] Conservatives 258; Liberals 159; Labour 191. There were many cross currents. The Conservatives lost 67 seats to Liberals and won 15; lost 40 to Labour and won 3. The Liberals won 11 seats from Labour and lost 21.

should take Baldwin's place as Conservative premier; Asquith should head a Liberal–Conservative coalition; McKenna should form a non-parliamentary government of 'national trustees'. None of these schemes came to anything. Asquith was clear that Labour should be put in, though he also assumed that he would himself become prime minister when, as was bound to happen soon, they were put out. In any case, George V took his own line: Labour must be given 'a fair chance'. On 21 January the Conservative government was defeated by seventy-two votes.[1] On the following day MacDonald became prime minister, having first been sworn of the privy council—the only prime minister to need this preliminary. George V wrote in his diary: 'Today 23 years ago dear Grandmama died. I wonder what she would have thought of a Labour Government!'; and a few weeks later to his mother: 'They [the new Ministers] have different ideas to ours as they are all socialists, but they ought to be given a chance & ought to be treated fairly.'[2]

MacDonald was a man of considerable executive ability, despite his lack of ministerial experience; he had also many years' training in balancing between the different groups and factions in the Labour movement. On some points he consulted Haldane, who became lord chancellor, principally in order to look after the revived committee of imperial defence. Snowden, MacDonald's longtime associate and rival in the I.L.P., became chancellor of the exchequer. MacDonald himself took the foreign office, his consuming interest; besides, he was the only name big enough to keep out E. D. Morel. The revolutionary Left was almost passed over. Lansbury, its outstanding English figure, was left out, partly to please George V, who disliked Lansbury's threat to treat him as Cromwell treated Charles I. Wheatley, a Roman Catholic businessman who became minister of health, was the only Clydesider in the government; to everyone's surprise he turned out its most successful member. Broadly the cabinet combined trade unionists and members of the U.D.C. It marked a social revolution despite its moderation: working men in a majority, the great public schools and the old universities eclipsed for the first time.[3]

---

[1] Ten Liberals voted with the Conservatives—a sign of things to come.

[2] Nicolson, *George V*, 384, 389.

[3] Seven trade unionists; 9 members of the U.D.C. Eleven were of working-class origin out of 20. The working-class preponderance is still greater if one ignores the peers brought in or created by MacDonald, none of whom had close connexion

The Labour government recognized that they could make no fundamental changes, even if they knew what to make: they were 'in office, but not in power'. Their object was to show that Labour could govern, maybe also that it could administer in a more warm-hearted way. The Left did not like this tame outlook and set up a committee of backbench M.P.s to control the government; it did not have much effect. The Labour ministers hardly needed the king's exhortation to 'prudence and sagacity'.[1] All, except Wheatley, were moderate men, anxious to show their respectability. They were willing to hire court dress (though not knee-breeches) from Moss Bros. It was a more serious difficulty that they lacked experience in government routine. Only two (Haldane and Henderson) had previously sat in a cabinet. Fifteen out of the twenty had never occupied any ministerial post. Inevitably they relied on the civil servants in their departments, and these, though personally sympathetic, were not running over with enthusiasm for an extensive socialist programme.

Wheatley was the only minister with a creative aggressive outlook. His Housing Act was the more surprising in that it had no background in party discussion or programme, other than Labour's dislike of bad housing conditions. Unlike Neville Chamberlain or even Addison, Wheatley recognized that the housing shortage was a long-term problem. He increased the subsidy;[2] put the main responsibility back on the local authorities; and insisted that the houses must be built to rent. More important still, he secured an expansion of the building industry by promising that the scheme would operate steadily for fifteen years. This was almost the first cooperation between government and industry in peacetime; it was also the first peacetime demonstration of the virtues of planning. Though the full Wheatley programme was broken off short in 1932 at the time of the economic crisis, housing shortage, in the narrowest sense, had by then been virtually overcome. Wheatley's Act did not, of course, do anything to get rid of the slums. It benefited the more prosperous and secure section of the working class, and slum-dwellers were lucky to find old houses which the council tenants

---

with the Labour party and two of whom were avowed Conservatives. Chelmsford became first lord of the admiralty only after securing Baldwin's approval.

[1] Nicolson, *George V*, 387.

[2] From Chamberlain's £6 a year for 20 years to £9 a year for 40 years; and the local authority could add a further £4. 10s. for 40 years if the controlled rent were not enough to meet the cost.

had vacated. The bill had a passage of hard argument through the house of commons. Hardly anyone opposed its principle outright. Men of all parties were thus imperceptibly coming to agree that the provision of houses was a social duty, though they differed over the method and the speed with which this should be done.

One other landmark was set up by the Labour government, again almost unnoticed. Trevelyan, at the board of education, was armed with a firm statement of Labour policy, *Secondary Education for All*, drafted by the historian R. H. Tawney, who provided much of the moral inspiration for Labour in these years. Trevelyan largely undid the economies in secondary education which had been made by the Geddes axe, though he also discovered that Labour would be effective in educational matters only when it controlled the local authorities as well as the central government. More than this, he instructed the consultative committee of the board, under Sir Henry Hadow, to work out how Labour's full policy could be applied, and he deserves most of the credit for what followed even though the committee did not report until 1926. The Hadow report set the pattern for English publicly maintained education to the present day. Its ultimate ideal was to raise the school-leaving age to 15. Failing this (and it did not come until after the second World war), there should be an immediate and permanent innovation: a break between primary and secondary education at 11.[1] Hence the pupils at elementary schools, who previously stayed on to 14, had now to be provided for elsewhere or, at the very least, in special 'senior classes'. Here was a great achievement, at any rate in principle: a clear recognition, again imperceptibly accepted by men of all parties, that the entire population, and not merely a privileged minority, were entitled to some education beyond 'the three R's'. It was less fortunate that the new system of a break at 'eleven plus' increased the divergence between the publicly maintained schools and the private schools for the fee-paying minority where the break came at 13.

The reforms instituted by Wheatley and by Trevelyan both had the advantage that, while they involved considerable

[1] Why at 11? Mainly because three years was the least which could be plausibly offered as secondary education, and, with the leaving age still at 14, 11 was the answer. Also most elementary schools had been built when the leaving age was 11, and their buildings were only adequate to provide classrooms to that age. Eleven has no particular virtue. The Scotch age was, and remains, 12—one of the points at which English and Scotch history diverge.

expenditure over a period of years, they did not call for much money in the immediate future. This alone enabled them to survive the scrutiny of Philip Snowden, chancellor of the exchequer. Snowden had spent his life preaching social reforms; but he also believed that a balanced budget and rigorous economy were the only foundation for such reforms, and he soon convinced himself that the reforms would have to wait until the foundation had been well and truly laid. His budget would have delighted the heart of Gladstone: expenditure down, and taxes also, the 'free breakfast table' on the way to being restored,[1] and the McKenna Duties—pathetic remnant of wartime Protection —abolished. No doubt a 'Liberal' budget was inevitable in the circumstances of minority government; but it caused no stir of protest in the Labour movement. Most Labour men assumed that finance was a neutral subject, which had nothing to do with politics. Snowden himself wrote of Montagu Norman: 'I know nothing at all about his politics. I do not know if has he any.' Far from welcoming any increase in public spending, let alone advocating it, Labour had inherited the radical view that money spent by the state was likely to be money spent incompetently and corruptly: it would provide outdoor relief for the aristocracy or, as in Lloyd George's time, undeserved wealth for profiteers. The social reforms in which Labour believed were advocated despite the fact that they cost money, not because of it, and Snowden had an easy time checking these reforms as soon as he pointed to their cost.

The Labour government were peculiarly helpless when faced with the problem of unemployment—the unemployed remained at well over a million. Labour theorists had no prepared answer and failed to evolve one. The traditional evil of capitalism had been poverty: this gave Labour its moral force just as it gave Marxists the confidence that, with increasing poverty, capitalism would 'burst asunder'. No socialist, Marxist or otherwise, had ever doubted that poverty could be ended by means of the rich resources which capitalism provided. Mass unemployment was a puzzling accident, perhaps even a mean trick which the capitalists were playing on the Labour government; it was not regarded as an inevitable outcome of the existing economic system, at any rate for some time. Vaguely, Labour held that socialism would get rid of unemployment as it would get rid of

[1] That is, a reduction in the duties on tea, coffee, cocoa, chicory, and sugar.

all other evils inherent in the capitalist system. There would be ample demand for goods, and therefore full employment, once this demand ceased to be a matter of 'pounds, shillings, and pence'. The socialist economic system would work of itself, as capitalism was doing. This automatic operation of capitalism was a view held by nearly all economists, and Labour accepted their teaching. Keynes was moving towards the idea that unemployment could be conquered, or at any rate alleviated, by means of public works. He was practically alone among professional economists in this. Hugh Dalton, himself a teacher of economics, and soon to be a Labour M.P.,[1] dismissed Keynes's idea as 'mere Lloyd George finance'—a damning verdict. Such a policy was worse than useless; it was immoral.

Economic difficulties arose for the Labour government in a more immediate way. Industrial disputes did not come to an end merely because Labour was in office. Ramsay MacDonald had hardly kissed hands before there was a strike of engine drivers—a strike fortunately settled by an intervention of the T.U.C. general council. Strikes first of dockers, then of London tramwaymen, were not dealt with so easily. The government planned to use against these strikes the Emergency Powers Act, which Labour had denounced so fiercely when introduced by Lloyd George. It was particularly ironical that the proposed dictator, or chief civil commissioner, was Wedgwood, chancellor of the duchy of Lancaster, who was generally held to be more an anarchist than a socialist. Here was fine trouble in the making. The unions provided most of the money for the Labour party, yet Labour in office had to show that it was fit to govern. Both sides backed away. The government did not actually run armed lorries through the streets of London,[2] and Ernest Bevin, the men's

---

[1] (Edward) Hugh John Neale Dalton (1887–1962): educ. Eton and Cambridge; son of a canon of Windsor; M.P., 1924–31, 1935–59; under-secretary for foreign affairs, 1929–31; one of the few Labour men to support rearmament, 1936; minister of economic warfare, 1940–2; president of board of trade, 1942–5; chancellor of exchequer, 1945–7; leaked budget detail and resigned, 1947; chancellor of duchy of Lancaster, 1948–50; minister of town and country planning, 1950–1; minister of local government and planning, 1951; life peer, 1960; voice of cavernous power and spirited teller of political anecdotes.

[2] Labour ministers seem to have turned a blind eye on the plans which were being prepared in government departments to deal with a general strike. At any rate, they did not pass on any information to the union leaders. In this, as in other ways, they respected constitutional convention. MacDonald, responsible as prime minister for the security services, asked to see the records kept about himself during the war. He was refused and did not insist.

leader, ended the strikes, though indignant at 'having to listen to the appeal of our own people'.[1] The dispute left an ugly memory. A joint committee of the T.U.C. general council and the Labour party executive condemned the government's proposed action. MacDonald replied that 'public doles, Poplarism,[2] strikes for increased wages, limitation of output, not only are not Socialism, but may mislead the spirit and policy of the Socialist movement'.

MacDonald would have been hard put to it to define that policy, and he did not try. His overriding concern was with foreign affairs. He had opposed entering the war in 1914. He had faced years of unpopularity and neglect for the sake of his principles. He believed that his time had now come. International difficulties could be resolved 'by the strenuous action of good-will'. He was fortunate in his moment. Both France and Germany were weary of the conflict in the Ruhr, though for different reasons. Both were ready for the practical approach which Lloyd George had always urged and never managed to achieve. MacDonald's advocacy was more convincing. Lloyd George had seemed to rely solely on expediency. MacDonald somehow transformed expediency into a high principle. He claimed to distribute even-handed justice between France and Germany. As he expressed it some years later: 'Let them [the French and the Germans] put their demands in such a way that Great Britain could say that she supported both sides.'[3] These words were a classic definition of British policy in MacDonald's time.

MacDonald, and the directors of British policy generally, claimed not to be anti-French or pro-German. Even their impartiality was a repudiation of the Anglo-French *entente* and an assertion that everything which had happened since 4 August

[1] F. Williams, *Bevin*, 122.

[2] In 1921 the Poplar borough council, led by Lansbury, protested against the inequality of rates in rich and poor London boroughs, and refused to pay its share of L.C.C. expenses. Thirty councillors were sent to prison. But they got their way: the rate burden in London was made more equal. Later 'Poplarism' became the name for any defiance by local (Labour) councils of the central government. Thus Poplar and other councils paid wages, and boards of guardians paid rates of relief, above the scales approved by the ministry of health. The defiant councillors were often surcharged (i.e. made personally liable for the unauthorized expenditure) and sometimes imprisoned for contempt.

[3] Minutes of Five Power Meeting, 6 Dec. 1932. *Documents on British Foreign Policy*, second series, iv, no. 211.

1914 had been mistaken. If there were nothing to choose between France and Germany, why have fought the war at all? In practice the British policy was nothing like as impartial as it claimed to be. It was always the French who seemed to be holding up the pacification of Europe with their demands for reparations and for security. It was the French who now maintained great armaments and encouraged their allies in eastern Europe to do the same. Occasionally the French ran into conflict with British imperial interests, as happened to some extent in the Middle East. Their air force, sometimes even their navy, was supposed to represent a danger to Great Britain. The feeling against the French extended beyond political circles. Pro-French emotion generally ran down sharply in the mid-twenties, and new sentiments sprang up of friendship and affection towards Germany—sentiments which even the rise of Hitler did not extinguish.

MacDonald would have been more than human if he had not inclined somewhat towards the German side. He recognized that the French had genuine, though in his opinion groundless, fears. He sought to remove these fears by promises of British support which, he was confident, would never be called on. The promises, 'black and big on paper', were a harmless drug to soothe nerves. MacDonald's policy had immediate success. A committee of experts under an American chairman, General Dawes, was already working out a scheme of reparations within Germany's capacity to pay. The Dawes plan was accepted, thanks to MacDonald's skilful mediation between France and Germany. He did right to boast that this was 'the first really negotiated agreement since the war'. The plan took reparations out of politics for the next five years. Germany paid, apparently of her free will; the French, with equal willingness, accepted less than their full claim. Great Britain, as honest broker, collected a percentage with general approval. Her share of reparations from Germany, together with a further share passed on by the French, enabled her to meet the debt payments to the United States. MacDonald also sought to make the League of Nations effective. He himself attended the League Assembly—the first British foreign secretary and the only British prime minister to do so. There he promoted the Geneva Protocol, the most ingenious of many attempts to reconcile the French and British views of the League Covenant. It pledged the signatories to accept arbitration in international disputes; pledged them also to disarm by agreement. In return they exchanged promises of mutual support in case of unprovoked aggression. This was a sweeping commitment, though one already laid down in the Covenant; strictly, it made Great Britain, along with the other signatories, guarantor of every frontier in Europe, if not all over the world. Some Labour men, including Arthur Henderson, maybe took this promise seriously. MacDonald urged it only so as to lure the French into disarmament and conciliation. These were the pre-conditions, and ensured, he thought, that the guarantors would never be called on.

The Protocol did not go through. The Labour government fell before it was ratified; the Conservatives dropped it. Nevertheless, MacDonald, during his short period of office, set the pattern of British foreign policy for years to come. This was markedly true of the way in which he treated the problem of European security as something concerning only France and Germany. Nearly all Englishmen agreed that French fears were imaginary; nearly all welcomed concessions to Germany and believed that with these concessions international tension would vanish of itself. Very few, perhaps none in the nineteen-twenties, advocated wholehearted backing of the French. Some, particularly on the Labour Left, wished to take the German side and were indignant at being associated with the treaty of Versailles, even though only to revise it. The Trades Union Congress, for instance, formally condemned the Dawes Plan for this reason; it still objected to reparations despite the fact that the Germans had agreed to pay them. Most Englishmen accepted Mac-Donald's argument that it was impossible to dictate to France and that therefore Versailles must be gradually whittled away.

MacDonald's attitude to the League also met with general approval. His readiness to accept commitments in the confidence that they would not amount to anything was shared by most Englishmen. Some Conservatives despised the League and wished to rely solely on the armed might of their own country. Mac-Donald's old associates of the U.D.C., on the other hand, deplored the reliance on sanctions, and hence on armed force, which the Protocol theoretically involved. One of them,[1] when a delegate at Geneva in 1924, voted for the Protocol, 'shrieking all the way'. The two views cancelled out; MacDonald rode

[1] Mrs. H. M. Swanwick, a founder of the U.D.C. and of the Women's International League. Norman Angell, *After All*, 242.

triumphant between them. In his own inimitable words: 'so soon as you aim at a guarantee by a body like the League of Nations you minimize and subordinate the military value of the pact and raise to a really effective standard the moral guarantees that flow from conciliation, arbitration, impartial and judicial judgment exercised by the body with which you are associated'. Lloyd George complained: 'The French are entitled to know what we mean. The British people are entitled to know what we mean, and I should not be a bit surprised if the Prime Minister would like to know himself what we mean.' Here Lloyd George was wrong. MacDonald did not want to know what he meant. Imprecision was the essence of his policy. The League was at once everything and nothing. This was the view of most Englishmen, and MacDonald's equivocations reflected the spirit of the time.

In another aspect of foreign affairs MacDonald was less successful. Labour had made a good deal, when in opposition, of its friendship with Soviet Russia. Some Labour men proposed to get rid of unemployment by a miraculous opening of the vast Russian market. MacDonald, long the principal target for Communist abuse both at home and in the international socialist movement, did not share these enthusiasms. Shortly after entering office, he recognized the Soviet Government,[1] though with none of the cordiality he showed towards Mussolini, the other old socialist now in high office. Deadlock followed. The British wanted payment, at any rate in part, of Russia's prerevolutionary debts; the Russians would consider this only if they were given a loan, guaranteed by the British government. On 5 August negotiations broke down. Some backbench Labour M.P.s, mostly of a Left-wing cast, then mediated between the two sides and produced an acceptable compromise. There was to be an immediate commercial treaty of the ordinary kind, later, a further treaty settling the Russian debts and then a guaranteed loan. This was a confused and complicated juggle, which could be still more discredited as having been dictated to the government by its Left wing.

The Conservatives attacked it at once. The Liberals hesitated. They themselves had advocated a loan to Russia. Besides,

---

[1] Lloyd George admitted a Soviet trade delegation to Great Britain in 1921, but without political recognition, and the Soviet behaviour at Rapallo the following year further hardened him against this.

Asquith, in his easygoing way, enjoyed being 'in power, but not in office'. Negation had always been his strong point. It was agreeable to feel that he could put Labour out; even more agreeable not to do it. Meanwhile, Labour would be tamed by responsibility. Lloyd George had no such nice feelings. Still dynamic, creative, and ambitious, he was interested in his own future, not in that of the Labour party, and he recognized that he would have no future if Labour made good. He was eager for combat and did not much care how things worked out so long as there was turmoil. The treaty with Russia gave him his opportunity. He could denounce it both ways round. It was shocking to lend money to the Bolsheviks; even more shocking when the loan was a pretence—'a fake . . . a thoroughly grotesque agreement'. During the summer recess Lloyd George swung the bulk of the Liberal party behind him. Asquith reluctantly agreed that the treaty should be attacked when parliament reassembled. It seemed that the days of the Labour government were numbered.

So they were, though over a more trivial affair than the Russian loan. On 5 August, the very day of hurry and scurry over the Russian treaty, a Communist called J. R. Campbell was charged under the Incitement to Mutiny Act of 1797, for publishing in the *Workers' Weekly* a Don't Shoot appeal to soldiers. Such appeals were routine stuff in the Labour movement. Backbenchers, who had often made such appeals themselves, protested to Hastings, the attorney general, and he, further prompted by MacDonald, dropped the prosecution. No doubt it was all a muddle. Hastings, a recent convert to Labour, realized belatedly that it was foolish for a Labour government to make a fuss over revolutionary phrases.[1] But the Conservatives were able to raise the cry of political interference with the course of justice. They put down a vote of censure when parliament met at the end of September.[2] It had been drafted by Sir John Simon, nominally still a Liberal.[3] Asquith tried to evade the issue by proposing a select committee. Labour were weary of being a minority government, and especially weary of being dependent on the Liberals. They rejected Asquith's compromise. The Conservatives voted for it. The government were defeated

[1] See Note B, p. 225.
[2] Parliament met in special session to carry an act, nominating a representative of Northern Ireland in the Irish boundary commission, when the Northern Ireland government refused to do so.
[3] Macleod, *Neville Chamberlain*, 167.

by 364 to 191.[1] Asquith's tactics of balancing between Conservative and Labour were thus thwarted. He had hoped that Labour would some time be defeated by Conservative votes, with the Liberals abstaining. Then he would become prime minister as the impartial third party. Instead, he seemed to have taken the initiative in defeating the government, and MacDonald was able to claim a dissolution, on the ground that both Liberals and Conservatives were clearly against him. Asquith's taste for a select committee again ruined the Liberal party, as it had done at the time of the Maurice debate, and this time for good. No doubt both Baldwin and MacDonald were not sorry to have compromised Asquith. The Liberal party would be squeezed out one way or the other.

The outcry over the Russian treaty and the Campbell case had a serious meaning behind the exaggerations. Both affairs raised the question: was Labour secretly sympathetic to the Communists despite its seeming moderation? The question was raised still more sharply, just before polling day, when a letter was published, allegedly from Zinoviev, president of the Communist International, to the British Communist party, with instructions for all sorts of seditious activities. The 'Red letter' caused a great stir. Labour was denounced as the accomplice of the Communists; alternatively as their dupe. Labour men replied, rather half-heartedly, that the letter was a forgery, which it may well have been.[2] The supporters of Labour were unshaken. Labour actually increased its total vote by a million.[3] The Zinoviev letter had its effect on Labour only after the election had been lost. It then became a cover against accusations of failure, and a bar against any attempt to face the problems of a future Labour government. Everything, it was supposed, had been going splendidly until Campbell and Zinoviev had cropped up. Labour had been tricked out of office. Hence there was no need to discuss such questions as unemployment or the relations between Labour ministers and the unions. Webb's law of the inevitable Labour majority would still operate when an election was held without such stunts. Moreover, MacDonald again became the hero of the

---

[1] Fourteen Liberals and two Conservatives voted with the government.
[2] See Note C, p. 225.
[3] This was partly due to Labour's running ninety more candidates, itself evidence of virility.

Left, whether he liked it or not. He had not received the 'fair play' which George V had promised.[1] He was once more the ostracized victim of capitalist unscrupulousness or even perhaps of intrigue by permanent officials in the foreign office. The Labour government acquired a posthumous repute among its own supporters from the way it fell.

The anti-socialist panic may have affected middle-class voters. Two million more people voted than in 1923 even though there were slightly fewer candidates, and mostly for the Conservatives. Voting Liberal in 1923 had put Labour in. Now the voters, including even Liberals, wanted Labour out. In June 1924 Baldwin had removed the greatest stumbling block against Liberals voting Conservative: he renounced Protection, and this time without even the conditional threat of reviving it after a further general election. Protection would have to wait for 'clear evidence that on this matter public opinion is disposed to reconsider its judgment'. This was economy of effort in Baldwin's best manner. First he used Protection in 1923 to detach its supporters, such as Austen Chamberlain, from Lloyd George; then he used its renunciation in 1924 to detach its opponents also. Winston Churchill was the great recruit here, now back as a Conservative after more than twenty years on the other side. With Free Trade secure, what was there left for the Liberal party to defend? The party was clearly in poor shape. It ran a hundred fewer candidates than the year before; its constituency organizations were falling to pieces; and Lloyd George refused to inject more money from his fund.[2]

The Liberal decline, not the Zinoviev letter, shaped the election. The Liberals lost a hundred seats, mainly to Conservatives. Asquith himself was defeated (by a Labour man) and departed to the house of lords. Though he remained nominally leader of the party, the Liberal remnant of forty in the commons found themselves marshalled behind Lloyd George, much to their discomfiture. Labour, losing 64 seats and winning 24, was still 10 better off (151 seats) than after the general election of 1922. The Conservatives scooped the pool: 419 members out of 615 and, with 48·3 per cent. of the total vote, the nearest

---

[1] The king, with his usual common sense, had doubts whether the Zinoviev letter was genuine. Nicolson, *George V*, 402.

[2] Lloyd George provided £50,000, with much grumbling.

to an overall Conservative majority between 1874 and 1931.[1]
The murmurs of criticism against Baldwin which had followed
the previous election were now stilled. He had led the Conservative party to victory. Hardly anyone noticed that he had done
this by not giving his followers what they wanted. There was to
be no Protection, no class war; if possible, there was to be
nothing at all. The repentant Coalitionists who now returned
to the fold were deliberately given posts unsuited to their
talents. Birkenhead, a great lawyer whose enduring monument
is the reform of the law of real property, was made secretary
for India. Austen Chamberlain, protagonist of Protection and
a former chancellor of the exchequer, was made foreign
secretary. Churchill, a Free Trader who understood nothing of
finance, became chancellor of the exchequer.[2] Only Neville
Chamberlain, relegated again to the ministry of health, knew
his business and supplied, as before, the creative element in the
government.

Churchill and Austen Chamberlain, though so oddly placed,
rounded off the restoration on which Baldwin had set his heart.
No more, of course, was heard of the Russian treaty, and
Chamberlain also rejected the Protocol—partly on the ground
that the Dominions were against it. But he made his own
contribution to the problem of European security. This was the
treaty of Locarno, negotiated over throughout 1925 and
finally signed (at London) on 1 December. Locarno was a pact
of non-aggression between France, Germany, and Belgium,
guaranteed by the two supposedly impartial powers, Great
Britain and Italy. Here at last was the evenhanded justice to
which Grey had aspired before 1914 and which MacDonald
had assiduously preached; not an alliance against a particular
country, but a guarantee against 'aggression' in the abstract.
British pledges under Locarno, like MacDonald's before them,
were black and big on paper, and only there. Though the
guarantee of the Franco-German frontier seemed a tremendous
commitment, in practice it amounted to nothing. No preparations were ever made to implement it. How could they be made?
The 'aggressor' would be known only when the moment for

[1] The Conservative majorities of 1895 and 1900 were attained with the help of
Liberal Unionists.
[2] It is said that Churchill, when offered the post of chancellor, thought that he
was being invited to become chancellor of the duchy of Lancaster, and accepted
gratefully.

action arrived. Locarno in fact ruled out any staff talks between Great Britain and France (or, of course, between Great Britain and Germany) so long as it existed, and no British strategist had to weigh the problems of Anglo-French co-operation until after Locarno collapsed. The guarantee was very much 'a harmless drug to soothe nerves' in the MacDonald manner.

Even this paper promise was made largely in order to emphasize that it was the limit of British commitment. Austen Chamberlain formally dissociated Great Britain from France's eastern alliances and described the Polish corridor as something 'for which no British Government ever will or ever can risk the bones of a British grenadier'.[1] Balfour called Locarno 'the symbol and the cause of a great amelioration in the public feeling of Europe'. It was more a symbol than a cause. The treaty of Locarno rested on the assumption that the promises given in it would never have to be made good—otherwise the British government would not have given them. From the British point of view, Locarno marked the moment when Great Britain regarded the European responsibilities which she had taken up in August 1914 as fully discharged. The British, by pledging themselves on the Rhine, turned their backs on Europe—or so they thought. Splendid isolation had come again.

Churchill's return to the gold standard completed the illusion of having done with the war years and their legacy. Later on, this return took on monstrous proportions of decision and error. Its significance was less clear at the time, or maybe was really less. Return indeed was implicit almost from the moment of abandonment. The act of 1919 suspending the gold standard applied only for six years, and the sterling–dollar exchange had moved steadily nearer to the old gold parity. Only C. H. Douglas, a retired major of engineers, advocated 'Social Credit' and paper money. Reputable economists, other than Keynes, held that gold was the only possible basis for currency, and even Keynes mainly opposed return to gold at the old parity. In his view there was a 10 per cent. discrepancy between

---

[1] The French gained one breach in the system of evenhanded justice. They reaffirmed their alliances with Poland and Czechoslovakia and wrote into the treaty a clause that action under these alliances would not constitute aggression against Germany. This breach was purely theoretical. The French army was equipped solely for defensive war and therefore really unable to invade Germany even while the Rhineland remained demilitarized, as it did until 1936.

British and American prices. Most judges put it much lower: $2\frac{1}{2}$ per cent. or none at all.[1] It was hardly worth while to quibble at so little. Things were different with countries like France and Italy which returned to gold, at a low rate, after really savage depreciation. Neither of these countries was a serious competitor against British exports. Germany and the United States—the other great exporters—were not gravely out of line. Industrialists often complained that the old parity made British prices too high, and therefore hampered exports. The real obstacle was that Great Britain was offering old-style products, which the rest of the world did not want more of even at lower prices. There was a compensating gain: Great Britain got her foodstuffs and raw materials even more cheaply than before.

Of course this was not the principal motive. British economic advisers were concerned to enhance the prestige of 'the City'; they exaggerated the profit which financial transactions brought and perhaps even their general importance in providing stability. The great, and in the end decisive, weaknesses in the gold standard lay elsewhere. Before the war, London had been a large net creditor. Now she tried to operate the gold standard with the assistance of foreign deposits which could be easily withdrawn. Moreover, the gold standard demanded flexibility on the part of both capital and labour: readiness of capital to move from old industries to new, readiness of labour to move also or to work for lower wages. Both were lacking: one form of stability defeated the other. For the time being, the return to gold was the least of Great Britain's difficulties, or even brought more gain than hardship.

On 28 April 1925 Churchill announced, as the highlight of his budget speech, that the government did not intend to renew the suspending act of 1919. With this Great Britain was automatically back on gold at the old rate. Not, however, in the old form. Gold currency was not restored. A few sovereigns were minted for the benefit of collectors. None passed into circulation. There was a gold-exchange standard purely for international purposes. At home Great Britain got a managed currency after all.[2] The gold standard was window-dressing, a

[1] Ashworth, *Economic History*, 387.
[2] To complete the illusion of an independent currency, treasury notes were ended in 1928, and the issue of paper money was confined to the bank of England.

doubtful gesture of respect to traditions which had already lost much of their force. Men with gold in their purses had taken the gold standard seriously. Now they attached more value to the stamps on their insurance cards. It was easy to guess which would win if it came to a clinch between gold standard and standard of life. The half-hearted gold standard was a symbol of the postwar restoration. To outward appearance, all troubles past, all passions spent: Free Trade, the gold standard, stability both at home and abroad. Underneath, an unformed belief was growing that men now counted more than money.

NOTES

NOTE A. *The appointment of Baldwin as prime minister.* It was believed until recently that George V chose the new prime minister without receiving any advice from Law. This, if true, was an independent exercise of the prerogative and, as such, an important episode in constitutional law. However, it is not true, and the precedent therefore disappears. The full story was told for the first time by Robert Blake in *The Unknown Prime Minister,* 518-27. Law expected Curzon to succeed him. He conveyed this expectation to Curzon by letter, and to Baldwin, Lord Crewe (ambassador in Paris), and Amery in conversation. He declined to give advice, and suggested that the king should consult Lord Salisbury, the lord president. Salisbury told Stamfordham, the king's secretary, that Law was 'disinclined to pass over Curzon', and added his own formal recommendation in Curzon's favour. But Stamfordham also received other advice. Waterhouse, Law's private secretary, brought Law's letter of resignation. He also brought a memorandum, supporting the claims of Baldwin, and stated that it 'practically expressed the views of Mr. Bonar Law'. It had in fact been drafted by Davidson, a leading Conservative and a close friend of Baldwin's. Two days later Stamfordham saw Waterhouse again. This time Waterhouse repeated what he claimed to be Law's own words: 'on the whole I think I should advise him [the king] to send for Baldwin'. Stamfordham also consulted the only other Conservative ex-premier, Balfour, and he, too, recommended Baldwin. There were as well the personal points against Curzon and Labour's objection to a prime minister in the house of lords. All the same, Law's supposed advice seems to have been the decisive factor, as was only natural. It is impossible to tell whether Law was a party to this advice. The members of his family, and Beaverbrook who was much with him at this time, are convinced that Law knew nothing of the memorandum or of Waterhouse's subsequent statement. On the other hand, Law told Tom Jones, deputy secretary to the cabinet: 'If the King asked for his advice as to a successor he would put Baldwin first'. Jones further recorded: 'The memorandum was drawn up last night at No. 10 by Amery and Davidson, and no doubt was seen by B.L.'.[1] Of course Jones was on the side of the officials, so

[1] Thomas Jones, *Whitehall Diary,* i, 236.

his evidence is not decisive. Either Law shrank from the responsibility of recommending a successor or feared Beaverbrook's indignation if he named Baldwin. Beaverbrook insists that Law, unlike all other politicians, was 'without guile'. Others have suggested that he performed some sleight of hand in December 1916 when he failed to communicate the memorandum of the three C's to Asquith. At any rate, Davidson received his reward. Baldwin made him chancellor of the duchy of Lancaster. Waterhouse also remained principal private secretary until 1928, when 'forces beyond his personal control' pushed him out.

NOTE B. *The Campbell case.* Campbell's alleged offence was the publication on 25 July of an appeal to soldiers to 'let it be known that, neither in the class war nor in a military war, will you turn your guns on your fellow workers'. Why was this published at this moment? There was no immediate prospect of soldiers being used in an industrial dispute, nor of war against Soviet Russia—the only war to which, according to Communist jargon, the latter part of the sentence could refer. Probably therefore it was published in order to embarrass the Labour government. The decision to prosecute was taken by the director of public prosecutions. Again, why? Perhaps stupidity (and the director of public prosecutions is usually a stupid man); perhaps also to embarrass the government. Hastings claimed, probably truly, that he had realized the significance of the case only at question time on 6 August. He consulted Maxton, a leading Clydesider. He learnt that Campbell was an ex-serviceman, with an excellent war record, crippled by war wounds, and that he was only acting editor of the *Workers' Weekly.* He therefore concluded that a prosecution before a jury was likely to fail. He was also told by MacDonald that 'the prosecution was ill-advised from the beginning'. Hastings therefore decided independently to drop the prosecution, and the cabinet merely endorsed his decision. MacDonald later denied that he had been consulted in any way; then denied that he had denied it. Hastings gave good reasons for dropping the prosecution, but there can be little doubt that they were excuses. Protests from Labour backbenchers were the decisive factor, and the Communists had ground for claiming that 'for the first time the course of justice in the Law Courts had been changed by outside political forces into a triumph for the working classes over the capitalist classes'. On the other hand, Liberals and Conservatives were going against their own practice when they complained of this political interference. Isaacs and Simon both sat in Asquith's cabinet as attorneys general, and that cabinet repeatedly discussed the political expediency of prosecuting Carson, F. E. Smith, and others. Douglas Hogg sat in Baldwin's cabinet of 1924 as attorney general, and that cabinet also discussed the political expediency of prosecutions—this time of Communists. The real justification for Hastings was that it was silly to have started the prosecution in the first place. This was not a justification which he could use unadorned. Probably he ought to have resigned. MacDonald, as usual the only man with any sense, seems to have suggested this. It sinned against trade union ethics, and the cabinet rejected it.

NOTE C. *The Zinoviev letter.* The authenticity of the letter is a curious little puzzle, though of no historical importance. There are strong arguments against its being genuine. No original was ever produced; some of the phrases are in the wrong jargon; individuals in it are wrongly described. On the other hand, there was nothing in it which flagrantly contradicted Communist policy, and the Communists were not sorry to embarrass the Labour government. The way in which it came into circulation counts strongly against its being genuine. If it had been intercepted by the secret service, as one story has it, or supplied by a British Communist leader (and one of them at this time was almost certainly a government agent), it would have come only into official hands. But copies reached the *Daily Mail* and the Conservative central office as soon as one reached the foreign office, or perhaps earlier. This points to its being the work of the well-known factory of documents run by White Russian émigrés in Berlin. The publication of the letter by the foreign office, together with an official note of protest, raises a further problem. MacDonald, who was away stumping the country, had known about the letter for a fortnight; he was obviously intending to keep quiet about it until after the election. Eyre Crowe, the permanent under-secretary, claimed to have been rushed into publication by the knowledge that the *Daily Mail* also had a copy. It is strange that he did not consult Ponsonby, the parliamentary under-secretary, or Haldane, who was acting for MacDonald at the foreign office. But Crowe always thought that he knew better than his political superiors.

VII

THE YEARS OF GOLD, 1925-9

BALDWIN'S second government passed five quiet years, with one alarming, and perhaps unnecessary, interruption: the General Strike. Otherwise, Baldwin got much of his way. Englishmen drew closer together; class conflicts were dimmed; the curves of production, wages, and standard of living, which had previously oscillated widely, now moved soberly upwards. Conservatives and Labour fell increasingly into agreement, at any rate at the top level. Baldwin would have been at home leading the Labour party, and MacDonald, with his romantic cast of mind, was well suited to lead the Conservatives. The things on which they agreed were becoming more important than those which divided them, and many great issues were settled far from the bitterness of party strife.

Defence was an outstanding example. The Conservatives were in theory the party of great armaments. Many Labour men opposed preparations for a 'capitalist war'. In practice Conservatives were eager for economy, and Labour maintained existing armaments despite the protests of its pacifist wing. The Labour government of 1924, for example, laid down five new cruisers to replace those which had become out of date. There was, after all, little to disagree about. Locarno seemed to have established a secure peace in Europe. More than this, the Great War had done its work. Great Britain was more secure than she had been for centuries. Germany had been defeated and disarmed; there was no longer a German navy. Russia had apparently ceased to exist as a great power after the Bolshevik revolution; Communist propaganda, though supposedly menacing, could not be combated by force of arms. Japan was a friend, even though no longer an ally. Few seriously maintained that France would resume Napoleonic ambitions, or that the United States would lay violent hands upon the empire. Thus no great power threatened, however remotely, the security of Great Britain or her empire. British disarmament, or rather reduction of armaments, was not initiated as an example to others. Still less, when originally planned, was it carried beyond the margin of safety. The great armaments of the war years were given up simply because it was held, quite correctly, that they were not required.

In 1919 Lloyd George told the service chiefs that they need not anticipate a major war within the next ten years. In 1925 the service chiefs asked again and were given the same answer: no major war within the next ten years. This answer was repeated in 1926 and 1927. Finally, in 1928, the service chiefs were told, on Churchill's prompting, that they need ask no more: the ten years' freedom from major war began automatically each morning. This instruction was revoked only in 1932. The ten years' rule came in for much criticism later, when it seemed that British disarmament had been carried too far or had gone on too long. Yet it was a sound political judgement when it started, and even its prolongation could be justified. There was not much point in maintaining great armaments when no conceivable enemy existed. Even the final guess of 1932 was not all that wrong. Both Hitler and Mussolini fixed on 1943 for the outbreak of the next great war, and the second World war might well have started then if it had not been for a series of accidents and misunderstandings. At any rate, the ten years' rule, while it lasted, was agreed doctrine between the party leaders.

Conservative and Labour both contributed also to shape the system which directed defence. Lloyd George had run defence in a muddle, despite his boasts of efficiency. His cabinets received no regular and coherent information on strategical questions. They lived from hand to mouth, with the chief of the imperial staff, a soldier, as sole adviser. The committee of imperial defence was kept in existence only to direct the writing of the history of the war. Law aimed to reduce the independent position of the prime minister in this, as in other, ways. He brought the committee back to life and left Curzon to preside over it. Haldane presided during the Labour government. In 1924 Curzon returned; next year he died. Baldwin then took the chair, as Balfour and Asquith had done before him. MacDonald was a more or less regular member, even when in opposition. The committee of imperial defence became once more the central point of British defence policy. It was now more efficient than before 1914, thanks to a casual legacy from Lloyd George. During the Chanak crisis, he sought combined advice from the three services for the first time. This joint chiefs of staff's committee was made a permanent institution by the two following governments. It has been called 'a Super-Chief of a War Staff in commission'. So it was in theory. The practice was different. The chiefs of staff's committee had no independent chairman: the senior chief of staff presided. The three members fought their battles privately and concealed their differences from prying politicians, even from their own civilian chiefs. Their recommendations to the cabinet were usually innocuous generalities.

The revival of the committee of imperial defence, and its reinforcement by the chiefs of staff's committee, killed the project of a Ministry of Defence, which was often aired after the war, particularly by the Geddes committee on grounds of economy. The open argument against this was that the job was too important for anyone except the prime minister himself. The real obstacle was mutual jealousy between the services. In particular, it was inconceivable that the admiralty would relinquish its traditional independence. The arrival of a new service helped to increase the jealousies. The Royal Air Force established its independence on 1 April 1918, when there was a delusive hope that strategical bombing might win the war. There was long dispute after the war whether this independence should continue. In 1919 Churchill combined the two posts of War and Air secretary, with the emphasis on the former. Later, though there was a separate secretary of state, he had no department of his own nor a seat in the cabinet. In 1922 the R.A.F. sensationally justified itself. There was a revolt in Irak. The R.A.F. bombed the villages of the turbulent tribes and quelled the revolt far more cheaply than a military expedition could have done. Here was an independent strategy of the air. From this moment, it was accepted that bombs could not only quell tribal revolts, but could win a great war. The R.A.F. became a fully independent service—the only such among the great powers. In May 1923 Sir Samuel Hoare received a seat in the cabinet as secretary of state for air.

Expenditure on arms went down in almost every year after 1922 and reached the lowest point in 1933. By then armaments absorbed little more than $2\frac{1}{2}$ per cent. of the national income, against $3\frac{1}{2}$ per cent. in 1913, and the expenditure was less than prewar, if the decline in the value of money be taken into account.[1] The three services had, however, different fates. The navy was always the least open to political attacks. It was, or seemed to be, a truly defensive service. The admiralty laid down absolute requirements—ships which would be needed for police work even if there were no other navy in the world. They also used other fleets as the yardstick against which to build, refusing to believe that even the most friendly power could be counted on to remain friendly unless outnumbered. The British battlefleet remained greatly superior to the French and Italian, its two nearest European competitors. The British maintained parity with the Americans, an expensive and futile procedure. Parity was really an excuse for the admirals to keep the big ships which they loved and which gave them an illusory sense of grandeur. The admiralty managed to spend roughly a quarter of its annual £50 million a year on ships and new equipment.[2]

Japan raised a special problem. However friendly, she had a dangerous supremacy in Far Eastern waters so long as the British had no dockyard east of Malta which could handle capital ships. After the Washington naval conference the admiralty proposed to create a first-rate naval base at Singapore. Yet this could be justified only by suspicion of Japan, which the British hardly felt and, in any case, hesitated to voice. Hence work at Singapore fell an easy victim to economy: it was stopped by the Labour government in 1924, half-heartedly renewed by the Conservatives in 1926, again stopped by Labour in 1929, and then further put off by the economizing National government until 1933. There was another odd feature about Singapore. It was exclusively a naval affair and was therefore defended only from naval attack. The admiralty refused to enlist air support. The chiefs of staff's committee made no protest. It was not after all a likely proposition that the admiralty should ask for money to be spent on the R.A.F., not on the navy.

The R.A.F., too, held the doctrine that overwhelming superiority was the only defence. Trenchard, who was chief of the air staff for ten years (from 1919 to 1929), set his stamp on

---

[1] If it had not been for the R.A.F., which did not exist before the war, expenditure would actually have been less than prewar in money terms.

[2] The highest sum spent on the navy was £59·7 million in 1926, the lowest £50·0 million in 1933.

British air-policy right up to the outbreak of the second World war and even during it. Bombing, he held, could win a war all by itself; it was also the only means of not being bombed by others. Trenchard and his successors persistently neglected air defence. If they once admitted that Great Britain could be defended from air attack, they would have to confess that other countries could be defended also, and hence that their policy of strategical bombing could be thwarted. The two other service chiefs did not like the idea that the role of the army and navy in a future war would simply be to guard Great Britain as a vast aircraft carrier. They even reinforced their objections by an appeal to moral principles. The argument was, however, confined to the chiefs of staff's committee, according to its usual practice of 'not before the servants', or, in this case, civilian ministers.

Superiority in the air became the accepted theory, and the R.A.F. formulated a requirement of fifty-two squadrons, which was supposed to give it this superiority over France, then the only competitor. The theory was not translated into practice. France could not be taken seriously as an enemy, particularly after 1925, and the R.A.F. remained not much more than a skeleton force. This apparent neglect turned out, in the end, to be a stroke of luck. Ships lasted for twenty years, rifles for fifty. Aeroplanes were obsolete by the time they had advanced from the drawing board to the airfield. France and Italy, who both accumulated large air forces in the twenties, found themselves lumbered with a host of antiquated machines when the second World war broke out. Even Germany began to arm in the air a bit too soon. Unintentionally and unwillingly the British came out best by waiting longest, though even so much of their air force at the outbreak of war proved out of date.

During the period of the ten years' rule the army suffered most. With a great war ruled out, there was nothing for it to do, except to guard the air bases from which the R.A.F. dominated the Middle East, or occasionally to quell civil disturbances at home or abroad. Though Great Britain had led in inventing the tank, these and mechanized transport also were laid aside, as weapons only for a great war. Cavalry again occupied a high place, perhaps because of its social attraction. 'New arms were neither ordered nor designed',[1] and the army spent nearly

[1] Postan, *British War Production*, 7.

all its not inconsiderable income on providing tolerable conditions for its long-term volunteers.[1]

Thus the ten years of genuine peace set the three services in entirely different patterns. The navy had plans and, though stinted, some equipment for a great war. The plans proved reasonably accurate when war came. The equipment could have been more up to date—for instance, the navy neglected aircraft carriers. Still, it just served. The air force had plans, though only for offence, and it had little equipment even for this until late in the day. Its defensive plans and equipment had to be improvised at the last moment. The army had neither plans nor equipment. Both had to be shaped amid the challenge of war, instead of being prepared beforehand. All such problems were remote in the nineteen-twenties. Arms were discussed solely in terms of what they cost, not of what they were needed for. Defence, or the lack of it, in the wider sense was agreed policy between the parties.

Agreement reigned also in another field, producing, without intention, a surprising contribution to British life. This was the transmission of words and sounds by wireless waves, 'broadcasting' as it was called. Northcliffe showed his usual flair in appreciating the new device. On 16 June 1920 the *Daily Mail*, at his prompting, sponsored a programme of songs by Dame Nellie Melba, the great operatic star. This was an historic date. Sponsoring, however, was not repeated. The Post Office, which was the licensing authority for wireless stations under an act of 1904, at first intended to license transmissions by rival manufacturers, who were concerned to sell their receiving sets. It soon had second thoughts. Competition for the limited wavelengths would raise awkward questions of favouritism. A single company would be easier to control. In this casual way, the Post Office decided for monopoly. At the end of 1922 the British Broadcasting Company, financed by a group of manufacturers, was given an exclusive licence to send out wireless programmes. Its manager was a Scotch engineer, John Reith. Calvinist by upbringing, harsh and ruthless in character, Reith turned broadcasting into a mission. It was to bring into every home 'all that was best in every department of human knowledge, endeavour and achievement'. He used what he called 'the

---

[1] The army's income ranged from £45 million in 1923 to £35 million in 1933. It never spent more than £2 million a year of this on new equipment.

brute force of monopoly' to stamp Christian morality on the British people. He stamped it also on his employees. Producers or even electricians found themselves out of a job if touched by the breath of scandal. Announcers had to put on dinner jackets before addressing the microphone.

In 1925 a committee of inquiry, under Lord Crawford, endorsed the moral case for monopoly. Parliament did not demur. Conservatives liked authority; Labour disliked private enterprise. The company had some difficulty in staving off government interference during the general strike, and this suggested that its independence should be strengthened, particularly no doubt against a future Labour government. Late in 1926 the company ceased to exist. The British Broadcasting Corporation was created by royal charter. It was financed by licence fees from the owners of wireless sets and had a board of distinguished governors nominated by the prime minister. These were agreeable sinecures. In practice Reith, as director general, had independence to impose his standards. This was a strange reassertion of authority just when intellectual freedom was supposed to be advancing in other spheres. The theatre, the music hall, and the cinema, all rested on private enterprise with varying degrees of censorship.[1] The printed word was free from control of any kind except the laws of obscenity and libel. Broadcasting became a dictatorship, as though Milton and others had never made the case for unlicensed utterance. In no time at all, the monopolistic corporation came to be regarded as an essential element in 'the British way of life'.

Like all cultural dictatorships, the B.B.C. was more important for what it silenced than for what it achieved. Controllers ranked higher than producers in its hierarchy. Disturbing views were rarely aired. The English people, if judged by the B.B.C., were uniformly devout and kept always to the middle of the road. Radio offered words without pictures, in this the counterpart of the silent film, which offered pictures without words. Both were

[1] Theatres and music halls in London operated under the censorship of the Lord Chamberlain. Elsewhere they were controlled by the local authorities, as heirs to the licensing justices. The film industry ran its own voluntary board of censors, the certificate of which was usually accepted. Technically, however, the local authorities were the licensing power, in this case as the fire authority (hence non-inflammable films were beyond their control), and could ignore the censors' verdicts. Thus Labour councils sometimes permitted the showing of Russian films which had been refused a certificate for political reasons. Private clubs were also formed to show banned plays and films.

lopsided arts, doomed to disappear when technical advance brought words and pictures together. The spate of words was delivered in the B.B.C. voice, which may have helped the standardization of English speech. Music was the other great standby of radio, and knowledge of classical music became more general, though at the cost of reducing live music in the home. The radio set replaced the piano in the front parlour. The corporation used its great financial resources to form its own symphony orchestra, with better pay and more secure conditions for its members. But the hand of bureaucracy lay heavy on creative art, and the B.B.C. orchestra never challenged the reputation of Manchester's Hallé—the one British orchestra of international standing in the interwar years. For that matter, a single man, Sir Thomas Beecham, did more for British music than was done by the massed battalions of the B.B.C. He was not only the greatest British conductor, he was also the greatest impresario of the age, endlessly stimulating and naturally disliked by everyone except his appreciative audiences.

The B.B.C. from its earliest days issued regular news-bulletins—short and, it was hoped, impartial summaries of news as supplied by the press agencies. This worked in well with the change which was coming over daily newspapers. The evening papers printed the racing results, and therefore still had news value; they remained predominantly local in circulation. The morning newspapers aspired to become national. They left late news to the B.B.C. and printed earlier, so that they could catch the mail trains to all parts of the country.[1] The local papers lost their virtue. One, the *Manchester Guardian*, became national in its turn, and ceased to be the voice of Manchester; the others dwindled in influence and circulation. This change reinforced not a little the uniformity of the English people.

Another change went with it. The news, to appear novel, had to be presented in a more lively, sensational way. The inspiring force in this transformation was Lord Beaverbrook, who succeeded Northcliffe as the giant of Fleet Street, though not on the same scale.[2] Unlike most press lords, including Northcliffe,

---

[1] Delane, when editor of *The Times*, rarely left the office until four in the morning. A modern editor goes home at ten p.m. and need hardly fear the ring of the telephone after midnight. Some papers extended their national coverage by printing a northern edition at Manchester.

[2] Northcliffe controlled at one time over half the London circulation; Beaverbrook never more than one fifth. He wisely limited his ambitions to three papers:

Beaverbrook was already a millionaire when he took to newspapers. He was in this world for political influence and for fun as much as for profit. His political axe was Empire Free Trade. It was never ground to success. Fun remained. Headlines grew larger; there were shorter sentences and paragraphs. Content changed also. The most successful journalists were feature writers, often men brought in from outside: Arnold Bennett the novelist; Inge, the 'gloomy Dean'; Lord Castlerosse, spendthrift Irish peer and prince of gossips; a little later, Tom Driberg, who invented 'William Hickey' and then became a solid Labour M.P. Northcliffe had triumphed by possessing, to perfection, the tastes and outlook of the ordinary man. Beaverbrook believed that what delighted his impish spirit would in time delight others, and success proved him right. His favoured writers were read by millions, but they wrote for 'one little old reader', Lord Beaverbrook.

The B.B.C. had an even more direct political impact: speeches could be delivered direct over the air. This took some time to get going. Politicians fought shy of the new instrument. They were at first chary of using a microphone even when speaking to a live audience. Gradually they succumbed. Men and women heard the voices of leading statesmen in their own homes. They ceased to attend political meetings, except those held by the advocates of minority views which were denied expression over the air.[1] Public opinion could no longer be gauged by public demonstrations. New, supposedly more scientific, tests had to be used. The character of oratory changed. Broadcasting demanded a gentler, more intimate style. The oldtimers, trained on audiences, could not manage this. Lloyd George and Ramsay MacDonald, once great magicians, were both ineffective on the air. Baldwin came into his own. At his first broadcast, he struck a match and lit his pipe as the green light flashed—or so it is said.[2] Thus relaxed, he played variations on the theme: 'You can trust me.' His plain direct speech carried a conviction which his acts did not always sustain.

the *Daily Express*, a derelict property which he raised to the highest circulation in Great Britain; the *Sunday Express* which he created; and the *Evening Standard*, also derelict when he acquired it.

[1] Hence the greatest orators of the interwar period were both extremists: Mosley, the Fascist leader, and Maxton of the I.L.P.

[2] A recording of the broadcast survives. It does not suggest that Baldwin spoke with the clenched teeth of a pipesmoker. Perhaps he took a puff at his pipe and then laid it down.

Baldwin wanted a quiet life for himself and for the country. His government has been called 'the rule of the old men'. Actually his cabinet was of the normal middle age, with Curzon and, after him Balfour, as elder statesmen.[1] Baldwin himself in 1924 was 57—only one year older than Asquith had been when he became prime minister. His colleagues were almost as much newcomers as the Labour ministers before them. Only two (Austen Chamberlain and Winston Churchill) had sat in cabinets before 1914; only six had sat in cabinet at all before Law's government of 1922, and it was not a recommendation for these to have served Lloyd George. The Conservative ministers were also new in character. Only Bridgeman, at the admiralty, was an old-fashioned country landowner. The others were cultivated businessmen, like Baldwin himself— the only industrial capitalist who has ever been prime minister.[2] If they proved unenterprising, this was rather because they reflected the spirit of the time than that they lagged behind it.

Baldwin soon showed the spirit in which he hoped to govern. On 6 March 1925 a backbench Conservative introduced a bill to abolish the political levy in the trade unions, which financed the Labour party. Baldwin swept the bill away in a speech which ended with the characteristic words: 'Give peace in our time, O Lord.' It seemed at first that his prayer would be granted. Many of the conflicts which tore prewar England apart, had now been stilled. The Irish question had been answered for good or ill. No one cared about Welsh disestablishment—the Church of Wales, now accepted as a national church among equals, least of all. Women had the vote, though not yet on the same terms as men. The Conservatives had renounced Tariff Reform. The social reforms, so bitterly contested when the Liberals introduced them, had become a habit, and the Conservatives even extended them. National Health Insurance was never disputed. Unemployment insurance was disputed only in detail. Labour wanted the rates of benefit raised. The Conservatives refused. On the other hand, in 1928 they jettisoned the insurance principle and made benefit for an unlimited

[1] The average age of politicians generally was a little higher now that fewer men of wealth or family entered the house of commons soon after reaching their majority. In the Labour party, particularly, men had to work for their reputations.
[2] Douglas Hogg, who had a seat in the cabinet as attorney general and became later lord chancellor, had not been educated at a university. Labour has never matched this democratic stroke.

period a statutory right so long as the applicant was 'genuinely seeking work'—as big a blow as any against the old poor law. Churchill, in his first budget, brought in contributory old-age pensions, which nearly doubled the income of the aged needy.[1] Education took 2·2 per cent. of the national income, as against 1·1 per cent. prewar. Public housing, mostly under Wheatley's act, provided nearly 100,000 houses a year. Great Britain was approaching the welfare state.

Churchill reduced income tax to 4s. in the pound. Otherwise he did little to reduce the heavy taxation of the rich which had come with the war. Death duties and supertax[2] remained at what had once been called 'punitive levels'. At the other end of the scale, gross poverty was declining. In 1899 Seebohm Rowntree had found that 15·46 per cent. of the working population of York were living in primary poverty; thirty years later the figure was 6·8 per cent., and hardly any of these were in regular work. The rise of real wages was one cause of this change; the decline in the size of families another, and probably a more important one. As well, there was now agreement among politicians, as there had not been a generation before, that poverty should be remedied by government action. Neville Chamberlain believed this as strongly as any Labour man and was indeed the most effective social reformer of the interwar years.

The difference between Conservative and Labour was more rhetorical than real. Chamberlain sounded mean, even when he was conferring benefits. Labour promised more and stuck to the existing rules in practice. Political Labour was buoyed up by the experience of 1924 and by the larger hope that the Liberals were on the way out. Labour leaders, with the dress of privy councillors hanging in their cupboards, had had their revolution and now looked forward to an automatic majority at the next election. MacDonald's prestige stood higher than ever. The I.L.P., it is true, was swinging left, and propounded the Living Wage as the main plank for the next election. Even this only meant that the attack on poverty should be accelerated, though with a hope that capitalism might be ruined by the exertion. In any case, the I.L.P. had lost its force. Its membership

---

[1] Churchill, though a Free Trader, met the cost of the pensions by restoring the McKenna duties which Snowden had abolished the year before.

[2] The name of this was changed to surtax in 1929.

steadily declined as the Labour constituency parties established themselves, and it became, in its final phase, what it had
never been before, a refuge for middle-class idealists, who
naturally favoured extreme courses once they took the jump
into socialism at all. The solid bulk of working-class Labour
supported moderation. Politics were set fair.

This happy prospect was disturbed by the shadow of mass
unemployment. Here was a new problem to which no one had a
ready-made answer. Cyclical unemployment was an old story,
and when unemployment soared in 1921 to two million, men
at first accepted this unprecedented figure as the consequence
of the worst depression since the industrial revolution. By
1925 there was recovery. Total industrial production in 1924
reached the level of 1913, and in 1925 was 10 per cent. higher.
There were more people in work than ever before, thanks to the
natural increase of the working population. Yet there were still
more than a million unemployed. Three quarters of them were
in the old staple industries, on which Great Britain's prosperity
had once rested. Industries producing for the home market
had recovered; imports had more than recovered—in 1925
they were 10 per cent. more in volume than in 1913;[1] exports
were trailing behind, 25 per cent. lower than the 1913
figure.[2]

We can now recognize the true causes of this. The export
trades were producing goods for which demand was not expand-
ing, and in any case the primary producers could not buy these
goods, because of the change in the terms of trade. At the time,
men saw only the decline in exports. They were alarmed,
though mistakenly, that Great Britain was not paying her way
in the world. They were convinced that unemployment could
be reduced only by increasing exports; convinced also that
exports could be increased if their prices were brought down;
and the employers at any rate were convinced that prices could
be brought down only by reducing wages. The complaint
against high wages was strengthened when Keynes and others
alleged that Great Britain had returned to gold at too high a rate.
The diagnosis seems to us faulty. Wages were already lowest
in the export industries, and further reduction, by weakening

[1] Taking 1938 as 100, the volume of imports in 1913 was 81; in 1925 it was 89.
[2] Again taking 1938 as 100, the volume of exports in 1913 was 173; in 1925 it
was 130.

the home market, would have caused more unemployment than it cured. This is wisdom after the event. Baldwin expressed the general view when he said on 30 July 1925: 'All the workers of this country have got to take reductions in wages to help put industry on its feet.'

Here was a direct challenge to the trade union movement. The union leaders were now, for the most part, skilled negotiators, not agitators. They regarded a strike as the ultimate weapon, much like the sanctions which the League of Nations flourished and hoped never to use. In 1925 days lost in strikes (just under eight million) were the lowest since the war: only a tenth of what had been lost in 1921, and somewhat lower than in 1913. Union leaders recognized that unemployment could not be solved, as perhaps poverty could be, by the methods of the class war. Many of them, like Ernest Bevin, were eager to cooperate with the employers in reorganizing industry for the common benefit of workers and employers. They drew the line at reductions of wages. They were ready to resist and did not mind if this cut across the moderation of the Labour politicians. The union leaders had found little joy in the Labour government of 1924, and Bevin had urged unsuccessfully that Labour should not take office again without a majority, or perhaps not even then. He and other union leaders were not sorry to show that 'direct action' could do more for Labour than all the rhetoric of MacDonald.

The coal industry was almost inevitably the field of conflict. It was by far the largest single industry, the only one employing more than a million workers.[1] It had always been the symbol of class struggle. Most industrialists seemed to earn a reward by their own skill, even if the reward was excessive. In working-class eyes, mine-owners had no skill and were being rewarded for the lucky accident that they were sitting on top of coal. Moreover, coal entered into every branch of industrial life. It was often difficult during a strike to recognize a 'black' article. There was no such difficulty with coal. Every worker in a factory or on a railway knew that he was using black coal and felt that he was something of a blackleg. To the workers, support for the miners was simply sympathetic action on a large scale, not a deliberate political threat like the projected general strike of 1920.

[1] Its nearest competitor was the textile industry, with half a million workers.

The coal industry had done unexpectedly well after the dispute of 1921. Its European competitors were hampered in various ways. Poland had not settled down after the war. German coal production virtually ceased during the French occupation of the Ruhr. In May 1924 the miners secured a more favourable wage agreement, thanks partly to the prompting of the Labour government. Then Polish and German coal knocked the bottom out of the European market. British mines were again running at a loss. The owners knew no remedy beyond lower wages and longer hours. The miners were as resolute as ever for a fight, or even more so. Herbert Smith was still their president. He replied to all attempts at compromise: 'Nowt doing.' Frank Hodges, who had favoured compromise, was no longer secretary.[1] His place was taken by A. J. Cook, an inspired orator, who interpreted his duty in a democratic way: to refuse all concession, as the miners wanted, not to get the best terms he could. The government, for their part, refused to help the reorganization of the industry by any fresh subsidy.

The general council of the T.U.C. sought a way out and thought they had found one. They calculated that, by offering to support the miners, they would break the existing deadlock. They, not the miners, would handle the negotiations and, in cooperation with the government, would lead both miners and owners to the compromise which they were incapable of reaching by themselves. This plan had two defects. The miners never accepted it, despite sometimes seeming to do so. In their view, the other unions should support the miners unconditionally, carrying on a general strike until complete victory—or complete disaster. On the other side, the government were incapable of imposing compromise on the owners. They therefore declared that the mining dispute was none of their affair. This produced a paradoxical situation. Government and general council implicitly admitted the other's case without meaning to do so. The government said that the mining dispute was

---

[1] Hodges resigned as secretary in 1924 to enter parliament, where he became a junior minister in the Labour government. The miners, who blamed him wrongly for Black Friday, did not keep his place open for him. He received later a sinecure on the Central Electricity Board and died, a wealthy man, in 1947—an interesting example of how THE THING, as Cobbett called the entrenched English system, looks after its own. What discredited Hodges with the miners was his making in other circles.

nothing to do with them. Support of the miners was therefore purely a sympathetic strike, not—as the government accused it of being—a political threat. But the general council were not really hoping to defeat the mine-owners. They wanted to push the government into taking part in the negotiations. So their action was a political threat after all. However, no one made these logical points. The general council talked about the miners; the government about the national interest—neither of which benefited much from what happened.

It seemed at first that the government would be the one to give way. On 30 June 1925 the owners gave a month's notice to end the existing agreement. Their new offer involved sharply reduced wages. The miners refused it. Lock-out threatened for 31 July. The general council issued instructions for an embargo on all movement of coal. The government, after again refusing a subsidy, climbed down twenty-six hours before the lock-out was due to begin. There was to be a subsidy for nine months, sufficient to maintain existing wage rates and standard profits;[1] meanwhile a royal commission would seek ways of raising the productive efficiency of the industry. Such was Red Friday—apparently an easy triumph for working-class solidarity. No one remarked that the government had still not accepted responsibility for the mining industry; they had merely bought time, perhaps in hope of conciliation, perhaps to prepare resistance, or may be from a mixture of both. The lockout was called off. The royal commission was duly set up under Sir Herbert Samuel, a former Liberal minister,[1] with three members (an economist and two industrialists), none of whom knew anything about the coal industry. It spent the winter hearing witnesses and preparing a report of some 300 pages. The unions and the general council did nothing.

But there was an unplanned shift of opinion. The railway and transport unions complained that operating an embargo on coal would fall solely on them; any new solidarity must be more

[1] The subsidy was expected to cost £10 million. It cost £23 million. Though usually described as a subsidy in aid of wages, it was just as much a subsidy in aid of profits.

[2] Herbert Samuel (1870–1963): educ. University College School and Oxford; president of local government board, 1914–15; postmaster general, 1915–16; home secretary, 1916, 1931–2; high commissioner of Palestine, 1920–5; leader of Liberal party, 1931–5; cr. Viscount, 1937; an amateur philosopher.

widespread. The other unions agreed, and thus stumbled towards a national, if not a general, strike. The government took sterner precautions. Some of these sprang from the strange Conservative delusion that the unions were influenced or even inspired by Communists. Joynson-Hicks, the home secretary, who saw a Communist under every bed, was the leading exponent of this view.[1] At his direction, twelve leading Communists were prosecuted in October under the Incitement to Mutiny Act of 1797. They were all found guilty and sent to prison, after an absurd offer by the judge to let them off with a caution if they would renounce their political opinions. This was one of the few occasions in recent English history when men were punished for their opinions, not for acts of practical significance. It bore striking testimony to the anti-Bolshevik panic of at any rate some Conservatives; or perhaps it was merely a demonstration by the preposterous 'Jix' (the home secretary's nickname) that, whereas Sir Patrick Hastings had failed to slay his Communist, Jix could slay his twelve.

The serious preparations were in the hands of the permanent under-secretary at the home office, Sir John Anderson, who had already had experience of civil war in Ireland and was to have more later in Bengal.[2] The plans for an emergency system of transport, originally made in Lloyd George's time, were dug out and elaborated. England was divided into ten areas, each under a civil commissioner, who could, if necessary, exercise all government power without reference to London.[3] The government had a great new asset in the rapid development of road transport. Previously a rail strike could paralyse the life of the community within a few days. Now road transport could maintain at any rate essential food supplies. The drivers were less organized than the railway workers. Moreover, anyone who

[1] William Joynson-Hicks (1865–1932): educ. Merchant Taylors'; postmaster general, financial secretary to the treasury (with a seat in the cabinet), 1923; minister of health, 1923–4; home secretary, 1924–9; cr. Viscount Brentford, 1929; a fervent evangelical and opponent of the revised Prayer Book.

[2] John Anderson (1882–1958): educ. George Watson's College, Edinburgh, and Leipzig; permanent under-secretary, home office, 1922–32; governor of Bengal, 1932–7; lord privy seal, 1938–9; home secretary, 1939–40; lord president of the council, 1940–3; chancellor of the exchequer, 1943–5; member of war cabinet 1940–5; cr. Viscount Waverley, 1952; recommended by Churchill as prime minister in case of his own death and that of Eden.

[3] Indirectly, the standing of parliament was maintained in that all the commissioners except one were M.P.s, and the exception, Lord Clarendon, was, of course, a member of the house of lords.

could drive a car could soon learn to handle a lorry. This made the general strike as antiquated as the tactics with which generals started the first World war. It was also an advantage for the government that few county boroughs had, as yet, a Labour majority; they could use the town clerk as their local agent without producing protests from the members of the town council.

The Samuel commission reported on 11 March 1926. It proposed various measures to improve the industry: nationalization of royalties; amalgamation of smaller pits; better working conditions, such as pithead baths. These were all for the future; the only present recommendation was for an immediate reduction of wages. The owners rejected any reorganization: they demanded not only lower wages, but also longer hours (which, since it involved legislation, brought in the government). The miners answered, in Cook's words: 'Not a penny off the pay, not a minute on the day.' Herbert Smith, when asked what the miners could offer to help the industry, replied: 'Nowt. We've nowt to offer.' Both Baldwin and the general council tried to lure the miners into accepting some reduction of wages, in the vague hope that they might then lure the owners into some concession also. The miners would not give way until the owners had done so—and perhaps not even then. Deadlock continued throughout April. The existing agreement in the coal industry ran out at the end of the month. The owners demanded district agreements and reduced wages. The miners refused. On 1 May they were locked out.

The same day a special trade union conference almost unanimously[1] placed authority in the hands of the general council and approved plans for a national strike on 3 May. There was still equivocation. The miners assumed that they had delegated power to the general council only to conduct a strike; they did not intend to authorize it to make any concession over their wages. The general council, on the other hand, would yield over miners' wages if the government would accept the Samuel report and agree to enforce it. They negotiated clumsily with the government throughout 2 May, each side hesitating to give way before the other did so. Shortly after midnight the government broke off negotiations on the grounds that there had been an 'overt act': the compositors had refused to set the

[1] Three and a half million to 50,000, i.e. all the large unions approved.

Daily Mail.[1] This refusal had nothing to do with the general council or even with the printers' union, whose officials protested against it.

The cabinet seem to have been divided until the last moment. Baldwin perhaps shrank from decisive action. Birkenhead was confident that the general council could be separated from the miners; when he heard that the *Daily Mail* leader had been stopped, he remarked: 'Bloody good job.' Churchill was the leader of those who wanted to fight, just as he had been the most aggressive minister against the workers when home secretary before the war and the most aggressive against the Germans during it. Fighting was his natural response to any challenge; as well, he may have hoped to oust Baldwin from the supreme position. If so, he failed; instead he implanted in Labour men a distrust of him which lasted until after the outbreak of the second World war. At any rate, the general council had now no alternative. A national strike duly began at midnight on 3 May. It was not intended to be general. Transport and railway workers were called out; so, to less purpose, were printers, workers in heavy industry, in building, and in gas and electricity undertakings. Other workers were held back in 'the second line'.

Plans worked fully on both sides, more fully even than had been expected. The response of union members was fantastic: all ceased work when called upon, and practically none returned to work until the strike was over. These were the very men who had rallied to the defence of Belgium in 1914. The voluntary recruitment of the first World war and the strike of 1926 were acts of spontaneous generosity, without parallel in any other country. The first was whipped on by almost every organ of public opinion; the second was undertaken despite their disapproval. Such nobility deserves more than a passing tribute. The strikers asked nothing for themselves. They did not seek to challenge the government, still less to overthrow the constitution. They merely wanted the miners to have a living

[1] The piece which provoked the refusal started as a government advertisement, appealing for volunteers. Other papers got it past the printers with the argument that they should not censor advertisements. Thomas Marlowe, editor of the *Daily Mail*, who was already in bad repute with the Labour movement from his publication of the Zinoviev letter, defiantly answered that he would endorse the advertisement in a leader. The compositors then stopped work, and Marlowe at once informed the cabinet by telephone. Maybe he had aimed deliberately at provocation, perhaps even with encouragement from inside the cabinet.

wage. Perhaps not even that. They were loyal to their unions and to their leaders, as they had been loyal during the war to their country and to their generals. They went once more into the trenches, without enthusiasm and with little hope.

The preparations made by the government worked also. Road transport did all that it had been expected to do, and on a voluntary basis. The road hauliers carried food supplies in the normal way, and the consumer paid the bill in the shape of higher prices.[1] The biggest single burden was the cartage of potatoes. A surplus of milk was produced by postponing the making of cheese, and the milk was brought to the towns by milk-trains— usually the only trains to run. Volunteer drivers for trains and lorries and special constables were recruited from ex-officers and from the universities. This was class war, in polite form.

Though each side attributed extremist policies to the other, neither meant it seriously. The general council assumed, correctly, that they would be able to communicate with their local officials by telegraph and to draw strike pay from the banks. The government assumed, also correctly, that there would be no serious violence nor attempts to interfere with the strike-breaking lorries. Troops were not called upon to preserve order except at the London docks, where industrial disputes always verged towards violence. Churchill tried to provoke conflict by parading armoured cars through the streets. He did not succeed. In places, particularly in the working-class suburbs of London, buses were obstructed or even wrecked. Some were withdrawn; some ran under police protection. Only one case is recorded (in Northumberland) of an attempt to sabotage a railway line. There was some violence in the mining districts, in Glasgow, and in a few other places—usually provoked by an attempt to run buses. Altogether about 4,000 people were prosecuted for violence or incitement to violence, and about a quarter of these received prison sentences. This was a trivial figure among millions of strikers.

Elsewhere police and strikers played football against each other. In one district collaboration went further. At Newcastle upon Tyne the local strike committee joined with the district commissioner to organize the unloading and delivery of food.

---

[1] Road transport cost the government £20,000. The total cost of the strike to public funds was £433,000 (£100,000 for extra police; £119,000 for the organization of food distribution).

The government did not like this arrangement and soon stopped it. The general council were equally disapproving. The maintenance of order and of supplies was the government's job, not theirs. A few extremists talked of creating an alternative, quasi-Soviet authority; this was far from the spirit of the general council. The strike of 1926 was no repetition of the threat which had prevented war against Soviet Russia in 1920. That threat had been a deliberate political act, and the union leaders had recognized that they might have to take over the running of the country. In 1926 their sole object was to ease the government into negotiations over the coal industry. When they failed in this, they had inevitably to retreat.

The caution of the general council was shown in other ways. They were hampered in appealing to public opinion by their own act in calling out the printers: even the *Daily Herald* was stopped. Churchill brought out an official government organ, the *British Gazette* (printed appropriately on the machines of the *Morning Post*), in which he denounced British workingmen as 'the enemy'.[1] He demanded 'unconditional surrender'—a demand he repeated, more appropriately, against the Germans in the second World war. The general council reluctantly answered with the *British Worker*; this was strictly a strike sheet and was debarred from giving ordinary news or even from making propaganda. Reith managed to preserve the technical independence of the B.B.C., not yet a public corporation. He did so only by suppressing news which the government did not want published. This set a pattern for the future: the vaunted independence of the B.B.C. was secure so long as it was not exercised. The ordinary newspapers gradually managed to come out in skeleton form, but with a much reduced influence. The voice of the government predominated, and this presented the general strike as a challenge to the constitution.

Pleas for conciliation and compromise were brushed aside. One such plea came from the archbishop of Canterbury with the general backing of other religious leaders. Lloyd George took the same line, to the annoyance of Asquith and other respectable Liberals; they thought that the time had come once more to drum him out of the party. In the house of commons, Sir John Simon, grasping at Lloyd George's vacant place, solemnly

---

[1] Baldwin later claimed that shunting Churchill on to the *British Gazette* was 'the cleverest thing I ever did'; probably he had no choice.

asserted that the strike was illegal and not protected by the act of 1906. This opinion, which was later torn to pieces by other legal authorities, does not seem to have shaken the general council, though it is sometimes alleged to have done so, and the government did not act upon it. An attempt to penalize the strikers or the unions was successfully resisted by George V who played throughout a moderating role. This ordinary little man (his own phrase), with his old-world Conservative outlook, yet recognized that the strikers were also his people—and good people at that. Nor were the general council frightened into surrender by the rumour that the government were planning to arrest a number of union leaders. They were, no doubt, harassed by the drain on union funds. But compromise and negotiation had been their aim before the strike started; they continued to pursue this aim when the strike was on.

Herbert Samuel was again the chosen instrument. He drafted proposals for a National Wages Board in the coal industry which would impose reductions of wages, but only when the recommendations for reorganization, made by the Samuel commission, were 'effectively adopted'. This was good enough for the general council, even though Samuel insisted that he was speaking only for himself, not for the government; public opinion, the union leaders believed, would enforce this compromise if the strike were called off. The miners dissented: they would still not yield an inch. On 12 May the general council called off the national strike unconditionally. They obtained no assurances that men would be taken back to work without victimization. When employers, particularly the railway companies, attempted to impose penalties and to reject active leaders, the strike was resumed —this time with some success. The government shrank from real class war, and Baldwin intervened to secure a fairly amicable return to work on the old conditions.

The miners, however, were ruined by their own obstinacy. Baldwin offered to operate the Samuel report, including a short-term subsidy, if the two sides in the industry would accept it first. The miners refused, and the government thus escaped the awkward, indeed insoluble, task of coercing the owners. After this the only contribution by the government was to pass an act suspending the seven-hour day in the coal mines for five years. The owners were free to impose their terms, undeterred by expostulations from Baldwin, who called them 'stupid and discourteous', or even from Churchill. The miners were driven back to work by starvation after holding out for six months. They had to accept longer hours, lower wages, and—worst of all—district agreements. Nothing was done to reorganize or to improve the industry. The owners had the whip hand and kept it, thanks to the pool of unemployed miners which longer hours brought into existence. Coal remained a great industry: the largest single employer of labour throughout the interwar years. Even in 1938 it produced four-fifths (227 million tons) of the record figure reached in 1913. Nevertheless, it was in slow decline, and the owners' victory in 1926 ensured that the price should be paid by the miners, who had to work under inhuman conditions. In the end, the owners were destroyed by their victory. The class war continued in the coal districts when it was fading elsewhere, and the miners insisted on nationalization as soon as power passed into their hands. No one mourned when the mine-owners disappeared; they were about the least worthy element in the British community.

The general strike had failed to help the miners. At first glance it seemed also to shake the trade union movement as a whole. Union membership fell to under five million for the first time since 1916; union funds were depleted by the drain of strike pay. All talk of a further general strike vanished. Even strikes in individual industries became rare. In the years before 1926 strikes involved an average of more than one million workers a year; in the ten years afterwards they never involved more than 300,000. All this was really due to a change of spirit rather than to defeat or to discouragement. The loss of membership and of funds was soon undone. The general strike brought to the front the very men, such as Bevin and Thomas, who put conciliation before conflict. Once the coal dispute was out of the way, they could follow their preferred course. Besides, the general strike was a warning to other employers, themselves wiser, more conciliatory, and of course less hard-pressed, than the mine-owners. Outside the coal industry there was little attempt to reduce wages. These remained stable for the next three years until the coming of the great depression, although the cost of living fell by fifteen points. As a result, the British working man, except for the miner, was better off in 1929 than he had ever been before. Even when the depression came and produced large-scale unemployment, employers shrank from conflict, and British wage rates declined far less than in other European countries. Wages came near to being a fixed charge on industry instead of the first thing to be cut at any sign of difficulty.

The export trades were still in trouble. At best, in 1927-9, exports reached only 84 per cent. of the 1913 figure, whereas imports had risen to 120 per cent. Unemployment apart, this did not seem to matter. Great Britain was again earning a comfortable surplus in the world, thanks to her invisible exports of shipping and other services and to the yield from her overseas investment. This surplus, though less than prewar (never much over £100 million a year as against £200 million prewar), was enough to replace, and a little over, the investments which had been lost during the war. But foreign investment now played a smaller part in the British economy.[1] Before the war 80 per cent. of new capital had gone abroad. In 1928 only 40 per cent. did so. The new industries, catering for the home market, were gradually pushing ahead. In 1930 well over one million private cars were registered, against 200,000 at the end of the war, and 60 per cent. of the motor-car output was in the hands of two firms. The heads of the new industries were themselves, for the most part, men of a new type. Where the old owners had created their industries and were ruthlessly eager for wealth, the new men were managing directors of limited liability companies, concerned more with efficiency than with their rights.

The first proposal for industrial collaboration after the general strike came from such a man, Sir Alfred Mond, head of Imperial Chemicals, and one-time follower of Lloyd George's.[2] On his initiative, a joint committee of employers and the general council explored in 1928 means for improving the efficiency of British industry. Though little came of these discussions at the time, they were a portent for the future. Ernest Bevin, in particular, was deeply influenced by them.[3] Many union leaders recognized that higher wages could come only from increased production,

[1] It was often said that greater exports would lead to more foreign investment. It is just as likely that the decline of interest in foreign investment was one cause of the decline in exports.

[2] Alfred Mond (1868–1930): educ. Cheltenham, Cambridge, and Edinburgh; creator of Imperial Chemical Industries and other great concerns; advocate of combination and conciliation; first commissioner of works, 1916–21; minister of health, 1921–2; cr. Baronet 1910, Baron Melchett, 1928; a keen Zionist.

[3] Though the meetings were known as the Mond–Turner talks, after Ben Turner the titular leader on the union side, Bevin did most of the talking.

not from industrial warfare. The mass of workers, it is clear, were no longer in a militant mood. The Communist party which had doubled its membership during the year of the general strike, lost all its new recruits soon afterwards. On a wider field, the general strike seems to have produced a lessening of class antagonism. The middle-class blacklegs, performing manual labour for the first and only time in their lives, learnt to respect those who did it always; the workers recognized that the leisured classes, too, were human beings. Hence the paradoxical outcome. The general strike, apparently the clearest display of the class war in British history, marked the moment when class war ceased to shape the pattern of British industrial relations.

This was less true in politics. Despite an appeal by the king immediately after the strike for 'a peace that will be lasting', the Conservatives in parliament were eager to enforce their victory over the unions. Baldwin acquiesced, thus throwing away much of the prestige which he had won by his seeming moderation. In May 1927 the government introduced a bill to amend the Trades Disputes Act of 1906 and carried it by means of the closure, which had not been used since 1921. Its principal clause made illegal any sympathetic strike or any strike 'designed or calculated to coerce the government'. As well, the government threw in other provisions which had nothing to do with the general strike, but dear to Conservative hearts. Civil servants were forbidden to join a union affiliated to the T.U.C. Members of unions who wished to pay the political levy had to contract in, instead of (as under the act of 1913) contracting out.[1] The bill aroused great bitterness in the Labour movement. It was fiercely contested in the house of commons, and its repeal followed close on Labour's victory in 1945. It was a futile measure. Men set on a strike, of whatever kind, are not deterred by a clause in a statute; you can no more indict a class than a nation. The clause against sympathetic and political strikes was never invoked during its nineteen years of existence: it was both unnecessary and useless. The attack on Labour party finance came ill from the Conservatives who depended on secret donations from rich men. It, too, had little effect in the long run. Though the income of the Labour party was reduced at the

[1] That is, each member had to sign a form expressing his willingness to pay the political levy, instead of paying it automatically, unless he insisted on signing a form refusing to do so.

time by more than one-third, it gradually recovered later.[1] The act was a vindictive stroke of no serious consequence: trade unions had become too essential a part of society to be shaken by it.

The act had one remote consequence of some importance. This was in connexion with the *Daily Herald*. In 1922 Lansbury had no longer been able to carry it on as a private enterprise. He therefore transferred it to the joint ownership of the Labour party and the T.U.C. The paper continued to run at a loss, despite a lavish recruiting of staff from the capitalist press, principally the *Daily Mail*—or perhaps because of it. The two owners had to meet the loss. In 1927 the Labour party, with its reduced income, could no longer pay its share. Ownership passed to the T.U.C. alone. Bevin took charge. He aspired to produce a newspaper worthy of the Labour movement, and selling on the scale of the great popular dailies. For this he needed a business partner. He found one in Odhams, a printing firm grown great on *John Bull*, which owned a popular Sunday paper, the *People*, and wished to keep their presses busy during the week.

The deal was completed in 1929. Odhams provided the business management; four directors, appointed by the T.U.C., had the decisive say in political questions. The *Daily Herald* duly became a mass organ. It had a unique character: the only British daily (other than the Communist *Daily Worker* with its trivial circulation) strictly tied to a political party.[2] Not that it won its place by this. Elias, the head of Odhams (later Lord Southwood), was the least political of men and sought readers by purely commercial devices. In this odd way, the most idealistic of newspapers established itself by the most materialist methods. The *Daily Herald* never acted as an intellectual centre for the Labour movement, and those who wish to understand the spirit of the movement must look elsewhere.

[1] The explanation is simple. In 1927 every union member had to be invited to sign a form, contracting in. It took some time for union secretaries to organize this, and many long-standing members naturally jibbed at taking on what seemed to be a new liability. As new members joined, they were given a variety of forms to sign and signed the lot without meticulous calculation of what they were doing. Hence, in time, the act ceased to make much difference.

[2] Though all British newspapers had a more or less precise political allegiance, this was determined solely by the whim of the proprietor and, to a lesser extent, the editor. The policy of the *Daily Herald* was defined in its articles of association: it was to be that 'laid down from time to time by the Labour Party Conference'. Even so the Labour party was not represented on the Board.

The general strike had, finally, an unexpected influence on the character of the Liberal party. During the strike Lloyd George took a bold line: support for the government, but also a demand for negotiations. 'I prefer the Liberal policy of trusting to conciliation rather than to force.' The elderly Liberal leaders forgot their liberalism when threatened by (imaginary) social revolution. Asquith (now Lord Oxford) excluded Lloyd George from the Liberal shadow cabinet. It looked as though Lloyd George was once more in the wilderness. Events took a different turn after the strike. Liberalism had no future if it merely said 'Me, too' to the Conservatives; its only chance was to find a radical, though non-socialist, solution for the economic problems of postwar Great Britain. Lloyd George was on the search for such a solution; the older leaders were not. He had on his side C. P. Scott and the *Manchester Guardian*; he had also, perhaps more importantly, the Lloyd George fund, while the official party was short of money. In October 1926 Asquith gave up. He resigned the leadership of the party, and Lloyd George took his place. The party was transformed. It became the source of new ideas in economic planning instead of relying on emotional appeals which had lost their force.[1] Lloyd George was lavish with his money; the Liberal party and its associate bodies received over £400,000 from him between 1927 and 1929. Others were lavish with ideas. Curiously enough Lloyd George's most powerful inspirer was his antagonist of 1919, J. M. Keynes. Here, it seemed, was a dangerous challenge to conservatism, and to Baldwin's policy, or no-policy, of 'safety first'.

The government, with their great majority, were secure while the present parliament lasted. The short-lived economic revival produced something like a golden age—the true 'age of Baldwin'. Unemployment fell to little over a million in 1928—its lowest point between 1920 and 1940. British production rose to record height, increasing by 14 per cent. between 1924 and 1929. The government stood complacently by and took credit for this last kick of individual enterprise. They lacked even a coherent financial policy, offering deflation with one hand and inflation with the other. Interest rates were kept high in order to protect the

---

[1] One symbol of this was the dismissal a little earlier (1923) of Massingham, an old-style radical, from the editorship of the *Nation*, and the appointment in his stead of the highly intellectual economist Hubert Henderson. At the same time, ownership passed from the Rowntrees, sentimental cocoa magnates, to a group of intellectuals, headed by Keynes.

gold standard of exchange. Yet, at the same time, Churchill's budgets were balanced only by sleight of hand. He raided the Road fund which had accumulated a surplus;[1] juggled with the Sinking fund; advanced the date for the payment of income tax; and allowed the unemployment insurance fund to run steadily into debt. His budget speeches provided much entertainment and some futile expedients, such as the attempt to tax betting. Churchill's years at the treasury were indeed the weakest in his varied career. His erratic finance discredited him in the eyes of more sober politicians and left the treasury weaker to face a period of real economic difficulty.

The government had some achievements to show. They tidied up imperial relations and thus made 1926 as much a landmark in the development of the Commonwealth as in industrial affairs. Since the Conservatives were shackled to Free Trade, the Imperial conference which met in that year for once kept off the barren topic of imperial preference. Instead it turned to constitutional questions. The demand for this came from the Canadian prime minister Mackenzie King, who believed (quite wrongly) that he had been victim of imperial interference.[2] He was determined that this should not happen again and that the independence which the Dominions enjoyed in practice should be defined in precise terms. The other Dominions wished to underline their detachment from the British foreign policy which had been expressed in the treaty of Locarno. South Africa and the Irish Free State perhaps foresaw the advantages to themselves which would follow from the ending of imperial sovereignty.[3] Balfour performed his last and most successful jugglery with high-sounding words. He defined Great Britain and the Dominions as 'autonomous communities within the British Empire, equal in status, in no way subordinate one to another in any aspect of their domestic or internal affairs, though united by a common allegiance to the Crown, and freely associated as members of the British Commonwealth of Nations'. This formula, though it

[1] When taxation was first levied on motor cars, a pledge was given that the yield would be spent on improving the roads. Since Churchill's time, no chancellor of the exchequer has kept this pledge.

[2] See Note A, p. 261.

[3] South Africa was restricted by the 'entrenched' clauses of the Union Act (1910); the Irish Free State by the treaty of 1921 and the subsequent constitution. These could be changed only with the cooperation of the British parliament. Once Dominion equality became absolute, the entrenched clauses probably and the Irish constitution undoubtedly could be changed unilaterally.

made no innovation in practice, emphasized how far practice had outstripped theory.

Now the theory was brought into line. The imperial parliament ceased to be sovereign over the Dominions. The imperial government became the government of Great Britain and of her colonies alone. The Crown was the only uniting link, and this more as symbol than reality. George V never visited any of his Dominions after he became king. Each governor general (henceforward appointed on the recommendation of the Dominion government concerned) acted as an independent constitutional monarch. The king exchanged friendly letters with them, as his predecessors had done with the now-vanished rulers of Europe. As a further gesture, a separate department of state was set up for relations with the Dominions, though Amery, the colonial secretary,[1] combined the two offices, as Passfield did in the Labour government which followed. Separate secretaries of state were appointed only in June 1930.[2] The first task of the new department was to translate Balfour's formula into a precise law, a task not completed until 1931 when the Statute of Westminster became the first general enactment for the constitution of the British empire since North's Regulating Act of 1778.

India was not affected by these discussions. There the old Raj continued unabated, with rumbling interruptions of political agitation and communal riots. The government flickered feebly towards concession. In 1926 Baldwin's friend Edward Wood (later Lord Halifax) became viceroy as Lord Irwin, and he was clear from the outset that the goal must be Dominion status. Late in 1927 a statutory commission was appointed under Sir John Simon to consider India's future. One member was C. R. Attlee—appointed for the simple reason that he could be easily spared from the house of commons. No one then foresaw that twenty years later he would be the prime minister who gave India independence, Attlee least of all. The commission duly visited India where it was greeted by crowds with banners inscribed: 'Simon, go back.' He went back and laboured on a

[1] Leopold Charles Maurice Stennett Amery (1873-1955): educ. Harrow and Oxford; *Times* correspondent in South Africa during Boer war; first lord of the admiralty, 1922-3; colonial secretary, 1924-9; Dominions secretary, 1925-9; secretary for India, 1940-5.

[2] Even this was for reasons of British domestic politics. J. H. Thomas had to be given an important post after his failure over unemployment, and Passfield, who had been greatly harassed over Palestine, was breaking up.

report which was ready only in 1930. Meanwhile, the government blamed Soviet propaganda for much of India's unrest.
Already, in May 1927, 200 police had raided the offices of Arcos,
the Soviet trading organization in London, in hope of discovering some evidence against the Communists. No evidence was
found.[1] To cover up their blunder, the government broke off
diplomatic relations with Soviet Russia. Later, in March 1929,
the Indian government began a long-drawn-out prosecution of
thirty supposed Communist agents in the Meerut conspiracy
case.[2]

The breach with Soviet Russia suited Austen Chamberlain's
foreign policy. The years after Locarno were the hey-day of
conciliation in western Europe. Germany was admitted to the
League of Nations; reparations were paid regularly under the
Dawes plan; the allied commission to control German disarmament was withdrawn, even though its task was not fully
accomplished. Chamberlain, Stresemann, and Briand always
attended the meetings of the League assembly at Geneva, which
was on the way to becoming the Areopagus of Europe. It seemed
all to the good that Soviet Russia was excluded from world
affairs, and the United States almost as much. A conference on
naval disarmament between Great Britain, the United States,
and Japan broke down in August 1927, when the admiralty
refused to reduce their demand for cruisers below seventy,
against American insistence.[3] Some extreme speculators, including Trotsky, foretold that the next great war would be between
Great Britain and the United States. This was folly; but the
directors of British policy assumed that civilized Europe, having
recovered from the last war, was again the centre of the world,
and that it could manage very well by itself, without thought for
the great isolationist powers elsewhere. There was no greater
praise in these years than to be 'a good European'. Sir Austen
Chamberlain, K.G., received this praise.

Austen Chamberlain's achievement was shortlived. His
brother Neville left a more lasting mark on British life as minister
of health. Neville Chamberlain, like his father before him, had

---

[1] The government were acting on a false tip, presumably (not for the last time)
from a double agent. It is said that the raid was decided on by Baldwin, Austen
Chamberlain, and Joynson-Hicks without consulting the cabinet.

[2] One of those prosecuted at Meerut became a Left-wing Labour M.P. from
1945 to 1950.

[3] It is characteristic that they only possessed fifty. The row was pure theory.

long experience of local government. Lloyd George described him, not unfairly, as 'a good lord mayor of Birmingham in a lean year'. He had efficiency, clarity, resolution; qualities marred only by his unsympathetic manner. It was typical of him that he announced twenty-five bills to the cabinet when he took office, typical also that he carried twenty-one. His first target was 'Poplarism'—the defiant way in which councils and boards of guardians with Labour majorities paid higher wages and rates of relief than those approved by the ministry of health, often with borrowed money. In July 1926 an act gave the minister of health power to supersede defiant guardians, and three such boards were duly superseded.[1] This was a warning to councils also. Neville Chamberlain thus confirmed the principle that social reform could go only as far as parliament approved. Lansbury, the originator of Poplarism, resisted Chamberlain's efficiency in emotional terms. Labour was deeply stirred, and Chamberlain was branded as the enemy of the poor. Yet even Labour ministers wanted to be obeyed when they came to office.

In any case, Neville Chamberlain was far from wishing to weaken local government. On the contrary, he did more to improve it than any other single man in the twentieth century. The poor law, and the boards of guardians which administered it, tangled hopelessly with the system of national health. Other *ad hoc* bodies cut across the work of the local councils. In 1928 Chamberlain made a clean sweep.[2] The boards of guardians were abolished, and their powers transferred to public-assistance committees of the counties and county boroughs, just as Balfour's act of 1902 had transferred education from the school boards to the local education committees.[3] A neat simple pattern was created. The sixty-two counties and eighty-four county boroughs[4] became the sole authorities, under the

---

[1] West Ham (which had a debt of £2 million) in 1926; Chester-le-Street and Bedwellty in 1927.

[2] His bill, introduced in Nov. 1928, became law in 1929.

[3] Ironically, Balfour's act, which was Neville Chamberlain's precedent, had been opposed by his father, Joseph Chamberlain.

[4] These figures are for England and Wales. The county boroughs reached eighty-four in 1926 when Doncaster was elevated to their ranks. This was the last creation of a county borough to date. Both counties and county boroughs were flagrantly uneven in size, the random product of historical accidents. The counties ranged (1931) from slightly over five million in Lancashire to 17,000 in Rutland; the county boroughs from one million in Birmingham to 26,000 in Canterbury.

ministry of health, for almost all local activities[1] along with the less important rural and urban district councils and non-county boroughs. Starting nearly a century before with such humble functions as streetlighting and the police, they had by now accumulated education, public assistance, welfare, public health, housing, slum clearance, roads, town and country planning. The county boroughs ran local transport, and provided gas and electricity; all except London, where the Metropolitan Water Board was allowed to survive, provided water.[2]

In few other European countries were the tasks of local authorities so wide and varied. For the ordinary British citizen, 'they' usually meant the town hall, not an agency of the central government. The post office, which distributed pensions on top of its postal duties, and the employment exchanges run by the ministry of labour were the only important exceptions, apart from taxation and justice. There was thus great prestige and much interest still in being a local councillor, though less room for independent initiative than in the nineteenth century. The councils became predominantly instruments of national policy. About two-fifths of their income came from government grants (£108 million in 1930 against receipts from rates of £156 million), and this in itself held them under central control without the need to invoke legal sanctions.[3]

Chamberlain carried this process further, rather against his will. His reforms of 1928–9 involved an extra cost to the exchequer of about £3 million. Churchill insisted on a bigger scheme of 'derating', by which agriculture was relieved entirely of rates, industry and the railways of three quarters.[4] The treasury made up the money lost by local authorities, at a cost of £24 million a year. This was a roundabout way of subsidizing industry at the expense of the taxpayer and also, since the government grant did not fill the gap completely, at the expense

[1] The watch committees, which ran the police, were supervised by the home office; the education committees by the board of education.
[2] London was an exception in many ways. The L.C.C. ran the trams, but not the tubes or buses; it did not provide gas or electricity. By a curious twist, Labour, formerly the protagonist of municipal enterprise, reduced local powers by nationalizing gas and electricity after the second World war.
[3] As well, the local authorities had receipts of some £150 million from their trading services. Most of this was spent on the services concerned, though there was sometimes a small profit.
[4] The railways were relieved on condition that they reduced their freight rates on coal and steel proportionately.

of ratepayers not fortunate enough to rank as productive—householders, shopkeepers, institutions. Chamberlain disliked this indiscriminate assistance to efficient and inefficient alike. However, Churchill got his way. He regarded derating as a substitute for tariffs, which was no doubt another reason why Chamberlain disliked it. Yet it was almost as much a departure from Free Trade principles: the ordinary taxpayer was relieving industry of financial burdens in the hope that it would then do better in foreign markets. Few disputed this idea.

A fundamental doctrine of public life was changing unperceived. Where the Victorians had advocated economy for the sake of the consumer, their successors were prepared to spend money in order to stimulate production. Poverty had been the great social evil of former times. Unemployment now took its place. The parties, still more the unions and the employers, were drawn together, where they had previously been in combat. Once they had fought over the division of the cake. Now they were more concerned to ensure that there was a cake to divide. Few were fully conscious of the changed outlook. Men still talked of economy, and even practised it, when they were also urging the government to assist industry. No one displayed these contradictions more clearly than Neville Chamberlain himself: zealous for recovery and yet hostile to public expenditure. Labour was soon to find itself as much mixed up over Planning and Free Trade. Men of all parties walked backwards towards Gladstone's old bugbear, 'constructionism'.

The parliament of 1924-9 did not spend all its time on such drab modern subjects as unemployment and derating. It had its great historic moments, when traditional cries came back in full force. In 1928 members of the house of commons championed an individual against the police, and forced a tribunal of inquiry to the discomfiture of Scotland Yard.[1] Generally, however, individual freedom was less secure than it once had been. The judiciary had tended, during the war, to become the watchdog of the executive, instead of its check, and this attitude was maintained afterwards. As England became more democratic, the judges—drawn exclusively from the privileged classes—became more conservative and construed executive action 'benevolently'. The legal outlook was changing, again without men appreciating what they were doing.

[1] See Note B, p. 261.

The great parliamentary stir of 1927 and 1928 was even more traditional, recalling the parliaments of Elizabeth I and Charles I. The Church of England had been labouring since before the war on the revision of the Prayer Book. The aim was to give greater latitude for the Anglo-Catholic practices and doctrines towards which most ordained members of the Anglican church now inclined. The revision was welcomed by the majority of the ordained. It was less welcome to lay members of the Church, who tended to be more 'protestant' the less they attended religious services. When the revised Book was submitted to parliament for approval, it was accepted by the house of lords and twice rejected by the house of commons. The majority against the Book was swelled by Scotch Presbyterians and by unbelievers (including the Communist Parsee, Saklatvala) who rallied to the 'protestant' cause. Two members of the government, Joynson-Hicks and Inskip, spoke powerfully against the Book. Experienced observers agree that the debate produced as fine a display of oratory as any which parliament has heard this century. Little came of the fuss. Convocation illegally authorized the bishops to allow the use of the revised Book 'during the present emergency'. Emergency and illegality have persisted to the present day. The outcry was the echo of dead themes. No one seriously regarded the Church of Rome, let alone the Anglo-Catholics, as 'papistical'. Moreover, England had ceased to be, in any real sense, a Christian nation. Only a minority of Englishmen attended any church, Roman, Anglican, or Free. The politicians were living in the past.

Of course there has always been a cleavage between the generations. It was probably deeper in the nineteen-twenties than at most times. The war dug an almost impassable ditch. Older men looked back to the years before the war and hoped for their return. Their minds were prewar, even if the fashion of their clothes had relaxed. Slightly younger men lived under the shadow of their wartime experiences, never ceasing to wonder that they had survived. For those who had grown up after 1918, the war was a memory, and soon hardly that. They aspired to make new standards, not to restore old ones. In 1919 Rutherford foresaw the splitting of the atom, though he did not suppose that this could be turned to practical use. The theories of Einstein shattered the Newtonian principles which had given a rational frame to the universe. Freud shook, in a similar way, the rational

frame of men's minds. Traditional values ran thin. The young
began to steer without a chart. Even the praetorian guard of the
established order turned traitor. Products of the public schools
could no longer be relied on to remain conventional. The
emancipation came first in private morals. Political revolt had to
wait until the next decade. The strange one-sex system of education at public schools and universities had always run to homosexuality. In Victorian times this, though gross, had been
sentimental and ostensibly innocent. At the *fin de siècle* it had
been consciously wicked. Now it was neither innocent nor wicked.
It was merely, for a brief period, normal. By the end of the
decade, even former public schoolboys were beginning to discover that women were an improvement on painted boys. This
fantastic epoch has been preserved for posterity in the rich early
farces of Evelyn Waugh.

There was a Golden Age; an illusion of rapture, soon to be
dispelled. The younger generation had escaped the war and
supposed that there would never be another. In 1928 all the
nations of the world signed the Kellogg Pact, renouncing war as
an instrument of national policy. Hatred for the Germans was
forgotten. Artists and writers went to Berlin and drew their
inspiration from Weimar Germany, instead of from Italy or
France. German expressionism dominated the advanced theatre
and advanced art. No one worried about politics or economics.
Noel Coward, for instance, the representative dramatist of the
decade, wrote (and composed) a succession of brilliant revues
for C. B. Cochran. None of them contained a sketch with any
political reference. The *Today and Tomorrow* series, which started
in 1924, depicted the endless improvement of everything—
science, morals, humour, and man himself. Utopia was not
something to be striven for; it would arrive automatically. The
old order, in Marx's phrase though not for his reasons, would
simply 'wither away'. These hopes were shortlived. Political
and social problems thrust forward uninvited, and men forgot
the time when they had been full of confidence. The last years
of the nineteen-twenties were seen through the mist of gloom
which characterized the following decade. Since they had not
been gloomy, they were condemned as frivolous. So no doubt
they were. All the same, they were a good time, or, at any rate,
a breathing space between two times of trouble.

NOTES

NOTE A. *The constitutional conflict in Canada.* In September 1925 Mackenzie King, then Liberal prime minister, asked the governor general, Lord Byng of Vimy, for a dissolution. This was granted. The Conservatives, under Meighen, won a majority of fifteen over the Liberals. King believed that he could maintain himself with the assistance of Labour and the Progressives; he therefore remained in office. In June 1926 he was threatened with a vote of censure and asked for another dissolution. Byng refused. Meighen became prime minister. Three days later he was defeated in the house of commons by one vote. Byng then granted to Meighen the dissolution which he had refused to King. At the ensuing election, the Liberals won a majority, largely by alleging that the influence of the crown had been used against them. King, restored as prime minister, claimed that he had been the victim of 'colonial' treatment. In reality Byng, though perhaps acting mistakenly, had done so with as much independence as a British sovereign; he even refused to consult the British government when King urged him to do so. However, King's unfounded grievance paved the way for the statute of Westminster. Probably King knew he was barking up a wrong tree. He was the smartest of political operators and not scrupulous in his means. It is not surprising that he held office for longer than any British prime minister since Walpole.

NOTE B. *The Savidge case.* Miss Savidge was conversing in Hyde Park with Sir Leo Chiozza Money, a junior minister of Lloyd George's and later a Labour authority on finance, when both were arrested and charged with indecent behaviour. Chiozza Money claimed that he had been advising Miss Savidge on her career. They were acquitted. Later Miss Savidge was taken from her place of work by detectives and interrogated at Scotland Yard for five hours. She complained to her M.P. There was a debate in the house, and the tribunal of inquiry condemned the police for excessive zeal. Four years later, Chiozza Money again conversed with a young lady, this time in a railway carriage. On this occasion he was not acquitted. It is consoling that, about the same time, Sir Basil Thomson, formerly director of intelligence at Scotland Yard, was found guilty of a similar offence.

VIII

UNEXPECTED CRISIS, 1929–31

THE British electoral system reached theoretical democracy only in April 1928. An act, promoted by the government for no particular reason,[1] then lowered the voting age for women from 30 to 21, and put them on the same straightforward residence qualification as men. One adult, one vote was at last attained except for the business and university franchises which together gave about half a million people (mainly males) a second vote until they were abolished in 1948.[2] The act of 1928 added about five million new voters to the register, and natural increase pushed up the total of 1924 by nearly two million more. The 'flapper vote' is supposed to have benefited the Labour party in the general election of 1929, but this is a guess. The increase of three million in the Labour vote may just as well have come from older electors. In the long run, more women voters probably benefited the Conservatives, and more voters altogether probably injured the Liberals, who were the least suited to become a mass party. In 1929 this last and least regarded extension of the franchise did not affect the character of the election. No party made a special appeal to women or to the young. All three parties used the old-fashioned means of the public meeting and the house-to-house canvass.

The general election of May 1929 was the only fully three-cornered contest in British history. For the first and last time, three parties—Conservative, Liberal, and Labour—fought on something like equal terms. Each of them ran more than 500 candidates—never before, and never again. Each had a coherent programme and fought, more or less unitedly, under a single leader. Each sought power. The Conservatives, as always, were the best supplied with money. Rich men subscribed to

---

[1] The usually obscurantist Joynson-Hicks promised the flapper vote in the excitement of a public meeting, and the government felt that they must honour his promise. Churchill and Birkenhead opposed the step.

[2] A small exception the other way: those (less than 5 per cent. of the adult population) who moved too frequently to satisfy the requirement of three-months' residence.

Conservative party funds from conviction as much as from hope of honours, though they often received some honour as well. Labour had a steady, though smaller, income mainly from the political levy in the affiliated unions, and the regularity of this income kept the party organization stabler between elections. The Liberals were in danger of wasting away from financial malnutrition, when they could hold out only slender prospect of rewards from a future government. In 1929 Lloyd George gave them a shot in the arm with over £300,000 from his political fund. This was a temporary, and a dangerous, remedy. While it helped the Liberals to fight the election, it gave little help to the local organizations in the constituencies.

It was these, rather than money alone, which sustained the parties and shaped the British political system. Conservatives and Labour had some sort of organization, though by no means always a paid agent, in nearly every constituency; the Liberals far fewer. Membership of the Conservative and Liberal parties is difficult to ascertain. Labour had about 300,000 individual members, sometimes more, sometimes less.[1] Not all of these were active, and, of course, the number varied greatly from one constituency to another—strong in most working-class areas and in some middle-class suburbs with Left-wing intellectuals, weak in the countryside. Probably a local party was lucky if it could count on fifty recognized figures, and could call on a couple of hundred more at a general election. Beyond this we can only guess at the strength of those who carried the political system.

It is easier to distinguish the character of the parties. The Conservatives had changed least with the passage of time. Their party remained much as Lord Randolph Churchill had shaped and failed to shape it in the eighteen-eighties. The constituency parties had little say in determining policy. The annual meeting of the National Union merely demonstrated confidence in the leader, or sometimes lack of it. On the other hand, the central office had little control over the constituency parties. A rich Conservative M.P., locally backed, could take an independent line, more or less with impunity—as some did by retaining their seats after being divorced. The Conservatives relied mainly on

[1] Labour had also about two million members in the affiliated trade unions. Not all unions affiliated to the Labour party, even when they belonged to the T.U.C.; nor did the affiliated unions pay for all the members who had paid the political levy, much of which they retained for their own use, e.g. supplementing the salaries of union M.P.s or subscribing to local Labour parties.

their natural advantages. Prominent local figures were nearly always on the Conservative side. Most of the national press supported it: in 1929 seven daily newspapers out of ten, and all the Sunday newspapers except one. The Conservatives appropriated patriotism. The Union Jack draped the table at their meetings. The Empire was their private estate. Universities, chambers of commerce, the civil service, the armed forces, nominally non-party organizations such as the Women's Institutes, and to a great extent the Church of England, were pillars of Conservatism in thin disguise. Other things being equal, those who rule go on ruling, and those who are ruled acquiesce. Habit was the great Conservative asset.

The Labour party had changed a great deal since its birth, or more accurately its christening, in 1906. This change was partly due to the institution of individual membership in 1918. It was due more to the tenure of office by Labour in 1924, to the confidence that there would soon be another Labour government, perhaps with a majority, and to the control by Labour of many local councils. Labour was no longer a propaganda association or a pressure group on authorities, local and national. It aimed at political power, and the views of its members had to take second place to this aim. Before 1918 the affiliated societies, political as well as industrial, could take their own line over policy without fear of embarrassing a future Labour government. The I.L.P., for example, could oppose the war; the miners could demand nationalization of the mines. Now the Labour leaders wanted loyal followers, and a free hand for themselves.

The I.L.P. sought to impose on the Labour party its own programme of the Living Wage. The annual Labour conference rejected this. The I.L.P. then retaliated by demanding from all candidates whom it endorsed, a pledge that they would carry out I.L.P. policy. The Labour party could not tolerate any pledge of loyalty in conflict with its own. Labour was the stronger financially. It had the subscriptions from the unions; the I.L.P. had only contributions from the faithful. Moreover, Labour, as a democratic party, asserted firmly the will of the majority, even though this majority was provided by the block vote of the unions. Acceptance of majority decisions had been devised originally against the Lib-Labs. Later it was used ruthlessly against the Communists. Now it was turned regretfully against the I.L.P., and with crushing effect. Though 140 Labour M.P.s elected in 1929 belonged to the I.L.P., only eighteen pledged themselves to support its policy, and some even of these did not honour their pledge.

This is not to say that Labour became, in later parlance, a monolithic party. There was still great divergence of outlook, ranging from extreme left to extreme right, among the union leaders, and even more among the constituency parties, though less divergence between the two groups than has often been alleged.[1] These divergencies were subordinated to party loyalty, as the only means of challenging 'the boss class'. The Labour party translated union practice into political terms, and the dissenter became a blackleg if he pushed his dissent too far. The argument was, to a great extent, over tactics. The leaders thought that Labour would win votes by conciliating moderate opinion. The critics wanted to inspire enthusiasm by a fervent socialist policy. Probably the argument was misconceived. Though Labour had men of middle-class origin among its leaders and sought, less successfully, middle-class votes, it was essentially a working-class party, and Labour voters responded to the class appeal, without inquiring what policy this committed them to. Still, Labour's moderation was, on the whole, a democratic decision. It represented what most Labour supporters wanted, and the 'democrats' of the Left were, like most extremists, officers without a rank-and-file.

In day-to-day affairs, Labour, despite its class character, had become part of 'the nation', almost without noticing it. For an ordinary man of modest ambitions, Labour, like the Conservative party, was the path to influence and honour—if he were a working man, the more rewarding path. A steadfast Labour worker in a constituency had less chance than a Conservative of receiving a knighthood or an O.B.E. He had almost as much chance of becoming mayor, a magistrate, or a governor of the grammar school. Broadly speaking, the Conservatives could count on more motor cars at general elections with which to take voters to the poll. Labour could count on more canvassers who induced voters to go there. In both cases, the organization was not created specifically for the general election. Local

---

[1] Commentators often make the mistake of assuming that the constituency parties, in contrast with the unions, represented the outlook of the individual members. This is not so. Constituency parties were themselves federal bodies, on which union representatives usually predominated. The Labour party had no machinery for ascertaining the distinctive views, if any, of its individual members.

politics sustained it all the time. There were municipal elections every year (in London, every three years), and, apart from these, there were endless local questions in which the local parties were involved. The caucus was not simply a machine for managing parliamentary elections. It had become, with both Conservative and Labour, an integral part of local administration.

The Liberals failed to transform themselves in this way. They had, of course, other weaknesses. They were hard hit by the fact that the nonconformists, their main interest group, had both lost bite generally, and had also lost interest in politics when education ceased to be a matter of sectarian dispute. The Liberals were confused and discredited by the feuds between their leaders which had gone on ever since December 1916. Their central fund was usually short of money. Nevertheless, their greatest handicap was that they were ceasing to make a distinctive contribution in local affairs. Formerly local authorities could strike out on their own, as the Radical Joseph Chamberlain, for instance, gave Birmingham many things not possessed by other cities. Now the local authorities had become agents of national policy and could only determine how this should be administered. Conservatives said, in the interests of the ratepayers; Labour, in the interests of the needy. Liberal councillors, sometimes masquerading as Independents, tended to go with the Conservatives.[1] The amalgamation of public assistance with the local councils by Neville Chamberlain increased the clear division. By 1930 local elections were being conducted openly on a party basis, and the two-party system triumphed in local politics even though there were still three parties at Westminster. Liberal organization in the constituencies languished between general elections and could rarely spring back into effective life. Liberalism became a national cause, increasingly cut off from its local roots.[2]

Lloyd George hoped to overcome this defect by making the Liberal party the party of ideas—a sort of non-socialist I.L.P. There was room for ideas. The two other parties deliberately steered clear of them. The Conservatives were strong in

[1] Except in Manchester, where there was for some time an unavowed Liberal–Labour alliance, thanks largely to Ernest Simon (later Lord Simon of Wythenshawe).

[2] The connexion between party organization and local affairs also worked against the I.L.P., which after 1918 surrendered local politics to the constituency Labour parties except in Glasgow.

resistance. They were stuck for a positive programme. Tariff Reform was the one cause which could stir their enthusiasm, also, however, the one cause which roused opposition even within their own ranks. Baldwin had burnt his fingers once. He refused to do so again, apart from cautious references to imperial preference—a policy in which he himself had little faith. Many Conservatives were impatient with Baldwin's inaction. They could do nothing against him. He was their only figure with a national appeal. Safety First, with a picture of Stanley Baldwin above it, was the full Conservative offer. The Labour party had also proved strong in resistance—in this case, resistance to promptings from the I.L.P. Labour must enter a future government with its hands free. MacDonald added: 'there must be no monkeying'—a blunderbuss levelled against both the I.L.P. and the unions. Instead of an election programme, the Labour party produced an essay on general principle, *Labour and the Nation*, which was written by R. H. Tawney. This was a popular version of Tawney's famous book, *The Acquisitive Society*, impeccably moral in tone and much vaguer than Webb's programme of 1918.[1]

The Liberals had more to offer, at any rate on paper. For years past, Lloyd George had been financing inquiries from his fund. Coal, agriculture, townplanning, and Britain's industrial future were all surveyed by economists, working at Lloyd George's inspiration. Early in 1929 he translated the conclusions into popular terms with the ringing title, *We Can Conquer Unemployment*. On 1 March he affirmed the pledge at a meeting of Liberal candidates. This was a dramatic event: the moment when the new ideas towards which economists were fumbling first broke on to public consciousness. Here, implicitly, was the end of Gladstonian finance and of the classical economics which followed in unbroken line from Adam Smith. Lloyd George's programme repudiated the system of *laissez faire* and balanced budgets, under which Great Britain had once grown great and was now, it appeared, stagnating. Instead there were to be great public works—roads, houses, electricity, telephones, railways—paid for by a deliberate deficit. Idle capital and, more

---

[1] Tawney was a moral educator, not a politician. He was a pioneer of the Workers Educational Association. His only public experience was to serve on the Sankey Commission in 1919. He never secured election to any popular assembly, though he was a parliamentary candidate for Rochdale and (while condemning university constituencies) for the university of London.

important, idle men would be set to work and would generate a prosperity which would ultimately absorb the expenditure involved. This was, in outline, the New Deal as applied later with some success by F. D. Roosevelt in the United States. Great Britain could have been first in the field.

In 1929 the new ideas were too new. Most economists were still unaffected by them. For instance, the accepted textbook of the nineteen-twenties, *Economics for the General Reader* by Henry Clay, contains no reference to them. Even J. M. Keynes, later regarded as the founder of the underlying theories, had not yet worked out his position fully. Though he already appreciated that savings tended to outrun investment (a discovery which Marxists had made long before), he had not hit on the 'multiplier' or snowball, by which putting one man to work not only benefits him but, by increasing his expenditure, puts half a dozen more men to work also. Hence finding work for the unemployed seemed more expensive than, in fact, it was. Neville Chamberlain made great play with this later. He pointed out that it cost £250 a year to find work for one man and only £60 to keep him in idleness, quite forgetting that the balance would be spent on employing others.

Where experts lagged, ordinary men were bewildered. The new ideas underlying Lloyd George's programme were difficult to grasp. It seemed common sense that a reduction in taxes made the taxpayer richer, and paradoxical to argue that individuals benefited more from increased public spending. The lessons of the war were all drawn one way. Nations were supposed to have been ruined by the vast expenditure. No one pointed out that they had also prospered while the war was on and had often benefited afterwards from its capital creations. Again, it was accepted doctrine that British exports lagged because costs of production were too high; and high taxation was blamed for this about as much as high wages. Thus there began in 1929 a cleavage between informed opinion and the assumptions of ordinary men which has lasted almost to the present day. The cleavage existed in many fields. Einstein, like Keynes, was incomprehensible, where Newton, like Adam Smith, had been neat and obvious. The concertgoer could hum the themes of Mozart and Beethoven, not those of Stravinsky. He never learnt to hum the themes of the new economics.

No doubt Lloyd George did not understand the theories

himself. He was interested in action, not in theory. His programme was sprung on the public with little preparation. The
schemes were concocted in secret. Lloyd George worked with
Seebohm Rowntree, the proponent of industrial welfare, and
with economists, such as Keynes and Hubert Henderson. There
was none of the simmering in public debate and newspaper headlines which usually precedes a great shift of opinion. As always,
Lloyd George was a bad party-man, even with a party which
he led and financed. He had little gift for working with colleagues. Some Liberal leaders, the old Squiffites, were, of all
men, the most wedded to the old economic order. Most Liberal
candidates in 1929 had little glimmering of the policy which
they were supposed to be advocating. If the impossible had
happened and the Liberals had won the general election, there
would have been no Liberal government in the ordinary sense.
Lloyd George would again have been dictator as he was during
the war, sustained only by backbenchers; he would have met
each problem with improvised action; and his agents would
have been detached intellectuals and non-party businessmen.

Lloyd George needed a new crisis to break the mould of
political and economic habit. Instead men regarded unemployment as a wasting disease, not as a crisis, and were glad that the
crust of habit had been reformed. The two other parties waved
Lloyd George's proposals aside. Each had a panacea, which it
dared not advocate. The Conservatives were indignant at the
suggestion that capitalism could be saved without tariffs;
Labour was indignant at the suggestion that it could be saved
at all. The arguments had little importance. The decisive thing
was the legacy of distrust which Lloyd George had accumulated
during his years of power after the war. Maybe the general
election of May 1929 ought to have been fought over unemployment and the New Deal. It was not. It was that rare thing, a
general election without a cause.

This was true in a technical sense. The parliament elected in
November 1924 was the first since that elected in 1886 to run
something like its full term.[1] Even in 1929 there was no reason except statutory enactment why it should end.[2] The government

---

[1] Except, of course, for the parliament elected in December 1910 which had its
life anomalously prolonged during the war years.

[2] The duration of parliament had been reduced from seven years to five by
the Parliament Act of 1911.

still had a great majority, despite steady losses at by-elections.[1]
There was no burning question to excite the passions of the
electors. The Conservatives did not threaten Free Trade;
Labour was clearly not a section of the Communist International; unemployment was an evil, but inevitable despite
Lloyd George's pledge. Nor was there a scare or stunt—no
Zinoviev letter; no khaki election or Hang the Kaiser. Though
the same proportion of electors voted as in 1924 (or in 1931),
they voted in an unexcited way. For once, the election turned,
as some modern theorists think all elections should turn, solely
on the question: who should be the next prime minister? Even
more unusual, the claimants were equally matched. It was not
a contest between a giant and apparent pygmies, as it had been
in 1918 with Lloyd George or was to be in 1945 with Churchill.
In 1929 MacDonald and Lloyd George were both great national
figures in their different ways; Baldwin was at any rate no
longer insignificant.

Thus free from the distraction of red herrings or red letters,
the electors voted much as they were to do thirty years later, in
the nineteen-fifties: they split evenly between Conservative and
Labour with the Liberals clearly in the third place. Both Conservatives and Labour polled over eight million votes, the
Conservatives 300,000 more than Labour. The distribution of
seats, however, being based on the census of 1911, was already
antiquated: it did not allow for the steady shift of population
from Scotland and the north of England to the south, and from
the centre of towns, including London, to the suburbs. As the
result, Labour won 288 seats; the Conservatives 260. Thus
Labour, supposedly the party of the people, owed its success to
comparatively rotten boroughs. The Liberals increased their
vote by over two million—from under three million to over five.
This was entirely due to the increased number of their candidates; their percentage of votes in contested seats actually declined (from 30·9 per cent. to 27·7 per cent.). The increased
vote brought to the Liberals only 19 extra seats—59 instead of
40.[2] As an added misfortune for Lloyd George, the successful
Liberals were predominantly men of the Asquithian old guard

[1] Between 1925 and 1929 Labour won 11 seats from the Conservatives and 2
from the Liberals. The Liberals won 5 seats from the Conservatives and 1 from
Labour. The Conservatives won 1 from the Liberals.

[2] These figures changed almost at once to 289 Labour and 58 Liberal, when
Jowitt, elected as a Liberal, became attorney general, and joined the Labour party.

who hated him, such as Runciman and Sir John Simon. The young adventurers failed. Still it was a new sort of parliament. Company directors, at ninety-six, were the lowest within living memory. Trade union officials were a minority among Labour members, for the first time in history. Both Conservatives and Labour were becoming parties of professional politicians, instead of being exclusively interest groups. This had been the Liberal pattern; and the others, by following it, perhaps made a distinctive Liberal party unnecessary.[1]

Labour, though the largest single party, was still in a minority. Baldwin, however, resigned at once. Anything else, he told the king, might seem 'unsporting'. His real reason was probably the old mainspring of his political life: distrust of Lloyd George. He was determined that Lloyd George should not get the credit for turning the Conservatives out—or, still worse, for keeping them in. On 5 June Ramsay MacDonald became prime minister for the second time. With some reluctance, he did not again take the foreign office also.[2] This went to Arthur Henderson after some jockeying with J. H. Thomas, who lightheartedly agreed instead to eclipse Lloyd George by devising schemes of employment. Sidney Webb, combining the posts of Dominions and Colonial secretary, went to the Lords as Lord Passfield. Margaret Bondfield, minister of Labour, was the first woman to enter the cabinet and to be sworn of the privy council. This time no Conservatives were recruited to fill up the list. Otherwise the second Labour government was much like the first— men of humble origin in a majority, not a single Etonian, and the cabinet, in Snowden's words, 'composed overwhelmingly of the Right section of the movement'.[3] Wheatley, who had been the greatest success of the first Labour government, was now ruled out by his loyalty to the I.L.P. and by a financial scandal in which his Glasgow firm had been involved. George Lansbury, first commissioner of works, took his place as spokesman of the Left. He got on surprisingly well with George V. The two men happily exchanged anecdotes about their respective illnesses. Lansbury also left his mark on English life by creating a

---

[1] Saklatvala, the one Communist in the 1924 parliament, was no longer unopposed by the Labour party and was defeated at Battersea. There was no Communist in parliament between 1929 and 1935.

[2] MacDonald told the king that he had offered to go to the foreign office and let someone else (presumably Henderson) become prime minister. Nicolson, *George V*, 435. There is no other evidence for this.   [3] Snowden, *Autobiography*, ii. 767.

somewhat tawdry Lido on the Serpentine—the only thing which keeps the memory of the second Labour government alive.[1]

With Labour again in a minority, there could be no question of a socialist programme, even if the leaders had believed in socialism or had known what it meant. Nevertheless the Labour government started with high hopes. When they took office, Great Britain was still prosperous, with unemployment under 10 per cent. Foreign policy seemed more pressing than economic affairs. Here MacDonald and Henderson improved even on the success of the first Labour government. Thanks to them, international agreement seemed nearer than at any other time between the wars. The impetus of Locarno had lagged in Austen Chamberlain's latter days at the foreign office. Now it was taken up again and carried further. In August 1929 a conference at The Hague endorsed a new arrangement, the Young Plan, for German reparations, which relieved Germany of allied control and thus restored her to equality with her former enemies. Snowden, attending the conference as chancellor of the exchequer, nearly wrecked it by refusing to accept a reduction (of £2 million a year) in Great Britain's share. For this 'the iron chancellor' received the Freedom of the City of London. Within less than three years, however, the money so heroically defended proved to be fairy gold. Henderson restored the conference to good feeling and secured the withdrawal of Allied troops from the Rhineland five years ahead of time.

At the League of Nations Henderson soon became the dominant figure. Stresemann died in October 1929; Briand was exhausted. Henderson took their place as the mainstay of the League. The French had never trusted MacDonald fully. They remembered his opposition to the war and suspected that he favoured the German side. Perhaps, also, his emotional oratory was too like their own. Henderson's record was beyond reproach —a supporter of the war while it was on and of conciliation afterwards. He spoke in straightforward simple terms, showing more sympathy than MacDonald did with the French craving for security. Hence he became the first, perhaps the only, British statesman between the wars who won the confidence of France and Germany. Henderson found the preparatory

---

[1] Apart from this, English cities made little provision for open-air bathing and sunbathing—an odd omission, unnecessarily depreciatory of the English climate.

commission on disarmament, which the League had set up, still dawdling over details. He pushed its work to a conclusion, and a world disarmament conference was summoned for February 1932. Henderson was elected President—a fitting tribute to a statesman of worldwide reputation. By the time the conference met, European affairs had taken a turn for the worse, and Henderson was no longer foreign secretary. But for a brief period high hopes had seemed justified.

MacDonald himself handled relations with the United States. The Conservatives always regarded America with some secret jealousy. They suspected that the Americans were seeking to carry off the British empire, or at any rate to dismember it; they resented the limitations on British naval power which the Washington naval treaty of 1922 had imposed. MacDonald, in contrast, was outstanding in his desire for Anglo-American friendship. He went to America in October 1929, and broke the deadlock on naval disarmament which had followed the failure of the conference at Geneva in 1927. Early in the following year he presided, with his accustomed skill, over a naval conference in London. He imposed a limit of fifty cruisers on a protesting board of admiralty and, armed with this concession, secured agreement between Great Britain, the United States, and Japan. The three Powers limited their cruisers, submarines, and destroyers on the Washington ratio of 5, 5, and 3. In addition, there was a holiday in the building of capital ships for five years. This success was little alloyed at the time by Italy's refusal to accept anything less than parity with France. The London naval treaty, like all such agreements, rested on continuing goodwill between the signatories, and this was lacking after 1931 so far as Japan was concerned. Still, in a longer perspective, the initiation of cordial relations with the United States counted for more than the dangers which were to follow from Japan.

Conciliation in international affairs reached its highest point under the second Labour government. Most English people agreed with MacDonald that nations had the same interests if they did but know it and that all conflicts could be dispelled by 'the strenuous action of good-will'. In 1909 the Liberals lost popular support by seeking a naval agreement with Germany instead of building more dreadnoughts; in 1927 the Conservatives lost popularity by proposing to build more cruisers instead of concluding a naval agreement with the United States.

The first World war was now believed to have started by mistake. As Lloyd George said: 'We all blundered into war.' The English historians who studied prewar diplomacy, with G. P. Gooch at their head, reinforced this belief. The course of the war, and its conclusion, pointed the same way. Men lamented that there had not been a negotiated peace of compromise in 1917. War, they said, settled nothing, and they were confident that everyone agreed with them. Ignorance was the only danger, and this ignorance could be dispelled by steadfast, impartial study. The Royal Institute of International Affairs was set up for this purpose shortly after the war and produced studies on many international problems—striking example of a view commonly held in the twentieth century that, if men accumulate enough information, they will inevitably find answers. Similarly on a larger scale, the League of Nations existed in order to damp down international conflicts in a warm current of discussion and investigation. Only disarmament was needed to round off the picture, and the Labour government had done their best to provide it.

There was one awkward flaw in this happy prospect. The Marxists who ruled Soviet Russia refused to acknowledge any community of interest with the capitalist world. Instead they preached international revolution, with tiresome results in Asia. They even supposed that one day the success of their socialist system would expose the defects of the economic order, or lack of it, elsewhere. Hence they suspected that the capitalist powers, led by Great Britain, were planning a new war of intervention. Here the Communists flattered themselves. The British government were not frightened of Soviet Russia; they were merely irritated and puzzled that she would not fit into their optimistic plans. They were glad no doubt to be spared the embarrassment of a Soviet representative at the League of Nations. On the other hand, the Labour government resumed diplomatic relations with Soviet Russia in October 1929, this time without fuss and for good.[1] Sokolnikov came to London as ambassador, despite George V's reluctance to receive the representative of his cousin's murderers. No more was said about a British loan to Soviet Russia and practically nothing about Russia's prerevolutionary debts. There was still suspicion and coldness on

[1] The recognition, accorded in 1924, was not withdrawn when diplomatic relations were broken off in 1927.

both sides. But at any rate a beginning had been made towards a restoration of normal relations.

The same spirit of conciliation was displayed in imperial affairs. Here, too, goodwill was expected to triumph. In 1931 the Statute of Westminster put the finishing touches to the process by which an empire, based on central authority, was transformed into a Commonwealth of independent states, cooperating in freedom. Many Englishmen, forgetting the troubles, presented Ireland as a further exercise in the virtues of conciliation. Now Egypt and India were supposed to be travelling the same road. Admittedly there were disputes—riots and imprisonments; they were disputes over timing only. The British authorities and those over whom they ruled had the same ultimate goal. This goal would be attained if the two sides met often enough at a round table. In the end, national claims would be satisfied. Yet no essential British interest would be lost. Labour practised this policy resolutely in regard to India. On 31 October 1929 Lord Irwin, the viceroy, made a public promise of Dominion status, without waiting for the report of the Simon commission.

The effect was the reverse of what had been intended. The Indian Congress answered in December with a declaration of independence. Gandhi started a new campaign of civil disobedience. He marched across India to the sea shore, where he defied the government salt monopoly by extracting, and tasting, some crystals of untaxed salt. He was imprisoned, and 50,000 Indians were soon sent to join him. The Labour government found themselves practising coercion, much as the Liberals had once done in Ireland. Nevertheless they persisted in conciliation also. In June 1930 the Simon commission produced its report. It recommended responsible government in the provinces, and negotiations between the British government, the Indian government, and the native princes on the future of the central power. Here was another opening for MacDonald's diplomatic gifts. A Round Table conference was held at London in November 1930. Congress refused to attend. Representatives of the princes attended and, what was more, agreed to enter a future Indian federation. This was tempting bait for Congress. Gandhi was released from prison and had a series of meetings with Lord Irwin. This was a strange conjugation and prelude to many other such meetings: the aristocratic ruler of a declining empire wooing the nationalist rebel. After prolonged and characteristically intricate discussion, Gandhi agreed to attend a second session of the Round Table. When the Round Table met again, Labour, as with the disarmament conference, was out of office. But in this case Labour's work was continued, however tardily, and ultimately bore fruit in Indian independence.

Negotiations with Egypt proved less rewarding. Henderson enforced the resignation of Lord Lloyd, the imperialist high commissioner, and, when attacked for this by the Conservatives, scored a hit in the house of commons by showing that Lloyd had already been at odds with Austen Chamberlain. Henderson then tried to secure a treaty with Egypt: Great Britain would give up her control of Egypt's internal affairs and would withdraw her troops to the canal zone. The Egyptians also demanded the restoration of their joint control over the Sudan, which had been forfeited in 1924, after the murder of Sir Lee Stack, the governor general of the Sudan, by an Egyptian nationalist. The British, however, were planning to turn the Sudan into a loyal dependency of their own. Negotiations therefore broke down. The British remained in Egypt, not much hampered by occasional demonstrations of nationalist discontent. They were still confident that their control over the Suez canal and Egypt's independence could be reconciled, and waited for time to bring wisdom.

Palestine raised a more difficult problem. The Balfour declaration committed the British to fostering a national home there for the Jews. At the same time they had to rule without offending the Arabs, who made up the large majority of the population. Jews came to Palestine, equipped with Zionist money. They bought land from the Arabs and made no secret of their intention to turn the national home into a Jewish national state. The Arabs resisted and rioted. Passfield, the colonial secretary, applied his dispassionate Fabian mind to the question. He reached the rational, though irrelevant, conclusion that it was impossible for more Jews to enter Palestine without displacing Arabs. In October 1930 a White Paper therefore announced that Jewish immigration must virtually cease. The Zionists raised an uproar. Poor Passfield found himself pilloried as the worst enemy of the Jewish people since Haman. MacDonald quietened the storm for the time being with soft words. The conflict between Jews and Arabs was postponed until the massive flood of Jews from central Europe, provoked by National

Socialist persecution, brought it to unescapable explosion. All
the same, Passfield had made an awkward discovery. He had
stumbled unwittingly on a question where the underlying philosophy of British Labour, indeed of nearly all Englishmen, did not
work. In Palestine, there was irreconcilable conflict between
Arabs and Jews, not a community of interests which the two
peoples merely failed to recognize by mistake.

In 1930 Palestine seemed a small affair, at worst an irritating
exception to an otherwise universal rule. Labour's foreign and
imperial politics were matters of general satisfaction. Conservatives applauded the three-power naval treaty of 1930 and
Henderson's work at the League almost as much as they did
Snowden's stand at The Hague. Baldwin was as deeply involved as MacDonald in the policy of leading India to Dominion
status. Disarmament was also an agreed question. In February
1931 a three-party committee of the Committee of Imperial
Defence discussed the forthcoming disarmament conference and
laid down the policy which the National government in fact
followed: 'Any further reduction of British armaments could
only be undertaken as part of an international agreement containing comparable reductions by other Powers, and after taking
into account the particular obligations and dangers of each
country.' This definition, despite the reserve in its second part,
accepted the principle that armaments should be determined
by agreement and not solely by British national needs—a
principle which before 1914 would have been repudiated by
nearly everyone.

A few Labour men objected that conciliation did not go
fast enough. On the Conservative side, Churchill stood almost
alone in attacking the Baldwin–MacDonald outlook. As usual,
Churchill wanted to take an aggressive line and to pursue the
Labour government with unrelenting opposition. He presented
himself in the new guise of imperial champion. He attacked disarmament. He criticized even the Statute of Westminster—on
the characteristic ground that the historic word Empire was to
be replaced by the newfangled word Commonwealth (which
had in reality as long a history). Most of all Churchill attacked
the conciliation of Indian nationalism. He took up the cause of
the Indian princes and evoked 'the warrior races'. In January
1931 he resigned from the Conservative shadow cabinet on this
issue, and thus began the years of isolation which ended only

with the second World war. Not only was his opposition ineffective, it established his reputation as a romantic sabre-rattler and
discredited him in advance against the time when he took up
worthier causes. Baldwin, we may be sure, was not sorry to
eliminate one whom he had regarded as a dangerous rival,
though no doubt his support for conciliation was also genuine
in itself.

In home affairs, there was the same tendency towards conciliation and agreement, though it was less avowed. Labour
men were agreed that socialism could be achieved by the democratic methods of a parliamentary majority and parliamentary
legislation. More than this, a belief came gradually into being
that in home, as in international, affairs there was no irreconcilable conflict. There was a further belief, still less consciously
formed, that those in a particular industry knew best how to run
it. Function, not property, as the basis of society was the central
point of Tawney's powerful teaching, and this doctrine, though
intended to benefit the workers, justified the director of industry also. Just as most Labour men rejected the Marxist view
that capitalist imperialism caused war, and blamed instead
international anarchy, so they moved gradually away from the
socialist indictment of decaying capitalism at home and blamed
only economic anarchy. All would be well, or at any rate better,
if the existing order were regulated—mainly by the producers
themselves.

Regulated capitalism had operated, without any clear design,
during the first World war. It had been dismantled afterwards.
The first peacetime model was the Central Electricity Board—
a public corporation set up in 1926 to organize the wholesale
distribution of electricity.[1] This was claimed to offer the advantages of socialism without the evils either of bureaucracy or
of workers' control. The Labour government carried the process further, though leaving more power to the existing owners.
The Coal Mines Act of 1930 was their most important domestic
achievement and a landmark in British history. Labour's immediate concern was to satisfy the miners by revoking the 8-hour
day which had been enacted in 1926. With characteristic compromise, the new act, instead of restoring the 7-hour day, settled
for $7\frac{1}{2}$ hours. The mine-owners were cajoled by being empowered

---

[1] The British Broadcasting Corporation also provided a public service, secured
against democratic control.

to fix minimum prices and quotas of production. More remotely, a reorganization commission was to devise schemes for closing the less efficient pits and amalgamating the others. The commission had no practical effect. On the contrary, the act protected the inefficient. It operated restriction and stable prices at the expense of the consumer. Here was the pattern for British capitalism in the thirties.

The Agricultural Marketing Act of 1931, devised by Christopher Addison, Lloyd George's former adherent, pointed the same way. This authorized boards of producers to fix prices and market their products. Their resolutions could be imposed by legal process on any dissenting minority. Herbert Morrison, the minister of transport,[1] worked out a similar public corporation for London transport. Its practical object was to make the buses, which ran at a profit, pay for the underground railways, which did not. The bill was not through parliament when the Labour government fell. It was enacted by the National government, with some slight changes, in 1933. The transport unions failed to secure any representation on the London Passenger Transport Board.[2] Nor did Labour raise any objection to the strange chance by which the chairman and manager of the private underground railways emerged, with increased powers, as the chairman and manager of the new Board.

Other Labour measures renewed the advances made in 1924. Arthur Greenwood, the minister of health,[3] rescued Wheatley's subsidies, which Neville Chamberlain had intended to terminate. Subsidized housebuilding continued until 1933. Greenwood struck a new note by instituting slum clearance in his Housing Act of 1930. Though this act was suspended by the National government, it began to operate in 1934. Then, thanks to Arthur Greenwood, more slums were cleared in the five years before the second World war than in the preceding fifty years. Trevelyan, at the board of education, attempted to improve on

---

[1] Herbert Morrison (1888–1965), son of a policeman: minister of transport, 1929–31 (in cabinet, 1931); minister of supply, 1940; secretary for home office and home security, 1940–5 (in war cabinet, 1942–5); lord president, 1945–51; foreign secretary, 1951; life peer, 1959.

[2] The members of the Board were appointed by five 'trustees': the chairman of the L.C.C., the heads of the London banks, the chartered accountants, and the Law Society, and a representative of the London Traffic Advisory Committee.

[3] Arthur Greenwood (1880–1954): minister of health, 1929–31; minister without portfolio (in war cabinet), 1940–2; lord privy seal, 1945–7; paymaster general, 1946–7; minister without portfolio, 1947; deputy leader of Labour party, 1935–45.

his work of 1924 by raising the school-leaving age to 15. His bill ran into difficulties from Roman Catholics on the Labour back-benches—a curious twist which indicated that, since Roman catholicism was mainly a lower-class religion, Labour had acquired its own sectarian lobby.[1] The education bill was re-jected by the Lords in March 1931, and Trevelyan resigned, as much out of general disagreement with the feebleness of the government as from disappointment at the loss of his bill.

The education bill was not the only one lost. An attempt to undo the trades disputes act of 1927 broke on Liberal resistance —evidence how some Liberals, at any rate, had moved to the right since 1913 when their own government brought in the act which Labour was now trying to restore. Electoral reform was another casualty. The Liberals wanted proportional representa-tion. Labour would offer only the alternative vote—a device for distributing the Liberal vote between the two other parties, and the Liberals reluctantly acquiesced. A bill struggled through the house of commons, with subsidiary wrangling over plural voting and the university constituencies, both of which Labour wished to abolish on the democratic principle of one adult, one vote. The Lords weakened it still further. In July 1931 the Labour government dreamt of carrying the bill by the machinery of the Parliament Act, thus envisaging another two years of minority government with Liberal support. Instead, the government fell a month later, and the bill perished with it. The Conservatives continued to benefit from plural voting and the university constituencies; Labour almost as much from the antiquated distribution of seats. The Liberals lost their last chance of reforming the electoral system in their favour. Proportional representation and the alternative vote alike vanished for ever.

These disputes were accompanied, and often overshadowed, by wrangles within the parties. All sprang from the same cause. The three parties, like the legendary Ford car, were running on their reputations. They divided on party lines when faced with traditional questions such as electoral reform. They were adrift in regard to the present. Conservatives endorsed Labour's foreign and imperial policy. Labour promoted capitalist monopolies. The Liberals—or at any rate Lloyd George—wanted more action, and even more socialism, than the Labour

---

[1] MacDonald's efforts to conciliate his Roman Catholic supporters on this occa-sion provoked Churchill's famous tribute to him as 'the boneless wonder'.

government would provide. Backbenchers stirred restlessly against the leaders who failed to give a clear lead. Liberalism, in a phrase attributed to Attlee,[1] was temporarily reunited in 1929 by a common distrust of their leader. Baldwin remembered 1931 as 'the year when my party tried to get rid of me'.[2] MacDonald had even more reason to remember 1931. It was the year when his party actually got rid of him—flung him, indeed, out of the party as well as out of the leadership. All three movements of discontent were expressed in personal terms. Lloyd George was unprincipled and motivated only by a love of power; Baldwin was lazy; MacDonald preferred high society, and in particular the society of Lady Londonderry, to that of his proletarian followers. Under the surface, all three parties were trying to discover reasons for their own existence.

Lloyd George was in the most difficult position: there was indeed little reason why the Liberal party should exist under his leadership. Free Trade was the one issue which gave the Liberals an uneasy semblance of unity. Yet it was irrelevant to the plans for economic expansion which Lloyd George advocated, even if it did not contradict them. The parliamentary situation, moreover, presented Lloyd George with an almost insoluble tactical problem. In previous periods of minority government, say between 1886 and 1895, the third party had been clear, despite their irritations, which government they wished to keep in. The Liberal Unionists sustained the Conservatives; the Irish Nationalists sustained the Liberals. Lloyd George wished to discredit the Labour government without discrediting himself. Instead, Baldwin forced him to support the government and so saddled him with responsibility for Labour's failures. Time and again, the Liberals split three ways—some voting with the government, some against, the rest abstaining. One group under Sir John Simon moved towards cooperation with the Conservatives; Lloyd George nibbled at joining the government; a pure remnant under Sir Herbert Samuel were left high and dry. Lloyd George was for ever offering to deliver the Liberal vote, if his advice were taken. He could not do so, and those with whom he bargained knew it.

Baldwin should have been pleased. He had consolidated his victory over the 'clever men' whom he had first defeated in

[1] Tom Clark, *My Lloyd George Diary*, 81. The grammar is presumably Attlee's.
[2] Young, *Baldwin*, 162.

1922. Churchill was isolated within the Conservative party; Lloyd George in difficulties at the head of the Liberals. But Baldwin had his own troubles. Beaverbrook, the king-maker, returned to his old trade; lacking a new Bonar Law, he played this time for his own hand. His weapon, too, was new: for the first and last time, a great attempt was made to change party leadership and party policy mainly by a battery in the columns of the popular press. Beaverbrook did not act simply from ambition. He had a genuine belief in a cause, Empire Free Trade. This programme was a fantasy and Beaverbrook, as an inspired journalist called him, was 'a pedlar of dreams':[1] the dominions were unlikely to lower their tariffs on British goods, though they might give a fictitious preference by increasing their tariffs still further against the foreigner. Still, the cause had a strong appeal for many Conservatives who wanted something more exciting than Baldwin's Safety First.

In July 1929, with the election hardly over, Beaverbrook launched his crusade for Empire Free Trade. He formed an alliance with another newspaper proprietor, Rothermere. The two men founded the United Empire party and threatened to run candidates against the official Conservatives. The alliance with Rothermere brought in more money and the backing of the *Daily Mail*. Otherwise, it was a source of weakness. Beaverbrook had serious pretensions to be a politician. Rothermere was a duller, heavier man, who aroused even more distrust than his dead brother Northcliffe.[2] Baldwin exploited this distrust to the full. At first he made tactical concessions. He agreed to a referendum on food taxes. He sacrificed his adherent, Davidson, as chairman of the party organization, and put in Neville Chamberlain. This was another brilliant stroke. Chamberlain was Baldwin's most dangerous rival—impeccably Protectionist, with a unique reputation for efficiency, and enjoying Beaverbrook's favour. He had also vulnerable points which Baldwin appreciated: a strong sense of loyalty, perhaps to atone for his father's strokes in the opposite direction, and a hatred of Churchill and Lloyd George, which kept him shackled to Baldwin.

---

[1] Howard Spring, the journalist, was at once appointed literary critic on the *Evening Standard*.

[2] Rothermere's other, more comical, excursion into politics was to take up the revisionist claims of Hungary. His son was allegedly offered the vacant Hungarian throne as reward. Rothermere contented himself with accepting the dedication of a fountain in Budapest. The name of the fountain has since been changed.

The storm within the Conservative party continued to rage, with occasional abatements, throughout 1930. In October an Empire Free Trade candidate defeated the official Conservative in a by-election at South Paddington. The party agents reported that the party despaired of winning a general election under Baldwin's leadership. On 1 March 1931 Chamberlain gave the message to Baldwin. He agreed to resign at once, and Chamberlain resigned the chairmanship of the party organization in expectation of an early call to the succession. Baldwin then decided to stay. On 17 March he repeated a manœuvre which Lloyd George had once used against Northcliffe: he appealed to the general prejudice against the press lords. Using a phrase supplied to him by his cousin Rudyard Kipling (curiously enough a friend of Beaverbrook's), he denounced Beaverbrook and Rothermere as wanting power without responsibility—'the prerogative of the harlot throughout the ages'. A few days later, the official candidate, Duff Cooper, won in a by-election at St. George's, Westminster.[1] Thus Baldwin triumphed. His leadership was never challenged again. Empire Free Trade became a dead cause. It was never much of a cause in the first place. Perhaps it was ruined by the support of the press lords. The popular newspapers supplied news and, more often, entertainment; they did not direct opinion. Parliament, not the press, remained, however inadequately, the forum of the nation. Chamberlain felt rightly that he had been tricked. There was nothing he could do. Though he was now Baldwin's predestined successor, he had to resign himself to waiting longer than he had expected.

The Labour government benefited from these Liberal and Conservative dissensions. Lloyd George did not want to put Labour out. Baldwin was in no position to come in. Labour's dissensions were, in comparison, small. The I.L.P. was a shrunken remnant, with little weight in party counsels. Ernest Bevin tried to establish the principle that the Labour government were merely the political agents of the T.U.C. MacDonald beat him down. Whatever critics might say later with the wisdom of hindsight, MacDonald retained an irresistible sway over the bulk of the party and over working-class audiences. He had only to draw out the stops of his rich eloquence for opposition

[1] Baldwin originally intended to fight the by-election himself, perhaps not very seriously.

to be silenced. Labour's difficulties came from events, not from internal quarrels. When Labour took office, the country was at a high tide of prosperity, even though over a million workers were still unemployed. J. H. Thomas set out to produce schemes for reducing unemployment, with the assistance of Lansbury and two junior ministers, Oswald Mosley and Tom Johnston. Few schemes were produced. Proposals to spend public money broke on the resistance of Snowden, chancellor of the exchequer, most orthodox of financiers. At best, the Labour government found work for some 60,000 men.

These trivial efforts were submerged by the great economic Depression which broke over the world in October 1929. The causes of this lay outside Great Britain, principally in the general reliance on American loans and American prosperity. On 24 October 1929 the speculative Bubble burst in the United States, and American money ceased to flow. The primary producers, already impoverished, were impoverished still further. They ceased to buy British goods, ceased to need the services of British ships. The British exporting industries, already in difficulties, saw their remaining markets disappear. Unemployment rose drastically, though less violently than in Germany or in the United States. There were over 2 million unemployed in July 1930, and $2\frac{1}{2}$ million in December. Three million were expected, incorrectly, for 1931.

The Depression was in Great Britain an odd lopsided affair. Though the price of imports tumbled catastrophically, the price of exports (mostly manufactured goods) did not. Within little more than a single year, 1930, the terms of trade turned 20 per cent. in Great Britain's favour. She was able to import as much as before at a greatly reduced cost. While the volume of exports was almost halved between 1929 and 1931 (from 141 to 88), the volume of imports remained exactly stable at 99 (1938 = 100). Yet the increased cost to Great Britain's international payments was only £25 million.[1] Wages remained stable. Indeed, with the fall of prices, real wages rose. Those in work (and there were always more of them than in 1924) were better off than they had ever been. Hence the problem of unemployment, though formidable as statistics and terrible of course for those who endured it, remained strangely remote from

[1] The value of British exports fell from £838 million in 1929 to £453 million in 1931. The value of imports fell from £1,200 million to £861 million.

the mass of the community, nor was it irrelevant that the areas of mass unemployment lay far from London, the political centre.

Labour was quick to blame the capitalist system. MacDonald, as usual, put it best: '*We* are not on trial; it is the system under which we live. . . . It has broken down everywhere, as it was bound to break down.' Few Labour men, however, knew what moral to draw. Passfield, the great Fabian, was at a loss. Ernest Bevin proposed currency devaluation; Lansbury, retirement pensions at 60 to help make the work go round. Only Oswald Mosley, a rich and relatively recent recruit to Labour, rose to the height of the challenge. His proposals were more creative than those of Lloyd George and offered a blueprint for most of the constructive advances in economic policy to the present day. It is impossible to say where Mosley got his ideas from. Perhaps he devised them himself. If so, they were an astonishing achievement, evidence of a superlative talent which was later to be wasted.

Mosley wanted planned foreign trade; public direction of industry; and a systematic use of credit to promote expansion. These ideas were beyond the grasp of J. H. Thomas. They were an outrage to Snowden and to the Free Trade sentiment which still lingered in the Labour movement; an outrage, almost as much, to orthodox socialists. In May 1930 the cabinet rejected them. Mosley resigned. Thomas, too, relinquished his task of combating unemployment and became Dominions Secretary (the first not to combine this with the colonial office). Mac-Donald himself took over responsibility for unemployment, though he did not discharge it. Mosley carried the fight to the parliamentary party. His speech there stirred general admiration. Nevertheless loyalty to MacDonald and distrust for the wealthy outsider were too strong. Mosley's proposals were rejected by 202 votes to 29. In the autumn of 1930 Mosley appealed to the party conference. MacDonald defeated him again. Mosley still believed that he could carry the party with him. In December he published a manifesto, which was backed by A. J. Cook and seventeen Labour M.P.s. In February 1931, losing patience, he founded the New Party. Only four M.P.s, one of them his wife, followed him. This was the greatest personal miscalculation since the fall of Lord Randolph Churchill. Mosley and his supporters were expelled from the Labour party. Even the most sympathetic Labour men would not forfeit their party backing. Mosley was ruined politically. His ideas were ruined with him. Labour drifted on without a policy.

The rejection by Labour of Mosley's programme was a decisive, though negative, event in British history: the moment when the British people resolved unwittingly to stand on the ancient ways. The very forces which made Great Britain peaceful and stable prevented her from becoming the country of the New Deal. Even if Labour had listened more receptively to Mosley, the obstacles would have been great. His ideas would have had to be applied by civil servants and industrialists who had no faith in them. British people needed years of economic debate and the impact of a second great war before they gave up the ideal of returning to the days of Queen Victoria. Those in authority had pride in the past; they had little belief that Great Britain could be even greater in the future. Neither Lloyd George nor Mosley could stir the enthusiasm for new ways which F. D. Roosevelt was to arouse a little later in the United States. The old outlook was too entrenched, and even the crisis, when it came, was not fundamental enough to shake men from their moorings.

The crisis did not come directly over unemployment. Difficulties over the budget prepared the way for it. Snowden inherited from Churchill a weak position—a budget not genuinely balanced even at a time of prosperity. He attempted to apply more orthodox principles.[1] Snowden's budget of 1930 increased income tax (to 4s. 6d. in the pound) and surtax. Snowden angered the Conservatives by equivocating over the safeguarding duties. He did not much mollify his own supporters by reviving the old Radical proposals for a tax on land values.[2] By 1931 the situation was worse. The yield from taxes had gone down; expenditure, particularly on unemployment, had gone up. Snowden believed fanatically that a balanced budget was the greatest contribution which a government could make to overcoming the Depression, and did not hesitate at the resistance this would provoke in his own party—indeed, he relished the prospect of being again an unpopular and heroic figure.

In February 1931 Snowden accepted a Liberal proposal for

[1] Even to the extent of restoring to its traditional position the furniture in the chancellor's room which Churchill had rearranged.

[2] No money was ever raised by this tax. Snowden had first to create the machinery for valuing the land. The National government suspended this valuation and, when Snowden resigned, abolished it.

an economy committee on Geddes lines. Its chairman, Sir George May, had been until recently secretary of the Prudential Insurance company. Four of its members were leading capitalists. Two were trade unionists. Snowden calculated that a fearsome report from this committee would terrify Labour into accepting economy, and the Conservatives into accepting increased taxation. Meanwhile he produced a stop-gap budget in April, intending to produce a second, more severe budget in the autumn. Snowden expected trouble and began to talk of 'national unity', meaning that the parties should unite to push through harsh measures.

Thus a crisis was more or less fixed for the autumn. It came sooner. In the summer of 1931 two committees reported. One on Finance and Industry had been set up by the treasury under Lord Macmillan in 1929. Keynes and Bevin were among its members. Their questions exposed the helplessness of orthodox financiers. In particular, Montagu Norman regarded unemployment with the fatalistic resignation which Jellicoe had shown towards the German submarines in April 1917. 'We have done nothing. There is nothing we can do.' The Macmillan report was to count later in preparing the way for a managed currency. At the time, it had a different effect. In discussing the international situation, it first drew general attention to Great Britain's balance of payments with the rest of the world. Awareness of this was new. Men vaguely assumed that Great Britain lived by trade, sending out manufactured goods which paid for the food and raw materials which came in, though in fact this trading account had never shown a credit balance since 1822. 'Invisible' items—banking, shipping, and the interest on foreign investments—had always put the balance right, except in 1847, 1918, and 1926. These were the very things worst hit by the Depression,[1] and the Macmillan report drew attention to the decline. Moreover, estimates of the balance of payments were being published for the first time and men treated these 'haphazard guesses' with exaggerated respect.[2] They were alarmed

---

[1] The receipts from shipping were £50 million less in 1931 than in 1929, and the return from foreign investment £70 million less.

[2] *The Banker* (Mar. 1948) described these estimates as 'little more than haphazard guessing, unworthy of the country and of the technical accomplishments of the men responsible for the task'. In the nineteen-sixties the treasury introduced a 'balancing item' (i.e. an allowance for its own errors) which might be as much as £100 million in a single year.

at the prospect that Great Britain was not paying her way in the world and easily confused the alleged deficit in the international balance with the budget deficit, though of course the two had nothing in common.

The alarm over the budget was therefore reinforced. It was made still more acute by the report of the May committee, a report compounded of prejudice, ignorance, and panic. Keynes called it 'the most foolish document I ever had the misfortune to read',[1] and an economic historian has said of it recently: 'The report presented an overdrawn picture of the existing financial position; its diagnosis of the causes underlying it was inaccurate; and many of its proposals (including the biggest of them) were not only harsh but were likely to make the economic situation worse, not better.'[2] The May report treated the sinking fund of £50 million a year (that is, the repayment of debt) as an untouchable charge on revenue; insisted that all unemployment relief must be paid for out of income; and thus arrived at an immediate deficit of £120 million, or £170 million in a full year. The five rich men on the committee recommended, not surprisingly, that only £24 million of this deficit should be met by increased taxation and £96 million by economies, two thirds at the expense of the unemployed whose relief should be cut 20 per cent. This outdid even the Geddes committee which had proposed economies only of £86 million. The two Labour men dissented from these conclusions and timidly advocated more government spending. Their dissent, again not surprisingly, was ignored. Snowden and the treasury had their ammunition for a stern budget.

The May report was published on 31 July, the day after parliament rose. The cabinet set up an economy committee of five to consider it.[3] There seemed no urgency before parliament resumed in the autumn. The ministers went on holiday. The first meeting of the economy committee was fixed for 25 August. On 11 August MacDonald was abruptly recalled to London. The assembled bankers told him that there was a run on the pound; 'we were on the edge of the precipice'. Foreigners were selling their sterling at a great rate. Technically, this had nothing to

[1] Dalton, *Call Back Yesterday*, 290.
[2] Ashworth, *Economic History*, 399.
[3] The committee was composed of MacDonald, Snowden, Henderson, Thomas, and Graham.

do with either the budget deficit or the deficit in the balance
of payments, still less with the general problem of unemployment. It sprang solely from the previous activities of London
bankers. Ever since the end of the war the City had been trying
to restore its old position as the centre of international finance
by accepting short-term deposits of foreign money. Some of this
was genuine trading money; much was 'hot' or 'funk' money,
moving at the first rumour from one capital to another. The
City also strove to restore the economic life of central Europe
by generous lending, usually on long term. No doubt this was
done from the highest motives, but it was also an inducement
that money could be borrowed, mainly from French depositors,
at 2 per cent. and lent to Germans at 8 or 10 per cent.

In 1931, when there was political tension between France and
Germany, many Frenchmen objected that their money was
being used to help Germany and withdrew it from London. At
the same time, there was a financial collapse in central Europe.
In May an Austrian bank could not meet its obligations. German
banks attempted to rescue it and were pulled down in their turn.
They repudiated their international liabilities by a moratorium.
The London bankers were then caught. They admitted to owing
foreign depositors £250 million; they probably owed £600 or
£700 million.[1] Much of their own money was frozen in Germany.[2] The rest could be called home only by transferring the
crisis elsewhere. The London bankers resolved to brave the
storm. The bank of England, itself directed by leading bankers,
allowed them to draw on the gold reserve and, as this ran down,
sought loans from the bankers of France and the United States.
They insisted that international confidence in the pound must
be restored by some dramatic act. That act had to be a balanced
budget.

This demand was irrelevant to the situation. Most men,
particularly the bankers, were misled by the previous wave of
financial upset after the war, when various European countries
—Germany, Austria, Hungary, France—had experienced inflation. In these countries, the governments had not balanced
their budgets and had paid their way by printing paper money.

[1] D. Williams (*Economic History Review*, xv) estimates London's short-term foreign
liabilities as £760 million in June 1930 and £411 million (i.e. after the run) in
Dec. 1931.
[2] At the outbreak of war in 1939, £94 million of British money was still locked
in Germany.

Their currencies had depreciated, in some cases catastrophically, and stability was restored only when their budgets had been balanced. In Great Britain prices were falling, not rocketing sky-high. The currency was backed by gold at the bank of England. The government deficit was small and, in any case, was being met by genuine borrowing, which removed money from the individual to the treasury just as effectively as taxation; often, indeed, the government were meeting deficits, particularly on the unemployment fund, by using money from other departments, such as the post office, which had credit balances. None of this was considered. Men were obsessed with the thought of the time, not long ago, when the German mark had stood at nineteen million to the pound. They were convinced that the same fate would overtake the pound, if the bank of England suspended the gold standard, though this classical remedy had in fact ended the domestic panics of 1847 and 1866. Montagu Norman, governor of the bank of England, reflected the general opinion when he insisted that ration books should be printed in case the currency collapsed and the country had to revert to barter.

A few people—Keynes, Bevin, and some Labour ministers—saw through the alarm about the unbalanced budget. They transferred the alarm to the supposed deficit in Great Britain's international balance of payments and proposed to remedy it by some restriction of imports such as a 10 per cent. revenue tariff—the word revenue being thrown in, like safeguarding before it, to conceal the fact that the tariff would be a tariff. This remedy, too, was irrelevant. The run on the pound was caused by movements of capital, not by British indebtedness, in any case trivial, for goods received. The run could have been stopped by the sort of measures which were being applied in Germany—control of the international exchanges and the blocking of foreign funds. Such measures were inconceivable in England: they would have meant the end of London as the world's financial centre, or so men thought. Hence the restoration of confidence was the only alternative, and the bankers, English and foreign, had to dictate terms whether they wanted to or not. The London bankers told MacDonald: 'The cause of the trouble was not financial, but political, and lay in the complete want of confidence in H.M.G. existing among foreigners.'[1]

[1] Feiling, *Neville Chamberlain*, 191.

Not only must the budget be balanced. The bankers, and most other people, believed that it must be balanced mainly by reducing government expenditure—'waste' as it was usually called, not by increasing taxation. They believed also that the gravest 'waste', crying out for reduction, was on unemployment relief, though the bankers, more generous than the May committee, were prepared to have their confidence restored by a 10 per cent. cut instead of 20 per cent. Behind this financial opinion, there was an unconscious moral judgement: the unemployed, living on the dole, were felt to be somehow unemployed through their own fault. Some businessmen went further. Cutting unemployment relief would not only reduce government expenditure. It would also break 'the rigidities' and open the way for a general reduction of wages. Faced with a crisis, the responsible authorities fled back to antiquated prejudices and practices which they had been unwittingly abandoning in easier times. Renewed class war seemed to them the only way out.

The Labour ministers returned to face the crisis. None dared to suggest that the gold standard be suspended or the budget left unbalanced. Some of them kicked against balancing it at the expense of the unemployed. The 10 per cent. revenue tariff was aired as an alternative. Snowden killed the proposal by threatening to resign. In any case, it would not have satisfied the bankers, at home or abroad. The 10 per cent. cut in unemployment benefit seemed inevitable if the pound were to be saved— and the Labour government agreed that it must be. The cabinet wrangled in vain from 20 to 24 August. Snowden was determined to enforce the cuts whatever his colleagues felt. MacDonald had no clear economic views. He supported the revenue tariff as well as the cuts. His aim was to lead the cabinet, or most of it, to an agreed programme, and then to carry this programme with the approval of the other parties. It looked at first as though he would get his way, as he had often done before. Resistance gradually hardened, particularly after 20 August, when the general council of the T.U.C., speaking through Bevin, firmly rejected the cuts in benefit and indeed the whole economy approach. Late on the evening of 23 August the cabinet finally failed to agree. Nine were determined to resign rather than accept the unemployment cuts. The other eleven were presumably ready to go along with MacDonald.

Six of these had a middle-class or upper-class background; of the minority only one. Perhaps it was no accident that he had started his career under Lloyd George.[1]

Clearly the government could not go on. Nine ministers were too many to lose. Besides they were formidable in quality. Clynes was deputy leader. Henderson carried almost as much weight in the party as MacDonald, and more with the unions. Yet even the minority assumed that the unemployment benefits would have to be cut, though not by them. They expected that the government would resign and a Liberal–Conservative coalition take its place. MacDonald seems originally to have shared this belief. The alternative of a National government under his leadership emerged without forethought. It was reinforced by the accident that Lloyd George, the only other man who could be cast as national saviour, was temporarily knocked out by a severe operation. MacDonald repeatedly saw the two opposition leaders, Baldwin and Herbert Samuel, who was taking Lloyd George's place: at first to secure their support for Labour's economies; then to warn them that they might have to take over; finally, to discuss what should happen when the Labour government broke up. Samuel was the first to suggest a National government led by MacDonald—no doubt in the hope that this would enable the Liberals to avoid becoming the prisoners of the Conservatives, as they had been under Lloyd George. Baldwin seconded the idea—again no doubt to spread the load of unpopularity which the economies were expected to provoke. This advice was welcome to the king. Always loyal to his prime minister of the moment, he was anxious to keep MacDonald whom he rated highly. Besides, coalition seemed to him the obvious step at a time which he, like others, regarded as one of national crisis.

This was, almost certainly, the determining factor for MacDonald also. Maybe he was aloof from his followers and impatient with their hesitations; maybe he often sought to conciliate the other parties. But he strove hard to keep the Labour government in being. When he failed, a government of national salvation on the French model appeared to be the most effective means of restoring financial confidence. MacDonald expected this to be a temporary expedient and assumed that he would return to the Labour party as Henderson and others had done after taking part in Coalition governments during the first World war.[1] His expectation proved false, and he was soon accused, unjustly, of betrayal long and deliberately planned. Unlike Henderson and the rest during the war, MacDonald failed to observe the 'democratic' practice of securing Labour party approval beforehand—rushed off his feet, of course, by events, though no doubt also reluctant to accept the dictates of a party meeting. More seriously, MacDonald did not grasp that the Labour movement, particularly in the unions, felt much more strongly and more unitedly about wage cuts (and so indirectly the cuts in benefit seemed to them) than they had done about supporting, or not supporting, the war; perhaps also that Labour had now acquired the habit of expulsion after dealing with the Communists and Mosley. MacDonald's largest miscalculation was the most excusable: he assumed that the Labour party, even if not actively supporting him, would at least not oppose an economy programme which the majority of the Labour cabinet had accepted.

At any rate, the decision was made. A National government was formed on 24 August, with MacDonald as prime minister. The cabinet was smaller than any in peacetime since the younger Pitt's: only ten members—four Conservatives, four Labour, two Liberals—with Snowden still in the most important place as chancellor of the exchequer. Lloyd George was not fit to take office, but he sent his blessing, and it was his Liberal associates (including his son) who joined the government, not the dissident Liberals grouped under Sir John Simon. Winston Churchill was also left out. He had excluded himself by resigning from the Conservative shadow cabinet, and no doubt both MacDonald and Baldwin were relieved at being able to pass him over. An official statement emphasized that this was a Government of Cooperation for a specific purpose: 'To deal with the national emergency that now exists.' The statement continued: 'When that purpose is achieved the political parties will resume their respective positions.'

The parties had a more urgent task: to define their attitude towards the National government. On 28 August the Liberals endorsed it with one dissentient: the Conservatives unanimously, though Amery and a few others regretted that Baldwin had not

[1] He might, however, have taken warning from the fate of Barnes and others who stayed with Lloyd George when the war was over.

formed a straight Conservative government with a Protectionist programme.[1] Labour was in a more difficult position. Three of Labour's 'Big Four' were in the emergency cabinet—Mac-Donald, Snowden, Thomas.[2] All three had a record of independence during the first World war, which until now brought them honour in the party.[3] Moreover, a majority of the late Labour cabinet had agreed to the proposals which the National government now intended to carry. On 24 August MacDonald addressed the junior ministers. In words more than usually ambiguous, he first invited them to support him and then warned them that they were 'putting their heads into a noose'. Only four Labour ministers went with MacDonald;[4] eight backbenchers followed them. On 26 August Labour was pushed towards uncompromising opposition by the general council of the T.U.C.; the economic basis of this was that sketched by Bevin on 20 August. Two days later the parliamentary party met. The members of the general council were also present, for the only time, 'to mark unity'. They are said to have taken no part in the proceedings, but even their silent presence must have been difficult to ignore. Neither MacDonald nor Snowden attended. Their defence was left to Sankey and to MacDonald's son Malcolm. Henderson covered his erring colleagues, and himself, by the argument that economy proposals had been aired, not decided; the cabinet, in his version, had suspended judgement until they could see 'the complete picture'. Henderson was elected leader in MacDonald's place. Labour was clearly in opposition; exactly what it should oppose—whether the whole economy programme or only certain details—remained an open question.

Labour opinion grew gradually more resolute. The crisis had revolved in a closed circle of bankers and ministers. Most

[1] Both meetings were attended by M.P.s, peers, and parliamentary candidates.

[2] Sankey, lord chancellor, was the other Labour minister in the National cabinet. Though respected, he carried no weight in the party.

[3] MacDonald and Snowden had been openly anti-war. Thomas, though supporting the war, refused to join Lloyd George's government, campaigned vigorously against conscription, and championed the conscientious objectors.

[4] Amulree remained secretary for air; Jowitt attorney general; Craigie Aitchison lord advocate; and Watson solicitor general for Scotland. Jowitt subsequently had a stroke of luck, though it did not seem so at the time. Almost alone among supporters of the National government, he failed to find a seat at the general election, or afterwards. In Jan. 1932 he resigned his post as attorney general. He was thus able to creep back into the Labour party unobserved, and lived to become lord chancellor in the postwar Labour government.

ordinary people did not understand what was happening, and the reaction of public opinion remained obscure, particularly in the working class. The Labour rank and file were naturally more uncompromising than those who had carried responsibility, and some of the leaders were tempted to think that an aggressive attitude would bring victory at a general election. The crisis was explained as a 'bankers' ramp' (which it was, though not in the conscious sense which the phrase implied). The acquiescence of most Labour ministers in the unemployment cuts was forgotten or brushed aside. MacDonald, and those who supported him, became not mistaken, but traitors.[1] The growing habit of cooperation was broken. The spirit of class war revived. This rising tide of bitterness caused a shift of ground. Only Mosley and Bevin grasped the creative alternative of expansionist economics and a managed currency. Mosley was an ineffective exile in his diminutive New Party; Bevin's influence did not extend beyond the general council, and his ideas were not understood even there. Most Labour people were content to assert that the crisis was unnecessary or a fraud. Still loyal to the fallen government, they soon found themselves arguing that that government had been right to do nothing, or at any rate right to do nothing within the capitalist framework, so long as Labour's minority position made a socialist remedy impossible. The financial crisis acted as the Zinoviev letter had done in 1924: it provided an all-embracing excuse to divert attention from Labour's own failings. Once more Labour claimed to have been intrigued out of office by a ruthless and unscrupulous capitalist class.

This attitude grew even stronger after parliament met on 8 September to pass Snowden's emergency budget. Ministers and ex-ministers wrangled over what had happened. They exchanged accusations of cowardice on the one side and treachery on the other. Snowden duly faced and conquered the prospective deficit of £170 million. He reduced the payment into the sinking fund by £20 million (which the Labour government had been told they could not do); increased taxes by £76 million, principally by raising income tax to 5s. in the pound; and

---

[1] On 31 Aug. the Labour party in Hampstead, where MacDonald lived, 'expelled' him. On the same day the executive of the N.U.R. accepted J. H. Thomas's resignation as political secretary and ruled that he was not entitled to his pension.

found the rest by economies to the tune of £70 million—
£8 million less than the minimum demanded from the Labour
government. All those paid by the state, from cabinet ministers
and judges down to the armed services and the unemployed,
were cut 10 per cent. The police by accident escaped with
5 per cent.[1] Teachers came off worst, as happened in every
economy drive: they lost 15 per cent. Maybe this indicated a
judgement that education was more of a luxury than other public services; maybe merely that teachers were thought less likely
to cause trouble.[2] Conservatives and Liberals supported the
economy programme almost unanimously.[3] They were joined
by twelve Labour men. Five more deliberately abstained. The
rest of the Labour party voted against, giving the government
a majority of fifty.

The formation of the National government brought its
reward. Paris and New York bankers provided a credit of
£80 million. For a few days the run on the pound was stayed.
It was soon renewed. The real causes of it, which had nothing
to do with the unbalanced budget, were as great as before.
Foreigners still wanted their money, still doubted whether the
London houses could recover their debts from Germany. Moreover, the speculator who sold sterling was betting on a certainty
once its stability was in question; at worst he risked only the
arbitrage rates. It is surprising that any Englishman with money
in the bank failed to turn it into dollars at this time. Ignorance
of financial principles perhaps prevented a strain on his patriotism. The strenuous Labour opposition raised further doubts.
The final blow to confidence came on 15 September when the
men of the Atlantic Fleet at Invergordon refused duty in protest
against the cuts in lower-deck pay, some of which exceeded
10 per cent. The board of admiralty hastily promised a revision,
and the more extreme cuts were in fact reduced.[4]

It was too late. The foreign holders of sterling were in wild
alarm. On 19 September the bank of England reported that the

[1] Samuel, the home secretary, mistakenly mentioned 5 per cent. and then
insisted on honouring his mistake. Perhaps, however, there was also a deliberate
intention to keep the police loyal.

[2] The judges raised the well-founded objection that the reduction in their
salaries was an attack on judicial independence as secured by the Act of Settlement.

[3] Five Liberals and three Conservatives were absent unpaired from the vote of
confidence on 8 September. It is not known whether their absence was deliberate.

[4] All cuts were strictly limited to 10 per cent. In this odd way the teachers were
the principal gainers from the 'mutiny'.

foreign credits were exhausted. Two days later an act suspending the gold standard was rushed through parliament. The value of the pound fell by more than a quarter on the foreign exchange.[1] Otherwise nothing happened. Englishmen had been using paper money for seventeen years. They had forgotten the gold sovereign, and their paper pound seemed to them just as valuable as it had been before. This anti-climax took everyone by surprise. Passfield spoke for all his late colleagues when he complained: 'Nobody told us we could do this.' The ministers of the National government could have said just the same. The 'mutiny' at Invergordon provoked a common-sense solution which the politicians and economists had been incapable of discovering for themselves. A few days before, a managed currency had seemed as wicked as family planning. Now, like contraception, it became a commonplace. This was the end of an age.

NOTE

NOTE A. *Fall of Labour government.* The incidents during the last days of the Labour government caused much recrimination later. The revelations of cabinet differences also provoked a tightening of the rules or conventions about cabinet secrecy, to the regret of historians. It is usually held that the cabinet does not 'vote'. This time there seem to have been at least two votes or at any rate definitions of opinion so sharp as to be next door to a vote. The first 'vote' (according to Passfield) was on 19 August over the revenue tariff. Six voted against: Snowden, Wedgwood Benn, Parmoor, Lees-Smith, Alexander, and Passfield. The second 'vote' (so described by Mac-Donald in his report to the king) was on 23 August over the unemployment cuts. The minority of nine were Henderson, Lansbury, Clynes, Graham, Alexander, Greenwood, Johnston, Adamson, and Addison (the only middle-class dissentient). Lees-Smith has sometimes been included in this list—wrongly. If there were no formal vote, but merely expressions of opinion, it may be that some of those in the apparent majority merely did not express their opposition. Certainly some of them afterwards did not regard themselves as committed to the cuts, to Snowden's indignation. Lansbury and Johnston were solidly in opposition from the first, and perhaps Greenwood. Clynes joined them fairly soon, and then Graham. Henderson came out slowly after 20 August. The others wavered until the last moment. Though the gallant nine failed at the time, they won the lasting admiration of the Labour movement, as their later careers showed. Their 'vote' on 23 August was a political bread-ticket for life.

[1] The pound fell first from $4.86 to $3.80, later to $3.23, then fluctuated around $3.40.

IX

HALF TIME

SEPTEMBER 1931 marked the watershed of English history between the wars. Though any division of time above a year is arbitrary, arising only from our habit of counting with arabic numerals by ten, decades take on a character of their own. What was at first merely a convenience for historians is accepted as a reality by ordinary men when they become more literate and judge the world more from books and newspapers than from their own experience. The 'twenties' and the 'thirties' were felt to be distinct periods even at the time, and September 1931 drew the line between them.[1] The break can be defined in many ways. The end of the gold standard was the most obvious and the most immediate. Until 21 September 1931 men were hoping somehow to restore the self-operating economy which had existed, or was supposed to have existed, before 1914. After that day, they had to face conscious direction at any rate so far as money was concerned.

By what was probably a coincidence, exactly the same sort of change took place in international affairs at exactly the same time.[2] Here, too, British policy in the nineteen-twenties had striven to erase the effects and even the memory of the World war. Peace was regarded as the natural rule, its operation impeded only by foolish suspicions. Even those who saw some good in the settlement of 1919[3] hoped that frontiers, and with them international resentments, would 'fade away'. On 10 September 1931 Lord Robert Cecil, speaking for the British government, told the League of Nations Assembly: 'there has scarcely been a period in the world's history when war seems less likely than

[1] The appropriateness of this starting date would be even clearer if men, by an understandable error, did not often count from 0 to 9, instead of from 1 to 10. Thus *The Thirties* by Malcolm Muggeridge includes 1930 and does not include 1940.

[2] It is tempting to conjecture that the Japanese took advantage of Great Britain's financial embarrassment when they occupied Manchuria. In fact the move seems to have matured gradually from internal politics and, to a lesser extent, from Japanese–American relations without any thought of what was happening in Great Britain.

[3] For example, Hugh Dalton in *Towards the Peace of Nations* (1928).

it does at present'. A week later, on 18 September, Japanese troops moved into Manchuria, which was nominally under the suzerainty of China. On 22 September China appealed to the League. This was not war by mistake. It was, or was supposed to be, deliberate aggression. Peace could no longer be relied on to happen of itself. International security had to be planned.

Reconstruction, Restoration, Recovery were the key words of the twenties, as an acute critic has remarked;[1] words of return. Nineteen-fourteen was the standard by which everything was judged. Planning was the key word of the thirties: planned economy, plan for peace, planned families, plan for holidays. The standard was Utopia. The distinction must not, of course, be drawn too sharply. There was some planning, or talk of it, before 1931, and much hope after it of returning to a world which would run itself. The British government had developed a conscious economic policy, to their own embarrassment, during the first World war. The Balfour committee on trade and industry, which produced a series of reports between 1925 and 1929, ranged far beyond tariffs in its constructive sugges-tions.[2] On the other side, few even in the nineteen-thirties went along with Amery in regarding Protection as merely the begin-ning of a planned economy. Neville Chamberlain, for instance, the most ardent Protectionist in the cabinet, was otherwise a pure Cobdenite in his reliance on 'natural' forces and individual enterprise. Great Britain's economic recovery after 1933 was indeed mainly 'natural', and the government deserved little of the credit.

Similarly, there had been plenty of talk during the twenties of universal guarantees for world peace; while during the thirties many, including those in charge of British policy, still expected peace to work of itself once some temporary difficulty from the Japanese, or later from Mussolini, or latest of all from Hitler, had been overcome. Even those most loyal to 'collective secur-ity'[3] were embarrassed at its logical consequences and shrank from preaching perpetual war for the sake of perpetual peace.

---

[1] E. H. Carr, *Conditions of Peace.*

[2] Sir Arthur Balfour, the chairman (later Lord Riverdale), was a Sheffield steel magnate and no relation of A. J. Balfour, the statesman.

[3] The principle of resistance to aggression was passed over so lightly in the twenties that the phrase 'collective security' was not used until 1932. It is said to have been coined by Beneš, foreign minister of Czechoslovakia. The French, though welcoming the principle, objected to the phrase as bad French.

When the *Manchester Guardian* asserted in November 1931 that acceptance of the Covenant meant 'in the last resort, war' against Japan, it was denounced by Gilbert Murray, spokesman of the League of Nations Union, and the paper then explained that it was not advocating war—merely pointing out, in an academic way, that this was what the Covenant involved. In short, men who had grown up with one set of conceptions were now being driven to operate others and did not change their natures merely because they were living in a new decade.

There was a deeper contradiction. While political leaders fumbled towards new outlooks, the English people were also changing, but in ways quite different from those towards which even the most enlightened politicians were moving. The economic plans of the thirties, so far as they existed, were designed to make the old industrial towns flourish again and to make Great Britain once more the workshop of the world. Politicians and planners scanned first the figures of British exports in order to learn whether their plans were succeeding. The object of rearmament, when it came, was that Great Britain should again play a leading part as a Great Power, in the Far East as well as in Europe. The people of Great Britain presumably approved, when they thought consciously of politics. They voted for politicians who pursued these aims. Their expressions of dissatisfaction—the hunger marches of the unemployed or the demonstrations to stand by some foreign cause or country— were demands that the aims should be pursued faster and more assertively.

Unconsciously, the people repudiated these aims without admitting or understanding what they did. They voted against them with their feet, as the Russian soldiers of 1917, according to Lenin, had voted against the war by running away. Politicians strove to revive the depressed areas; the inhabitants left them. Public policy concentrated on the staple industries and on exports. Capital and labour developed new industries which provided goods for the home market. The government tried to promote new investment abroad. The individual spent his money on domestic comforts—indeed, with the growth of hire-purchase, spent other people's money also. Similarly, the people lost interest in the empire and showed it in a practical way. Whereas in the nineteen-twenties something like 100,000 people went overseas each year, in the thirties an average of over

20,000 returned home.[1] In the words of Geoffrey Crowther, the English people were 'more planned against than planning'.

A new England was coming into existence which owed nothing to the planners, which indeed created itself in defiance of their efforts. J. B. Priestley, author of the *Good Companions*, was the first man to discover this new England. When he made his *English Journey* in the autumn of 1933, he found, as he expected to find, two Englands. He found the traditional England of literature and the history books, complete with squires, fox hunting, and gnarled yokels; sustained no doubt more from dividends than from agricultural rents, but tolerably resembling Shakespeare's England all the same. Priestley also found the bleak England of harsh industrial towns, by now hardly less traditional: the rows of mean streets, the factory hooters sounding before dawn, trams clanking, and grime everywhere. The majority of English people still lived in one or other of these Englands, and they could be described in terms hardly changed from an earlier period. The gentry still followed country pursuits, still belonged to west-end clubs, still upheld social standards. Working men still went to the public house. Railwaymen still cultivated their allotments, miners still kept whippets; pigeon racing still flourished.

Priestley also found, to his surprise, a third England, which appeared haphazard and in unexpected places, the England of the twentieth century, shapeless, unplanned, yet representing the ideal towards which all Englishmen unconsciously moved.[2] When a new England previously came into existence during the industrial revolution, this was largely the creation of genuinely new people. At any rate, there were a great many more people than before. The new Englishmen of the twentieth century were converts. They came from a population almost stationary in numbers. The population increased between the wars at the slow rate of less than 0·5 per cent. a year. By 1931 there were just under forty million people in England and nearly forty-five million in Great Britain.[3] The birth rate went down to just

---

[1] These are, of course, net figures. Far more people moved one way and the other. Total net overseas emigration for the twenties: 1,013,000. Total net immigration for 1931–8 (the figures for 1939 and 1940 are not available): 184,000.

[2] Priestley distinguished a fourth England: the England of 'the dole'. This was surely a subdivision of England No. 2.

[3] England and Wales: 39,952,000. Great Britain: 44,795,000. The population of England and Wales is estimated to have passed the forty million mark in 1932.

over 16 per thousand in the nineteen-twenties, and fell to under 15 per thousand for most of the thirties.

Experts, who had once sounded the alarm of over population, swung round and foresaw a steep decline until England would be no more densely populated than Denmark—a prophecy falsified by the rise in the birth rate after the second World war. The same experts, being themselves from a supposedly superior class, were also gloomy over the fact that the birth rate declined at each step upwards in the social scale, with the two odd exceptions that coal miners and aristocrats were prolific beyond all others. The decline was recorded. Its motive remained obscure. Was it an instructed preference for the pleasures of copulation over the pains and burdens of childbirth? Was it psychological—a backwash perhaps from the common talk that England was no longer a great country with a great future? Or was it economic—a calculation that children cost money which could be spent more agreeably on an increasing range of goods? This was the explanation favoured at the time. The baby Austin[1] ousted the baby. The nursery gave place to the garage.

The motor car was undoubtedly the great formative influence of the new England, transforming social life even more fundamentally than the railways had done before it. In 1920 the number of private cars registered was under 200,000. Ten years later it exceeded a million and reached nearly two million before the outbreak of the second World war. The motor car enjoyed an extraordinary freedom. Virtually no roads were barred to it. Anyone over the age of 17 could drive one. The sole requirement (and that only after 1931) was an unsupported declaration of physical fitness. There were no driving tests until 1934, and then only for newcomers; thirty years later there must still be many thousands of 'ancient right' drivers.

In 1930 the obsolete speed limit of 20 miles per hour was abolished, and for four years drivers were free from all restriction.[2] In 1934 a speed limit of 30 miles per hour was imposed in built-up areas—areas conveniently defined by (usually inadequate) street lighting. Like other measures of control, the speed limit was rarely enforced, and then more to add to police funds than in the interests of safety. No special body of motor

---

[1] A 7 h.p. car first put on the market by Austins in 1922.
[2] Local authorities were empowered to impose a speed limit in their own areas. Only one (Oxford) did so.

police was created. The local police simply added the enforce-
ment of the Road Traffic Acts to their other duties. Not much
was enforced. While private cars increased ninefold between
the wars, the number of those charged for offences against the
Road Traffic Acts only doubled. The number of those killed
on the roads in 1934 was actually greater than those killed
thirty years later when the number of cars had increased six
times.[1] Public opinion endorsed this attitude. In an accident,
it was the driver, not the person killed, who was felt to have had
'bad luck', and the pedestrian was often condemned for his
obstinacy in being on the road at all.

The social function of the motor car changed basically between the wars. Earlier it had been exclusively an instrument
for pleasure, and largely confined to the rich. The car owner
took 'drives' or occasionally made 'tours'. Now, though still a
prestige symbol, it was used for day-to-day transport. The
system of motor-taxation made the car a characteristically
middle-class possession. Taxation, being based absurdly on horse-
power until after the second World war, artificially encouraged
the smaller car. Manufacturers had to concentrate on the home
market, and a mass market at that. As a further result, road
surfaces had to be better than in other countries. England spent
proportionately more than other countries on maintaining
existing roads and less on improving them or making new ones.
High speeds were rarely possible. The cheap underpowered car
first kept the antiquated roads in existence and then was further
stimulated by them.

The Englishman, commuting to work in his own car, was still
far from being the normal pattern between the wars. Here the
new formative influence was the public-service vehicle, called
the bus. Buses were unknown outside urban areas before the
end of the first World war, and virtually unknown in them
except in London. Though hardly any new railways were laid
down after 1914, tram lines reached their peak of length in
1928. Then the tide turned. In 1928 the manager of Manchester's transport system—a pioneer enthusiast for buses—was
the first to supersede an existing tram service by buses. Soon
tram lines were being torn up instead of more being laid down.
The halfhearted compromise of trolley buses, using the old

---

[1] 1934: 7,343 road deaths and 1·3 million cars. 1963: 6,922 road deaths and
7·3 million cars.

electric wires in a patriotic preference for home-produced electricity over foreign oil, prolonged the rigidity for a few years. Essentially the old pattern of civilized life was breaking down. By 1932 buses were carrying more passengers than trams. Country buses were catching up on the railways and penetrating where the railways had failed to do.

Englishmen were emancipated from the iron frame of railways and tram lines which had previously dictated their lives. The map of any town shows the change. The towns of the early twentieth century centred on the railway station and radiated outwards from it along the tram lines. The country began roughly where the tram lines ended. Now men could live wherever cars or buses could carry them. New houses spread along the main roads in the ribbon building characteristic of the period, with little stabs a hundred yards or so down the side roads. These new settlements had no centres, no sense, no communal spirit. They were composed of little more than individual motor cars come to rest. Nor was it only private houses which straggled along the road. New factories followed the same ribbon.[1] This was partly to escape the heavier rates in urban areas; partly to escape the stronger trade unionism of the old towns. Predominantly it represented the new motive which shaped the pattern of industry: pursuit of the consumer.

Previously factories had grown up near raw materials and coal fields, or near ports. The new factories used lighter materials, were powered by electricity, and delivered their products by road, not by rail or sea. Their main interest was to be as near a prosperous mass market as possible. This market was largely near London, and inner Britain, grouped round London, increased its share of insured workers from 46 per cent. in 1923 to 54 per cent. in 1938. The pull worked for great cities even in the depressed areas. Manchester, for instance, developed new industries and continued to grow when Blackburn or Colne was in decline. This growth was everywhere on the fringes. The centre of every city, including London, was steadily depopulated to the advantage of the outer suburbs.

The new industries produced amenities for the home, not basic goods for export. Between 1924 and 1935, for example,

---

[1] With characteristic anarchy, the few arterial roads built for the new traffic were at once lined with factories and thus became more congested than the roads which they had been designed to relieve.

cotton fell from third to eleventh place among British industries in value of net output. The motor industry moved up from eighth to fourth. Coal, though still the greatest single industry by the same standard, earned three times as much as its nearest competitor in 1924; only 20 per cent. more in 1935. Workers, though often unemployed, stuck to the old industries until the great Depression and even during it. Recovery from 1933 pulled them rapidly away. In the interwar period, cotton, shipbuilding, and coal mining each lost a third of their labour force, wool lost a quarter.[1] The workers making electrical apparatus multiplied three times; those making motor cars by two and a half; building workers increased by a third. Bernard Shaw was not far wrong when he prophesied in *The Apple Cart* that soon England would live solely by producing chocolate creams.[2]

The new light industries were little affected by the Depression, sustained no doubt by the fact that the general level of wages hardly fell. The service industries (hotels, restaurants, entertainments) actually increased their employment figures throughout the Depression and when, with recovery, general employment rose by about 10 per cent., employment in these industries rose by 40 per cent. This was clear evidence that English people were enjoying themselves more despite the public gloom. It was evidence also that more of them were taking holidays away from home. In the nineteenth century this had been almost exclusively a middle-class habit, and even in 1939 less than half the population left home even for a single night in the year. These stay-at-homes often had their first taste of sea or country in day trips on a charabanc[3]—another work of emancipation achieved by the internal-combustion engine. But even in the working classes many more took real holidays. By 1939 eleven million had secured holidays with pay. Holiday camps catered for broader sections of the community. All this was communal service.

The number of private domestic servants did not increase even during the Depression. Only about 5 per cent. of private households had a resident domestic between the wars. The cynical observer will not forget this fact when he reads lamenta-

---

[1] 'Lost' is, of course, the wrong word as applied to individuals. The older workers stayed in the industry. Their children did not enter it, or only for a short time.

[2] For chocolate creams, read motor cars, washing machines, spin dryers, television sets, and the prophecy has already come true.

[3] An open motor coach.

tions from the comfortable classes about the decline of civilization. The lamentations only mean that professional men were
having to help with the washing-up.

Rich people still lived in the west end of London, though they
were moving from houses into flats. Otherwise men worked in
cities and aspired to live outside them. The 'new' Englishman
lived in a new house[1] within sight of green fields, though these,
smeared with ribbon building, could hardly be called the
country. The house was usually his own in the sense that he was
buying it on instalments with the aid of a building society. For
that matter, he was buying his furniture, kitchen-equipment,
and car by instalments also. Hire-purchase was a striking innovation of the nineteen-thirties, enabling men without capital to
buy ten times more household goods than they had done before
and a potent stimulus therefore to the home market. It was still
not quite respectable. The leading hire-purchase firm guaranteed to deliver their furniture 'in plain vans', much as contraceptives were delivered by post in plain covers.

There was little modern about the new house except its date.
Architects were rarely employed—not that they kept up with
the times. Speculative builders ran up the houses, just as they
had run up the industrial dwellings of the nineteenth century.
Each house had its private garden and whispered the last
enchantments of the middle ages. It was a baronial mansion on
a tiny scale. It still had a hall and a drawing-room (now called
the lounge). There was still a separate kitchen for the non-
existent domestic servant, and the family spent most of their
time in it during the week. The rooms upstairs were deserted in
the daytime. 'Bedsitter' was a term of horror. Windows and doors
did not fit. Draughts were everywhere. Chilblains remained
a unique English malady. One room was heated by an open
coal fire. The rest of the house was unheated. Central heating
was virtually unknown except in luxury flats and hotels. Though
electricity eclipsed gas for lighting, only a minority used it for
cooking, and only a very small minority had electric fires. Other
electrical devices were creeping in slowly: electric irons fairly
common, vacuum cleaners increasing,[2] refrigerators still rare.

[1] This gives an indication how many 'new' Englishmen there were. Nearly four
million houses were built between the wars, nearly half of them away from the old
centres. In 1939 there were more than ten million households.
[2] Production of vacuum cleaners increased twelvefold between 1930 and 1935
(from 37,550 to 409,345).

The one universal feature was the wireless set, symbol of the interwar period, especially towards the end when nine million sets were licensed; in other words, in nine homes out of ten. Television, though provided by the B.B.C. from 1936 until the outbreak of war, was little regarded until its postwar revival. Still, the world was now in men's homes instead of being outside them. Attendance declined at the old social centres. Churches, chapels, clubs, and literary societies were all affected. The public houses were emptier. Though prosperity increased during the nineteen-thirties, the consumption of beer did not increase with it. Beer drinking was mainly a social activity. At home English people drank only tea, and their home habits conquered even in communal life. The typical factory worker now had his tea break, not a midday visit to the pub. Only the miner and the worker in heavy industry still got through six or eight pints of beer a day. Convictions for drunkenness were more than halved, and it was unusual to see a drunk man in the streets.

The Englishman still belonged to a community, though shut up in a box listening to a tinier box. There is little to be learnt about him from the wireless set, his constant companion. The B.B.C. had been born to caution out of bureaucracy, and, as its bureaucrats swelled, became more cautious still, controllers set on top of producers, and senior controllers, who were often retired admirals, on top of these. Religion, society, public affairs, were discussed in well-bred undertones. In 1932 King George V took to broadcasting a message on Christmas afternoon to families replete with turkey and plum pudding. Amateur Freudians were not slow to remark that the king had become a father figure; with his old-fashioned beard and guttural pronunciation, grandfather figure would have been nearer the mark. George VI's coronation provided one of the few incidents which disturbed the peace of the air. The naval commentator at the night review of the fleet, overcome no doubt by meeting his old shipmates again, repeated in broken tones: 'The fleet's lit up . . . Now it's gone . . .', until his microphone was abruptly stilled. There is no means of knowing whether the listeners would have liked the performance to continue. Perhaps listeners, too, were mainly concerned not to be offended, and preferred wireless programmes suited to children below the age of consent. Perhaps they did not care what they heard so long as some noise from the little box gave them a substitute for human society.

The printed word remained the serious means of communication. The English people were now universally literate, or as nearly so as mass education could make them. The great majority were not much more. The Fisher Act of 1918 was the only educational advance. The school-leaving age remained stuck at 14 between the wars. Its raising to 15 was often promised and as often postponed. Finally, it was settled for 1 September 1939, a date which turned out singularly unsuitable. By that time, there were some achievements to record. Classes of over sixty in primary schools had practically disappeared,[1] and classes of over fifty were on the way out. Two thirds of the children over 11 were in some sort of senior department. Education over the compulsory age showed little increase. In 1931 only one adolescent in five received any secondary education (nearly half of them assisted from public funds), and the proportion declined slightly during the thirties. University education was still more stagnant and still more selective. Three university colleges were created between the wars;[2] one, at Reading, became a university. Otherwise, there was little expansion. The secondary schools, supported by public funds, sent only six from every hundred pupils to a university. Out of every thousand children at an elementary school only four managed to reach a university; less than one in a thousand reached Oxford and Cambridge. Of course, even this made some difference to the composition of the universities, though not to their character. One third of those entering universities in 1934 came from grant-aided schools; nearly half these, or one seventh of the total, had started at elementary schools.

The run down of education as age advanced can be shown in another way. In 1931 there were five and a half million children in elementary schools; something over 600,000 in some form of secondary school (not all, of course, over 14); and just under 30,000 undergraduates at universities. These figures define class distinctions which endured through life. Yet, by a brilliant twist, the universities which catered predominantly for a narrow privileged class were presented as national institutions and

---

[1] In 1938 only fifty-six remained.
[2] Swansea, Leicester, and Hull.

received slightly more than half their income from public funds. Not only this. The newer civic universities, which had often started in aggressive repudiation of Oxford and Cambridge, either secular or Dissenting, now strove to resemble them and increasingly offered an imitation or echo of upper-class education. In most countries and at most times university students lived under hard conditions, probably lower than they were accustomed to at home. In England they came to live above their station, the teachers even more so. It is not surprising that the vast majority of Englishmen were unaffected by such remote institutions. Though nearly all Englishmen could read, they did not read what the universities produced, and the universities produced little.

Ordinary men and women read mainly newspapers and more of them than ever. The circulation of newspapers had been advancing for about a century in a series of jumps. Each jump came when papers offered more interesting things to read—more news more effectively presented by Northcliffe, more lively features prompted by Beaverbrook. The papers sold on their contents and derived their profits from the pennies or halfpennies paid by the readers. Gradually there came a change, almost without the proprietors noticing it. The papers came to depend increasingly on the money which they received for advertisements. Larger circulation meant higher advertising rates. Hence circulation mattered in itself, even when each additional copy sold involved a slight additional loss. The reader no longer bought newspapers. Newspapers bought readers. Elias of Odhams hit on this device. He was saddled with the *Daily Herald*, and, being a printer, not a newspaper man like Northcliffe or Beaverbrook, had no idea how to make a newspaper sell. He therefore won readers for the *Daily Herald* by door-to-door canvassing, much as for insurance policies or vacuum cleaners. The *Daily Mail*, then at the top of the circulation tree, was alarmed at this novel competition. It retaliated by pushing up the free insurance which it already offered to registered readers.

This began the great newspaper war. The other popular dailies, the *Daily Express* and the *News Chronicle*,[1] joined the battle. A registered reader who got in at the top of the struggle might provide £250,000 for his bereaved heirs. In 1932, the

[1] The *Daily News* absorbed the *Daily Chronicle* one afternoon in 1930.

newspaper owners made a self-denying ordinance against insurance policies, only to embark on a new war with free gifts.
Registered readers stocked up with silk stockings, household
goods, encyclopaedias, sets of Dickens—apparently the only
writer of universal appeal. Each new reader cost the *Daily
Herald* £1, and the *Daily Express* 8s. 3d. Nor was the reader a
freehold. He needed only to register for one month, and could
then switch to another paper with another flood of free gifts.
In 1933 this race was called off also. When the fighting died
down, the *Daily Express* and the *Daily Herald* had both gone to
over two million, a circulation which the *Daily Express* retained.

The *Daily Express* was distinguished not only by its circulation.
It was unique also in the universality of its readership. All other
newspapers were associated with a particular social level from
The Times at the top to the *Daily Herald* for trade unionists. The
Daily Express drew its readers impartially from every group—
about a third of each of them. Beaverbrook, its Canadian proprietor, was not confined by the English social system and had
the New World view that there was no difference between rich
and poor except that the rich had more money. The *Daily
Express* was what England would have been without her class
system.

Educated Englishmen derived their ideas more from weekly
journals than from daily newspapers. These journals had great
influence, though small circulations. The *Spectator* continued to
appeal to enlightened Conservatives. Its editor, Wilson Harris,
was a strong proponent of the League of Nations and became
a genuinely Independent M.P. The *Saturday Review*, earlier a
stalwart and lively organ, fell on evil days. Its editor, Gerald
Barry, quarrelled with the proprietor and started the bright
Weekend Review overnight. This failed to prosper and was eaten
up by the *New Statesman*, which had already absorbed the
Radical *Nation*.[1] Keynes was the principal controller of the *New
Statesman and Nation*, which did not, however, become a coolly
rational weekly as he had intended. Kingsley Martin, the editor
whom Keynes chose, though an intellectual socialist, came of
Radical stock[2] and continued the warm radicalism which

---

[1] The *Nation* had itself absorbed the *Athenaeum*, a literary journal of distinction,
in 1920. For some years, the *New Statesman* displayed the cannibalistic masthead:
The New Statesman and Nation, including the *Athenaeum*: *The Weekend Review*.
[2] His father was a nonconformist minister and a leading pro-Boer.

Massingham had displayed in the *Nation*. No man expressed better the confused emotions of the nineteen-thirties—collective security and pacifism, hostility to the German Nazis and hatred of war all in the same parcel. He was a compendium of the time, or at any rate of the Left. For that matter, the literary section of the *New Statesman* gave the best general reflection of English culture.

It would, however, be rash, indeed mistaken, to assume that literary taste and popularity indicate what ordinary people were thinking. The assumption perhaps works in earlier periods, when history deals only with the upper, cultivated classes, and great works therefore can be regarded as the mirror of the age. Even this assumes that works which have survived or are rated highly by posterity were necessarily the most influential or the most representative in their own time. At any rate, literature tells us little when we deal, as we must in the twentieth century, with the people of England. The novels of Virginia Woolf, for example, were greatly esteemed by a small intellectual group, and their destruction of the tight narrative frame has influenced later writers. They are irrelevant for the historian. Again, the thirties produced a school of poets deeply concerned with social and political questions, and it is tempting to regard their leader, W. H. Auden, as the characteristic voice of his time, in the way that, say, Tennyson had once been. Maybe Auden expressed in poetic form what many Englishmen were thinking. This does not mean that they read his poems or had even heard of him. The decade was indeed short of literary pundits. No one took the place of Bernard Shaw or Arnold Bennett, men who pronounced without hesitation on every great question.

There were, of course, successful writers, and of a more sober cast than in the preceding decade. The nineteen-twenties produced three outstanding best sellers of gilt gingerbread. *If Winter Comes* by A. S. M. Hutchinson was praised at the time for its 'high ethical quality, power and beauty'. The *Annual Register* for 1922 called it 'the year's most arresting achievement in fiction'. It is now incomprehensible in appeal and sentiment, as though H. G. Wells had lost his mental faculties and yet gone on writing. *The Constant Nymph* by Margaret Kennedy was the day-dreaming of an adolescent girl presented in literate form: Lolita with the sex left out. *The Green Hat* by Michael Arlen, even more unreal, was the deliberate fabrication of a hardheaded

Armenian. It was solemnly accepted by social critics as
a picture of contemporary manners. These fantasies had no
successors, unless Priestley's *Good Companions* can be regarded as
a last splash in 1929, despite its genuine characters, and *Rebecca*
by Daphne du Maurier as a solitary revival in 1938. The best
sellers of the thirties were predominantly realistic in tone.
Priestley, Cronin, Louis Golding, offered chunks of ordinary
life, usually in drab surroundings. Perhaps English people were
dreaming less. Perhaps they were trying to catch up with what
was going on around them. More probably, the writers changed,
not the readers.

One development in reading habits was curious, though
maybe not enlightening. This was a new twist to the adventure
story, or thriller. The less literate classes had always read
thrillers when they read anything. Sexton Blake continued his
fortnightly adventures until the outbreak of the second World
war—read by boys in the more educated classes and by adults
lower down. Sapper, Dornford Yates, and John Buchan provided thrillers at a slightly more sophisticated level, with fine
old-fashioned codes of morality merging into dislike of foreigners
and Jews. If plot were all, P. G. Wodehouse (also originally a
writer of tales for boys) would count as an author of adventure
stories. In fact, what mattered with Wodehouse was his style.
He ranked with Congreve and Ronald Firbank as a master of
exquisite, fantastic prose. Presumably this is what Oxford
University had in mind when it frivolously gave him an
honorary degree. The new development was the detective story:
a sober, solid narrative in which ordinary people had extraordinary experiences—usually murder. Agatha Christie was the
acknowledged queen in this art, with no rival in the ingenuity
of her plots. Serious writers, including Priestley, anticipated that
the detective story might supersede traditional fiction altogether.
Certainly these stories often provide for the historian clearer and
more accurate social detail than can be found in more literary
works. Otherwise they were without significance: an intellectual
game like the crosswords, which became a universal feature in
the newspapers at this time. Still, the picture of the interwar
Englishman, particularly of the middle class, is incomplete,
unless we see him reading thrillers, detective stories, and P. G.
Wodehouse.

Reading took up, of course, little of his time except on train journeys. The Englishman still ran after public entertainment. Improved communications, greater leisure, newspaper publicity beat up crowds for royal weddings and for the film stars who visited London. Sport, or rather the watching of professional sport, mounted steadily. Horse racing continued to provide the main outlet for gambling. £200 million is said to have gone on bets in 1929.[1] The pools—betting attempts to foretell the results of football matches—expanded steadily during the nineteen-thirties. The elaborate forms were, of course, filled up at home during the evenings. Greyhound racing, introduced in 1926, gave the masses a more public, cheap version of the green tables at Monte Carlo. Cricket was watched for its own sake and stood high in the social scale. One writer, Neville Cardus, devoted to it the literary gifts which he kept sharp during the winter on classical music. No professional cricketer was allowed to captain his team. Command remained, as in most walks of English life, an amateur occupation. Tennis spread to the working class—of course, the younger members. Watching it remained a middle-class taste, as amateur Rugby football had always been except in Wales. The professional Rugby form was as exclusively working class, principally in the north of England.

Association football united all classes—partly no doubt because the grandest public schools had been above following the example of Rugby and Dr. Arnold. The king himself took to attending the Cup Final, when he presented the Cup to the captain of the winning team. When George V first did this at Wembley in 1923, the crowd was larger than the stadium could hold and burst on to the field. Association football was the most democratic game, and also the most international. By it the mark of England may well remain in the world when the rest of her influence has vanished. The continent supplied in return the *palais de danse*. This spread more widely the romance which balls had previously brought for the rich.

Though large crowds watched Association football on Saturday afternoons and attended the *palais de danse* on Saturday evenings, they were dwarfed by the crowds who attended the cinemas every night of the week. The cinema was the essential social habit of the age, a compensation perhaps for the private boxes: doll's house at one end of the scale, cinema palace at the other. The cinema slaughtered all competitors. The music halls

[1] This is a gross figure. Some punters, of course, got their money back.

were worst hit. Outside London, nearly all closed their doors. Gracie Fields of Rochdale was the only new star, last of a long line, and even she had to use films and the radio to sustain the fame she had won on the boards. Provincial theatres vanished almost as fast. They survived only in a few great cities, and even here presented only London successes or pre-London rehearsals. In the nineteen-twenties there were still touring companies: two in Shakespeare, one in Shaw, two (one conducted by the last great actor-manager, Martin Harvey) in romantic plays. These all expired. Shakespeare dwindled to the London Old Vic and the Memorial Theatre at Stratford upon Avon, which was sustained mainly by American tourists and parties of school-children. It was incidentally one of the few buildings in a contemporary style, when rebuilt after destruction of the mid-Victorian theatre by fire in 1927.

Some repertory theatres kept going, not without difficulty. Birmingham and Liverpool were thus distinguished. Man-chester, on the other hand, was distinguished by failure, after possessing in Miss Horniman's Gaiety the greatest of repertories. Perhaps the Hallé orchestra exhausted the appetite of Man-chester citizens for culture. The London theatres offered fewer new plays of distinction. The literary renaissance of drama, which marked the earlier years of the century, virtually ended. Galsworthy died in 1933. John Drinkwater followed Stephen Phillips into oblivion. Shaw was in his dotage: verbal felicity and nothing to say. Noel Coward turned to the patriotic display of *Cavalcade*—begun, it is said, though not completed, tongue in cheek. The cinema threatened humbler forms of entertainment. Children's parties had private film shows, usually of Charlie Chaplin, instead of a conjuror. Punch and Judy wilted before the cinemas for children on Saturday mornings. The barrel-organ or hurdy-gurdy, with attendant monkey, vanished from the streets.

Glittering cinema palaces went up everywhere, even in the most impoverished areas. In Liverpool, it was calculated, 40 per cent. of the population went to the cinema once a week, 25 per cent. went twice. The cinema was church and theatre in one, though with no communal reality. The watchers in the darkened halls remained individuals, unknown except to their neighbour in the next 'stall' or 'fauteuil'. Laughter had to be cut short as the film remorselessly proceeded. Towards the end of the nineteen-twenties the cinemas tried to atone for their silence by installing monstrous electric organs which rose from the bowels of the earth. Their torrent of glutinous sound was short-lived. In 1927 an American film producer, threatened with bankruptcy, gambled on a soundtrack synchronized with the pictures, and won. Al Jolson, a 'black-face' performer, conquered the world as *The Jazz Singer*. Even more sensational than his singing were the words spoken by accident: 'Come on, Ma, listen to this!'

Within three years everyone was listening. The 'talkie' triumphed. The silent film was dead. The new form was less sensational and less emotional than the old. Crowd scenes became too expensive when sound had to be provided as well as pictures.¹ Besides, the special feature of the talkies was to talk. Most of the talk was American. In 1927 a quota of British films was imposed on the cinemas by law—a Protectionism allegedly as much cultural as economic. It had little serious effect. Few British films made their mark. The actors were borrowed from the theatre and soon departed for Hollywood if they achieved any reputation. Only two British directors reached the front rank: Alexander Korda, an expatriate Hungarian, and Alfred Hitchcock, a successful maker of silent thrillers, who went on to equal success in talkies. Otherwise the Americans had it all their own way.

The American hold created alarm among the self-appointed guardians of British culture. The alarm had little justification. There was some increase in American phrases, but little in American habits as depicted on the screen—no cigar-chewing, no gangsters. Few learnt their morals, good or bad, from the cinema; fewer still followed the stars in the morality of their private lives. The barrier of language may have turned English people away from the Continent and may have strengthened the illusion of a special relationship with the United States—an illusion reciprocated by few Americans. The real effect of the cinema went deeper: it provided a substitute for real life and helped people to become watchers instead of doers. The unemployed man could forget, for a few pence, his harsh surroundings and could move into a world of palatial halls, obsequious

¹ D. W. Griffiths used 10,000 extras in *The Birth of a Nation*. The British film, *Henry V*, had to present the battle of Agincourt with 500 extras, supplied by the Irish army. Admittedly this was an extreme example in wartime.

servants, and marble baths (though no lavatories). Why should he bother with political demonstrations? Real life was itself turned into a spectacle. The newsreels, which were then part of every programme, presented current events in the same intense, dramatic way. It is hard to distinguish between shots of a genuine Nazi rally and the same theme treated by Chaplin in *The Great Dictator*. During the second World war film units operated in the front line, and the battles of El Alamein or Stalingrad only became fully authentic when they appeared on the screen. Politics seemed more passionate; international events were more widely discussed than ever before. Yet with it all was a feeling that these great happenings had no more connexion with real life than those seen every night in the cinema palaces.

The new communal activity had one curious conflict with the older religious beliefs. Many local authorities assumed that their licensing power extended so far as to permit the opening of cinemas on Sundays. In 1930 a common informer caught them out under the Sunday Observance Act of 1782. After some fuss, a characteristic compromise was reached. The ninety local authorities who had broken the law were allowed to go on doing so. Elsewhere Sunday opening was authorized only after a local poll. Not many such were held before Sunday opening became general during the second World war. As a further tribute to God from Mammon, a proportion of the takings on Sunday nights were to go to charity. Most cinemas therefore put on inferior films when they opened at all. As appropriate retribution, the Church itself provided material for Sunday entertainment. The proceedings in its consistory courts were not covered by the ban which had been imposed in 1926 on the publication of proceedings in divorce courts. They became the richest source for the popular Sunday newspapers. The greatest sensation of the decade was the trial in 1932 of Harold Davidson, rector of Stiffkey, who devoted more time to chorus girls than to his parish. He was unfrocked and became a public entertainer like the Tichborne claimant before him, until mauled and killed in 1937 by a lion, with whom he was exhibiting himself. Davidson offered a parable of the age. He attracted more attention while he lived than, say, Cosmo Gordon Lang, archbishop of Canterbury. Which man deserves a greater place in the history books?

The same sort of problem arises at every turn. Public affairs were harsh and intense; private lives increasingly agreeable. The nineteen-thirties have been called the black years, the devil's decade. Its popular image can be expressed in two phrases: mass unemployment and 'appeasement'. No set of political leaders have been judged so contemptuously since the days of Lord North. Yet, at the same time, most English people were enjoying a richer life than any previously known in the history of the world: longer holidays, shorter hours, higher real wages. They had motor cars, cinemas, radio sets, electrical appliances. The two sides of life did not join up. The public men themselves had the air of appearing in a charade. The members of the National government may be seen in a newsreel, assembling for discussion: stern features, teeth clenched, as they face the crisis. They would hesitate at nothing to save the country, to save the pound. The result of their courage was that the children of the unemployed had less margarine on their bread. After this resolute decision, ministers dispersed to their warm comfortable homes and ate substantial meals. Such was 'equality of sacrifice'. At the end of the decade an academic writer, F. L. Lucas, published a diary covering the last year of peace. It was entitled *A Year under the Terror*. The nearest that the author came to Dachau or Vorkuta was the senior common room of a Cambridge college.

In theory England was still a Christian country. All school children started the day with Christian instruction; doubters were allowed no say on the radio; great issues such as capital punishment or the monarchy were discussed in terms of fundamentalist Christianity. Yet only one prime minister between 1916 and 1945 (Baldwin) was a Christian in any strict sense. Again, every politician extolled the virtues of democracy, especially at the expense of Soviet Russia. Despite this rhetoric, MacDonald wrote friendly personal letters to the Fascist dictator Mussolini; Austen Chamberlain exchanged photographs with him and joined him in family holidays; Churchill sang his praises—and those of Hitler—in newspaper articles.

The contradiction was shown especially over foreign affairs. Churchill said in 1932: 'I cannot recall any time when the gap between the kind of words which statesmen used and what was actually happening was so great as it is now.'[1] Of course there

---

[1] Churchill, *Arms and the Covenant*, 43.

had always been wishful thinking in such matters. Perhaps it was only that now the penalties for mistake were greater. In theory, Great Britain was committed to disarmament and to reliance on the League of Nations. In practice, the League was treated as an extra, providing an agreeable meetingplace for statesmen and handling questions remote from power, such as the white slave traffic. When British interests were threatened, as at Shanghai in 1927, the British defended them in the old-fashioned way, by force of arms. The British government did not invoke the League in their disputes with Egypt, a nominally independent country. Still less did they think of entrusting the League with control, say, of the Suez canal. British armaments were determined solely with reference to British needs. The chiefs of staff never asked specifically: 'what armaments do we need in order to discharge our commitments under the Covenant?' They used support for the League as an argument only when they wished to advocate increased armaments for some other purpose. Privately they regarded the League as a nuisance or even a danger. Statesmen equivocated. The League became in their speeches 'the sheet anchor of British policy'. Baldwin won a general election in 1935 by appearing to support the League of Nations. He himself had no faith in it. He never attended the League assembly, and he once attributed his political misfortunes to the League of Nations Union, which had tried to make him take the League seriously.[1]

The advocates of the League did little better. They never faced the problem that adherence to the Covenant might involve Great Britain in war. They were concerned, for the most part, that Great Britain should not act in defiance of the Covenant, and therefore did not consider what she should do if some other Power so acted. Thus, in 1926, the Labour party at its annual conference passed a resolution supporting the League of Nations, and followed this by another, declaring that the workers would meet 'any threat of war, so-called defensive or offensive, by organising general resistance, including the refusal to bear arms'. Support for the League and opposition to almost any British armament went hand in hand. Wars, it was supposed, started by mistake. Therefore, if Great Britain had no armaments, she at least could not contribute to these mistakes. Even those who thought more realistically claimed that moral

[1] Young, *Baldwin*, 129.

disapproval would of itself check aggression. If not, fantastically exaggerating the lessons of the first World war, they relied on 'the economic weapon', the blockade. As late as 1933 Arthur Henderson, by no means a pacifist and as near a realist as a Labour man could be, explained collective security to the Labour annual conference as 'the obligation to withhold all support from a Government that breaks its pledge to keep the peace . . . a common refusal to assist the international criminal who breaks the peace'.

Later on, when all was over, rulers and ruled exchanged accusations. According to one version, the rulers were 'Guilty Men', at best incompetent, more often deliberately deceiving the British people. Churchill described Baldwin[1] as 'putting party before country'. According to the other version, much formulated by Baldwin himself, the fault lay with 'democracy', which was reluctant to make exertions, sacrificing the future for the sake of the present, 'always two years behind the dictator'. Both accusations missed the truth. The statesmen were indeed incompetent, probably more so than usual. Baldwin made this a virtue. 'I always make mistakes', he said in 1935. Equally English people showed little enthusiasm for a dynamic leadership even if it were offered to them. Essentially rulers and ruled had the same outlook and belonged to the same decade. Both were trying to operate old concepts in a changing world. Both hoped that the storm would not blow or that at least it would blow elsewhere.

In his lazy fashion, Baldwin truly represented the decade. The ordinary Englishman, never attending church or chapel, probably without a Bible in his house, and yet expecting his children to swallow unquestioningly a Christian education, was an exact parallel to the statesman who made speeches supporting the League of Nations and never thought of asking the chiefs of staff how the League could be supported. Façade became reality for a generation trained in cinema palaces. Men believed the phrases which they heard and themselves used. Churchill really thought that there was a glorious Indian empire still to be lost; Baldwin really imagined that he was defending democratic virtues; Left-wing socialists really anticipated a Fascist dictatorship in England. So the watchers in the cinemas really felt that life was going on among the shadows of the screen. Of course no

[1] In the index of the *Second World War*, i.

one supposed that the tinny words would take on substance or that even the most menacing figures among the shadows could reach out and hit the audience on the head. This is what happened before the decade ended. The pretence turned out to be no pretence. Or perhaps it merely eclipsed the real life underneath.

X

THE NATION SAVED: ECONOMIC AFFAIRS, 1931-3

THE new age got off to a good start. A crisis of muddle which no one properly understood led to a general election of unrivalled confusion. A National government, which had been formed to save the pound, failed to save it; presented themselves as the saviours of the country on the basis of this failure; and had their claim accepted by a great majority of the electors. The government was a demonstration of national unity. This unity was shown in practice by public declarations of disagreement over fundamental issues among the leading members of the government—declarations in which indeed they were more anxious to emphasize the disagreements with their colleagues than to indicate what remedies they proposed themselves. It was also odd that the first clear call for a general election in order to strengthen the National government and introduce Protection was made on 8 September by Winston Churchill, who was not a member of the government and was a lifelong Free Trader; while the most uncompromising defence of Free Trade came from Lloyd George, a man who had never made a god of Free Trade in its great days. The accepted landmarks were down, and men reacted to a contradictory situation in contradictory ways.

The National government had been formed, as the political leaders repeatedly insisted, for 'a limited period' and 'a specific object': to balance the budget and so to save the pound. The budget had been balanced, though the pound had not been saved. No one, however, suggested that the National government should now disappear. Labour could hardly take office again as though nothing had happened. International confidence had to be won for a pound depreciated to two thirds of its former gold value. Besides, the immediate financial crisis had been provoked by larger problems; or at least men thought so. The run on the pound was explained by the budget deficit and by the deficit in the balance of payments. Behind these lay the chronic unemployment of the nineteen-twenties and the greater unemployment caused by the world Depression. Most men assumed that somewhere was to be found a solution to all four problems at once. The failure of the Labour government to deal with the larger problems was supposed to have brought on the financial crisis. A National government, formed to meet the financial crisis, should therefore deal with the larger problems.

No one except Mosley had shown much idea how to do so in the preceding two years. But crisis was expected to produce new ideas of itself, as had happened during the first World war. The politicians, like everybody else, hoped to be pushed into a new age backwards. Unemployment seemed the overriding problem. More work would mean a greater yield from taxes, and less expenditure on unemployment relief; the budget therefore would be secure. It would also presumably mean more exports. The balance of payments would be redressed, and the pound would be strong. The National government would have saved the country after all. How was this miracle to be accomplished? A few daring speculators talked of autarky, a closed economic system sheltering Great Britain from the storms of the world. Most people still believed that Great Britain lived by exports. In their eyes, the remedy was Protection. Fewer imports would give British industry a wider home market, and on this secure basis it would become a more powerful competitor in the markets of the world. In practice the arguments were mixed up: sometimes implying that foreign goods would be kept out, sometimes that more British goods would go abroad.

There were also more mundane calculations. The Conservatives were confident that they could win an election on the National cry; confident too that they could win it in such a way as to enter at last the promised land of tariff reform. Their great asset was to have a remedy, even though it might be the wrong one, while others had no remedy at all. MacDonald was firmly pledged against a general election. On the other hand, he was even more firmly convinced of the need for a National government with himself at the head and would accept an election if this were needed to preserve it. His prime motive was patriotism, though no doubt vanity also entered in. Few repudiate the title of saviour when it is offered to them. The national executive of the Labour party gave him a further push when they resolved on 28 September that those associated with the National government thereby ceased to be members of the Labour party. This decision broke with the precedent of the wartime Coalitions. It implied that there was a political intrigue, not a real crisis. In this way a sponge was passed over the record of the Labour government. From this moment, not earlier, MacDonald, Snowden, and Thomas became 'traitors', their work for Labour henceforth ignored as though it had never been. All the rest were in the clear; the embarrassing support which many of them had given to the 10 per cent. cut in benefit was not mentioned again.[1] At any rate, MacDonald had now no future except as National leader, and he had some cause for resentment against his former colleagues and admirers.

The Liberal ministers were in great difficulty. They could hardly swallow an election campaign under the banner of Protection. Equally they were lost if they fought against the National appeal. They were further weakened by dissension. Some twenty Liberals, led by Sir John Simon, went over to Protection and were for the National government at any price. Curiously most of these enthusiasts for national unity, including Runciman and Simon himself, had been the outstanding 'Squiffite' opponents of it fifteen years earlier. On the other side, Lloyd George, once the advocate of a Centre party, was now against National government at any price, particularly when it involved association with MacDonald and Baldwin, the two men who had supplanted him.

There was much coming and going: visits to Lloyd George by Samuel, the acting Liberal leader, and by MacDonald; Simonites waiting on the mat outside the cabinet room in the vain hope that Samuel and his supporters would resign; prolonged wrangles within the cabinet. This seems incidentally to have been the last occasion when cabinet, not prime minister, determined a dissolution of parliament. The exceptional circumstances were justification enough. On 5 October someone—perhaps Neville Chamberlain, perhaps Snowden, perhaps no one in particular—came up with a solution: a general election with each party putting forward its own programme under a blanket of words provided by MacDonald. This task was easy

[1] Henderson, with his usual puzzled honesty, was the only member of the executive to vote against the resolution. Technically a declaration that supporters of the National government had ceased to be members of the party was not the same thing as expulsion. It was more on an analogy with similar previous declarations in regard to Communists.

for the master of imprecision. MacDonald had no strong feelings on Protection and Free Trade. In his view, conflicts, whether international or domestic, sprang from misunderstanding, not from a clash of interests, and could therefore be ended by good will. If Germany and France could be reconciled, why not Protectionists and Free Traders? Somewhere, somehow, a formula could be found. This view, however absurd, was generally held at the time; MacDonald, in expressing it, was representative of the age.

In more popular terms, MacDonald asked for 'a doctor's mandate'—a blank authority for the National government to do whatever they could agree on. The phrase was significant in another way, more so than MacDonald or anyone else realized. In those days, before the development of modern remedies, all a doctor could prescribe for most ailments was rest, while natural recovery took its course, and this was much what the National government did in the end. All else was the 'quackery' which MacDonald threatened to expose. A general election was embarked on at once, perhaps for fear that the compromise between the parties might break down. Parliament was dissolved on 7 October. Anyone who reflected for a moment knew that Protection would follow a Conservative victory. Yet the question of abandoning the system which had served Great Britain well for three generations was never submitted frankly to the electors. The Conservatives had to make out that there would be a solemn inquiry, impartial and of open mind, before tariffs were introduced; the Liberals had to pretend to believe them.

The result on the other side was also curious. Labour defended the cause of Free Trade in the hope of winning Liberal votes, though its hastily drafted programme, which few Labour candidates understood, contained sweeping proposals for a planned economy. Lloyd George tried to pull the cause of Free Trade out of the bag; the other Liberal leaders indignantly pushed it back again. As a result, they got no money from Lloyd George's fund and were only able to contest 122 seats. The Liberals had to pretend, in any case, that this was not a 'coupon' election, and could therefore not complain when Conservatives ran against them. In practice, there were many Conservative withdrawals,[1] leaving 409 straight fights against

---

[1] And some Labour withdrawals also, to encourage straight fights between Liberals and Conservatives in constituencies hopeless for Labour.

102 in 1929. The Liberals came out badly more from their own lack of candidates and money than from Conservati malignancy.

The campaign resembled that of 1918 in other ways. There was the same cry of emergency, the same demand for new ideas; above all, the same emphasis on the past record of the contesting parties. This was the decisive issue. The conflict between Free Trade and Protection was not merely hushed up. It was dead now that men thought in terms of employment, not of cheap prices, which were only too cheap. The yardstick of the age was production, not consumption, at any rate in public. This developed a common interest between employers and employed. There were scares, made much of by Labour. MacDonald brandished million-mark notes from the time of German inflation to show what he had saved the country from, though paper money was in fact the benefit which he had undesignedly provided. Snowden achieved the first political sensation ever made on the radio by describing the Labour programme (not markedly different from that which he had helped to draft in 1929) as 'Bolshevism run mad'. Runciman raised the alarm that money from the post office savings bank had been used to bolster up the 'bankrupt' unemployment fund, though government departments had borrowed from the post office bank ever since it was first created. All these were irrelevancies, and Labour evaded its own failure by attributing defeat to them. The election campaign was not particularly scurrilous, apart from Labour attacks on MacDonald. On the contrary, it was rather quiet, and the turnout on 27 October, election day, was no higher than in previous elections. The voters judged in simple terms. Labour had run away; the National government had faced the crisis. Electors responded to an appeal for disinterested sacrifice, as the young men had done over Belgium in 1914. Whatever the party calculations of politicians behind the scenes, the people put country before class.

This patriotic interpretation of the voting should not be carried too far. On a more prosaic level, the Liberal vote mattered most. Some three million Liberals, who had no longer a candidate of their own, presumably voted solid for Conservatives. MacDonald, not Lloyd George, had caught the right tune: national emergency eclipsed Free Trade. Labour polled nearly two million votes less than in 1929. About half a million of these voted 'National'; they are said to have been mainly women. The rest merely did not vote. Thus, even in the most decisive election of modern times, the swing of the pendulum was less than 2 per cent., so far as the essential question, Labour versus the rest, was concerned. Workers lost faith in the Labour party; they did not get it in anyone else. Even so the results were dramatic enough. The Conservatives, with their inseparable allies, National Labour (the MacDonaldites) and National Liberal (the Simonites), received slightly over 60 per cent. of the vote—the only victors ever to top this mark—or with their less inseparable allies, the 'pure' Liberals, 67 per cent. The system, as often, exaggerated the effect of the voting. The Conservatives and their allies won 521 seats.[1] Labour, with a third of the total vote, held only fifty-two. All the members of the former Labour cabinet lost their seats except George Lansbury. The Liberals got their deserts: thirty-three seats, which was about right for their vote. The Communists and Mosley's New Party did not win any seats. Lloyd George was reduced to a family party of four: himself and his son, daughter, and son-in-law. His day was over.

The National government were clearly there to stay. The emergency cabinet was succeeded by one of normal size, and this inevitably meant Conservative predominance—eleven out of twenty members. There was really no one else of ministerial capacity. Individual changes shifted the balance still more. Snowden went to the house of lords, as lord privy seal, and combined his new dignity with proletarian ruggedness, singing 'On Ilkla Moor baht 'at' or even 'the Red Flag' in a Yorkshire accent. Neville Chamberlain, Protectionist by heredity, took Snowden's place as chancellor of the exchequer. The Simonite Runciman went to the board of trade, in the hope that he would resist Protection; he disappointed this hope as McKenna had done before him. Simon himself became foreign secretary.

A legend grew up later that the ablest men had been left out. This has no foundation. No one suggested bringing in Lloyd George. It was a kindness to pass over Austen Chamberlain, whose powers were failing. Churchill was in violent disagreement with the policy of conciliation in India; it was partly to sustain this policy that MacDonald and Baldwin had come together and now continued to cooperate. Soon Churchill was

[1] Conservatives 473; National Liberal 35; National Labour 13.

to make himself even more unpopular with enlightened opinion by his contemptuous opposition to disarmament. Amery was the only other notable absentee: he, too, an opponent of 'National' government and of most of the things which MacDonald and Baldwin stood for. Also, if the truth be told, he was, though able, a long-winded bore, and those with whom he had sat in cabinet must have rejoiced that he did so no longer. The National government owed its electoral success to Liberal votes and, still more to liberal spirit, quite as much as to patriotism. There was no room in it for the pugnacious Imperialists, Amery and Churchill.

The new house of commons presented a strange appearance: more new faces than after any previous general election, and the Opposition benches emptier than in any parliament since the days of Charles James Fox and the war against revolutionary France. Labour, unlike Fox, never thought of seceding, and Baldwin praised them later for having 'helped to keep the flag of Parliamentary government flying in the world'. Most Labour men still assumed that they would win at some time in the future. The general election of 1931 soon joined its predecessors of 1918 and 1924 as a fraud and a freak. Labour even welcomed 'emergency' measures—for economy now, one day for socialism. The diminutive party had a changed character. Union officials had suffered at the polls much like others: they were little more than half the Labour M.P.s (32 out of 52), and all were of the second rank. J. H. Thomas was the last leader of a great union to sit in parliament, except for Bevin in the unusual circumstances of the second World war. Union secretaries henceforth went their own way, negotiating directly with the employers. The general council of the T.U.C. never recovered the confidence in the parliamentary party which had been shattered by the events of August 1931. It formulated its own policy, in both economic and international affairs, sometimes more extreme, sometimes more moderate than that of the political wing of the movement. The Labour party took a further step towards becoming, except in income, a political party of the normal type.

Lansbury, the only ex-cabinet minister to survive the general election, was the obvious choice as leader. This was less strange than it seemed. His humble position as first commissioner of works did not represent his real standing in the Labour movement. He had long been a national figure, who could command audiences as big as MacDonald's, and would have been a member of Labour's Big Four or Big Five if it had not been for MacDonald's dislike of him. He had edited and sustained the *Daily Herald*; he had had, in the nineteen-twenties, his own Left-wing organ, *Lansbury's Labour Weekly*. As the hero of Poplarism, he had a unique skill in local government and was, in his own way, a master also of parliamentary tactics. As the ringleader against the cuts, he was the appropriate leader for Labour so long as economic questions came first. Things were different when international affairs took the centre of the stage. Two survivors among the junior ministers assisted him on the front bench: Stafford Cripps, then almost unknown except as a successful company lawyer, his main interest hitherto in the reunion of the Churches;[1] and C. R. Attlee, also a middle-class man, with considerable experience of the east end and some slight pretensions to be an 'intellectual'. No one then foresaw that Cripps would succeed Lansbury as the leader of the Left, still less that Attlee would one day be prime minister of the first Labour government with a clear majority.

What the Labour party did was, at the time, of little moment. The National government had the power and the authority to do whatever they wished, with some slight deference perhaps to 'national' unity. The Conservatives were clear what they wanted to do: they wanted Protection. An Abnormal Importations Act was at once passed (November 1931) to stem the imports which naturally came flooding in at the rumour that tariffs were to be imposed. Then a cabinet committee on the balance of trade was set up to maintain the appearance of an impartial inquiry. Neville Chamberlain was in the chair, and Protectionists had a secure majority. The inquiry was, in Samuel's words, 'merely perfunctory'. The committee was packed.

In any case, it was difficult for anyone to discuss economic policy except in terms of existing prejudice. Basic information was lacking. There was no central department of statistics. Government departments collected figures at random to suit their own needs. Four separate departments collected industrial

---

[1] Richard Stafford Cripps (1889-1952): educ. Winchester and London; solicitor general, 1929-31; expelled from Labour party, 1939 (readmitted, 1945); ambassador to Russia, 1940-2; lord privy seal and leader of the house of commons (member of the war cabinet), 1942; minister of aircraft production, 1942-5; president of board of trade, 1945-7; chancellor of the exchequer, 1947-50.

statistics;[1] five classified employers of labour;[2] two produced
rival and conflicting figures concerning overseas investment.[3]
Officials from the treasury and the board of trade dogmatized
without much knowledge. During the first World war the board
of trade had attempted to create a sort of civilian general
staff, called the General Economic Department. In 1919 this
dwindled into the Power, Transport and Economic Department
and was then slaughtered by the Geddes axe. All that remained
was a Chief Economic Adviser, who was not equipped to give
advice and in fact gave none. MacDonald, with his usual faith
in agreement among men of good will, set up in 1930 an Economic Advisory Council, composed of four capitalists, two trade
union leaders, and three economists. The experiment was not
a success. The businessmen advocated lower wages and public
economy; the trade unionists and economists advocated more
public expenditure; some of them advocated tariffs and devaluation. The Council did not meet again after the summer of
1931.[4]

The cabinet committee had therefore little before it other
than the bare bones of the balance of payments. It could not
seek advice from economists, most of whom were still Free
Traders. The few, like Keynes, who had gone over to tariffs,
were even more ruled out by the fact that they coupled tariffs
with increased spending and an unbalanced budget. The case
for Protection seemed to Conservatives so obvious as to be
hardly worth making. Tariffs would reduce British imports
without affecting British exports. Runciman added the argument, quite in contradiction to this, that the yield from customs
duties would be substantially increased and the budget therefore strengthened—foreign goods, in fact, would come in much
as before.

The arguments hardly mattered. Protection was advocated
for its own sake. The majority of the committee returned their
verdict early in January 1932. Once more Liberal ministers
resisted, and Snowden along with them. Again they threatened

---

[1] The registrar general, the board of trade, the inland revenue department,
and the ministry of labour.

[2] The board of trade, ministry of labour, census office, inland revenue, home
office.

[3] Board of trade and inland revenue.

[4] It remained theoretically in existence and even circulated some papers. In
Nov. 1939 it was replaced by the Central Economic Information Service.

to resign. Once more a solution was found, this time by Hailsham, the secretary for war. There should be 'an agreement to differ'. The dissentients remained in the government, free to attack its most vital point of policy. There had been nothing like this since the agreement long ago to differ over Catholic emancipation; even that had been only an 'open question'. It was a last, and rather absurd, obedience to the façade of national unity.

Neville Chamberlain introduced his Import Duties bill on 4 February, complete with pious references to the memory of his father. The Liberals duly opposed it, as Snowden did in the Lords. It was carried by crushing majorities,[1] and came into operation on 1 March. There was to be an immediate general tariff of 10 per cent., and an advisory committee under Sir George May, hero of the report which had touched off the financial crisis in the previous year, to recommend changes. This it speedily did, nearly always in an upward direction. Empire goods escaped for the time being. So did raw materials, and nearly all foodstuffs: 'stomach taxes' still cast a long shadow. Imports under the old McKenna and Safeguarding duties were also unaffected. In the end, about a quarter of British imports still came in free of duty; about half were paying between 10 and 20 per cent. Forty or fifty years before, the change to Protection would have been sensational, almost revolutionary. There would have been wide public controversy. Now no one displayed emotion except Neville Chamberlain; even his display was unconvincing. There were no victory rallies by triumphant Protectionists, no demonstrations of protest by indignant Free Traders. The heart had gone out of the quarrel. In its great days, it had been as much a battle over political power as over economics, if not more. The Anti-Corn Law League had been out to end the political domination of the landed aristocracy, not just to repeal the Corn Laws. Tariff reform sprang from the sentiment of imperialism, and was defeated by Liberal idealism. Now no great principle was at stake. The idea of Protection had long been accepted—for the sick, for the aged, for the unemployed. It was a comparatively trivial extension of this principle when ailing industries were protected also. Some Conservatives thought that British industries could be

[1] In the Commons by 454 votes to 78, i.e. all the Labour members plus 32 Liberals.

reconstructed, or as it was called rationalized, behind the tariff walls. A few welcomed tariffs as a way of increasing the cost of living, and so of reducing real wages unperceived. These were refinements beyond ordinary comprehension. Protection was not even a deliberate turn away from the world market by British industry, though this indeed was happening under the surface. On the contrary, the world market had turned away from British industry, and tariffs were imposed ostensibly to turn it back again. The tariffs were put on, according to Neville Chamberlain, so that they could be taken off again by bargaining with other countries—a hope largely unfulfilled. To judge by what men said, the whole affair was topsy-turvy. Protection was carried by the Conservatives who claimed to believe in free enterprise. It was opposed by Labour, whose programme demanded a planned economy. Once the gesture had been made, the National government went back to relying on the forces of natural recovery and continued to take advice from rigid Free Trade economists, so far as they took advice at all.[1]

The budget, which Chamberlain opened on 19 April 1932, was more representative of what the National government stood for, claiming to outdo Snowden's emergency budget in its rigour. Even this was more phrase than reality. Despite all the previous talk of economy, Chamberlain could find little to economize on. He enforced belatedly the additional 5 per cent. cut in police pay which had been left out by accident in September 1931. He allowed for the lowest arms estimates between the wars,[2] thus carrying British disarmament further than any Labour government had dared to do—a clear indication that this disarmament sprang more from economy than from pacifist agitation. Otherwise he changed little, relying on tariffs to bring in new revenue. As a matter of fact, he got his calculations wrong, and ended the year with a deficit of £32 million, which he cheerfully added to the national debt. Thus even Chamberlain's finance turned out to be mildly inflationary after all—a process which he carried further in 1933 when he suspended the sinking fund altogether.

There was not much here of the financial orthodoxy which

---

[1] It is a curious academic point that economic historians were more flexible than economists. In the early twentieth century they provided the first Protectionists (Ashley, Cunningham, Hewins); between the wars they were usually social reformers or socialists (Tawney, the Hammonds, Cole).

[2] £103 million.

had brought the Labour government down. In one way, how-ever, Chamberlain's budgets, with their reliance on the yield from protective duties, were truly reactionary. They reversed the trend towards direct taxation which had been going on for nearly a century. This trend reached its height in 1917–18, when 82 per cent. of government revenue came from direct taxes; then the figure settled down at precisely two thirds until 1932. Chamberlain pulled it down to 55 per cent. This benefited the moderate middle class. Even in 1937, when taxation had again increased, a man with £500 a year was paying no greater proportion of his income in tax (5½ per cent.) than before the first World war. The really poor man, with only £100 a year, was paying twice as much.[1] To this extent the National government earned their majority.

This was more than balanced by Chamberlain's most con-siderable achievement: converting the mountain of War Loan (over £2,000 million) from 5 per cent. to 3½ per cent. Snowden had been planning to do this in his emergency budget. The plan was resumed in the more favourable atmosphere of eagerness for patriotic sacrifice. In any case, investors were grateful for a safe 3½ per cent. at the height of a depression where many industrial shares were showing no yield at all. Probably these are vain speculations. The psychology of investors was no longer decisive. The money market, like other things, no longer worked in the world of free enterprise. Rates of borrowing could be 'made' by the bank of England, once it had the will to do so. At all events, the rate was pulled down, and War Loan successfully converted. Politicians and lenders exchanged mutual con-gratulations.

The immediate result was a saving of £23 million. By 1936 the general reduction in interest rates was saving the national finances £86 million a year.[2] Thus, the principal economy of a government, for which we can be sure all bondholders had voted, was made at the expense of bondholders, not of the un-employed; yet with none of the outcry against confiscation which would have greeted the same economy if made by a

---

[1] The really rich, over £10,000 a year, of course paid much more (39 per cent. as against 8 per cent. prewar). This increase in taxation did not much change the ownership of capital. In 1913, 0·4 per cent. owned 55·6 per cent. of total capital; in 1937, 0·95 per cent. owned 55·68 per cent.

[2] Morton, *British Finance 1930–1940*, 274. Another authority (Hicks, *Finance of Br. Govt.*, 380) gives the saving between 1929 and 1935 as £131 million p.a.

Labour government. This seems to confirm Bismarck's rule that in England a progressive government is always put in to carry reactionary measures, and a reactionary government to carry progressive ones. The change was, of course, made purely to save money and to reduce taxation. Later on it was dressed up in high principles and presented as inaugurating an era of cheap money for the sake of industrial revival. Here again, the politicians were pushed into enlightenment backwards, so far as they got there at all.

The greatest of Chamberlain's ambitions still lay before him: to fulfil his father's dream of Empire Free Trade. It was to prepare for this that empire goods had been temporarily exempted from the general tariff in April, on the urgent plea of the Canadian government. Now the grandiose vision was to be fulfilled: Great Britain the workshop of the Empire, if no longer of the world; the grateful Dominions supplying the mother country with food and raw materials. As a display of sentiment towards these Dominions, an Imperial conference was held outside London for the first and only time. It met at Ottawa from 21 July to 20 August. Baldwin, Chamberlain, J. H. Thomas, Runciman, and three other cabinet ministers crossed the Atlantic. MacDonald remained in London to conduct the government almost alone. The great gathering was a failure, the end of an illusion. The Dominions, themselves devastated by the Depression, were as much concerned to protect their own industries as to benefit their farmers. Baldwin was firmly against 'stomach taxes'; the other British ministers, except Chamberlain, secretly agreed with him. Bennett, the prime minister of Canada, who presided, thought only of Canada's troubles, not of the Imperial cause which he had once preached. No food taxes on the one side; preferences for British industry only in the sense of increasing Dominions tariffs against foreigners on the other—these two things firmly barred the way against Empire Free Trade.

In the end there was no great charter of empire, only twelve individual agreements over details of preference between Great Britain and the Dominions, and between the Dominions themselves. The agreements made it more difficult for Great Britain to strike tariff bargains with foreign countries, though this had been a considerable object originally in introducing tariffs. Otherwise 'Ottawa' was merely a symbolic gesture towards the idea of a closed empire; a repudiation of Free Trade principles in theory, though not in practice. As such it was too much for the Liberal ministers and Snowden. Having swallowed in January tariffs which really amounted to something, though not as much as Protectionists claimed, they now strained at the gnat of Imperial unity. Despite pleas from MacDonald that his position would become 'more and more degrading',[1] if he were left alone surrounded by Conservatives, they insisted on resigning. Snowden was soon attacking his recent colleagues as virulently as he had attacked his old ones. The thirty odd Liberals who followed Samuel went into a state of suspended animation. Theoretically they supported the government on every issue except tariffs until November 1933; then they finally avowed general opposition on the ground that the government were not promoting disarmament strenuously enough.

The Liberals, looking back, attributed their eclipse to the selfish party manœuvres by the Conservatives during the crisis of 1931 and afterwards. This explanation did not cut deep enough. The Liberals were brought down by their lack of strong organization in the country; by shortage of money, which supplies from the Lloyd George fund could not conceal; and, most of all, by their own disunion. If Samuel had spoken for seventy-two Liberals after the general election of October 1931, he would have counted for something. As it was, he was supported in the house of commons by less than half of those who called themselves Liberal. The National Liberals became, as they have remained, Conservatives in all but name. MacDonald saw his own prophecies of isolation and humiliation fulfilled. He was the scapegoat for the failures of others: to Labour the traitor who had planned the disaster of 1931; to Conservatives the symbol of national pretence, which excused their own shortcomings.

MacDonald himself fell into the vagueness of despair. He had a last moment of aspiration, though not of success, seeking to end the economic troubles of the world at a great international meeting, much as Lloyd George had done before him at Genoa in 1921. This was the World Economic Conference which met in the Geological Museum at South Kensington on 12 June 1933. It was opened by the king, and attended by representatives

[1] MacDonald to George V, 11 Sept. 1932. Nicolson, *George V*, 498.

of every extant government, not excluding Liberia. MacDonald presided. For the last time, in his words, the lion (whichever was the lion) lay down with the lamb (whichever was the lamb). All the representatives deplored tariffs, exchange restrictions, and unstable currencies. All of them clung to one or other of these devices. The principles of Free Trade had become fossils, suitably preserved in the Geological Museum. On 5 July President Roosevelt killed the conference by refusing to stabilize the dollar, which he had previously taken off gold and devalued as part of the New Deal. After some lamentations, the conference adjourned for ever. The age of pious platitudes, as MacDonald once called it, was running down. The British government, who had themselves helped to speed up tariffs and devaluation, claimed that they would have returned to the course of virtue if others had done the same. They were secretly relieved when no one responded to their prompting.

The British indeed gave a further kick at the system of international obligations, appropriately at America's expense, and once more with the plea that it was done unwillingly. Baldwin's settlement of the British war debt with the United States in 1923 had been a striking symbol that the old world was being restored; repudiation of this debt now became an equally striking symbol that the restoration had not succeeded. In 1931 British payments had been suspended by the general moratorium on international debts which President Hoover promoted. A year later, the moratorium ran out. By then, the payment of German reparations had been virtually ended by the Lausanne conference of June 1932. Nor would France and other British debtors, lacking these, resume their payments. The British government were therefore in the position which they had tried to resist ever since the Balfour note, of having to pay the United States when no one was paying them. In December 1932 they paid their instalment in full as a gesture of solvency. At the next half year they tried a token payment, to be told by President Roosevelt that they were not in default, then by Congress that they were. At this the British gave up. No further payments were made. The British government felt that they had a good case. Great Britain had renounced her claims on others; she had borrowed the money to fight a common war; American tariffs made payment difficult; the transfer of gold threatened the stability of the pound. All the same, the British had practised the unilateral repudiation of an international agreement which they were to condemn so sternly when practised against them by de Valera or Hitler.

Throughout 1932 the British government were trying to discharge their 'doctor's mandate'. They sought means for lifting Great Britain out of the Depression. By the end of the year the new system, most unsystematically arrived at, was complete. After this, it was worked out, not added to. The following year, 1933, seemed to bring the merited reward. Unemployment reached its all-time peak of just under three million in January 1933.[1] It fell by half a million during the year. Production recovered to the level of 1930 and, by the end of the year, outtopped that of 1929. Great Britain's international payments exactly balanced, though more from a further decline in the cost of imports than from an increase of exports.[2] The government naturally took the credit for this recovery. Probably the claim was unjustified. World trade generally recovered somewhat in 1933 for no apparent reason. Both Germany and the United States, who had been worse hit than Great Britain by the Depression, also began to recover during 1933, though using means entirely different from those used by Great Britain or by each other.[3] It seems that statesmen can do nothing right when the economy is going wrong, and nothing wrong when the economy is going right. However, the policy of the National government certainly affected the pattern of British economic life, whether it brought benefits or no.

That policy had three principal branches: devaluation and a managed currency; cheap money; tariffs. The British government had arrived at the first unwillingly; at the second by accident; at the third with determination. Devaluation, or rather detaching the pound from gold, had been the obvious answer to the financial panic of August 1931. It was soon being hailed as something much more—a heaven-sent device with which to rig international prices in favour of British exports.

[1] These were the registered unemployed. If those who had ceased to register are included, the peak was reached in September 1932 with three and three quarter million unemployed. Conversely, when recovery came, the number of those employed increased faster than the number of registered unemployed declined.

[2] In any case, the exact balance was a coincidence so freakish as to raise a suspicion that the figures had been rigged.

[3] Soviet Russia, which had also been hard hit by the Depression despite the closed economy of the Five Year Plan, also recovered in 1933.

Even the government practised this secretly, despite its professions of financial orthodoxy, like a teetotaller sneaking into the private bar of a public house. In April 1932 an Exchange Equalization Fund was set up[1] ostensibly to smooth out temporary fluctuations in the rates of international exchange. Behind the scenes, the Fund deliberately kept the pound down, actually accumulating large quantities of gold as a result.[2] The manœuvre brought little lasting advantage. For one thing, British customers abroad got less for the goods they sent to Great Britain when the pound was devalued, and hence could buy no more than before, indeed probably less. More important, others could play the same game. In April 1933 President Roosevelt deliberately devalued the dollar as part of his New Deal, ultimately to 59 per cent. of its gold parity. The pound rose embarrassingly to $5.13, then settled at just under $5. In 1936 France and other members of the gold block also went off gold.

By then the British government preferred stable exchanges to competitive devaluation, and a Tripartite Agreement with the United States and France created a gold standard of a kind until the outbreak of war. The advantage of stable exchanges had come on a smaller scale long before. Most Dominions and some foreign countries followed Great Britain off gold in 1931. Together these constituted the Sterling Area, in which the bank of England performed its historic role on a more modest field. In theory, detachment from gold meant that the price-level at home could be 'made' without worrying about the effect on international exchange, and the other way round. In practice, the government and its financial advisers shrank from such a daringly modern idea. The currency was managed internationally, not at home.

There was, however, one important domestic consequence. The traditional device for protecting the pound was to raise interest rates. This was now abandoned.[3] Bank rate was pushed

[1] Originally with an endowment of £175 million in treasury bills; £200 million more were added in May 1933, and a further £200 million in 1937.

[2] In 1939 the gold reserve was £650 million, as against £130 million when Great Britain left the gold standard, and around £150 million when she tried to operate it. (Before 1914 the bank of England worked the gold standard with a gold reserve of £30–£40 million.)

[3] Even in the crisis of 1931 Montagu Norman hesitated to raise the bank rate for fear of the domestic effects. The device was in any case pointless. 'Hot' money— the curse of the thirties—moved from one capital to another for political reasons, not in search of higher rates of interest.

down to 2 per cent. in June 1932, where it stayed until 1951 except for a few weeks of alarm after the outbreak of the second World war. The original motive was simply to clear the way for converting War Loan. Next the government realized that low rates helped to reduce their own expenditure. Perhaps, too, they were nibbling at Keynes's doctrine that the rentier was doomed to the gas-chamber, or rather to an ultimate reward of 0 per cent. Finally, in 1933 they stumbled on the claim that cheap money would stimulate recovery: industrialists would be encouraged to embark on new projects. Authorities now seem agreed that the claim had little foundation. Industrialists will not borrow, cheap or dear, unless they see the chance of a profit. In 1933 few saw this chance. Investment which had fallen catastrophically since 1930 did not move up again until well on in 1934. Those who had money to spare put it in gilt-edged stocks, thus pushing rates down still further.[1]

The government themselves prevented the benefits of cheap money as far as they were able. Having secured cheap money, they refused to use it, and prevented those whom they controlled from doing so. The budgets of 1932 and 1933 were meant to balance, though they did not according to the strict doctrine of financial purity. Even so, they helped to create a psychology of economy, not of spending. The government refused to contemplate a deficit, or even public works on any large scale for the relief of unemployment. Such schemes as the Labour government had inaugurated were cut off. Local authorities were sternly told to limit their expenditure. The building of new schools practically stopped. The making of new roads stopped altogether. A later generation paid a bitter price for this in traffic congestion. It inherited many new roads from the nineteen-twenties;[2] from the thirties hardly any. Later on, when the economy recovered, the government authorized more public spending. Thus their use of cheap money was directly contrary to modern theory. They refused to spend when the economy was going down; spent when it was going up; and so exaggerated the respective trends instead of smoothing them out. More sensible behaviour came unwittingly from local authorities who

[1] In 1936–7 cheap money even worked to check expansion. Rates were kept so low that lenders were unwilling to come forward even though borrowers were eager for their money.

[2] For example, the Liverpool to East Lancashire road; the Great West road; the North Circular road; to say nothing of the Mersey tunnel.

embarked on large-scale schemes which could not easily be suspended. The reward was to be much condemned for 'waste'.

Tariffs were the most deliberate innovation of the National government, and the one of which they were proudest. The results did not come up to expectations. In the words of one authority:[1] 'There is no sign that these protective devices improved British foreign trade as a whole at this time.' The foreign manufacturers whose goods were excluded from Great Britain simply became fiercer competitors against British goods elsewhere—the Germans in South America and the Balkans, the Japanese in the Far East. The bulk of British imports were food and raw material. These could not be reduced much. They came mostly from poor countries which could buy little of the finer, and more profitable British goods; yet the proportion coming from these countries was deliberately increased. The reduction in manufactured goods imported, on the other hand, meant the loss of valuable markets in richer countries. In the end, therefore, tariffs actually reduced British exports more than they reduced imports.

Tariffs were more important politically than in economics. They shifted, or helped to shift, British trade away from foreign countries to the Dominions and colonies. The Dominions had agreed on this at Ottawa. The crown colonies, governed from Downing Street, were 'invited' to give preference to British goods, and had no choice but to do so. Cheap Japanese goods were kept out; British goods were too expensive to take their place. Thus the British who had always claimed to run their Empire for the benefit of the native inhabitants now belatedly exploited it in crude mercantilist fashion—death-bed wickedness instead of death-bed repentance. Yet they were aggrieved when others complained of their selfishness. Here again the gain was relative. Though trade within the Empire markedly increased its share in British overseas trade,[2] the total of this trade was every year a diminishing proportion of British trade as a

---

[1] Ashworth, *Economic History of England*, 404.

[2] U.K. imports from the Dominions, India, and colonies increased from 24 per cent. of total overseas trade in 1931 to 37 per cent. in 1937; exports from 32 per cent. to 39 per cent. The Dominions benefited more than the mother country. British imports from the Dominions increased from 18 per cent. to 25 per cent.; exports from 24 per cent. to 29 per cent. British imports from India and the colonies increased from 10 per cent. to 14 per cent. British exports to them did not increase at all.

whole.[1] The two things—the increase in Imperial trade and the decline in the importance of overseas trade—were part of a process which Protection merely helped on its way. Nevertheless, the National government, so far as they achieved anything, contributed to the nationalist economics and autarky which they deplored when practised by others.

Tariffs had indeed been promoted for another, more strictly nationalist reason: to assist the replanning of British industry behind the tariff wall. This wall was reinforced by the new device of quotas, an even more brutal instrument. There was a good deal of this replanning during the nineteen-thirties. All of it reflected the current spirit of the time which favoured producers, that is both employers and workers, as against consumers, among whom the unemployed man was numbered as soon as he fell out of work. The schemes showed two constant features. They were carried through by the producers themselves, often with legislative backing; and they aimed to reduce the productive capacity of an industry by a general levy on its members so that the survivors should make higher profits, though producing fewer goods. This method was applied ruthlessly in shipbuilding, where berths with over one million tons building-capacity, were destroyed, and in cotton, where six million spindles were destroyed. Even so destruction could not keep up with the decline in markets. At the end there was as much redundant plant in shipbuilding as there had been when destruction started, and in cotton more.

In coal a similar scheme, though strongly pushed, did not work. The owners of smaller, less efficient pits refused to be bought out and had to be carried by the more efficient districts. The government blustered and did nothing until almost the end of the decade. Then their nationalization of mining royalties in 1938 set a precedent both in principle and in method. In principle, because if royalties could be nationalized, so could the mines. The method was compensation, fixed by arbitration, when government and owners failed to agree.[2] Iron and steel

[1] British exports had been 33 per cent. of the total national product in 1907 and 27 per cent. in 1924; they were 15 per cent. in 1938. Imports had been 31 per cent. of the national income in 1913 and 25 per cent. in 1929; they were 16 per cent. in 1938.

[2] The owners demanded £112 million. The government offered £75 million. The arbitrators awarded £66·5 million, and the government added £10 million in order to propitiate Conservative opinion.

were the show piece of rationalization. This was a declining
industry in some areas, a progressive one in others. Not surprisingly therefore it showed some advance in production and
efficiency. Planning, however, retarded the decline as much as
it helped the advance. The historian of the steel industry
describes the nineteen-thirties as a period of 'retarded development', and the community at large paid the cost of reconstruction in the shape of excessively high prices for steel.[1]

Agriculture provided a strange story, in which emotion
played as much part as economics. Antagonism to the landed
interest had always been at the heart of the Free Trade movement; enthusiasm for it inspired the Protectionists. Even Protection for industry did not seem to justify 'stomach taxes', and
direct tariffs on foreign food played little part in agricultural
policy, though they played some. Quotas counted for more,
with the great advantage that they could be varied with the
seasons. Most striking were subsidies, once so condemned for
coal, soon a permanent feature in agriculture, and costing by
1936 £40 million a year. They had the great advantage of
benefiting the farmer without directly increasing the price of
food. As well, the agricultural marketing boards, created by the
second Labour government, were given greater powers. They
worked successfully with milk and potatoes, less successfully
with bacon and meat. The whole process was a dramatic
reversal of the secular trend by which Great Britain had become
predominantly industrial, while drawing food from the rest of
the world. The reversal was peculiarly perverse at this time.
The world was overflowing with food, prices were excessively
depressed, and Great Britain could best contribute to the recovery of world trade, including her own, by increasing her
purchases of food from the impoverished countries. Instead she
did the exact opposite.

What was the explanation? The strategic need of being self-
sufficient in wartime was hardly mentioned, at any rate until
1937. Only the encouragement of sugar-beet, which cost £5½
million a year, was occasionally justified on this ground. In any
case, as one economic historian has pointed out,[2] England still

[1] D. L. Burn, *Economic History of Steelmaking*, 483.
[2] A. J. Youngson, *The British Economy*, 120. Of course, as Mr. Youngson goes
on to observe, the admiralty would probably not have built more aircraft carriers
even if they had had the money. One was ready in 1939. Four came into service
during 1940 and 1941. None was laid down between 1939 and 1942.

needed to import much of her food, and half the money spent on agricultural subsidies would have provided the much greater security of four aircraft carriers. No doubt it was felt that agriculture could not be left out when other industries were being protected. Also, in an odd way, the demand of the Dominions for food preferences strengthened the claim of British agriculture. Dominion producers, it was felt, should benefit only if British farmers benefited still more.

The deeper motives were political and social. Though few constituencies were exclusively agricultural, the agricultural vote was decisive in many, and both parties wooed it, the Conservatives more blatantly than Labour. Again, agricultural prosperity meant higher, or more secure, rents for landlords, the traditional core of the Conservative party, and for many cherished institutions, such as Oxford and Cambridge colleges. Deepest of all, though rarely avowed, was a belief in the superior virtue of country life. The rural communities were supposed to enshrine historic England. An England which increasingly emphasized its historic character was anxious to preserve them. The results were disappointing. Agricultural production rose during the thirties by one sixth, though even so it hardly reached the prewar level. The rural communities were not preserved. The increased output came from improved methods and more mechanization, not from putting more workers on the land. Quite the contrary. Agricultural employment fell by a quarter of a million between 1920 and 1938. Workers left the industry at the rate of 10,000 a year. Here as elsewhere, the people of England voted against the plans of their own government by running away.

Thus, though the measures laboriously devised by the government modified the character of the British economy, they contributed little to recovery. Yet in 1933 England began a recovery which carried production and employment to an all-time peak by 1937. This was done against the government, not by their aid. The people of England defied the principles which the government were seeking to impose and which they themselves extolled in theory. Instead of economizing, they spent. Instead of making sacrifices for the national cause, they improved their own living conditions. Wages remained stable when economists insisted that they must go down. Prices went down despite the efforts of the government to push them up. Foreign producers contributed to this process. The terms of trade were not affected by the devaluation of the pound. The primary producers, desperate from poverty, would take paper pounds rather than nothing at all. The terms of trade continued to move in Great Britain's favour. In 1929 exports had bought 14 per cent. more imports than prewar. In the mid-thirties they bought 40 per cent. more and slipped down only to 30 per cent. more in 1938.

English people further impoverished the primary producers by investing less abroad. Only once after 1930 did the balance of payments show a surplus, and that a trivial one—£32 million in 1935. Economists and politicians shook their heads over this. It was evidence of British decline, 'an indication of greater insecurity',[1] the end of British greatness. On the contrary, it was evidence of greater sense. English people were not too poor to lend abroad; they merely did not want to do so. An Englishman who put his money into tin mines, Argentine rails, or foreign government-bonds in the nineteen-twenties, found himself in the nineteen-thirties with a stack of worthless, highly decorative share-certificates. An Englishman who built a fine modern house found himself with a fine modern house. A favourable balance of payments looked impressive in a table of statistics. For the individual it meant that he had been presenting goods to foreigners instead of acquiring them himself. The National government told English people that their own country came first. English people unconsciously drew the moral. Domestic conditions worked the same way. Increased social security meant that individuals saved less against misfortune and old age. Increased equality of incomes, or rather lessened inequality, meant that there were fewer rich people with an automatic surplus available for investment.

At any rate, the result was unmistakable. Increased consumption by individuals pulled England out of the slump. All the growing industries produced mainly for individual consumers at home. This was true, for instance, of the electricity supply industry, which increased its consumers from three quarters of a million in 1920 to nine million in 1938, with a consequent boom also in electrical goods. It was true of the automobile industry, which increased its production, almost exclusively for the home market, in every year except 1932. It was true of artificial silk, and of the two even newer products which

[1] Ashworth, *Economic History*, 351.

were developed fully only after the second World war—nylon and plastics. Private housing eclipsed them all. The building boom was the outstanding cause for the recovery of the thirties.

The government did not launch this boom. On the contrary, they had tried to prevent it. They ended building under Wheatley's act in 1932; they never began the building projected by Greenwood in 1930. They did not begin slum clearance until 1934, and then demolished only a quarter of a million houses up to 1939—half the figure which Greenwood had laid down for urgent immediate action. Meanwhile, individuals built nearly three million houses during the nineteen-thirties without government aid—nearly twice as many as had been built with government aid during the preceding decade. Even the government's cheap money contributed little to this boom. The building societies hardly reduced their rates. Cheap money worked at best only in a negative way. Houses built for rent were a more profitable investment than money lent to the government. New houses therefore represented one quarter, or perhaps more, of the total capital investment of the country during the nineteen-thirties.

When recovery came, activity in the building trade increased at about twice the general rate, and the building boom accounted for 30 per cent. of the increase in employment between 1932 and 1935. The indirect effects went wider. Men with new houses bought radio sets, electrical equipment, and new furniture. They raised their general standard of living. Many of the houses had their own garages, and this went along with the sales of motor cars. Most of the unsubsidized houses were built in new districts. When men broke away from their old houses, they usually broke away also from their old occupations and their old regions. The south of England, like the new houses and the new industries, was more high class. Hence there was a demand for new roads, new shops, new schools, new public buildings and cinemas; and these had to be of a higher standard. This was the new England which saved itself by its own exertions, or rather by preferring new amenities to exertions of the old type. Yet it received blame, not praise, when it was noticed at all. As an 'image' of society the new houses and their inhabitants had a great defect, as the new industries had also. Each of them individually was small. They looked unimpressive when set off against the massive picture of the great staple industries in decline and against the old industrial towns. Moreover, the new England was uninspiring. It seemed wrongheaded and selfish for men to promote recovery by spending money on themselves, when there were still nearly two million unemployed living in harsh circumstances. This obstinate mass of unemployment and the stagnation of British exports made the nineteen-thirties 'the black decade' as much for those living in them as for posterity.

The government continued to rely on the forces of 'natural recovery'. In February 1933 Chamberlain said that they must keep 'pegging away'—more economy, cheaper money, lower taxes. Their hope was for the recovery of old industries, not the development of new ones. 'Natural forces' worked in the opposite direction, but they did not work fast enough. It had taken sixty years or more in the first Industrial Revolution, before the surplus agricultural population moved into the industrial towns. Now a new industrial revolution could not happen in a single decade. English economy had been coasting for a long time. The need for change had been obscured by the misleading boom before 1914, then by the first World war, and after it by the belief that all would be well on the old lines if the effects of the war could be undone. Though change imposed itself all the same, the new industries and the demand for their products increased less rapidly than the old industries, and the export trade on which they had depended, declined. Men saw that the race was being lost. They did not appreciate that ultimately it would be won.

Most of all, perhaps, the change was retarded by the very success of social reform. The victims of the Industrial Revolution left nothing except a tumbledown cottage. The unemployed miner or cotton worker, previously the aristocrat of labour, had a decent, though old-fashioned, house in a reasonably well-kept town. He belonged to a community with a flourishing life and strong loyalties. He had paid trade union dues for years, had an account at the local cooperative store. He sang in the Methodist or Baptist choir. Though unemployed, he received 'the dole', which enabled him and his family to keep alive. He had been promised recovery, and he waited for it. It was calculated towards the end of the nineteen-twenties that 800,000, or more than half, of the unemployed were due to the decline in the export trades. Ten years later these same permanently unemployed were still almost half a million, or nearly a third of the total.

The division came also with age. The man over 45 whose place of employment closed, fell out of work for good. The young man without a job tended, in the end, to change his trade or go elsewhere. Class loyalty counted too. The unions were strong in the declining industries, weaker in the new ones. The new towns were less distinctively working class in character. Even the social services often did not benefit the workers. Subsidized houses went to the prosperous artisan and the lower middle class. Public education brought its greatest benefit still higher on the social scale. Even the things which benefited the workers—public health and unemployment relief—were largely paid for by the workers themselves, thanks to the principle of insurance, or poll tax, which Lloyd George had regretfully accepted in 1911. The workers had hoped to be emancipated. Instead the new England was being made against them, and at their expense—or so it seemed.

Hence recovery did not bring with it a softening of class antagonisms. Rather there was a more aggressive tone of class war. This took on a new form. In the old days, or even in the nineteen-twenties, the unions had been the instruments of class war, and the Labour party had been more moderate, particularly under the leadership of MacDonald. Now it tended to be the other way round. Under the influence of Bevin and Citrine, the unions continued throughout the thirties the line of collaboration with the employers which they had adopted after the general strike—assertive and pugnacious no doubt, but set on compromise, not conflict, in a hard-headed, practical way. In this decade there were no great strikes with union approval, as there had been between 1911 and 1926. The Labour party, on the other hand, became more consciously socialist than it had been before. This was partly a natural reaction to the experiences of the second Labour government. Labour had tried to make capitalism work and had paid a bitter penalty. Now, according to a resolution passed at the annual conference in 1932, the next Labour government must introduce 'definite Socialist legislation immediately', whether it had a majority or not. As always, the members of the Labour party were more anxious to decide what they should do when they came to office than to determine how they should get

there. The old faith was still strong. Labour was the party of
the people, and a majority would appear automatically when
the people came to their senses.

The new line had also a more specific cause. It was, in large
part, the creation of a new element in the Labour party: the
left-wing intellectual. In remote Victorian times many of the
socialist pioneers had come, of course, from the educated,
established class. The Labour party, however, had been almost
exclusively a working-class affair, led by working men or at
any rate men of humble origin. Comparatively few intellectuals
joined the party, and these, except for Webb and other Fabians,
usually for reasons of foreign policy. The extremists of the nineteen-twenties were either union leaders like A. J. Cook (many
of whom, though not Cook, had been members of the Communist party) or men deeply embedded in working-class life
like Lansbury and Maxton of the I.L.P. The Communist party
was itself almost exclusively working class in leadership. Of
the twelve Communists sent to prison in 1925 only one, T. H.
Wintringham, was middle class, and he had been pulled in by
mistake. The intellectuals of the twenties—Webb, Dalton,
Tawney, even Cole—were regarded as shockingly moderate
even by the I.L.P. Marxists were to be found only among the
advocates of 'independent working-class education'—the Plebs
League and its offshoot, the National Council of Labour Colleges—virtually none of whom had been at a university.[1]
The few English textbooks of Marxism were crude exercises by
working men, ruthlessly disregarding the capitalist economics
and political theory of the universities.[2]

The new development was basically a revolt of social conscience by intellectual members of the educated class, ashamed
of 'poverty in the midst of plenty'. The younger poets—Auden,
Day Lewis, and Spender—showed this revolt in its literary
form. Most of them learnt their Marxism in Berlin, during the
struggle of Communists and National Socialists before Hitler
came to power. *Mr. Norris Changes Trains* (1935) by Christopher
Isherwood best recaptures the spirit of that time. The theo-
reticians, however, were directly inspired by the example of

---

[1] Walton Newbold, a Marxist of a sort and the first Communist M.P., had been
educated at Manchester University. This, and his personality, deprived him of all
influence inside the Communist party.

[2] e.g. *The State* by William Paul.

Soviet Russia, where the Five Year Plan, started in 1928, seemed to show a way of escape from the evils of capitalist anarchy. Keynes did not work out his ideas for the overcoming of cyclical unemployment until 1936; the future New Dealers of the United States had not fumbled into action; Swedish experiments in planned economy were little regarded. Therefore, once men talked of planning, many of them regarded communism as the only way of getting it.

The new enthusiasts for communism had different starting points. Some had been Fabians, including the Webbs themselves, who discovered in Soviet Russia a new civilization.[1] Others arrived at Soviet planning after previously associating with Mosley. This was true, for instance, of John Strachey whose book, *The Coming Struggle for Power* (1932), was the most influential work produced by the new movement and the best Marxist exercise written in English. Strachey had actually been a candidate of Mosley's New Party in the general election of 1931. Laski, another moderate who now swung left, followed a path of his own. His conversion sprang from politics, not from economics. He worked up the legend that the constitution had been manipulated against Labour during the crisis of 1931 and drew from this the conclusion that socialism could not be introduced with the existing machinery of parliamentary democracy. Whatever their background, these representative figures all had the same character: they were highly educated intellectuals whose ideas and writings appealed to others of the same sort.

Few of these middle-class Marxists joined the Communist party, at any rate openly. Maybe they disliked its aridity and dogmatism; maybe they wanted to be leaders, not political cannon-fodder. Most of them hoped to find 'an English way', somewhere short of total dictatorship. Accident provided them with a political home. In 1932 the I.L.P. finally broke with the Labour party. It had been increasingly restive during the second Labour government, and now, refusing to accept Labour-party discipline in the house of commons, voluntarily disaffiliated from the Labour party. The more intellectual

---

[1] Their book with this title was published with a question mark in 1935, without one in 1937. It is, despite severe competition, the most preposterous book ever written about Soviet Russia. Probably the best is by Beatrice Webb's nephew-by-marriage: Malcolm Muggeridge, *Winter in Moscow* (1933).

members of the I.L.P. refused to cut themselves off in this way[1] and formed a new organization, the Socialist League, designed to continue the work of the I.L.P. in association with the Labour party. The Socialist League was the I.L.P. with a difference. The I.L.P. had been predominantly working class in composition, despite some intellectuals near the top. The Socialist League was intellectual and nothing else, all leaders and no followers. Its branches counted for little; its programme of ideas was all that mattered. It claimed to be thinking for the Labour party, though in practice much of the thinking met with Labour's disapproval.[2]

This thinking, when it started, was almost entirely on economic questions. Unemployment was the spur towards a more aggressive socialist policy. It also provided the opening through which Communist influence broke into the middle classes. In the nineteen-twenties Communist efforts had gone mainly into the trade unions. Their organization for disruption, the Minority Movement, was now on the point of collapse. The National Unemployed Workers' Movement provided a welcome, and more successful, alternative. Leadership of this movement fell inevitably into Communist hands. The Socialist League was too remote; the unions frowned on separate organizations for the unemployed. The Communists stepped eagerly into the vacant place. Wal Hannington, their nominee for leadership, hit on the device of 'hunger marches'—an echo of the old Blanketeers. Select bands of unemployed from the depressed areas marched on London, where they demonstrated to little purpose. Their progress through the country, however, was a propaganda stroke of great effect. The hunger marchers displayed the failure of capitalism in a way that mere figures or literary description could not. Middle-class people felt the call of conscience. They set up soup-kitchens for the marchers and accommodated them in local schools.

The Communists did not need to argue. Their case was

[1] Membership of the Labour party was always more urgent for middle-class people than for workers. A working man does not need to join the Labour party in order to prove that he belongs to the working class. A middle-class man can prove it in no other way.

[2] The foundation of the Socialist League had an important personal consequence. The seceders from the I.L.P. joined with another body, the Society for Socialist Information and Propaganda, of which Bevin was chairman. Bevin hoped to be chairman of the new body. The ex-I.L.P.ers insisted on E. F. Wise. Bevin, though himself an intellectual lone wolf, never forgave the 'intellectuals' for this.

ready made. The great Depression, and the mass unemployment which accompanied it, proved that capitalism had broken down. Class war, fought to a finish, would automatically end capitalism and all its evils. The Communists did not so much preach a policy as sound a call to action. Early in 1933 events provided them with a reinforcement. On 30 January Adolf Hitler became German chancellor. Soon he established a National Socialist dictatorship. In Marxist eyes, he was capitalism's last throw, and the British capitalist government were supposed to be aiding him. Consciences which had been already stirred by the unemployed grew even more insistent at the tyrannies of Nazi rule. The two emotions merged into one. Hunger marchers filled the streets one day; demonstrators against Fascism followed on the next. Economic discontent was no doubt still the main driving force, with anti-fascism as a top-layer. But there was a change of tone and emphasis. Social questions, though still important, slipped into second place. Those who had begun by applauding the hunger marchers, were now concerned to arrest capitalism's march to war.

XI

THE NATION NOT SAVED:
FOREIGN AFFAIRS, 1931–6

WHEN the National government was formed in August 1931, the nation seemed to be endangered from economic, and particularly financial, weakness. By the time MacDonald ceased to be prime minister in June 1935, the danger came from abroad. The change of emphasis was gradual, though Hitler's coming to power may appear in retrospect as the decisive moment. At the time, men blinked at the mounting difficulties of the Disarmament conference and at the great debate whether peace could be preserved by means of the League of Nations. Foreign affairs were all along the interest of a minority. For most men, economic questions came first, and foreign policy was debated in such moments as could be spared from wrangles over unemployment. The government were content to have balanced the budget, somewhat mis-leadingly, and waited for 'natural recovery'.

In 1934 Chamberlain announced that the country had finished the story of Bleak House and could now sit down to enjoy the first chapter of Great Expectations. The public, their houses stocked with free copies of Dickens after the newspaper war, no doubt took the allusion. Chamberlain reduced the standard rate of income tax to 4s. 6d., restored the cut in unem-ployment benefit and half the cut in government and local government salaries.[1] In 1935 he claimed: 'Broadly speaking, we may say that we have recovered in this country 80 per cent. of our prosperity.' The claim was unduly modest. Production was ten points higher than in 1929; wage rates had fallen since then by 3 per cent., the cost of living by 13 per cent.

Mass unemployment in the old industrial areas still clouded this cheerful picture: villages in Durham, South Wales, and Lancashire with practically the entire adult male population out of work, Jarrow ('the town that was murdered') with two thirds permanently unemployed. Unemployed became in these

---

[1] The other half was restored in 1935.

towns a way of life, commemorated in *Love on the Dole* by
Walter Greenwood (1933), one of the few genuinely 'proletarian' novels written in English.[1] The government were stirred
into action against their principles, and half-heartedly. In
November 1934 they acknowledged the existence of four
Depressed, or as the Lords tactfully renamed them, Special
Areas—Scotland, South Wales, West Cumberland, and Tyne-
side. Two commissioners[2] were appointed to revive these areas,
with an initial grant of £2 million. Not much came of this.
The old industries could not be pulled back to life by a little
judicious prodding. In 1936 the English commissioner, Sir
Malcolm Stewart, reported that he had 'generally speaking . . .
failed'. He wanted powers with which to attract new industries.
His successor was given these powers in 1937; and industrial
estates were started in South Wales and near Gateshead. In
all, work was found for 12,000 men, an unimpressive total.
The unemployment figures in these areas improved much
more because of the movement of workers to prosperous
districts, some with assistance from public funds, most without.
The Special Areas scheme was a mere gesture towards planning,
and, as usual, went against the grain. It might have had some
use in 1932. Its operation in 1937 slightly retarded migration
to more secure jobs elsewhere at better pay.

The government never cared for the scheme and seemed to
expect its failure. They were more concerned to tidy up the
chaos of unemployment relief. Here Neville Chamberlain, who
was again the driving force, crowned the reform of local government which he had carried through in 1929. Unemployment
insurance, in the strict sense, was never a problem after the
cuts of 1931: the Fund was kept solvent at whatever hardship
to the unemployed. The difficulty lay with the long-term
unemployed who had exhausted their contributions and who
received relief, disguised as some form of 'benefit'.[3] The money
came directly from the Exchequer, and the government imposed a 'means test' as one of the economies in 1931. The
Ministry of Labour was not equipped to carry out this test,

[1] Its only rival is *The Ragged Trousered Philanthropists* by Robert Tressell.
[2] One for England, one for Scotland.
[3] 'Uncovenanted benefit' from 1921 to 1924; 'extended benefit' from 1924 to
1928; 'transitional benefit' from 1928 to 1934; 'unemployment assistance' (the
most accurate name for it) after 1934. It was not, of course, 'benefit' in any
insurance sense.

which was therefore entrusted to the public assistance committees of the local councils. The means test became the central topic of social controversy. The taxpaying classes were indignant if men received relief from public funds when they possessed resources of their own. The working classes were equally indignant that a man who had the misfortune to be out of work should be penalized because he had been provident or because other members of his family were in work. The public assistance committees of Labour-controlled councils would not carry out the means test, or carried it out evasively. Rules for the test and rates of relief varied widely from district to district. Poplarism was back more obstinate than before. The breaking point had again been reached for the basic assumption on which modern English administration rested— the assumption that men in public life would carry out rules with which they did not agree until these were changed by parliament.

The Unemployment Act of 1934, which Neville Chamberlain inspired, ended all this. The act took unemployment 'out of politics'—away from the Ministry of Labour at the top and from the public assistance committees lower down. A statutory committee was to run unemployment insurance in the strict sense, with a Fund designed to break even at an unemployment rate of $16\frac{3}{4}$ per cent., the rate of 1934. In fact, this rate was never reached again, and workers thus paid to keep the Fund solvent against a day which never came. 'Benefit', now renamed assistance, was transferred to an Unemployment Assistance Board of six members remote from politics, with its own offices and full-time staff throughout the country. This was a striking break from the normal pattern by which local elected authorities acquired ever wider functions though with ever narrowing power to decide how to use them. Instead an autonomous system was created, such as Chadwick had dreamt of a century before, and the U.A.B. was more formidable than the Bashaws of Somerset House. However, the problem was not spirited out of politics so easily.

The new national rates were due to be introduced on 7 January 1935. They turned out to be in many cases less than those fixed by the local public assistance committees, particularly of course in the most distressed areas. There were public demonstrations, renewed hunger marches. The government ran away from their high principles; interfered with the Board that was supposed to be above politics; and forbade any reduction of the previous rates. Perhaps they were conscious that a general election was approaching; perhaps they were flexing their muscles for appeasement elsewhere. At all events the second 'appointed day' did not come until 1 April 1937. By then the Board had learnt to walk more tactfully. No rates were reduced. There was no new outcry. Soon the Board took over responsibility for further categories of unemployed. In 1940 it became the Assistance Board pure and simple. The public assistance committees of the local councils were left only with tramps and the aged. Thus Neville Chamberlain realized the Fabian ambition. The Poor Law was dead.

The prolonged dispute over the means test did more than anything else to keep alive the political bitterness which had been caused by the events of 1931. The trenches of class war ran along the floor of the house of commons. In theory Labour condemned the entire system of unemployment insurance. It wanted work or maintenance as a national charge. Until that happy day (which did not dawn even under a Labour government), it pressed any claims for more generous relief which came to hand and saw in Neville Chamberlain the principal enemy of humane practice. He, on his side, was equally ready to dismiss Labour men as sentimental idealists.

Over planning the parties fought less fiercely, or divided less sharply. There were planners on the Conservative side: Amery as part of his old Protectionism, Harold Macmillan and others in a more cautious, and of course more democratic, version of the ideas which Mosley had originated.[1] Many Labour men regarded planning with distrust. Trade unionists saw in it something near direction of labour, to which they were fundamentally opposed. The Labour planners, Strachey and the Socialist League, used Marxist terms which roused the distrust of their moderate colleagues. The academic economists, who were moving towards planning with Keynes at their head, were discredited by their old association with Lloyd George. Moreover, they were curiously blinkered in their enlightenment. Shaw's saying applied in economics as much as in other walks of life: 'Those who can, do; those who can't,

[1] Allan Young, originally economic adviser to Mosley and a candidate of the New Party in 1931, became thereafter economic adviser to Harold Macmillan.

teach.' Even Keynes, who had more business experience
than most economists of the time, knew only the world of
finance. He had worked at the treasury, was chairman of an
insurance company, and speculated in commodities. He had no
feeling for industry except as figures in a book. Lloyd George
had denounced 'the penguins of the city'. Keynes was a here-
tical penguin, not a bird of a different species.

Hence the new ideas only got as far as a rigged or managed
currency and the use of credit for economic expansion. The
plans aimed solely at reducing unemployment. Increased production, not what was being produced, became the guiding
factor, and wealth, the preoccupation of older economists,
went into second place. This emphasis was not surprising in a
period of great unemployment. Its legacy was shown in a later
generation which made production a god for its own sake.
Moreover, Keynes and his school did the wrong sum so far
as Great Britain was concerned. They saw the problem as a
permanent pool of unemployed men and unemployed resources,
and proposed to dry out this pool by planned expenditure from
public funds. This analysis was correct for the United States
and still is. The British problem was at once simpler and more
intractable. The old England of the declining staple industries
had a surplus of resources which could not be brought back into
use even by a lavish credit policy. The new England had
reached, in a later phrase, something like full employment
except during the world Depression. Public spending stimulated industries which were already prospering, without doing
much to reduce unemployment in those industries which were
in decline. Yet prevailing opinion, including that of Keynes, rejected the alternative course of a directed, or planned, economy.
Under such circumstances, the endless economic debates in
parliament fumbled in the dark, occupying much time, creating much passion, leading to little result.

Yet another issue diverted men's minds from foreign affairs.
This was India. Indeed, if the importance of a subject were to
be measured by the columns which it took up in Hansard,
the entire nation would seem to have been obsessed with the
intricacies of India's constitutional future. This was not so.
India was a specialist affair, an important one all the same.
MacDonald and Baldwin were both committed to Dominion
status, and held tightly together. They stepped cautiously: a

second session of the Round Table conference[1] in the autumn of
1931, with Gandhi demanding Dominion status or even external association at once; a third session, to little purpose, in
1932; a joint select committee deliberating throughout 1933.
The Government of India Act was introduced late in 1934 and
became law in August 1935. There was to be responsible
government, or something near it, in the provinces, where
Congressmen could play politics without causing harm; a complicated jugglery with communal electorates; and a central
Power still safely under the control of the British Viceroy.
The British government claimed to care for the minorities,
especially for the Moslems. In practice, they clung to the
Raj, until that impossible day when communal jealousies
ceased to exist. Yet the old Raj was vanishing before their
eyes. English people had lost interest in India. Japan, not
Lancashire, provided such cotton goods as the Indians could
not make for themselves. Indians were beginning to enter the
civil service and the judicature. The future of India lay with the
brown Britons, especially with Nehru the old Harrovian, and
the Government of India Act was a temporary brake of little
relevance.

Its real significance lay in home politics. Churchill was the
remaining giant in politics after the eclipse of Lloyd George.
Isolated and resentful, he thought that with the debate over
India his chance had come. He would attempt the task which
had defeated Beaverbrook and drive Baldwin from the leadership of the Conservative party. Of course there was conviction
in his resistance as well. Churchill always responded to the
glittering words of history, to the call of drum and trumpet;
perhaps most of all now, when he was writing the life of his
ancestor, the first Duke of Marlborough. The Union Jack was
unfurled. An India Defence League, paid for by the Indian
princes, was set up. Little came of the turmoil except a spate of
words. Most Conservatives wanted a quiet life and were won by
Baldwin's advocacy of cautious, gradual concession. Besides,
they distrusted Churchill as they always had done—too clever,
too erratic, no Conservative in the narrow sense. Baldwin never
worried during this conflict, as he had done during the conflict
with Beaverbrook. He won almost without effort and carried the
Government of India Act to triumph for what that was worth.

[1] For the first session, see above, p. 275.

Churchill acknowledged defeat. He had estranged the
Conservatives and had also deepened the profound hostility
which practically all Labour men felt towards him. In 1935 he
seemed a man without a future. When, at this time, Baldwin
and Chamberlain thought of strengthening themselves against
the coming election, they dangled a fly towards Lloyd George,
not towards Churchill. Lloyd George unfolded his plans for a
British New Deal. To no good purpose. Lloyd George, too, was
a man without a future. Neville Chamberlain never forgot his
humiliation of 1917 and insisted that if Lloyd George entered
the government, he would go out. Chamberlain stayed. Lloyd
George attempted to wield his old power, if only for destruction.
Though he had now no followers and few friends, there was
still much money in the Lloyd George fund, and he was always
inclined to believe that money could work miracles. He created
a thread-bare agency, entitled the Council of Action—bizarre
echo of 1920 when the real councils of action had been effective against himself, and spent on it £400,000. He tried to woo
the Nonconformist conscience, his original love. This existed
no longer or could not be rallied as a political force. Lloyd
George spoke in the void. It was now his turn to wait at the
telephone for the call that never came.

One other question stirred in these years, hardly coming
back to life, but making a sort of posthumous reappearance.
When the Statute of Westminster was being debated, critics
pointed out that its provisions for unfettered Dominion sovereignty would enable the Irish to repudiate the treaty of 1921.
Cosgrave, then prime minister of the Free State, answered with
an assurance of Irish good faith. This could be no more than
a personal pledge. In 1932 de Valera, who had swallowed his
objections to the oath and entered the Dail, became prime
minister of the Free State. He recognized no obligation to the
treaty, and at once worked towards his doctrine of external
association. Coolly and legally, he chipped away the restrictions of the treaty. He abolished the oath which had once
caused such bloodshed; reduced the office of governor general
to a nullity; created a separate Irish citizenship—an example
followed by all other members of the Commonwealth after the
second World war.

The British government were indignant and helpless. The
judicial committee of the privy council ruled that the legal

weapon had broken in their hands and that de Valera well understood the Statute of Westminster. He offered to submit the disputed questions to an international tribunal. The British government, still clinging to the shadow of phrases, would accept only a tribunal confined to members of the Commonwealth. This de Valera, in his turn, rejected. The British therefore fell back on a method much valued in these years—'the economic weapon' as it was called or, in League of Nations parlance, 'sanctions'. De Valera refused to hand over the land annuities which in the treaty the Free State had undertaken to collect.[1] J. H. Thomas, the Dominions secretary, displayed an unwonted aggressiveness. A 20 per cent. tariff was slapped on imports from Ireland. The Irish retaliated in kind. Trade between the two countries was abruptly reduced. Increased separation was achieved, exactly as de Valera wanted.

At the end of 1934 the Irish agreed to take more British coal, and the British took more Irish cattle. This was an agreement between two independent countries to all intents and purposes. Ireland had become a member of the Commonwealth only in the most nominal sense. The civil war which followed the treaty thus proved to be the most futile struggle in Ireland's tragic history; Michael Collins and others had died in vain. Moreover, sanctions, far from being successful, had merely increased mutual hostility and had caused mutual impoverishment—a lesson, totally ignored, which had its application in the wider field of international relations.[2] The affair was a last kick of the old rule that English statesmen took leave of their senses when dealing with Ireland. Most English people, except for the small

[1] By the various Land Purchase Acts of 1870–1909 Irish tenants bought their land from the previous owners with money advanced by the British government and were to repay it, with interest, in annual instalments. The British government in their turn applied the annuities to servicing the loans which they had contracted. De Valera argued that the English had stolen the land from the Irish in the first place and were therefore not entitled to compensation. His case was as good as the British government's in refusing to pay their war debt to the United States, if not better. The British ignored this analogy. They could sin and retain their virtue. No one else was allowed to do so. De Valera kept the annuities for the Irish exchequer and in 1936 halved the claim made from the owners.

[2] Sanctions had one success. In 1933 the Soviet government accused some British engineers of 'wrecking'. Two of them were sentenced to imprisonment. The British government imposed an embargo on trade with Soviet Russia. The Soviet government first answered with a counter-embargo; then, having plenty of their own citizens in prison, quietly released the two engineers. After this the two embargoes were removed.

Ulster lobby, no longer cared about the question at all. Even
J. H. Thomas kept it going mainly to prove that he was
still politically alive. The proof did not help him much. In
1936 he leaked budget secrets, probably to his own financial
advantage, certainly to that of others, and vanished from
the scene[1]—the biggest fish ever caught by the machinery of
a judicial inquiry.

All these questions—unemployment, India, Ireland—kept
politicians busy and filled the newspapers. Foreign affairs
got in at the cracks. Yet there was mounting controversy here
also, and mounting difficulties as well, far more so than in the
preceding decade. Indeed, foreign policy had been largely an
agreed matter between the parties after the fall of Lloyd George,
except in regard to Soviet Russia, and even here the differences
were smaller than they seemed. Most Labour men disliked
Soviet dictatorship more than they liked Soviet socialism;
the Conservatives sought Soviet trade, despite their dislike of
Soviet policy. Both hoped that the Soviet Communists would
become, in time, more moderate and less troublesome. Labour
did not plan an alliance with Soviet Russia, nor did the Conservatives plan a war against her.[2] In any case this was a fringe
question. Over the really great questions—reconciliation with
Germany and cautious support for the League of Nations—
there was at most a difference of emphasis.

Baldwin and MacDonald agreed more with each other than
Baldwin did with the pro-French 'Die-hards' among the Conservatives or than MacDonald did with the pro-Soviet 'Reds'
in the Labour party. This applied equally to Austen Chamberlain and Arthur Henderson, as was shown over the question
of relations with Egypt. Chamberlain, too, had rebuked the
Imperialist Lord Lloyd, proconsul of Egypt, whom Henderson
dismissed; Henderson, too, held on to the Suez canal. Labour,
on the whole, accepted Locarno, objecting, if anything, that
it committed Great Britain too much, not too little. The

[1] It was normal at this time for the stock exchange to gamble on budget changes.
It was also normal for income tax to go up or down by 6d. In 1936 Chamberlain
put it up by 3d. Those who betted on this unprecedented change were clearly not
guessing. There was an outcry, and the leak was traced to Thomas. One of those
who had made money on the gamble paid Thomas £20,000 for his unwritten autobiography, and he may have received other rewards as well.

[2] Though a few Conservatives talked of such a war, no military preparations
were made for it, except in the sense of defending India, and the question was
never discussed by the chiefs of staff.

Conservatives welcomed the London naval treaty, despite complaints from the admirals. All parties looked forward to the Disarmament conference and were agreed as to the line Great Britain should take there. Whatever doubts Mac-Donald may have had about agreement on economic matters when he became National prime minister, he was confident that he would still be the national leader in foreign affairs.

This did not happen. Instead the parties divided deeply and bitterly over foreign affairs, as much as at any time in English history, and perhaps more so. This was in part a legacy of the way in which the National government had been formed and an extension of the disputes over economic matters. The rancour was generalized. Once Labour men saw MacDonald as a 'traitor' in his immediate acts, he became a traitor over everything. Equally the Conservatives became the agents of 'capitalism', not of the people, in foreign policy as elsewhere. Conversely, the supporters of the National government believed that a Labour party which had run away from its national responsibilities in an economic crisis would be equally unpatriotic and unrealistic in foreign affairs. Personalities also counted. Henderson virtually withdrew from politics in order to preside over the Disarmament conference, and played little part in them, even when he re-entered parliament in September 1933. The new leaders of Labour were not admitted within the charmed circle of the governing class and were, in any case, determined to keep out of it. Obviously there could never be the confidence between Lansbury, as leader of the Opposition, and MacDonald, as prime minister, that there had previously been between Baldwin and MacDonald when they were still on opposite sides.

Besides there was a far wider divergence of outlook. Lansbury was a pacifist, or next door to it. Of his two lieutenants, Cripps took up Marxism with the rigidity of a convert. Attlee, though not a Marxist, also held that there was 'no agreement on foreign policy between a Labour Opposition and a Capitalist Government'.[1] The result was startling. Before 1914 Balfour had sat on the committee of imperial defence when the Liberals were in office. MacDonald, when in opposition, had been consulted by Baldwin. Baldwin and Chamberlain, when in opposition, had been consulted by MacDonald. Even Churchill, though a

---

[1] C. R. Attlee, *The Labour Party in Perspective* (1937), 227.

bitter critic of government policy, served on secret government committees after 1935—originally at MacDonald's invitation. Labour was neither consulted nor informed. Baldwin once thought of meeting the leaders of the T.U.C. He did not do so. No Labour man received any confidential information about foreign policy or the state of British armaments until the spring of 1939, and then only in the most general terms. Great Britain never knew less national unity than in the days of the National government.

The cleavage far transcended personalities. Views about war which had been held during the nineteen-twenties only by a minority now became more widespread. Indeed, for a little while, they were the accepted orthodox opinion of the decade. The end of the twenties saw a sudden rush of war books. By the sort of odd chance which sometimes happens with literary fashions, practically all the books on the first World war which have remained famous to the present day—novels, memoirs, and a play (*Journey's End*)—were published between 1928 and 1930.[1] All preached the same lessons: the futility and dreariness of war, the incompetence of generals and politicians, and the ordinary men on both sides victims of this incompetence. The lessons were reinforced on an academic level by American and British historians who studied the diplomatic origins of the war and repeated, with a more scholarly equipment, the views first put forward by E. D. Morel and the U.D.C.

Few educated people now believed that the war had been caused by a deliberate German aggression,[2] though one or two still held that Germany had been more militaristic than others.[3] In the general opinion, wars started by mistake—the view of Lord Grey; the negotiating machinery of the League would prevent these mistakes in the future. Or they were caused by great armaments, the view of Lloyd George; the remedy for this was disarmament. Or they were caused by 'grievances';

---

[1] 1928: *Undertones of War* by Edmund Blunden; *Journey's End* by R. C. Sherriff. 1929: *Death of a Hero* by Richard Aldington; *All Quiet on the Western Front* by E. M. Remarque (translated from the German); *Goodbye to All That* by Robert Graves. 1930: *Memoirs of an Infantry Officer* by Siegfried Sassoon; *Her Privates We* by Private 19022 (Frederic Manning).

[2] Sir Robert Ensor still did, perhaps to atone for the fact that he had been secretary of an anti-Grey committee before 1914.

[3] E. L. Woodward demonstrated this in *Great Britain and the German Navy*. Though a distinguished work of scholarship, it passed almost unnoticed as he records in his autobiography, *Short Journey*.

the clear moral here was that these, now predominantly German, should be redressed. Or finally they were caused by 'capitalism'; hence Labour's contribution to peace was to bring capitalism to an end. A refinement of this last view was the doctrine, widely held in the thirties, that wars were deliberately fostered by the private manufacturers of armaments—a doctrine which produced a royal commission on the 'war traffic' in this country in 1935 and a Senate inquiry in the United States.

These explanations were usually mixed together. Whichever were adopted, it led to much the same conclusion. Since there was nothing to choose between the governments of each country and since war was always a purposeless evil, the duty of those who wanted peace was to see that their own government behaved peacefully and, in particular, to ensure this by depriving their government of arms. Hence the famous resolution at the Oxford Union in February 1933 that 'this House will not fight for King and Country' was a gesture of loyalty towards world peace rather than an act of disloyalty in the ordinary sense.[1] Disarmament became, as it were, the higher loyalty—the best thing not only for one's own country, but for all the world. This sentiment took on a more practical, urgent form with the opening of the Disarmament conference in February 1932. From this moment, Labour and Liberals alike pressed for disarmament as the main element in British foreign policy and developed their opposition to the government mainly on this issue. Samuel and his Liberals went into formal opposition because of the government's hesitations. Labour denounced the government as apologists for 'the merchants of death'.

The government and their followers moved tardily in the opposite direction. During the nineteen-twenties successive

[1] This resolution, which was carried by a substantial majority, caused a sensation, and the sensation was increased when some old members of the Union tried unsuccessfully to have the resolution expunged. The resolution became and remained a potent source of myth. There is, for instance, no documentary evidence that foreign governments noticed it or drew from it the moral that Great Britain had ceased to count in the world. On the other hand, the argument that it was really a vote for collective security, not for pacifism, cannot be pressed far. C. E. M. Joad, the principal speaker in favour of the resolution, certainly made a pacifist speech. At this time, early 1933, collective security was not yet a live issue. The only war which anyone envisaged was a so-called imperialist war, and pacifism seemed to be the only alternative. Pacifists cheerfully supported the League of Nations, just as those who opposed disarmament assumed that this made them opponents of the League of Nations also.

British governments had promoted disarmament, or rather a low level of armaments. Great Britain and her empire were unquestionably secure, and the chiefs of staff protested ineffectively in the void. They found practical arguments when Japan invaded Manchuria in September 1931 and when Hitler became German chancellor in January 1933 with an avowed programme of making Germany once more a great power. The chiefs of staff could now point to the Japanese navy in the Far East and to the coming shadow of a German air force. Like the 'pacifists', they regarded armaments as themselves the cause of war, except, of course, when they were in British hands. They assumed that any Power other than Great Britain, which built up great armaments, intended to use them. Great Britain therefore must also rearm either to deter the approaching war or to meet it if it came. Moreover, to be on the safe side, they usually exaggerated the armaments of others and then put in a large claim of their own, knowing that it would probably be cut down. The chiefs of staff, despite their talk of deterrence, were more or less convinced that the guns would go off of themselves once they were loaded, and this conviction helped to make war more likely, as it had done in 1914. Before both wars, the service experts gave a technical opinion that Germany, at a certain moment, would be ready for a great war. Unconsciously, this slipped, both with themselves and others, into a political opinion that Germany, being ready for war, would inevitably launch it.

The chiefs of staff, as was their duty, judged the international situation solely in terms of armaments. It was the fault of others if their technical opinions took the place of policy. The three chiefs of staff, sitting together, by-passed their political heads—the secretaries of state for war and for air and the first lord of the admiralty. These became little more than agents for those who were in theory their subordinates. The foreign secretary also was pushed aside, conducting diplomacy instead of defining policy. The chiefs of staffs reported directly to the prime minister, who was expected to act as a minister of defence[1] on top of his other duties. He did this

---

[1] It was a minor curiosity of the time that preparations for war were always known as 'Defence'. Of course this was true in the wider sense that they were designed to defend an existing empire, not to add to it. But most of them were offensive in their application—capital ships, a bomber force, ultimately an expeditionary force on land. Strictly defensive measures, such as radar and fighter

half-heartedly, acting more as a mediator between the chiefs
of staff and the political world than as the spokesman for defence needs. He skimmed through the recommendations of the
chiefs of staff and watered them down in his own mind. He
watered them down further for submission to the cabinet, and
the cabinet watered them down again at the thought of difficulties in parliament and in the country.

MacDonald was still pinning his hopes to the Disarmament
conference. Baldwin, who often acted for him in defence
matters, regarded the prospect of a future war with despair.
In November 1932 he told the house of commons: 'the bomber
will always get through', and concluded with the extraordinary
remark that, if war came, the youth of the world would be to
blame for allowing older men to make a mess of things. 'When
the next war comes . . . then do not let them lay blame on the
old men. Let them remember that they, they principally or they
alone, are responsible for the terrors that have fallen upon the
earth.' This was next door to an invitation for undergraduates
to vote for the 'King and Country' resolution.

In such circumstances, the chiefs of staff kicked in vain.
The prime minister and the cabinet accepted their advice as
theoretically sound and then did not act on it. On paper the
chiefs of staff got their way. In March 1932 the government
cancelled the rule that no great war need be expected for the
next ten years and instructed the chiefs of staff to make recommendations for remedying the worst deficiencies. Immediately
afterwards, Neville Chamberlain, chancellor of the exchequer,
introduced the lowest arms estimates between the wars. The
government had been formed to restore sound finance and
were almost as reluctant to spend money on armaments as on
the unemployed. In any case, the chiefs of staff took almost two
years to prepare their recommendations. Ministers still professed faith in disarmament, though secretly acquiescing in the
warnings from the service chiefs. At the same time, they sought
ways of evading the recommendations from the chiefs of staff
when these came. They were cheating both sides, to their own
bewilderment, and naturally transferred to their critics the

aeroplanes, were made belatedly and with difficulty. The choice of name was partly
technical, due to the fact that the political head of the army had already carried
off 'war'. But it was also part of the general reluctance to call a spade a spade, or
war war.

resentment which they really felt against circumstances or themselves. Hence the myth that British rearmament was prevented by a Labour party which had only fifty members in the house of commons.

The question came gradually into the open after the Disarmament conference began its discussions in February 1932. The British government ought to have had an easy time of it. They had no axe to grind over the navy, the strength of which was already defined by the Washington and London treaties, to the satisfaction of everyone except the admirals. With an army which did not exist from a European point of view, they had no interest in land forces except to secure an agreement between France and Germany. And, since London was supposed to be peculiarly vulnerable from the air, they might have been expected to jump at the idea of abolishing all aerial warfare. They made a mess of their case. Negotiations over disarmament, by getting down to details, usually reveal dangers which have not been noticed before and send the participants away eager for greater armaments. This conference was no exception. The service chiefs had no faith in international agreements, believing, in the British way, that no one except the British would keep their promises. The R.A.F. feared that a ban on bombing would mean the end of the R.A.F. and therefore insisted that bombing villages in the Middle East was an essential, indeed a beneficent, measure of police—an argument loyally voiced at Geneva by Lord Londonderry, the secretary for air. This aroused much indignation among British opponents of the government. It had little to do with the failure of the Disarmament conference.

The real deadlock, existing from the first day, and never solved, was between France and Germany. The Germans wanted equality; the French wanted security. The deadlock was not conjured away by the ingenious compromise of December 1932, promising Germany 'equality of status within a system of security'. The British government did not believe that France was in any danger from Germany—at any rate this is what they said in public in order to keep the Germans in a good temper. On the other hand, they could not bring themselves to order France to accept equality, nor would the French have obeyed such an order. In September 1933 the French produced a solution which was even more abhorrent to the British government than a breakdown. Germany should be given equality, and the British should then guarantee France against German bad faith, guarantee it, moreover, with real military preparations, not with the paper promises of Locarno.

The British government rejected this proposal. Their immediate motive was financial: with British economy just approaching convalescence, the government could not swallow any expense which might disturb the precariously balanced budget. More deeply, military commitments on the continent would have met with unanimous opposition from all schools of British opinion, from imperialists as much as from pacifists. The French therefore offered equality only after a trial period of four years, during which Germany should prove her good faith. Hitler rejected the offer. On 14 October 1933 Germany withdrew from the Disarmament conference. A week later, she left the League of Nations. The Disarmament conference was virtually dead, though it dragged on a shadow existence until April 1934, when the French themselves ended its misery.

A detached observer might have blamed the French for this failure. He might have blamed the Germans. Or he might philosophically have dismissed as hopeless any possibility of agreement between them. English people were not detached observers. They, or rather the believers in disarmament, blamed the British government. After all, there is nothing to be gained by blaming foreign governments; it is only the policy of one's own government that one can change. Again, it was easier to pick on superficial explanations of failure, such as the cool logic-chopping of Sir John Simon or the supposed intrigues of armament manufacturers, than to face the real difficulties. Besides, the British government were, in a sense, to blame: they had undertaken to reconcile France and Germany, and they had failed. Even now they could not justify themselves. Still hoping for reconciliation, they hesitated either to denounce French obstinacy or to express distrust of Germany. On the other side those who blamed the government most sharply for the failure of the Disarmament conference would have been even more indignant if the government had underwritten a Franco-German agreement by giving a pledge to France of military support, let alone taking steps to make this pledge effective. There was again a competition in equivocation. The government secretly agreed with their service advisers that more arms were needed, and dared not say so, did not even dare to think so;[1] the Opposition denounced the government for doing nothing and yet would have condemned even more severely the only things which the government could do.

The Opposition won the competition, at any rate for the time being. Twelve days after Germany left the Disarmament conference, the Labour candidate in a by-election at East Fulham turned an adverse majority of 14,000 into a victory by 5,000. This was universally regarded as a triumph for 'pacifism'. The view was probably mistaken. Neville Chamberlain suspected that at East Fulham 'the main attack was on the means test',[2] and later investigation has confirmed this judgement. Electors, as distinct from politicians, were interested in housing and unemployment, not in foreign affairs. In any case, there was a natural swing back to Labour after the freak results in 1931. A few days later, on 1 November, Labour won control of 200 boroughs at the municipal elections, and in the following March captured the L.C.C. These successes obviously had nothing to do with disarmament. The main outcome indeed of Labour's victory in London was that the L.C.C. pulled down Rennie's Waterloo Bridge, despite the desire of parliament that it should be preserved.[3]

However, East Fulham frightened the government out of what senses they had, Baldwin most of all. In his own words, 'it was a nightmare', and his biographer adds: 'I always felt that the nerve, injured in October 1933, the East Fulham nerve, never quite healed.'[4] Of course it was not really as simple as that. The government would have given a resolute lead, if they had seen clearly what lead to give. They did not. Ministers, too, were men of the time. The crisis of 1931 had been their supreme experience, and they could not help believing that economy and a balanced budget were more important than armaments. They still hoped that disarmament might succeed after all; they still professed in the League of Nations a faith which they rarely felt.

[1] G. M. Young's phrase about Baldwin, *Baldwin*, 200.
[2] Macleod, *Neville Chamberlain*, 179.
[3] The bridge was inadequate for modern traffic. The L.C.C. wanted to pull it down and build a new one. Parliament, wishing to have the bridge reconstructed, refused a grant for a new bridge. Finally, the L.C.C. went ahead on its own, without assistance from national funds.
[4] G. M. Young, *Stanley Baldwin*, 200.

The League was the other great issue in foreign policy in these years, disputes regarding it gradually eclipsing the disputes over disarmament. Here again the nineteen-twenties had enabled men of widely differing outlooks apparently to agree without really doing so. The League then provided a useful meeting-place where statesmen could express benevolent sentiments about nothing in particular. MacDonald best expressed the feeling of the time when he spoke of men getting the League habit. Wars, he held, would simply fall out of fashion. The discussions about 'putting teeth into the Covenant', though prolonged, were academic. For, though no teeth were put in, there was also no one whom it was necessary to bite. Successive governments, Labour as much as Conservative, regarded the League as an alternative to armaments, not as a reason for having them. Underneath there was precious little faith in the League except among a few dedicated enthusiasts, of whom Robert Cecil and Gilbert Murray were the chief. Many socialists still held that wars were inevitable under capitalism. Many Conservatives regarded the League as a hangover of the wartime idealism to which they had paid grudging lip-service. Generals and admirals, at bottom, saw in the League an instrument which threatened to put them out of business, not a cause which offered them a nobler and wider appeal. Still, in theory all three parties were committed to the League.

By 1933 or thereabouts, the existence of the League might have been expected to resolve the disputes over disarmament. Labour might have swallowed more arms, if these were to be used in support of the League; the government, by professing faith in the League, might have found a non-controversial reason for more arms. Exactly the reverse happened. Practically no one said: Rearm in order to support the League of Nations.[1] Support for the League of Nations—'collective security' as it was called—and rearmament were regarded as rival policies, mutually incompatible. Attlee defined the Labour outlook precisely in May 1935: 'We stand for collective security through the League of Nations. We reject the use of force as an instrument of policy. . . . Our policy is not one of seeking security through rearmament but through disarmament.'

[1] Though Churchill said something like this by 1936, he certainly did not say it in 1932 or 1933. At that time, no one was more outspoken in denouncing League of Nations 'illusions'.

Collective security, though impressive as a phrase, made sense only if the fifty-two members of the League had agreed to pool their military resources. Labour did not make any practical proposals to achieve this. Indeed, successive British governments, Labour as much as Conservative or National, had rejected anything in the nature of a League army. In any case—a point ignored by supporters of the League—none of the League powers except Great Britain and France had any serious naval forces to pool.[1] Disarmament was the central demand in Labour policy, and collective security not much more than a cover for it. The opposite attitude was equally clear in Baldwin's speeches defending the first timid steps towards rearmament, speeches phrased in terms of national security and with little reference to the League of Nations. The service chiefs were even blunter. If the League were ever mentioned, metaphorically they spat. Those who relied on armaments had no faith in the League, indeed much contempt for it. Naturally, therefore, those who supported the League distrusted armaments and, still more, the arguments of those who relied on them.

In practice both sides hedged their bets. Only a few Labour men, headed by Lansbury, were out-and-out pacifists. Only a few Conservatives, such as Amery and Lord Lloyd, repudiated the League openly. Nearly everyone believed that blockade—'economic sanctions' in League parlance—would be a let out. Labour would not have to support a war; Conservatives would not have to use their precious armaments for an idealistic cause. Peace would be maintained without effort. Blockade would stop any aggressor in his tracks. This belief sprang partly from an exaggerated recollection of what the blockade against Germany had accomplished during the first World war—an exaggeration encouraged by the Germans themselves from a desire not to admit that their army had been defeated. It sprang also from the circumstances of the time. In a world reeling under the impact of a great Depression, when economic problems seemed so much more important than anything else, it was easy to suppose that a nation would be brought to the ground if its foreign trade were cut off.

The League had a dummy run while the Disarmament conference was in progress or lack of progress, over the Japanese

---

[1] Italy had a fairly serious navy, but not in the Far East and in any case was not likely to cooperate for League purposes.

invasion of Manchuria. The affair did not attract much attention at the time, when men were consumed with economic anxieties and thought only about disarmament in the few moments which they could spare for foreign affairs. Later on, it became encrusted with myths, and assumed legendary importance as the first step on the road to the second World war. As often happens, these later judgements came to count for more than what actually happened. On 18 September 1931 Japanese forces seized control of Manchuria, a province which was theoretically part of China. The Chinese government appealed to the League for redress. Responsibility for League policy fell largely on the British government. Great Britain and France really ran the League, despite the nominal presence of three other Great Powers—Germany, Italy, and of course Japan. In this case, British leadership was especially predominant. Great Britain was the only League Power with a serious stake in the Far East.[1] The British aim was conciliation—ending the conflict on almost any terms. British statesmen were not interested in asserting a moral principle, or rather they thought peace a more important principle than abstract justice.

Resolute action could not be expected from the National government at the exact moment when they were being forced off the gold standard and facing a contentious general election. Besides, action was impossible. The Washington naval treaty gave Japan a local supremacy in the Far East, and successive British governments had confirmed this supremacy when they postponed the building up of Singapore as a naval base. Not that the British statesmen weighed these practical difficulties. All of them regarded the League as an instrument of conciliation, not of resistance, and they recognized that the weaker Power—in this case China—would have to pay the price. So it had been in the dispute between Greece and Italy in 1923: Greece paid a penalty because she was the weaker. Even the high-minded Sir Edward Grey took the same attitude towards Serbia, though not towards Belgium, in the crisis which led up to the first World war. Serbia, he thought, must save the world from war by agreeing to the Austro-Hungarian demands, however unjust some of these were.

[1] Though the French were also a Far Eastern power, their stake was limited to Indo-China, despite the French concession at Shanghai, and Indo-China seemed at that time remote from the field of Japanese action.

This time, even the arguments of justice were not all on one side. The authority of the central Chinese government, nowhere strong, did not run in Manchuria, which was in a state of lawless confusion. Japanese trading interests had suffered greatly. There were, too, many precedents in China for independent military action—the last being a landing of British troops at Shanghai in 1927. The Japanese, as Sir John Simon put it, were wrong in taking the law into their own hands, but it was law—the restoration of peaceful conditions in Manchuria—which they took into their own hands all the same. No doubt many British people involved, with their own experiences of the troubles in China, sympathized with Japan more than abstract justice demanded. Nor did the British government hesitate to send troops and ships to Shanghai, despite their supposed weakness, when the Japanese extended the conflict there in March 1932. Still, Sir John Simon, the foreign secretary, could assume that he was acting in the highest tradition of British policy, and one previously approved by all parties, when he strove at Geneva to reconcile China and Japan. On his initiative, the League set up a commission under Lord Lytton to inquire into the rights and wrongs of the affair; meanwhile it postponed judgement. Nor did Simon neglect the claims of morality. Again on his initiative, the League Assembly in March 1932 passed a unanimous resolution pledging its members not to recognize any changes brought about by force.

The Lytton commission laboriously toured the Far East. At the end of 1932 it reported. It found that many of the Japanese grievances were justified. At the same time it condemned the Japanese method of redressing these grievances. On Simon's initiative, the League adopted this report. Japan was censured for resorting to force before all peaceful means were exhausted. No one at Geneva proposed to condemn Japan as an aggressor within the meaning of the Covenant. No one proposed to invoke Article XVI—the sanctions article—against her. There is not a fragment of evidence to suggest that the statesmen of other countries were deterred from making such proposals by British pressure. They recognized that the policy advocated by Simon was the only possible one to follow. Japan withdrew from the League in protest when the Lytton report was adopted. Nevertheless, the object of British policy was attained. The Chinese reconciled themselves to the loss of a province which they had not controlled for many years. In May 1933 China and Japan signed the truce of Tangku which virtually restored peace in the Far East. This was not a glamorous settlement: the stronger party got its way. Still, it was a settlement. Moreover, the League had behaved honourably. It had offered the chance of conciliation, and when this was rejected, it had refused to condone the use of force.

Criticism built up gradually while the affair was going on. Simon, with all his gifts, had one defect which made him unfit to be British foreign secretary. He was too cool and rational. He lacked the air of puzzled rectitude which enabled a Grey or a Halifax to lapse from the highest moral standards without anyone complaining or even noticing. Simon angered idealists by keeping calm and by seeing both sides of the case. Yet the critics had no alternative to offer except some display of world indignation such as the withdrawal of ambassadors from Japan. Many members of the Labour party even suspected that the government were exploiting the League in order to defend British interests at Shanghai. Their favoured solution was an embargo on the supply of arms to the Far East—a solution which they advocated as much because it would injure British manufacturers of arms as because of any effect it would have on the conflict.[1] Once the affair was over, those who advocated collective security as an alternative to rearmament had to explain why collective security had failed. They answered that it had never been tried, and that this was the deliberate fault of the British government. If only something or other had been done—usually a blockade of Japan with American cooperation—Japan would have run away.

The assertion was almost certainly untrue, to the extent that any untested assertion can be so described. Apart from anything else, there was never at any time the slightest chance that the United States would cooperate in any action. Americans had a far larger share of Japan's foreign trade than had any other country, and the American government repeatedly made clear that they would not tolerate any interference with this trade.[2] Defenders of the British government did not,

[1] The government imposed an embargo of this kind in Feb. 1933—to Labour's approval and surprise.

[2] One myth was especially tenacious. In Feb. 1932 Stimson, the American secretary of state, announced that the United States would not recognize territorial

however, like to blame the United States, particularly when they were just wrangling over the war debt. They therefore replied with another unprovable assertion: that Japan would have answered a blockade by going to war against the League Powers. This assertion, too, was probably untrue. But such was the legacy of the Manchurian affair. On the one hand, idealists who believed that the British government had deliberately betrayed the League of Nations; on the other, practical men who believed that support for the League would have landed Great Britain in an unnecessary war.

This legacy became important after Hitler's rise to power and, with it, the prospect that Germany would rearm. Before that time, Labour had a simple solution for the German question: Germany should be trusted. Most Labour men thought that the Germans had lost interest in dominating Europe; a few believed, along with Keynes, that German economic domination was the best answer to Europe's difficulties. In either case, the same conclusion followed: Germany should be treated as an equal. Reparations should be ended; Germany should be allowed to rearm, or rather others should disarm down to her level; Austria should be allowed to unite with Germany; the frontiers of Poland and Czechoslovakia should be revised to Germany's advantage; her former colonies should be restored to her. Many Conservatives disliked this programme, particularly as regards the German colonies. They had no answer of principle to it. They, too, wanted to keep clear of Europe; they, too, regarded the French as unreasonable and difficult. Among many sayings of Churchill's which made him unpopular, none outraged opinion more even among Conservatives than his cry, on 23 March 1933: 'Thank God for the French army.' Conservatives, in fact, followed the Labour line, though hoping that they would not have to go very fast or very far.

The appearance of Hitler might have been expected to push

changes brought about by force and invited other countries to accept this doctrine. Simon put off endorsing it until he could carry the other members of the League with him, which he did in March. 'Non-recognition' became a League principle. Meanwhile, President Hoover rebuked Stimson for running the risk that the United States might become involved in international affairs and warned him not to do it again. When Simon reported to Stimson his success in getting non-recognition accepted by the League, he received a dusty answer. Nevertheless, a legend was soon established that Stimson had proposed joint action against Japan and that Simon had turned down the proposal. The legend was totally untrue and was made no truer by Stimson's repeating it later.

English people together. Labour disliked his dictatorship; Conservatives disliked his threat to British security. Once more, however, as with disarmament and collective security, Hitler pushed English people apart. They disliked him for different reasons, and this increased their mutual suspicion. Labour men still sympathized with German grievances, indeed believed, not altogether wrongly, that these had helped Hitler to power. They therefore went on preaching that these grievances should be redressed. Their dislike of Hitler was, in a phrase of the time, ideological. Hitler was a 'Fascist', and Great Britain should lead an anti-Fascist crusade, an idealistic campaign unsullied by anything so sordid as the defence of British interests or British security. Yet even this did not make Labour advocate increased armaments. Fascism was supposed to be a confession that capitalism was about to collapse, and Hitler therefore would soon tumble down if he were not being secretly financed by the city of London. This outlook infuriated Conservatives. They did not want to be involved in any ideological crusade.[1] A few of them sympathized with Hitler's national assertiveness, as Churchill had done at one time. Most of them preferred national socialism to the communism which was supposed to be the alternative.

Even at home Conservatives still regarded Communists as the greater danger. In 1934 the government undid John Wilkes's achievement and restored general warrants as a precaution against Communist propaganda in the armed forces.[2] The British Union of Fascists, which Mosley founded in 1932, was at first applauded by many respectable Conservatives, and also by Lord Rothermere. The members of the Union (some 20,000 at its highest point) wore blackshirts and uniforms on the Italian model. They relied on marches and violence, not on speeches. In time this violence was too much even for Conservatives. The Public Order Act of 1936 virtually killed the movement by prohibiting political uniforms and empowering the police to forbid political processions. The attitude of

---

[1] It is ironical that many of those who now preached non-intervention, such as Sir Samuel Hoare, had been crusaders against Soviet Russia in 1919, while Labour had then been on the side of non-intervention.

[2] The Incitement to Disaffection Act allowed a general search warrant to be issued by a judge of the High court—the bill had originally said by any magistrate. Academic authorities still went on teaching that general warrants had been declared illegal in 1765. Little use was in fact made of the power.

Conservatives towards Hitler was much of a piece. They began by welcoming him as the saviour of Germany from communism. They were estranged by his brutal methods and particularly by his treatment of the Jews. Gradually they took precautions of the old style—some increase in armaments, some attempts to conciliate Hitler, some attempts to construct a defensive alliance against him. Labour, on its side, went on saying that all would be well if the British government pledged themselves to collective security and disarmed at the same time.

The cleavage grew deeper throughout 1934. The chiefs of staff increased their warnings, and now with a different emphasis. In 1932 they had asserted that Japan was the more immediate danger, though Germany would be ultimately the greater one. Their immediate concern therefore was with the navy. By the end of 1934 the chiefs of staff were coming to believe that Germany was the more immediate, as well as the greater, danger. For this and for other reasons,[1] Baldwin pledged the government to maintain parity in the air, that is, an air force as large as Germany's. This had an unforeseen consequence. The navy and the air force had kept up their capital equipment better than the army even during the years of disarmament.[2] Now the decision to maintain a great navy and to create a great air force put the army yet further down the list. The government, still anxious to maintain economy, virtually decided not to have an army at all. There was to be a 'limited liability' army, fit only for colonial defence. In this odd way, the practical effect of rearmament was actually to increase British isolation: not only the will, but the means, for British intervention on the continent were lacking.

The preparations for rearmament were still largely on paper. The arms estimates barely moved. In 1934 they were still lower than they had been ten years before; in 1935 not appreciably higher. Leading civil servants disliked this position, as did the chiefs of staff. They were drawing up plans for total war—rationing, exchange control, mass evacuation from large towns, conscription of labour. Yet the public, who would be involved

[1] The British government hoped to 'deter' Hitler by this warning that they would keep up with him. They were also badgered by Churchill's exaggerated estimates of the German air force—estimates which, of course, made him more unpopular than ever with the Labour party.

[2] The navy never sank below £10 million a year on armaments, the air force never below £8 million. The army was lucky when it got £2 million.

in these plans, were being told nothing. Senior civil servants therefore drafted a White Paper, depreciating collective security and explaining that German rearmament made British rearmament necessary. Underlying this was the unargued assumption held by nearly all the government's professional advisers: that once Germany had rearmed, war would more or less follow of itself.[1] The White Paper was a remarkable innovation. Government servants, civil and military, had, of course, often taken the initiative over policy. They had done so behind the scenes. They persuaded the responsible minister, and it was his task to present the policy to the public. With the White Paper, civil servants addressed themselves directly to public opinion, not to a minister or even to the cabinet.

Ministers acquiesced. The cabinet watered down the blunt hostility to Germany expressed in the White Paper, for fear of offending Hitler. Then they allowed it to be published. The *Statement Relating to Defence*, issued on 4 March 1935, was a landmark in British policy. It announced that the British government had ceased to rely on collective security and were now going to rely on the older security of armed force. The White Paper was initialed by MacDonald—almost his last act as prime minister. This seemed bitter irony: the man who had earlier been accused of pacifism, however wrongly, now gave the signal for a renewed race to war. In fact MacDonald had always held, more clearly than most, that rearmament and war would inevitably follow if the Disarmament conference failed.

The White Paper did not produce the explosion which the civil servants had hoped for. Ministers themselves were only half-convinced by it. Those who had previously opposed rearmament were not shaken at all. It needed more than a few pages of official prose to reverse the thinking habits of a generation, and the remoteness of high civil servants from public opinion was shown when they imagined otherwise. Observers might complain that civil servants were encroaching on policy and that administration had taken the place of government, as it did in old Austria. The complaint was not unfounded. All the same, the civil servants had one great handicap: they could not make their words carry beyond the confines of their offices.

---

[1] Sir Horace Wilson, chief industrial adviser to the government, did not share this view. Hence Chamberlain's reliance on him later.

Many civil servants were men of first-rate ability; some cabinet ministers were next door to dim-witted. But when it came to managing the public or even the house of commons, ministers took it in their stride, and civil servants were nowhere. Later, during the second World war, some civil servants actually became ministers; as such, they were political failures. Ministers were still essential in the British parliamentary system. Unless they led, no one would follow. So it happened now. The White Paper passed over the heads of the politicians and the public.

It had, however, an unwelcome effect elsewhere. Hitler used the British White Paper as his excuse for restoring conscription in Germany on 16 March. The National government, on their side, accepted this as a justification for their new line of policy. In April MacDonald, still just on his feet, met Mussolini and Laval, the French prime minister, and the three set up the 'Stresa front' against breaches of the international order. The meeting was a last echo of the great international gatherings with which Lloyd George had once dazzled Europe, and an odd meeting at that—three renegade Socialists defending the results of 'the war to end war and to make the world safe for democracy', two of whom had opposed the war, while the third had destroyed democracy in his own country. The 'Stresa front' was a front in the sense of a 'bold front' to conceal inner quaverings, not in the sense of 'front line', as Hitler correctly assumed. The National government soon added their own proof. In June they concluded a private deal with Germany, limiting the German navy to 35 per cent. of the British, with submarines at 45 per cent. or even 100 per cent. in case of danger from Russia. This, though defended as better than nothing, was an open repudiation of disarmament by international agreement and of the treaty of Versailles.[1]

The government sounded the national appeal in a more glamorous way. On 6 May George V was given the unprecedented honour of a Jubilee to celebrate the twenty-fifth anniversary of his accession. This was a deliberate attempt to revive past glories, echoing the Jubilees of Queen Victoria; an assertion also of traditional loyalty against the 'King and

---

[1] It was also argued that there was no point in making a bargain with a man who would not keep his word. In fact, Hitler kept this word—perhaps in hope of cajoling the British into neutrality, perhaps because he was trying to economize on his navy, as the British did with their army.

Country' resolution of two years before. The Jubilee had little political significance when it came to the point. Labour men and League of Nations enthusiasts joined in with equal zest. English people, very sensibly, turned the Jubilee into a personal tribute to a king who, in a modest conservative way, had a better record as constitutional sovereign than any monarch since William III.[1] Otherwise, for most people there seemed little to celebrate: still a million and a half unemployed; international difficulties on the increase; and the Commonwealth by no means stalwart. There was something shaky here, when relations with Australia, for example, could be endangered by rough play at a Test match—Larwood's body-line bowling in 1933.[2] Probably most people accepted the Jubilee as another agreeable occasion for a public holiday. They were not celebrating the rule of MacDonald or even of Baldwin.

The Jubilee was positively MacDonald's last appearance as prime minister. His physical powers were failing: his political influence was exhausted. On 7 June he and Baldwin changed places. MacDonald became lord president of the council. Baldwin became prime minister and so at last accepted responsibility for the power which, like other 'harlots', the press lords, he had previously exercised from behind the scenes. Simon, who had been discredited, however unjustly, by his handling of the Manchurian affair, went to the home office. Hoare became foreign secretary, with a liberal reputation secured by his work in carrying the Government of India Act. Londonderry, also discredited by his defence of the bombing aeroplane, was replaced at the air ministry by Cunliffe-Lister, once called Lloyd-Greame, soon to be called Lord Swinton and soon also to be as discredited as his predecessor. The 'National' balance was precariously maintained by making MacDonald's son Malcolm colonial secretary to set off the disappearance of Sankey, whom Lord Hailsham insisted on ejecting from the woolsack. Otherwise the only concession to youth was the elevation of Anthony Eden to the cabinet as

[1] George V's Jubilee speech in Westminster Hall to the two houses of parliament expressed admirable Whig sentiments. This was not surprising. It had been written for him by G. M. Trevelyan, great-nephew of Macaulay's.
[2] Larwood was alleged to bowl at the batsman instead of at the wicket. He was dropped from future Test teams on the insistence of J. H. Thomas, Dominions secretary—the only occasion on which a cabinet minister has chosen a cricket eleven, even negatively.

'Minister without portfolio for League of Nations Affairs'. Thus collective security was openly acknowledged as a fifth wheel of British policy, added for ostentation not for use.

The fifth wheel, however, took charge in an unexpected and unwelcome way. The advocates of disarmament, too, had not been inactive while the plans for rearmament and the White Paper were being prepared. They, too, appealed to public opinion, and more skilfully than the civil servants. The League of Nations Union organized a house-to-house canvass, as a sort of unofficial referendum. Householders were asked five questions, phrased, of course, to elicit a favourable response. In October 1934, when the questions were framed, disarmament still seemed the burning issue. Only question 5, thrown in as an afterthought, asked whether an aggressor should be stopped by economic measures and, if necessary, by war. This was not, as it was abusively called, a Peace Ballot, if by this was meant a ballot for pacifism. It was a ballot for international disarmament and collective security, though no doubt pacifist sentiment was mixed in with it. Those who conducted it were not pacifists. Most of them were non-party men or former Liberals. All were from the middle class, and the ballot was actually opposed by the Left wing of the Labour party. The response was formidable. Over 11½ million replied—a substantial majority of all householders. More than ten million answered Yes to every question except to the second half of the last—whether the aggressor should be stopped by war. Here six and three quarter million said yes; over two million said no; another two million did not answer. The results were announced on 28 June 1935. By then international disarmament was a dead cause. Only the answers to question 5 mattered. The Peace Ballot had become un-designedly a ringing assertion of support for collective security by all means short of war, and a more hesitant support even for war.

Here was a conundrum for the National government to solve. They were backing away from collective security; their professional advisers were urging them to champion rearmament and national defence in the general election which could not long be delayed. Yet they needed Liberal votes, and still more liberal sentiment, if they were to maintain their great majority. Besides, most ministers were less clear cut in their outlook than the civil servants and service chiefs. Some of them still hankered after collective security; a few, more cynically, hoped to twist it against Germany. Pious and abstract phrases of loyalty to the League of Nations in Baldwin's best manner would have satisfied them. Unfortunately these did not meet the situation. A concrete case of aggression was in the offing. Mussolini, for motives which need not be discussed, had resolved to attack Abyssinia, a member of the League of Nations. The National government had not the slightest wish to go against Italy. They had none of Labour's hostility to Mussolini as a 'Fascist'. He was their prized partner in the Stresa front. The service chiefs, with the problems of Japan and Germany on their hands, were insistent that Italy should not be added to the list of possible enemies. Eden, the supposed champion of collective security, went to Rome and attempted to buy Mussolini off. Italy could have the lowlands of Abyssinia without war; Great Britain would secure Abyssinia's agreement by surrendering part of British Somaliland to her. Mussolini rejected the offer: Italy, he insisted, must have the position in Abyssinia which Great Britain had in Egypt—an awkward analogy for a British government to reject.

The National government were caught between practical calculations and the Peace Ballot. Hoare, fresh from his jugglings over India, came up with an ingenious solution. Great Britain should announce her wholehearted support for collective security, on condition that all other members of the League were as wholehearted as she was. Hoare always suffered from excessive cleverness, and never more so than on this occasion. He seemed to be betting on a certainty either way. If collective security worked, the prestige of the National government would be enhanced and the League could then be used effectively against Germany; if it failed, others could be blamed and the way would be open for rearmament.

Hoare announced his policy at Geneva on 11 September 1935. The League was now in better shape for action. The organization of economic sanctions had been worked out in detail after the Manchurian affair. They were applied after 3 October when the Italian armies attacked Abyssinia. Italian credits were cut off; all imports from Italy and some exports to her were banned by virtually all members of the League.[1]

---

[1] Italy's three satellites—Albania, Austria, and Hungary—refused to operate sanctions. Germany and the United States, being outside the League, were not

Tories in England were dismayed. The service chiefs grumbled, and the foreign office with them. Winston Churchill kept out of England throughout the autumn and so avoided pronouncing for or against Italy. Amery denounced the League and championed the Italian side. These voices were hardly heard. The liberal repute of the National government was restored. Collective security was in action at last. The aggressor was being resisted by 'all sanctions short of war' or most of them, exactly as the voters in the Peace Ballot had demanded.

The Labour party, in their turn, were now landed in an awkward predicament. Hitherto they had been coasting happily along, confident that the sentiments expressed in the Peace Ballot would automatically wash victory into their hands. Instead Baldwin and the National government had casually stolen their thunder. What should they do? Outbid the government by demanding further sanctions, even at the risk of war, and thus estrange the pacifists? Or denounce the League as a sham, and thus lose the support of the enthusiasts for it? In the end, Labour did both and thus gave the impression of sincerity in neither. The Trades Union Congress, meeting early in September, returned a clear answer: restraint of Italy even at the risk of war. The Labour party conference, at the beginning of October, had a rougher passage. The official resolution endorsed 'all the necessary measures provided by the Covenant'. Dalton, Morrison, and, more grudgingly, Attlee, supported this. There were formidable voices on the other side. Cripps took the traditional Marxist line[1] that the League of Nations was 'an International Burglars' Union': 'every war entered upon by a capitalist government is and must be an imperialist and capitalist war'. Or, as Mellor, another member of the Socialist League, put it, 'our enemy is here'. Lansbury, still technically leader, voiced the pacifist principles which he had previously choked back; if others did not practise these principles, he declared, he would answer only by passive resistance.

Such sentiments had always been held by a minority in the Labour movement. This minority had been respected, though its line had not been followed. Lansbury, in particular, was

committed. In practice, they doubted Italy's ability to pay and therefore cut down their trade with her also. The sanctions were enough to cause Italy grave economic difficulties.

[1] No longer taken by the Communist party, which supported the League unreservedly once Soviet Russia became a member in 1934.

loved as no Labour leader had been since Keir Hardie. On the other hand, Labour men were on edge after the split of 1931, and irritated, too, by the impracticality of the idealists. Ernest Bevin expressed this irritation when he answered Lansbury with a brutality such as had never been directed against Ramsay MacDonald during the first World war. Bevin sounded the old Labour cry of loyalty—loyalty to the League as to a sort of trade union, loyalty to party decisions settled by the votes of the large unions which Bevin and a few others controlled.[1] On paper Bevin won. Support for the Covenant was carried by two million votes against 100,000.

The decision was much applauded, especially outside the Labour party, as the beginning of a more realistic approach to foreign affairs by Labour. Underneath nothing was changed. The Left, though defeated, were not silenced, and the Labour party remained what it had been before—an alliance of men with widely differing views, not a disciplined army. The victory was barren even in regard to the immediate issue. The great question of peace or war—or rather of peace by means of war—was not faced. Nearly all Labour supporters of collective security continued to say: collective security will stop the aggressor, therefore rearmament is unnecessary. A few recognized that collective security might lead to war; even they were not ready to place arms in the hands of the National government. The confusion was shown at once. Lansbury resigned as leader after the annual conference. The parliamentary party elected Attlee, then the only possible claimant with Cripps also out of the way, to succeed him, and Attlee criticized every demand for arms made by the National government until after the outbreak of war in 1939.

Things had turned out nicely for the National government. They could condemn Labour both as 'pacifists' and as 'warmongers', basing both accusations on quotations from the brawling Labour leaders themselves. They could claim to be supporting the League and could use this claim to justify rearmament. It is not surprising that Baldwin had parliament

[1] Bevin played loyalty both ways. Lansbury was denounced for remaining on the party executive when he disagreed with its policy; Cripps was denounced for resigning from it for the same reason. Bevin claimed to be against 'intellectuals'. Yet he himself ran a highly intellectual and impractical line—that wars could be prevented by the international control of raw materials. He objected to ideas only when others had them.

dissolved on 25 October, and the general election fixed for
14 November. It was a confused election. Essentially both
Labour and the National parties, apart from a few extremists
on either side, were saying the same thing: all sanctions short
of war. Labour implied that the government were not operating
sanctions seriously; Conservatives alleged that Labour, if in
power, would topple over into war. Both sides were in a muddle
themselves and therefore muddled their charges against each
other. The National government wanted a mandate for rearmament and in theory asked for it. In practice, they spoke the truth
in an undertone, much as Lloyd George had done over reparations in 1918, hoping that no one would hear. Baldwin asked
only for power 'to remedy the deficiencies which have occurred
in our defences', and added: 'I give you my word that there
will be no great armaments.' Because of this, he was accused
later of having deceived the electorate.[1] The truth was rather
that neither he nor the other members of the government,
perhaps not even the service chiefs, realized what lay ahead.
Neville Chamberlain, for example, was much more anxious
than Baldwin to make rearmament the central issue of the election. Yet even he only supposed that it would be necessary to
spend an extra £120 million over the next four or five years.[2]
By the time he became prime minister in May 1937, the estimate
had swelled to £1,500 million over the next five years, and that
proved to be not enough.

In any case, rearmament and foreign policy were pushed into
the background once the election campaign started. The electors
showed little interest in these questions, and the arguments of
the rival parties at best cancelled out. Housing, unemployment,
and the special areas were still the dominant themes. The Conservatives lacked a panic; Labour lacked enthusiasm. Baldwin
was the only 'national' figure, and he inspired calm, not excitement. The turn out on election day was lower than at any
election since December 1923. The Conservatives held almost
exactly their vote of 1931; Labour recovered those who had
then not voted. This brought a hundred odd gains to Labour,
less than they deserved on the figures,[3] giving 154 Labour
members and 432 supporters of the National government.

---

[1] See Note A, p. 387.
[2] Chamberlain's diary, 2 Aug. 1935. Macleod, *Chamberlain*, 182.
[3] Conservatives 11·8 million; Labour 8·3 million.

The Liberals slipped down further, from 33 to 20, and 4 of these were Lloyd George's family connexion. National Labour also suffered. Ramsay MacDonald and his son Malcolm both lost their seats, though both crept back at by-elections, Ramsay for one of the university constituencies which he had previously denounced. As a minor oddity, one Communist, William Gallacher, was returned; he provided the only unwavering voice of resistance to Hitler, until that unhappy day of 23 August 1939, when the Nazi–Soviet pact revealed that the second World war was not an anti-Fascist crusade after all.

The National government now had their mandate for rearmament. They also still had the Abyssinian affair on their hands. Economic sanctions had been intended as a bluff, a solemn warning to Mussolini. The bluff had not worked. Now more would have to be done against Italy, or a way out would have to be found. It was generally held that stopping oil supplies to Italy—the 'oil sanction'—would do the trick. The government hesitated. Mussolini, it was alleged, would answer the oil sanction by war—the spook which had formerly been raised in regard to Japan. France would not support Great Britain. The British navy would have to fight alone, and it was apprehensive of the Italian air force. It was maybe a little unreasonable for the British to claim the mastery of the Mediterranean and then to complain that fighting there would fall on them. Such is the price of Empire. These were not much more than rationalizations. The government, and the British people, had said: all sanctions short of war. Therefore any sanctions which raised the shadow of war were automatically ruled out. Besides, the British government had no wish to topple Mussolini. On the contrary, the foreign office wanted to enlist him as an ally against Hitler. Compromise on the Manchurian model was the only alternative—some settlement favourable enough to persuade Mussolini to stop the war.

Hoare dug out the offer which had been made to Mussolini before the war; improved it to Italy's advantage; and on 7 December crossed to Paris with Baldwin's blessing. Laval made the offer still more favourable to Italy. She would receive the fertile plains. The emperor of Abyssinia would keep his old kingdom in the mountains. The two men endorsed the 'Hoare–Laval plan'. The British cabinet approved it. Mussolini was ready to agree. The next step was to present it at Geneva. Then the emperor would have to accept it or could be abandoned to his fate. Hoare departed cheerfully for a holiday in Switzerland, confident that he had pulled off a great stroke. Things went wrong. Someone leaked the plan to the Paris press. In England the storm blew. The high minded supporters of the League had just helped to return the National government. They felt cheated and indignant. The League of Nations Union, the two archbishops, *The Times* newspaper, Sir Austen Chamberlain, and many younger Conservatives protested. The government tried to brazen things out; then put the blame on Hoare, who had been 'tired', 'a sick man'. Halifax, formerly Irwin, who had just joined the cabinet as lord privy seal, devised this let-out. Hoare returned from Switzerland, sobbed, resigned. Eden took his place as foreign secretary. The Hoare–Laval plan was dead.

The League died with it. The outcry in England against the Hoare–Laval plan was the greatest explosion over foreign affairs for many years, perhaps the greatest since the campaign against the 'Bulgarian horrors' in 1876.[1] Like that campaign, it was effective only in negation. It subsided once the Hoare–Laval plan was withdrawn. The problem remained just what it had been before: how to stop Mussolini without war. No answer was found. The oil sanction was repeatedly proposed and as repeatedly put off when Mussolini objected to it. Compromise was still in the air: another version of the Hoare–Laval plan waiting to be produced when rain closed the campaigning season in Abyssinia. Instead Mussolini whipped his armies on and won the war in a hurry. On 1 May 1936 the Emperor Haile Selassie left Abyssinia. A week later Mussolini proclaimed the foundation of a new Roman empire. Haile Selassie appeared at Geneva to protest in person; was welcomed at Victoria station by Anthony Eden; and settled as an exile in Bath. On 10 June Neville Chamberlain, acting on his own in foreign affairs for the first time, condemned the continuance of sanctions as 'the very midsummer of madness'. On 18 June they were withdrawn.

Before then the Abyssinian affair had been eclipsed by greater events. On 7 March 1936 Hitler sent German troops into the demilitarized Rhineland. He had only a token force and assured

---

[1] The outcry of 1876 was widespread throughout the country, more so indeed than in the house of commons. The outcry of 1935 was strongest in political circles. The mass of people were little concerned, and there were few demonstrations of public protest.

his generals that he would withdraw at the first sign of opposition. There was none. The French had an army equipped only for defence, and a political outlook even more defensive. They passed the problem to London.[1] On paper the British were deeply involved. Great Britain and Italy were the guarantors of Locarno. This was a guarantee against 'flagrant aggression'. Was it flagrant aggression for the Germans, in the phrase of the time, 'to walk into their own backyard'? Few English people thought so. Baldwin confessed, with tears in his eyes, that Great Britain had no forces with which to sustain her guarantee, and that, in any case, public opinion would not allow it. Baldwin was right. Hugh Dalton, the most strenuous of Labour politicians for resistance to Germany, said on 26 March: 'Public opinion in this country would not support, and certainly the Labour party would not support, the taking of military sanctions or even of economic sanctions against Germany at this time.' The British government could only offer France and Belgium a renewed guarantee against German aggression, thus escaping from a promise now by giving a less effective one for the future. The example was to be followed later.

The guarantee was expected to be temporary, even though it was reinforced by staff talks—the first such since the end of the first World war. Germany, it was hoped, would settle down now that her unequal conditions had been ended. Arthur Greenwood, deputy leader of the Labour party, for example, found the situation 'pregnant with new and great possibilities for the future of the world'. The hope was not fulfilled. The Council of the League met in London. Only Litvinov, the Soviet representative, proposed sanctions against Germany. His advocacy was enough to damn the proposal. The Council resolved, though not unanimously, that the treaties of Versailles and Locarno had been broken. Hitler was invited to negotiate a new arrangement for European security, to replace that which he had destroyed. He responded to the invitation: he had 'no territorial claims in Europe', wanted peace, proposed a twenty-five year pact of non-aggression with the Western Powers. The British government sought further definition with a list of precise questions. To this Hitler did not reply. Silence followed. 'International Anarchy' had come again.

[1] Note B, p. 387.

NOTES

NOTE A. *Baldwin and rearmament.* Baldwin was a sly operator on many occasions, but the charges against him on this subject have been exaggerated. He has been accused of keeping quiet about the need for rearmament until after the general election. What he actually said (on 12 November 1936) was that he could not have campaigned for rearmament at the time of the East Fulham by-election; he had to wait until 1935 when public opinion had woken up. Then he got 'a mandate for doing a thing that no one, twelve months before, would have believed possible'. He might also have said that there was not much sense in campaigning for rearmament until the plans for it were ready.

He has also been accused, particularly by Churchill, of underrating the German air force, in a speech of 28 November 1934; and on 22 May 1935 Baldwin himself confessed that he had been wrong. He had said that the German air force was weaker than the British, and it had in fact achieved parity. The absurd part of the story is that Baldwin had been right. Parity is a difficult thing to judge. Do you weigh front-line strength, total number of planes, number of pilots, capacity of aeroplanes? The possible juggles are endless. However, on any comparable basis, the German air force had not achieved parity with the R.A.F. in May 1935. The only evidence to the contrary came from Hitler himself. On 2 May 1935 he told Sir John Simon that his air force was as strong as, if not stronger than, the British. Hitler's assertion was at once accepted as true by everyone concerned, and has been generally accepted to the present day. Usually governments armed more than they admitted. This might be to cheat foreign governments, as the German government maybe tried to cheat the British over their navy in 1909; or it might be to cheat their own people, by no means an unusual experience in a democracy. It was unprecedented for a statesman to confess to more arms than he had. But this was Hitler's way: he hoped to win by bluff. British Intelligence estimates of German spending on armaments before the war were consistently nearly twice what was actually being spent, and much of this information was fed to the British from German sources. At first this played into Hitler's hands: there was an exaggerated fear of him. Maybe later it worked the other way: exaggerated precautions were taken against him.

NOTE B. *France and the reoccupation of the Rhineland.* It is now clear from the French documents published in 1964 (*Documents diplomatiques français 1932–39*, second series, i) that the French never had any intention of opposing the German reoccupation of the Rhineland. The French military authorities held that, since their army was incapable of invading even the demilitarized Rhineland, the reoccupation would make no real difference. The French politicians were only concerned to exploit the affair by extracting a promise of future support from the British. There is therefore no foundation for the version, built up later by some Frenchmen, that the French government were eager to resist and were held back by the British. Nor is there any justification for the belief that this was a great 'lost opportunity'—the last chance to overthrow Hitler without a large-scale war. The French army was the only means available and, in the judgement of its leaders, not equipped to do it. In the years before the second World war, there was always a divorce between diplomacy and strategy. The diplomatists, or rather the more enterprising of them, and unofficial critics such as Churchill, talked in terms of imposing the will of the Western powers on Hitler—how to forbid his reoccupation of the Rhineland, for example, or his invasion of Poland. The military leaders were concerned to prevent Hitler imposing his will on them—how to prevent especially the invasion of France. The contradiction was already shown at Stresa. The political agreement there was to oppose further breaches of the treaty-settlement. The military plans (never operated) were for the mutual defence of Alsace and south Tyrol.

XII

APPEASEMENT, 1936-9

THE prestige of Ramsay MacDonald dwindled gradually. Baldwin's shrank overnight. His biographer writes of him in the spring of 1936, perhaps with some exaggeration: 'From the highest place in public esteem and confidence he had sunk to very nearly the lowest.'[1] National governments did not live up to their promises either in 1931 or in 1935, but with a different outcome. Though MacDonald's National government did not save the pound which they had been formed to save, this failure actually worked out to their credit. Baldwin's National government won a general election as supporters of collective security, failed to support it, and there was nothing to redeem the failure. Baldwin himself was bewildered by his estrangement from public opinion. He lost his hold over the house of commons, hesitated and blundered when dealing with trivial issues. He had to appeal for a vote of confidence, always a bad sign for a government, and got it only by the strenuous exertions of the Whips. In oratory he was outmatched. A coalition of national defence seemed to be forming against him. Inside parliament were the elder statesmen, Churchill, Austen Chamberlain, and Amery, with Lloyd George explosive on the wings; outside it, trade unionists led by Bevin.

Yet Baldwin survived. Most Conservatives still distrusted the 'clever men' whom they had turned against in 1922; Labour distrusted them still more. It was the old complaint: brilliant leaders and few followers. Ironically, much of the turmoil was misplaced. Nineteen-thirty-six saw the beginning of British rearmament, though few people appreciated this at the time. The advance was not shown in the arms estimates which went up only to £159 million[2]—according to contemporary calculations, one fifth of the German expenditure; according to later and more correct information, still less than half. Nor was it shown when Baldwin yielded a little to the clamour for a ministry of supply, and created in March 1936 a

---

[1] G. M. Young, *Baldwin*, 226.
[2] The actual expenditure on arms in 1936-7 was £186 million.

minister for the coordination of defence. For this minister was not Winston Churchill, whose appointment, it was feared, might provoke Hitler, nor even Sir Samuel Hoare, though he bid hard for the job. The minister was a routine lawyer, Sir Thomas Inskip,[1] and the appointment was described justifiably, though without originality, as the most extraordinary since Caligula made his horse a consul. Nor did the new post carry any weight. Inskip had one room, two secretaries, and no powers. In practice, he became little more than a fresh treasury brake on the demands of the services.

Real events happened in the back rooms. In November 1935 the armament plans were recast in order to prepare for a great war, not merely to fill a few gaps. Effective rearmament began soon afterwards. No doubt it proceeded slowly. Before this time it had not happened at all. Later even the critics could only have speeded it up—they could not have produced results at once. The foundations for effective power were thus being laid at the very time when the government were most discredited. Even more important, a few scientists changed the face of history. It had been universally assumed, ever since the first World war, that there was no defence against bombing from the air. Anti-aircraft guns were virtually ineffective. Fighter aeroplanes, though perhaps effective, could not be on patrol in the air all the time. 'The bomber will always get through.' The greatest cities would be speedily razed to the ground. This doctrine was preached by General Billy Mitchell in America. It was formulated at length by the Italian general, Douhet.

The leaders of the R.A.F., trained by Trenchard, had the same outlook. They pointed to their success in bombing the villages of Irak, and claimed that the only defence was a bomber force which could answer terror with terror, or perhaps even get its blow in first. A single scientist sapped this doctrine. In 1935 Watson Watt invented a device, later known as 'radar', by which radio instruments could detect distant objects in the air. Watson Watt took his invention to Sir Henry Tizard, a skilled middleman between scientists and the services. Radar was developed, thanks to Tizard. By 1939 it covered most of

[1] Thomas Walker Hobart Inskip (1876–1947): educ. Clifton and Cambridge; solicitor general, 1922–3, 1924–8, 1931–2; attorney general, 1928–9, 1932–6; minister for coordination of defence, 1936–9; dominions secretary, 1939, 1940; lord chancellor, 1939–40; lord chief justice, 1940–6; cr. Viscount Caldecote, 1939.

the eastern approaches. The arrival of enemy bombers could now be precisely foreseen. Fighter planes would have time to rise into the skies. In addition, these planes were independently improved at this time by Mitchell's development of the Spitfire. Defence in the air was at last possible. The strategy of aerial warfare was revolutionized.

The revolution was hardly appreciated even by those who knew what was happening. The chiefs of the R.A.F. could not bring themselves to renounce their belief in bombing. They yielded slowly, grudgingly, and little. In the course of 1936 the air defence of Great Britain was divided into Bomber Command and Fighter Command, with Dowding at the head of the fighters. The main weight of preparation was still on bombers. Late in 1937 Inskip insisted that the proportion of fighters be increased. The cabinet endorsed his decision. This was not from any strategical understanding: it was simply because fighters were cheaper to produce than bombers. When in 1939 the R.A.F. had more money allotted to it, the air staff reverted to their old love and spent the money on more bombers. Absurdly enough, the projected bomber force could not perform the task which it was being built for. The original plans of 1923 had been laid against France, and they still shaped preparations against the new, and more distant, potential enemy, Germany. Until shortly before the outbreak of war, hardly any of the bombers in service could reach Berlin. Two sevenths of them could reach the Ruhr from British airfields. Three sevenths of them would have to use French or Belgian bases, though expenditure on aeroplanes had made it impossible to provide an army with which to protect these bases.[1] Quite apart from this, the air staff ignored the improvements in defence which the Germans, too, had made, except that they did not possess radar.

In this paradoxical way the leaders of the R.A.F. preferred an offensive strategy which, when put to the test, failed, to a defensive strategy which, when tested, succeeded. The preference was as much psychological as informed, much like the generals' dislike of machine guns in the first World war. To lay the emphasis on defence, it was claimed, would sap the will to victory. Yet the R.A.F. had only the will, not the means.

---

[1] The remaining two sevenths of the bomber force could not reach important German targets even from French soil.

When war broke out, 'Bomber Command was incapable of inflicting anything but insignificant damage on the enemy'.[1] Perhaps it was no accident that Dowding almost alone among commanders of the R.A.F. had started his career as a gunner. Nearly all the rest, from Trenchard onwards, had been cavalry officers, and their strategy was the last charge of the Light Brigade.

Ministers, too, did not understand the changed position. Swinton, the secretary for air, provided the money for radar and perhaps took in Tizard's explanations. Most ministers did not, even if they troubled to listen. They went on believing that the bomber would always get through. Churchill had always been quick to appreciate new inventions, and he became a member of Tizard's secret committee, despite his public attacks on the government. Churchill brought his own scientific adviser, Lindemann,[2] with him, and Lindemann, though with a more original mind than Tizard's, was rough, impatient, and intolerant of any ideas except his own—some of which were crackbrained. The brawls between Tizard and Lindemann broke up the committee. Tizard used his influence with civil servants, and renewed the committee without Churchill and Lindemann. The development of radar went on. The price was paid later. Churchill, now relatively uninformed, continued to believe in bombing, and this belief had decisive effect on British strategy during the war. There was a personal price to be paid also. When Churchill became prime minister, Lindemann came in too, and Tizard was eclipsed for the duration. Yet Tizard, Watson Watt, and their associates laid the foundations for victory. Without them, success in the Battle of Britain, and so survival, would have been impossible. In the words of an official historian, 'radar was possibly the best investment ever made by a British government'.[3]

All this was, of course, unknown in 1936. Baldwin and his government rode out the days of unpopularity for quite other reasons. One was the ally on which Baldwin had often relied before: the passage of time. The house of commons could not go on debating the lack of armaments for ever. Sooner or later, members got back to the themes which really interested them—

---

[1] Webster and Frankland, *The Strategic Air Offensive*, i. 125.
[2] Later Lord Cherwell.
[3] Collier, *Defence of the United Kingdom*, 430.

the means test, the special areas, the condition of British agriculture. Moreover, Baldwin's enemies were divided. Conservative critics attacked him for not rearming faster; most Labour men still attacked him for rearming at all. Bevin and a few other union leaders might support rearmament, as did Dalton. Attlee, who had been re-elected leader after the general election,[1] continued to oppose it, and was in this more representative of the Labour party. In June 1936 Baldwin brought Hoare back into the cabinet as first lord of the admiralty. This was a significant gesture. The betrayal of the League by the Hoare–Laval plan was forgotten, if not forgiven. Middle-class idealists had refused to go over to the Labour party, perhaps from class consciousness, perhaps more from Labour's failure to provide a clear lead. In the long run therefore they had no alternative but to slip back into questioning support of the National government.

In the summer of 1936 a new question came to divide Baldwin's enemies still more. This was the Spanish civil war. Spain had become a republic in 1931. Early in 1936 a general election, of somewhat doubtful validity, gave a majority to the Left-wing coalition of 'the Popular front'. On 16 July Spanish generals, controlling most of the regular army, raised the standard of rebellion, and marched on Madrid. They expected an easy victory, and others expected it for them. The republican government armed the factory workers and, to everyone's surprise, held the rebels under General Franco at bay. The civil war was thus prolonged. Fascist Italy and, to a lesser extent, Nazi Germany sent military aid to Franco. A little later, Soviet Russia replied by sending military aid, on a smaller scale, to the republic.

These interventions transformed the civil war into a great international question, a question sharply posed to the British and French governments, as the two Western Powers and

---

[1] This was the first contested election for the party leadership since MacDonald was elected in 1922. Attlee's challenger was Herbert Morrison, his senior in the second Labour government but out of parliament since 1931, and a man of working-class origin, though not a trade unionist. Arthur Greenwood, a highly respected though ineffectual figure, split the vote. When he came third most of his votes were transferred to Attlee. Attlee's election was a victory for the moderate Left and, of course, for the old-stagers who had been in the 1931–5 parliament. Morrison's defeat lost him for ever the chance of becoming prime minister. Though an abler administrator than Attlee, he lacked Attlee's gift for keeping the party together and giving a lead, in Attlee's own words, 'slightly left of centre'.

Spain's neighbours. Both governments wanted to turn their backs on Spain, and wished that other countries would do the same. Their principal motive was no doubt the desire to avoid a general war—a danger obviously threatening when foreign 'volunteers' were fighting on opposing sides in Spain. There were less noble motives as well. In France, too, a government of the Popular Front had just taken office under Léon Blum, and they feared that French military aid for the Spanish republic might provoke a similar civil war in France. The British government had no love for the Spanish republic. Most British 'experts' on Spain—diplomatists, army officers, businessmen—inclined to Franco's side. Léon Blum first agreed to supply arms to the Spanish republic, then hesitated at warnings from his more moderate supporters, and the British government encouraged his reluctance.

The British and French governments proposed a general agreement not to aid either side in Spain, and the other Powers acquiesced. Significantly, no one thought of appealing to the League of Nations, which limited its activities to housing the Spanish pictures from the Prado. A non-intervention committee was set up in London, and solemnly laboured. Its proceedings were a farce, bringing all international agreements into contempt. Italy and Germany cheated openly from the beginning. Soon the Soviet government announced that they would cheat in favour of the republic so long as others did so for Franco. Foreign arms went to both sides in Spain, though more to Franco than to the republic. Italy sent him whole divisions, numbering some 100,000 men in all. Here was stuff for controversy—the British government once more taking a timid line at the expense both of international obligations and apparently of British interests. The Labour party originally supported non-intervention at Blum's request. They swung against non-intervention when it was obviously not working. Their opposition would not have mattered much if it had remained within the framework of conventional politics. The official leadership of the Labour party was somewhat embarrassed at having to take a line which seemed to raise the danger of war. The union leaders were particularly embarrassed by the Roman Catholics among their members, who tended to favour Franco or, at any rate, to dislike the republic.

But the Spanish question far transcended politics in the

ordinary sense. The controversy provided for the generation of the thirties the emotional experience of their lifetime. It has been rightly said that no foreign question since the French revolution has so divided intelligent British opinion[1] or, one may add, so excited it. The rebellion was generally supposed to be part of a coordinated Fascist conspiracy against democracy, with Franco as Mussolini's or Hitler's puppet. The belief was in fact unfounded. Franco was nobody's puppet. He had acted without prompting from Rome or Berlin, and displayed later a remarkable obstinacy in asserting Spanish independence. Nor could the causes disputed in Spain really be interpreted in simple terms of fascism and democracy, still less of socialism and capitalism. However, what men believed at the time was more important than what was actually happening. Spain was transformed into the battleground of rival ideologies. Sentiment in England was not all one way. Opponents of 'socialism', many of them Roman Catholics, found in Franco a safe champion, where they had hesitated to extol Hitler, a possible enemy even on purely patriotic grounds. Wyndham Lewis, for instance, backed Franco, as a change from attacking his fellow artists and writers. Mostly, the intellectual current ran in the opposite direction. The Spanish civil war at last enabled men to wage the fight against fascism literally.

Hitherto the opportunity had been wanting. The struggle against fascism had been a popular phrase among intellectuals ever since 1931, and particularly since Hitler came to power in January 1933. It had been little more. There was, in England, not much fascism to fight. Though fifteen well-known writers complained, in a book of essays, that the Mind was in Chains, because of 'a dying social system', most of them had secure employment at good salaries. Intellectuals turned out to cheer the hunger-marchers or occasionally to harass Mosley's Blackshirts in the east end of London. Otherwise, they had only, in Auden's words, 'the flat ephemeral pamphlet and the boring meeting'—mortifications of the flesh which soon palled. Former public schoolboys could contribute little to the working-class struggle, nor enter working-class life. The Etonian, George Orwell, for instance, did not become a working man by living in Wigan instead of London. Now, with the Spanish civil war, there was something real to do. Intellectuals demonstrated in

[1] Graves and Hodge, *The Long Week-End*, 337. 'Intellectual' would be a truer word.

favour of the Spanish republic. They demanded 'arms for Spain'. Some of them visited Spain. Some of the younger ones fought for the republic. Some, of high intellectual lineage and achievement, were killed. 'Bloomsbury' rallied to Spain where it had once held aloof from political questions. This enthusiasm was by no means exclusively middle class. The working class, too, had its intellectuals of a vaguely Marxist cast. Of the 2,000 odd British citizens who fought for the Spanish republic, the great majority were workers, particularly unemployed miners. The middle-class men are more remembered only because they had already made a mark.[1] All alike went off on a crusade.

> What's your proposal? To build the just city? I will.
> I agree. Or is it the suicide pact, the romantic
>   Death? Very well, I accept, for
> I am your choice, your decision. Yes, I am Spain.[2]

The Spanish civil war provided inspiration for the Left. It brought difficulties for the Labour party. It raised again the spectre of association with communism. Spanish Communists were prominent on the republican side and soon established control over it. Communist Russia sent aid to Spain. The British Communist party was active for the Spanish cause. An agency of Communist influence had been established fortuitously just before the Spanish civil war broke out. This was the Left Book Club, the creation of an enterprising publisher, Victor Gollancz. The Club 'chose' two new books each month which were sold, at a cheap subscription rate, to members. Three men selected the books. Gollancz, at this time, saw no enemies on the Left; Strachey took his instructions from the Communist party, if not himself a member; Laski, the third, was a Marxist, though he combined this with being a prominent member of the Labour party. The books chosen usually followed the Communist line.

The Club had something like 60,000 members. Many of them set up local groups, which discussed the monthly choice and expressed Left-wing views. Gollancz catered for them further with a periodical of political instruction, *The Left Book*

---

[1] Five hundred British members of the International Brigade were killed. At first Communists predominated among the dead. Later the party realized that it was losing its best members and pulled them out of the front line into positions of command.

[2] W. H. Auden, *Spain*.

Club News. Altogether, this was a formidable achievement—a membership ten times greater than the I.L.P. or the Communist party had ever secured, solidly based on intellectuals, particularly school teachers, throughout the country.[1] For the Labour party, the Left Book Club was an exasperation. It had always been a critical problem for Labour how to win strong middle-class support, and the party had counted largely on foreign affairs to do this. Now the Left Book Club was diverting highminded school teachers into reading Communist tracts when they ought to have been joining the Labour party and working for it.

The Spanish civil war raised a further menace. Support for the Popular Front in Spain seemed to imply the Popular Front at home—again, in practical terms, association with the Communists. The Abyssinian affair had split the Left. The Communist party had supported sanctions, in obedience to Soviet policy; the I.L.P. opposed them on pacifist grounds; the Socialist League opposed them with Marxist arguments. The Spanish civil war pulled the three groups together again. Pollitt, the Communist leader, Maxton of the I.L.P., and Cripps of the Socialist League launched a Unity Campaign and appeared together on the platform of the Manchester Free Trade Hall. The Labour party hit back at once. The Socialist League was expelled from the Labour party on 27 January 1937. The League, to save its members from further trouble, dissolved itself two months later.[2] Individuals who supported 'Unity' were then threatened with expulsion. The campaign ran down, and disappeared. Its legacy remained. There was an enduring suspicion that the Labour leaders were more concerned to assert party discipline than to conduct 'the fight against Fascism'. The anti-Fascists responded often enough by fighting the leaders of the Labour party.

The dispute over the Spanish civil war had wider effects. The attempts at national unity against Hitler were sharply arrested. None of Baldwin's Conservative critics had any

[1] Another instrument of Communist penetration into the intellectual middle class was *The Week*, a cyclostyled sheet which claimed to give the news behind the news. Sometimes it did so; sometimes it drew on the inner consciousness of its editor, Claud Cockburn. Cockburn, a former *Times* correspondent, was now also a leading writer for the *Daily Worker* under the name of Frank Pitcairn.

[2] The League, at its dissolution, had 3,000 members, few of them industrial workers.

sympathy with the Spanish republic; some indeed great hostility to it. In the house of commons, Labour, pushed on by its own Left, accused the government of favouring fascism. Baldwin and his ministers retaliated by describing Labour men as warmongers. One accusation was about as well founded as the other. These controversies distracted attention from greater problems of foreign policy. Conservatives talked as though the peace of the world would be secure if the pretence of non-intervention were continued until Franco won. Labour men of the Left seemed to believe that the victory of the Spanish republic would overthrow Hitler also. Politicians wrangled over the Spanish question and had little time to look at the state of British armaments. Yet it remained very much a question for the few, an episode in intellectual history. It would be hard to decide who was the strangest recruit to the anti-Fascist cause: Chalmers Mitchell, a former director of the London zoo; Collingwood, the philosopher, who turned the end of his autobiography into an aggressive anti-Fascist manifesto; or Vaughan Williams, the composer, who abandoned folk music for anti-Fascist symphonies. Most English people displayed little concern. They wanted peace. They disliked communism. Baldwin gave them what they wanted. His hard times were over.

Events ran still more on Baldwin's side at the end of 1936 and in an unexpected way. The monarchy became a topic of dispute for the first time since the death of Queen Anne, or at any rate since the widowhood of Queen Victoria. George V died on 20 January 1936 after a brief illness. His last reported words were: 'How is the Empire?' He had been a model of constitutional rectitude and a model of conservative respectability also in his private life. The new king, Edward VIII, had built up a stock of popularity as prince of Wales. In a rather feckless way, he wanted to make the monarchy more adventurous, and the country with it. He resented the staid tepidity of the 'old men', his ministers. They resented him. In the early days of the reign, Neville Chamberlain drafted a memorandum of complaint, urging the king to 'settle down'. He should wear drabber clothes, work at his 'boxes', and not make public remarks about the slums or unemployment. Baldwin suppressed the memorandum. As always, he made time his ally, and waited on events.

Edward's position had a fatal flaw. He was still a bachelor at 41. He now intended to marry. Mrs. Wallis Simpson, his proposed wife, was gay, witty, attractive. As a royal consort, she had every conceivable disadvantage. She was an American; she was a commoner—and truly common at that, not even a millionaire's daughter, let alone an untitled member of an aristocratic family; she had a former husband living, whom she had divorced; and a present husband, Ernest Simpson. The king and Mrs. Simpson had been on affectionate terms for some time. Like other sons with an overbearing father, Edward had let things drift during his father's lifetime. Now he wanted the glamour of his royal position; he even wanted to do his duty, though with some impatience at its formal side; most of all, he wanted to marry Mrs. Simpson as soon as she had divorced her husband. He had apparently no inkling of the difficulties which he would encounter. His personal friends were out of touch with respectable opinion. Mrs. Simpson knew only the American code, in which marriage was essential and divorce a harmless formality. So far as Edward thought at all, he assumed, like many of his generation, that he could keep his private life entirely distinct from his public image. Also, like others of his generation, he exaggerated the decline in traditional standards of behaviour.

England was a laxer country than she had been thirty years before. But appearances were kept up in public. Divorce still carried a moral stigma and still drove men from political life. It was especially damaging for a king. The monarchy was inextricably entangled with the Established church, and the church had grown increasingly rigorous against divorce— perhaps in feeble competition with the Roman church's stand against birth control. The directors of British public life had invested much emotional capital in Edward's popularity, when he was prince of Wales. They did not want this investment to be wasted. It would be wasted if he ceased to be king; but still more, in their opinion, if he threatened the façade of accepted morality. There was nothing that ministers could do while the king and Mrs. Simpson remained merely on friendly terms. The example of Edward VII prevented any objection. Besides, many public men had worse skeletons of this sort in their cupboards. Throughout most of 1936 therefore the king and Mrs. Simpson went openly together everywhere. The British press kept news of their doings out of its columns—apparently by a voluntary agreement to avoid an embarrassing subject, and not because of any official, or even unofficial, request. Foreign newspapers were censored by the wholesalers before they reached the British public.

On 27 October Mrs. Simpson obtained a decree of divorce *nisi* from her husband at Ipswich, where she had established a rather fictitious residence. The way for her remarriage was being opened. The cohorts of morality now mobilized. Sir Alexander Hardinge, the king's private secretary, was the first to expostulate—a curious little indication that this once personal post had acquired constitutional standing.[1] Baldwin himself was pushed into action by Dawson, editor of *The Times*, who produced evidence that American opinion was disturbed. Baldwin posed a stern choice: renunciation of Mrs. Simpson or abdication. Mrs. Simpson posed an equally stern choice on the other side: marriage whatever the price. Her firmness over this made things easy, and she deserved more gratitude from the respectable than she received. For the king wavered. He wanted to have his cake and eat it—somehow to marry Mrs. Simpson and yet to remain on the throne.[2] He shrank from any clear-cut action, much as the union leaders had done during the general strike. Baldwin, as then, was determined not to yield. Though usually slow and inactive, there was no one better at forcing a decision when he set himself to it.

Edward was overawed by 'the constitution'. He bowed to Baldwin's ruling that the question should be settled quietly behind the scenes, and settled without delay.[3] He proposed to

---

[1] Later private secretaries have been appointed, like bishops and other public officials, on the advice of the prime minister.

[2] Edward's wavering had a practical cause, unknown at the time. He spent his days during the crisis at his private house, Fort Belvedere, in Windsor Great Park, withdrawn from all society. There he received Baldwin and often seemed to weaken. Late each night, he motored to London and joined Mrs. Simpson. Then his resolve to marry was renewed.

[3] There is no clear evidence why the king allowed himself to be rushed in this way. Baldwin threatened that the cabinet would resign if their advice against marriage were not accepted. It would have been difficult, indeed impossible, for them to resign if Edward had merely declined to give a promise against a hypothetical marriage at some time in the future and had then withdrawn to Windsor or Balmoral. On the other hand, ministers had a powerful weapon at hand, though there is little evidence that they threatened to use it. In the then state of English law, Mrs. Simpson's decree could not become absolute for six months. Until then it could be challenged. A law clerk called Stephenson duly 'intervened' and withdrew

put his case before the nation in a radio address. Baldwin forbade it. The king gave way. Eager for compromise, he suggested some form of morganatic marriage—Mrs. Simpson to become his wife, but not queen. Baldwin consulted the governments of the Dominions and reported that they were unanimously against this idea. Remorselessly, the king was driven towards abdication. On 1 December an obscure bishop, who knew nothing of Mrs. Simpson, casually remarked that the king was in urgent need of God's grace. The editors of the leading provincial newspapers used this as an excuse to break their long silence. The London newspapers followed them the next day. By then, the affair was practically settled, even though Mrs. Simpson left the country and announced that she had 'withdrawn from the scene'. Edward was only anxious to follow her.

There was a belated attempt to drum up support for Edward VIII or even to form a King's Party. Rothermere and Beaverbrook backed the morganatic marriage in their newspapers. Churchill, responding as usual to the call of romance, pleaded in parliament for delay. There were demonstrations in favour of the king outside Buckingham Palace, Communists and Fascists marching for once on the same side. Such support did the king no good. Baldwin stood impregnable. Most Conservatives supported him. The Labour party was virtually united[1] on the constitutional doctrine that the king must always accept the advice of his ministers. Some sixty M.P.s were reputedly ready to support a 'king's government'. This was probably an exaggeration. Members of parliament, visiting their constituencies at the weekend, learnt the strong feeling against Edward, particularly, it is said, in the north of England. No doubt the feeling was all the stronger from the suddenness with which the news had been sprung on the public, as

his intervention after Edward's abdication. Stephenson was a clerk in a firm sometimes employed by Baldwin. However, the most probable explanation is that Edward was in a hurry to get married. As part of the price for abdication he was promised a special act of parliament, making Mrs. Simpson's divorce absolute at once. At the last moment, the cabinet decided that this would have the appearance of a corrupt bargain, and the promise was not fulfilled. Edward and Mrs. Simpson did not marry until 3 June 1937.

[1] Josiah Wedgwood, one of the few exceptions, had himself been divorced. The other sceptics on the Labour side were republicans who regarded the monarchy and its affairs with indifference. They pointed the contrast between the former adulation of Edward and the present criticism of him.

happened with Parnell long before. Longer debate might have modified it.

Duty, rather than divorce, was the deciding factor. If 'they' thought that Edward should not marry a divorced woman, it was his duty to accept this ruling, just as the ex-servicemen, whose representative he was supposed to be, had once gone blindly to the slaughter when instructed to do so by their officers. It was Edward's weakness that he shared this feeling. He was not the man to shatter the Establishment, at best only to niggle at it. He was now impatient to go quietly, and nothing in his short reign became him like the leaving of it. On 11 December Edward VIII abdicated[1] and was succeeded by his brother Albert, duke of York, who took the title of George VI. Queen Mary, widow of George V, remarked: 'The Yorks will do it very well.' And so they did. George VI followed his father's example devotedly. Frail, highly strung, and inexperienced, he did his duty to the best of his limited ability and worried himself to an early death.

Many people feared, a few hoped, that the abdication of Edward VIII would permanently weaken the monarchy. It did not do so. Edward's former popularity turned out to be as evanescent as the enthusiasm for a film star. He left England; and, though he was created Duke of Windsor, the title of Royal Highness was refused to his wife, when he married Mrs. Simpson (with the assistance of a clergyman of the Established church). The fallen king attached importance to such trifles and therefore remained a resentful exile, casually consoled by being made governor of the Bahamas during the second World war.[2] Edward VIII and his abdication were almost forgotten by the time that George VI was crowned on 12 May 1937. George had none of his brother's glamour. He liked a quiet life, and an impediment in his speech, though partly overcome, caused anxiety on his public appearances. Still, he had more solid things to show. He had seen active service at Jutland. He had run, for many years, the Duke of York's camps, at which public schoolboys and boys from the lower classes were brought together. He gave unquestioning support to his ministers, as

[1] The abdication was given legal effect by an act of parliament, which passed through all its stages in a single day.

[2] He was also consoled by a large sum, said to be £25,000 a year, which George VI paid to him by private arrangement.

his father had done before him, and set a high example when war came. He and Queen Elizabeth clocked in at Buckingham Palace each morning in order to run the risk of bombs and lived on austere rations, eating spam off a gold plate.

The abdication was a strictly English affair. The question of Edward's marriage was discussed solely in English terms, related to the English Established church. No one would have supposed from these discussions that the king had among his subjects many hundred million Moslems and Hindus, who would be unruffled by a divorced woman as queen, nor even that he was king also of Scotland, where the Established church had no objection of principle to divorce. The English people behaved as though they lived in an isolated community, and others accepted this assumption. The inhabitants of India received a new emperor overnight (the last as it turned out). The Dominions, being now sovereign states, passed their own legislation to give effect to the abdication. In the Irish Free State, de Valera took the opportunity to complete his doctrine of 'external association', and the crown disappeared from the Irish constitution except as an anonymous 'organ' for international relations. In this odd way, a divorce once more shaped Irish history. The private life of an English king sapped the Irish treaty of 1922, or what remained of it.

The stir against a divorced queen might have been expected to inaugurate a period of moral rigidity. The men who had worked for Edward's abdication—Baldwin, Dawson, and, most of all, Lang, archbishop of Canterbury—talked as though they had triumphed over the laxity inherited from the frivolous nineteen-twenties. Little came of their triumph. Indeed, 1937 saw a move the other way, which might even be regarded as a gesture of atonement and apology. A. P. Herbert, Independent representative of Oxford University, had the rare success of actually carrying a private member's bill, which brought some relaxation in the marriage laws almost for the first time since divorce became a recognized legal process in 1857. Desertion and insanity were added to adultery as grounds for divorce; the waiting period was reduced from six months to six weeks.[1] One other man received his reward. When the salaries of ministers were rationalized in 1937, the leader of the Opposition,

---

[1] Herbert had to pay a price, and to make marriages indissoluble for their first three years.

too, was given a salary of £2,000 a year.[1] He had supported the constitution in 1936. In return the constitution formally recognized him.

The abdication left its principal mark in the world of practical politics. By toppling Edward VIII off his throne, Baldwin restored his own moral prestige. Though no doubt intent to out-manœuvre the king all along, he gave the Cromwellian impression that he was the instrument of a harsh necessity. Reluctantly, it seemed, he had voiced the conscience of the nation. The highminded men who had insisted on the abdication, such as Dawson and Lang, were exactly those who had cried out against the Hoare–Laval plan twelve months before, just as Edward's support came from the disreputable elements which had been sceptical or contemptuous about the League of Nations. The abdication was Baldwin's atonement for the Hoare–Laval plan. His opponents were routed, Churchill most of all. Churchill made every possible blunder during the crisis. He misjudged public opinion—or the skill of those who manipulated it; he counted wrongly on the king's resolution; he was shouted down in the house of commons. He had grasped at any means to overthrow Baldwin and his government of feeble men. Instead, the gates of power seemed to close against Churchill for ever. It was now his turn to be a broken man.

Baldwin survived in glory until the Coronation. Then he departed with adulation from the public scene. Ramsay MacDonald went less ostentatiously at the same time.[2] In a personal sense, the interwar era ended appropriately with the two men who had characterized it. Neville Chamberlain at last reached the supreme position for which he had waited so long. He was the least glamorous of prime ministers: efficient, conscientious, and unimaginative. His was a humdrum government with none of the glow which Baldwin and MacDonald had occasionally provided. The ministers were the 'old gang' slightly reshuffled: Sir John Simon at the exchequer in place of Chamberlain was the most substantial change. The government were 'National' only in name. Simon (the only minister incidentally to have held office before 1914) had nothing distinctively Liberal about

[1] The Ministers of the Crown Act has other constitutional interest. It gave statutory recognition to the cabinet for the first time and made one of the rare references to the existence of a prime minister.

[2] Baldwin was created an earl and a knight of the garter. He died in 1947. MacDonald accepted no honour and died at sea later in 1937.

him, nor Malcolm MacDonald anything distinctively Labour. The other ministers, for that matter, had little distinctively Conservative. Only Halifax had an historic title, and it derived from a nineteenth-century Whig.

The ministers were respectable administrators like Chamberlain himself, and most of them had made in home affairs such reputations as they possessed. Only Eden felt at home with the professional members of the foreign office. The others looked at diplomatists with distrust—an attitude especially strong perhaps with Simon and Hoare, the two former foreign secretaries who were regarded as failures. In return the staff of the foreign office had little confidence in the government. Sir Robert Vansittart, the permanent under-secretary, was set on resisting Germany. He paraded his resolution in an ornate literary style and also in more irregular ways, such as passing information to Churchill and stirring up opposition to the government in the press. Yet the attitude of Vansittart and the other professionals was singularly impractical. They could only reiterate that Hitler should be resisted and had no idea how to do it. Not surprisingly, Chamberlain wearied of this carping, and Vansittart was pushed aside with the high-sounding meaningless title of Chief Diplomatic Adviser.

The coolness between ministers and the foreign office has promoted the belief that Chamberlain and his colleagues were irresponsible amateurs. On the contrary, in practical matters, few governments have got on better with their professional servants, or worked more closely with them. Sir Horace Wilson, technically Chief Industrial Adviser, became Chamberlain's closest adviser on practically everything, especially foreign affairs, and had more influence than many members of the cabinet. In 1938 the need to direct air-raid precautions actually carried a prominent civil servant, Sir John Anderson, into the cabinet (as lord privy seal)—the first such translation in modern times. To some extent, it may be, civil servants were pushing politicians aside. At any rate the technical requirements of war and its preliminaries inevitably gave greater influence to the men who understood these requirements. The decision between war and peace rested with the politicians. The shape of the war, if it were decided on, was largely determined in advance by officials.

Chamberlain's government had a good administrative

record, as could be expected from his previous reforms of local government and public assistance. In quieter days, their Factory Act, Housing Act, Physical Training Act, and projected reform of criminal justice would each have rated a paragraph. In 1939 they made passenger air services a public corporation—directed, appropriately, by Sir John Reith. Their nationalization of mining royalties in 1938 was prelude to the nationalization of the coal mines after the war. The government prepared to raise the school-leaving age to 15 on 1 September 1939. Chamberlain himself had further plans in mind for local government. He was a meticulous housemaid, great at tidying up. In his narrow, rational way, he believed that most resentments and disputes could be ended by a sensible process of compromise.

Chamberlain grappled firmly with what remained of the Irish problem. In 1937 a new constitution, devised by de Valera, made southern Ireland or 'Eire' independent for all practical purposes. The British government accepted this constitution without demur, as did the Dominions. They continued to treat Eire as a member of the Commonwealth and gave Irishmen the advantages of citizenship—a compliment which Eire reciprocated. Why bother about the last trifles? Early in 1938 the disputes were duly wound up. The land annuities were settled for a single payment of £10 million—Great Britain thus renouncing theoretical claims to £100 million which she could not enforce. Most obstacles to trade between Eire and Great Britain were removed. These were reasonable bargains.

Chamberlain also made a larger concession. The three naval bases in southern Ireland, which Lloyd George had insisted on retaining, were handed over to the Eire government. Some Englishmen were bitter at this surrender. Churchill complained that the loss of these ports would be a disastrous handicap on the British navy in time of war. It could be argued on the other side, as the chiefs of staff argued, that the ports would be useless if Eire were hostile and that it was worth giving them up to make her friendly. This was Chamberlain's intention. By an ironical twist, he, the son of Joseph Chamberlain, put the Irish question on a purely practical basis, and so removed it from British politics. He imagined that the Irish would do the same. Chamberlain did not appreciate that practical grievances, though real, were often the cover for deeper sentiment, which could not be so easily satisfied. So it was with Ireland. De

Valera would be content with nothing less than the reunifica-
tion of the whole island—an idea which the Unionist government of Northern Ireland rejected with unslackened vigour. The
agreements of 1938 were for Chamberlain a final settlement, for
de Valera a payment on account. The negotiations provided in
fact an object lesson in the merits of 'appeasement' and also in
its limitations—a lesson which Chamberlain ignored to his own
undoing elsewhere.

Palestine provided a further lesson. Here, as in some parts
of Europe, two peoples, in this case Arabs and Jews, were living
in the same community, and their mutual hostility could not
be assuaged by the rational inquiries of a detached mediator.
The hostility grew worse during the nineteen-thirties, as anti-
semitic measures in Germany and other countries pushed up the
numbers of Jewish immigrants. The Arabs rioted and resorted
to violence on the old Irish scale. In July 1937 a royal commission under Lord Peel recommended the partition of Palestine
into an Arab state, a Jewish state, and a British mandate for
Jerusalem and Bethlehem with a corridor to the sea. Zionist
opinion was indignant. The British government were much
badgered on the mandates committee at Geneva by states
which did not have to carry the burden of maintaining order.
In 1938 a partition commission, under Sir John Woodhead,
reported that the two peoples were inextricably tangled up and
that partition was impossible. In March 1939 the British government tried the resort of a Round Table conference—an expedient which proved as barren as it had done for Ireland and
India. Finally in May 1939 there came a White Paper, promising the end of Jewish immigration after a further 75,000 Jews
had been admitted. The Balfour declaration was thus abandoned, after twenty years of attempting to reconcile the
irreconcilable. It was no doubt unreasonable that the Arabs of
Palestine should pay the whole price for what was a world
problem, anti-semitism. On the other hand, British governments had made repeated promises to the Jews. Now the
promises were broken—too difficult to carry out, too expensive
and worrying. Above all, the Arabs caused the more trouble,
and the British needed, or imagined that they needed, the
friendship of the Arab states in order to maintain their position
in the Middle East. They surrendered to violence, and wrapped
up this surrender in ethical phrases. Here was another object

lesson. Appeasement in practice meant endorsing the claims of the stronger and then making out that these claims were just.

These questions provided much stuff for parliamentary debate. The old topics of housing, education, and the obstinately depressed areas were still alive. But foreign affairs kept breaking in, as never before in peacetime.[1] During the first session of MacDonald's National government (from November 1931 to November 1932), the house of commons devoted two half-days to foreign affairs, and one to the Disarmament conference. In Chamberlain's first session (November 1937 to November 1938), foreign affairs occupied the house for thirty-one full days, and this does not include the days spent on discussing armaments. Similarly, questions of foreign policy dominated the annual meeting of the Trades Union Congress and the conferences of the Labour party. Newspapers and weekly periodicals were equally obsessed. More pamphlets and books on foreign affairs poured from the press than at any previous time in English history. In the great divide between war-mongers and appeasers, men broke with old friends. Social life was disrupted, as it had only been earlier during the bitterest days of the Irish question.

This preoccupation with foreign affairs still affected only the conscious nation: politicians, trade union secretaries, writers and readers of sophisticated journals—those whom Keynes called 'the Ins'. Ordinary men and women had little idea that a great European war might be imminent until they were caught up in the crisis over Czechoslovakia at the end of September 1938. Even after this, the recruits for civil defence and the territorial army came mainly from the educated middle class. The *Evening Standard* published each day cartoons by David Low, which depicted Hitler and Mussolini as war-mongers. The *Daily Express*, true to its principle that a favourable forecast produced good weather, ran across its front page after Munich: 'Great Britain will not be involved in a European war this year or next year either', and the *Daily Express* had eight or ten times the circulation of its evening stable-companion. Though foreign affairs occupied the centre of the stage, the play was performed in a theatre which was

[1] Certainly not before the first World war. In the two and a half years between the Agadir crisis in 1911 and the outbreak of war in 1914, the house of commons did not have a single full-dress debate on foreign affairs.

almost empty and where the stagehands took little notice of
what was going on. Full national participation in public affairs
began only in May 1940, when these affairs went disastrously
wrong.

The arguments and acts were on two levels: armaments
(usually called 'rearmament' or 'defence') and policy. Though
the two levels were obviously related, they rarely overlapped.
The service chiefs took German armament, or supposed
German armament, as their yardstick and set out to counter it.
They did not speculate on the causes of possible conflict between
Great Britain and Germany, or on how these might be removed.
They assumed that, since Germany was again becoming a
military power, war with her would follow, once the armament
plans of both sides matured. They also assumed, less consciously, that in this war Great Britain would have to rely
mainly on her own strength. They rarely considered possible
allies, and then usually to depreciate them. In February 1939,
for example, when the government were drawing the ties of
alliance with France tighter, the chiefs of staff anticipated that
the French army might be defeated. On the other side, foreign
policy, as such, was determined with little reference to the
state of armaments. Concession or resistance were decided on
for their own sake, and military reasons, if adduced at all,
were called in afterwards to justify what had been decided.
There are thus two different stories of how Great Britain moved
towards the war of 1939—both true in their own terms and yet
seemingly contradictory. One is the story of steadily accelerat-
ing preparations for an inevitable war. The other is of groping
attempts to prevent war—attempts which failed regretfully
and by mistake.

Armament on a large scale was begun after the general election of 1935, though it had, of course, been theoretically propounded before it. Political motives entered in. The election
itself gave the government some sort of mandate for armaments. The Abyssinian crisis, and thereafter Germany's
reoccupation of the Rhineland, shattered the easy security of
the postwar years. The principal motive, however, was technical: the need to counter Germany's growing strength, particularly in the air. The British air chiefs pushed up their
demands by jerks, as they revised, time and again, their estimates of German arms. From that terrible day in March 1935

when Hitler told Sir John Simon that Germany had reached parity in the air with Great Britain, the British service chiefs took German figures at their face value, or rather regarded them as less than the reality. The truth was exactly the reverse: Germany never had the arms she claimed to have. American investigators surveyed the German economy immediately after the war. They concluded: 'The world greatly over-estimated Germany's [air] strength.'[1] This conclusion, though put correctly by the official historians, has not yet penetrated the popular versions of prewar history.

In fact, Germany was busy preparing to become again a military power in the continental fashion, though even here she was less busy than men at the time made out. Her efforts aimed almost exclusively at creating a force for land operations. Until 1940 she made no direct preparations for war against England. She had no battle fleet, no landing craft, very few submarines. Her air force was designed for cooperation with the army, not for use as an independent weapon. Of course it was still assumed, by the Germans as by everyone else, that almost any aeroplane could go off and bomb towns when it had nothing better to do. However, the German *Luftwaffe* had no plans or training for this, despite Hitler's threats of indiscriminate destruction. The British air staff took these threats seriously. They assumed, without discussion, that all the German bombers could be used against British targets and that they would be so used. They further overrated the number of aeroplanes which Germany possessed and, still more, of those which she would soon possess. In 1938, for example, they estimated the German frontline strength at twice the British, and future German production at twice the British also. Actual German superiority then was only 60 per cent. in front-line strength; reserves were less than the British; trained pilots equal. British production of aeroplanes had almost reached the German level and surpassed it in the course of 1939.[2]

[1] United States Bombing Survey.

[2] The exaggeration extended to German rearmament generally. In 1936, according to Churchill, Germany was rearming at an annual rate of 12,000 million marks. The actual rate was 5,000 million. Hitler himself boasted that he had spent 90,000 million marks on rearmament. His actual expenditure in the six years up to March 1939 was 40,000 million marks. In 1938 Germany was supposed to be devoting to arms 25 per cent. of her gross national product, and Great Britain 7 per cent. The actual German figure was 15 per cent., reduced by a third after Munich, and the British figure reached 15 per cent. by the end of the year. The

British experts also exaggerated the effect of bombing—their own, of course, as much as the German. In 1937 they expected an attack continuing for sixty days, with casualties of 600,000 dead and 1,200,000 injured. The ministry of health, advised by these experts, calculated in 1939 that from one million to three million hospital beds would be needed immediately after the outbreak of war. Actual civilian casualties from air attack in Great Britain during nearly six years of war were 295,000, of whom 60,000 were killed.[1]

The air chiefs insisted that massive retaliation was the only defence, and that bombers must take precedence over all other forms of armament. The heads of the army and navy tried to resist this doctrine, fearing for their own programmes. They resisted in vain. In 1935 the R.A.F. received only half the money spent on the army and less than a quarter of that spent on the navy. By 1939 it was receiving more money than either of the other forces.[2] Ministers accepted the R.A.F. doctrine in principle and limited its application only on grounds of expense. In their view, a stable currency and foreign credits were as important as fleets of bombers. Sir John Simon, shortly after the outbreak of war, called finance 'the fourth arm of defence'.[3] Moreover, ministers shrank from the unpopularity which, they imagined, would follow a great increase in taxation. They shrank, too, from disturbing civilian prosperity and wanted armaments as a sort of 'extra' which no one would notice. They yielded slowly to the terrifying figures which the air chiefs put before them, and less than they were asked to do.

Even then, ministers and air chiefs alike misunderstood the problem involved in manufacturing aeroplanes. They were misled by the naval race with Germany before 1914, which most of them remembered, and imagined that, if the money were provided, aeroplanes would appear of themselves. This

story of tanks is similar to that of aeroplanes. By the outbreak of war, British production of tanks was greater than the German, which was in fact only 45 per cent. of the figure estimated by British Intelligence. Burton Klein, *Germany's Economic Preparations for War*, 17–20.

[1] Titmuss, *Problems of Social Policy*, 13, 324–6. See Note A, p. 437.

[2] 1935: air, £17 million; army, £40 million; navy, £56 million. 1939: air, £133 million; army, £121 million; navy, £127 million.

[3] An economist, writing late in 1939, pointed to the large total of British gold reserves and of overseas securities, and concluded: 'Such a reserve of financial strength gives Britain an enormous, if not deciding, advantage in the conduct of hostilities.' E. V. Francis, *Britain's Economic Strategy*, 382.

had been true, or almost true, of battleships in the old days. Great Britain had then an almost inexhaustible reserve of shipyards and shipbuilding labour, which only needed government orders to set to work. It was not true of aeroplanes. There was no large aircraft industry, based on a vast civilian market. Resources and workers had to be diverted from other work. The very factories had to be built. Indeed, the larger the service programme, the fewer were the aeroplanes actually produced. Everything had to go on preparations; there was little left over for production. Ministers were baffled that, the more money they poured out, the less apparently they had to show for it.

There were four clear steps in the advance of British armament after the change of principle announced in the White Paper. First had been the decision to arm fully in the autumn of 1935. This produced many figures on paper and few results. Baldwin thus kept his promise that there should be no great armaments, no doubt to his own surprise and regret. Next, Neville Chamberlain, in his last budget (April 1937), abandoned orthodox peacetime finance, and devised a special tax, the National Defence Contribution, on those who were profiting from the manufacture of arms.[1] He also laid down that £400 million of the extra cost should be met by borrowing, spread over five years, instead of being paid for by taxation—the first time this had been done, when the country was at peace, since the Naval Defence Act of 1889.[2] On each occasion the assumption was the same (and on each occasion wrong): that this was a once-for-all expense. The additional aeroplanes, or, in 1889, ships, were expected both to be enough and to last more or less for ever.[3] At any rate, the money was now there.

The aeroplanes, however, continued to lag. A year later, the government took a third, more drastic step. On 22 March 1938 the services were freed from the restriction not to interfere with 'normal' trade. Henceforward, for example, manufacturers could be induced to switch their works to making aeroplanes, despite the civilian demand for motor cars. On the following

[1] There was an outcry against the tax, which was denounced as unworkable. Chamberlain withdrew it and substituted a straight tax of 5 per cent. on all profits.

[2] The amount to be raised by borrowing was increased in 1938, and again in 1939.

[3] The word 'rearmament', commonly used at the time, itself carried an implication that one day armament would be completed.

day the leaders of the T.U.C. came to No. 10 Downing Street for the first time since 1931 and agreed to relax craft restrictions in the engineering industry. This was the equivalent of Lloyd George's treasury agreement on 27 March 1915—this time eighteen months before the outbreak of war instead of seven months after it. The two decisions marked the real beginning of a war economy. Though they came ten days after Hitler's incorporation of Austria into Germany, this was a pure accident. The technical arguments happened to mature at that moment.

The fourth and final date did not coincide with any political event. On 22 February 1939 the government authorized aircraft production 'to the limit', that is, as much as industry could produce without regard to the money being available.[1] The outbreak of war, on the other hand, made no mark on the economic record. Production went on at an uninterrupted rate from 22 February 1939 until the acceleration provoked by the catastrophes of May 1940. Indeed, if one were to judge British policy solely from the story of armaments (as Hitler's policy is often judged solely from his armaments), it would appear that Great Britain was marching consciously towards a war on which she was all along resolved.

Politics, however, provide a different story. Of course some politicians believed that the armaments race would produce war of itself. Churchill came near to believing this. He and his few supporters held that Germany was set on a great war and that Great Britain must simply prepare to resist her. A few Labour men also continued to regard armaments as the cause of war, though they drew an opposite conclusion. They wanted to cut down British armaments in the hope that then all would be well. The general Labour view was more equivocal. The party officially now accepted the view that some increase in armaments was necessary in order to support the collective security in which Labour still believed. In July 1937 the parliamentary party decided henceforward to abstain over the armament estimates instead of voting against them. In this way, they hoped to escape the reproach that they were preaching strong action without providing the means for enforcing it, and yet to show their lack of confidence in the government's policy.

[1] The one remaining restriction was on spending dollars, which were still rationed to the equivalent of £150 million a year.

Even this change of line was less striking than it seemed. The majority for it was small (45 to 39) and was provided mainly by inarticulate trade unionists. The leaders were mostly still on the other side.[1] Attlee himself voted against the change, as did his two principal lieutenants, Morrison and Greenwood, and so, of course, did the members of the Left, such as Cripps and Bevan. These were the spokesmen of Labour in the house, and they could not change their tune. Sometimes they argued that armaments would never be used for any good purpose, that is, for collective security; sometimes that they would be used for a bad one, that is, for assisting Germany against Soviet Russia. In either case, the impression on public opinion was the same. Labour seemed to be opposing armaments. Hence it remained vulnerable to the reproach of preaching a strong policy, supported only by strong words.

Labour's confused attitude barred the way against any attempt at national collaboration, and, of course, the more Labour was spurned, the more suspicious it became. Neville Chamberlain did not repine at this: he liked to make differences sharper, where Baldwin had sought to smooth them over. Chamberlain took a practical line in foreign policy as in everything else. He had long groaned under Baldwin's drift and delay. He was impatient with words and phrases, whether those of the Labour party or all that structure of pacts and treaties, on which the French relied. He disliked pretence and uncertainty. He had been the first minister to advocate the abandonment of sanctions against Italy, when they had obviously failed, just as he had been the most rigorous in pressing Edward VIII. He had led every step towards rearmament and, indeed, more than any other man, laid the foundations for British fighting power during the second World war. On the other hand, he resented the money wasted on armaments and resented, too, the way in which foreign affairs distracted him and his government from their projects of domestic reform. He believed that the European dictators, Hitler and Mussolini, were rational statesmen like himself, or at any rate must be treated as such, and that their discontents could be appeased by rational discussion. He was therefore eager to start this discussion and to get Europe resettled on new lines.

[1] Hugh Dalton's was the Labour voice most powerful (in more senses than one) in favour of large armaments.

Chamberlain's asset was his sharp rationalism. He beat down critics with the question: what is the alternative? Hardly anyone now believed that the League of Nations could be effective in its existing form, though many shrank from admitting it—Germany, Italy, and Japan outside the League; sanctions shattered by the failure over Abyssinia. Churchill tended to talk as though Great Britain and France could still lay down the law to Europe; some members of the foreign office thought that Hitler should be 'hit on the head'. Chamberlain had no faith in this policy. Though he regarded France as secure from invasion behind the Maginot line and Great Britain as equally so behind the shield of sea power, he believed that Germany was also secure on her side. At least, she could be tamed only by a great war, lasting for years and tearing Europe to pieces. Such a war he and nearly all Englishmen wished to avoid.[1] The few who suggested that Hitler was bluffing could be answered by the estimates of the service chiefs—or, for that matter, of Churchill himself. Nor did Chamberlain regret the decline of Anglo-French influence in eastern Europe. This was precisely what British statesmen, including his own brother Austen, had advocated ever since the end of the first World war.

It was, of course, obvious to him, as to everyone else, that Germany would become the predominant power in eastern Europe and the Balkans; there was no escape from this, once she was acknowledged as a Great Power at all. Did Chamberlain go further and look forward to a war between Germany and Soviet Russia as a way of getting the British empire out of all its troubles? This sophisticated explanation was put forward, to

[1] The opponents of appeasement and, for that matter, its supporters often failed to distinguish between 'stopping' Hitler and defeating him in a great war. Hitler could be stopped only in areas directly accessible to Anglo-French forces, particularly to the French army (assuming, as was not in fact the case, that it was capable of offensive action). For instance, Hitler's reoccupation of the Rhineland could have been stopped theoretically by the French army. German and Italian intervention in Spain could have been stopped by the British and French navies. Hitler's annexation of Austria could have been stopped by the French and Italian armies, if Mussolini had still been on the side of the Western Powers. Austria was the last occasion when direct opposition was possible. Great Britain and France could not have stopped a German invasion of Czechoslovakia. They could only threaten to attack Germany's frontiers, which they believed, rightly or wrongly, to be heavily defended. Similarly, they could not stop the German invasion of Poland. They could only begin a general war which brought no aid to the Poles. There were thus two different questions. At first: shall we go to the aid of this country or that? Later: shall we start a general war for the overthrow of Germany as a Great Power? In practice, of course, the two questions were always mixed up.

Chamberlain's discredit, by a few extreme socialists at the time, and has occasionally been put forward, to his credit, later. There is little evidence for it. Chamberlain lived in the present. He wanted to settle immediate problems and did not much peer beyond. No doubt he hoped that Germany and Soviet Russia would balance out and hold each other in check. A war between them would be a catastrophe also for Great Britain, if it ended in a decisive victory for either. On this subject, Chamberlain kept his fingers crossed, if he thought about it at all.

It is possible to speculate whether Chamberlain ever envisaged an alliance with Germany against Soviet Russia. It is certain that he abhorred alliance with Soviet Russia against Germany. This was the favourite idea of the extreme Left— of the Left Book Club, of the unavowed Popular Front, and of those who were fighting for the Spanish republic. The bulk of the Labour party shuffled towards it more reluctantly. It is a reasonable surmise that most English people came to regard Communist Russia as less wicked than Nazi Germany only late in the day, perhaps not until Hitler's attack on Russia. Besides, there were in 1937 and the years immediately after it practical objections. Russia was in the midst of Stalin's great purge, and it was difficult to take her seriously as a military power when all her principal military leaders had just been shot. The British service chiefs rated Russia's power very low, and their opinion carried weight even if it sprang as much from political prejudice as from knowledge. Again, Soviet Russia could not act effectively against Germany even if she had the power, so long as the *cordon sanitaire* of eastern European states was in existence—and anti-Russian. The settlement of Europe had to be revised one way or the other. It was plausible to argue that a revision to suit Germany would be less drastic than one to suit Russia, and the outcome less painful. Russia would want to communize Europe. Germany sought the redress of her national grievances and would then settle down to a happy partnership in prosperity with the Western Powers.

These were more or less rational calculations which Chamberlain made to himself. The great debate over British foreign policy did not revolve round them. It was conducted in moral terms. Most English people still assumed that Great Britain was a power of the first rank, despite the deficiencies in her armaments.

Hence she was free to choose the moral course, and, if she did so, this course would inevitably triumph. English people were in fact more concerned to be on the side of God than to keep their powder dry. One moral argument told strongly in Germany's favour: the argument which had been pressed, particularly by the Left, ever since the end of the first World war. The treaty of Versailles had been presented as unjust, punitive, and unworkable. Germany was entitled to equality in armaments and everything else. The Germans of Austria, Czechoslovakia, and Poland were entitled, like other nationalities, to self-determination, even if this meant an increase in German power. More broadly, Germany was entitled to a place in Europe and in the world commensurate with her greatness in population, economic resources, and civilization. This doctrine had long been the stock-in-trade of Labour foreign policy. Labour was still solid for it when Hitler reoccupied the Rhineland. Even later, Labour men could not bring themselves to renounce it altogether. They felt, with a puzzled embarrassment, that Germany's demands were just, even though Hitler was not entitled to make them.

Conservatives took up Germany's moral claims just as Labour was backing away from them. The Conservatives of the nineteen-thirties were no longer the fire-eating imperialists of the first World war. They, too, had been gradually educated by Keynes in his denunciation of the peace settlement. The first World war, it seemed, had shaken Great Britain's position both at home and abroad. No sensible man wanted another. Again, there had always been something strained and artificial in the *entente cordiale* with France. Some army men of the type who always dislike their allies, were accustomed to say that Great Britain had fought on the wrong side. Businessmen preferred the hard-working Germans to the unreliable French. They admired Hitler for his economic achievements, just as earlier they had been impressed when Mussolini allegedly made Italian trains run to time. There was, of course, apprehension of Germany's power and of her economic competition. But meeting her just grievances seemed the most sensible way of taming her—certainly much more sensible than a great war. Guilty conscience was undoubtedly the strongest factor: a desire to atone for the mistakes of the past and a hope that this atonement would settle things. Geoffrey Dawson, editor of

The Times, was a striking example. Like most of Milner's kindergarten in South Africa long ago, he had always tended to sympathize with the Germans—this was why Northcliffe had dismissed him as editor in 1919.[1] Dawson was superbly confident in his own righteousness. He had been implacable against Edward VIII. He was now equally ruthless for reconciliation with Germany. He turned *The Times* into a propaganda sheet and did not hesitate to suppress, or to pervert, the reports of his own correspondents.

For there was also a strong moral argument on the other side: the character of the German government. Germany ceased to be a democratic country after Hitler became chancellor in January 1933. She was, in the contemporary phrase, a totalitarian state. All political parties, other than the National Socialist, were suppressed. Political opponents were sent without trial to labour camps—called by the Nazis, in wicked echo of British practice during the Boer war, concentration camps. Religion was hampered. General elections became artificial plebiscites for a single party. British and American reporters did full, and perhaps more than full, justice to what was happening in Germany. The Nazi dictatorship was no worse than that in some other countries, particularly that in Soviet Russia, with whom, all the same, the Left were advocating an alliance. But events in Germany were reported much more fully. Besides, Germany had once been democratic and law-abiding; Russia had not. It was Germany's lapse from her high estate which constituted her special crime.

The Labour Left, spurred on by the Communists, had denounced German fascism from the first day. Few of them openly preached a crusade or war of liberation. But they came near to it. Just as they had exaggerated the effect of economic sanctions against Italy, so they seemed to imagine that moral disapproval and economic boycott would bring down German fascism. In any case, most of them accepted the current Marxist doctrine that fascism inevitably led to war, thus finding themselves in unwelcome agreement with the service chiefs, who regarded war as inevitable on other grounds. There was not

[1] Northcliffe said: 'Dawson is naturally pro-German. He just can't help it.' The first act of Astor and Walter was to restore Dawson as editor when they acquired *The Times* after Northcliffe's death. Lord Lothian (formerly, as Philip Kerr, one of Lloyd George's private secretaries) and Lionel Curtis were also members of Milner's kindergarten who now supported appeasement.

much difference in practice between regarding war as inevitable and advocating it. This anti-Fascist crusade deepened the cleavage between Labour and the supporters of the government. Conservatives had no desire to be taken for an ideological ride. They reacted by finding apologies for Hitler and were the more provoked to do so, when socialists discovered 'fascism' even in the policy of the National government. Most Englishmen had no desire to interfere in the affairs of other countries and held that what went on in Germany was 'no business of ours'.

This aloofness broke down at one point. Englishmen of all classes and of all parties were offended by the Nazi treatment of the Jews. Here again, Jews were treated as badly in other countries, and often worse—in Poland, for example, with whom, nevertheless, Great Britain remained on friendly terms. For that matter, there was a good deal of quiet anti-semitism in England. Jews were kept out of many social organizations such as golf clubs, and some of the most famous public schools exercised a *numerus clausus* against them. Indeed, until Hitler's time Germany had probably been an easier country than most for Jews to rise high in industry and the professions. Once more, it was the reversion to barbarism almost as much as the barbarism itself which made Nazi Germany peculiarly hateful, and some English people were no doubt the more annoyed at having to repudiate the anti-semitism which they had secretly cherished.

Besides, the German Jews were not poor people, like most Jews in Poland or Rumania. They were famous authors, musicians, bankers, and scientists. There was now a planned exclusion of them from public life. Many left Germany—particularly those who could afford to do so. They received a warm welcome in England. As early as 1933, a fund was opened to place academic refugees in English universities. Some refugees set up their own businesses, to British advantage. Some became journalists and writers. Every refugee was walking propaganda against the Nazis, even if he never opened his mouth—propaganda which often reached people remote from the Left. The most non-political professor was moved by the sufferings of those who were now his colleagues. Even city bankers became champions of freedom when a Rothschild was imprisoned in Vienna. After the incorporation of Austria into Germany, Sigmund Freud, founder of psychoanalysis, was admitted into

England with none of the usual formalities, and, against all the rules,[1] was made a British citizen the next day. The membership roll of the Royal Society, which had never left the Society's premises before, was taken to Freud's house for his signature. Baldwin's only speech on the radio after his retirement was in aid of a fund for resettling the Jews. Nazi treatment of the Jews did more than anything else to turn English moral feeling against Germany, and this moral feeling in turn made English people less reluctant to go to war.

Chamberlain shared this feeling. But he rarely allowed emotion to determine his policy. In any case he believed that appeasement was the best way of bringing Germany back to civilized behaviour. It is a fair guess that his outlook was shared by the great majority of English people outside the Labour party, and Labour was ruled out of court by its seeming advocacy of collective security, unsupported by arms. Chamberlain was further sustained by the representatives of the Dominions, when an Imperial conference was held in May 1937 during the coronation. They were unanimously for appeasement of the European dictators. Australia and New Zealand were especially anxious to see Europe settled, so that more British power could be built up against Japan in the Far East, and their anxiety grew greater in July 1937 when fighting was renewed between China and Japan. It is not surprising that the son of Joseph Chamberlain responded to this prompting. Chamberlain also received strong support from the leading members of his own cabinet; nothing could be further from the truth than the idea that his policy was a one-man affair. The two former foreign secretaries in the cabinet, Simon and Hoare, worked closely with him; they were joined by Halifax, now lord president of the council, who had learnt the virtue of appeasement during his long negotiations with Gandhi. Eden, the actual foreign secretary, stood practically alone against this formidable combination, with some feeble support occasionally from junior members of the government.

Eden's previous record was not marked by resolute action. He had been the conciliator in chief, travelling across Europe with disarmament conventions and peace pacts in his bag. As

---

[1] Legally naturalization was granted at the unfettered discretion of the home secretary. The invariable practice was to require five years' residence and evidence of good character.

foreign secretary, he had provided the idealistic smokescreen with which to save Baldwin after the outcry against the Hoare–Laval plan. He had acquiesced in the Italian conquest of Abyssinia and had deterred the French, so far as they needed it, from action in the Rhineland. He sponsored the pretences of the Spanish non-intervention committee. He relied on moral disapproval: strong words and no acts. Sooner or later, he believed, Hitler and Mussolini would come begging for forgiveness, if Anthony Eden continued to wag his finger at them. This worked out in practice as a grumbling retreat. The dictators got what they wanted and grew increasingly confident that, by threats, they could get more. Honour perhaps was saved. Everything else was being lost. Chamberlain disliked this attitude. Like a good businessman, he was anxious to cut his losses in order to be in a better position for the future.

In the summer of 1937 Eden for once stirred himself to action. 'Unknown' submarines, actually Italian, sank British, French, and Russian ships which were carrying food and civilian supplies to the Spanish republic. Great Britain and France summoned a conference of Mediterranean powers at Nyon and set up anti-submarine patrols. The sinkings stopped. Here was a demonstration that firm action would work in favourable circumstances, and in fact Hitler and Mussolini often told their own advisers that they would cease to intervene in Spain if the Western powers ordered them to do so. The lesson was not heeded. Italian divisions continued to serve with Franco. Eden continued to complain. He was to write in his memoirs: 'If I had had to choose, I would have preferred a [Spanish] Government victory.'[1] He did not choose, or rather he chose a line which led in practice to the victory of Franco.

In November 1937 the emptiness of talk was again exposed. The Chinese appealed to the League of Nations against Japan. The League hastily passed the hot potato to a conference of Nine Powers at Brussels. This time, the British government got their blow in first: they offered to support any action in which the United States would take part. The United States, though lavish in words, would do nothing—except to continue their profitable trade with Japan. In the usual manner, the conference registered disapproval, and dispersed. Eden continued to have faith in words. He believed that a talk between President

[1] Avon, *Facing the Dictators*, 441.

Roosevelt and himself would make the dictators hesitate.[1]
In January 1938 Roosevelt moved towards the idea of a world
conference to air every grievance under the sun, though again
without an assurance that the United States would act in any
way. Eden was on holiday in the south of France. Chamberlain
had more hope from direct negotiations with the dictators.
On his encouragement, Halifax had already visited Germany
and had assured Hitler that Danzig, Austria, and Czechoslovakia could be settled in Germany's favour, provided that there
were no 'far-reaching disturbances'—that is, without war.
Chamberlain therefore replied discouragingly to the Americans,
and they, who had never meant anything in particular,
acquiesced gladly enough. Eden, on his return, was angry.
He thought mistakenly that Chamberlain had missed a great
opportunity for enlisting American support.[2] He was still more
angry on the personal ground that a decision had been taken in
foreign policy without his being consulted.

A sharper conflict followed in February. Independent Austria
was running into difficulties. Chamberlain believed that Mussolini might be induced to moderate Hitler, if not to save Austria.
Eden stuck to his line of impotent disapproval. There had already been a 'gentleman's agreement'[3] between Great Britain
and Italy in January 1937, promoted by Eden himself, when
both sides agreed to respect the *status quo* in the Mediterranean;
and Chamberlain had exchanged friendly letters with Mussolini
shortly after becoming prime minister. Chamberlain now proposed to go further; Eden to stand still. Their dispute was within
a narrow compass. Mussolini wanted *de jure* recognition for the

---

[1] 'Its steadying effect upon the dictators could have been important.' Avon,
Facing the Dictators, 530.

[2] The American offer is still often regarded as another great 'lost opportunity'.
Langer and Gleason, the best informed American historians, write of Roosevelt's
proposal (*The Challenge to Isolation*, 31–32): 'Conceivably a really strong stand by
the United States Government in support of the British might have changed the
course of events, but . . . nothing of the kind was even remotely envisaged in
Washington. Mr. Roosevelt and his advisers sympathized with the British and
wished them well in whatever efforts they might feel constrained to make in the
direction of peaceful adjustment; but there was never any question of approving or
supporting their specific policy and certainly no thought of assuming any political
or military commitment in connection with it.'

[3] This absurd phrase was taken by Papen from business usage to describe the
agreement between Austria and Germany in July 1936. It was much used hereafter
for an agreement with anyone who was obviously not a gentleman and who would
obviously not keep his agreement.

Italian empire in Abyssinia. Both Chamberlain and Eden were ready to grant it, once the Italian 'volunteers' had been withdrawn from Spain. Chamberlain wished to put this conditional agreement on record; Eden objected. That was all. There was no suggestion of action on Eden's part—no stopping of the Italian supplies to Spain, still less any counter-intervention on the side of the Spanish republic. The dispute was over words—whether or not to pronounce a particular formula. Preoccupation with words was a foreign office habit, no doubt a necessary one. Chamberlain, though claiming to be a practical man, had caught it too. He even enlisted the assistance of Grandi, the Italian ambassador, in an effort to convince Eden that the proposed incantation would work. Eden merely took further offence that the prime minister should talk to foreign ambassadors.

Chamberlain appealed to the cabinet. No member supported Eden, though some of them wanted to hush the dispute up—or perhaps did not understand what the fuss was about. Chamberlain insisted on a decision.[1] On 20 February Eden resigned. Halifax reluctantly became foreign secretary. Looking back to his time as viceroy, he had said: 'I have had enough obloquy for one life-time.' However, in the end he did well enough and alone emerged from appeasement with a reputation unsullied or even enhanced. Hitler and Mussolini boasted that they had forced Eden from office, and many English people believed their boast. Eden, the man of strong words, acquired retrospectively a mythical reputation as the man who had favoured strong acts and became a symbol of resistance to Chamberlain's policy. Twenty-five Conservative M.P.s abstained from voting after the debate on Eden's resignation—the first breach in the government's majority.

This was a bad start for appeasement. Chamberlain had intended a grand design for ending European tensions. Instead he appeared to be conceding timorously, and in vain. Mussolini was not won over by the shadowy formula.[2] He did nothing to

---

[1] According to Chamberlain, '14 supported me without qualification, 4 . . . with some qualification or reserve. None supported Anthony.' Macleod, *Chamberlain*, 216.
[2] Nor can he be altogether blamed. British diplomacy moved slowly, despite Chamberlain's insistence on the need for haste during his argument with Eden. The new agreement with Italy was not signed until 16 Apr. and was not to come into force until the 'Spanish question' had been settled, i.e. the Italian volunteers

save Austria. On 13 March Hitler entered Vienna and incorporated Austria into Germany. Once this would have been hailed as a triumph for self-determination. Now many English people accepted Churchill's warning to the house of commons on 14 March that Europe was 'confronted with a programme of aggression, nicely calculated and timed, unfolding stage by stage'.[1] Chamberlain, too, believed that Hitler would strike again unless his justified grievances were met in advance. Chamberlain also agreed with the general view that Czechoslovakia was next on the list. Here he was anxious to satisfy Hitler. Chamberlain did not regard the independence of Czechoslovakia as a British interest, and he shared Hitler's dislike of her alliances with France and, especially, with Soviet Russia.[2] He also believed that she had a shaky position, both in morals and in power, while three million Germans remained within her borders.

These views were not personal quirks. They had been held until not long before by nearly all politically minded Englishmen, especially on the Left. They were still held by most Conservatives, belatedly converts to enlightenment. Of course Chamberlain had practical motives also. He did not believe that Great Britain and France could do anything for Czechoslovakia from a military point of view. He doubted indeed whether, in the present state of their air forces, they could do much even for themselves. The chiefs of staff agreed. In their opinion, 'to take offensive against Germany now would be like "a man attacking a tiger before he has loaded his gun" '.[3] Chamberlain does not, however, seem to have sought formal

withdrawn. On 2 Nov. 1938, however, the British government waived this condition. Halifax explained that, in Mussolini's view, only Franco's victory would settle the Spanish question; the British government were ready to agree with him and would therefore tolerate the continued presence of the Italian volunteers until the end of the war.

[1] Churchill, *Second World War*, i. 212. This view was, in my judgement, wrong. Hitler, it seems to me, had no precise plans of aggression, only an intention, which he held in common with most Germans, to make Germany again the most powerful state in Europe and a readiness to take advantage of events. I am confident that the truth of this interpretation will be recognized once the problem is discussed in terms of detached historical curiosity, and not of political commitment. However, an historian of England fortunately need not debate the subject. The contemporary estimates of German armaments and of Hitler's supposed plans shaped British policy, and it is irrelevant to this policy whether the estimates were right or wrong.

[2] The Czecho-Soviet pact was to operate only if France acted first. Hence French hesitations left the Soviet government in the clear.

[3] Minney, *Private Papers of Hore-Belisha*, 146.

guidance from his service advisers. He used the military arguments as an afterthought, to sustain a policy on which he had already decided. His overriding motive was the conviction that peaceful revision could avert a second European war.

British foreign policy has usually been content to react to the behaviour of others. In the Czech affair, for once, the British took the initiative. Chamberlain tried to get ahead of events, instead of waiting for them to happen. He did not act alone. Policy was conducted by the foreign secretary and the foreign office until Chamberlain intervened in the middle of September. The policy was endorsed by the leading British ambassadors— some, particularly Nevile Henderson at Berlin, eagerly, some regretfully. It was British policy in the fullest sense. Its object was to extract from the Czechoslovak government concessions which would satisfy the German inhabitants before Hitler imposed a solution by force. One part of this policy was easily accomplished. The French did not need much encouragement to back away from unreserved support of Czechoslovakia. Though they claimed that Hitler was 'bluffing' and would run away if faced with united opposition, they would not call this bluff without a firm promise of support from Great Britain. They acquiesced in extracting concessions from Czechoslovakia when this promise was refused.[1] The rest of the policy broke down. President Beneš of Czechoslovakia and his Germans were not genuinely seeking agreement. They negotiated solely with the object of discrediting each other in the eyes of the Western powers and were not brought together even when Lord Runciman was sent as a mediator to Prague in July. On the other side, Hitler was not much impressed by warnings that France might support the Czechs if negotiations broke down, and that Great Britain might then support France, when he saw the British assiduously thrusting concessions on the Czechs.

In September the crisis exploded. On 4 September Beneš

[1] Here again, hindsight makes it difficult to understand how things looked at the time. The French were in fact right. Hitler often told his intimates that he would act against Czechoslovakia only if he were certain that Great Britain and France would not intervene. He made virtually no preparations even for a defensive war against them. But those, such as Churchill, who had sounded the alarm over German armaments were the least entitled to assert that Hitler was bluffing. Could Hitler be safely opposed because he was weak? or should he be opposed because he was overwhelmingly strong? Both arguments were used, often confusingly by the same person.

agreed to all the demands which the Czechoslovak Germans chose to make; he did so only when he knew that even this would not satisfy them. On 13 September the Germans of Czechoslovakia attempted to revolt. The attempt failed. The Czechoslovak government restored order without difficulty. In Paris the nerve of the French government collapsed.[1] Daladier, the premier, sent an urgent message to Chamberlain: 'Entry of German troops into Czechoslovakia must at all costs be prevented.' Chamberlain had a free hand to redress German grievances. This, he believed, would give Europe a stable peace. On 15 September he flew to Munich,[2] and saw Hitler at Berchtesgaden. His sole companion was Sir Horace Wilson. Chamberlain at once offered the separation of the Sudeten Germans[3] from the rest of Czechoslovakia. Hitler accepted, though doubting whether Chamberlain could carry out his offer.

Chamberlain returned to London. Some junior ministers disliked the apparent surrender to Hitler's dictation. Against them Runciman now wrote a report, recommending self-determination for the Germans.[4] The idea was strongly supported in the press, by the *New Statesman* and *The Times*, for example, papers not usually in agreement.[5] The British cabinet wrangled, and acquiesced. The French were more difficult. Daladier and Bonnet came to London on 18 September. Daladier argued that Hitler's real aim was the domination of Europe. If Chamberlain believed in Hitler's good faith, would he, Daladier asked, guarantee the new, truncated Czechoslovakia? Chamberlain was trapped by his own argument. He and his three colleagues[6] gave the guarantee apparently without

---

[1] Actually six French ministers were for resistance, four for surrender. The four included Bonnet, the foreign minister. Daladier, the prime minister, after failing to give a lead, came down on their side.

[2] This was his first journey by air (at the age of 69), though not his first flight in an aeroplane.

[3] The Germans of Czechoslovakia were usually called 'the Sudetens' at this time, though many of them lived in areas remote from the Sudeten mountains. Chamberlain's actual words were: 'I didn't care two hoots whether the Sudetens were in the Reich or out of it according to their own wishes.' Macleod, *Chamberlain*, 238.

[4] Runciman's report was bogus. As first drafted, it outlined arrangements by which Germans could be satisfied within Czechoslovakia. He then rewrote the report when told that Hitler wanted self-determination and had been promised it.

[5] The *New Statesman* on 27 Aug.; *The Times* on 7 Sept. Dawson, the editor, wrote the decisive sentence into *The Times* leader with his own hand.

[6] Halifax, Simon, and Hoare.

consulting the cabinet. In this strange way, the British government guaranteed a weak, defenceless Czechoslovakia, where they had previously declared it impossible to assist a heavily armed one. Finally, President Beneš was driven to agree on 21 September by an ultimatum that otherwise Great Britain and France would not support him.

Chamberlain thought he had won. On 22 September he again flew to Germany, where he met Hitler at Godesberg on the Rhine. Chamberlain imagined that he had come only to settle the details. Hitler was no longer satisfied with the transference of territory after negotiation; he wanted immediate occupation. It is impossible to tell why Hitler put up his demands—perhaps to humiliate the Western powers, more probably because, with the Poles and Hungarians now also making claims, he expected Czechoslovakia to fall to pieces. Deadlock followed. In the end Hitler promised not to act before 1 October, before which in any case his military plans would not mature. Chamberlain once more went home. It seems that he intended to acquiesce. He said to reporters on leaving Godesberg: 'It's up to the Czechs now.'

In London he found a changed atmosphere. Most people had not noticed the Czech affair until the middle of September. Now they snatched at the idea that a small democratic state was being bullied, just as, in earlier days, they had snatched at the idea that the Germans had justified grievances. The Labour party and the trade unions were for resistance. Halifax was always sensitive to the conscience of the nation and took the moral line, as he had done at the time of the Hoare–Laval plan.[1] Simon and Hoare both held that the Godesberg demands would not do. Preparations were made for war. Primitive trenches, for air-raid precautions, were dug in the London parks. The few anti-aircraft guns were trundled out—forty-four in all. Warning sirens were tried over the radio. Regional commissioners, on the general strike model, were sent to their posts 'in secret'. Thirty-eight million gas masks were distributed to regional centres.[2] An emergency scheme was botched up for evacuating

---

[1] It was Halifax who then insisted that Hoare must resign, even though the government had endorsed the plan. 'Unless Sam went, the whole moral force of the Government would be gone.' Macleod, *Chamberlain*, 189.

[2] Fear of gas attack from the air was an acute element in the apprehension before 1939. In fact gas was never used by any of the belligerents during the second World war. The reasons for this are not discussed at length by any authority. It may

schoolchildren from London. Eighty-three per cent. of parents applied for their children to go.

On 26 September the foreign office issued a warning: 'If German attack is made upon Czechoslovakia ... France will be bound to come to her assistance, and Great Britain and Russia will certainly stand by France.'[1] On 27 September the fleet was mobilized, on Chamberlain's order. Underneath, his view was unchanged: nothing could be done to assist the Czechs. The French were in the same confused state as before: Bonnet eager for surrender; Daladier advocating resistance, and not knowing how to resist. They were greatly relieved when Chamberlain sent Horace Wilson to plead with Hitler once more. This direct approach failed. In England the national mood had changed again. The trenches in the park had done the trick. Apprehension took the place of resolution. On 28 September Chamberlain spoke in the house of commons, which had been recalled from holiday. Members sat tense, believing, as most of their constituents did, that London was about to suffer the fate of Guernica and other defenceless villages of Spain. Chamberlain drearily recounted the negotiations, his grating voice growing ever more melancholy. He had good news up his sleeve. He had already appealed to Mussolini and knew that Mussolini's mediation with Hitler was likely to be successful. At the last moment, a message was passed to Chamberlain along the benches.[2] The answer from Mussolini had arrived. On his urging, Hitler had agreed to a four-power conference at Munich. Members rose to their feet, cheering and sobbing.[3]

be that all the Powers involved were too moral to use gas, though in view of other ruthless methods from which they did not shrink this seems unlikely. It is possible that the Germans were deterred by the repeated British threats of retaliation. Most probably the explanation was the simple calculation that, weight for weight, high explosive was more effective than gas in killing people.

[1] The statement was drafted by a member of the foreign office, at Churchill's prompting and in Halifax's presence. Halifax 'authorized' the statement, but did not sign it. In Paris, Bonnet repudiated it as a forgery. Chamberlain virtually disavowed it by announcing that the British government were still ready to fulfil Hitler's demands. Halifax made no protest. A characteristic transaction.

[2] It came from Halifax, who was sitting in the peers' gallery. It was passed from Chamberlain's parliamentary private secretary, Lord Dunglass (later Lord Home, later still Sir Alec Douglas-Home), to Hoare; from him to Simon, who thrust it on Chamberlain. The chain of appeasement was complete.

[3] Who remained seated? Certainly Gallacher. According to Seton-Watson, who was in the gallery (History of the Czechs and Slovaks, 367), Churchill, Eden, and Amery. According to Wheeler-Bennett, who was not present (Munich, 170), 'Eden walked out of the Chamber, pale with shame and anger ... Harold Nicolson,

Attlee, Sinclair the Liberal leader, and Maxton of the I.L.P. blessed Chamberlain's mission. Only Gallacher, the Communist, spoke harshly against it.

On 29 September Chamberlain flew to Munich once more. He refused to coordinate policy with Daladier. The conference rattled through its work in a few hours. Mussolini played the impartial mediator, though the plan he produced had in fact been supplied to him by the German foreign ministry. Chamberlain wrangled over the financial details. Otherwise the plan was adopted unchanged. It differed from Hitler's demands at Godesberg only in the sense that the occupation of the Sudeten territories was spread over ten days, instead of taking place at one bound—an operation which was in any case technically impossible.[1] Diminished Czechoslovakia was to be guaranteed by the four Powers when the question of the Polish and Hungarian minorities was settled. The agreement was signed shortly after midnight. Chamberlain and Daladier then saw Czechoslovak representatives who had been waiting in the lobby, and told them that their government must accept unconditionally and without delay. Chamberlain yawned. He was 'tired, but pleasantly tired'.

The next morning Chamberlain saw Hitler again. He brought with him a statement: 'We regard the agreement signed last night and the Anglo-German Naval Agreement as symbolic of the desire of our two peoples never to go to war with one another again. We are resolved that the method of consultation shall be the method adopted to deal with any other questions that may concern our two countries.' Hitler welcomed the statement enthusiastically. The two men signed. When Chamberlain arrived at the airport in England, he waved the statement which he had signed with Hitler, and cried: 'I've got it.' Later in the

despite the threats of those surrounding him, remained seated'. Nicolson had no recollection of remaining seated, though he remembered being rebuked for it the next day by a Conservative M.P. (Nicolson was National Labour—the only new recruit of 1935). There was little stir on the Labour and Liberal benches. When Attlee spoke, Conservatives cheered again, and this forced Labour M.P.s to their feet. The *Annual Register* (which was hostile to Chamberlain) says: 'Members on the Ministerial side and many persons in the strangers' gallery rose and cheered wildly.'

[1] The Munich agreement worked out territorially worse for the Czechs than the Godesberg demands. These defined the German claims precisely. The Munich agreement left the details to be settled by a commission of the four powers, meeting at Berlin, and this commission, dominated by the German and Italian representatives, decided every disputed point against Czechoslovakia.

evening he appeared at the window of 10 Downing Street, and told the cheering crowd: 'This is the second time that there has come back from Germany to Downing Street peace with honour. I believe it is peace for our time.'[1]

All the press welcomed the Munich agreement as preferable to war with the solitary exception of *Reynolds News*, a Left-wing Socialist Sunday newspaper of small circulation (and, of course, the Communist *Daily Worker*). Duff Cooper, first lord of the admiralty, resigned and declared that Great Britain should have gone to war, not to save Czechoslovakia, but to prevent one country dominating the continent 'by brute force'. No one else took this line in the prolonged Commons debate (3–6 October). Many lamented British humiliation and weakness. All acquiesced. Some thirty Conservatives abstained when Labour divided the house against the motion approving the Munich agreement; none voted against the government. The overwhelming majority of ordinary people, according to contemporary estimates, approved of what Chamberlain had done. The governments of the Dominions were equally approving. If war had come in October 1938, South Africa and Eire certainly, Canada probably, would have remained neutral; Australia and New Zealand would have followed the mother country with reluctance.

Yet the triumph of appeasement also marked its failure. Everything had happened in the wrong way. Appeasement had been designed by Chamberlain as the impartial redress of justified grievances. It became a capitulation, a surrender to fear. This was largely Chamberlain's own doing. He was never much good at the moral line, even though he no doubt felt it. He slipped easily into practical arguments, whether he was dealing with the unemployed, de Valera, Edward VIII (whose hesitations were 'holding up business and employment'), or Hitler. He himself 'didn't care two hoots' about the Sudeten Germans one way or the other. He was more at home arguing that he had saved the Czechs,[2] the French, or finally the British people themselves from the horrors of war; and most at home

---

[1] Chamberlain was referring to the treaty of Berlin which Beaconsfield brought back in 1878.

[2] It is often overlooked that he succeeded in this. Great Britain refused to support Czechoslovakia. Some 100,000 Czechs were killed in the second World war; Prague was undamaged. In 1939 Great Britain guaranteed Poland. 6,250,000 Poles were killed in the second World war; Warsaw was destroyed.

of all arguing that the state of British armaments made war impossible. He relied on these arguments in the Commons debate. Only Sir John Simon tried to make the old moral case, now discredited.

Most English people probably judged in the same practical way. The crisis was sprung on them unawares,[1] much as the marital affairs of Edward VIII had been, and they reacted with the same exasperated impatience. They could not see the sense of going to war 'because of a quarrel in a far-away country between people of whom we know nothing'.[2] Yet they were ashamed, too, at what they had done. Hitler himself helped to wreck Munich and the policy of appeasement. His treatment of the Czechs was far from the evenhanded justice which he had earlier claimed for Germany. He presented Munich as a triumph of German might, not as a highminded redress of wrong, and who was Sir John Simon to disagree with him? Even Chamberlain deep down did not know what to think. He professed both belief and disbelief in Hitler's good faith. He claimed that Munich was the first step towards a new system of peace in Europe and also excused it as a device for buying time until British armaments were greater. A few hours before proclaiming 'peace for our time', he allegedly said to Halifax among the cheering crowds: 'all this will be over in three months'.[3] Chamberlain was not being dishonest or two-faced. He reflected the muddle in most English minds. Munich sprang from a mixture of fear and good intentions. In retrospect, fear predominated.

The clearest lesson to be drawn from the crisis over Czecho-

---

[1] Was this deliberate? It is tempting to suggest that the air-raid precautions of late September were designed to cause panic and that the dramatic arrival of Mussolini's message at the end of Chamberlain's speech on 28 Sept. was a stage effect. No evidence is ever available on such points. Probably men, fearful themselves, took steps which caused fear in others. On 28 Sept. Chamberlain knew that a message from Mussolini was due to arrive at any moment. He was fairly sure that it would contain good news. It would be nice to know whether Halifax in the gallery really received the message at the end of Chamberlain's speech or whether he sat on it until the moment of drama. At any rate, either events or men squeezed every ounce of sensation out of what was happening.

[2] Chamberlain's words in a broadcast on 27 Sept.

[3] Feiling, *Chamberlain*, 382. Halifax, the only possible witness, later denied the story in a letter to *The Times*. Halifax, according to his own account, urged Chamberlain not to exploit his popularity by holding a general election and to admit Eden and Churchill into the government. Chamberlain accepted the first part of the advice and not the second.

slovakia was that Great Britain should be more heavily armed, whether for negotiation or for war.[1] Chamberlain, a persistent advocate of rearmament, emphasized this lesson strongly and gave Hitler some excuse for complaining that Chamberlain was as insincere in appeasement as Hitler himself was accused of being. British armaments undoubtedly increased a good deal in the twelve months between Munich and the outbreak of war, and this gave the misleading impression that the increase was due to the Munich alarm. In fact most of it came from the maturing of plans which had been started long before and would have happened automatically, with Munich or without. For instance, factories projected in 1936 and 1937 raised the production of aircraft from 240 a month in 1938 to 660 a month in 1939. Designs drawn even earlier gave the R.A.F. 26 squadrons of efficient fighters in September 1939 (and 47 in June 1940) against 6 in September 1938. Again, radar extended purely from its own momentum. In September 1938 it covered only the Thames estuary. Twelve months later, the chain ran from the Orkneys to the Isle of Wight. Naval plans, too, were virtually unaffected by the Munich crisis. The British navy was already overwhelmingly superior to the German and reasonably superior to the German and Italian navies combined, even if the French were not counted in. There was some increase in defensive measures against submarines. Otherwise the only change in naval policy before the outbreak of war actually implied that the danger in European waters could take second place. This was the decision, made in the early summer of 1939, to go over to a two-ocean standard, that is, to establish an independent fleet in the Far East as a counter to Japan.

Munich seemed, at first sight, to have a more direct effect on plans for the army. The French were quick to urge that

[1] The argument over relative strengths in Sept. 1938 was confused from being conducted on two separate levels. The main argument against war was that Great Britain was defenceless against air attack. This was correct. There were hardly any modern fighters, virtually no air-raid precautions, and few means of retaliation. No one appreciated that the German bombers were much less effective at long range than was supposed. The main argument for war was the great superiority of the Allied land forces. This, too, was correct, at any rate on paper. The French had 80 divisions, the Czechs 36, without counting the Russians. The Germans had 21, with 14 in process of formation. Only 2 German divisions were on the Western front, facing France. The real question, though unspoken, was whether the French were willing, or even able, to take the offensive. The answer was: almost certainly not. The Czechs would have had to fight unaided. No one can tell whether they would, or could, have done so.

British forces should replace the thirty-six divisions, lost by the ending of their alliance with Czechoslovakia. The army chiefs seconded French promptings. They had always kicked against the doctrine of 'limited liability', which virtually eliminated the army as a major weapon of war. Now they were ready to assert that neither bombing nor the French army unaided could knock Germany out. They even hinted that France might be defeated and that Great Britain would have to fight alone. In either case, she would need an army fit for a continental war, though not on the scale of the first World war. These arguments were, however, frills, agreeable additions thrown in to make weight. The real case of the army chiefs was that, as the navy was satisfied and the air force nearly satisfied, it was now the army's turn to spend money. The government accepted this case. The great jump was made in February 1939. Limited liability was abandoned. A target was set of thirty-two divisions—six regular and twenty-six territorial.

The decision had little immediate result. Factories had to be created for making tanks and guns. Labour and capital had to be diverted, or bribed, from working on aeroplanes. There was no interference with civilian industry except in theory. The target was to be reached only in September 1941, or even some time in 1942. The army chiefs made two further recommendations. Once the army really began to grow, they could not rely on voluntary recruits. They therefore wanted some measure of compulsion to provide a reservoir of half-trained men for the army of the future. They also wanted a minister of supply to handle the new orders to industry which the army was distributing. The government walked warily round these two proposals and reached no decision. Great Britain pottered along, confident that large-scale fighting would come, if at all, only when it suited her convenience.

The one direct impact of Munich was on measures for the security of the civilian population: air-raid precautions (A.R.P.). The topic had been discussed in an academic way for many years. The home office had been preparing schemes on paper since 1935. No action had followed. For one thing, the home office was remote from the two departments, the ministry of health and the board of education, which would be most concerned as dealing with casualties and schoolchildren. For another, the magnitude of the problem seemed overwhelming. Officials contemplated the prospect of millions of casualties with helpless dismay. The few steps, hastily improvised at the end of September 1938, only emphasized the lack of any real preparations. Something had to be attempted even if it could never be enough. In November 1938 Sir John Anderson was brought into the cabinet as lord privy seal and put in charge of A.R.P. He was the outstanding administrator of his generation and soon produced results. Expenditure on A.R.P. went up from £9½ million a year before Munich to £51 million (including the fire services) in 1939-40. The ministry of health strove to provide some 300,000 hospital beds—a long way from the desired aim of some millions, but better than nothing.[1]

A firm decision was taken to move from the great cities all who did not need to stay. The country was divided into evacuation, neutral, and reception areas. All schoolchildren and mothers with children under 5 were to be moved from the great cities and billeted in private houses in the reception areas. Provision was made for special trains and for supplies of food during the journey. The plans were made public only in a cautious, hesitant way. Urgency, it was feared, would cause alarm, and the government had a terrified vision of panic-stricken mobs fleeing from the great cities on the outbreak of war. They envisaged using troops to master these crowds and actually called in a former Indian officer to advise on the handling of crowds out of control. The lists of those to be evacuated therefore remained sadly incomplete. Only a third of the mothers with children under 5 registered. In London 69 per cent. of schoolchildren were registered; in Sheffield only 15 per cent. Newcastle and Gateshead did best with just under 80 per cent. No one knows the reason for these variations. A.R.P., however, in practice, did not cause panic. On the contrary, like most precautions, it stilled alarm, just as a householder, taking precautions against burglary or fire, becomes more confident that his house will not be broken into or burnt down. Fear of attack from the air had been decisive in September 1938. A year later, the authorities, and probably the people, were less fearful.

The service chiefs treated war as more or less inevitable.

[1] When the ministry surveyed the problem, it discovered that it had no idea how many hospital beds there were in the country and, given the tangle of voluntary and local government hospitals, no means of finding out at all accurately.

Critics raged against the slowness of British rearmament. The government remained unmoved. Chamberlain resisted any drastic steps which might increase European tension. At least, this was the reason he gave publicly. Actually, he was determined not to confess that he had been wrong, and he would certainly appear to make this confession if he brought Eden, or still more Churchill, into the government.[1] Besides, most people, including even many critics, assumed that Munich had done what was claimed for it. Though craven and perhaps immoral, it had averted war. The principle had been accepted that the peace settlement of 1919 should be revised in Germany's favour, and with this Germany would be content. Of course, the lesser powers of eastern Europe would abandon their alliances with France, as Poland was assumed to have done already.[2] They would fall into Germany's economic sphere. Germany would grow stronger. But Great Britain and France would remain secure particularly as British armaments increased. The storm of war, if it came, would blow eastwards, against Soviet Russia. Many English people assumed that Hitler could somehow attack Soviet Russia without conquering eastern Europe first.[3]

This outlook was not universally accepted. The opponents of Hitler plucked up courage when the excitement of Munich died down. There was renewed stir for united political action. This time it took a rather different form. The campaign of 1937 had been for unity of the extreme Left, working-class unity as it was called—Labour, Communists, and the I.L.P. The 'Popular Front' in the winter of 1938 was to be between Labour, Liberals, and even Conservative critics of Chamberlain. The Conservatives did not come in. Even Churchill never voted or spoke against the government, though he often criticized them. He strove always to change the government's policy, not to throw them out. The 'Lib–Lab' combination showed more

---

[1] Chamberlain's only invitation was to Lord Samuel, the Liberal leader in the Lords—a harmless gesture. Samuel declined, as he had declined a similar invitation from Lloyd George in Dec. 1916.

[2] In the words of Halifax: 'Poland can presumably only fall more and more into the German orbit.' Halifax to Phipps, 1 Nov. 1938. *British Foreign Policy*, third series, iii, no. 285.

[3] So to some extent he did. Neither Rumania nor Hungary needed conquest by Germany to bring them into the war against Soviet Russia. Croatia and Slovakia were also willing associates.

life. It enforced united action at two by-elections, in one of which the government candidate was actually defeated.[1]

Thereafter the campaign declined. It bubbled up with the indignation against Munich and lacked positive content. Resistance to Hitler seemed a lost cause, and the concern of the Popular Front was rather to prevent British participation in Hitler's war against Russia—a remote peril for most English people. Besides, the Labour leaders disliked the movement. 'Lib–Lab' was to them another version of the old evasion by which middle-class voters could turn against the National government without going over to Labour. They stood firm on the doctrine that a Labour government was the only alternative to Chamberlain, and they had massive support from their paymasters in the unions. Local Labour parties, supporting the Popular Front, were broken up and reorganized by 'loyalists'. Cripps was expelled from the party when he refused to give up his advocacy of the Popular Front and was followed into exile by other prominent Left-wingers, such as Aneurin Bevan and Charles Trevelyan. In this odd way, the Labour party entered the war against Hitler, locked in conflict with his most vocal opponents.

This internal strife left the government with a free hand. Rearmament proceeded on its gentle way. Staff talks were renewed with the French and provided for a British Expeditionary Force on the French left wing, just as in 1914. In January 1939 Chamberlain and Halifax visited Mussolini. They came away fairly confident that he would exercise a moderating influence on Hitler. Mussolini got his reward. On 27 February the British government recognized Franco as the rightful ruler of Spain, though the republicans did not give up the fight until the end of March. The Left lamented this final betrayal of democracy. The government were confident that they could acquiesce in a Fascist victory without danger to peace or to British interests—a belief which proved correct so far as Spain was concerned. They were less confident about Hitler. His stock fell sharply even among British sympathizers, when in November 1938 he launched a sharper pogrom against

[1] The Popular Front was unsuccessful at Oxford, where A. D. Lindsay, Master of Balliol, was its candidate, and Quintin Hogg (later second Lord Hailsham and later still Quintin Hogg again) the champion of Munich. It was successful at Bridgwater. Vernon Bartlett, the victor here, was the only man to win a seat in parliament before the war solely on the strength of his talks on the radio.

the Jews. Experts in the foreign office attributed to him plans, which he did not possess, for immediate aggression—perhaps against Soviet Russia, perhaps against Holland, Switzerland, or even, most absurdly of all, against the British fleet. In fact, Hitler remained quiet: no new demands, no new threats. The corner seemed to have been turned: the dictators could be contented without a general war. Idealists despaired at the prospect of a Fascist Europe. Auden, the most powerful literary figure of the Left, departed for the United States, where he soon lapsed from political commitment. Dylan Thomas, the new poetical genius, never showed any in his writings. On 10 March Hoare, precipitate as ever, told his constituents at Chelsea that a new Golden Age was approaching: British rearmament was complete, and cooperation between the Great European Powers (including strangely Soviet Russia) 'would raise living standards to heights we had never before been able to attempt'. Appeasement had done its work.

NOTE

Note A. *The effects of bombing.* The miscalculation of the effects of bombing had cumulative causes. Firstly, the number of German aeroplanes was exaggerated, as described in the text. Secondly, it was assumed that all the supposed German bombers could reach England and that all of them would be devoted to this purpose. The experts anticipated that the Germans would drop 100,000 tons of bombs on London in fourteen days. The actual total dropped on London throughout the war did not reach this figure. Thirdly, the effect of bombs dropped was exaggerated. The experts assumed a 'multiplier' of fifty, that is, each ton of bombs would cause fifty casualties. This figure was derived from inadequate, and incorrect, statistics about German bombing in the first World war, when one lucky hit caused one tenth of the total casualties suffered. Every bomb was expected to fall on a densely populated area. Nothing was allowed for bombs falling in open spaces; for a second bomb falling where a first had already killed all the available victims; for evacuation of the population; or for shelters. Experience in the Spanish civil war gave a multiplier of 17·2. This experience was ignored. Instead all the emphasis was laid on Guernica, where nearby German aeroplanes bombed a defenceless village on a crowded market-day. The actual multiplier in London during the second World war was between 15 and 20.

The exaggeration had been implicit in all discussion of air strategy from the early days. It was now given more plausible precision because this was in everyone's interest. The air chiefs wished to justify their demands for more bombers; the government wished to justify appeasement; the critics of the government wished to justify their demands for more expenditure on armaments or on air-raid precautions. As always, the technical estimates were shaped by non-technical predilections. But even the most detached judges were mistaken. Thus Liddell Hart, a cautious and independent authority wrote in 1939 (*The Defence of Britain*, 154): 'Nearly a quarter of a million casualties might be anticipated . . . in the first week of a new war.'

In strange contrast, the experts greatly underrated the material damage, especially to houses, which bombing would cause. Virtually no preparations were made to repair houses or to rehouse those who had lost their homes. British air strategy had to be hastily remodelled during the war in order to aim at destroying houses rather than at killing civilians.

XIII

RELUCTANTLY TO WAR, 1939-40

CZECHO-SLOVAKIA had been diminished and weakened by the Munich settlement. On 15 March 1939 it fell to pieces.[1] Slovakia became an independent state. Sub-Carpathian Ukraine was seized by Hungary. Hacha, who had succeeded Beneš as Czechoslovak president after Munich, placed the destinies of his country in Hitler's hands. Bohemia or 'Czechia' became a German protectorate. German administrators, including the Gestapo, moved in and established the same Nazi dictatorship as in Germany. Hitler himself spent the night of 15 March in the palace on the Hradčany at Prague—his only recorded visit. The collapse of Czecho-Slovakia was not all Hitler's doing. Indeed, its abruptness took him by surprise. The Slovaks, or many of them, had always kicked against the unitary republic, and it was difficult to hold them once the Munich crisis had destroyed Czech authority. No doubt Hitler encouraged them, but they needed little encouragement, and he would probably have been content with an obedient satellite. When the Slovaks broke away, Hitler did the first thing that came to hand.

The English people saw things differently, and events were shaped by what they believed, not by what happened. They had been told by Chamberlain, by other ministers, by Hitler himself, that Munich was a final settlement. The Sudeten territories were Hitler's 'last territorial demand in Europe'. He wished only to include all Germans in the greater Germany, and Czecho-Slovakia, relieved of her embarrassing German minority, would henceforth enjoy a modest independence. The guarantee, offered so lightheartedly in September 1938, was unnecessary—a harmless gesture of conscience more to the French than to the Czechs. Now Hitler had dismembered his small neighbour without warning or provocation and had

[1] The hyphen was itself warning of things to come. The Czechs, led by Masaryk, insisted that Czechoslovakia was a unitary state, and the Czechoslovaks a single people. The Slovaks denied this, and the hyphen, inserted in October 1938, accepted their denial.

carried off the most valuable, industrial part for himself. Here was clear proof of planned aggression. Hitler's word could never be trusted again. He was on the march to world domination, like the Kaiser before him. Nothing would stop him except a firm front of resistance. Such was the almost universal reaction of English opinion. The great majority of Conservatives had backed Chamberlain. They had loyally voiced the arguments of appeasement, had brushed passionately aside the charges of cowardice and betrayal. Now it seemed that Churchill, Duff Cooper, the Liberal and Labour oppositions, had been right. Great Britain and her powerful National government had been made fools of, or ministers had fooled their followers. There were deeper factors at work. Appeasement never sat comfortably on Tory shoulders. It was in spirit and origin a Left-wing cause, and its leaders had a Nonconformist background.[1] True Conservatives reverted easily to a belief in British might.

The government moved more slowly. Halifax was relieved at escaping from 'the somewhat embarrassing commitment of a guarantee, in which we and the French had been involved'.[2] In the house of commons on 15 March, Chamberlain speculated that the end of Czechoslovakia 'may or may not have been inevitable', and Simon explained that it was impossible to fulfil a guarantee to a state which had ceased to exist. The underground rumblings soon broke to the surface. Perhaps the government whips reported discontent on the backbenches. Perhaps Halifax heard the call of conscience in the watches of the night.[3] Probably there was nothing so clear-cut, only a succession of doubts and resentments which shook Chamberlain's previous confidence. On 17 March he addressed the Birmingham Conservative association. He was among his own people—jewellers, locksmiths, makers of pots and pans. His prepared speech was an elaborate defence of Munich: no one 'could possibly have saved Czechoslovakia from invasion and destruction'. At the last moment he threw in a reference to what had happened two days before. The audience applauded his protest, and with each

[1] Neville Chamberlain was a Unitarian; Sir John Simon the son of a Congregationalist minister; Sir Samuel Hoare a member of an anglicanized Quaker family. Halifax was the exception. He was an Anglo-Catholic. For this, as for other reasons, he was always an in-and-out member of the appeasement group.

[2] Halifax to Phipps, 14 Mar. 1939. *British Foreign Policy*, third series, iv, no. 234.

[3] This is Wheeler-Bennett's version (*Munich*, 355). He learnt it, and other similar stories, from Halifax at the British embassy in Washington during the war years.

roar Chamberlain's improvisations grew stronger. 'Any attempt to dominate the world by force was one which the Democracies must resist.' Appeasement and Munich were eclipsed. The apologies which Simon was still making in the house of commons seemed a world away. Chamberlain had turned British foreign policy upside down.

The revolution was not so fundamental as it seemed at first sight, or as many English people took it to be. No doubt Chamberlain shared the general indignation at Hitler's occupation of Prague, just as he had been angered by the German annexation of Austria a year before. No doubt he thought that Great Britain was stronger, now that more money was being spent on armaments.[1] The old restraints soon came flooding back into his mind. War still seemed to him an unmitigated disaster. Great Britain had nothing to gain by war and much to lose. The defeat of Germany would leave eastern Europe helpless before Soviet Russia. Appeasement remained the wisest course, if it could be brought about; only now the alternative of war must be put more clearly before Hitler. As Hoare wrote later: 'The lesson of Prague was not that further efforts for peace were futile, but rather that, without greater force behind them, negotiations and agreement with Hitler were of no permanent value.'[2] British ministers hoped that there was a sane Hitler who could be deterred (and also, of course, rewarded). They feared that there was an insane Hitler who might be provoked. They steered uneasily between hope and fear. What followed after 17 March was a change of emphasis, not a change of course.

The immediate emphasis was on firmness, and no wonder.

[1] This is sometimes treated as the main reason for Chamberlain's change of policy. There is, however, no evidence that he consulted the chiefs of staff in the hugger-mugger between 15 and 17 Mar. A more sophisticated explanation has also been put forward. The British government, it is suggested, had been expecting Hitler to attack Soviet Russia, using Czechoslovakia as a corridor. Hungary's seizure of Sub-Carpathian Ukraine closed this corridor. The British expectation, or hope, was thus belied; and the British government now anticipated that Hitler would strike against the West. This view, too, rests on little hard evidence. It derives solely from the Communist obsession that British policy in these years worked consciously for a German attack on Soviet Russia. The British, judging from the record, lived from hand to mouth and had no 'grand policy' of this or any other kind. In any case, after Prague they still expected Hitler to go East—against Poland or Rumania. A direct German attack on the West was among the least of their immediate anxieties.

[2] Templewood, *Nine Troubled Years*, 377.

New alarms came tumbling in. On 16 March Tilea, the Rumanian minister in London, told the foreign office that his country was about to be invaded by Germany. This is a mysterious episode. There was no such German plan or preparation. The alarm was denied by the Rumanian government and by the British minister at Bucharest. The British government preferred to believe Tilea. On 19 March Chamberlain drafted a declaration of joint resistance which the French, Polish, and Soviet governments were invited to sign. The French agreed. The Russians agreed, on condition that France and Poland signed first. The Poles refused: they would not take sides between Russia and Germany. The British government had now fresh cause for alarm. Poland was essential if a second front, or any sort of resistance, were to be raised in eastern Europe against Germany. Yet the Poles seemed to be again playing along with Germany as they had done during the Munich crisis, when they seized Tĕšín from Czechoslovakia. This was indeed the Polish intention. Though they were negotiating secretly with Hitler over Danzig (the Free City created in 1919), they believed that they could hold their own in these negotiations without outside assistance. Beck, the Polish foreign minister, would accept an individual agreement with Great Britain. He rejected association with Soviet Russia, even if it were dressed up as collective security.

At this uneasy moment, the British were further alarmed by rumours, unfounded it now appears, of German troop movements against Poland. They feared that Poland was about to be forced on to the German side. On 29 March the Berlin correspondent of the *News Chronicle*, who had just been expelled from Germany, brought the rumours to London. He was interviewed by the cabinet. His story, which came from German generals, was believed. Somehow the Polish slide towards Germany must be arrested. On 31 March Chamberlain wrote an assurance to the Poles with his own hand: if their independence were threatened, 'His Majesty's Government and the French Government would at once lend them all the support in their power'. That same afternoon Beck accepted the British offer 'between two flicks of the ash off his cigarette'. He was too proud to be content with a one-sided guarantee. He insisted on alliance between equal partners, and the British agreed.

A peacetime alliance with an east European Power had no

precedent in modern British history. The guarantee of post-Munich Czechoslovakia had been a vague diplomatic gesture with no practical consequences. The Polish alliance embedded Great Britain in east European affairs. Yet the British government had no means of fulfilling their bargain. In practical terms, their promise could only mean that the French, who had been committed without prior consultation, would not desert Poland, as they had deserted Czechoslovakia. But Chamberlain and his associates were not thinking in practical terms. They wanted some gesture which would incline Hitler towards moderation and would keep Poland available for a second front, if needed. They had no intention of underwriting the Polish obstinacy over Danzig and, indeed, sympathized with Hitler's demand for revision there, which seemed the most justified of all his claims.

The British government did not consider how to put teeth into the alliance with Poland. They had no teeth for this purpose. Obviously they could not provide military aid. The Poles asked for financial assistance. The British were evasive. The Poles wanted a loan of £60 million in cash. The British first replied that they had no cash and could only offer credits; then they insisted that the credits must be used in Great Britain; finally, having reduced the figure to £8 million, they explained that British armament factories were fully employed and that the credits therefore could not be used. No credit had passed by the time war broke out; not a single British bomb or rifle went to Poland. Equally, the British stalled on the political side, and the alliance was not formally confirmed until 25 August, less than a week before the outbreak of war.

Nevertheless, the alliance with Poland was a decisive event, against the intention of the British government. Hitler used it as excuse for repudiating on 28 April both his non-aggression pact with Poland of 1934 and the Anglo-German naval agreement of 1935. This may have been, as is often suggested, a declaration of delayed war. Alternatively, Hitler may have hoped that either British or Polish nerves would crack. He had often won before by subjecting his opponents to the agony of suspense, and maybe he relied on this method now. Having delivered his stroke, he withdrew into silence. He made no new proposals, formulated no new demands. The diplomatic machine spluttered in the void. There were no further German exchanges with Poland over Danzig or anything else before the outbreak of war, and none directly with Great Britain until the middle of August.

The alliance had its deepest effect in British politics. The advocates of a strong line supposed that they had been vindicated. Hitler, it seemed, had been 'hit on the head' at last. The British lion had roared, and the sound cheered even those who had supported appeasement. It cheered Chamberlain. All public men like applause, and Chamberlain enjoyed his new role of strong man, almost as much as he had enjoyed that of appeaser. Besides, this was a good opportunity to take the steps for which the army chiefs had been pressing, and from which the government had previously shrunk for fear of alarming the public. At the end of April, they announced their intention to set up a ministry of supply and to institute compulsory military service. Both were greeted as further gestures against Hitler. So they were: preparations no doubt as well for a distant future, irrelevant to the immediate crisis which was supposed to be approaching.

The minister of supply was not appointed until July[1] and did not set up his office until August. Even then he was far from being the grand director of a war economy whom the critics had wanted. The admiralty insisted on their traditional independence. The R.A.F. followed suit. The new ministry was therefore left only with supplies for the army, exactly like the ministry of munitions in the first World war. Its powers were slightly more extensive than its predecessor. It took over army clothing, which the war office had previously retained. It handled the supply of stores common to all three services, though with no power to decide whether a service was ordering too much—or too little. The minister of supply was at first not much more than a buying agent, and the vaunted innovation was only a change of office boy.

Compulsory military service was also little more than a gesture. It applied only to future age groups, as they reached 20 years.[2] The first (and, as things turned out, the only)

---

[1] To please the Liberals, who had been particularly keen on a minister of supply, the new minister was a National Liberal, Leslie Burgin. This was not a dynamic appointment, rather another horse from Caligula's well-stocked stable.

[2] Compulsory military service never extended to Northern Ireland, a curious exemption which annoyed those who escaped and which was maintained in order to please Eire.

'militia-men' did not register until June. They were not called up until July and were to serve only for six months, as preparation for their real call-up, if needed, in 1941 or 1942.[1] Even so, peacetime conscription was too much for both Liberals and Labour. The two Opposition parties resisted it strenuously, with much outcry against this surrender to militarism. Bevan exclaimed: 'We have lost, and Hitler has won.' Attlee said much the same in more moderate tones: 'It is very dangerous to give generals all they want.' Labour was again exposed to the reproach of advocating resistance to Hitler and yet of refusing the means to resist, and the reproach was especially plausible when it came from Churchill. Labour men had an answer: Great Britain needed allies, not future conscripts, if she were to deter Hitler in time.

Foreign policy remained the great topic of debate. If Hitler attacked Poland, Great Britain and France could perhaps defend themselves. They could perhaps bring some economic pressure on Germany. They could not provide any real aid to Poland, unless Soviet Russia were also on their side. Hitherto the British government had evaded the Soviet problem. They had hoped, like the Poles, to get through without deciding between Germany and Soviet Russia. They made no serious effort to enlist Soviet support during the Czech crisis. They were relieved that there was no Soviet representative at Munich. Now the question was decisively posed. It was raised immediately on 3 April, when the guarantee to Poland was announced in the house of commons. Churchill said: 'Having begun to create a Grand Alliance against aggression, we cannot afford to fail. We shall be in mortal danger if we fail.' Lloyd George was more emphatic still: 'If we are going in without the help of Russia we are walking into a trap', and he wanted to tell the Poles that they would get no British aid unless they accepted aid from Russia also. The idea of a Soviet alliance was a god-send for Labour. It helped to resolve their internal difficulties. Even the opponents of an 'imperialist' war changed their tune at the prospect of alliance with 'the Socialist sixth of the world'. The war would be a people's war after all. Still, geography was the decisive consideration. The map lay open for all to see, and the practical arguments on which Chamberlain relied now turned

[1] Further to placate public opinion, they also received amenities (pyjamas), never provided before for common soldiers.

against him. Previously his critics could be accused of advocating an ideological war against Hitler. Now Chamberlain seemed to be rejecting the invaluable Soviet aid on ideological grounds.

Confused events had already rushed the government into a guarantee of Poland, in which they did not much believe. Now public opinion was pushing them into an alliance with Soviet Russia, in which they did not believe at all. Their scepticism was both practical and ideological. Chamberlain expressed this clearly in private on 26 March: 'I must confess to the most profound distrust of Russia. I have no belief in her ability to maintain an effective offensive, even if she wanted to. And I distrust her motives, which seem to me to have little connection with our ideas of liberty, and to be concerned only with getting everyone else by the ears.'[1] The chiefs of staff confirmed the doubts about Soviet military strength, though not on the basis of much evidence. All the same, these doubts would probably have been less strong had there not been the shadow of communism.

Of course, the British government welcomed a vague Soviet menace which could be evoked, at a desperate moment, against Hitler. In the words of Halifax: 'It was desirable not to estrange Russia, but always to keep her in play.'[2] But it was to be a one-sided transaction. Soviet assistance was to be available 'if desired'—a tap to be turned on and off at will by the British, by the Poles, by almost any small state, not, however, by the Soviet government themselves. Soviet policy at this time is a matter of total obscurity. Some writers think that Stalin and his associates intended to do a deal with Hitler all along; others that they hoped for a 'peace front' and abandoned it gradually as they were disillusioned. One conjecture may be ventured. The only offer which the Soviet government might have accepted was a straight military alliance with Great Britain and France—an alliance which allowed each of the three partners to decide if its interests were endangered. This offer the British government were firmly resolved not to make.

In retrospect the prolonged negotiations therefore seemed doomed to failure from the start. They were in three stages. The first ran from 15 April to 14 May. The British sought

---

[1] Feiling, *Chamberlain*, 403.

[2] Halifax, conversation with Gafencu, 26 Apr. 1939. *British Foreign Policy*, third series, v, no. 280.

openly for a one-sided Soviet pledge of assistance 'if desired'. The Soviet government demanded 'reciprocity'. In mid-May the negotiations reached deadlock. The French, who did not share the British belief in Poland's strength, pushed the British government to try again. British public opinion pushed also. In the second stage, from 27 May to 23 July, the British tried to devise a formula which would look like a straight alliance and which yet would bar a Soviet initiative. The ostensible stumbling-block was 'indirect aggression'—whether Soviet Russia should be entitled to rescue any Baltic state from Hitler, even if it did not want to be rescued. The real obstacle lay deeper: the British would cooperate with Soviet Russia only if Poland were attacked and agreed to accept Soviet assistance. This deadlock, too, could not be broken. Molotov, who had become commissar for foreign affairs on 3 May, then suggested that they should proceed to military talks and hope that the question of indirect aggression would somehow settle itself. British and French military missions were appointed, and proceeded leisurely to Leningrad by sea.

The military talks from 12 to 21 August were the final stage. The British representatives had been instructed to 'go very slowly. . . . Agreement on the many points raised may take months to achieve.'[1] The British government in fact were still chalking a Red bogey on the wall in the hope that Hitler would then run away. Voroshilov, the Soviet leader, however, sprang the decisive question on 14 August: 'Can the Red Army move across North Poland . . . and across Galicia in order to make contact with the enemy?' The British and French could not answer. The talks ran to a standstill.[2] The Poles refused to admit the Red Army. Beck said: 'It is a new partition of Poland that we are being asked to sign.' The French tried to turn the obstacle by telling the Russians that they were free to go through Poland without Polish permission. The British declined to be associated with this move. In any case, it did not interest the Russians. Voroshilov said: 'We do not want Poland to boast

---

[1] Instructions to British military representatives, Aug. 1939. *British Foreign Policy* vi, appendix v.

[2] In 1942 Stalin told Churchill (*Second World War*, i. 305) that the Russians would have had to provide 300 divisions, while the British provided two, and two later. This disproportion might have become the decisive stumbling block if the point had ever been reached. It was not. The talks broke down on the question of Polish permission.

that she has refused our aid—which we have no intention of forcing her to accept.' The military representatives met for the last time on 21 August, only to record that they had nothing to say.

No alliance has been pursued less enthusiastically. The British government acted as though they had all the time in the world. They held every Soviet formula up to the light and took days, sometimes weeks, to answer. Halifax was invited to Moscow. He declined the invitation, and Chamberlain denied in the house of commons that it had been made. Eden offered to go to Moscow on special mission. Chamberlain turned the offer down. The British government were mainly concerned to conciliate public opinion. As well, they hoped to give Hitler a vague fright. They did not at any time seek Soviet military aid in practical terms. Not only did they fear the consequences of Soviet victory and German defeat. They were hoping all along to strike a bargain with Hitler when the prospect of resistance had made him more moderate, and kept the door open for agreement. Like many people at that time, they imagined that Germany's real grievances were economic and therefore thought of proposing a sort of Anglo-German economic partnership: Germany to be predominant in eastern and south-eastern Europe; a colonial condominium for the exploitation of tropical Africa; and a British loan to Germany of £1,000 million to tide over the difficulties of disarmament. In this happy atmosphere, political problems would lose their force: the British would forget their guarantee to Poland, Germany would treat the lesser races of Europe in a more civilized manner, and Danzig would fall into her lap from heaven. Universal prosperity would reign, exactly as Hoare had foretold on 10 March. These projects were repeatedly aired to the Germans in the course of the summer.[1] It is not clear whether they reached Hitler. If they did, they probably served to strengthen his belief that the British government would bid still higher when faced with a crisis. At any rate, he made no response.

Thus the British government came away emptyhanded. They failed to secure alliance with Soviet Russia. They failed to convince Hitler that they would resist him. Equally they failed to win him with plans of appeasement. Of course they were not alone in error. The Soviet government blundered in imagining

[1] See Note A, p. 475.

that Great Britain and France were strong enough to hold the balance against Germany and that therefore they were free to choose whether to come in or to stay out. Hitler blundered in supposing that he could attack Poland without provoking Great Britain and France. An historian of England has to look at things from the English side, and finds there blunders enough. The incompetence displayed seems to have had no equal since Lord North lost the American colonies. On both occasions, men sought personal explanations. Chamberlain was alleged to be blinkered, narrow, impatient of criticism; Halifax to be lazy, easygoing, and evasive. The appeasers generally were accused of lacking all sense of British greatness, or even of being cowards.

These charges ignored the difficulties which confronted the government. Chamberlain and his colleagues were not below the average of normal times. But the times were not normal. The freak period in which neither Germany nor Russia counted as a Great Power was at an end. The system of Versailles was in ruins, and British ministers did not know what to put in its place. They would probably have welcomed partnership with a civilized Germany. This was not on offer. They did not believe that alliance with Soviet Russia would bring any improvement on Hitler—rather the contrary. They were faced with unwelcome alternatives and chose neither. But they could not stand still. The stir of British public opinion made them pretend to seek a Soviet alliance. Their own distaste for this made them dream of reconciliation with a reformed Hitler, and this was almost as much a pretence. They drifted helplessly, waiting on events, or rather hoping that there would be none.

This hope was disappointed. Though Hitler remained silent, tension mounted at Danzig. The British government sent no new warning to Hitler. Nor did they urge the Poles to give way. Late on 21 August the mine exploded. It was announced that Ribbentrop, the German foreign minister, had been invited to Moscow. On 23 August he and Molotov signed the Nazi–Soviet pact. Soviet Russia promised to stay neutral if Germany were involved in war; there were also secret clauses limiting the gains which the Germans could make in Poland. Hitler assumed almost certainly that, without the Soviet alliance, the Western Powers would run away. Stalin probably made the same assumption. Both seem to have expected that Poland would be diminished or dismembered without a general war. The French almost came up to these expectations. Bonnet, the foreign minister, proposed to repudiate the alliance with Poland and to renew the military talks with Soviet Russia at a more favourable moment. This was too strong meat for the other French ministers. They made no attempt to warn the Poles or consult the British government. They merely decided to do nothing. Decision was left to the Poles or to the British. French statesmen stood aside and let things happen during the days which settled France's destiny.

The British reaction was different. The Nazi–Soviet pact was regarded as an affront, a challenge to British greatness. The government had always claimed that alliance with Soviet Russia was not much more than an unnecessary luxury. This compelled them now to appear undismayed. Conservative backbenchers who had regarded Hitler as the champion of Western civilization, were now indignant against him. Labour turned with equal bitterness against Stalin. Even members of the Left Book Club were determined to show that they, at any rate, were sincere in their anti-fascism. The stir was mainly confined to parliament. There were no great public meetings in the week before the outbreak of war, no mass marches demanding 'Stand by Poland'. It is impossible to tell whether members of parliament represented the British people. At any rate, the M.P.s were resolute and the government tailed regretfully after the house of commons.

On 22 August the government announced that the Nazi–Soviet pact would not change their policy towards Poland. On 24 August parliament met, and passed an Emergency Powers Act through all its stages. On 25 August the Anglo-Polish treaty of mutual assistance was at last signed. A secret clause extended the guarantee to cover Danzig. Yet Chamberlain, Halifax, and perhaps other senior ministers were still eager to give way. The secret clause was kept secret so as not to annoy Hitler. Chamberlain implored Roosevelt to put pressure on the Poles, since he could not do it himself. Kennedy, the American ambassador, reported: 'He says the futility of it all is the thing that is frightful; after all, they cannot save the Poles.'[1] When these approaches failed, Chamberlain and Halifax employed a

---

[1] Kennedy to Hull, 23 Aug. 1939. *Foreign Relations of the United States, 1939*, vol. i. General.

Swedish businessman, Dahlerus, to spread out before Hitler the rich banquet which he could enjoy if he refrained from war.

Hitler responded. In the first exuberance of the Nazi–Soviet pact, he had fixed the German attack on Poland for 25 August. News of the Anglo-Polish alliance made him call it off.[1] He demanded that a Polish plenipotentiary should come to Berlin. Nevile Henderson thought the German terms for a settlement 'not unreasonable': 'They sound moderate to me and are certainly so in view of German desire for good relations with Britain.'[2] Halifax agreed. His last act before the outbreak of war was to urge the Poles to negotiate with Hitler. Beck refused. On 31 August Hitler gave the order to attack Poland.[3] At 4.45 a.m. on 1 September German troops crossed the Polish frontier. At 6 a.m. German aeroplanes bombed Warsaw. The Poles appealed to their ally. They met with a cool response. The cabinet decided that if Germany would suspend hostilities and withdraw her troops, a solution without war would still be possible. A warning to this effect ('not to be considered as an ultimatum') was sent to Hitler in the course of the evening.[4]

On 2 September Halifax had new resources. Mussolini was reported to be on the point of proposing a conference. Bonnet was eagerly seconding this idea. Moreover, the French generals, fearful of German air attack, wished to complete mobilization before declaring war. This gave an excuse for postponement; it was also a cover for the hope that Mussolini's mediation might prevent war after all. The British cabinet was more obstinate. It insisted that German troops must be withdrawn from Poland before a conference could be considered. On the afternoon of 2 September it met again and lost patience: 'Unanimous decision was taken that ultimatum should end at midnight.'[5] No ultimatum was sent. Halifax went on negotiating for a conference with no time limit attached for the withdrawal of German troops. Chamberlain feared to get ahead of the French and was not sorry, until afterwards, to be held back by them.

[1] At least this seems the most likely explanation. No one knows for certain.
[2] Henderson to Halifax, 31 Aug. 1939. *British Foreign Policy*, third series, vii, no. 587.
[3] See Note B, p. 476.
[4] Minute by Cadogan, 1 Sept. 1939. *British Foreign Policy*, third series, vii, no. 652. Halifax to Henderson, ibid., no. 664.
[5] Minney, *Private Papers of Hore-Belisha*, 226.

At 7.30 p.m. he appeared in the house of commons. Members expected to be told of the ultimatum. Instead Chamberlain entertained them with prospects of a conference: if the Germans agreed to withdraw their forces (which was not the same as actually withdrawing them), the British government would forget everything that had happened, and diplomacy could start again. Chamberlain sat down without a cheer.[1] When Arthur Greenwood, acting Labour leader,[2] rose to speak, Amery shouted from the Conservative benches: 'Speak for England, Arthur!' Greenwood did his best. 'Every minute's delay now means the loss of life, imperilling of our national interests' and, as an afterthought,[3] 'imperilling the very foundations of our national honour.' The house broke up in confusion. Greenwood went to Chamberlain and told him that, unless war were declared next morning, 'it would be impossible to hold the House'.[4] Some ministers[5] met in Sir John Simon's room, and Simon carried their message to Chamberlain: war must be declared at once. Thus the man who had been on the point of resigning in protest against the first World war gave the final push into the second. The cabinet met at 11 p.m. Some members of it declared that they would not leave the room until an immediate ultimatum was sent. Chamberlain gloomily agreed. Halifax delayed once more and put off the ultimatum until the next morning—presumably from habit, not with any hope of escape.

The British ultimatum was delivered to the German government at 9 a.m. on 3 September 1939. The Germans made no reply, and the ultimatum expired at 11 a.m. The French limped regretfully after their ally and declared war at 5 p.m. The British declaration of war automatically brought in India and the colonies as it had done in 1914. The Dominions, however, were now free to decide for themselves. The governments of Australia and New Zealand followed the British example at once without consulting their parliaments. The Canadian

[1] In the interests of national unity, it later became the agreed version that Chamberlain was merely covering up for the French and himself had no hope of a peaceful settlement. This is not what appears from the contemporary record.

[2] Attlee was absent at this time, convalescing after an operation.

[3] Greenwood added these words only when prompted by Boothby, a Conservative supporter of Churchill's.

[4] Amery, *My Political Life*, iii. 324.

[5] Simon, Hore-Belisha, Anderson, de la Warr, Burgin, Colville, Dorman-Smith, Stanley, Wallace, and Elliot. Minney, *Private Papers of Hore-Belisha*, 226.

government waited for their parliament and declared war on 10 September. In South Africa, Herzog, the prime minister, wished to remain neutral. Parliament resolved on war by 80 votes to 67; the governor general refused Herzog a dissolution; Smuts became prime minister and declared war on 6 September. For Eire the opportunity had now come fully to apply de Valera's doctrine of external association. Eire declared her neutrality and remained throughout the war a thoroughgoing neutral.

What caused the second World war? There can be many answers: German grievances against the peace settlement of 1919 and the failure to redress them; failure to agree on a system of general controlled disarmament; failure to accept the principles of collective security and to operate them; fear of communism and, on the Soviet side, of capitalism, cutting across ordinary calculations of international policy; German strength, which destroyed the balance of power in Europe, and the resentment of German generals at their previous defeat; American aloofness from European affairs; Hitler's inordinate and unscrupulous ambition—a blanket explanation favoured by some historians; at the end, perhaps only mutual bluff. The question of its immediate outbreak is easier to answer. The house of commons forced war on a reluctant British government, and that government dragged an even more reluctant French government in their train. The British people accepted the decision of parliament and government without complaint. It is impossible to tell whether they welcomed it or whether they would have preferred some other outcome. Argument was almost stilled once the war had started, and, if doubts existed, they were kept in the shadows.

There was much talk later of a world crusade for freedom and against fascism. France, Great Britain, and the Dominions were, however, the only powers who declared war on Germany. All other countries which took part in the war waited until Hitler chose to attack them, the two World Powers, Soviet Russia and the United States, as supinely as the rest. Perhaps the difference was no more than technical. Perhaps the British and French could boast that they alone joined the crusade for freedom of their own free will. Probably the British people were surprised at the noble part which events had thrust on them.

The opening of the second World war surprised the English

people in another way. Though war was declared, little war followed. Sirens sounded their first air-raid warning on 3 September soon after Chamberlain had announced his tardy act. The population of London trooped obediently to the shelters. The fate of Warsaw, they thought, was upon them. It was a false alarm. No bombs fell on English soil then, or for many months thereafter. Hitler needed his air force for the Polish campaign, and in any case hoped that Great Britain and France would call off the war once Poland had been conquered. Hence he did not provoke them. The 'phoney' war was deliberate on his side. The Allied governments were equally anxious not to provoke German attacks and wrapped this up in morality. In March 1939 they had agreed that they 'would not initiate air action against any but purely military objectives in the narrowest sense of the word . . . objectives attack on which would not involve loss of civil life'.[1] The British and French governments set up a Supreme War Council, composed of the two prime ministers, their staffs, and such other ministers as they chose to invite, and the council endorsed this air stategy at its first meeting on 12 September. The British government declared that even if they went over to unrestricted air-warfare, they 'would refrain from attack on civil populations for the purpose of demoralisation'.[2] Thus the R.A.F. was debarred from operating the only sort of campaign for which it had prepared—though, as later events showed, one which it was incapable of conducting.

Nevertheless, precautions against air attack were fully applied. Gas masks were issued to all civilians and were duly carried in their cardboard cases for many months. Street-lighting was extinguished on 1 September. A blackout began which lasted until the defeat of Germany. Motor cars were forbidden to use their headlights, and deaths on the roads increased 100 per cent. during September.[3] The greatest operation was the evacuation from the supposed danger areas of primary schoolchildren, complete with teachers, and of mothers with children under 5. Four million had been planned for; only a million and a half went—47 per cent. of the schoolchildren, and about one third of the mothers. As well, two million people moved out privately. This was a stupendous

---

[1] Butler, *Grand Strategy*, ii. 17.
[3] After this, masked headlights were authorized.

[2] Ibid. 20.

migration. The special trains ran to time; the emergency feeding arrangements worked successfully. Difficulties started when the evacuees reached their reception areas. The city children had no warm clothes or strong shoes, let alone rubber boots, to protect them against the country mud. The overburdened rural authorities had no funds from which to make clothing grants; the parents in the towns often refused to contribute, even when they could be traced; the foster parents were themselves usually too poor. The city children were often verminous. Many, far from home, relapsed into bed-wetting.

These troubles fell upon those least able to cope with them. The poor housed the poor. The wealthier classes, as an official historian remarks, evaded their responsibilities throughout the war.[1] English devotion to local autonomy added its own quirk. The evacuees remained the financial responsibility of the local authority from whose area they had come, and some thousands of clerks were busy for years trying to recover sums which had been spent in the reception areas.[2] Conditions for those who remained behind were also bad. Social services ceased—no free milk, no school dinners. The city schools were all closed until November, and over half the schoolchildren in London were not receiving full-time instruction even in the spring of 1940. Hospital beds were kept empty for the air-raid casualties which never came. Even the maternity wards were barred against expectant mothers. When no bombs fell, people voted against evacuation with their feet. By January 1940 nearly one million had returned home. Nevertheless, country people, and to a certain extent even the wealthy, learnt for the first time how the city poor lived. English people became more mixed up than before. When air raids produced a second evacuation, this time unplanned, there followed also a social revolution. The *Luftwaffe* was a powerful missionary for the welfare state.

Many other administrative preparations had been made before the war—a 'shadow' system of war-government similar to the shadow factories for aircraft and armament production.

---

[1] Titmuss, *Problems of Social Policy*, 393.

[2] The confusion was particularly great when primary schoolchildren reached the age for secondary education. This was the financial responsibility of their home authority. The children could only remember where they came from, if that. This was often not the 'settlement' district of their parents, who had now moved again. As well, the secondary school appropriate to them had often been evacuated to a different part of the country.

These shadows now took on substance. Chamberlain asked for the resignation of the existing cabinet and set up a war cabinet in its place. New ministries sprang, fully staffed, into existence: economic warfare, to conduct the blockade; food, with ration books already printed; shipping, to direct the merchant ships and to build more; information, to supply the press, to conduct propaganda against the enemy, and to raise morale at home. Two other new ministries were joined with existing ones. Home security was amalgamated with the home office under Sir John Anderson. The ministry of labour was already operating the registrations for compulsory military service. It was therefore made the ministry of national service also and thus acquired far greater powers than it had exercised in the first World war, particularly as military conscription was now extended to the age of 41. The treasury imposed exchange control and set up a committee to check capital issues. On paper the government were more effectively and more ruthlessly equipped for war than Lloyd George had been at the height of his power. It was only on paper. The war machine resembled an expensive motor car, beautifully polished, complete in every detail, except that there was no petrol in the tank. In 1936 a government adviser had pointed out that there could be no adequate manpower policy (nor, indeed, war policy of any other kind) without 'a general recognition of the issue before the country, popular support of the Government, and a Government strong enough and decisive enough to make use of this popular support'.[1] All these were lacking in the first nine months of the second World war.

Chamberlain had often lamented the hard lot which diverted him to foreign affairs and preparations for war when he was cut out to be a great peace-minister. Fate took him at his word, and he remained a peace-minister even in wartime. The war cabinet behaved much like any ordinary cabinet except for being somewhat reduced in size. It was composed of the old inner ring of appeasers (Halifax, Hoare, Simon) and the three service ministers, with Hankey, now minister without portfolio, to recall the traditions of the first war.[2] Other ministers attended

[1] Hancock and Gowing, British War Economy, 62.

[2] Lord Chatfield, first sea lord 1932-8, who had succeeded Inskip as minister for the coordination of defence, was also a member, though his task had been to stand in during peacetime for the future war cabinet. He had now no function. He resigned in April 1940, and his post was abolished.

and brought the number to fifteen or so. Executive conduct of the war was left to the chiefs of staff, who in practice ran three separate wars much as they had run three separate schemes of rearmament.

In civil affairs the cabinet waited for proposals from the departments and usually turned them down for fear of alarming the public. It refused at first to sanction food rationing. It made no attempt to curtail civilian industry or to direct labour. Rich people could still move their money to the United States, and many did. Military conscription moved slowly.[1] There was no point in calling up men until the army was equipped to receive them, and it was hard pressed to provide for the existing territorial divisions. One negation proved lasting. Plans had been laid to move the seat of government from London—parliament to one place, the war cabinet to another, ministries scattered all over the country. These plans were put off when no bombs fell, and ultimately few of them operated. A section of the admiralty went to Bath. The ministry of food found itself in Colwyn Bay. Queen Mary was persuaded to take up residence with the duke of Beaufort at Badminton. Otherwise London remained the capital.

The declaration of war had received almost unanimous support in parliament and was, it seems, accepted almost unanimously in the country also. The prewar pacifists, though still numerous, were no longer influential. Some 58,000 men, and 2,000 women, applied to be registered as conscientious objectors during the second World war. Forty thousand of these were given conditional, and 2,900 unconditional exemption. About 5,000 were prosecuted and for the most part sent to prison. But there was little of the previous bitterness. The public looked on the conscientious objectors with tolerance, and they repaid this by dissenting from their fellow countrymen regretfully. Besides, the division between civilian and combatant was less sharp than in the first war, and conscientious objectors who played a heroic part in the 'Blitz' could not be labelled shirkers. Their objection was nearly always to war in general, not to this particular war,[2] and the political opposition which there

---

[1] Only men to the age of 27 had registered by May 1940.
[2] A few socialists pleaded that they could not take part in a capitalist war. They, too, were given exemption, whereas in the first World war only religious objections had been recognized—and that rarely.

had been during the first war hardly existed. The I.L.P.,
which continued to take this line, was a spent force. The
Communist party at first approved the war as an anti-fascist
crusade, then reversed its attitude a few weeks later on orders
from Moscow. Pollitt, the party leader, was degraded and
compelled to confess his error. This only served to discredit the
party. Its membership fell by a third (from 17,000 to under
12,000), and its Left-wing associates, such as Gollancz, swung
violently away. The Communist party had an unrivalled con-
sistency before the war in opposition to Hitler. Now it forfeited,
and never regained, this prestige.

The government made nothing of the national mood. They
remained a government of National pretence. Chamberlain
brought in the two Conservatives associated with resistance to
the dictators. Churchill became first lord of the admiralty;
Eden Dominions secretary. Liberals and Labour refused to join
the government, and Chamberlain was not sorry. He was never
one to forgive those who had criticized him. There was more
than personal resentment in Chamberlain's failure to unite the
country. He and his fellows were at a loss to explain why
they were at war or what they were fighting for. Their policy
was in ruins. They had wanted to settle with Hitler on reasonable terms or, failing that, to shift the brunt of the fighting
on to Soviet Russia. Now they were pledged to the defence of
Poland—a pledge which they could not fulfil. Hitler offered
peace when Poland had been conquered. The government, after
some hesitation, turned down the offer formally in both houses
of parliament. But what now? Did the British government seek
to overthrow fascism throughout Europe?, to destroy Germany
as a Great Power?, or merely to substitute Goering or some other
Nazi for Hitler as dictator of Germany? They did not know,
and the British people were more or less told that they should
not ask such questions. It was hardly surprising that in return
the bulk of people came to feel that the war was little concern
of theirs.

The government were incapable of enlisting popular support.
What was more, they did not want it. A war, based on popular
enthusiasm, seemed to raise the ghost of the Left-wing Popular
Front. It would be the Spanish civil war all over again. Maybe
not the burning of churches or the raping of nuns. But the
unions and shop stewards would have to be brought into part-

nership; the social order would be threatened; something like socialism would reign. Better far that ordinary citizens should carry their gas masks, read official instructions, and proceed quietly with their affairs. A poster appealing for national savings was as characteristic of the second World war at this period as Kitchener's glowering face had been of the first: 'YOUR resolution will bring US victory.' The men of the first World war had fought for King and Country; the men of the second were expected to conform to the requirements of the higher civil service.

Popular support seemed unnecessary. The war was running satisfactorily all by itself. There were no air raids. The R.A.F. made some ineffectual attacks on the German fleet and then contented itself with dropping propaganda leaflets. Kingsley Wood, secretary for air,[1] met a proposal to set fire to German forests with the agonized cry: 'Are you aware it is private property? Why, you will be asking me to bomb Essen next.'[2] Nor was there any fighting on land. An expeditionary force of four divisions duly crossed to France. Hore-Belisha, the secretary for war,[3] was on bad terms with Gort, the C.I.G.S., and hastily shipped him off to command the B.E.F. Ironside became C.I.G.S. instead; he was equally unsuited to the post, and spent his time railing against the politicians. Warning had been taken from the inter-allied confusions of the first war. The B.E.F. was placed unreservedly under Gamelin, the French supreme commander.[4] Then nothing happened. French forces tiptoed across the German frontier while Hitler was busy in Poland. They withdrew a little later when German soldiers

[1] Howard Kingsley Wood (1881–1943): educ. Central Foundation Boys' School; son of a Wesleyan minister; insurance expert; Kt., 1918; postmaster general 1931–5 (in cabinet 1933); minister of health, 1935–8; advised Chamberlain to hold a general election after Munich; secretary for air, 1938–40; lord privy seal, 1940; chancellor of the exchequer, 1940–3; in war cabinet, 3 Oct. 1940–19 Feb. 1942.

[2] Spears, *Prelude to Dunkirk*, 32.

[3] Leslie Hore-Belisha (1893–1957): educ. Clifton and Oxford; National Liberal M.P.; minister of transport, 1934–7, when he gave his name to the beacons which marked pedestrian crossings; secretary for war, 1937–40; minister of national insurance, 1945.

[4] Gort, like Haig before him, had the right to appeal to the British government if he thought the safety of his army endangered. He used this right in May 1940. The British assumed that Gort was directly under Gamelin's command. Gamelin, however, delegated his authority to General Georges, commander of the land forces on the north-east front, and he in turn delegated it to the commander of the northern group of armies. Hence Gort never knew from whom he was supposed to receive orders.

opened fire upon them. That was all. The French army garrisoned the Maginot line. A few British soldiers took their turn in it, and the first of them was killed there on 13 December. The B.E.F. casually threw up some defences on the unfortified French frontier with Belgium. When Hore-Belisha raised an alarm that these defences were inadequate, the generals complained, and Chamberlain dismissed him.[1]

The British and French governments had settled their grand strategy before the war started. They would build up their military resources in an unhurried way. Meanwhile, there would be diversionary attacks on Italy, the weaker member of the Axis, first in Abyssinia and North Africa, then perhaps in Italy itself. This was called 'knocking down the props'. Actually it was intended to provide the sensations of war, and of victory, on the cheap. Finally, at some remote time there would be a victorious attack on Germany herself—an attack again almost without effort, since Germany was supposed to be already on the point of economic collapse and the Allies had hardly started. This strategy was now applied. The British government announced that they were planning for a three-year war: seemingly a heroic resolve, really only an assurance that nothing serious, such as the 32-division army, need be ready until 1942. General Sir Archibald Wavell, an associate of Allenby's, was placed in command of the Middle East.[2] British stores and forces were accumulated in Egypt. A considerable proportion of the British navy was centred in the Mediterranean. Unfortunately Mussolini did not oblige the Allies by presenting them with an easy target. Instead he announced his 'non-belligerence', thus performing a greater service to Hitler than he did by joining in the war later. Soon the Allies forgot their plans against Italy and were back at the old will-o'-the-wisp of securing Mussolini's neutrality or even his benevolent mediation.

The British government remained blindly cheerful. Time,

[1] Chamberlain proposed to make Hore-Belisha minister of information. Halifax overruled this 'because H. B. was a Jew'. Macleod, *Chamberlain*, 286. Hore-Belisha then refused the board of trade. He had appealed to Churchill for support. Churchill, himself insecure, failed to give it, and counted the appeal against Hore-Belisha. Hence Hore-Belisha remained out of office throughout the war.

[2] Archibald Percival Wavell (1883-1950): on Allenby's staff, 1918; commander-in-chief, Middle East, 1939-41; commander-in-chief, India, 1941-3; supreme commander, South-west Pacific, 1942; viceroy of India, 1943-7; cr. Viscount, 1943; cr. Earl, 1947.

they believed, was on their side. Ministers shared the general delusion that economically Germany was at the end of her tether.[1] The experts at the ministry of economic warfare ran over with confident assurances that Germany's military machine would bog down from lack of oil in the very near future and her entire industry grind to a halt from lack of other essential raw materials. Blockade would win the war by itself. It was, as Chamberlain called it in March 1940, 'the main weapon'. These calculations were fantasy. German economy had hardly begun to mobilize at the outbreak of war. Indeed, it remained 'a peacelike war economy', in Klein's words,[2] until 1943. The Germans were not short of raw materials and had learnt from the first war to manufacture substitutes for those, such as rubber, of which they might run short. Moreover, the British blockade had little existence except on paper. Italy provided a leak difficult to control; Soviet Russia one which could not be controlled at all. During the period of the Nazi–Soviet pact, the Germans acquired from Soviet Russia many of the reserve stocks which they (like the British) had failed to build up before the war. The ministry of economic warfare, like some other repeat performances, probably did more harm to the British, who staged it, than to the Germans, against whom it was supposed to operate.

The British soon discovered, to their surprise, that they, not the Germans, were running into economic difficulties. They had assumed before the war that imports could be maintained practically at the peacetime level. The government had made little attempt to build up reserve stocks, despite promptings from Sir Arthur Salter. Petrol rationing, on a generous scale, was the only encroachment on civilian consumption. The admiralty were confident that Asdic, their device for submarine detection, would master the U-boats. There was supposed to be a surplus of shipping. The reserves of gold and foreign currency were large. These high hopes did not work out. The U-boats,

---

[1] Thus Liddell Hart wrote in the summer of 1939 (*The Defence of Britain*, 41): 'If war came now these nations [Germany and Italy] would be starting from the same point of undernourishment that Germany reached after two or three years of the last war.' In fact the Germans had in 1939 a higher standard of life than they had ever had before, and this standard was hardly reduced until the autumn of 1943. German production of civilian goods declined less than the British until the closing months of the war.

[2] Burton Klein, *Germany's Economic Preparation for War*, 173.

though few in number, did much damage. Sinkings of merchant ships were heavy, and the navy was struck also. In September a U-boat sank the aircraft carrier *Courageous*. In October another penetrated the defences of Scapa Flow, a feat never accomplished in the first World war, and sank the battleship *Royal Oak*. Once more the fleet had to withdraw to the west coast of Scotland until the new year.

The German pocket battleship *Graf Spee* raided the South Atlantic and sank eight cargo ships. In December a British force found her. The British ships, though less heavily armed, damaged her in daring attacks and forced her to seek refuge in Montevideo. There the *Graf Spee* was scuttled on Hitler's order. This was a noble exploit, as cheering as the battle of the Falkland Islands in December 1914. The war against the U-boats was less successful. In addition, the Germans did much damage with a magnetic mine, the secret of which was not broken until the end of the year. The British lost 800,000 tons of merchant shipping in the nine months before the real war started. This was not in itself catastrophic. Ships were hired from neutrals. Laid-up ships were brought into commission; new ships were built. By 1940 Great Britain had actually more shipping than at the outbreak of war.

Carrying capacity, not shipping, was the grave shortage, unforeseen before the war. Convoy was instituted immediately on the outbreak of war and proved as successful as in the first World war.[1] But it meant that ships made fewer voyages and took longer over them. A little later, ships had to be kept in port while they were protected from magnetic mines by 'degaussing'—a strip of wire run round their hulls. Central Europe and the Baltic were closed to the British. Hence supplies had to be brought from further afield. The treasury, thinking in terms of a three-year war, rationed expenditure in the United States to £150 million a year. Supplies had to be sought in the sterling area, i.e. those countries which were prepared to accept payment in sterling instead of demanding British goods, and they were usually remote—another cause of longer voyages. Even so, the stock of foreign currencies soon ran short. Early in 1940 the government launched, rather ineffectually, an export drive—still another diversion from bringing in essential supplies.

[1] 229 ships were sunk by U-boats between Sept. 1939 and May 1940. Only twelve of these were sailing in convoy.

There was one unexpected relief. Before the war it had been assumed that bombing would put London and the east coast ports out of action from the first day. The shipping which used these ports was therefore to be diverted to the west coast. This diversion was operated for a fortnight. Then London and the other east coast ports were brought back into service. This relief concealed future danger. The calculation that the west coast ports could handle 75 per cent. more than their normal peacetime traffic, though confidently held by nearly all experts, was, in the words of one ministry of transport official, 'absolute nonsense',[1] and his judgement was amply confirmed a year later. As it was, the railways ran much as usual—theoretically under government control, conducted in fact by a committee of railway managers.

The country was ill-prepared for war, despite all the previous work on paper, and the historian of Food has said that, if there had been air or submarine attacks on the scale of 1940–1, 'the country might have looked defeat in the face before the first Christmas of the war'.[2] Even the peacelike situation brought difficulties enough. The ministry of shipping was at first confident that British ships alone would bring in 48 million tons a year and that neutral ships would raise this to the normal average of 55 million tons. Before long it reported that 47 million tons was the most that could be expected from all sources, and even this estimate proved too optimistic.[3] There was no machinery for allocating imports. The ministry of shipping arbitrarily limited food to 19·8 million tons and supply to 23·9 million. Neither department took any notice. On the contrary, each stepped up its orders in order to guard against the future shortage.[4]

The ministry of food raised the alarm and called for rationing. The government trembled and gave way only when a public-opinion poll revealed that the public actually wanted rationing. The ministry of food then discovered that rapid

[1] The miscalculation sprang from an accumulation of errors. The basic error was the failure to grasp that, while each port could handle 75 per cent. more when considered in isolation, their equipment (particularly of railways taking goods inland) would break down when all of them were working at the higher level.

[2] Hammond, *Food*, i. 77.

[3] Actual imports between Oct. 1939 and June 1940 ran at a yearly average of 45·4 million tons.

[4] Food cheated more successfully than Supply. Food's annual rate (Oct. 1939–June 1940) was 22 million tons; Supply's was 22·6 million.

action was impossible. Though the ration books were already printed, no decision had been taken whether to rely on individual rationing by coupon or to revive the retailer–consumer tie which had been used in the first World war. S. P. Vivian, the man who had devised the abortive national scheme for individual coupons in 1917, was now registrar general and urged the claims of his old love. He could offer a ready-made instrument: the national registration of all British citizens, carried through on 30 September, which incidentally imposed identity cards on English people—an indignity which they had escaped during the first war.

The ministry of food had a confused memory that Vivian's scheme had proved unworkable in 1917. Moreover, they thought that, since national registration was the basis for compulsory military service, any link with it would make food rationing unpopular—another strange and characteristic misjudgement of popular feeling, which preferred an orderly call-up to the volunteer chaos of the first war. The ministry of food therefore insisted on the consumer–retailer tie when rationing began in January 1940. Yet it used national registration as the basis for distributing the ration books, and this really made the consumer–retailer tie unnecessary. As a result, Great Britain was saddled throughout the war with a slow, clumsy system of rationing, 'eminently suited to a war of attrition',[1] and thousands of clerks were kept uselessly at work tracing the movements of consumers, because of a vague tradition left over from the first World war.

The ministry of food promoted rationing solely as a means of distributing supplies more efficiently. Others, including some members of the government, thought in terms of reducing consumption—'tightening our belts' (or, more strictly, the belts of others) as it was called. The ministry of health replied that less food would mean less production in the factories. Scientific advisers of the ministry had devised a sensible and more economical diet, but this involved a reduction in the good red meat which many, including Churchill, equated with a proper meal. Besides, the ministry of agriculture was set on producing more meat, despite protests from the ministries of food, health, and shipping. Not until the second year of war did it acknowledge the simple principle that cereals for direct human consumption

[1] Hammond, *Food*, ii. 756.

had exactly ten times the food value of feedingstuffs for animals. Thus, in food as elsewhere the months of waiting were wasted.

Virtually the only adventurous step was to make summer time last all the year round for the duration of the war.[1] This was a trivial improvement. Otherwise ordinary life was little affected. Industry still laboured on luxury goods. In spring 1940 there were still over one million unemployed. On 4 May 1940 Churchill complained, this time with more justification, that manpower in the munitions industries had increased only 11 per cent., one sixth of what was required. Skilled labour was running short. Yet the ratio of women and young workers to mature men in munitions was only 1 to 12; in the first war it had been 1 to 3. The government dared not go against the unions and would not cooperate with them. 'The historian finds himself oppressed by a feeling of lost opportunity.'[2]

Finance reinforces this feeling. The treasury had expounded the bases for 'a level economy' in 1929; heavy taxation, control of prices, profits and wages, consumer rationing. Little of this was applied. Taxation was pushed up timidly: income tax to 7s. 6d. in the pound, a penny on beer, an excess-profits tax of 60 per cent. Less than half the cost of the war was met out of taxation, and even this was achieved only because industry failed to deliver the munitions which the government had ordered. Only 20 per cent. of goods were brought under any sort of price control. In any case, import prices were beyond control and went up fast. Nor could the government resist demands for increased wages. Prices and wages both rose more in the early months of the second World war than they had done in those of the first.[3]

The government, in their weakness, stumbled on one innovation of decisive importance. In November 1939 the ministry of food reported that it must raise food prices and so send up the cost of living index by 7 points; otherwise it would lose £60

[1] In 1941 and subsequent years double summer time was introduced during the summer months.

[2] Hancock and Gowing, *British War Economy*, 149. The writers add: 'Government and people were out of tune with each other, the nation was divided within itself, men and women were divided within their own minds.' Only the first part of the sentence seems true.

[3] Wholesale prices: July 1914, 100; July 1915, 129; August 1939, 100; July 1940, 142. Wages: July 1914, 100; July 1915, 105–10; September 1939, 100; July 1940, 112–13.

million a year. This would certainly have started a general round of wage increases, just when the government were trying to stabilize wages. They therefore agreed to bear the loss 'temporarily'. In January 1940 the government prolonged food subsidies for a further four months, though with a warning that, if they were continued, 'there would be nothing to prevent the cost mounting until it reached figures completely outside our power to control'. The warning was not heeded. Food subsidies went on throughout the war, at an ever-increasing cost (£72 million in 1940, £250 million in 1945), and the cost of living was held fairly stable at about 25–30 per cent. above prewar.[1] As a result, peace reigned almost unbroken in industry. This was probably the most valuable, though involuntary, legacy of Chamberlain's war government.

The government were still moving into war backwards, with their eyes tightly closed. Churchill was the one exception, a cuckoo in the nest, as restless against inaction and as fertile with proposals as Lloyd George had been in Asquith's war government. There were great differences between the tactics of the two men. Lloyd George already enjoyed great reputation and commanded a strong following in the Liberal party before the first World war. He did not need to conceal his discontent, though he trembled when it came to decisive action. Churchill had stood almost alone until the outbreak of war, his personal following reduced to two. His name was tarnished by Antwerp, the Dardanelles, and other outbursts of supposed irresponsibility. Conservatives remembered his campaign against the India bill and his support of Edward VIII at the time of the abdication. Labour remembered his aggressiveness during the general strike and harked back even to Tonypandy (when he had sent troops to South Wales during a mining dispute).

The parliamentary situation was also unfavourable to Churchill. In the first war, the two major parties almost balanced, and Lloyd George could rule with Conservative backing once the Liberals were split. In 1939 the Conservatives had a crushing majority, and Churchill could have made nothing against them if backed only by the two Opposition parties—itself an unlikely hypothesis—and some Conservative rebels.

---

[1] Strictly the cost of living index was kept stable, and this was based on an out-of-date estimate of personal expenditure. Hence the government sometimes deliberately subsidized items which carried more weight than they deserved.

He had to carry the entire Conservative party, not to split it. This was, in any case, what he wanted to do. Years of bitter experience—Lloyd George's as well as his own—had taught him the need for organized support. Besides, he was now himself a Conservative, whatever radical impulses he had shown in the past. Fresh from writing a four-volume history of the English-speaking peoples (published only after the war), his mind ran over traditional values. Though passionately intent to save England, it was the England of the old order that he wanted to save, or as much of it as he could.

Churchill therefore walked warily. He did not intrigue. He was a loyal colleague. Chamberlain had talked of making him virtually minister of defence by putting him, alone of the three service ministers, in the war cabinet; then demoted him by bringing in the other two also. Though Churchill did not complain, he could not keep his hands off the general conduct of the war. He harangued the war cabinet and bombarded Chamberlain with long papers. He had two immediate proposals for increasing Germany's supposed economic difficulties. One was to launch floating mines down the Rhine from Alsace. The other was to mine the leads—the long strip of Norwegian territorial waters which German ships, carrying iron ore from Sweden, used in the winter when the Baltic was closed by ice. The French government also welcomed action, if only to stir up some support for the war in their own country. But they wanted to keep the war as far from France as possible—hence mines on the Rhine were ruled out. Also they dreamt of switching the war from Germany to Russia, a dream not altogether foreign to some Conservatives in England, and produced a fantastic plan for bombing the oil wells at Baku—ostensibly to lessen Germany's supplies of oil. The British government did not care for this, Churchill least of all. He always persuaded himself easily into believing anything which he wanted to believe, and he now wanted to believe that Soviet Russia was a patriotic national state, not—as he had formerly alleged—the centre of international revolution. In October 1939, when Soviet forces occupied eastern Poland, Churchill applauded: 'Hitler's path to the east is closed.'

Thus, with mines in the Rhine ruled out by the French and bombs on Baku ruled out by the British, only the Norwegian leads remained. Events increased the attractiveness of the extreme North. Soviet Russia was anxious about her security in the Baltic, as she had shown during the negotiations for an alliance with Great Britain and France. Now she acted by force, not diplomacy. Three Baltic states—Latvia, Estonia, Lithuania—fearfully accepted Soviet military control. Finland refused and on 30 November was invaded by Soviet troops. The League of Nations, which had ignored the German aggression against Poland, stirred on its deathbed and expelled Soviet Russia—the only aggressor to be thus treated. The Finns resisted successfully and defeated the Soviet forces. Enthusiasm for Finland mounted. Conservatives naturally applauded her defiance of Red Russia. Most Labour men joined in, to show their freedom from Communist ties. The few who dissented were expelled from the Labour party.[1] Aid for Finland became the general cry. The Allied governments responded, and an Anglo-French expeditionary force of 100,000 men was hastily assembled.

The French ministers hoped to lead an anti-Bolshevik crusade and even had a far-fetched vision that the Germans might overthrow Hitler in order to enlist under the French banner.[2] Some British Conservatives, too, were not sorry to go against Soviet Russia or regarded her as another German prop waiting to be knocked down. Others thought that it would show Great Britain's impartial hostility towards dictatorships, Communist and Fascist, if she took on both Soviet Russia and Germany at once. Churchill had a more subtle intention. The expeditionary force would have to cross Norway and Sweden before reaching Finland. On the way it would seize Narvik, the Norwegian port from which the iron ore was shipped to Germany, and would then go on to wreck the Swedish iron mines. In this ingenious way, the French, thinking to go against Soviet Russia, would go against Germany after all. The supply of iron ore to Germany would be stopped. German industry would be crippled. It was a matter of less moment whether the expeditionary force reached Finland. The project was debated between the allies in a confused, muddled way: anti-Soviet at one moment, anti-German at the next. There was much talk, not welcomed by the admiralty,

---

[1] Some of those now expelled, e.g. D. N. Pritt, never rejoined the party.

[2] Other recruits to the crusade were supposed to be waiting for the call. Americans were strong for Finland, the only country which had continued to pay its war debt. Fascist Italy sent aeroplanes and munitions to Finland, until Hitler forbade it.

about exploiting the strategical advantages of sea power. The decisive argument was simply the need for some action, never mind where or who against. The Finnish campaign was Gallipoli again, and worse.[1]

The plans, too, were run up in the slapdash spirit which had characterized the expedition to the Dardanelles. Once more there were no maps, no intelligence reports, no systematic preparations. It would take three weeks to put the expeditionary force ashore at Narvik, and eleven weeks before it could move forward. Meanwhile, Soviet Russia and Germany were expected to do nothing. There was only one railway line, and no road, from Narvik into Sweden. The operation could work, if at all, only with the active cooperation of the Norwegian and Swedish governments. Neither was likely to welcome the destruction of invaluable economic assets nor be eager to bring down the united wrath of Germany and Russia. The Allies brushed aside these trivial difficulties. In January 1940 the Norwegian and Swedish governments were invited to authorize the passage of Anglo-French forces and to join in staff talks. Both refused.

The war cabinet continued to dither round the problem and debated it on sixty distinct occasions. Early in March a decision was reached to go ahead, and the commanders were cheerfully told that serious opposition need not be expected. At the last moment the bottom fell out of the plan. On 12 March Finland agreed to the Soviet demands and made peace. The British and French governments were humiliated. Once more they had paraded their intention of aiding a small country which was the victim of aggression. Once more they had failed

---

[1] The motives for the projected expedition to Finland defy rational analysis. For Great Britain and France to provoke war with Soviet Russia when already at war with Germany seems the product of a madhouse, and it is tempting to suggest a more sinister plan: switching the war on to an anti-Bolshevik course, so that the war against Germany could be forgotten or even ended. Some leading Frenchmen certainly inclined towards this, enough at any rate to confirm the suspicions which the Soviet government had expressed during the negotiations for an alliance. British ministers, too, were not sorry to parade their anti-Soviet feelings—feelings which had become general in the country since the Nazi–Soviet pact. Still, their main impulse was simply a vague longing for action. The 'phoney' war discredited ministers and exasperated the public. Finland seemed to offer an opening to start fighting somewhere, with the added advantage of being far from the Western front. A full examination of the British and French records may some time make the affair clearer. At present, the only charitable conclusion is to assume that the British and French governments had taken leave of their senses.

to do so. In France those who had wanted to fight Russia joined
in discontent with those who wanted to fight Germany. Daladier's government fell. Reynaud, the new premier, was more
resolute, though his political position was weaker. Almost his
first act was to conclude with the British an agreement, hitherto
overlooked, to make war and peace in common.

British opinion was also stirred. On 4 April Chamberlain
sought to calm it. He ran over the march of rearmament and
announced: 'Hitler has missed the bus.' Narvik and the leads
remained a temptation. Reynaud pressed hard for the operation. Churchill seconded him. The war cabinet agreed and
resolved to mine the leads on 8 April.[1] The expeditionary force,
which had been disbanded, was hastily recalled: it was to go to
Norway only if mining the leads provoked a German intervention. This came, and sooner than expected. Hitler had long
anticipated some Allied act in Norway, particularly after 16
February, when a British force stopped the *Altmark*, a German
ship, in Norwegian territorial waters and rescued the British
prisoners of war whom she was carrying. Hitler planned a
full-scale occupation of Denmark and Norway. The German
move was also timed for the night of 8 April. The British,
engaged in their own minor illegality of mining the leads,
were taken completely by surprise. The Germans took
over Denmark unopposed and seized every important
Norwegian port from Oslo to Narvik. The British had imagined,
mistakenly, that they controlled the North Sea. Now their
sea power was openly defied. Churchill announced: 'Every
German ship using the Kattegat will be sunk'—a boast that
was not fulfilled.

Inevitably the British government responded to the Norwegian appeal for aid. After all, Norway, unlike Czechoslovakia
or Poland, seemed within range. Everything went wrong. The
land forces were unprepared for an opposed landing or for
immediate action; they were composed mainly of territorial
units which were only half trained. The Germans already held
most of the air fields in Norway, and the British discovered, to
their surprise, that their navy and army could not operate
within range of the German air force. This was the decisive

---

[1] In exchange the French agreed to launch mines on the Rhine, then backed
out of their promise. The dispute over this postponed the mining of the leads from
5 to 8 April—as events worked out, a vital delay.

cause of failure. Confusion of counsels made things worse. Churchill wanted to concentrate on recovering Narvik. The war cabinet insisted on attacking Trondheim, the ancient capital of Norway, as a political demonstration. The chiefs of staff agreed, had second thoughts, and fell back on an enveloping movement from Namsos and Aandalsnes—two fishing ports which could hardly handle even small landings. The admiralty and war office issued contradictory orders to their respective subordinates. Outside Narvik, for instance, Lord Cork and Orrery, the admiral, wished to attack, as he had been instructed to do. Mackesy, the general, refused to land in face of opposition, which accorded with his instructions.

Narvik was in fact not captured until 28 May. By then it was eclipsed by greater events. Holding Narvik would clearly impose too great a strain on the British navy and on shipping resources. It was evacuated on 8 June. The aircraft carrier *Glorious* and two destroyers were sunk during the evacuation. Narvik was a postscript. The main operation at Namsos and Aandalsnes had already failed disastrously: the British forces were finally withdrawn on 2 May. There were some gains to set off against this dismal record. The king of Norway and his government came to England as allies. More than a million tons of Norwegian shipping were added to British resources. The German navy had suffered heavily. It lost three cruisers and ten destroyers; its two heavy cruisers and one of its two pocket battleships were put temporarily out of action. In the summer of 1940 the effective German fleet was reduced to one 8-inch cruiser, two light cruisers, and four destroyers. The successful British withdrawal from Dunkirk and the German failure to invade England both owed something to the Norwegian campaign.

These were poor consolations to British opinion in the opening days of May. The failure had solid technical reasons: inadequate forces, lack of air power. This is not how English people saw it. They blamed the men at the top. Their wrath turned against Chamberlain; their enthusiasm towards Churchill. This was wrongheaded in terms of the immediate past. Churchill had far more to do than Chamberlain with the Norwegian campaign. Many of the wildest impulses came from him, and Chamberlain, no mean tactician in politics, had already given him much of the responsibility for defence, though little power over it.[1] Public opinion ignored these niceties. It judged men by their spirit. Chamberlain paid the penalty for appeasement. Churchill reaped the reward for his years of solitary warning. Still it was a nice twist that a campaign, directed largely by Churchill, should bring Chamberlain down and raise Churchill up.

On 7 May Chamberlain opened a two-day debate on the Norwegian campaign. The strongest attacks on him came from the Conservative backbenches. There were many territorial officers among the younger Conservative M.P.s, and they spoke for the territorial units which had suffered in Norway. Sir Roger Keyes, hero of Zeebrugge, denounced the government, wearing the uniform of an admiral of the fleet. Amery, sensing the mood of the house, ended with Cromwell's words to the Rump: 'Depart, I say, and let us have done with you. In the name of God, go!' The Labour party had not intended to force a division, fearing that the Conservatives would obey the whips and that a great majority would perpetuate Chamberlain's government. They plucked up courage during the night.[2]

On 8 May Morrison announced that Labour proposed to divide the house. Chamberlain fell back on party loyalty; he appealed to 'his friends'. This roused Lloyd George. He had his revenge at last for years of exclusion. Lloyd George warned Churchill 'not to allow himself to be converted into an air-raid shelter to keep the splinters from hitting his colleagues'. He told Chamberlain to make an example of sacrifice, 'because there is nothing which can contribute more to victory in this war than that he should sacrifice the seals of office'. Churchill remained faithful to his old line and made the best case he could for the government. It was no use. Resentment and humiliation had cut too deep. At the division,[3] 41 of those who usually supported the government voted with the Opposition,

[1] On 4 April Churchill was made chairman of the Military Co-ordination Committee. This gave him no real authority over the army or air force. Ten days later he called in Chamberlain to support him—a confused arrangement. On 1 May Churchill was made the prime minister's deputy with special responsibility 'for giving guidance and direction to the Chiefs of Staff Committee'—again more responsibility than power.

[2] Their hand was forced—a little-known fact—by the women M.P.s. These had an all-party room of their own and, in discussion there, some of them resolved to force a vote if no one else did so.

[3] Many writers describe this as a vote of censure or of no confidence. This is technically incorrect. It was a division on the motion that 'this house do now adjourn'. In practice, of course, it came to much the same thing.

and some 60 more abstained.[1] The government's majority of about 240 fell to 81 (281 for, 200 against).

On 9 May Chamberlain tried to win over Amery and other Conservative rebels. They refused to join the government unless Labour and Liberals were brought in also. Chamberlain, though still anxious to remain prime minister, appreciated that Labour and Liberals might refuse to serve under him. In that case, whom should he recommend to the king as his successor? Churchill was the obvious man. Yet there were plausible reasons for hesitation: his rashness; the hostility to him of many Conservatives and, it was supposed, of Labour; perhaps a fear that he would not wage a respectable moderate war. An alternative lay ready to hand: Lord Halifax, prince of appeasers and yet adroitly free from blame. All the political leaders, we now know, would have accepted Halifax; most of them, including Chamberlain and Attlee, actually favoured him. The only obstacle to Halifax was Churchill himself, and he seemed defenceless. He had repeatedly declared that, in this national emergency, he would serve with or under anyone.

Attempts were made to shake Churchill's high-minded resolve. Beaverbrook returned to his old trade of kingmaker. Wiser than Chamberlain and the old gang, he realized that Churchill was the only saviour, even for Conservatives. He argued in vain: Churchill would not be moved. New urgings came from Brendan Bracken, Churchill's most stalwart supporter in the lean years. He brought tidings: he had learnt from Attlee that, though Labour preferred Halifax, they would not refuse to serve under Churchill.[2] Reluctantly Churchill agreed that, if asked to serve under Halifax, he would make no reply. On the afternoon of 9 May, Chamberlain met Churchill, Halifax, and Margesson, the Conservative chief whip.[3]

[1] The figures usually given of 44 voting against and 80 abstaining were guesses made on the night. The division lists show that 33 Conservatives, 4 National Liberals, 2 National Labour, and 2 Independents who usually supported the government voted against them, and that 65 Conservatives were absent unpaired. Eight Labour members were also absent unpaired. The voluntary Conservative abstentions were therefore probably about 60.

[2] Amery, *My Political Life*, iii. 371. Spears, *Prelude to Dunkirk*, 130–1. Attlee, characteristically, cannot recall any conversation with Bracken. Dalton, *The Fateful Years*, 309.

[3] Wheeler-Bennett, *George VI*, 442. Churchill (*Second World War*, i. 597–8), wrongly puts the meeting on 10 May. The mistake, no doubt unconscious, is easy to explain. When the book was written, Churchill was Conservative leader. By dating the meeting 10 May, he made it appear that Hitler, not his own implicit

Chamberlain asked: what should he say to the King? Margesson advocated Halifax as prime minister. Churchill, the master of eloquence, remained silent. The silence lasted for two minutes. During that time, the 'decayed serving men', as Amery had called them, faced truth. Churchill held them in the hollow of his hand. If he stood out of the government, they would all be swept away in a storm of national indignation. Halifax broke the silence with the modest remark that it would be difficult for a peer to be prime minister 'in such a war as this'. With that, the phantasm of prime minister Halifax vanished for ever.

Now only Chamberlain himself could keep Churchill out. Later in the afternoon he met the two Labour leaders, Attlee and Greenwood, and invited them to join his government. They shrank from responsibility and declined to answer until they could consult the national executive at Bournemouth, where the party was assembling for its annual conference, but they expected the answer to be 'No'. Chamberlain then grudgingly asked whether they would serve under someone else. Here the answer was left open. During the night a last chance was offered to Chamberlain. The Germans invaded Holland and Belgium. Surely this was no time to rock the boat; the government should go on. Chamberlain appeared at the cabinet 'in good form; the news from the Low Country had stimulated him. . . . He was ready for action if encouraged and authorised to act.'[1] Kingsley Wood shattered the dream: now more than ever, he insisted, Chamberlain must go. Wood had started his career as an insurance expert. Though hitherto Chamberlain's Sancho Panza, he knew when to take out a cover note for the future. He reaped his due reward when the new government was formed. In the afternoon Labour's answer came from Bournemouth. They would serve 'under a new Prime Minister'. This was the final blow. Chamberlain went to Buckingham Palace and resigned. The king suggested Halifax. Chamberlain replied 'that H. was not enthusiastic'.[2] The king then agreed that it must be Churchill. At 6 p.m. Churchill became prime minister. The next day the king

threat, brought him to power. For the same reason, he omitted Margesson from those present at the meeting.

[1] Reith, *Into the Wind*, 382.
[2] Wheeler-Bennett, *George VI*, 444.

met Halifax: 'I told him I was sorry not to have him as P.M.' The sorrow was not widely shared.

Though Churchill had some faithful followers, in the last resort he succeeded by calling in the people against the men at the top. The words which he applied to Lloyd George were true of himself: 'He seized power. Perhaps the power was his to take.' Chamberlain was more generous than Asquith had been in December 1916 and agreed to serve under the man who had supplanted him. The Conservatives who had backed Chamberlain to the last did not forgive so easily. When the house met on 13 May, they rose and cheered Chamberlain. Cheers for Churchill came only from the Labour benches. In a speech, which combined echoes of Garibaldi and Clemenceau,[1] Churchill said: 'I have nothing to offer but blood, toil, tears and sweat. You ask, What is our policy? I will say: It is to wage war, by sea, land, and air, with all our might and with all the strength that God can give us. . . . You ask, What is our aim? I can answer in one word: Victory—victory at all costs, victory in spite of all terror; victory, however long and hard the road may be.' This was exactly what the opponents of Churchill had feared, and even he hardly foresaw all that was involved. Victory, even if this meant placing the British empire in pawn to the United States; victory, even if it meant Soviet domination of Europe; victory at all costs. This was probably the will of the British people. At any rate, Churchill's words on 13 May charted the history of England for the next five years.

NOTES

Note A. *The Wohltat–Wilson conversations.* These Anglo-German negotiations were conducted in a secret unofficial way. British businessmen approached Goering, supposedly the economic dictator of Germany. Swedish businessmen acted as intermediaries. The most serious talks were with Wohltat, commissioner under Goering for the German four-year plan. He was in London from 18 to 21 July. He met Sir Horace Wilson and R. S. Hudson, parliamentary secretary at the department of overseas trade. According to

[1] On 2 July 1849 Garibaldi said in Rome: 'I offer neither pay, nor quarter, nor provisions; I offer hunger, thirst, forced marches, battles and death.' Clemenceau said on 20 Nov. 1917: 'Finally you ask what are my war aims? Gentlemen, they are very simple: *Victory*', and on 8 Mar. 1918: 'My formula is the same everywhere. Home Policy? I wage war. Foreign policy? I wage war. All the time I wage war.' Churchill never believed in wasting a phrase. Thus in Jan. 1940 he said, challenging Hitler: 'Let us go forward together and put these grave matters to the proof.' He first used the phrase early in 1914, but then in challenge to Ulster and the Unionist party, of which he was now a distinguished member.

his account (*German Foreign Policy*, series D, vi, no. 716), both men placed before him detailed programmes for Anglo-German cooperation. Wilson claims that he only gave Wohltat a copy of a speech which Halifax had made a few days before and that a second meeting on 21 July, which Wohltat describes, never took place (Gilbert and Gott, *The Appeasers*, 226). Hudson only denied that a precise figure of £1,000 million had been set for the loan. Possibly Wohltat exaggerated the formality of the British proposals. On the other hand, Wilson repeated the heads of his programme to Dirksen, the German ambassador, on 3 August almost word for word (*Dirksen Papers*, ii, no. 24–II). This conversation has not been questioned.

Note B. *Hitler's decision for war*. It is not clear why Hitler made this decision. Of course there is no problem for those who regard Hitler either as a madman or as set on a world war all along. But these views do not accord with his previous behaviour. Hitler had been a skilful, though unscrupulous, tactician and had carried Germany nearer to domination of Europe by threats and bluff. His military preparations also seem to suggest that he intended further bluffs or, at worst, brief wars against minor opponents. It is hard to believe that he wanted a full-scale war against Great Britain and France. Perhaps therefore (and this is the view towards which I incline) he misjudged the situation. He thought that the British had already deserted their Polish ally or were on the point of doing so and that an attack on Poland would rush them into a new Munich, just as threats to attack Czechoslovakia had done the year before. There is an alternative explanation. The German generals had been told to prepare the invasion of Poland for 1 September. They had none of the reluctance which they profess to have felt in regard to attacking Czechoslovakia. Hitler had until 1 September to succeed by diplomacy. Then he had to order the invasion or be discredited in the eyes of the generals, and he had at this time by no means the complete dominion over them which he secured by 1944. However, we cannot tell for certain and shall never be able to do so, just as we cannot be sure why the rulers of Germany made the decision for war at the end of July 1914. The greatest decisions are nearly always the ones most difficult to explain simply.

XIV

FINEST HOUR, 1940-1

CHURCHILL was swept to power by a revolt of the back-benches as Lloyd George had been in December 1916. The revolt this time was open, displayed in the division lobbies. There was no element of intrigue—or not much. Yet the consequences were strikingly modest, at any rate in appearance. Lloyd George wished to show that he was making all things new and exaggerated his innovations. Churchill was anxious to conceal that anything unusual had happened. He venerated traditional institutions and sought to keep them alive. Throughout the war, he courted both king and parliament with romantic respect, which was more than Chamberlain had done.[1] Moreover, Churchill held firmly to his belief that no individual was strong enough to go against the party system. His government, as Lloyd George complained, was 'a Coalition of Parties and their nominees. . . . Not a War Directorate in the real sense of the term.'[2] Though Churchill was clearly a national leader above party when he formed his government, he escaped from this position as soon as he could. In October 1940, on Chamberlain's resignation, he had himself elected leader of the Conservative party; while, on the other side, Attlee, leader of the Labour party, was the only man, apart from Churchill, who sat in the war cabinet from the first day to the last. The Conservative and Labour chief whips set up a joint office. The senior Labour ex-minister (at first Lees-Smith and later Greenwood) acted as leader of the Opposition only to expedite the business of the house. There was again an electoral truce. The major offices went to recognized politicians in accordance with party strength. Though there was equality in the war cabinet (two Labour and two Conservatives plus Churchill), outside

[1] Chamberlain, for instance, went to see Hitler at Berchtesgaden without obtaining the king's permission to leave the country and resented parliamentary criticism or inquiry.

[2] Owen, *Tempestuous Journey*, 748–51. This was the ostensible reason why Lloyd George did not join Churchill's government. A deeper reason was dislike of Chamberlain, and deeper still his failing powers.

it fifteen offices of cabinet rank went to the Conservatives and their allies, only four to Labour and one to a Liberal.[1]

There was no inrush of new men. Churchill set his face against proscription of the appeasers. Only Hoare was again the fall guy as he had been during the Abyssinian affair. He was packed off to Madrid as ambassador. The others survived in glory: Simon at last lord chancellor after twenty-five years of waiting; Chamberlain and Halifax both in the war cabinet. Churchill even intended to make Chamberlain leader of the house of commons. Labour objected, and Churchill took the job himself.[2] The Conservative opponents of appeasement received few rewards: Duff Cooper, the true hero of Munich, for instance, only got the ministry of information. Churchill brought in two new men: Beaverbrook, now his intimate adviser, as minister of aircraft production; Bevin, secretary of the transport and general workers' union, as minister of labour.[3] It was no accident that these two provided, after Churchill himself, most of the drive and also most of the trouble during the next two years. Of course the neat party deal was somewhat deceptive. The Labour masses, though not the Labour leadership, wanted more than a mere change of government, and the Conservatives sheltered under Churchill's national prestige. He, on his side, hoped to use this prestige for Conservative purposes at the end of the war—a hope not then fulfilled.

There were few changes of system just as there were few changes of men. The instruments of war government were already there from the war cabinet to local agricultural committees and only needed to be infused with a new spirit. Churchill created one ministry against Lloyd George's half dozen: aircraft production, to do for the R.A.F. what the ministry of supply was doing for the army—an obvious enough innovation and, if it had not been for the new minister, an

[1] The Liberals came off badly in this manœuvring of the massed battalions. Sinclair, their leader, was not in the war cabinet, though told that he could attend 'when any matter affecting fundamental political issues or party union was involved'. Churchill, *Second World War*, ii. 8.

[2] In practice Attlee usually acted for him and also took the chair at the war cabinet when Churchill was absent.

[3] Some 'non-party' men (usually of Conservative allegiance) had already been brought in by Chamberlain: Sir John Anderson, now home secretary, before the war; Sir Andrew Duncan, president of the board of trade, and Sir John Reith, now minister of transport (previously minister of information) in Jan. 1940; Lord Woolton, minister of food, in April.

innocuous one.[1] Similarly, the government already possessed, on paper, all the powers which had to be created, with much travail, during the previous war. Rationing, compulsory military service, exchange control, licensing of imports, were in operation. Other plans, as for the direction of labour and for effective wartime finance, had been shaped, though not applied. On 22 May an Emergency Powers Act, passed in a single day, gave the government practically unlimited authority over all British citizens and their property. This, though a noble gesture of defiance, really added little to the existing powers of government, and new encroachments, when they came, were fully debated as though the Act of 22 May had never been.

There were great changes despite the seeming moderation— as Churchill has called them 'more real than apparent'.[2] The greatest was deceptively simple: Churchill gave himself the additional title of Minister of Defence. He did not seek parliamentary approval for this. He acquired no statutory powers. He had no staff other than the military wing of the war cabinet secretariat, the head of which, General Ismay, became a member of the chiefs of staff's committee as Churchill's watchdog. The name was enough by itself. It made Churchill supreme director of the war on the military side. The three service ministers were excluded from the war cabinet and lost their directing powers. They became little more than superior civil servants administering the forces under their control, so much so that in 1942 a civil servant, Sir James Grigg, was made secretary of state for war without anyone's noticing the difference. Churchill announced losses and victories in the house of commons, appointed and dismissed generals, admirals, and field marshals. The orders to them were issued in his name or with a 'we' which was more regal than collective. The chiefs of staff's committee could no longer claim autonomy nor doubt to whom it was subordinate.

Churchill, as minister of defence, was no innocent civilian, criticizing strategy from outside, in the way that Lloyd George had been. He was himself an expert on war, or so he believed. He had been a serving army officer; had directed the admiralty

[1] There were also few new ministries later. Only the ministry of production, created in 1942, was of real importance. The others were either rearrangements or preparations for postwar.
[2] Churchill, *Second World War*, ii. 15.

in two world wars—trespassing into operations more than any
other first lord had ever done; and now often wore the uniform
of an air commodore, complete with honorary 'wings'—the
only prime minister, not excluding Wellington, to wear military
uniform while in office. He had written on great commanders
from Marlborough to Foch. His mind teemed with original,
often with dangerous, ideas, and he could sustain them with
technical arguments. The chiefs of staff had difficulty in resisting him. No British general, until late in the war, had the
prestige of Kitchener, Haig, or even French. They were names
to the public and no more, expendable as everyone else was
except Churchill. The chiefs of staff had to answer Churchill's
proposals with objections equally technical and even more
carefully thought out. This was a wearing business, especially
when Churchill, in his romantic way, suggested that the conduct
of the war would be much improved if some generals, or even
some chiefs of staff, were shot. Still, this was not the division
between Frocks and Brasshats which had characterized the first
war. It was a conflict between an amateur strategist and professionals within a service framework. The chiefs of staff admired Churchill, were indeed devoted to him, even when they
railed against his impulses. He, on his side, deferred to professional views when they were expressed as coherently as his
own—a hard condition to fulfil.

Churchill's impact was different on the three services. The
admiralty was itself an operational headquarters, issuing orders
directly to the home fleet and sometimes even to the fleet in
the Mediterranean—an authority not always used to good
purpose. Churchill was perhaps a little in awe of Admiral Sir
Dudley Pound, the first sea lord. In any case, naval strategy
largely determined itself. There was no need to remodel the
navy or to ask—what shall we do with it? Its tasks were clear:
to contain the enemy forces and to keep the seas open, as much
as it could, for British ships. The air force also tended to go its
own way. Its two chief forces, fighter command and bomber
command, both had their headquarters near London,[1] and
their commanders could bypass the chiefs of staff. Dowding,
commander-in-chief of fighter command, was the only officer
who ever appealed to the war cabinet against a directive of
Churchill's—and got his way. Later Sir Arthur Harris, who

[1] Fighter command at Stanmore and bomber command near High Wycombe.

became commander-in-chief of bomber command in 1942, exploited the nearness of High Wycombe to Churchill's weekend resort at Chequers and promoted his strategy by personal approach to the minister of defence. Here, too, strategy largely determined itself, given the character of the air force as shaped before the war. The R.A.F. was set on independent, or as it came to be called 'strategic', bombing once the German attack on England had been beaten off. Harris preached this strategy. Churchill agreed with it. So, too, with some reservations, did Sir Charles Portal, who was chief of the air staff from October 1940 onwards, and there were no serious disputes until the Allied invasion of France.

Military plans were, however, often in question. In June 1940 the British army was thrown out of Europe with the loss of nearly all its equipment. It had to be remade as an offensive force. There was prolonged debate where it should strike or indeed whether it should strike at all. Churchill was offensively minded even at the darkest hour. His restless promptings fell upon the C.I.G.S. The strain wore down Sir John Dill, who was C.I.G.S. from May 1940 until the end of 1941. Sir Alan Brooke, his successor, held out more successfully and discharged his resentment only in the harmless form of postwar memoirs. Beneath the arguments, there was fundamental agreement. Churchill remembered the Somme and Passchendaele. He wanted an offensive without great casualties, a way round in fact, a backdoor into Germany. This time, the C.I.G.S. wanted it also. The conflict of principle between direct and indirect attack was fought out later with the Americans. It was not in dispute between minister of defence and C.I.G.S.

Churchill did not run the war immune from civilian supervision. In theory he deferred elaborately to the war cabinet. On its authority, he presided over a Defence Committee (Operations)—composed of two members of the war cabinet,[1] the chiefs of staff, and the service ministers. This committee met a good deal in the early days, though it seems to have done little more than endorse Churchill's proposals. Later it almost faded away as he tightened his grip and as decisions of principle became less necessary.[2] A similar Defence Committee

---

[1] At first Chamberlain and Attlee, later Attlee and Beaverbrook.

[2] The Defence Committee (Operations) held 52 meetings in 1940 and 76 in 1941. It held 10 in 1944, and then only to discuss minor topics. Similarly the meetings

(Supply) was supposed to coordinate the needs of the three forces. In practice the rival services still scrambled for everything they could lay their hands on.

The civil side of war had an even more elaborate organization with no less than five committees, all but one under a member of the war cabinet.[1] Churchill seems to have started out with the idea that, while he directed the military side of the war, Chamberlain, as lord president, would be virtually civilian prime minister. The lord president's committee was therefore set up to control and to coordinate the others. Chamberlain, a dying man, made little of this. When he died, Anderson was made lord president. His committee eclipsed the others, and all except one were, in time, abolished. Anderson gradually became the supreme figure in civil administration and ran the war on the civil side so far as any one man could be said to do so. Churchill acknowledged this pre-eminence in 1945 when he nominated Anderson as prime minister in case both Eden and he himself were killed.[2]

This extraordinary suggestion indicated how much politicians and the political system were pushed aside during the war, despite Churchill's attempts to nourish them. Even so, the suggestion had an incurable defect. Anderson had no independent existence. He was unknown to the public, almost unknown to his colleagues, a mere agent for the prime minister, and had to call in Churchill when any grave decision was taken. Indeed, all the ministers except Bevin were in practice Churchill's instruments. All the committees, military and civil, acted ultimately at his direction and submitted to his verdicts. Churchill was a good committee-man, even when he growled against the system. Unlike Lloyd George, he did his work on paper. Even his speeches were either read or memorized beforehand. He ran the war with a flow of 'chits', provoking memoranda, to which he made further written replies. At meetings he did not discuss. He harangued, and others contributed by listening, patiently or not, to his monologues.

of the Defence Committee (Supply) declined from 18 in 1940 to 8 in 1944. The chiefs of staff, on the other hand, had more than 400 meetings each year and in 1942, 573. Ehrman, *Grand Strategy*, vi. 325, 331.

[1] Home policy, abolished 1942; food policy, abolished 1942 (both under Attlee); production council, abolished 1941; economic policy, abolished 1941 (both under Greenwood); civil defence, under Anderson. A production executive was substituted for the production council from 1941 to 1942 and then abolished in its turn.

[2] Wheeler-Bennett, *George VI*, 545.

Churchill has described his method in an engaging phrase: 'All I wanted was compliance with my wishes after reasonable discussion.'[1] This applied even to the war cabinet. In theory it was supreme. In practice, its decisions were prepared by Churchill or some committee, and it was invoked only to give a final ring of authority, much as the Jacobin deputies on mission spoke 'in the name of the republic' during the French revolution. Lloyd George's war cabinet had been a true committee of public safety, running all great affairs in common. Churchill's war cabinet rarely initiated, and overruled him even more rarely. Indeed, it is difficult to discover from the record[2] what the war cabinet did during the war except, like the abbé Siéyès, keep alive. Churchill carried the war on his shoulders. These shoulders were broad. But the burden was excessive. Churchill provided political inspiration and leadership. He determined strategy and settled the disputed questions in home policy. Later in the war he conducted the diplomatic relations with the great allies and sometimes with the small ones as well. Not content with this, he concerned himself in every triviality from the size of the jam ration to the spelling of foreign place-names. He never drew breath. In this turmoil of activity he made some great mistakes and many small ones. The wonder is that he did not make more. No other man could have done what he did, and with a zest which rarely flagged.

Events thrust on Churchill far greater power and responsibility than had been envisaged at the time of his accession. The Norwegian fiasco, which brought Chamberlain down, was after all a comparatively trivial affair—not even a Gallipoli, let alone a threat of total defeat. That came soon afterwards, and it was Hitler rather than the British people who transformed Churchill into a dictator. In the early hours of 10 May German armies invaded Holland and Belgium without warning or excuse. The attack had been long prepared by the Germans and, by the allies, long expected. Hitler feared that Holland and Belgium, with their frontiers as much undefended on the German as on the French side, would give the Allies an easy road to the Ruhr, heart of industrial Germany—a road for

[1] Churchill, *Second World War*, iv. 78.

[2] The qualification is important. While the work of most departments has been described by official historians, that of the war cabinet remains shrouded by secrecy, presumably until the opening of the archives by the thirty-year rule in 1970–5. Thus secrecy, as often happens, injures those whom it is supposed to protect.

bombing aircraft if not for armies. His original intention in
October 1939 was to overrun the two countries and so close the
road. He planned to attack on the extreme right, according to
the Schlieffen model, and then to swing left, thus meeting the
Allied armies head-on. Gradually his plan changed. Hitler now
put his main weight in the centre, where the Maginot line gave
out. There he would break through the French defences and
go straight to the sea. Holland and Belgium would be cut off
from Allied help. Hitler did not foresee that the main fighting
strength of the Allies would be cut off also and that he would
win the war in the west at one blow. He collected more gains
than he had expected, as he had often done before, now for the
last time.

The Allies had puzzled, since before the war, what to do
about Holland and Belgium. The obvious course was to concert
defence with them beforehand. But the governments of the
two countries refused to depart from their neutrality. The
Allies threatened to refuse all aid and could not enforce their
threat. There was, for one thing, an obligation of honour.
The Great Powers, Great Britain and France, who had promised to aid Poland and had tried to aid Norway, could not
turn away from small countries on their very doorstep. Gamelin,
the supreme commander, had practical motives also. An advance into Belgium would shorten the Allied front and so save
manpower. Joining up with the Belgian and Dutch armies would
redress the Allied inferiority against Germany still further.[1] The
issue was never properly debated by the Allied supreme council.
Gamelin's authority was unquestioned. Gort raised no objection, and the British government therefore acquiesced also.
Gamelin made another fateful decision. His reserve army, with
the heaviest armour, was on the extreme left of the Allied front
between the B.E.F. and the sea. He resolved to send it forward
into Holland, and again no one questioned his decision. Great
Britain and France paid bitterly for this civilian loyalty to
the supreme commander.[2]

[1] In May 1940 the Germans had 134 divisions on the western front. The French
had 94, the British 10. The Belgians had 22, the Dutch 8, the Poles 1—a total of
135 if they had cooperated effectively and had all been equipped at full strength.
Both French and Germans had about 2,500 tanks. Butler, *Grand Strategy*, ii. 177.

[2] Some authorities, such as Churchill and Montgomery, lament the advance of
the B.E.F. from its prepared defences. Others, such as Kennedy and Ellis, believe
that it would have been cut off there by the Germans and unable to retreat to the
coast. These speculations cannot be resolved.

On 10 May the Allies duly advanced into Holland and Belgium. They could do nothing for Holland. The Dutch army capitulated on 15 May. Queen Wilhelmina set up her government in England. The Dutch East Indies and merchant marine were added to British resources. The Germans bombed Rotterdam during the offensive and killed many civilians. The British, in return, felt free to attack industrial targets and on 15 May bombed the Ruhr. The strategic air offensive, far removed from the field of military operations, thus casually began. In Belgium the Allies at first held their own. Then on 14 May the Germans broke through at Sedan. The French had no reserve with which to oppose them. Within five days the Germans took Amiens and reached the sea at Abbeville. The Allied forces in Belgium were cut off. Gamelin and the French government watched this advance with helpless dismay. Reynaud appealed for more British aeroplanes, and Churchill agreed. Dowding resisted successfully, though only after appearing in person at the war cabinet and threatening to resign.[1] In any case, the Germans soon overran the airfields from which fighters could work, and the British, in their obsession with independent bombing, had no tactical bombers, such as the French really needed.

On 16 May Churchill went to Paris. Gamelin explained the situation with cool detachment: the French had no strategic reserve; the Germans would be in Paris within a few days. Churchill urged a combined attack on the flanks of the German corridor. Gamelin agreed and did nothing. Three days later he was replaced by Weygand, Foch's old assistant, who postponed action still further while he surveyed the situation. On 19 May the British government learnt that Gort was preparing to retreat to the sea. Ironside, still C.I.G.S., was sent over with the firm order that Gort should attack southwards towards Amiens. Gort explained that, with seven out of his nine divisions engaged against the Germans on the Schelde, a southern offensive was impossible. Ironside agreed with him. Gort thus initiated the end of the Anglo-French alliance and saved the British army.

Weygand produced belated plans for a combined offensive.

[1] When argument failed, Dowding laid down his pencil on the cabinet table. This gentle gesture was a warning of immeasurable significance. The war cabinet cringed, and Dowding's pencil won the battle of Britain.

Churchill, once more in Paris, endorsed them on 22 May. No action followed: Weygand's offensives existed only on paper. By 25 May Gort had abandoned any attempt to cooperate with the imaginary strategy of the supreme commander.[1] On 27 May the British government, too, faced reality: Gort was told that his sole task was 'to evacuate the maximum force possible'. This seemed a hard order. On one British flank Calais had fallen after resisting stubbornly. On the other, the Belgian forces capitulated in the early hours of 28 May.[2] 'Operation Dynamo'—the evacuation from Dunkirk—began on 27 May, though on that day only 7,000 men were moved. Churchill warned the country to prepare for 'hard and heavy tidings'.

Operation Dynamo succeeded beyond all expectation. The forces of fighter command were thrown in without reserve and tempered the weight of German bombing on the beaches. Destroyers, which brought off most of the men, were aided by every sort of vessel—pleasure boats, river ferries, fishing smacks. Altogether 860 ships took part. As a further advantage, the weather was uniformly benign. On 31 May Gort, as his force shrank, handed over to General Alexander,[3] the senior divisional commander, in accordance with orders.[4] On 3 June the last men were moved. In all, 338,226 men were brought to England from Dunkirk, of whom 139,097 were French. Dunkirk was a great deliverance and a great disaster. Almost the entire

---

[1] On 23 May the German armour to the south of the British halted. Why it did so is a problem in German, not in British, history. Some have blamed the commanding general, Rundstedt; others have blamed Hitler. Perhaps it was a combination of both. The Germans had not gauged the extent of the French collapse and wished to husband their strength for further battles. They were made apprehensive of loss by a combat against the British armoured brigade at Arras on 21 May. Goering claimed that the *Luftwaffe* could destroy the British forces at Dunkirk without assistance from the land forces. Hitler is also alleged to have treated the British gently in preparation for a compromise peace. There is no evidence for this. It probably did not occur to him that they would fight on if France were defeated. On 23 May the British army seemed hopelessly done for, and the decision to halt the armour took on significance only when the British got away.

[2] King Leopold, unlike Queen Wilhelmina and other rulers, remained in his country. The Belgian government disavowed him and came to London, bearing with them the riches of the Congo.

[3] Harold Leofric George Alexander (1891–   ), field marshal; commanded 1st division, 1938–40; Southern Command, 1940–2; Burma Command, 1942; Commander-in-Chief, Middle East, 1942–3, North Africa, 1943, Allied Armies in Italy, 1943–4; Supreme Allied Commander, Mediterranean, 1944–5; cr. Viscount, 1946, Earl, 1952.

[4] Gort was governor of Gibraltar 1941–2, and of Malta 1942–4.

B.E.F. was saved.[1] It had lost virtually all its guns, tanks, and other heavy equipment. Many of the men had abandoned their rifles. Six destroyers had been sunk and nineteen damaged. The R.A.F. had lost 474 aeroplanes.

The rest of the French campaign was little more than an epilogue. The French had only fifty divisions left with which to hold the line of the Somme. On 31 May, when Churchill again went to Paris, he found Weygand and Marshal Pétain, who had joined Reynaud's government, already talking of an armistice. Churchill insisted that in any case Great Britain would fight on. The British government did what they could to sustain French spirit. Two divisions were all that remained of British fighting strength. They were sent to France under General Sir Alan Brooke. He soon grasped that the French campaign was over, and on 14 June was authorized to act independently. Fog prevented evacuation from St. Valery, where the 51st division was lost on 12 June. The rest of the British forces were brought successfully away, and 20,000 Poles with them.[2] It was almost precisely four years before British troops were on French soil again.

Meanwhile Churchill was repeatedly called over by Reynaud (on 11 June, 13 June, and for an abortive meeting on 17 June). The discussion was no longer on resistance, despite futile appeals for American aid. Weygand and Pétain wished to conclude an armistice; Reynaud hoped somehow to stave this off. The overriding British concern was that the French fleet should not fall into German hands. In the hugger-mugger this was never put properly to the French. On 16 June, when the French government were deliberating at Bordeaux, a stern message was sent demanding that their fleet should go to British ports. At the last moment this message was withdrawn, and there went instead a proposal for indissoluble union of the two countries—a single government, common citizenship, and associated parliaments.[3] The proposal was poorly received

[1] The total casualties of the British army during the French campaign of May–June 1940 were 68,111.

[2] 191,800 men were brought to Great Britain from the area between the Somme and Bordeaux; 144,000 of these were British—some from the force under Brooke, more of them men who had been serving in the rear of the B.E.F. (transport, administration, communications, medical). The grand total of men brought back to Great Britain during the battle of France was 558,032, of whom 368,491 were British.

[3] The proposal was drafted by Vansittart, de Gaulle, and Jean Monnet, the

by the French, who saw in it only a humiliating offer of Dominion status. Reynaud resigned. Pétain formed a government and at once asked the Germans for an armistice, which was concluded on 22 June. Northern France and all her coastline down to the Pyrenees fell under German occupation. Great Britain now faced a hostile continent, the more so as Italy, fearful of being too late for the spoils, declared war on 11 June.

The British people remained unruffled. The historically minded remembered the long years when Great Britain had stood alone against Napoleon, whereas the French, recalling 1814, 1815, and 1871, had assumed that an armistice of surrender must follow defeat in the field. Dunkirk brought a misleading confidence: after the early forecasts of disaster, nearly all the expeditionary force had been saved. The old faith in sea power and the moated island were not forgotten in an hour. No doubt many went on with their routine tasks and would have acquiesced in a compromise peace as quietly as they acquiesced in continued resistance. Still, a considerable number went on record, and the record is consistent: a simple, human feeling that the British, or some of them, had rebuked others for failing to resist Hitler and that it was now up to the British to do better. Few at first supposed that Great Britain could actually win the war. Not many perhaps supposed that she could even hold out. Very many wanted to try. Churchill expressed the spirit of the hour. He had not been rated highly before the war as a radio speaker. His resonant voice and rotund phrases were out of keeping with the fashionable radio undertones. But the prime minister had obviously to deliver some messages over the air in the dark days of May and June 1940, and Churchill repeated there speeches which he had given to the house of commons earlier in the day.

His speeches succeeded, to the surprise of experts. They were rhetorical and cheeky at the same time, Macaulay and contemporary slang mixed together, much as Churchill sometimes wore a Victorian frock-coat and more often an extremely practical siren-suit reminiscent of a child's 'rompers'.[1] Churchill was no longer a radical, if he ever had been. He was an eccentric, which exactly suited the mood of the British people.

French economic expert, who later devised the Common Market. Churchill accepted it without much enthusiasm or faith.

[1] These suits had been devised for the use of wardens during air raids. The siren was the warning that hostile aircraft were approaching.

They welcomed his romantic utterances, though themselves still speaking in more prosaic tones. Their formidable enemy was diminished into 'little old Hitler'—a figure of contempt or even of fun. Churchill did not speak alone. J. B. Priestley, the novelist, commanded almost as large an audience on the air, and his speeches were more representative in their cheerful understatements, more representative also in their assumption that a people's war would be followed by a people's peace.

The continuance of the war was never formally debated. On 27 May, after the war cabinet had rejected a French idea of making concessions to Italy, Halifax speculated what answer they should give if Hitler offered reasonable terms of peace. Churchill said that this was unlikely, and there was no further discussion. However he took precautions that the discussion should not be renewed. On 28 May he met all ministers of cabinet rank and, after surveying the situation, remarked casually: 'Of course, whatever happens at Dunkirk, we shall fight on.' Ministers shouted: 'Well done, prime minister.' Some burst into tears. Others slapped Churchill on the back.[1] This was the nearest approach to a discussion or a decision. On 19 July Hitler offered peace in a public speech.[2] Churchill wished to put down formal motions of rejection in both houses of parliament. Chamberlain and Attlee advised against this,[3] and Halifax was appropriately given the task of brushing Hitler's offer aside on the radio. A few days later, Churchill sent out a general instruction which defined British war aims until the end of the war. There must be total victory or, put the other way round, unconditional surrender. The Germans must relinquish all their gains and give 'effective guarantees by deeds, not words' that nothing of the kind would ever happen again, before Great Britain would condescend to negotiate with them.[4]

[1] Churchill, *Second World War*, ii. 88. Dalton, *The Fateful Years*, 336. Dalton gives a different and less probable version of Churchill's remark.

[2] Hitler, though 'recognizing' the British empire, proposed to collect Irak and Egypt for himself. He also played with the idea of restoring the duke of Windsor and looked forward to Hoare or perhaps Lloyd George as prime minister.

[3] Their ostensible reason was that a formal motion was 'making too much fuss about it'. Perhaps also they did not want to draw attention to it. Hitler was treated at this time as a devil or a joke. Either interpretation ruled out any thought of doing business with him.

[4] Churchill defined the British terms on 3 Aug. (*Second World War*, ii. 231): 'effective guarantees by deeds, not words, . . . from Germany which would ensure the restoration of the free and independent life of Czechoslovakia, Poland, Norway, Denmark, Holland, Belgium, and above all France, as well as the effectual security of Great Britain and the British Empire in a general peace'. A German request for

The British government, and presumably the British people, did not waver from these terms in good times or bad.

This may be judged inspiring, arrogant, or merely inevitable in the circumstances of mid-summer 1940, when the British were also debating whether they could survive the next few weeks. On 27 May the chiefs of staff submitted a prosaic estimate. They expected Hitler to attempt a serious invasion. The British navy, they reported, could not hold up an invasion indefinitely without air support; the land forces were not strong enough to repel the Germans if they were once securely ashore. 'The crux is air superiority'; and, while Dowding regarded his front-line strength as adequate, the chiefs of staff feared that German bombing might cripple the factories on which the R.A.F. depended.[1] As usual, the service advisers exaggerated the effects of bombing—German as much as their own.

More aircraft were clearly the crying need, and Beaverbrook, as minister of aircraft production, was the man of the moment. He produced aircraft as he had previously produced newspapers. He appointed new men; inspired them by personal direction over the telephone; and planned only in the sense of setting goals almost impossible to attain. 'Action This Day' was his constant message. He tore up the previous schemes for the methodical expansion of a balanced air force and aimed to turn out fighters there and then. He enforced priority against the claims of other departments and laid hands on the accumulating stock of spare parts, 'cannibalizing' them into aircraft. As one historian has put it, 'The flood of Lord Beaverbrook's forceful, personal onset foamed against what he considered the obstruction of the Civil Service and the Air Marshals',[2] to which may be added another official verdict: 'The most spectacular, as well as the most important, single incident in the history of war production was crowned with success.'[3] Beaverbrook no doubt disrupted civil service plans and retarded the growth of a great bomber force. But, thanks largely to him, fighter command had more aeroplanes when the battle of Britain ended than when it started.

an armistice would be considered only when these guarantees, 'by deeds', had been given. The terms thwarted in advance the later approaches from the so-called German resistance. These Germans wanted assurance of generous treatment for Germany before they would move against Hitler. The British attitude was always that Hitler must be overthrown and the conquered countries restored before any negotiation could take place.   [1] Churchill, *Second World War*, ii. 79.

[2] Butler, *Grand Strategy*, ii. 253.   [3] Postan, *British War Production*, 116.

Beaverbrook had an impact on the public also. He appealed for scrap metal. Gardens lost their iron railings; kitchens lost their aluminium pots and pans. Labour regulations were ignored. Men in the aircraft factories worked 10 hours a day seven days a week. Bevin counted for much in securing this new spirit of cooperation. He was determined to be the dictator of labour[1] and enforced this position throughout the war. He moved warily, resolved always not to use legal powers until labour opinion was ready for it. Men took long to grasp economic realities even in wartime and were more willing to sacrifice their lives than their standard of life. There were many instances of this. Kingsley Wood, now chancellor of the exchequer, imposed a purchase tax in July on most consumer goods. Labour members growled that the masses were being reduced to poverty and were little mollified by the raising of the income tax to 8s. 6d. Public finance remained feeble in this period of national inspiration. The deficit for the calendar year was £2,115 million. Earnings went up, unemployment disappeared, and the pressure of increased purchasing power was hardly checked by an answering increase in taxes. The financial battle was won only in 1941, not in 1940.

The British people were in too exalted a mood to be interested in increased taxation. On 18 June Churchill warned that a German attack was imminent and concluded: 'Let us therefore brace ourselves to our duties, and so bear ourselves that, if the British Empire and its Commonwealth last for a thousand years, men will still say: "This was their finest hour".' The public responded. Few of them grasped that the decision would lie with the air force and, in any case, there was little that any except factory workers could contribute to this. The British people wanted to do something dramatic themselves. With their heads full of what was supposed to have happened in the Low Countries and in France, they foresaw German tanks rolling over the country, aided by fifth-columnists and parachutists.[2] All German subjects in Great Britain were hastily interned, regardless of the fact that nearly all were Jewish refugees and most of the rest political opponents of the Nazis.[3] Some British

[1] One of his first acts was to take over factory inspectors from the home office.

[2] Parachutists played a part in the capture of Rotterdam. The fifth columnists, or traitors, were the products of heated imagination, as shown in de Jong, *The Fifth Column in Holland.*

[3] The suspicion of refugees had one strange result. When the war started, most British physicists were put on to radar, which was regarded as the most urgent and

Fascists and pro-Germans were interned also; they included Sir Oswald Mosley, his wife, and an M.P.[1] Elaborate precautions were taken to ensure that the invading Germans should not know where they were. Road signs and names of railway stations were removed. Place-names were painted out even on shop fronts. Booksellers destroyed their stocks of maps, though the Germans would presumably have had maps of their own and been able to read them.

An auxiliary force had been inaugurated at the beginning of the French campaign: at first known as the Local Defence Volunteers, soon receiving the more dignified title of the Home Guard. Over a million men enrolled by the summer of 1940. This provided a welcome activity for veterans of the first war. It had less value as a fighting force. There were few rifles to spare for it until the late summer and, even when these were issued, there was no ammunition. The Home Guard harassed innocent citizens for their identity cards; put up primitive road blocks, the traces of which may delight future archaeologists; and sometimes made bombs out of petrol tins. In a serious invasion, its members would presumably have been massacred if they had managed to assemble at all. Their spirit was willing though their equipment was scanty. Churchill proposed to launch the slogan: 'You can always take one with you' if the Germans landed. This policy of slaughter and destruction might have been applied. We cannot be sure.

Those in authority showed a misplaced lack of confidence in the British people. Grumblers were prosecuted for causing disaffection and discontent until Churchill put a stop to it. Duff Cooper, the minister of information, sent round investigators to probe public opinion (dismissed by those investigated as 'Cooper's snoopers') and sought to rouse the nation by reciting Macaulay's poem on the Armada over the radio. Some indications suggest that the fearful were themselves in high

also the most confidential task. Refugee scientists were excluded from this work and were thus free to continue their research in nuclear physics, which was not expected to have any practical application to the war. They discovered how to control a nuclear explosion—the vital step towards the atomic bomb. When the refugee scientists made this discovery, they were still forbidden to possess bicycles and had to obtain special permission from the local police when they went to London in order to report their discovery to the government's scientific advisers.

[1] Altogether 1,769 British subjects were interned, of whom 763 had been members of the British Union of Fascists; 1,106 were later released. Herbert Morrison, the home secretary, released the Mosleys in 1943, despite outcry from the extreme Left. Beaverbrook prompted this act, and Churchill applauded it.

places. The government attempted, reasonably enough, to send children from London's east end overseas. There was shipping space only for 2,664. Meanwhile 11,000 women and children from the richer classes went privately at their own expense. Members of the government and university professors sent their families on this unseemly scramble.[1] This flight, too, was stopped on Churchill's order. Three or four respectable citizens were secretly nominated in each district to keep life going under the invader, and it is impossible to tell how far they would have collaborated. The Germans found some local agents in every country they conquered. Maybe England would have been an exception, but the example of the Channel Islands is not encouraging. They were the only part of the king's dominions to fall under German occupation. About half the population was brought to England. The rest remained. The police and the administration continued to function throughout the war. The law courts still acted in the king's name, though on German orders, and at the liberation men who had been imprisoned for offences against the Germans were sent to complete their sentences in Winchester jail.[2] It was perhaps fortunate that British patriotism was not put to the supreme test.

The Germans did not come with an immediate rush as had been expected. Hitler was taken unawares by his own success. He had made no preparations for invading England and waited a month or so after the fall of France before deciding what to do next. Meanwhile the British government strove to consolidate their position both for the impending struggle and for more distant campaigns. Their most urgent anxiety was over the French fleet. Its powerful battleships would turn the balance at sea against the Royal Navy if used on the enemy side. The armistice provided that the French ships were to be disarmed under German and Italian control and would not be used by the Germans during the war. The French commanders had received secret instructions to sink their ships rather than let them fall into German hands. This was unknown to the British.

[1] The royal family set a spotless example. The queen said: 'The children can't go without me. I can't leave the King, and of course the King won't go.' The king practised revolver-shooting in the grounds of Buckingham Palace and intended to die there fighting.

[2] The offences were, of course, ordinary criminal acts, especially smuggling. But while the Germans ruled, all crimes were acts of resistance.

Germany's word seemed their only security, and this was not a security which they valued.

The war cabinet resolved that the French fleet must be put out of action. Churchill has called this 'a hateful decision, the most unnatural and painful in which I have ever been associated'.[1] The French ships in British ports and, after some negotiation, at Alexandria were reduced after a short struggle. The main force at Mers-el-Kebir (Oran) was more obdurate. The French officers resented the implied slur on their honour. They resented also the British patronage of an insubordinate officer, Charles de Gaulle, who was attempting to recreate 'Free France' from London. The British admiral, Sir James Somerville, disliked the operation almost as much and, in his trouble, failed to make clear the possible alternative of removing the ships to American waters. Orders from London were implacable, and on 3 July Somerville destroyed two French battleships and a battlecruiser, with considerable loss of life among their crews. The French were understandably bitter at this attack and broke off diplomatic relations, though they did not declare war. In November 1942 the French duly sank their remaining ships when the Germans moved into unoccupied France, and the terrible affair at Oran was then criticized as unnecessary. The event could not be foreseen in July 1940. The British government strengthened their sea power by ruthless means and showed to the world that they would stop at nothing in their defiance of Hitler. It was unfortunate that the demonstration was made at the cost of their former ally. The British people certainly approved. When Churchill announced the action at Oran in the house of commons, he received full-throated applause from the Conservative benches for the first time. 'All joined in solemn stentorian accord.'[2]

The British were acquiring new allies while losing an old one. The governments of Poland, Norway, Luxembourg, Holland, and Belgium were on British soil, bringing with them fighting men, financial resources, and 3 million tons of shipping. On 3 July Beneš, the former president, was recognized as head of a provisional Czechoslovak government.[3] General de Gaulle, though not the head of a government, was organizing a Free

---

[1] Churchill, *Second World War*, ii. 206. [2] Ibid. 211.

[3] The British government did not, however, repudiate the Munich agreement until Aug. 1942.

French movement, on which the British at first pinned exaggerated hopes. The Dominions were inspired by British determination,[1] though they had as yet little to offer. Great Britain turned also to the two great neutrals, Soviet Russia and the United States. Cripps was sent to Moscow as ambassador, in the mistaken belief that a Left-wing socialist would get on well with Communists. Stalin explained frankly that he expected a German attack in 1941 and meant to keep out of trouble as long as he could.[2] There was nothing more to be done here.

Churchill's thoughts were set from the first moment on the United States, arsenal of democracy.[3] He had begun a private correspondence with President Roosevelt while at the admiralty, and this personal approach, now greatly expanded, became the vital channel for Anglo-American relations throughout the war.[4] The relations were one-sided from the start. The British might take the view that defence of freedom was a common cause. In fact Great Britain was at war and a suitor for American assistance. The United States were neutral and anxious to remain so, though alarmed at the prospect of German victory. Roosevelt himself doubted at first whether Great Britain could survive and tried to extract an assurance that the Royal Navy would be sent across the Atlantic if the German invasion succeeded. Even when he grew more confident, he doubted whether he could carry his people into war and perhaps did not wish to do so.

The British had to convince Americans that they could fight on. They had further to show that for this they needed American assistance. The American government were still bound by the cash and carry legislation: the British could take away in their own ships armaments and other goods which they bought

[1] The Dominions were not altogether in line. Some of their governments had wished to reply in a conciliatory way to Hitler's peace offer in Oct. 1939. Canada maintained diplomatic relations with Pétain's government at Vichy. Australia and New Zealand were anxious that the security of the Far East should not be jeopardized for the sake of Egypt.

[2] Langer and Gleason, The Challenge to Isolation, 644.

[3] The arsenal was potential, not actual. American industry was not yet geared for war production and, even when it developed, the demands of the American services increasingly took priority. As with Great Britain earlier, it was difficult to grasp that a great industrial power could not produce armaments overnight.

[4] The correspondence had also the advantage for Churchill that, being private, it escaped the restrictions of the Official Secrets Act and so provided him with the principal material for the six volumes of his Second World War.

with their own money. Ships were not yet a problem. Money was: the cherished reserves of dollars and saleable securities would not stretch far. The British could only gamble that something would turn up. Churchill cancelled the previous restrictions on spending dollars and wrote to Roosevelt on 15 May: 'We shall go on spending dollars for as long as we can, but I should like to feel reasonably sure that when we can pay no more you will give us the stuff all the same.'

This was easier said than done. Roosevelt hesitated to take any decisive action before the presidential election in November. The British had to plunge on without regard to the future. Arthur Purvis, a Canadian businessman, headed their purchasing commission in Washington and gradually brought the chaotic orders of the rival services under some control. He took over at a moment's notice all the contracts which the French had previously placed in the United States—a commitment of £650 million.[1] Purvis was a negotiator of genius and stood in the first rank among British makers of victory until his death in August 1941. But he could not accomplish miracles, though he came near to it. Orders were one thing, deliveries another. American industry was not equipped for war, and British money went largely into building factories, not into buying aeroplanes or tanks. This washed still further back: the new factories increasingly absorbed the machine tools which the British would have liked for themselves. The outcome was ironic. The expenditure of British treasure served to rearm the United States rather than to strengthen Great Britain.[2] Roosevelt found one loophole. He could certify some arms as 'surplus to American requirements' and transfer them to Great Britain. This provided half a million rifles for the Home Guard. The British also wanted fifty over-age destroyers and got them in September, after a complicated swap allowing American bases in the British West Indies and Newfoundland. Only nine entered service before 1941. Like much else, the destroyers were a gesture of sympathy, promising great things in the future. The Americans had virtually nothing to provide for the present. Great Britain faced the immediate peril on her own.

[1] Not all the orders matured. The British finally spent some £350 million under this head.

[2] Until the end of 1941 the Commonwealth had received only 7 per cent. of its munitions from American sources, despite an expenditure of nearly £1,000 million.

British defences improved somewhat during the weeks of waiting. Ironside, commanding the home forces,[1] started with fifteen divisions at half strength; his tanks were less than half the equivalent of one division. He planned defence in the old linear style and ran primitive anti-tank obstacles across southeast England.[2] Brooke, who took Ironside's place on 20 July, was more experienced in modern war. He pulled his forces back from the coast and intended to throw the Germans out by a counter-offensive, though this was probably asking too much of his ill-equipped divisions. The navy was overwhelmingly superior to the German and decided not to risk its capital ships unless heavy German units appeared; these, though the British did not know it, were out of action. Sea defence was left, fairly confidently, to light cruisers and destroyers.

Fighter command remained the decisive instrument. Dowding had fifty-five squadrons, a number which he regarded as adequate, and we now know that the Germans had little superiority in modern fighter aeroplanes. Dowding's worst shortage was in the reserve of trained pilots, not in aeroplanes, and this weighed on him as the battle proceeded. He had two invaluable assets. The first was radar. This chain was now in full working order and enabled the British pilots to take the air only when raiders were approaching instead of wearing themselves out on ceaseless patrols.[3] The second asset was himself. Like all great commanders, he had a clear picture of the battle which he was about to fight and of how he would win it. He and his subordinate Air Vice-Marshal Park, commanding No. 11 Group, were determined to husband their strength and to engage the Germans on favourable conditions. The highest authorities, including Churchill and the chief of the air staff, often prodded them towards more dramatic action. They remained firm. One historian has given this explanation of the British victory: 'Whereas Dowding and Park proved capable of standing up to men who wanted them to do the wrong things, their German counterparts proved incapable of standing up to Goering.'[4]

[1] Sir John Dill, a more competent soldier, succeeded Ironside as C.I.G.S. on 27 May.
[2] Some may still be seen, much overgrown, in the valley of the upper Thames.
[3] The Germans are commonly supposed not to have known about radar. This is incorrect. They knew and attached no importance to it.
[4] Collier, The Battle of Britain, 19.

On 16 July Hitler directed that preparations should go forward for invading Great Britain. The German generals proposed to land on a broad front from the North Foreland to Lyme bay.[1] Raeder, the German naval commander-in-chief, declared that he could support only a narrow landing around Beachy Head and demanded air superiority even for this. The generals ostensibly acquiesced, though they regarded Raeder's plan as a recipe for disaster and still accumulated forces for a landing in Lyme bay. Hitler tried to allay the generals' fears by an assurance that landing would take place only when air attack had worn down the British defences. Indeed, he sometimes supposed that the German forces would merely have to occupy a country which had already surrendered. Hitler, too, exaggerated the effects of bombing, and, like Goering, exaggerated the strength of the *Luftwaffe*, which had never yet encountered a serious enemy. The *Luftwaffe* was saddled with three tasks in ascending order of difficulty. The first, difficult enough, was to deprive the R.A.F. of air superiority, so that a landing would not be harassed by attack from the air. The second was to establish its own superiority so that it could batter the British army and navy. The third was to reduce Great Britain by air bombardment alone. The first might have been temporarily achieved if the *Luftwaffe* had concentrated on it. Muddle between the three aims, combined with Dowding's resolute strategy, brought complete failure.

The battle of Britain began, by British reckoning, on 10 July, by German on 13 August.[2] In the preliminary phase, the Germans attacked the convoys of merchant ships which the admiralty were still trying to send through the straits of Dover. Dowding was much pressed to throw in everything for their defence. He refused. The convoys had to be ended—seemingly a German victory. Against this the Germans had lost 300 aeroplanes, the British 150—and Dowding had received 500 new

[1] The British chiefs of staff at first expected German landings in East Anglia and set up there what defences they could. Many can still be seen. The East Anglian beaches were indeed the only ones suited for a large-scale invasion, but they were nearer to the Home Fleet at Scapa Flow, beyond the range of German air-cover, and, lacking sea power, the German generals could not face the long voyage. They chose the Channel, which they claimed was no more than an anti-tank ditch. As German preparations went forward, the British appreciated that East Anglia was not threatened and shifted their defences to the south coast.

[2] The first serious 'incident' was in fact reported from Cambridge on 19 June, when nine people were killed.

fighters from the factories. On 13 August the Germans began their full attack on south-east England with fleets of bombers protected by fighters. Dowding concentrated on destroying the bombers. By 18 August it was clear that the *Luftwaffe* could have no easy victory. The Germans had lost 236 aeroplanes against 95 British. They could not hope to secure air superiority until fighter command had been eliminated.

The Germans now adopted their most dangerous tactic. They set out to destroy the fighter bases in Kent and nearly succeeded. Losses were nearly equal (225 German and 185 British between 30 August and 6 September). Dowding had grave cause for anxiety. On 7 September there came a miraculous release. The Germans turned aside to bomb London. This was implicitly confession of defeat, though the *Luftwaffe* excused it with the argument that Dowding would have to use his fighters in the defence of London. Besides, Hitler was now in a hurry: he wanted to bring about the collapse of British spirit before unfavourable autumn weather made invasion impossible. He had a more immediate motive. On 25 August the British began the night-bombing of German towns, including Berlin, and Hitler felt that he must retaliate for the sake of his prestige.[1] The German bombing of London disrupted civilian life and caused many casualties. But it saved the Kent air fields.

The British believed that the crisis had come. They knew that hundreds of barges had been accumulated along the hostile coasts. They calculated correctly that tide and moon made invasion possible only during the next few days. By an odd mischance, the chiefs of staff had no means for ordering the army to 'instant readiness'. They had only the signal 'Cromwell', which meant 'invasion imminent', and this was sent out at 8.7 p.m. on 7 September. The Home Guard stood to arms. In some districts church bells were rung—the sign that the Germans were already here. Then nothing happened. The German invaders never came. The *Luftwaffe* made its last great effort on 15 September, the day now traditionally associated with British victory. The British lost 26 aeroplanes, the Germans between 56 and 60. The pride of the British public was swollen by the mistaken claim that 185 German aeroplanes had been

---

[1] The British act, though a logical development of their strategy, was itself a retaliation for bombs dropped on London on 24 Aug. The German pilot concerned had dropped them against his orders.

destroyed.[1] Even the correct figure was enough: the *Luftwaffe* had not won air superiority. On 17 September Hitler postponed invasion 'until further notice'. On 12 October he cancelled it for the winter.

Some German preparations were maintained until March 1942, and the British kept up their defences, particularly with an enormously reinforced Home Guard, for long after that.[2] But 15 September was the moment of decision: Great Britain would not be brought down by military conquest. The fighter pilots received due acknowledgement. Churchill said what everyone felt: 'Never in the field of human conflict was so much owed by so many to so few.' One man was left out. Dowding had resisted Churchill successfully. He had offended some air marshals by his defensive strategy.[3] On 25 November 1940 Dowding was relieved of his command and passed into oblivion. Yet he was 'the only man who ever won a major fighter battle or ever will win one'.[4]

The war now took on a new shape. Germany and Great Britain were the only antagonists. Neither, it was clear, could strike a quick final blow against the other. The Germans could not invade Great Britain. The British had no forces with which to invade the continent. Both sides were driven back to attrition, with air power now seconding the previous weapon of blockade. This was a tall order. The Germans had hardly begun to develop their economic power for purposes of war and, as well, could draw on the resources of conquered Europe, to say nothing of the remaining neutrals, including Soviet Russia.[5] Great Britain was rapidly developing her economic mobilization, so much so that by 1941 her production of munitions greatly surpassed that of the Germans in many spheres, including

---

[1] Pilots on both sides naturally exaggerated their claims in the heat of combat. The British claimed to have destroyed 2,698 German aeroplanes during the battle of Britain and actually destroyed 1,733. The R.A.F. lost 915 aeroplanes. Fighter command had 656 aeroplanes on 10 July, and 665 on 25 September.

[2] In 1942 the Home Forces had 850,000 men, and the Home Guard numbered 1,600,000.

[3] His successor operated a daylight offensive over France which cost more pilots than the battle of Britain (426 pilots lost against 414), merely to keep a few hundred German pilots from the eastern front. He claimed to have killed 731 German pilots; it appeared after the war that the actual German loss was 103.

[4] Collier, *Battle of Britain*, 158.

[5] The conquered countries had to be supplied and kept down. Germany did her best business with the neutrals, Sweden and Switzerland, who, among other advantages, were safe from British air attack.

tanks and aeroplanes. She could draw on the resources of the outer world and had the fairly secure prospect that the industrial might of the United States would soon be freed for her from financial restrictions. Still she had a hard time to survive in the winter of 1940–1.

The Germans struck their most dramatic, though not their most dangerous, blow with night bombing, soon to be known in popular English parlance as 'the Blitz'.[1] This grew by accident out of Hitler's earlier attempt to secure immediate surrender and went on in retaliation for British bombing as much as for any other reason. It was an improvised affair. The Germans had no aeroplanes specifically designed for independent long-range bombing, no pilots trained for it (particularly at night), and no clear picture of what they were attempting to do. At first they concentrated on London which was bombed every night from 7 September to 2 November. Then they switched mainly to industrial centres in the provinces and finally to the western ports. 16 May 1941 saw the last heavy German attack—on Birmingham. Thereafter the *Luftwaffe* was busy preparing to cooperate with the army against Soviet Russia, and in England precautions against air raids became more of a burden than the air raids themselves.

At the outset the British were as ill-equipped for defence as the Germans were for attack. Their fighters were almost useless at night, and the anti-aircraft guns, too few in any case, nearly as ineffective. Techniques were gradually improved as the winter wore on. Physicists, sustained by Professor Lindemann, Churchill's personal adviser, invented radar assistance both for the fighters and the guns. When the Germans began to navigate by radio beams instead of by the stars, the British were already prepared to divert the beams, and many German bombs fell harmlessly in the open country.[2] The Germans erred by failing to repeat their attacks on a chosen target, such as Coventry. They could not bomb with any precision and thus failed, for instance, to destroy vital railway junctions. Most of all, their attack lacked weight. A major raid meant 100 tons of bombs. Three years later the British were dropping 1,600 tons a night on Germany—and even then not with decisive effect.

[1] Popular parlance was, of course, wrong. 'Blitz' was lightning war. This was the opposite.
[2] On 30 May 1941 Dublin was bombed, in mistake, it is said, for Belfast.

Fifty-seven raids brought 13,561 tons of bombs on London. Later the British often exceeded this total in a single week.

Still, the Blitz caused much destruction, particularly when the Germans turned from high explosive to incendiary bombs. Over three and a half million houses were damaged or destroyed. For every civilian killed, thirty-five were rendered homeless. The house of commons was destroyed;[1] Buckingham Palace was damaged. The City of London, the east end, and many provincial cities, with Coventry the most famous, were devastated. Often an observer could only tell by the line of the streets that houses and commercial buildings had once stood in the empty acres. The effect on production was less serious. The ministry of home security reported that 'effective damage has not been serious in relation to the national war effort'. Even in ravaged Coventry the factories were back to full production five days after the raid. Beaverbrook gave the order for dispersal of factories in October 1940 and, though this brought an immediate decline in production, it led later not only to greater security but also to much increased production when the older factories could be used as well. Loss of life, though much less than had been feared, was heavy enough. Some 30,000 people were killed during the Blitz, slightly more than half of them in London, and until September 1941 the enemy had killed more civilians than combatants.

Civilian morale had been Hitler's original target and was now the government's main anxiety. There was again evacuation from the great cities, this time voluntary and almost unplanned. About a third fewer people left London than on the outbreak of war. In the country as a whole about one million and a quarter moved. In the provinces many trekked into the country every night,[2] and the men returned for work in the morning. Londoners broke into the underground stations against official resistance and set up their nightly abode there—often for the duration of the war. They were, of course, a minority—one in seven of the population; six Londoners out of ten slept at home even during the worst days of the Blitz. Much was done to raise their spirits. Churchill or the king was usually on the scene after a severe air raid, and on 23 September

[1] The commons moved to the house of lords, and the lords to Church House, Westminster.

[2] Thus 50,000 left Plymouth each night after its heavy raid.

George VI instituted the George Cross for deeds of civil bravery. Herbert Morrison, who succeeded Anderson as home secretary in October, gave a firm lead. To answer the incendiary bombs, he ordered compulsory fire-watching of commercial and other buildings previously left unguarded at night. The fire brigades, previously under local control, were reorganized as the National Fire Service.[1] Moreover, evacuation was itself a disguised welfare scheme, and the most dangerous period of the war became paradoxically the most fruitful for social policy. The standard of school meals was raised; cheap milk was instituted for children and expectant mothers; vitamins and cod-liver oil became part of their ration (though only 49 per cent. of those entitled took them up).

The unshaken spirit of the British people may be inferred from two examples. In December 1940 the I.L.P. members of parliament brought forward a motion for a negotiated peace. It was rejected by 341 votes to 4. In January 1941 the Communist party summoned a 'People's Convention', ostensibly to demand better air-raid shelters, really to agitate against the war. Morrison banned the *Daily Worker*, and not a dog barked.[2] The most stalwart members of the party were busy as air-raid wardens or instructing the Home Guard in guerrilla warfare.[3] Of course the raids caused much suffering and hardship.[4] In the long term they cemented national unity. They were a powerful solvent of class antagonism and ensured, too, that

[1] All the anti-air-raid services started by voluntary recruitment. All were gradually 'frozen', i.e. their members were not allowed to resign: the police and firemen on 20 June 1940; rescue and first-aid parties on 9 July; air-raid wardens in October; part-timers on 22 Jan. 1942. Later these services got members by compulsion, though this power was used mainly to resist the claims of industry and of the armed forces.

[2] The house of commons approved the ban by 297 votes to 11.

[3] The banning of the *Daily Worker* proved an undesigned blessing for the British Communist party. Unlike the American party, it escaped the embarrassment of actually opposing the war right up to the day on which Hitler attacked Soviet Russia.

[4] Only the direct effects of the raids were recorded: deaths, injuries, destruction of houses and public buildings. Their indirect effects cannot be estimated. Some people went mad; health was affected, as may be seen in the increase, for example, of tuberculosis; statesmen, staff officers, and civil servants had to do their work in unfavourable conditions. Many government offices went underground, with bad lighting and ventilation. Others had no windows and little heating. Travel was difficult to and from work, and there was a shortage of public eating places. An uninterrupted night's rest was possible only for those who could go to the country at weekends. None of this can be set down in figures or percentages.

there was none of the hostility between fighting men and civilians which had characterized the first World war. The fading of the Blitz inspired a mistaken feeling that Hitler had shot his bolt, and English people believed that, by showing that they 'could take it', they were already on the way to winning the war.

The German attack at sea though less sensational than the air raids, presented in fact a graver threat to British survival. Here, too, the Germans were badly prepared. At the outset of war they had only twenty-two ocean-going U-boats and few trained crews. Hitler did not authorize new construction until July 1940 and cut it down again in December when the army prepared to attack Soviet Russia. The *Luftwaffe* had not been trained to attack ships nor to cooperate with submarines. The big surface ships, though extremely effective as commerce-raiders, were regarded by Hitler as precious possessions, and he pulled them home after short periods at sea. Against this, the Germans had a great geographical advantage which they did not possess in the first World war: they could operate from the French Atlantic ports and so could strike far out into the ocean. The British had a corresponding disadvantage: the former naval bases in southern Ireland were now closed to them, and the government of Eire remained implacably neutral, despite much British and even American prodding. The British had other weaknesses. The French had betrayed that most prized equipment, asdic, to the Germans. It could not detect a vessel on the surface. The U-boats therefore shadowed a convoy by day and attacked on the surface at night. The British remained acutely short of destroyers for convoy work until the end of 1943. Moreover, fear of the German surface ships meant that a battleship had to accompany important convoys. The air ministry, set on bombing Germany, grudged supplying aeroplanes for coastal command and agreed even more reluctantly that this command should be put operationally under naval direction. Every now and then, during the worst moments of the shipping war, the war cabinet intervened on the naval side; in no time at all, the air ministry pulled things back to their standing obsession of the strategic bombing offensive.

This was not the only strategical obsession. Convoy, though the most effective way of bringing in ships and even the most effective way of destroying U-boats, seemed unenterprising and defensive. Churchill, often seconded by the admiralty, wanted more aggressive methods. Destroyers were encouraged to leave their convoys for a futile hunt after U-boats, and bomber command complained, this time rightly, when it was diverted to attacks on the submarine bases in France. The attacks killed many Frenchmen. Many British aeroplanes and pilots were lost. One U-boat was destroyed by these attacks in the whole course of the war. The British gradually learnt their lesson. The Americans insisted on learning it all over again for themselves when they were drawn into the war. The conflict at sea had no neat beginning and end as the Blitz had. It went on with ups and downs throughout the war. It reached its first peak between March and July 1941, the period when Churchill proclaimed 'the battle of the Atlantic'. In April alone nearly 700,000 tons of shipping were sunk. By the autumn the immediate crisis was overcome.

The reduction in sinkings had many causes. The greatest was convoy which became increasingly successful as the protecting ships and the aeroplanes of coastal command learnt to work closely together. Sinkings were pushed away from British ports out into the Atlantic. There the U-boats encountered a new enemy, the American navy, which extended its patrols on Roosevelt's orders. In June 1941 the Americans took over the garrisoning of Iceland, which the British had occupied in the previous year. In September the Americans had their first engagement with a U-boat. Hitler averted his eyes from these unneutral acts. These measures would have been useless without the unbroken spirit of the merchant seamen. Over 30,000 lost their lives in the course of the war,[1] and they deserved the tribute paid to them in 1942: 'Morale has so far not been affected, and the only thing one can say with conviction on the subject is that it is admirable and indeed wonderful.'[2]

In May 1941 the home fleet had its most substantial engagement of the old sort. The German battleship *Bismarck*, of 45,000 tons, was the most heavily armoured ship afloat. Accompanied by the heavy cruiser *Prinz Eugen*, she broke out into the Atlantic. The entire home fleet put to sea against her and called on the resources of Gibraltar as well. The *Bismarck* justified her

---

[1] Behrens, *Merchant Shipping*, 184. Miss Behrens calculates that the true total, including deaths indirectly due to the war, should be 50,525.

[2] Deputy-Director-General of Ministry of War Transport. Ibid. 176.

power. On the first contact she damaged the battleship *Prince of Wales* and sank the battlecruiser *Hood* which blew up at the fifth salvo. Though also damaged in her oil supply, the *Bismarck* broke away from the British ships converging upon her and vanished into the Atlantic. There was gloom at the admiralty. The *Bismarck* seemed on the track of a large convoy. At the very least she would escape to a French port. She was found again on 26 May by aircraft from the *Ark Royal* and damaged by their torpedoes. The next morning the big British ships closed and finished her off. This was a great relief. The Germans had only one battleship left, the *Tirpitz*, and she was never put to full use. There were less cheerful points on the other side. The *Hood* had been lost from exactly the same defect as had been shown by British ships at Jutland nearly thirty years before. The might of the British navy would have failed without the aeroplanes of the *Ark Royal*. British sea power appeared to be restored. In reality, the sinking of the *Bismarck* gave a disregarded warning that sea power in the old style was drawing to an end.

Destruction by air raids and losses at sea were not the only causes of economic difficulty. The railways, too, faced crisis in the winter of 1940-1. They had to carry more and different traffic over different routes and were not equipped to do so. Actual bomb damage was the least of their worries; indeed, it caused less dislocation than the air-raid warnings which accompanied it. The long-threatened shift of imports to the western ports now took place, and the disregarded bottlenecks soon made themselves felt. The railways had to handle freights such as frozen meat and steel, for which they had little proper equipment.[1] The ministry of supply laid its hands on far more wagons than it really needed. Coal traffic was the greatest burden. The east coast and the Channel were closed, and the railways had to provide south-east England with the coal which had previously come by coastal steamers. On top of this, passengers used the railways more as private motoring was cut down. The Severn Tunnel was congested with the coal from South Wales and the industrial traffic to it. The Thames bridges, endangered by air raids, were in any case too few for the new

---

[1] Crude steel could be carried only in special long wagons, of which there were few. The monthly average of steel imports between Sept. and Dec. 1940 was 1,163,000 tons against 50,000 tons prewar.

demands. As well, England paid a heavy price for maintaining four independent railway systems, with inadequate links between them, particularly between Lancashire and Yorkshire and in the Midlands at Banbury and Rugby. Loaded wagons accumulated at the ports or near them, and every such wagon meant further delays in unloading.

Thus bombs, blockade, and strain on the railways brought accumulating shortage. At the same time there was increased demand, as British industry set out to produce aeroplanes and equipment for a great army. As well, the people had to be kept reasonably fit and cheerful. All this produced a revolution in British economic life, until in the end direction and control turned Great Britain into a country more fully socialist than anything achieved by the conscious planners of Soviet Russia. The process was in one sense easy. No one now believed that *laissez faire* was the best method of conducting a war, or even a possible one. British industrialists had got into the habit during the interwar years of turning to the state when they ran into difficulties and now welcomed control for increased production as they had previously done for restriction. The workers did not feel this time that they were being exploited for a bosses' war. They, too, were ready for sacrifice, though they expected a policy of 'fair shares' and, on the whole, got it. War socialism was socialism by consent, that is to say, socialism with the difficulties left out.

The administration of war socialism was vastly more efficient than it had been during the first World war. Then everything had been improvised at random. Now most plans had been laid years before, even if some had not been laid right. Moreover, in the first World war there had been a three-way pull: the established civil servants; the recruits from business; and the intellectuals, mostly university teachers. The three groups had little in common and fought domestic wars against each other. Now administration was in the hands of much the same three groups, with the addition this time of trade union officials. But they were no longer at odds. They had grown closer during the interwar years. The civil servants had experience of working with industry and had encountered modern ideas, especially in economics. The businessmen were no longer pirates, with the exception of Beaverbrook and the few men he brought in personally. Most were managing directors of large companies, and it made little difference to them when they ran a government office instead of a business concern. Equally, the university teachers had studied practical affairs and had often taken part in them. Many had been parliamentary candidates, and many showed their contentment with the civil service by remaining permanently in it after the war. The union officials were skilled administrators, not class warriors. Thus there was a common doctrine and outlook, a readiness to use the same methods and to move towards the same conclusions, and a will to cooperate. Everywhere in England people no longer asked about a man's background, only what he was doing for the war. This was especially true in the civil service.[1]

The fighting services were also affected. The regulars were much less suspicious of the temporary officers than they had been during the first World war. The commanders recognized that they needed scientists and intellectuals to advise them. The R.A.F. in particular was always turning to the scientists for new devices, and the other services were not far behind. Mountbatten, when head of combined operations, relied on two scientists, J. D. Bernal and Solly Zuckerman, and sent them into the front line. Montgomery had a university teacher, E. T. Williams, as his chief Intelligence officer. Of course many mistakes were made. But by and large the second World war was as well arranged on the British side as human intelligence could make it.

On the other hand, higher direction was still sporadic and chaotic. Plans for the future could not be worked out on precise estimates of either resources or requirements. The last census of production had been taken in 1935, and confusion was made worse by Churchill's private intelligence staff under Lindemann which often mistook assertive guesses for facts. The board of trade had no idea how many retail shops there were when it set out to regulate retail trade. In any case, the upheavals of war made much prewar information useless. Thirty-four million changes of address (often, of course, the same people) were recorded in England and Wales in the course of the war. Evacuees had new sorts of demands. So had the two million

[1] The numbers holding responsible positions were comparatively small. The top (administrative) grade had just over 2,000 members at the beginning of the war and just under 5,000 at the end. Non-industrial civil servants, excluding also the post office, were over 2 per cent. of the employed population in 1945.

servicemen, quite apart from their military equipment. The service authorities themselves were greedy. In 1941, for instance, the army demanded 100 million shells for 1942, which was 25 per cent. more than had been used in 1916 and 35 per cent. more than in 1918. By 1942 it had rifles for ten years ahead and troop-carrying vehicles for four. There was still no supreme coordinating authority other than Churchill himself. A Production Executive was set up in January 1941, composed of the three supply ministers[1] and Bevin, the minister of labour. This turned into a battleground between Beaverbrook and Bevin. The two men carried the war into the war cabinet of which both were now members.[2] The causes of conflict remain obscure until the records are explored. Probably Beaverbrook wished to disregard the established rules for labour as he had done for everything else, while Bevin would allow no encroachment on his domain. Perhaps there was antagonism of principle between the improvising individualist Beaverbrook and the slow-moving Bevin with his ingrained suspicion of all capitalists, especially press lords.

At any rate, this battle was the great undisclosed theme of British government throughout 1941. Churchill favoured Beaverbrook, at this time his most intimate friend, and would have liked to make him overlord of production. The idea broke down, perhaps because of Beaverbrook's precarious health, more likely because of Bevin's objection.[3] Beaverbrook could produce the goods. Only Bevin could produce the labour, and this gave him the whiphand. Beaverbrook had to be content

[1] The minister of supply, the minister of aircraft production, and the first lord of the admiralty.

[2] Beaverbrook joined the war cabinet in August 1940, as Churchill's personal adherent and inspirer. In October, when Chamberlain resigned, Wood took his place as Conservative representative, and Bevin was brought in at the same time. In December there was a further change. Halifax became ambassador at Washington, though remaining in theory a member of the war cabinet. Eden succeeded him both as foreign secretary and in the war cabinet. Eden was interested only in foreign affairs. Wood was too cautious to be drawn into brawls. On the other side, Greenwood was ineffective, and Attlee cast himself as deputy prime minister. Hence Beaverbrook and Bevin inevitably became the principal antagonists, quite apart from their clash of personality and outlook.

[3] On 1 May 1941 Beaverbrook ceased to be minister of aircraft production. On 29 June he became minister of supply. In the intervening period he was 'minister of state'—the first to possess this meaningless title, which subsequently became common. Presumably it was an imitation of the French, like 'minister' before it. Beaverbrook, when offered the title, replied that he was prepared to be 'minister of church' as well.

with the ministry of supply, where he stamped tanks out of the ground as he had previously stamped aeroplanes. In such circumstances, plans merely projected existing achievements upwards—what Beaverbrook called the carrot principle—and then waited for the sparks to fly, as the demands of one department hit those of another.

Somehow everything was sorted out. Port directors were set up as dictators at the docks, distributing imports in a coordinated way. Railway wagons were pooled. Through trains were worked across the once-rival systems. In May 1941 Lord Leathers became minister of war transport, uniting the two departments of transport and shipping. New marshalling yards and linking lines were commissioned to the tune of £5 million.[1] By the summer of 1941 the railways had been cleared. The board of trade undertook the gigantic task of regulating retail trade, a task never attempted in the first World war, and did it with a staff increased only from 2,000 to 6,500. Civilian industry was concentrated, mostly by voluntary agreement. Some factories worked fulltime. The unemployed factories were turned to other work or used for storage, particularly of tobacco. A Consumer Needs department was set up to discover the most urgent shortages. The board of trade devised 'utility' schemes for furniture and many other domestic articles—uniform goods of a reasonably sound standard.

The board's most remarkable achievement was clothes rationing, which ensured that the reduced supplies were fairly distributed—a striking instance of how wartime pressures and welfare were often combined. The rationing was by individual points, and the ministry of food took belated notice that this system could work after all.[2] It, too, relied on points when it extended rationing to jam and tinned goods. The ministry of food became more constructive in other ways. It planned to produce the most scientific diet, not merely to make supplies go round; and this time, thanks to the advance in understanding of nutrition, it succeeded. The British people were better fed than before the war, though not so agreeably. The ministry of agriculture played its part. It grudgingly recognized that crops were more economical than animals. Nearly four million

[1] In all, £11·5 million were spent on railway improvements during the war.
[2] Woolton, the minister of food, having been in retail trade, always thought that points would work and finally imposed them on his ministry.

acres were ploughed up between 1939 and 1941, again mostly by voluntary agreement, and the increase of food for direct human consumption is calculated to have saved 22 million tons of shipping by the end of 1941.[1]

Finance took on a startlingly new shape. Though Wood, the chancellor, had himself little grasp of principle, he was shrewd enough to listen to Keynes and other economists. His budget of April 1941 abandoned the narrow conception of government income and expenditure, and presented instead a survey of the national income—based, of course, on intelligent guesswork. Wood now openly accepted the principle that subsidies (extended, if necessary, to other goods than food) should keep the cost of living at 25 per cent. to 30 per cent. above prewar. He did not try to balance his budget, though this time the British people paid for 55 per cent. of the war in taxes—a much better figure than in the first war. Wood's main concern was to close 'the inflationary gap' between what the government was spending and what it received in taxes—a sum Keynes and others guessed to be about £500 million. Half the gap was met by raising income tax to 10s. in the pound and by reducing the allowances, thus bringing most industrial workers into the class of income-tax payers for the first time. Some of these increases were credited to the taxpayer, to be repaid after the war—a device which Keynes advocated as a means of combating postwar unemployment and which Wood accepted, on the more humdrum ground, that it made increased taxation more palatable.[2] The rest of the gap, Wood hoped, would be met by voluntary savings, and the hope was more or less fulfilled. People saved partly for patriotic reasons and more because rationing and general shortage made it difficult for them to spend their money. Personal consumption was 14 per cent. less in 1941 than prewar, and people spent less on everything[3] except beer, tobacco, the cinema, and public transport. Wood's calculation was not watertight: the gap was never fully closed. Still his

---

[1] More speculatively the saving throughout the war has been estimated at 43½ million tons.

[2] Unemployment was never serious after the war, and the postwar credits have therefore remained a tiresome burden on the exchequer. They were, in any case, a clumsy device. By their nature, their repayment would tend to benefit the better off (i.e. payers of income tax), not those in real need.

[3] Twenty per cent. less on food, 38 per cent. less on clothes, 43 per cent. less on household goods, 76 per cent. less on private motoring.

finance ensured that queues and wage increases—the two symptoms of inflation—never took on threatening size.

This was a decisive achievement. It made labour relations easy, and these were the critical point of the war economy. Though the ministry of shipping could bring in only 30·5 million tons of imports in the second year of the war, this proved enough. Rations never ran short, and 'the war machine at no stage threatened to come to a halt for want of raw materials'.[1] The ministries of food and supply were both astonished at this. Both had lamented the cut in imports and had declared that their work had been made impossible. Both were saved by their own blunders: 'minimum food requirements were considerably, and raw materials requirements wildly, overstated'.[2] The plans succeeded by mistake, as often happens. The shortage of labour could not be conjured away so easily. By the summer of 1941 Great Britain had 49 per cent. of her total occupied population employed upon government work of one kind or another.[3] The demand was still growing. Soon there would be a labour famine. With Churchill's approval, the army was put at the end of the queue: henceforth it must make do with two million men. Still more was needed.

Two great innovations met the extremity. First was the direction and allocation of labour; second, at the end of the year, the conscription of women. Neither was attempted systematically in any other belligerent country. Both worked smoothly, thanks to Bevin's tact in administering them—his great contribution to the war. Bevin was insistent that control and recruitment of labour should not be used as devices for controlling wages, and wage incomes[4] went up 18 per cent. between 1938 and 1947, while the income from property was reduced by 15 per cent. and from salaries by 21 per cent. Not surprisingly there was a contented labour force. More important was the general willingness to cooperate. Workers wanted to be told what to do and welcomed their mobilization for war production. A further advance was prepared in 1941, though not yet applied. Sir John Anderson worked out a manpower budget, and this became the determining factor of the British

[1] Hurstfield, *The Control of Raw Materials*, 245.
[2] Hancock and Gowing, *British War Economy*, 267.
[3] The United States in 1944 had only 40 per cent. of their labour force in the armed services and civilian war employment combined.
[4] Calculated at constant (1947) prices.

economy in the later stages of the war—conscious recognition
for the first time of the socialist doctrine that labour lay at the
root of all wealth.

Such were the elements of siege economy, when Great
Britain survived against great odds. The British people were
keyed up by a hope that they would not stand alone for ever.
President Roosevelt recognized Great Britain's financial need.
On 17 December 1940 he propounded the idea of 'lend-lease',
by which American goods could be provided without cash
payment. On 11 March 1941 it became the law of the United
States.[1] This was a great promise for the future: Great Britain
would not fail from lack of dollars. It offered little help in the
present. Long and complicated negotiations were needed before
the American goods were released. Even then they had to be
ordered and manufactured. British imports from the United
States only increased by 3 per cent. in 1941, as compared with
the last four months of 1940,[2] and this increase was mostly in
foodstuffs and steel. Throughout 1941 Great Britain still bought
with cash most of the American arms which she obtained.
For instance, only 100 out of the 2,400 American aeroplanes
which went to Egypt in 1941 came from lend-lease.

There was, moreover, a high price to be paid on the other
side. Lend-lease was an act 'to promote the defense of the
United States'. Great Britain was still a poor relation, not an
equal partner. There was no pooling of resources. Instead Great
Britain was ruthlessly stripped of her remaining dollars. The
Americans insisted that they were aiding Great Britain so that
she should fight Germany and not to maintain her as an industrial power. No lend-lease goods could go into exports, and
even exports not made from these had to be cut down for fear of
outcry from American competitors. Thanks to lend-lease Great
Britain virtually ceased to be an exporting country.[3] She
sacrificed her postwar future for the sake of the war. As Keynes
put it, 'We threw good housekeeping to the winds. But we
saved ourselves, and helped to save the world.'

Lend-lease enabled Great Britain to turn all her resources
to the business of war. Even so, she could hardly match

---

[1] See Note A, p. 533.

[2] British imports from the United States were 51 per cent. of her total in Sept.–
Dec. 1940, and 54 per cent. in 1941.

[3] Taking 1938 as 100, British exports were 29 in 1943, when imports were still 77.

German power which rested on an almost united, though conquered, Europe. In such circumstances, survival was itself a
remarkable achievement and, as events proved, Great Britain's
decisive contribution to the defeat of Germany. But the
British people and their government were not content to hang
on until somehow Soviet Russia and the United States became
involved and so turned the balance against Germany. The
British wanted to win and, still more remarkable, believed that
they could do it. This was in part an echo from the first war
when Germany appeared to be victorious for four years and then
cracked suddenly within three months. Whether mistakenly
or not, the British still regarded themselves as a Great Power
of the first rank, capable of defeating any other. They exaggerated their own strength and, still more, the strength
which came from their empire. This, of course, provided
something both in manpower and in economic resources.
Canada, for instance, first with a thousand million dollar gift
and then with mutual aid, supplied more proportionately to
her strength than the United States did with lend-lease. The
sterling area became a one-way system, by which its members
accumulated unlimited sterling balances in London. These
were virtually forced loans, and £1,138 million was no small
contribution to be levied from the impoverished people of India.

On the other side, British authorities persistently exaggerated
Germany's economic weaknesses and the extent to which these
could be intensified. There was an almost universal dogma
among economists that Nazi autarky was itself a symptom of
impending breakdown,[1] and the dogma was sustained by
information from German refugees, who naturally gave Hitler
no credit for anything. An official historian says: 'The guesses
by the Ministry of Economic Warfare during this early period
of the war tended to be far too optimistic.'[2] The Germans were
comparatively ill-supplied with oil, and air attacks on their
synthetic oil-plants brought catastrophe for them in the last
stages in the war. Such action was beyond the capacity of the
R.A.F. in 1940 and for long afterwards. Apart from this, German
economy was secure and under little strain. Indeed, the hope of
defeating Germany without enlisting the full strength of Soviet

[1] The exception was C. W. Guillebaud in *Germany's Economic System, 1933-38*.
His reputation never recovered from this recognition of the truth.
[2] Hancock and Gowing, *British War Economy*, 216.

Russia and the United States appears in retrospect a fantasy. But the fantasy had great historical importance. No people or government can keep going without some prospect of ultimate victory, and it is better to do the wrong thing in wartime than to do nothing at all.[1] The illusion about Germany's weakness buoyed up the British people in their darkest hours. Moreover, the decisions taken as a consequence of it continued to shape British strategy even when circumstances had changed. The manufacture of tanks and landing-craft could not be substituted for that of bombers at a moment's notice; nor could a campaign in the Mediterranean be broken off in order to prepare a landing in France.

British confidence showed itself in a remarkable way: on 27 May the chiefs of staff submitted their plans for winning the war, when the bulk of the British army seemed lost at Dunkirk; a revised version was ready on 4 September, just before climax in the battle of Britain.[2] The basis of both plans was the same: the expectation that Germany's economic difficulties would cause crisis and collapse by the end of 1941. The British army therefore would not have to face battles on the scale of those in the first World war. It need only be ready in 1942 to restore order in a continent where German power would already have disintegrated. This was in part a rationalization. Given the demands on industry for aeroplanes and ships, an army of thirty-two divisions—the figure already settled on[3]—could not be equipped before 1942, and the chiefs of staff were making the best of things. Meanwhile the process of German disintegration had to be speeded up. The chiefs of staff proposed to do it in two ways: subversion and bombing. The British exaggerated a good deal the discontent in the conquered countries of Europe and still more its effectiveness. Churchill, for instance, supposed that the German army could be defeated by arming the local population once a landing had taken place.[4] High hopes were placed at first in de Gaulle and

[1] This was, of course, the case for the Somme and Flanders offensives in 1916 and 1917.

[2] The report of 27 May is summarized in Butler, *Grand Strategy*, ii. 212–15; and that of 4 Sept. in ibid. 343–5.

[3] Or with Indian and Dominion forces, fifty-five divisions.

[4] 'It need not be assumed that great numbers of men are required. If this incursion of the armoured formations is successful, the uprising of the local population for whom weapons must be brought, will supply the corpus of the liberating offensive.' Churchill, memorandum, 18 Dec. 1941. *Second World War*, iii. 583–4.

his Free French movement, particularly as the French empire was beyond German control. In September 1940 a British expedition, cooperating with de Gaulle, attempted to seize Dakar, an important French port on the west coast of Africa. The attempt was beaten off with some loss and much discredit.[1] Even after this the British continued to believe that other French colonial authorities would respond eagerly to the Free French appeal. In May 1941 the Germans seemed on the point of taking over Syria as a base for their air force. Once more the British relied on the Free French. Once more they were disappointed and learnt that British forces were needed, though this time successfully. British troops conquered Syria, and soon de Gaulle was quarrelling over infringements of French sovereignty.

These experiences did not weaken the British belief that Hitler's empire could be shaken by words. A special Executive was set up for Political Warfare. The B.B.C. sent out programmes in forty-three languages. Many aeroplanes were risked, and many lives lost, in supplying the various resistance movements. There was little to show for all this effort. The reliable news, broadcast by the B.B.C., no doubt helped to sustain spirits in conquered Europe. The resistance was a rich source of intelligence and information. But the Germans did not have to increase their occupying forces except possibly later in the mountainous regions of Yugoslavia. They had in any case to keep these forces, which were mostly composed of middle-aged men, unfit for active service. Hitler's 'New Order' could be overthrown only by defeat in the field, not by the activities of the political warfare executive. However, its activities did no harm and maybe a little good. They were conducted largely by refugees and thus cost little more than keeping the refugees in internment camps. They also provided a useful distraction for politically minded Englishmen and planners who might otherwise have been a great nuisance. The Germans waged political war with equally little success. William Joyce, their principal English broadcaster (known as 'Lord Haw-Haw' from his supposed way of speaking), excited amusement, not alarm, though this did not prevent his

---

[1] The French defence was strengthened by ships which had recently passed the straits of Gibraltar. The British admiral who allowed them to pass was made the scapegoat for failure and was dismissed without a hearing.

being executed on a trumped-up charge at the end of the war.[1]

British bombing of Germany was a more serious story, a powerful element during the war and fateful also for the future of mankind. Bomber command claimed the largest share of Great Britain's war-production and provided the most distinctive part of her strategy during the second World war. Though experts in many countries had argued that a war could be won solely by bombing, the R.A.F. alone made this doctrine the basis of its strategy. The *Luftwaffe*, for instance, was designed as an auxiliary to the army and improvised the Blitz with difficulty. The chiefs of the R.A.F. always put independent bombing first and grudged the tiresome distractions of fighter and coastal command. Great Britain, they argued, had two special assets: her island position and her industrial strength. These would enable her to defeat a continental enemy by air power. There was equivocation over the objectives. Sometimes the air chiefs implied that they would destroy the enemy's armed forces; sometimes that they would destroy his industry. Essentially they aimed at destroying the enemy's will to fight, and this meant indiscriminate attacks on the civilian population. The British government and the chiefs of staff, though not the chief of air staff, shrank from saying this openly.

At the beginning of the war, the chiefs of staff laid down that Great Britain would always observe the principle of 'refraining from attack on civil population as such for the purpose of demoralisation', and Chamberlain declared in the house of commons: 'Whatever be the lengths to which others may go, His Majesty's Government will never resort to the deliberate attack on women and children, and other civilians for purposes of mere terrorism.' The British gradually retreated from this high position. They claimed that the Germans had set the example and deserved to be repaid in kind. The argument was doubtful if applied only to bombing,[2] but the British justified it to themselves on general grounds of Nazi wickedness. Concentration camps, aggressive war, ill-treatment of the conquered peoples, and later mass extermination made the Nazis the common enemies of mankind, and Great Britain was entitled to use any weapon against them. The groups in England who were usually the guardians of morality had been the first

[1] See Note B, p. 533.   [2] See Note C, p. 534.

to turn their moral indignation against the Nazis, and there was virtually no one left to speak with a higher conscience. So far as air strategy was concerned, the British outdid German frightfulness first in theory, later in practice, and a nation which claimed to be fighting for a moral cause gloried in the extent of its immoral acts. By 1945 all attempts to civilize air war or to control its effects had been rejected, and the British took the lead in this rejection.

Practical arguments pushed the British the same way. Under the impact of the Blitz, the British people demanded retaliation and did not stop to ask whether they or the Germans had started it. Moreover, with the fall of France, bombing seemed to be the one resource left to the British. Churchill wrote on 8 July 1940: 'There is one thing that will bring Hitler down, and that is an absolutely devastating, exterminating attack by very heavy bombers from this country upon the Nazi homeland. We must be able to overwhelm them by this means, without which I do not see a way through.'[1] Bombing would show that Great Britain was still in the war and determined to win, even if it did nothing else. Maybe, at this high time of national inspiration, the British were also anxious to show that they would jettison even morality in their determination to bring Hitler down. The most powerful reason for indiscriminate bombing was, however, the simplest: in 1940 and 1941 bomber command was incapable of anything else, though as events proved, not even capable of that. Before the war air-strategists had assumed that bombing would take place in daytime. Fleets of bombers, unassailed by enemy fighters, would strike with unfailing precision at their defined targets. Experience showed at once that daylight bombing was impossible without command of the air, and the R.A.F. did not believe that this could be attained: long-range fighters would never be able to defeat short-range fighters. Bomber command had therefore to go over to night attacks without command of the air, without the necessary equipment, and with little training.

There was at first an attempt, or perhaps a pretence, to operate against military targets. The British raids in the autumn of 1940 were supposed to be directed against German marshalling yards and synthetic oil-plants—sensible targets if

[1] Churchill, *Second World War*, ii. 567.

only the R.A.F. could have hit them. Gradually the aim was shifted, partly to satisfy the public demand for retaliation, partly from recognition that the precise targets were not being achieved. On 30 October 1940 the war cabinet agreed that 'the civilian population around the target areas must be made to feel the weight of the war'. Six weeks later it sanctioned a 'crash concentration' against a single German city. The ministry of information was confident that 'the Germans, for all their present confidence and their cockiness will not stand a quarter of the bombing that the British have shown that they can take'. The high hopes of bomber command were not fulfilled. For a long time it accepted the reports of pilots at their face value and was convinced that enormous destruction was being achieved. Doubts accumulated.

In August 1941 Butt, of the war cabinet secretariat, made an independent survey, reinforced by study of air photographs. He reported that one third of the aircraft dispatched did not attack their target and of those which did only one third got within five miles of it; without a moon the proportion fell to one-fifteenth. Information collected after the war shows that 'the German war economy was but little, if at all, affected by the strategic bombing that took place during these years'[1]— at most there was a loss of under 1 per cent., perhaps not even that. Against this, the R.A.F. in 1941 lost a bomber for every ten tons of bombs dropped; and the strategic air-offensive of 1940–1 killed more members of the R.A.F. than German civilians. Add to this the manpower, industrial resources, and raw materials devoted to producing bombers, and it seems clear that the offensive did more damage to Great Britain than to Germany.

Not all this was recognized at the time. Enough was recognized to break off the air-offensive in November 1941. The official historians write: 'This was no less than a formal expression of the belief that the results which Bomber Command was achieving were not worth the casualties it was suffering.'[2] It did not, however, mean that strategical bombing was written off as a method of war. The contrary lesson was drawn that bomber command must be made much greater and more powerful before it returned to its allotted task. The demands on the

[1] Webster and Frankland, *The Strategic Air Offensive*, i. 299.
[2] Ibid. 187.

ministry of aircraft production were violently increased during 1941 and still more with reference to 1942. In February 1942 bomber command was given a new, more aggressive chief: Air Chief Marshal Sir Arthur Harris, the supreme advocate of strategical bombing. The decision to pursue strategical bombing on a far greater scale was one of the two vital legacies from the period when Great Britain stood alone.

The other legacy, arrived at even more haphazard, was that which made the Mediterranean a hub of British naval and military endeavour. At the beginning of the war the British had a considerable naval force there and a small army in Egypt. If Italy entered the war, these forces, in cooperation with the French, would dominate the Mediterranean and would thus secure both French communications with North Africa and British communications with India and the Far East. In June 1940 Italy duly entered the war, but France fell out. There were now no French communications to secure, and the Mediterranean was also closed to British merchant ships.[1] Malta lay under the shadow of Italian air-attack, and the Mediterranean fleet had already withdrawn to Alexandria, which was by no means equipped as a first-class naval base. Pound, the first sea lord, was apprehensive that the fleet was not secure from Italian aeroplanes even at Alexandria. On 16 June he therefore invited Admiral Sir Andrew Cunningham, the Mediterranean commander-in-chief, to block the Suez canal and to withdraw the bulk of the fleet to Gibraltar and the rest to Aden. Cunningham objected that this would be a grave blow to British prestige; Churchill objected also. Pound did not insist, and the question of remaining in Egypt was never discussed in principle either by the chiefs of staff or by the war cabinet. The three commanders-in-chief there[2] declared that they could hold their own only if they received reinforcements. On 16 August the war cabinet decided to reinforce them. From this moment Great Britain was committed to a campaign in the Mediterranean on an

[1] From this time until May 1943, all British shipping to Egypt, India, and the Far East went round the Cape—a considerable drain on carrying capacity.

[2] The idea of appointing a supreme commander was aired and rejected. Running a war by committee was very much in the British tradition. It had special difficulties in Egypt. Cunningham was at Alexandria and often went to sea with the fleet. General Wavell and Air Chief Marshal Longmore were at Cairo. As well, each commander had his own interests which were not easily reconciled.

ever-increasing scale. There was also implicit in this a negative decision. Though Australia and New Zealand were told that, if Japan attacked them, Great Britain would cut her losses in the Mediterranean and 'sacrifice every interest, except only the defence and feeding of this island' for their defence,[1] the British government had in fact decided to gamble that Japan would remain neutral, and the Far East was from this moment neglected.

More subtle arguments than prestige could, of course, be found for remaining in Egypt. Germany was supposed to be short of oil. Hitler therefore was expected to lay hands on Irak and Persia, and the British must stand in his way. The argument was in fact unfounded. Hitler had no plans for conquering the Middle East—a project which looked attractive only on small-scale maps. His later interventions in Greece and in North Africa were defensive—responses to British threats, not part of an aggressive design. When Hitler attacked Russia, there were fears that he would break through to Persia, and this fear had more justification. Persia and the line of the Caucasus needed direct defence, and the desert war, far from helping this defence, pulled away the only forces available for it. The British themselves recognized that they would have to abandon Egypt if the Germans reached the Caucasus—hence their presence there was no obstacle to Hitler whatever else it may have been.

The British also hoped that, by remaining in the Mediterranean, they would somehow acquire allies: the French in North Africa at one end, Turkey at the other. These hopes, too, were unfounded. Weygand, the ruler of French North Africa, though anti-German, was loyal to the Vichy government and in any case meant to maintain the independence of North Africa against all comers. He would join the British only when they were overwhelmingly strong, and then his assistance would be unnecessary. Moreover, as the British and later the Americans failed to recognize, North Africa had few assets for war. The French there had to be rearmed from American resources after the Allied landings of November 1942, and this rearming was more trouble than it was worth except from a political point of view—the Americans had plenty of men of their own whom they could arm more simply. The Turks had a substantial army but few modern weapons. They had no

[1] Churchill, *Second World War*, ii. 386.

intention of drawing the might of Germany on to themselves if this could be avoided, and they too would come over to the British side only when the war was already won. The Turkish alliance was a will o' the wisp which Churchill pursued with unshakeable constancy. It was probably fortunate that his dream never came true. Turkish neutrality was a stronger barrier against the Germans than her belligerency could ever have been.

The presence of Italian troops in Libya and Abyssinia was a stronger reason for remaining in the Middle East. The British could not strike at Germany except in the air. They could strike at the Italians and, what was more, would be taking on an opponent of their own size. Victory over the Italians would provide some cheer for the British, from Churchill downwards, even if it did nothing else. It was claimed that it would do more. The defeat of Italy would be a blow against Hitler's prestige; it would even be a weakening of his power—a perverse argument considering that the British felt stronger at having shaken off their alliance with France. Moreover, victory in the Mediterranean would enable the British to invade Italy herself and would thus open a door into Europe. New Gallipolis lay tantalizingly on the horizon. Tradition played its part. For long years the British had been taught that the Suez canal was the key-point of the British empire, and they continued to believe this even when the canal was not being used as a trade-route. Naval domination of the Mediterranean had been regarded as decisive in more than one great war—against Napoleon as well as against the Kaiser. In truth these were all rationalizations. The British were in the Mediterranean because they were there. This simple statement of fact determined the main weight of Great Britain's military effort until the late days of the second World war.

In August 1940 even the defeat of Italy seemed far off. The British expected to stand on the defensive. The Italians had 300,000 troops in Libya and another 200,000 in Abyssinia. Wavell had in all less than 100,000 men, only 36,000 of them in Egypt. The Italian navy and air force were also markedly superior on paper.[1] On 19 August the British withdrew from

---

[1] The Italians had 6 battleships, 7 8-inch and 12 or more 6-inch cruisers, 50 destroyers. The British had 4 battleships, 8 6-inch cruisers, 20 destroyers, and 1 aircraft carrier. The Regia Aeronautica had over 600 bombers in Africa. The R.A.F. had 96.

British Somaliland—their only African territory to fall under enemy occupation, though only for seven months. Early in September the Italians invaded Egypt[1] and advanced as far as Sidi Barrani. There they stopped. Their forces were not equipped for long transport across the desert, and their convoys across the Mediterranean were harassed by British submarines and aircraft based on Malta. The British government resolutely sent an armoured brigade to Egypt round the Cape, even though a German invasion of England was expected at any moment—an indication perhaps that they did not rate the chances of invasion as highly as they claimed to do or perhaps a tacit admission that all would be lost if fighter command were defeated.

Churchill impatiently 'prodded' the British commanders—a prodding which ignored their difficulties and which they deeply resented. Cunningham, in any case, needed no prodding. He repeatedly led the fleet into dangerous waters. The Italians were obsessed with the doctrine of 'a fleet in being' and therefore, despite their apparent superiority, always turned away when they came within range of the British battleships. Cunningham pressed harder. On 11 November aircraft from the carrier *Illustrious* attacked the Italian fleet in its harbour at Taranto. Three battleships were torpedoed; half the Italian battlefleet was put out of action. The British believed that they had recovered command of the sea. They did not reflect that they had won it by air power and that others might in turn use this against them.

Wavell moved more slowly. He was, by all accounts, a general of the first rank. But he was weighed down by the paucity of his resources and by his immense responsibilities. Though officially only one commander-in-chief among three, he had in fact to provide both strategical decision and political guidance throughout the Middle East[2]—a vast area which included the eastern half of the Mediterranean, East Africa, and all Asia

[1] A minor oddity of the war in the Mediterranean was that Egypt remained technically neutral throughout. The king of Egypt was, however, more than once compelled to dismiss a prime minister who took this neutrality too seriously. Egypt reaped a reward of £500 million in sterling balances.

[2] The Near East disappeared by chance during the second World war. Originally Wavell's Middle East command was concerned with Egypt and Palestine, where it linked up with the French in Syria. The changed circumstances after June 1940 extended it to the Equator, the borders of Tunis, and Greece. The Near East was squeezed out.

up to the confines of India. He was also, like many generals, taciturn and obstinate in personal discussion. In July 1940 he was called home in order to be instructed, and Churchill at once doubted his offensive spirit. However, he was sent back to his command. In October Eden, secretary for war, arrived in Egypt to prod Wavell personally. This proved unnecessary. Eden returned with the great secret that Wavell was preparing to strike. The result exceeded all expectation. Wavell intended only a spoiling offensive, 'a raid in force'. Instead the entire Italian army collapsed under the impact of a small armoured force. The desert army under General O'Connor attacked on 8 December with a total strength of 25,000 men. Sidi Barrani fell within three days; Bardia on 5 January 1941; Tobruk on 22 January; Benghazi on 5 February. With this the whole of Cyrenaica was in British hands. They had taken 113,000 prisoners, 1,300 guns, and had destroyed 10 Italian divisions; 438 British soldiers were killed, 355 of them Australians. This was a great triumph. It also brought retribution. German forces now entered the Mediterranean campaign.

Mussolini had been under few illusions about Italy's strength in June 1940. But he supposed that he was taking on two dead ducks and, once in the war, his vanity swelled. He insisted that he could invade Egypt without German help and in October, largely to spite Hitler, launched an attack on Greece as well. Greece had received a British guarantee in April 1939. However, the Greeks held their own alone and did not invoke British aid, for fear of provoking German intervention. Hitler on his side never took the Mediterranean and Middle East seriously, and his elaborate plans to drive east existed only in British imaginations. In September 1940 he played with the idea of moving through Spain on to Gibraltar, but soon dropped this when Franco proved obstinate. Nor was he sorry maybe to see Mussolini in difficulties. Hitler's mind was, however, now set on the invasion of Russia, and he could not risk dangers in his rear. At the beginning of 1941 he decided that he must rescue Mussolini after all. Squadrons of the *Luftwaffe* were sent to Sicily, where they soon shook British control of the central Mediterranean; an Afrika Korps under Rommel was prepared for Libya; and Hitler also prepared to knock out Greece. Bulgaria was already favourable to him; Yugoslavia, Greece's other neighbour, seemed to be inclining the same way.

The British government were aware of these German preparations. Their resources were fully stretched in Libya and East Africa. Now they were faced with the prospect of a Greek campaign as well. Eden, now foreign secretary, and Dill, the C.I.G.S., were sent out to stir up the Middle East commanders. Confusion of counsels followed. Eden and Dill wanted to show that they could be as daring as Churchill. Wavell was worn down by the earlier reproaches of excessive caution and thought only of avoiding new ones. When Churchill and the war cabinet for once hesitated, the men in Egypt regarded this as a challenge, which it was no doubt intended to be, and declared their readiness to go forward. No systematic military appreciation was ever made. The decision to intervene in Greece was taken on political and sentimental grounds—Norway all over again. Failure to aid Greece would be bad for British prestige. Intervention there would inspire Turkey and Yugoslavia; it would give the British an opportunity to fight the Germans. When Yugoslavia broke with Hitler on 27 March, the desire for some dramatic British action became irresistible. The Greeks, to make disaster certain, refused to withdraw to the defensive line on which Wavell had at first insisted. Smuts, arriving in Cairo, contributed the loud-sounding nothings of which he was a master: 'Which course would put heart into the freedom-loving nations?'—and so on.

Everything went wrong. Rommel, intending only a raid in force like Wavell before him, attacked on 30 March. He, too, was surprised into success. The British front collapsed. By 11 April they had lost all Cyrenaica with the exception of Tobruk, which remained as an isolated garrison to their subsequent embarrassment. Even graver was the revelation that British tanks were too slow and their engines too weak to compete with the Germans. The British were now paying for their neglect of tanks between the wars. The campaign in Greece was equally catastrophic. Early in April the Germans overran Yugoslavia and arrived in Greece before the British had begun to move. The inferior British forces never came to grips with the enemy. They were retreating and being withdrawn almost as soon as they landed. Sixty-two thousand men were put ashore in Greece; 50,000 were taken off; most of their equipment was lost. It is difficult to believe that even a refusal to help Greece could have been such a grave blow to British prestige. The high hopes which had followed Wavell's earlier successes in Cyrenaica were dispelled. The British seemed to be back where they had started: obstinately on the defensive and with little prospect of ultimate victory.

There was discouragement in England, and it turned against Churchill. He believed in challenging his critics. On 7 May the house of commons gave him a vote of confidence by 477 votes to 3 and 'an ovation such as he had never yet received'.[1] It was an ovation with a difference. Churchill had been revealed as the old Churchill of Gallipoli: a gambler for high stakes who tried to do too much with inadequate resources. The British people did not doubt that Churchill was the best war prime minister they had or could possibly have. But henceforth they accepted him despite his faults. They expected him to make mistakes, and he made many. In regard to Greece he stood by no means alone. But the ultimate responsibility was his in more than one sense. Commanders knew that they would be applauded if they took risks and condemned if they hesitated. They needed political skill in order to survive. Longmore, the air commander in Egypt, was recalled on 17 May. 'He had incurred the displeasure of the Prime Minister for appearing to doubt that the utmost was being done to help him.'[2] Cunningham, too, was in trouble. On 27 March his fleet had sunk three Italian heavy cruisers and two destroyers at the battle of Matapan. This did not help him when he defied an order to block the port of Tripoli. He escaped only by bombarding Tripoli—an operation attended surprisingly by little loss and also with no effect. Churchill's fiercest goads fell on Wavell. He was expected to act in every sphere with virtually no forces. Wavell, too, had a success to his credit. The Italian forces in East Africa had been routed. On 5 May the emperor of Abyssinia re-entered his capital—the first victim of Axis aggression to be restored. Apart from this, Wavell felt fully stretched in defending the frontiers of Egypt.

This would not do for Churchill. A government friendly to the Axis had been set up in Irak; Wavell must intervene. German aeroplanes were using air-bases in Syria; Wavell must

---

[1] *Annual Register, 1941.*
[2] Playfair, *The Mediterranean and Middle East.* ii. 236. Longmore's successor, Tedder, was more politically adroit. He was also that rare thing: an air-commander who believed in cooperating with the army.

intervene there also, in cooperation with the Free French. The Germans were preparing to attack Crete, where the British had established a naval base; Wavell must defend it. Wavell did not believe that any of these operations was possible. Over both Irak and Syria he offered to resign; over both he was overruled, and submitted. Two of the operations proved less onerous than he had expected. In Irak the pro-Axis government collapsed almost without a struggle. In Syria the French forces, though loyal to Vichy, were defeated by British troops.[1] Crete was a different story. The British had been there for six months, but, with all their other pressing anxieties, had done little to make the island secure. They relied on sea power and did not foresee an air-borne invasion. In any case they had no aeroplanes to spare, but the failure to garrison the Cretan air-fields adequately with ground troops sprang from pure blindness. The German attack on Crete was indeed a new sort of war: for the first and, so far as the Germans were concerned, the only time, the air beat the sea. The Germans attacked on 20 May with parachute forces. Two days later, these established control of an air-field at Maleme. With this, the battle for Crete was lost. On 27 May the British forces were withdrawn. Twelve thousand were left behind and became prisoners. The navy had lost three cruisers and six destroyers. The German parachute strength was also shattered, though this was not known at the time.

There was renewed discouragement in England, once more a grumbling debate (on 10 June), though this time no division. Churchill himself was deeply dissatisfied with the conduct of affairs in the Middle East. Wavell appreciated that he was in danger. He wished to stand on the defensive for the next three months. Churchill demanded immediate action. On 15 June Wavell launched an offensive against Rommel with the grandiose title of 'Battle Axe'. It was a total failure and was broken off within two days. This was the end for Wavell. On 21 June he was sent to India as commander-in-chief, and General Sir Claude Auchinleck,[2] the previous commander-in-chief there,

[1] Support for de Gaulle turned out to be illusory, and German use of Syria turned out to be an illusion also. All German aeroplanes had left before the British attacked.

[2] Claude John Eyre Auchinleck (1884–   ), field marshal; G.O.C. North Norway, 1940; commander-in-chief, India, 1941, 1943-7; commander-in-chief, Middle East, 1941-2.

came to the Middle East in his place. As often happened after an upheaval of this kind, Auchinleck was then given everything which had been denied to Wavell. Political and economic affairs were taken off his shoulders, and Oliver Lyttelton came out to Cairo as minister of state, representing the war cabinet. Even more ironical, Auchinleck postponed the desert offensive for five months, where Wavell had asked for three.

Auchinleck had a new, and much stronger, reason for his hesitation. On 22 June, the day after his appointment, the Germans invaded Soviet Russia.[1] Most British authorities expected an early Russian defeat, and Auchinleck, influenced particularly by his Indian experience, looked with great apprehension at the line of the Caucasus. The British hoped, at most, for a short breathing-space. Churchill had decided his policy in advance,[2] and announced it over the radio the same evening: unreserved solidarity with Soviet Russia in the war against Hitler. 'The Russian danger is our danger, and the danger of the United States, just as the cause of any Russian fighting for his hearth and home is the cause of free men and free people in every quarter of the globe.' No doubt the decision came easily to Churchill. He had long advocated alliance with Soviet Russia. He was pledged to victory at all costs and, as he said in private, 'if Hitler invaded Hell I would make at least a favourable reference to the Devil in the House of Commons'.[3]

In any case Churchill had no choice. The British people were in no mood to reject any ally after the Blitz and the failures in the Middle East.[4] Many of them had been championing the Soviet alliance long before Churchill. The decision was a momentous step in world history all the same. Fear of communism was laid aside for the duration. The great debate between Germany and Russia which had haunted British policy since the beginning of the century and had bedevilled it before the war was now determined in Russia's favour, determined as events turned out once and for all. If Russia

---

[1] Napoleon invaded Russia virtually on the same date. There is no evidence that Hitler knew of this discouraging coincidence.

[2] According to Hopkins, Churchill conferred principally with Beaverbrook and Cripps. Sherwood, *Papers of Harry Hopkins*, i. 305.

[3] Churchill, *Second World War*, ii. 331.

[4] Some Conservatives took the line, which Senator Truman did in the United States, that Germans and Russians should be left to cut each others' throats. Moore-Brabazon, the minister of aircraft production, indiscreetly said this in public, and protests from the workers in aircraft factories forced him to leave office.

survived the German attack, she would become a World Power with British and American acquiescence, even with their backing. Churchill's radio speech of 22 June settled the fate of the world for many years to come.

The British could do little to help their new ally. They certainly could not provide the second front—an invasion of Europe—which Stalin at once demanded. They could not even conduct an effective air offensive against Germany. They could only offer supplies, and these mostly in the future. Beaverbrook, with his usual enthusiasm, became the leading advocate of the Soviet cause—first for aid and soon for the second front also. In September he went to Moscow with Harriman, Roosevelt's representative, and won Stalin's heart by the lavishness of his promises. Others grumbled. 'The Service departments felt that it was like flaying off pieces of their skin.'[1] Even those who hoped most for Russia's success doubted whether it were possible, and the likelihood of her defeat opened up a catastrophic prospect. Germany, it seemed, would soon be impregnable economically. Hence the need for American assistance was greater and more urgent than ever.

In August 1941 Churchill had the first of his nine meetings with Roosevelt, at Placentia Bay, Newfoundland. The British were keen to discuss future strategy. The Americans refused to be drawn. They condemned the Middle East as 'a liability from which the British should withdraw'.[2] They refused to believe that bombing could defeat Germany without a great engagement on land. Otherwise they contributed nothing. Roosevelt, too, would not discuss the war except in terms of supply to Soviet Russia. He wanted a resounding declaration of principle. The British had a draft ready. Roosevelt endorsed it after inserting a harmless blow against the Ottawa agreements and Imperial Preference.[3]

Such was the Atlantic Charter. No doubt it was useful for the Americans to learn that this time Great Britain had not entered into any secret treaties. Maybe it was a gesture of some value that belligerent Great Britain and the neutral United States had joined in any declaration, however innocuous. Otherwise the Atlantic Charter left little trace. Few references were made to it in discussions of postwar policy; the

[1] Churchill, *Second World War*, iii. 402.
[2] Gwyer, *Grand Strategy*—iii, i. 126.   [3] See Note D, p. 534.

Russians, if they noticed it at all, were not attracted by the Anglo-American proposal to determine the future of the world without them; and the British people were equally little impressed. They wanted practical aid from the United States, not moral blessings. Arthur Purvis in his last days (just before being killed in an air crash) did more than all the glittering pilgrims at Placentia Bay for future victory. He presented the Americans with a statistical balance sheet: requirements on the one side, British and American contributions on the other. The contrast between the great British effort and the lagging American shocked the American experts, and they produced in return the Victory Programme, which charted American economic expansion in the following years. Beaverbrook, too, contributed to this. At Placentia Bay he told the Americans to set their sights far higher, and they followed his lead in bewildered surprise.

What Russia did was more important at this moment than what Americans said or even planned. Despite great defeats and terrible losses, their front held. By October it was clear that the Germans would not reach the Caucasus, at any rate until the new year. Auchinleck, though still reluctant, decided to risk a desert offensive. The British army attacked on 18 November. Its attack did not prosper. The field commander, General Sir Alan Cunningham (conqueror of Abyssinia and brother of the admiral), wished to break off. Auchinleck could not agree, for fear of roars from the government at home. He came up to the battle front; dismissed Cunningham; and ordered the offensive to continue under his own chief of staff, Ritchie—a general with no experience in command. Rommel, wiser than Auchinleck, decided to conserve his forces, and withdrew from Cyrenaica. By January 1942 the British were back where they had been after Wavell's victory a year before.

The success was illusory. The British had not broken the enemy forces or secured a firm defensive position. Their line of supply was long and inadequate, while Rommel was back at his home base. Moreover, during the autumn, the Mediterranean fleet had suffered catastrophic losses. The aircraft carrier *Ark Royal* and the battleship *Barham* were sunk by German U-boats. Two more battleships were put out of action in Alexandria harbour by Italian 'human torpedoes'. The cruiser force was virtually eliminated by striking mines. Cunningham's total fleet, apart from destroyers, was reduced to three light cruisers and an anti-aircraft cruiser.[1] It was impossible to pass supplies to Malta, which, far from harassing Axis supplies, was now itself in danger. Meanwhile Hitler had dispatched a whole air corps to Sicily and North Africa. The stage was set for British disasters in 1942.

This was by no means the only British anxiety. Russia's defeat by Germany still seemed only to have been postponed, not averted. The Caucasus and Persia were still threatened. The United States drew no closer towards entering the war. In September a close observer noted that President Roosevelt 'was afraid of any assumption of the position that we must invade Germany and crush Germany'.[2] Hitler did not oblige by declaring war against the United States even when American ships attacked U-boats. There was a new, and even worse, shadow. In the Far East the Japanese had been taking steady advantage of the European war. They controlled French Indo-China. They were impatient to bring their war with China to a victorious end. In July 1941 the American government banned virtually all trade with Japan. The British and Dutch governments dutifully followed America's example. Japan was poorly supplied with oil and raw materials. She would have to strike out somewhere, unless she accepted the American terms of complete withdrawal from China, and this was unlikely. The rich prizes of Malaya and the Dutch East Indies were within Japan's grasp. Only the British base at Singapore stood in her way.

Singapore had been neglected before the war and still more during it. The original assumption had been that, with Japan thousands of miles away, the main British fleet could arrive at Singapore from European waters in case of danger, before the Japanese had time to strike. Now the Japanese were in Indo-China, on Singapore's doorstep. It was therefore decided to rely on air protection. But few aeroplanes could be spared from the Middle East and from the bomber offensive against Germany. In any case, there were also few troops to spare for the defence of the airfields, and the construction of these actually worked out to Japan's advantage—her forces seized them immediately after the outbreak of war. At Churchill's prompting,

[1] The Italians had at this time 4 battleships, 7 heavy and 12 light cruisers.
[2] Langer and Gleason, *The Undeclared War*, 735.

the battleship *Prince of Wales* and the battlecruiser *Repulse*
were sent out to provide 'a vague menace', though it should
have been clear that they would have to withdraw from
Singapore in case of war.

Only firm support from the United States might make the
Japanese hesitate, and the Americans were hard to draw. On
10 November Churchill made the ringing promise that 'should
the United States become involved in war with Japan a British
declaration of war would follow within the hour'. The American
government did not return the promise. They did not even
respond to a suggestion that their fleet should make a friendly
call at Singapore by accident. The British had a nightmare
that the Japanese might attack Singapore without provoking
the United States into war. They had a further nightmare
that the Americans might be drawn into war against Japan,
while still neutral towards Germany, and would therefore devote
all their fighting strength to the Far East. Neither nightmare
was all that remote from reality.

The worst fears were soon dispelled. On 4 December the
German attack on Moscow was halted. The Russians, for a short
time, took the offensive. On 7 December the Japanese attacked
the American fleet at Pearl Harbour and sank most of it. Hitler
declared war against the United States in support of his Japanese ally,[1] and Mussolini followed suit. Terrible events followed.
The Japanese struck great blows also against the British and
destroyed British power in the Far East. But the losses were
worth while. No greater service than Pearl Harbour was ever
performed for the British cause. The doubts of President

---

[1] Hitler's declaration of war against the United States was an act of gratuitous
loyalty. He was not pledged to support the Japanese, who had told him nothing
of their plans. He had skilfully avoided war against the United States despite many
provocations. But he was angry with the Japanese for failing to support him against
Russia and wished to show that he had more sense of honour than they had.
Maybe, too, he wished to match Churchill's promise of support to the United
States. Hitler's declaration of war was a romantic, empty gesture. Germany could
do nothing to aid Japan. On the other hand, Hitler did not believe that the United
States could do any more against Germany than they were doing already. In
reality, Hitler's declaration of war ranks second only to Pearl Harbour as a service
to Great Britain. Nearly all Americans were eager to throw the whole military
might of the United States against Japan, and it was only thanks to Hitler that
Roosevelt was able to establish the principle of defeating Germany first. Those
who like the 'ifs' of history may speculate on what would have happened if Hitler
had done nothing or even, raising the cry of the Yellow Peril, had declared war
on America's side.

Roosevelt and of the American people were resolved for them: they were in the war whether they would or no.[1] The private war between Great Britain and Germany was ended. A true World war began, and the outcome of that seemed sure. Churchill made the only appropriate comment: 'So we had won after all!'

NOTES

NOTE A. *Lend-Lease.* The aim of lend-lease was, in Roosevelt's phrase, 'to eliminate the dollar sign'. The act provided that the President, when he deemed it in the interest of national defence, might authorize, to the extent to which funds were available, the production or procurement of any defence article for the government of any country whose defence the President deemed vital to the defence of the United States and might 'sell, transfer title to, exchange, lease, lend, or otherwise dispose of' any such defence article to any such government. The terms and conditions of such aid 'shall be those which the President deems satisfactory and the benefit to the United States may be payment or repayment in kind or property, or any other direct or indirect benefit which the President deems satisfactory'.

The act had important consequences: (i) The American government procured the supplies through the service departments or special buying agencies. The recipient governments could only state their requirements; they could not insist on them. (ii) The cash was made available by Congress in specific sums. (iii) No cash could be transferred to the recipient governments—hence Great Britain still had a dollar problem for goods not provided under lend-lease. (iv) The American government never claimed any repayment in cash. The return in kind was principally to fight the common enemy, and this was the only obligation which Soviet Russia undertook. The British government were, however, required, by the Master Agreement of 23 February 1942, to promise the reduction of trade barriers and the elimination of discriminations after the war.

British reciprocal aid and Canadian mutual aid did not demand any consideration in return. They were 'unsordid' from the start.

NOTE B. *The killing of William Joyce.* Joyce was born in New York. His father was a naturalized American citizen. Joyce never acquired British nationality, though he spent most of his life in England and was a rabid patriot. He became a Fascist, for whom Sir Oswald Mosley, the 'Bleeder', was too moderate. In 1938 Joyce applied for, and obtained, a British passport, stating falsely that he was a British subject. In August 1939 he renewed this passport for one year and went to Germany. In September 1940 he became a naturalized German. As Joyce had never been a British subject, it seemed that he was secure from a charge of high treason. It was, however, argued that Joyce

[1] Churchill's promise to declare war against Japan in support of the United States was more than fulfilled. Owing to the time difference between London and Washington, the British declaration of war against Japan on 8 Dec. actually preceded the formal resolution of Congress by a few hours.

had sought the protection of the Crown by acquiring a British passport and therefore owed allegiance while he retained it. Even on this tawdry basis, the charge against Joyce was not proved. It was not shown that he had retained his passport once he was in Germany, though he probably did; nor was any satisfactory evidence produced that he had broadcast for the Germans during the period of the passport's validity. Technically, Joyce was hanged for making a false statement when applying for a passport, the usual penalty for which is a small fine. His real offence was to have attracted to himself the mythical repute of Lord Haw-Haw. Most of the broadcasts attributed to Joyce were not in fact made, either by him or by anyone else. No German broadcaster, for instance, ever gave the names of British towns which the *Luftwaffe* would bomb the next night nor state that the clock at Banstead was ten minutes slow. These legends were the manufacture of war-nerves.

Broadcasting from enemy stations produced other outbreaks of hysteria. The novelist P. G. Wodehouse was captured by the Germans and interned. He gave a lighthearted talk over the German radio, describing life in the internment camp (where he continued to write novels under difficult conditions). The Germans released him when he reached the age of 60, and he returned to France. At the liberation, orders were given to arrest him and to send him to England for trial. A sensible British Intelligence officer sheltered him until he could be smuggled into Switzerland. But for some years English publishers fought shy of Wodehouse's novels, and he never returned to his native country.

Note C. *Indiscriminate bombing.* Since all war involves wickedness, perhaps no good purpose is served in trying to run a competition of wickedness between the belligerent countries. Certainly if Hitler neglected the means of indiscriminate bombing, this was because of a strategical judgement that aeroplanes cooperating with the army were more useful and not from any moral repugnance. Still, the British initiative is fairly clear. The German bombing of Warsaw and Rotterdam was part of a military campaign, an extension of previous artillery bombardments against defended towns. The Blitz began only after the British had been bombing German towns for five months, and it, too, was designed as preliminary to a military occupation. J. M. Spaight, principal assistant secretary to the air ministry, writes: 'We began to bomb objectives on the German mainland before the Germans began to bomb objectives on the British mainland.... Germany would have called a truce if she could . . . she did call one in effect, whenever she saw the ghost of a chance' (*Bombing Vindicated*, 73–74). Similarly, Liddell Hart (*The Revolution in Warfare*, 85): 'Hitler, during the time when he had immensely superior bombing power, was remarkably reluctant to unleash it fully against his opponents' cities, and repeatedly sought to secure a truce in city bombing during the peak days of his power.'

Note D. *The Atlantic Charter.* 'The so-called Atlantic Charter was apparently a by-product of the conference rather than its primary objective.'[1] The Americans wished to guard against any new 'secret treaties' and also against

[1] Langer and Gleason, *The Undeclared War*, 677.

any continuation of autarky by the British after the war. The British wanted to commit the United States to some form of international organization. On 10 August Sir Alexander Cadogan of the foreign office produced a British draft:

1. Their countries seek no aggrandizement, territorial or other;
2. they desire to see no territorial changes that do not accord with the freely expressed wishes of the peoples concerned;
3. they respect the right of all peoples to choose the form of government under which they will live; . . .
4. they will strive to bring about a fair and equitable distribution of essential produce. . . .;
5. they seek a peace which will not only cast down for ever the Nazi tyranny, but by effective international organization will afford to all states and peoples the means of dwelling in security. . . .

The Americans disliked article 4 as too vague and 5 as too precise. After some negotiation, the Anglo-American declaration came out in eight articles:

1. Their countries seek no aggrandizement, territorial or other;
2. they desire to see no territorial changes that do not accord with the freely expressed wishes of the peoples concerned;
3. they respect the right of all peoples to choose the form of government under which they will live; . . .
4. they will endeavour, with due respect to their existing obligations, to further the enjoyment by all States . . . of access, on equal terms, to the trade and to the raw materials of the world . . .;
5. they desire to bring about the fullest collaboration between all nations in the economic field . . .;
6. after the final destruction of the Nazi tyranny, they hope to see established a peace which will afford all nations the means of dwelling in safety . . .;
7. such a peace should enable all men to traverse the high seas and oceans without hindrance;
8. they believe that all the nations of the world . . . must come to the abandonment of the use of force. Since no future peace can be maintained if land, sea and air armaments continue to be employed by nations which threaten, or may threaten, aggression outside of their frontiers, they believe, pending the establishment of a wider and permanent system of general security, that the disarmament of such nations is essential. . . .

The British reservation in article 4 protected the Ottawa agreements. Article 8 pleased them by its implication of an Anglo-American police force after the war and by its still vaguer implication of a future international organization. The Charter 'technically was nothing more than a press release, of which there was no official copy, signed or sealed.'[1]

[1] Ibid. 688.

XV

THE GRAND ALLIANCE, 1942-4

FROM the fall of France until Pearl Harbour Great Britain had conducted war against Germany and Italy on her own. Russia was also at war with Germany, and theoretically with Italy, from 22 June 1941, and Great Britain early joined with the United States in sending supplies to her. But there was no coordination of plans then or for long afterwards; there was not even a formal alliance until June 1942. Great Britain and the United States had drawn closer together. They had made a joint declaration of principles in the Atlantic Charter. The United States provided supplies and some naval assistance. There were Anglo-American staff talks between 29 January and 27 March 1941 to consider joint strategy 'should the United States be compelled to resort to war'; and it was agreed that 'since Germany is the predominant partner of the Axis Powers, the Atlantic and Mediterranean area is considered to be the decisive theatre'.

This agreement, known as ABC-1, was important for the future. It had no bearing on the present, and throughout 1941 Great Britain went on alone. Pearl Harbour changed the face of the war. The strength of the United States was now engaged and held out the promise of final victory over the Axis Powers. Great Britain had kept the war going until the United States were drawn in, and with that her unique contribution was ended. Churchill recognized that his great work was done and spoke, perhaps not seriously, of withdrawing from the scene. He soon thought again and found a new role as partner and diplomatist: the man who held the Grand Alliance together.

On 13 December Churchill, accompanied by the chiefs of staff,[1] went to Washington for 'Arcadia', the first conference of the true World war.[2] Here, Great Britain and the United States

---

[1] Brooke, who had just been appointed C.I.G.S., remained behind 'to mind the shop'. Dill, his predecessor, came instead and so was fortunately available to serve as principal British member of the Combined Chiefs of Staff's Committee which was set up at Washington.

[2] The conferences and operations of the second World war all received code names, partly for convenience, partly—though surely not very skilfully—for security. Churchill's literary gift can also be detected in the choice of names.

merged more fully for war than perhaps two countries had ever done, certainly far more than the Axis Powers did.[1] This was accomplished in casual and personal ways. There was no revival of the supreme war council which the Allies had set up towards the end of the first World war, and Great Britain and France during the early months of the second. Anglo-American partnership was cemented round the personal relations between Roosevelt and Churchill, each of whom could commit his country, with the added advantage that the other Associated Powers could be kept out. There was never a formal alliance between Great Britain and the United States except in an indirect way. Roosevelt invented a grander name, the United Nations, for the associated powers, and on 1 January 1942 all joined in a declaration that they would wage war together and not make a separate armistice or peace.[2] Apart from this, the United Nations, other than Soviet Russia, conformed to Anglo-American plans. The directorate for these plans also emerged casually. The Americans, unlike the British, wanted unity of command in each theatre, and in particular a supreme commander for south-east Asia. The British acquiesced reluctantly in this novel idea, and a little less reluctantly when the Americans nominated Wavell for the post. Who should give orders to Wavell? The British said: nobody. The Americans suggested a joint committee. Roosevelt widened its powers to cover all spheres of war. Thus the Combined Chiefs of Staff were born.

They soon became the pivot of a united war. The political chiefs decided a strategy; the combined chiefs of staff carried it out.[3] In theory, their committee was composed of the two chiefs of staff's committees sitting together.[4] In practice the British

[1] There was never any coordination of plans between Germany and Japan. There was not even a joint strategy between Germany and Italy. Germany merely went grudgingly to Italy's rescue now and then.

[2] The declaration put the United States, Great Britain, Soviet Russia, and—on American insistence—China ahead of the other Associated Powers and thus foreshadowed the predominance of these Powers, with the addition of France, in the postwar United Nations Organization.

[3] The operational direction of each campaign was usually left, under the direction of the combined committee, to the national chiefs of staff's committee concerned. Thus the Americans issued the orders in the Far East; the British in the Mediterranean and in regard to the bombing of Germany.

[4] To meet this arrangement, the Americans had first to create their own Joint Chief of Staff's Committee, an institution which they had previously lacked. They had only two chiefs of staff (army and navy). A general of the air (Arnold) was added to conform to the British pattern. The American navy objected that the

and Americans could meet only during a great conference. At other times, the combined committee met regularly in Washington, the Americans present in person, the British represented by a joint staff mission with Dill, Churchill's personal representative, at their head. For this and for other reasons, the United States were clearly the predominant partner. They had the massive resources for the future. On the other hand, Great Britain alone was at present engaged against the enemy except in the Far East, and the Americans had to fit into a war which was already in progress. Thus Great Britain, by her solitary war between June 1940 and December 1941, pegged out her claim to remain a Great Power under changed circumstances.

Anglo-American inequality was clearer still when it came to the allocation of war supplies. The Americans had much to give or soon would have. The British were at the receiving end. They even feared that the American services would demand everything for themselves. This fear proved excessive. Roosevelt recognized the need to keep Great Britain going and did something to hold the services in check. Still, there were plenty of difficulties. The American services refused to produce an order of battle or to define their needs. They merely demanded everything and fought with the civilians to get it. The British, on the other hand, had to justify every claim.[1] Again British representatives, authorized by the war cabinet, could commit their government. American representatives could only offer an 'arrangement' which they would try to smuggle past Congress and the services. There was never a true pooling of resources. Lend-lease remained the legal basis for aid, and in American eyes this had always been an act of charity towards a poor relation. The British tried to change the atmosphere by themselves behaving in a spirit of unreserved cooperation. Their aid to the United States, which became in time considerable,[2] was not lend-lease in reverse, but reciprocal aid with no strings attached.

army had now two members to their one. Fortunately Leahy, chief of Roosevelt's personal staff, was an admiral. He was made head of the joint committee. Honours were even. (Joint was used for national committees; Combined for Anglo-American.)

[1] Unlike the Russians, who were given, without scrutiny, everything they demanded up to the limit of supplies and carrying capacity.

[2] The total American expenditure on lend-lease was $43,615 million. The British empire received $30,073 million and of this the United Kingdom probably $27,025 million. The British contributed £1,896 million to reciprocal aid, of which the United States received £1,201 million, that is roughly $5,667 million, or

The British made other gestures. In September 1941, to meet American complaints, they voluntarily issued a White Paper which laid down that no lend-lease supplies would be used for exports. The only thanks they got was the setting up of an American committee to see that the promises of the White Paper were kept. More striking still, the British handed over to the Americans a mass of scientific secrets for war, including that for a controlled nuclear explosion. The Americans had the industrial resources to develop this and, armed with the British secret, had atomic bombs ready by 1945. The British received no acknowledgement or reward, other than a personal promise from Roosevelt to Churchill that Great Britain should share fully in all nuclear advances. This promise lapsed on Roosevelt's death, and the British had to start out again on their own. The British in fact assumed a more or less permanent merger of the two countries. The Americans accepted only a short-term combination and tried to put it on a business footing. This brought trouble later. It mattered less during the war. The Americans appreciated that Great Britain must be kept afloat as a major belligerent, and, of course, many of them wanted to do so in any event.

The Arcadia conference also determined future strategy. The British were apprehensive that the Americans, under the impact of Pearl Harbour, would turn their main strength against Japan and would leave the European war to carry itself. This was a false alarm. The Americans stuck to the ABC-1 doctrine that Germany, as the principal enemy, must be defeated first. This decision determined the shape of the second World war. It seems to have been taken almost without discussion, and there is no evidence how it was reached. It followed naturally enough from previous habits of thought, when Germany had been at war and Japan had not. It may have been influenced also by the mistaken belief that there was a grand Axis design. Perhaps, too, the British and Americans were frightened of what might happen in Europe if they stood aside. A German victory, a Russian victory, or a compromise peace, were alike abhorrent to them. Probably the motives were simpler and more practical.

between one fifth and one quarter of what they provided under lend-lease. The United States contributed 11 per cent. of its war expenditure to the United Kingdom; and the United Kingdom contributed 9 per cent. of its war expenditure to the United States. Both countries devoted 4¾ per cent. of their national income to aiding others, including, of course, each other.

War in the Pacific was the navy's affair, and the American army wanted to get into action. With its own mobilization hardly begun, it could do this only by supporting the British, and they were committed to the European theatre. The consequences were odd. British forces were not fighting Germany except in the air. They were fighting Italy. Thus the Americans, by deciding not to go against the less important enemy, Japan, were in fact drawn into going against Italy, who was less important still.

Churchill returned from Washington well pleased. He had secured full cooperation with the United States and a decision for early action in French North Africa. This decision did not work out. Disasters in the Far East forced a diversion from it. The first disasters came even before Churchill left for America. On 8 December Admiral Tom Phillips at Singapore learnt that the Japanese were about to land on the coast of Malaya. There were few British aeroplanes at Singapore. Phillips himself had no aircraft carrier and recognized that he should at once remove his two big ships to Port Darwin in Australia out of harm's way. But, with the other two services already engaged, it was inconceivable that the navy should go off without striking one blow against the enemy. Phillips decided to attack the Japanese invaders, 'relying on surprise to off-set the weakness and unsuitability of his force'.[1] He at once put to sea. Shortly afterwards he received a message that, as the Japanese were overrunning the airfields in north Malaya, no air cover could be provided. On 9 December Japanese aeroplanes sighted the British ships. Surprise was lost. Phillips turned back, then decided to bewilder the Japanese by going forward after all.

On 10 December Japanese bombers attacked the British force. Within two hours the *Prince of Wales* and the *Repulse* were sunk. Over 2,000 men were saved. Six hundred, including Phillips and his flag captain, were lost. Britannia no longer ruled the waves of the Far East. In England 10 December 1941 was the darkest day of the war. The British people, conditioned by their past, could stomach military defeats. They were shaken by the loss of two great ships. The gloom was overdone. British sea power had never been a reality in the Far East during the twentieth century. The British had relied first on the Japanese alliance and then on a vague hope that, if things went wrong,

[1] Gwyer, *Grand Strategy*, iii, i. 308.

the main fleet would somehow arrive at Singapore in time. Nor did it need this disaster to show that the day of battleships, unsupported by aircraft, was over. Even the sinking of the two ships was not decisive. The critical shortage in the Far East was in fighter aeroplanes, not in capital ships; and this was due in its turn to the concentration on heavy bombers. This strategical obsession was the main cause of British misfortunes in the second World war.

Further disasters followed. In Libya Auchinleck had been driven forward beyond his resources by Churchill's goadings, and his situation was made worse by Malta's weakness, also in fighter aeroplanes. Rommel was able to bring in reinforcements. The British army, badly led and equipped with inferior tanks, was driven out of Cyrenaica at the end of January, back to the line of Gazala and Tobruk. No new supplies could be sent. With the Japanese on the march, forces were being belatedly pushed into Singapore. Now indeed came a penalty for neglect and for the admiralty's insistence that Singapore should be exclusively their affair, fortified only against attack from the sea. The Japanese advanced down the Malayan peninsula, superior in fighting skill, though not in strength. The Australian government set up a cry of imperial betrayal, and more troops were poured in, even when it was clear that Singapore was doomed. On 15 February General Perceval and 60,000 British troops surrendered. This was the greatest capitulation in British history, a blow, according to some judges, from which British prestige in the Far East never recovered.

That prestige had long rested on bluff. The British hoped to maintain it by the shadow of a great name and a fleet which was not there. Once at war with Germany, they gambled, and had to gamble, that Japan would remain neutral. Before Pearl Harbour, Singapore came inevitably at the bottom of the list. Churchill had contributed characteristic faults. He tried to deter the Japanese with hard words and then with two battleships, not supported by air power. Overburdened with other work, he failed to inquire into Singapore's defences and, as so often, took his will for the deed.[1] At the end, he sent further troops into certain captivity in order to appease the Australians. Once more, he had attempted too much with inadequate

---

[1] 'I ought to have known. My advisers ought to have known and I ought to have been told, and I myself ought to have asked.' Churchill, Second World War, iv. 43.

resources, but this time he was not alone. In trying to remain a World Power in all spheres, the British people, or at any rate the government, were bidding above their strength. All the same, the fall of Singapore would have brought ruin to any lesser man.

As it was, it brought trouble enough. The months from February to November 1942 were politically the most disturbed time of the war. During this period the parties supporting the government lost four by-elections to Independents. There was general dissatisfaction with failure and, among some of the politically informed, a desire for an independent minister of defence, with Churchill retained only as an oratorical figure-head. Churchill challenged this underground muttering imme-diately after his return from Washington and obtained a vote of confidence on 29 January by 464 against 1.[1] Whatever Churchill's mistakes, there was no one better to put in his place —certainly not Shinwell or Lord Winterton, the ill-assorted leaders of an unavowed Opposition.[2] Hence Churchill survived the innumerable setbacks of the time—Singapore, the loss of Malaya and Burma, no victories in the Middle East. British opinion, ever set on the sea, was more outraged on 12 February, when the two German battlecruisers, the *Scharnhorst* and the *Gneisenau*, withdrawing from Brest to Germany, sailed through the English Channel in defiance of the R.A.F. and Royal Navy. As a matter of fact, this was a German retreat, which brought the British great alleviation of their Atlantic anxieties.

There was, however, a deeper cause of discontent which re-vived class antagonisms and the prewar conflicts. This was the tug of loyalties between the United States and Soviet Russia. Churchill, and with him nearly all those in responsible positions, staked everything on the Anglo-American partnership. Those lower down, particularly the factory workers, were enthusiastic only for Soviet Russia, once more restored to her idealistic pedestal by Hitler's attack. The Communist party increased its membership threefold after 22 June 1941. Communist shop-stewards were now strikebreakers where they had previously been troublemakers. They, and Left-wing opinion generally,

---

[1] Only three members of the I.L.P. (two of whom acted as tellers) voted against the government.
[2] The two men were known as Arsenic and Old Lace, the name of a play then running in London.

wanted 'a Second Front now', an immediate invasion of the continent. There were no doubt sound technical reasons why this was impossible. These reasons could not be publicly displayed, and in any case ordinary people usually explain failure by lack of will, not by lack of means. The governing classes were suspected of being indifferent to Russia's need and fearful of her success. These suspicions could not be lightly brushed aside: without contented and cooperative munition workers, no war. There were sentimental gestures of friendship towards Russia. Mrs. Churchill raised a fund for Russian aid. Red Army day was celebrated by generals, bishops, and lord mayors. The B.B.C. added the *International* to its nightly roll-call of Allied anthems.[1] The demand for a second front went on unallayed.

At this moment Sir Stafford Cripps returned, without authorization, from his post as ambassador to Russia. He enjoyed wide esteem, altogether undeserved, as the man who had brought Russia into the war. He had a high, indeed an excessive, confidence in his own powers. Though still excluded from the Labour party—or perhaps because of that—he became the hero of the discontented Left. Churchill attempted to buy him off with an offer of the ministry of supply. Cripps demanded increased powers and a seat in the war cabinet. Churchill had quite other intentions. A minister of production was needed, if only to coordinate plans with the Americans, and here was the opportunity to revive the former project of a supreme minister, determining priorities and allocations of raw materials. The minister of supply, along with the minister of aircraft production and the supply department of the admiralty, would dwindle into an administrator, as the service ministers had done. Cripps refused this diminished post. On the other hand, Beaverbrook's chance seemed to have come again. On 4 February 1942 he became minister of war production and so virtual dictator of Great Britain's war economy. This was a short-lived triumph.

Beaverbrook fought to control war transport. He won. He fought to control labour. He lost. His improvising zest broke on the rock of Ernest Bevin. Beaverbrook had a fatal weakness. He had no political following. He commanded no wide popularity in parliament or in the country. He was, in his own words, a court favourite, who owed his position to Churchill's friendship.

[1] The B.B.C. soon escaped from this embarrassment by deciding that the roll-call had now grown too long to be played every night and so did not play it at all.

The protecting hand was now withdrawn. Beaverbrook's defeat was cloaked by the excuse of physical illness. No doubt more lay behind. Churchill could not go into battle against Bevin. Besides he did not want to. Beaverbrook was as enthusiastic for Soviet Russia and the Second Front as any factory worker. Churchill resisted these enthusiasms. This brought Beaverbrook down. He left the government. Oliver Lyttelton became minister of production[1] in his place. Lyttelton belonged to the modern type of managing director who cooperated with trade union leaders. He made no claim to control labour. He did not at first even claim to control priorities and allocations, though he gradually gained this by his control of supplies from America. At the same time, Churchill found a way of making Cripps harmless or even useful. He was given the limelight instead of power and became leader of the house of commons. The gestures to Left-wing opinion went further. Attlee was officially named deputy prime minister. Kingsley Wood, the only solid Conservative in the war cabinet, was ejected from it, on the pretext that Greenwood, who had failed, was being ejected also. Despite Churchill's respect for the party system, the war cabinet after February 1942 was made up of individuals. Attlee was the only party wheel-horse; all the others were outsiders or former rebels.[2] The need to conciliate public opinion triumphed over the parties, as it did during the first World war.

Cripps was, for the moment, the dominant figure. He told the house of commons in his prim voice: 'Personal extravagance must be eliminated altogether', and he rejoiced at introducing measures of austerity: no petrol for pleasure motoring, the clothes ration cut down, sporting events curtailed, a limit of 5s. on meals in restaurants. Churchill gave him rope enough to hang himself. A really thick rope was soon offered. The tale of disaster in the Far East mounted. The attempt to create a naval front against the Japanese in the Dutch East Indies collapsed on 9 March after the battle of the Java Sea. The Japanese invaded and overran Burma. They penetrated into the Indian Ocean with a fleet far superior to that now commanded by Somerville. It was feared that they would strike across the Ocean and take Ceylon. In early April the flood was

---

[1] For some reason, 'war' disappeared from the title.

[2] Cripps was a Labour rebel. Churchill was a Conservative rebel; Eden a Conservative rebel of a sort. Bevin, Anderson, and Lyttelton were gatecrashers.

unexpectedly stayed. The Japanese were concerned mainly with the Pacific. India and its ocean did not interest them except as securing their flank. They never contemplated the far-fetched plan, attributed to them by the British, of joining hands with the Germans across the wide expanses of the Middle East. A few British fighter aircraft, which they encountered near Colombo, deterred their fleet from further advance. After April 1942 the Japanese navy attempted no offensive action in the Indian Ocean, and their army on the frontiers of India attempted none until 1944. India was not, as was supposed, in imminent danger. The Japanese were too busy elsewhere.

This could not be appreciated at the time. It seemed urgent to win over Indian opinion. There was another motive for a con-ciliatory gesture. Roosevelt, like most Americans, was deeply suspicious of British imperialism. If the united nations were fighting for freedom, India too, he thought, should be free. Cripps was clearly the man for the situation. He was a Left-wing socialist and had long been friendly with the Indian Congress leaders. On 22 March he flew to India, armed with a draft declaration that the British government would grant full independence to India if demanded by a constituent assembly after the war. His discussions were fruitless. The old insoluble conflict between Moslems and Hindus again raised its head. As well, Congress demanded immediate self-government with a minister of defence in full independent control. Gandhi said: 'This appears to be a post-dated cheque.'[1] On 10 April the talks broke down. Cripps returned to England. Congress opinion was in fact divided. Nehru was ready to support the war against Japan if self-government were granted. Gandhi, and with him the majority of Congress, would have tried to make peace and, failing this, would have relied on non-resistance.

The failure of the negotiations with Cripps thwarted Nehru's patriotism. He joined with Gandhi, and Congress proclaimed civil disobedience against the British authorities. There were fresh disorders. In August Gandhi, Nehru, and many other Congress leaders were again imprisoned—this time for the duration of the war. The British insisted on defending India, against the will of her political leaders, and paid for the privilege of doing so. All the costs of the war in India were debited to

---

[1] A bystander added: 'and drawn on a crashing bank!'

Great Britain and produced sterling balances at the rate of one million pounds a day. This was a curious outburst of imperial obstinacy: the British incurred a vast debt and many casualties for the sake of a country which they had promised to leave when the war was over. Of course, the British needed India as their base for the reconquest of Burma and Malaya, and this reconquest in turn had to be pursued in order to demonstrate that Great Britain was still a world Power. But essentially the defence of India sprang from habit. As in the Mediterranean, the British remained in India because they were there already and continued to behave in the fashion of an imperial power, even though they had formally announced that the fashion was soon to be given up. Nothing else could be expected of Churchill, but the Labour leaders, including Cripps, also responded to the last call of the Raj.

Cripps returned from India with his position shaken: admired now by Conservatives, but less so by the Left. Conservatives, too, soon proved restless. America's entry into the war brought no improvement in British conditions. On the contrary, the shipping position became worse. The Americans neglected convoy, and the U-boats had an easy time sinking their ships. American shipyards could not cover the losses until December 1942. There was nothing left over for British needs. As well, British resources were strained in running convoys to Russia and, as the nights drew shorter, losses increased. In June the admiralty ordered the most unfortunate of these convoys, P.Q. 17, to disperse on a false alarm that the big German ships were at sea, and twenty-three out of thirty-four defenceless ships fell easy victims. Total British imports for the year fell under 25 million tons, and the British scraped by only because the food and supply ministries had, as usual, greatly overestimated their requirements.[1] Even so life became harsher. In March the extraction rate for wheat was raised to 85 per cent. The British people did not eat white bread again until after the war.

A new shortage now menaced. Coal was the overriding problem of 1942, as the railways had been in the winter of 1940-1. Both mines and miners were growing older. The labour force was down 10 per cent. on prewar, and not surprisingly. The

---

[1] Food demanded 12·4 million tons, and supply 15·1 million. The actual realized figures were 11·4 million tons for food and 13·3 million for raw materials. Yet there were no unmanageable shortages.

miners were badly paid: in 1938, out of 100 industries they
came 81st, and their position had not much improved four
years later. Younger miners were going into munitions; 80,000
were in the armed forces. Coal output had been 227 million
tons in 1938. Now it threatened to fall under 200 millions, while
the demand from the factories was constantly rising. Though
the mines were still in incompetent private hands, the responsibility lay on socialists: Cripps as leader of the house, Dalton
now president of the board of trade. In March Dalton commissioned the indefatigable planner Sir William Beveridge to
prepare a scheme for rationing domestic consumers. It was
ready in May and, unlike other rationing schemes, leaked out
before it could begin to operate. The Conservatives raised a
howl. Beveridge's plan hit the dwellers in larger houses and the
possessors of electric fires, in other words, the richer classes. As
well, the Conservatives, always most combative over coal,
suspected that Dalton was preparing to smuggle in nationalization by the back door.

This was the only successful Conservative revolt of the war.
The government ran away. Rationing of coal was scrapped.
Instead there was to be control, that is, consumers simply got
less than before.[1] But the mines did not escape entirely. A new
ministry of fuel and power, detached from the board of trade,
was set up under a safe Liberal, Gwilym Lloyd George, who
soon found himself directing coal-production despite his
protestations of anti-socialist virtue. More immediately, a committee under Lord Greene gave the miners a substantial increase in wages and a national minimum. Discontent was
allayed, though output did not go up. Respectable opinion was
irritated that the miners did not now run over with patriotic
energy. Why should they? They had previously been among the
most impoverished elements in the community and were not
much impressed at being put more nearly on a level with others.
They wanted security for the future, and this they could not be
given by a government dependent on Conservative votes.

There was little economic discontent outside the coalfields
except over occasional specific grievances. On the essential

[1] Domestic users of coal ultimately received two-thirds of their prewar consumption, whereas the consumption of electricity went up 10 per cent. The
abandonment of coal-rationing was, however, probably wise. Rationing implied a
guarantee of supplies, and with coal this could not be given. 'Fair shares' broke
on physical obstacles.

matter of the war, national unity was greater than in any previous period of British history, and as great as has ever been achieved in any country. The I.L.P. members of parliament opposed the war on pacifist grounds, and some high-minded men believed that the Germans would turn against Hitler if offered generous enough terms. They preached in the void. A British statesman who had pursued anything less than total victory would have been swept away by a storm of public indignation—a storm in which factory workers and housewives would have been as resolute as journalists or politicians. This patriotism was not only deep. It was also sane. The women who distributed white feathers in the first World war worked part time on munitions in the second. There was no new Bottomley. The independents who broke the electoral truce, though critical of the way in which the war was being run, were otherwise not much different from the ordinary run of M.P.s. One of them, W. J. Brown, had been a Labour M.P. from 1929 to 1931; another, Tom Driberg, subsequently rose to respectability as chairman of the Labour party.

There was no cheap organ of hate on the *John Bull* model. The war had one important outcome in the newspaper world. For the first time the masses—other ranks in the forces and factory workers—read a daily newspaper, and this carried the *Daily Mirror* to the top of the circulation list. The *Mirror* was popular in a special sense. Previous popular newspapers, the *Daily Mail* and the *Daily Express*, were created by their proprietors, Northcliffe and Beaverbrook—men not at all ordinary. The *Mirror* had no proprietor.[1] It was created by the ordinary people on its staff and especially by Harry Guy Bartholomew, a man who worked his way up from office boy to editorial director. The *Mirror* was, in its favourite word, brash, but it was also a serious organ of democratic opinion and owed its success as much to its sophisticated columnist Cassandra[2] as to Jane, its strip-tease strip-cartoon. The *Daily Mirror* gave an

---

[1] In March 1942 the *Mirror* provoked the government by its demagogic demands for a more energetic conduct of the war. They attempted to discover the proprietor or principal shareholder (in the absurd belief that he might be an enemy citizen) and found that there was none. Churchill then wished to suppress the paper. Morrison, the home secretary, seconded by Beaverbrook, reduced this to a solemn warning.

[2] Cassandra (William Connor) started in charge of an astrology column and gradually transformed himself into a distinguished writer.

indication as never before what ordinary people in the most ordinary sense were thinking. The English people at last found their voice, and the historian is the more grateful for this voice, since the second World war, unlike the first, produced no distinctive literature. There were no war poets during the war, and few war novels or memoirs after it.[1] There were no war songs—only *Lili Marlene*, which was borrowed from the Germans. The silence was itself significant. The fighting men grumbled as they always had. But they did not feel this time the futility of war. They even had confidence in their leaders or at least in some of them. The war was a people's war in the most literal sense. The Englishman who fought the second World war believed that the war was worth fighting. They also believed by and large that they would win it.

The fighting men were much more part of the community and much less a race apart than they had been in the first World war. A great many of them were stationed in Great Britain —a large part of the navy and the air force all along, and then the army accumulating for the invasion of France; while on the other side civilians in the Home Guard, civil defence, or merely being bombed, were clearly in the war. The servicemen overseas, in Egypt or India, had a link with England provided by shortwave radio and heard the same programmes as listeners at home. Of these programmes one was pre-eminent: second only to Churchill's speeches in influence and inspiration, or even ranking ahead of them in the later years of the war. ITMA (It's That Man Again) characterized the second World war as, say, Mademoiselle from Armentières characterized the first, indeed a good deal more so. ITMA was a nonsense programme, impossible to describe, centred on Tommy Handley. The entire nation listened. Everyone knew the imaginary figures: Colonel Chinstrap, Mona Lot, Funf, Mrs. Mopp. Everyone repeated their signature-phrases: 'I don't mind if I do'; 'Don't forget the diver'; 'Can I do you now, sir?' Handley could not sing nor even, in any serious sense, act; but he deserved, though he did not receive, a place in Westminster Abbey.

[1] Some young men who were already poets continued to write poetry when they were in the services. This did not make them war poets in the sense that Blunden, Sassoon, or Owen had been. Similarly, there are memoirs of adventures during the second World war, but not memoirs in the Montague, Graves, Manning spirit.

One other radio programme distinguished the second World war. This was the Brains Trust, started for a few experimental weeks in 1941 and continued throughout the war. Listeners sent in questions. Three men answered them. The classic three were Julian Huxley, scientist; C. E. M. Joad, philosopher; and Commander Campbell. The early questions were factual. Later they grew speculative and moral. The talkative trio were never at a loss.[1] Though the Brains Trust was entertainment, it was also part of the increased intellectual and cultural activity which went on during the war. Other signs of this were the lunchtime concerts which Dame Myra Hess ran at the National Gallery[2] and, even more remarkable, the Army Bureau of Current Affairs (ABCA). The Bureau sent fortnightly pamphlets to army units, which met under the guidance of a subaltern and discussed them. Of course there was an element of pretence in this. Most other ranks were merely glad to sit down and smoke for half an hour, just as clerical workers in London welcomed somewhere to go at lunchtime. But these enterprises, or the more elaborate activities of CEMA (the Council for the Encouragement of Music and the Arts), were also real. There was a genuine will to bring the best of everything to the people, and the people on their side raised their standards. Patriotism and the Brains Trust, fighting the Nazis and lunchtime concerts were different expressions of the brief period when the English people felt that they were a truly democratic community.

Of course people were not contented solely out of patriotism and democratic spirit. Most of them were also better off. While the true cost of living had risen in 1942 by 43 per cent. since 1938, average weekly earnings were 65 per cent. higher, and the disproportion increased thereafter—in 1944 the cost of living was 50 per cent. higher than in 1938 and weekly earnings were 81½ per cent. higher. Broadly speaking, the entire population settled at the standard of the skilled artisan. This was a comedown for the wealthier classes: no private motoring or foreign travel, few domestic servants or none, far fewer clothes and these less smart. It was security for the masses such as they had not known before. From the middle of 1942 onwards the health of

---

[1] The original three were gradually diluted and, though the Brains Trust lingered on for years, it was never the same again.

[2] The pictures from the National Gallery had been sent to a cavern in Wales for shelter, and the building stood empty.

the nation showed a steady, striking improvement. No one knows why. Was it due to more use of medical services? better food? or merely less worry? Of course there were many hardships. Housing conditions were probably the worst. Building of private houses had virtually stopped,[1] and even the repair of houses damaged by bombs was not begun seriously until 1943. The daily routine of the housewife became hard. There were shortages in the shops despite rationing, and fewer shops. Most purchases had to be carried home instead of being delivered. Still, as the historian of transport remarks, 'the schemes worked because of the public conviction that they were both reasonable and necessary'.[2]

Occasionally the public jibbed. They refused to spend their holidays at home, despite government exhortations and the withdrawal of holiday trains. Another little breaking-point was reached in the autumn of 1942. The ministry of transport stopped the special trains bringing cut-flowers from Cornwall and the Scilly Isles. The ban was defied. Enterprising traders travelled on passenger trains, their suitcases loaded with flowers. In March 1943 Churchill intervened and had the special trains restored. After all, if unlimited tobacco was being provided (largely on lend-lease), why not cut-flowers? Horse racing, too, was treated gently. In May 1944, 10,000 tickets for Ascot were issued on a single day, and traffic for Newmarket clogged Liverpool St. station at the very time when steel production was being cut because of transport difficulties. As the official historian says, 'Horse racing must have been among the few activities to escape through the now tightly-drawn net of war transport.'[3] These were trivial exceptions in a nation geared for war.

The Arcadia conference had confirmed British strategy: Europe first, despite the crumbling of empire in the Far East. The British chiefs of staff reviewed their detailed plans. They reached one negative decision: in March 1942 they abandoned subversion as an effective weapon. Churchill may still have dreamt of arming the insurgent populations. The chiefs of staff took a more realistic view. Positive decisions were more important. On 14 February 1942 the air ministry issued a new directive to bomber command. The primary object 'should now be focused on the morale of the enemy civil population

[1] Only 9,000 houses were built in 1943 against 360,000 in 1938.
[2] C. I. Savage, *Inland Transport*, 506.   [3] Ibid. 599.

and, in particular, of the industrial workers'. The immediate impulse for this directive was the introduction of a navigational device, known as *Gee*, which, it was calculated, would baffle German defences for the next six months. The deeper foundation was the belief in an independent strategical bomber offensive which would win the war all on its own. The directive did not pass uncontested. The admiralty wanted the main weight of bombing attack on enemy warships and submarines. The war office grudged the resources of industry and shipping, when it was building up an army for land operations. Churchill himself was sceptical and tended to regard independent bombing as something Great Britain had fallen back on when she stood alone. There were formidable advocates on the other side. Lindemann, now Lord Cherwell, Churchill's confidential adviser, produced powerful arguments, based on fallacious statistics.[1] Sir Arthur Harris, the new chief of bomber command, was a fierce fighting man, whose passionate advocacy overwhelmed rational calculation. Above all, there was the argument, that unless Great Britain conducted a bomber offensive, she would do nothing against Germany in the long months before any invasion was possible anywhere. This was unanswerable. Harris went ahead.

Harris pressed for indiscriminate or as he called it 'barnyard door' bombing on two grounds. He genuinely believed that the German people could be cowed from the air as he had once cowed the tribesmen of Irak. He also recognized that his hastily trained crews could not bomb with precision and that they must hit a barnyard door if they were to hit anything at all. This argument was self-defeating: the more crews were used on indiscriminate bombing, the more precision bombing was postponed to an indefinite future, indeed to the never-never. Harris knew that he could not achieve decisive results in 1942 with his existing force, but he could not afford to wait for a larger one. Unless he acted at once, his bombers would be put at the

---

[1] Cherwell has sometimes been given sole, or main, responsibility for the bombing offensive. This is an exaggeration. He merely provided arguments to sustain a case which was already being strongly pressed by the air ministry and the chief of bomber command. Cherwell exaggerated the number of bombers available and the accuracy with which they would reach even the target of a large town. Further, like nearly everyone else, he assumed that German economy was already fully stretched and that workers, put on house repairs, would have to be taken off munitions. He also assumed, wrongly, that German morale was inferior to British.

service of the admiralty, and production would be shifted from bombers to fighters, tanks, and landing-craft. His offensive was therefore an advertising campaign to impress the government, the public, and the Americans. The effect on the Germans was less important. The targets were deliberately chosen for their publicity value. Lübeck (28 March) and Rostock (24–27 April) were not important in the Germany economy. But they were medieval towns, full of wooden houses, and burnt well. On 30 May, even more dramatically, Harris put a thousand bombers into the air over Cologne. This was sensational news. The Germans retaliated by 'Baedeker' raids on historic English towns, Exeter being the worst hit—also a waste of their re-sources. Otherwise little was achieved. By the autumn of 1942 bomber command had outrun its strength. Losses were once more becoming unmanageable. The German economy, accord-ing to the postwar American survey, suffered a loss of produc-tion in 1942 of 2·5 per cent. The British survey reduced this estimate to 0·7 per cent. of total production and 0·5 per cent. of war production.[1] Though these figures were not known at the time, enough was known to point the inexorable conclusion that the independent bombing offensive was not in sight of winning the war.

Thus invasion of somewhere came back to the top of the pro-gramme. But where? At the Arcadia conference the Americans had light-heartedly endorsed the idea of a landing in French North Africa. They had assumed that this would take place almost at once. The Japanese attack diverted resources to the Pacific. As well, the Americans discovered that forces even for an unopposed landing—and it was by no means certain that the French would not oppose—could not be conjured out of the air. Most American leaders, including Marshall, chief of the army staff, and Stimson, the secretary for war, had no interest in the British policy of nibbling at the edges. They wanted a direct onslaught on Germany, and their advocacy was strengthened in May 1942 when Molotov, the Soviet foreign minister, came to London and Washington with an urgent demand for a second front. Churchill dared not go directly against the Americans. If he did, they might turn their backs on Europe and concentrate on the Pacific war. On 14 April therefore the British and American staffs agreed to prepare for a large-scale

[1] Webster and Frankland, *The Strategic Bombing Offensive*, i. 479.

landing in France. The Americans admitted that this could only be ready in 1943. They also wanted a smaller landing on the Cotentin peninsula, to take Cherbourg, in 1942. The British agreed, but with the unspoken reserve that it should take place only if Germany were already in collapse. Meanwhile, Churchill prodded Auchinleck to take the offensive. Victory in the western desert would eclipse the demand for a second front. Auchinleck refused. With Malta out of action and supplies pouring into Rommel, the British army was in no state to attack.

Churchill determined to get his way by a direct appeal to Roosevelt. On 17 June he went to Washington for the second time. He brought with him a bait: further details of the British advances in nuclear research. He brought also a demand: invasion of North Africa, not of France. Churchill's plan miscarried. Fighting had already started in Cyrenaica late in May, on Rommel's initiative, not on Auchinleck's. After a month's fighting, the British position broke. On 20 June Tobruk fell. Thirty-three thousand men surrendered. This was no moment for Churchill to impose a strategy on the Americans. He returned home with no decision reached.

Yet events had begun to impose a decision. To aid Auchinleck, the Americans diverted 300 Sherman tanks to Suez—tanks superior to the Germans', but also tanks subtracted from the second front. Churchill found political trouble waiting for him in England. The fall of Tobruk increased the dissatisfaction caused by the fall of Singapore, and there was as well a justified suspicion on the Left that no second front would be launched in 1942. The critics ventured this time on a vote of no confidence —a demonstration of hostility never attempted in the first World war. This was debated on 1 and 2 July. The attacks were rambling and confused. The leading critic, Sir John Wardlaw-Milne, an influential Conservative, spoilt his case by suggesting that the duke of Gloucester be made commander-in-chief. At this the house dissolved in laughter. Apart from the record of failure, the critics were girding against the way in which Churchill did everything himself. They wanted an independent minister of defence and could not find the man. Churchill, sustained by the party machines, stood firm. The motion was defeated by 476 to 25, with some 40 deliberate abstentions. But the cloud was still there. Churchill had to produce success, not a majority in the voting lobbies.

The worst was in fact over. Auchinleck went up to the front himself and took over command from Ritchie. The British army retreated to El Alamein, a position easily defended and only 60 miles from Alexandria. It was now Rommel's turn to outrun his supplies. Mussolini crossed to Libya and prepared to lead the triumphal entry into Cairo on a white horse. He was disappointed. On 25 July Rommel attempted to break through the British lines at Alamein and failed. He had reached his highest point. Churchill also scored a triumph in the field of strategy. Early in July he and the chiefs of staff formally ruled out a landing in France in 1942. This was open defiance of the Americans. Their chiefs of staff proposed to switch to the Pacific. Roosevelt rejected their advice. He wanted a dramatic military operation, if only to influence the approaching elections for Congress, and, if northern France were ruled out, 'then we must take the second best—and that is not the Pacific'.[1] Marshall, Admiral King, chief of naval operations, and Hopkins, Roosevelt's intimate, came to London with instructions to press for a landing in France. The British explained that they could not do it, and the Americans had no resources, particularly no ships, to do it themselves. Marshall continued to insist.[2] Roosevelt refused to back him and on 25 July decided firmly in favour of a landing in North Africa.

Strategical arguments could be paraded for this decision. Mastery of the Mediterranean would save shipping, though of course the shipping was being consumed mainly because of the African campaign. Conquest of North Africa would give the British and Americans some compensation, if Russia collapsed and Hitler remained in permanent control of Europe. Moreover, the Germans would have to go to the rescue of the Italians. Their military and air resources would be diverted from the Russian front and from northern France. The North

---

[1] Sherwood, *Papers of Harry Hopkins*, ii. 603–4.

[2] Marshall even quoted against Churchill a passage from Sir William Robertson's book, *Soldiers and Statesmen, 1914–1918*, condemning the Dardanelles expedition. Churchill replied neatly: 'Soldiers and statesmen here are in complete agreement' (Butler, *Grand Strategy* iii, ii. 633). In the first World war British staff officers, directed by Robertson, demonstrated to their own satisfaction that the Germans could move forces to the Balkan or Italian fronts by land faster than the British could move them by sea. In the second World war British staff officers, directed by Brooke, demonstrated to their own satisfaction that the British and Americans could move forces to North Africa and Italy by sea faster than the Germans could move them by land.

African campaign would thus be both an effective substitute for the second front and a preparation for it.[1] These arguments were really irrelevant. Churchill wanted a victory to still the discontent in England. Roosevelt wanted some 'action' for the American army in 1942. North Africa was the only place where their wishes met. The combined chiefs of staff recognized that this decision put off a true second front until 1943. Events soon proved that it had been postponed until 1944. Political needs came ahead of strategy and determined it, as often happens in war.

To please the Americans, Churchill asked them to provide a supreme commander for North Africa. General Eisenhower was appointed. Churchill had less congenial tasks. He had to break to Stalin the news that there would be no second front in 1942. He had also to stir up the British army in Egypt. For the sake of British prestige, and his own, Churchill needed a victory there, not merely a successful landing in French North Africa under American command. Early in August Churchill flew to Cairo. He found the British army bewildered by retreat and confused leadership. He found Auchinleck overburdened with responsibilities and looking apprehensively over his shoulder for the arrival of a German army on the Caucasus. Preparations had been made to abandon Egypt and the Suez canal.[2] Auchinleck refused to be prodded into a premature offensive. Churchill determined to restore confidence by changing the leaders. Maybe he hoped, too, to get more amenable ones. General Sir Harold Alexander was summoned from the frontier of Burma to replace Auchinleck. General Sir Bernard Montgomery[3] was called from England to command the eighth

---

[1] The idea of preparing for a second front by weakening the Germans elsewhere reflected the difference between the British and American outlooks. The British wanted to land in France only when Germany was already on the point of collapse. The Americans wanted to defeat Germany by attacking her at her strongest point. There were also differences within the British ranks. Brooke, the C.I.G.S., was anxious to avoid heavy casualties and advocated action in the Mediterranean largely to put off the second front, which he really did not want at all. The only positive gain he saw in it was the relief to shipping when the Mediterranean was opened. Churchill, with his old Gallipoli outlook, tended to believe that the Mediterranean backdoor was an easier way into Europe.

[2] Auchinleck has been sometimes blamed for this. In fact he was only carrying out instructions received from the chiefs of staff at the end of July: 'Should the worst arise . . . you must hold on to the Abadan area in the last resort—even at the risk of losing the Egyptian Delta.' Playfair, *The Mediterranean and the Middle East*, iii. 365.

[3] Bernard Law Montgomery (1887–   ), field marshal; commanded 3rd division, 1939–40; South East Command (England), 1942; commanded eighth

army.[1] This was a good combination. Nothing ruffled Alexander, neither the enemy, politicians, nor his own generals. Montgomery was the best British field-commander since Wellington: the only British general of the twentieth century who knew how to inspire enthusiasm among his men, and the only one also who conducted a battle instead of merely fighting it.

From Cairo Churchill went to Moscow. He had four meetings with Stalin. A strange encounter: Churchill who had once promoted the wars of intervention against bolshevism; Stalin who now personified bolshevism in the eyes of the world; old enemies who were soon to be enemies again. These first meetings proved surprisingly successful. No practical political questions were discussed. Stalin, though complaining at the failure to open a second front, warmed to the landing in North Africa. Perhaps he thought it was a considerable achievement to get the British and Americans engaged anywhere. Perhaps he was misled by Churchill's talk of 'a deadly attack upon Hitler next year'.[2] Probably both men, still intent solely against Hitler, had the sense not to quarrel. At any rate, all went well to the accompaniment of a lavish hospitality unknown in the West. Churchill hoped that he had established a genuine personal relationship with Stalin. He was probably wrong. But at least his freedom to move round the world—to Washington, to Cairo, and now to Moscow—enabled him, and through him Great Britain, to play a decisive part as intermediary between East and West until the following year, when Roosevelt, overcoming constitutional and physical difficulties, began to move around the world also.

Back in Cairo Churchill learnt news which seemed to confirm the British rejection of a second front in 1942. On 19 August British and Canadian forces landed at Dieppe. The attack was a failure and brought heavy losses. Over half the Canadians involved were killed or taken prisoners. The raid on Dieppe had been in contemplation for many months, partly to get experience of an opposed landing, partly to give the Canadian

army in North Africa, Sicily, and Italy, 1942–4; commander-in-chief, British Group of Armies and Allied Armies in Northern France, 1944; commanded 21st Army Group, 1944–5; cr. Viscount, 1946.

[1] Churchill's first nominee for the post was General Gott, who had distinguished himself in desert fighting. Gott was killed in an air accident two days later. He was in any case a tired man and probably without the gift of high command.

[2] Churchill, *Second World War*, ii. 433–4.

troops, who were kicking their heels in England,[1] something to do. Montgomery, who had been in charge originally, had insisted on air cover and a heavy naval bombardment. Then the R.A.F. announced that they had no aeroplanes to spare, and the admiralty refused to supply any big ships. Montgomery, fortunately for his reputation, left for the Middle East. The plans went on of their own momentum, and the raid was undertaken despite the lack of all the conditions which had been laid down for its success. The old story of Gallipoli, Norway, and Greece was told once more: improvised muddle again brought discreditable failure. It was alleged that the raid on Dieppe provided valuable lessons for future landings. The practical lessons could have been learnt much more cheaply. But a great general lesson was learnt, though it, too, should not have needed this fresh experience. The Dieppe raid showed that it was not enough to say: 'Things will be all right on the night.' Courage and initiative were no substitutes for detailed planning. In this sense, failure at Dieppe was the preliminary for success at D-day. For once, British strategists actually thought ahead. Otherwise Dieppe was irrelevant to the question of a second front. The question was answered decisively in the negative by lack of equipment. A Left-wing government, intent on aiding Russia, might have shifted the priorities from bombers to landing craft. As it was the independent bomber offensive and the campaign in the Mediterranean kept the second front on a starvation diet.

At any rate, the decision in favour of the Mediterranean had been taken. Men had now to wait for the plans to mature. There was again a period, as Churchill has called it, of 'suspense and strain'. On 30 August Rommel made a last attempt to break the lines of Alamein. His attempt was defeated. Montgomery refused to be hurried in his own offensive. As often happened after one general had been dismissed for being too slow, his successor proved to be even slower. In England Cripps lost control of the house. On 8 September he rebuked members who had shown their boredom during a speech of Churchill's. Leading members answered him sharply. Cripps had his own complaints. He wanted the war cabinet to be in real control of the war, as it had been in Lloyd George's time. He also wanted a war-planning directorate which would leave the chiefs of staff

---

[1] The Canadian government refused to allow their forces to be used in the Middle East campaign, an affair which did not interest them.

free for detail and routine. This had a plausible appeal. The chiefs of staff, with their immediate responsibility for every operation, had little time to survey the general shape of the war. But it would have ended Churchill's dictatorship, and he would have nothing to do with it.

Cripps resigned, though he agreed to postpone his resignation until after the approaching battle in Egypt. The enthusiasm for him had already proved 'a fleeting passion', as Beaverbrook had foretold it would.[1] After Montgomery's victory, Churchill did not need a cover, and in any case Cripps had none to give. He left the war cabinet, gave pious addresses on moral leadership, and took over the ministry of aircraft production, where he produced order, though also a slower rate of production, after the chaos which Beaverbrook had left.[2] Eden became leader of the house, and Morrison, the home secretary, succeeded Cripps in the war cabinet—a return to the principle of party balance. The war cabinet thereafter kept the position on the side lines, from which Cripps had tried to rescue it.

Montgomery waited obstinately until he had built up a crushing superiority in tanks and guns. On the night of 23 October he began the battle of Alamein. Unlike previous commanders who had sent tanks over the desert in the spirit of cavalry, Montgomery planned a setpiece battle. He put all the weight of his armour into a slogging match against the enemy's strongest point. It was Robertson's old doctrine of 'the longest purse'. Montgomery lost more tanks than the Germans and Italians did. The proportion of casualties among men actually engaged was as heavy as on the Somme.[3] Montgomery could afford these losses, thanks to the flow of supplies through the Suez canal. Rommel could not, thanks to the destruction from Malta of Axis convoys. Montgomery began an encircling movement only when the enemy had been worn down.

On 4 November Rommel defied Hitler's order and began to retreat. In pursuit Montgomery was less successful, or maybe the British army was too tied to routine. Rommel abandoned Cyrenaica and Tripoli, but he and his army got away. Still, it was a great victory. Egypt was secure for good. The eighth

[1] Beaverbrook to Churchill, 17 Feb. 1942. Churchill, *Second World War*, iv. 73.
[2] Cripps substituted a minimum programme of what M.A.P. could actually do for Beaverbrook's 'carrot' programmes.
[3] Far more men were now engaged in supplying the fighting line. Hence the overall percentage of losses was much smaller.

army began an advance which ended only in Italy. Alamein came only just in time.[1] It was won on 4 November. On 7 November Anglo-American forces landed in French North Africa, and with that British military action was finally merged into the coalition war. On 15 November the church bells were rung in England—significantly for Alamein, not for the landing in North Africa. They were celebrating victory; they were also ringing out the end of British strategic independence.

The landings in French North Africa took place ironically four days after the elections to Congress which they had been expected to influence. Their success was also slower than had been anticipated. Reversing the usual roles, the British had wanted to push more deeply into the Mediterranean. The Americans had insisted on cautiously hanging back. The Germans took over unoccupied France. The French fleet escaped them by scuttling itself at Toulon. But the Germans had time to establish their control of Tunis. The six weeks which had been anticipated by Marshall for securing North Africa turned into six months. There were political troubles. Admiral Darlan, one of Pétain's closest associates, was in Algiers when the Allies landed—perhaps by chance. The Americans, after some bargaining recognized him as the representative of French authority. This was a purely military decision. The Americans wanted a quick end to the resistance by the French forces in North Africa, and only Darlan seemed powerful enough to issue the necessary orders.[2] But it provoked an outcry in England. Even the king was perturbed.[3]

There had always been a suspicion that Churchill was only fighting a nationalist war against Germany, not an ideological war against 'fascism'.[4] The deal with Darlan, a French 'Fascist', seemed to confirm these suspicions. They were, on this occasion,

[1] Whether the victory was strategically desirable is another matter. Rommel would have been more precariously placed if his lines of communication had still run to Alamein when the British and Americans had established control of French North Africa.

[2] The Americans had at first intended to use Giraud, a general of the first World war who escaped from a German prison in the second. It soon turned out that he had no authority, and the Americans were resolute against de Gaulle.

[3] Wheeler-Bennett, George VI, 556.

[4] It is true that Churchill was only interested in overthrowing Hitler. He had no desire to disturb Franco in Spain nor much in overthrowing Mussolini. He wrote: 'Even when the issue of the war became certain Mussolini would have been welcomed by the Allies.' Second World War, v. 48.

misplaced. Churchill, too, distrusted Darlan and was embarrassed at being carried along by the Americans—particularly when British troops were doing most of the fighting. The worst sting was removed when Darlan was assassinated by a French royalist on Christmas eve. But clearly the British and Americans needed to sort out their political intentions—both in regard to France and over a wider field. More urgently, they had to decide their future strategy, now that the campaigns in North Africa and the western desert seemed within sight of success.

Stalin declared that he could not leave Moscow. The Russians had just destroyed a German army at Stalingrad and were beginning to prepare for victory. Roosevelt and Churchill, with their accompanying flock of advisers, therefore met at Casablanca from 14 to 25 January 1943. The two men laboriously reconciled the rival French generals, Giraud and de Gaulle. This proved a pointless operation. Giraud had no political skill. De Gaulle had much and soon made himself sole leader of resurgent France. The other act of high policy was perhaps of greater importance. Roosevelt produced his terms for ending the war: 'Unconditional Surrender.' Churchill endorsed the phrase, after trying, unsuccessfully, to exclude Italy. The war cabinet endorsed it also.[1] Much controversy centred later on the phrase. It perhaps gave Stalin some security against a compromise peace between the western Powers and Germany. It provided public opinion with an assurance against any new Darlan deal. It prevented any inter-allied wrangling and German complaints such as there had been over the Fourteen Points. On the other hand, it has been urged that it took the heart out of the moderate elements in enemy countries who wished to end the war and gave Axis propagandists an invaluable weapon. Probably there was not much in this. A leading American historian has written: 'In my opinion, "unconditional surrender" did not prolong the war a day.'[2]

The Allied Great Powers were already committed to total victory. Germany and Japan would lose all their conquests, and Italy her colonies; all three would be disarmed. Against this, as Churchill said later (22 February 1944): 'Unconditional surrender means that the victors have a free hand. It does not mean that they are entitled to behave in a barbarous manner. ... If we are bound, we are bound by our own consciences to

[1] See Note A, p. 576.   [2] Morrison, *The Two Ocean War*, 239.

civilization.' The leaders of the Axis Powers went on dreaming
that they would get compromise terms, and in fact both Italy
and Japan surrendered on elaborate conditions. 'Unconditional
surrender' perhaps led the Allies to neglect their consideration
of postwar policy. Otherwise it was important, if at all, only by
completing the oblivion into which the Atlantic Charter had
already fallen. Fundamentally it changed nothing. In the first
World war it had seemed necessary to answer the question:
'what are we fighting for?' In the second the answer was
obvious: victory. The Allies wanted nothing except to be rid of
the nuisance which the Axis Powers had caused.

The strategical decisions were what mattered at Casablanca,
as at other conferences. The British and Americans had to face the
fact that the North African campaign was going to take longer
than they had expected—though how much longer they did not
yet realize. They were back at the old question: what next? It was
pretty clear that the continuing drain of supplies to North
Africa made any massive invasion of France impossible in 1943.
Marshall therefore proposed to shift American resources to the
Pacific. Churchill tried to hold him to Europe by offering a
landing in northern France after all. Marshall did not believe
him. But Roosevelt, as usual, would not turn his back on
Europe. The result was a compromise. The Mediterranean
campaign was to go on until Sicily was conquered. Then the
British and Americans would think again. The Americans intended to stop at this point; the British hoped for further distractions. At the same time, the Americans would move forward
in the Pacific, and the British promised to undertake an offensive in Burma also—a promise which they were unable to keep.

Germany was not altogether neglected. The American air
force was to join the strategical bomber offensive from Great
Britain. Here again there was equivocation. Harris and perhaps
some American airmen assumed that this offensive was intended
to defeat Germany without any action on land. Marshall and
most others regarded it as preparation for invasion. There was
another topic at Casablanca, the most urgent of all, though not
the most discussed. The shortage of shipping was 'a stranglehold
on all offensive operations'. Roosevelt, without warning his
shipping authorities, promised to transfer some American
shipping from the Pacific to the British. Churchill had already
withdrawn some ships from military use in order to build up

stocks. Now he cut down sailings to the Indian Ocean from 100 a month to 40 in order to sustain the Mediterranean campaign. This decision had disastrous consequences. The harvest had failed in Bengal. Imports of food were urgently needed and did not come. A million and a half Indians died of starvation for the sake of a white man's quarrel in North Africa.[1]

Victory there was delayed. Rommel, driven from Libya, took up a new defensive position on the borders of Tunis. Hitler sent in fresh forces. The Allied forces advancing from the west were driven back. The situation was redeemed only when Montgomery arrived across the desert. The two armies were then amalgamated: Eisenhower still as supreme commander, with Alexander as his deputy and in command of the land forces.[2] Axis resistance ceased only on 12 May. Over a quarter of a million prisoners were taken (about one third of them German), an uncovenanted mercy owed to Hitler's obstinate reinforcement of Tunis, on the Singapore model, when defeat was already certain. In England the church bells were rung again.[3] On 17 May the first convoy through the Mediterranean since 1941 left Gibraltar. On 26 May it reached Alexandria.

There was renewed debate over what to do next. Churchill again went to Washington (12–25 May). He urged anew the attack on Sicily, and thereafter an invasion of Italy. The Americans demanded that everything be subordinated to preparations for the second front. Churchill had still some assets. The bulk of the forces in North Africa was British, and the British could claim how they should be used. Moreover, there would be no serious fighting in 1943 unless they were used. The Mediterranean campaign had in fact created its own momentum, exactly as Marshall had feared. Once more there was a compromise. Eisenhower was instructed to make plans for invading Italy, though without any assurance that they would be acted on. In return the British were pinned down to Overlord,

---

[1] Behrens, *Merchant Shipping and the Demands of War*, 345–53. Some famine was inevitable in India when the supplies of rice from Burma were cut off, and the full extent of the failure of the harvest in Bengal was not known. Still, 'The North African campaign doomed almost inevitably to starvation any deficit area in India where the harvest failed'.

[2] The air commander, Tedder, and the naval commander, Cunningham, were also British. The appointment of Eisenhower was mainly windowdressing to please American opinion.

[3] Their sound was less sensational than after Alamein. The ban on ringing church bells for service had been removed on 19 April.

an invasion of northern France, on 1 May 1944. Churchill
pushed things a little further. He persuaded Marshall to accompany him to Algiers. Marshall found even the American generals
there eager to invade Italy. He grudgingly agreed to consider
their plans favourably. The British still seemed to be shaping
the course of the war.

The sands were shifting under them. 1943 was the year when
world leadership moved from Great Britain to the United
States. British strength was running out. American strength was
growing on a massive scale. The summer of 1943 saw the
decisive turn in the war at sea against the U-boats. March 1943
was the worst month of the war: 477,000 tons of shipping
sunk and only twelve U-boats destroyed in the north Atlantic.
Then there was a dramatic change. In July only 123,000 tons of
shipping were sunk, and thirty-seven U-boats. In the last quarter of the year 146,000 tons of shipping were sunk and fifty-three
U-boats. This victory had many causes. The Americans provided a flood of destroyers for convoy—260 in all during 1943.
The British, despite protests from Harris, diverted bombers to
escort duties and to attacking U-boats in the bay of Biscay. A
little later, the Americans actually provided aircraft carriers,
from their limitless resources, for escort duties. Finally, Portu-
gal, Great Britain's oldest ally, who had behaved in a far from
allied fashion earlier in the war, allowed the British and
Americans to use the Azores as an air base and so closed the gap
in mid-Atlantic. The German surface ships were also put out of
action. Germany's only battleship, the *Tirpitz*, was severely
damaged on 23 September by two British midget submarines,
while she lay at anchor in Alten Fiord, and was never again fit
for action.[1] Germany's only remaining battlecruiser, the
Scharnhorst,[2] was sunk by the *Duke of York* on 26 December.
Thanks to these various successes, British imports at 27 million
tons were a great improvement on the previous year.

Imports were also more needed. Great Britain could no longer
maintain herself as a Great Power from her own resources. The
determining shortage was manpower. British mobilization had
been more complete than that of any other belligerent and now

---

[1] The *Tirpitz* was repeatedly attacked thereafter by bombers and finally sunk
on 12 Nov. 1944.
[2] Her sister ship the *Gneisenau* had been irremediably damaged while passing
through the Channel on 12 Feb. 1942.

could not be carried further. Human beings, the foundation of all power, were running out. When the first manpower budget was drawn up in 1942, this was merely to allot labour according to requirements. The government still supposed that they were living within their manpower income and had only to determine how to spend it most usefully. Early in 1943 a fresh review revealed a different situation. The services and the munitions industries were demanding a labour increase of over one million. These demands could not be met. The total labour force was 150,000 down. Older men were falling out and, thanks to the declining birth rate between the wars, the young were too few to replace them. There were no more women to be mobilized, even part-time. Nor could more labour be taken from civilian industry. Rather civilian production had to be reinforced, now that household stocks—the spare suit in the cupboard for instance—had been used.

Civil defence was run down in the justified belief that there would be no more heavy raids by German bombers. In many spheres the production of munitions could be reduced. The services, in their usual fashion, had demanded too much of nearly everything, and industry had then provided more than they had demanded. The production of bombs, for instance, tailed off after the end of 1942, that of guns early in 1943, that of tanks a little later. Shells had been produced on a greater scale than in the first World war, though there was much less heavy fighting. As a result, there were far too many of them. The side of every country road had to be turned into a shell-dump. The occasional motorist drove for mile after mile past these neat heaps. Some of them were drawn upon after the landing in northern France. Most remained unused at the end of the war.

Still, despite these alleviations, there were vital shortages of war equipment, which the British could not supply without reducing their armed forces. Only American assistance kept British forces going at their high level. In the early days of lend-lease, the British brought in food, tobacco, and machine tools. They remained self-sufficient in munitions, apart from aircraft. Now they came to rely on the Americans for essential military requirements.[1] The Americans provided half the

[1] In 1941 munitions made up only 31·7 per cent. of American lend-lease to Great Britain (itself only a quarter of what it became in 1942 and one eighth of

British tanks, three-quarters of the tank transporters and two thirds of the transport aircraft. They provided most of the landing-craft and restored the losses of British merchant and naval ships. In 1941 the United States provided only 10 per cent. of the munitions for the British empire.[1] In 1943 they provided 27 per cent. and in 1944 28·7 per cent. They could easily afford to do so. In 1943 the American mercantile marine surpassed the British for the first time. In the early part of 1942 American munitions production was still less than British. By the end of 1943 it was four times as great, and in 1944 six. Yet the Americans also enjoyed a higher standard of life than before the war, while in Great Britain the production of consumer goods had shrunk to 54 per cent. The future was even darker. The British had run through their currency reserves, and the Americans, armed by the lend-lease agreement, refused to allow them to accumulate afresh. Sterling balances had been piled up to nearly £2,000 million. Exports were less than a third of prewar. Thus Great Britain could keep going as a Great Power during the war only with American assistance and seemed to have no chance of remaining a Great Power after it.

The British people did not appreciate this. Even Churchill assumed that confidence, and his personal relations with Roosevelt, would somehow carry the day. No one suggested that the United States and Soviet Russia should be left to finish off Hitler, while the British licked their wounds. Yet there was an unconscious withdrawal—due in part to weariness, in part to a renewed interest in home affairs. The victories in North Africa and later in Italy were too remote to revive men's spirits. Between mid-1943 and the landing in France on 6 June 1944 there were as many strikes as in the worst period of the first war. The Communist shop stewards could not stop them. Prosecutions of so-called Trotskyites by the ministry of labour were equally ineffective. The miners were again restless. Nothing would satisfy them short of nationalization. On 13 October Churchill rejected this. He said: 'Everything for the war, whether controversial or not, and nothing controversial that is not needed *bona fide* for the war.' The miners got only increased

---

what it became in 1943). In 1942 munitions made up 53·6 per cent. of lend-lease supplies and in 1943 70·3 per cent. In 1944 many civilian supplies, including tobacco, were cut out of lend-lease altogether.

[1] Only 2·4 per cent. under lend-lease.

wages on a national scale.[1] In many spheres Churchill's rule was not observed. Men talked of reconstruction as they had done during the first World war. This time they were determined not to be cheated, and therefore demanded the formulation of practical schemes while the war was on.

This demand was hard to resist. The governing classes were on their best behaviour, from conviction as well as from calculation. It was difficult to realize in a time of national inspiration and unity that this inspiration and unity would ever fade. The British people had risen, without fuss, to unparalleled heights of sacrifice and resolution. They deserved a reward. The most substantial of these rewards was a plan for universal social security, worked out by Sir William Beveridge.[2] This fulfilled at last the Fabian plans laid down by the Webbs before the first World war. It came some forty years too late and provided, as might be expected, against past evils: abject poverty and mass unemployment, one the great social evil before 1914 and the other between the wars. Neither was to present a problem after 1945. Moreover, Beveridge, the Liberal planner, assumed the continued working of capitalism and finally rejected the socialist doctrine of a social security provided by society. He took over the principle of flat-rate contributions, which Lloyd George had unwillingly accepted in 1911, and so perpetuated, seemingly for ever, the retrograde principle of the poll-tax, against which Englishmen had revolted as long ago as 1381.

Even so the Beveridge report seemed a great advance. In February 1943 the government gave it only faint blessing. Labour demanded more and revolted for the only time in the war. An amendment demanding stronger approval was defeated by 338 to 121. With two exceptions all Labour members not in office voted for the amendment. There was fresh pressure in the autumn. A new party, Commonwealth, came into existence on an idealistic socialist programme and won three by-elections. Some gesture had to be made. In November 1943 Lord Woolton, who had been a successful minister of food, became minister of reconstruction with a seat in the war cabinet, and thereafter spoke more favourably about the Beveridge plan.

---

[1] To deal with national wages, the miners' federation of Great Britain turned itself into the national union of mineworkers in Nov. 1944.

[2] Beveridge got the job against his will. He wanted to plan labour. Bevin did not like him and wished him on to Greenwood.

The government, in a fine fling of noble resolve, also pledged themselves to 'the maintenance of a high and stable level of employment after the war.'

Other projects were aired, and some accomplished. When men began to talk of economic planning, they went on to talk of planning in more practical forms: town planning and the use of land. A ministry of town and country planning was set up early in February 1943. An act of November 1944 proposed to secure development rights for the community—a revised version of the old radical proposals for the taxation of land values. Later events were to show the emptiness of these projects. One advance was real. The Education Act of 1944, promoted by R. A. Butler, outdid Fisher's act of 1918. The school-leaving age was to be raised to 15[1] and later to 16.[2] Secondary education of three types—grammar, technical, and modern—was to be free, without means test or other restriction. This unwittingly created a new class division between those who were clever enough to get into a grammar school at 'eleven plus' and those who were not. There was one other significant provision. Makers of previous education acts had assumed that all schools could be counted on to provide religious worship without being told to do so. Education acts were only concerned to ensure that the worship in schools, maintained by public money, was not denominational. The 1944 act made religion compulsory for the first time. Every state-aided school, primary or secondary, must begin each day with an act of non-denominational collective worship. This clause could hardly spring from stronger Christian conviction. The explanation was surely the reverse. The Christian devotion of teachers, or of parents, could no longer be relied on. Christianity had to be propped up by legislative enactment. The British people were, however, to show that they were more concerned with this world than with the next.

There was less need for political reform in the second World war than there had been in the first. The franchise was already fully democratic, with the two exceptions of the vote for business premises and in university constituencies. Labour would have liked to get rid of these and also to reduce further the powers of the house of lords. The Conservatives were reluctant. There were fruitless discussions between the two parties. In the end

[1] This came into force in 1947.   [2] Due in 1970.

a temporary measure merely brought the electoral registers up
to date and split constituencies with more than 100,000 electors
in two, thus creating twenty-five new seats at the 1945 election.
The completion of democratic franchise had to wait until 1948.[1]
In this odd way, Labour achieved its first great majority (in
1945) on a franchise which was not strictly democratic.

One political decision was of great negative importance. This
was the failure to make permanent the new system of local
administration which had developed during the war. The
regional commissioners, appointed in 1939, fortunately never
had to perform their allotted task of wielding executive powers
in case of a German invasion. Nevertheless, they became the
central figures of a vast regional system. The ministries engaged
in planning the life of the nation—food, transport, fuel and
power, labour, supply, the board of trade, information, and
others—set up regional offices, and these were coordinated by
the regional commissioners. If the board of trade closed a
civilian factory, the supply office knew that more workers were
available for a munitions factory; labour knew that a new
munitions factory would be opened; food knew that the demand
for rations would increase in a new area. A crisis, such as
followed heavy bombing, was at once met by the regional
authorities without waiting for the central government:
emergency supplies of food and clothing, emergency housing,
and advice from the local information office were all laid on.
War socialism could not have worked without this system.
Administratively it was a vast improvement on the historic
arrangement, where nothing was interposed between the central
departments in Whitehall and the elected local authorities of
the counties and county boroughs. But the regional commissioners savoured of emergency; Labour was suspicious of
dictatorship by officials; and the local authorities were jealous
at the encroachment on their powers. As a result, the regional
commissioners were abolished at the end of the war, and, though
many government departments kept their regional offices, the
chance was lost to give England the blessings of regional
government.

At the time, winning the war still took first place. With the
second front postponed until 1 May 1944, the British way of war

[1] The Conservatives argued later that the compromise of 1944 was binding on
Labour for all time.

had a last chance to prove its worth, though it was now under notice to quit. The months until March 1944 were the full and, as it proved, the final test of independent strategic bombing. Harris claimed that the Casablanca directive authorized his policy of indiscriminate area bombing.[1] The Americans did not agree. They believed that their heavily armed bombers could operate in daylight and therefore against precise targets. Sir Charles Portal, chief of the air staff, who was in operational control under the combined chiefs of staff, could not decide between the two strategies. The Americans were too independent to be overruled. In any case, Portal was less certain than Harris about the efficacy of area bombing, though—being somewhat in awe of Harris—he dared not say so.

There were therefore two separate air offensives, not a combined operation. The American offensive was a failure. Even their Flying Fortresses were no match for the German fighters. Harris drew the conclusion that the Americans should join in the night attacks. The Americans drew a different conclusion: that the air battle should be waged immediately against the German air force, and this policy was laid down at the Washington conference of May 1943 in the Pointblank directive. Harris, however, was undismayed. He argued that area bombing was also a contribution to defeating the German air force. In any case, the 'main aim' was still the destruction of German industry, and it made sense to get on with this instead of wasting time ineffectively against the German air force. He continued to dismiss selective bombing as the pursuit of 'panaceas', and experience seemed to prove him right.[2]

British bombers still went in therefore for indiscriminate destruction throughout 1943, and this was great. The industrial towns on the Ruhr were attacked from March to June; Hamburg from July to November; Berlin from November 1943 to

---

[1] Harris skilfully perverted the directive. It read: 'Your main aim will be the progressive destruction and dislocation of the German military, industrial and economic system and the undermining of the morale of the German people.' Harris substituted: 'progressive destruction and dislocation of the German military, industrial and economic system aimed at undermining the morale of the German people'. Webster and Frankland, *The Strategic Air Offensive*, ii. 14.

[2] Two 'panaceas' were attempted in 1943. The British bombed the Ruhr dams. Two were breached. The third was not. It held back the flood water, and nothing was achieved. The Americans bombed the ball-bearing factory at Schweinfurt. The Germans discovered, to their own surprise, that they had supplies for six months in the pipeline, and before then the factory was restored.

March 1944. Of this last attack Harris wrote: 'We can wreck Berlin from end to end if the U.S.A.A.F.[1] will come in on it. It will cost us 400–500 aircraft. It will cost Germany the war.'[2] These expectations were not fulfilled. Indiscriminate bombing could aim only at the centres of towns, and most factories were in the suburbs. Many houses were destroyed, and few factories. Of the factories destroyed, most were old ones, producing civilian goods. The war factories had already been safely dispersed. The British calculations assumed that the German economy was fully stretched, whereas it had in fact plenty of slack. The air offensive of 1943 compelled the Germans to take in some of this slack, and the civilian standard of life declined for the first time, though never, of course, to the British level.[3] Against this, the bombing created resentment and a revived morale, with greater readiness for work. German munitions production doubled between the beginning of 1942 and the end of 1943. It went on rising until the third quarter of 1944. In June 1944 Germany was better stocked with munitions than at any time in the war.

Of course German war production might have increased still more if it had not been for the bombing, and the need for air defence diverted this production to fighters and anti-aircraft guns and away from bombers. Against this, the damage to German war production was at most 9 per cent. and probably less. The demands of bombing on Allied war production were much greater: about 25 per cent. in Great Britain and 15 per cent. in the United States.[4] The official history has passed judgement in excessively moderate terms: 'The area bombing was very far from inflicting any crippling or decisive loss on the

[1] United States Army Air Force.

[2] Harris to Churchill, 3 Nov. 1943. Webster and Frankland, *Strategic Air Offensive*, ii. 190.

[3] German production of consumer goods fell to 91 in 1943 and to 85 in 1944, against 100 in 1939. The British figure in both years was 54.

[4] The British Bombing survey (Webster and Frankland, *The Strategic Air Offensive*, iii. 287) gives a different calculation: 'The British strategic air offensive over Western Europe cost, on an average, 7 per cent. of the manpower effort directly absorbed by the fighting services during the war.' It is difficult to understand what this means. Even on this favourable estimate, British bombing did more damage to Great Britain than to Germany until the autumn of 1944. The official history seems to argue that the repeated failures and disappointments were justified as preparations for the final success, just as the Somme and Passchendaele were justified by 8 Aug. 1918. The official history delivers this concluding oracular verdict: 'Both cumulatively in largely indirect ways and eventually in a more immediate and direct manner, strategic bombing and, also in other roles strategic bombers, made a contribution which was decisive' (ibid. 310).

enemy and had not prevented the great increase in armaments carried out in this period.'[1] In March 1944 Harris was still unmoved, though even he admitted that the rising casualties, caused by the German night fighters, made further attacks on the existing model impossible.[2] In any case, Harris's day was over. There was a technical reason. The Americans had perfected what the British had always dismissed as inconceivable: a long-range fighter aircraft, and direct combat with the German air force now became possible. The strategical reason was even more telling. The time for the invasion of northern France was fast approaching. On 13 April 1944 Harris was informed, much to his indignation, that bomber command had been placed under Eisenhower, the supreme commander of Overlord. The independent bombing offensive was ended.

The British and Americans arrived in France crablike, after many dissensions and delays. On 9 July 1943 Allied forces landed in Sicily. The Italians appealed in vain for German help. On 25 July Mussolini was overthrown. The new Italian government, under Marshal Badoglio, soon put out feelers for peace. It seemed that the Allies might win the whole of Italy almost without fighting. At any rate, the temptation to move from Sicily to the mainland was irresistible. Churchill and Roosevelt, with their advisers, met at Quebec from 14 to 24 August. The Americans agreed to land in Italy. But they exacted a price. Not only was Overlord given 'priority'. The detailed plans, prepared by General Sir Frederick Morgan in London, were approved, and orders were given that they should go forward. The Americans insisted also that there must be a landing in southern France.[3] As well, they demanded British action in Burma—another diversion, they hoped, of landing craft from the Mediterranean. Churchill gloomily acquiesced. But he was not convinced. When the conference ended, he trailed back to Washington with Roosevelt and the American chiefs of staff, in the hope of shaking their rigorous determination on Overlord after all.

---

[1] Webster and Frankland, *Strategic Air Offensive*, ii. 268.

[2] In a raid on Nuremberg on 28 Mar. 1944, bomber command lost 94 aeroplanes out of 795.

[3] As usual, there was equivocation in this. The Americans proposed it in order to prevent any Churchillian action in the eastern Mediterranean. Churchill agreed to it because it would keep landing craft in the Mediterranean and away from the Channel.

The news from Italy grew better and worse. On 7 September the Italians signed an armistice. The Italian navy sailed for Malta and surrendered. But the Germans had had time to move forces into Italy. The Allied forces could land only in the extreme south. They could not take Rome. They were lucky to take Naples. In Washington Churchill pleaded for a more flexible strategy, to exploit the changing situation in the Mediterranean. He was rebuffed. Roosevelt abruptly went to his country home and left Churchill to wrangle fruitlessly with Marshall. Overlord retained its dogmatic priority. Churchill's attempted insistence on the Mediterranean did not spring from any desire to forestall Russia in the Balkans.[1] Indeed, he did not advocate an invasion of the Balkans. He merely retained his illusion, now thirty years old, that there was somewhere an easy backdoor into Germany and hoped to win the war by some unexpected miracle instead of by heavy fighting. Gallipoli was never far from his mind—as an example, not as a warning. Even now, he was unrepentant. He stirred up General Sir Henry Maitland Wilson, the commander in the Middle East, to seize the Italian islands in the Aegean. Wilson obeyed. The Americans refused to authorize reinforcements. The British forces were overwhelmed by the Germans. Most of them were taken prisoner. This was not only an unnecessary misfortune. It shattered another of Churchill's dreams: that of bringing Turkey into the war.

On paper, at any rate, the second front was now firmly resolved on. There was striking confirmation when Churchill returned to England. Beaverbrook came back to office as lord privy seal. He had been a symbol of the 'second front' agitation, his newspapers conducting a radical campaign against the government, much to the disapproval of the respectable classes.[2] Now he seemed to have won. His return was disguised as part of a general reshuffle. Kingsley Wood died suddenly on 22 September.[3] Sir John Anderson took his place as chancellor

---

[1] See Note B, p. 576.

[2] A little episode illustrated this. Lord Astor, proprietor of the *Observer*, had tolerated for years the vagaries of Garvin, its editor. When in 1942 Garvin urged the return of Beaverbrook, Astor dismissed him. Gollin, *Proconsul in Politics*, 379 n.

[3] Wood left a legacy, 'Pay as You Earn' (P.A.Y.E.), a scheme by which the employer worked out each week the employee's liability to income tax and deducted it from his wages. This was recognition that the working classes had now come permanently within the income-tax range. Less fortunately, it increased the

of the exchequer. Attlee took over Anderson's directing responsibilities as lord president of the council.[1] Beaverbrook's return
was hardly noticed in comparison. So low had the war cabinet
sunk that he did not even bother to rejoin it. This did not prevent his being put in charge of ministerial committees on any important question. Indeed, Beaverbrook was soon re-established
as Churchill's intimate adviser, as was to be shown ultimately
in the general election of 1945. Only one thing still lay between
them. Churchill was still not fully committed to the second
front, and Beaverbrook had been brought in partly as window
dressing.

Churchill appreciated indeed that time was running out for
Great Britain. On 1 November he asked the fateful question:
could they assume the defeat of Germany in 1944? In that case,
they could maintain the armed forces at their existing level and
neglect any future supply of munitions. If not, the armed forces
would have to be cut at once. The British decided to gamble on
victory in 1944. This might have been expected to make
Churchill eager for the second front. On the contrary, his persistence for the Mediterranean was undimmed. Yet one more
meeting with Roosevelt, he hoped, might secure kinder treatment for the Mediterranean after all. The opportunity for a
meeting was there. Roosevelt had long waited to get on terms
of personal friendship with Stalin. Obviously Churchill would
have to come also. Churchill proposed that he and Roosevelt
should first meet at Cairo to coordinate their future strategy.
He intended in fact to wheedle Roosevelt against Overlord.

Roosevelt's intention was quite other. He did not return the
affection which Churchill felt for him. He had used Churchill
as a convenient instrument and was now out after bigger game.
He would not 'gang up' against Stalin. When Churchill arrived
in Cairo, he found Chiang Kai-shek, the Chinese dictator, there
also, and the time was consumed in discussions, highly distaste-
ful to the British, for an operation against the Japanese in the
Indian Ocean. Nothing had been agreed on European strategy
when Roosevelt and Churchill met Stalin at Teheran from
28 November to 1 December. Roosevelt presided. He sat back

rigidity from which the British tax-system already suffered: future changes of rate
and still more of general principle were made more difficult.
[1] Anderson, however, took with him to the treasury his direction of the manpower budget.

and asked Stalin, the great authority on defeating the Germans, for strategical guidance. Stalin said firmly: Overlord. If there were any secondary operation, it should be a landing in southern France, not further east. Churchill argued volubly and was beaten down. The United States and Soviet Russia had imposed an unwelcome strategy on Great Britain.

Back in Cairo, the Americans agreed not to insist on an operation in the Indian Ocean, even though Roosevelt had promised it to Chiang Kai-shek, now that they had got their way in regard to Overlord. Roosevelt and his staff departed. Churchill remained behind—at first voluntarily, then because of illness. He did not waste his opportunity. Now that landing craft were not needed in the Indian Ocean, they should, he argued, be used once more in the Mediterranean before being sent back to England for Overlord. He ingeniously discovered a new margin of time. The Russians had been promised a second front on 1 May 1944. This seemed too tight. Moon and tide would be favourable again only in early June, but this could still be described as 'within the May period'. The evasion was accepted. Eisenhower was just off to England as supreme commander of the second front.[1] He did not like to interfere. Alexander, his successor, was ready, as ever, to do what Churchill wanted. The deadlock in Italy should therefore be broken by a landing behind the German lines. Amphibious strategy was to be attempted once again. There would be a quick rush. Rome would be taken. Then the landing craft would be free for Overlord.

The plan did not work out. British and American forces landed at Anzio on 22 January 1944. The American commander was concerned to establish his position instead of rushing forward. Alexander was too courteous to push him on, just like Hamilton at Gallipoli many years before. Anzio was indeed Gallipoli all over again: inspired by the same man and with the same result. The Germans had time to counter-attack. The Allied forces were nearly pushed into the sea. Prestige forbade

[1] The Americans had wanted a single supreme commander for all operations against Germany both in northern Europe and the Mediterranean. Marshall would have been given the job. The British objected that this would virtually eliminate the combined chiefs of staff. The Americans acquiesced and fell back on Eisenhower. The Middle East and Italian commands were united under Maitland Wilson, with Alexander in command in Italy. Thus the Mediterranean became, in command, a purely British affair.

a withdrawal. Casualties mounted. Landing craft could not be released for Overlord. The plans for a landing in southern France had to be put off. In the end, far from the operation at Anzio's aiding the main Italian front, it was the armies there which broke through and rescued the forces at Anzio. On 11 May the Allied armies launched an offensive. It was successful. On 4 June Allied troops entered Rome. This should have been sensational news. It was not. It was eclipsed by greater events. The taking of Rome provided an historical stroke of irony for the second time. In the nineteenth century Italian nationalists had presented the taking of Rome as the climax of their endeavour which would dazzle the world. On 20 September 1870 Italian forces entered Rome. No one noticed except the pope. The German armies had defeated the French at Sedan a fortnight before, on 3 September, and this occupied universal attention. So now. Two days after Alexander announced the taking of Rome, Allied armies landed in northern France. With this, the taking of Rome, and indeed British strategy in the Mediterranean, lost all significance.

NOTES

Note A. *Unconditional Surrender*. Many incorrect statements have been made about the birth of the phrase. Roosevelt himself said that it came into his head suddenly just before he announced it at a press conference. Churchill said that Roosevelt's statement at the press conference took him by surprise. Bevin alleged (in the house of commons on 21 July 1949) that the war cabinet had not been consulted. All three were wrong. Roosevelt mentioned the phrase to his military advisers before leaving for Casablanca.[1] He told Churchill, who in his turn informed the war cabinet, proposing, however, that Italy should be left out.[2] The war cabinet replied that Italy should be included.[3] Churchill did not pass this message to Roosevelt—evidence how lightly he treated the war cabinet. However, Roosevelt included Italy at his press conference, without consulting Churchill further, and Churchill thought it best to endorse his statement.

Note B. *The Balkans in Allied strategy*. The policy of forestalling Soviet Russia in the Balkans was an invention of the postwar years, partly encouraged by Churchill himself when he became anti-Russian in 1946. There is no contemporary evidence for it. On the contrary, all the strategies—Soviet, British, and American—were designed with the sole object of defeating Germany, however much they differed on the way to do it. The postwar outcry sprang from the belief that the Balkans and east-central Europe were

[1] Clive, *Washington Command Post*, 217.
[2] Churchill, *Second World War*, iv. 613.   [3] Ibid. 614.

important in the Balance of Power. This was an illusion. They had perhaps some strategic value, though only in the sense that, if Soviet armies were on the Danube, an invasion of Russia by the Western Powers would have to start from further off. Otherwise the states concerned were liabilities, not sources of strength. Rumanian oil supplies were almost exhausted. The Balkan countries strictly speaking—Yugoslavia and Bulgaria—were pure burdens. Czechoslovakia had some economic resources, though less than Belgium; Hungary about as much as Luxembourg. The only great prize in Europe was western Germany, and especially the Ruhr, as anyone can see for himself by visiting the Ruhr and then, say, Macedonia or the Hungarian Puszta. Bismarck said the last word on the Balkans: they are not worth the bones of a Pomeranian, or any other sort of, grenadier.

From a postwar point of view, the Americans were acting rightly when they insisted on driving into Germany, though of course this was not why they did it. If Stalin had been preparing for the cold war when he was still fighting the hot one, he would have urged the British and Americans to concentrate on south-east Europe. They would have ended up with the Balkans, and Soviet forces would have been on the Rhine instead of on the Elbe. In fact, Stalin urged the Americans to attack Germany directly. This was the best strategy for war, but, from Stalin's point of view, the worst strategy for postwar. Other Soviet acts have been similarly misinterpreted. In August 1944 the Soviet armies halted outside Warsaw and did not renew their offensive against the German armies until January 1945. Meanwhile other Soviet armies conquered Rumania and Hungary. It has therefore been alleged that Stalin collected his prizes in east-central Europe, once the British and Americans were safely pinned against the Germans in the west. This, too, is wrong. The German armies were still too strong for the Russians in August 1944, particularly now that their communications were much shorter. The Russians halted until they could bring up reinforcements and attacked further south in order to pull German forces away from the vital front.

After the war, when the Great Powers fell out, men everywhere accused the other side of manœuvring for future advantages while the war was on. All the accusations were unfounded. But there can be no doubt which powers derived most advantage from the way the war worked out, however much they tried not to. Soviet Russia did most of the fighting against Germany, sustained nine tenths of the casualties, and suffered catastrophic economic losses. The British suffered considerable economic loss and sustained comparatively few casualties. The Americans made great economic gains and had a trifling number of casualties fighting against Germany— their main losses were in the war against Japan. In short, the British and Americans sat back, though not of malice aforethought, while the Russians defeated Germany for them. Of the three great men at the top, Roosevelt was the only one who knew what he was doing: he made the United States the greatest power in the world at virtually no cost.

XVI

ENDING, 1944–5

THE Allied landing in northern France on D-day, 6 June
1944, was the third great milestone in British history
during the second World war. Dunkirk began the period
when Great Britain stood alone. Pearl Harbour inaugurated the
Grand Alliance.[1] After D-day, British and American armies
were fighting a substantial part of the German army for the
first time,[2] and their success, combined with that of the Russians,
brought final victory. Despite the demands for starting the
second front earlier, D-day, it seems, came at the right time
or, at any rate, at an appropriate one. It could not have been
launched until the U-boats were mastered in the summer of
1943—too late to mount a landing that year. The Americans
had just put into the air a long-range fighter which could, at
last, defeat the German air-force directly. The detailed consideration of the problems involved had gone on long enough
to produce answers for most of the difficulties.

D-day came at the right time also in regard to the future. In
1944 Germany, though hard-pressed, was by no means finished.
Not only was her war production still increasing. She was also
preparing new weapons—fast U-boats equipped with 'schnorkel',[3]
jet-aircraft, pilotless aeroplanes, and rockets—weapons which
the Allies could not have answered, or only after another long
period of setbacks and delays. Allied unity and the resolution of
the Allied peoples, particularly of the British, would have been
dangerously strained. As it was, Germany's new weapons came
too late. The fast U-boats and the jet-aircraft never operated on
any large scale. The use of the pilotless aeroplanes and of the
rockets was delayed, first by bombing the stations where they
were being prepared and then by bombing their launching sites
in France. Both weapons came into action, with much suffering

---

[1] The German attack on Russia, though it made a more decisive change in the
general war, was less significant in British history.

[2] In France, the Allies fought fifty and later sixty German divisions, in Italy
only twenty and usually less.

[3] A breathing tube which enabled the U-boat to remain under water for long
periods.

to the inhabitants of London, but only after D-day, and the Allies, advancing through France, overran most of the launching sites before life in London became intolerable. The final victory of May 1945 came only just in time. It was touch-and-go, not a foregone conclusion.

The D-day operation was a remarkable breach with British tradition. Every previous combined operation from Gallipoli to Anzio—or, going further back, Walcheren in 1809 and La Rochelle in 1629—had run true to form: no proper survey beforehand, confusion of command, improvization leading through muddle to failure. This time everything was done right, and the British deserved most of the credit, though they were no doubt on their best behaviour under American scrutiny. Preparations had been pursued in detail ever since April 1943 when General Sir Frederick Morgan had been appointed chief of staff to a non-existent supreme commander.[1] The French Channel coast had been precisely surveyed, and solutions devised for each particular obstacle. Two artificial harbours, known as 'Mulberries', had been designed.[2] A pipeline, 'Pluto', was ready to carry oil under the Channel.[3] Immense forces had been assembled: 1,200 fighting ships, 4,000 assault craft, and 1,600 merchant vessels; 13,000 aircraft; and Allied armies of more than three and a half million men. As Eisenhower remarks with unusual wit: 'Only the great number of barrage balloons floating constantly in British skies kept the islands from sinking under the seas.'[4]

This was a truly combined operation, with British and American staffs more mixed up than they ever were in the Mediterranean. Eisenhower, the supreme commander, was American. Tedder, his deputy, was British. The air commander, Leigh-Mallory, and the naval commander, Ramsay, were also British. The command on land was more equivocal. Montgomery was brought back from Italy to command the initial landings, both British and American. Once the build-up made

[1] Hence his shortened designation: COSSAC. When Eisenhower became supreme commander, he chose an American, Bedell Smith, as his chief of staff, and Morgan was set aside.

[2] Only one was brought into use. The Mulberry on the American sector was destroyed during the great storm of 19–22 June.

[3] Pluto did not in fact begin to function until after tankers were bringing over adequate supplies.

[4] Eisenhower, *Crusade in Europe*, 63.

the Americans preponderant, Montgomery would revert to
command only of the British army group, and Eisenhower would
himself act as land commander-in-chief. This imperfect arrangement was inevitable for political reasons. The British would not
accept an American land commander-in-chief as well as an
American supreme commander; the Americans would not
accept a British land commander-in-chief once they had the
larger forces engaged.[1]

Eisenhower was also empowered to issue directions to the
strategic air forces and delegated this power to Tedder, his
deputy. The power was not exercised without difficulties. Harris,
the British commander, still hankered after area bombing
and dismissed precision bombing as impossible. Spaatz, the
American commander, though ready for precision bombing,
proposed to concentrate on German oil. Tedder wanted
attacks on the German communications in France and, after
some dispute, got his way to a considerable extent. The Transportation plan, as it was called in deference to American taste
for polysyllables, was given first place, and Harris and Spaatz
were left free to pursue their particular hobbies with anything
that was left over. A political obstacle then appeared. Churchill
feared that many French lives would be lost during the bombing
of railways and that a legacy of bitterness would be caused. The
war cabinet was called in for once[2] and supported Churchill's
objection. It was overruled by Roosevelt who insisted that military needs must come first—he was in any case less regardful
of French feelings. The bombing took place, with less loss of
life than had been feared,[3] and was a triumphant success.
Nearly every bridge over the Seine was destroyed. The German
armies in France were cut in two for lack of communications.
Even Harris had to admit that his bombers had done what he
had thought them incapable of doing.

The overriding problem was where to land. The choice lay
east or west of the Seine. The coast east of the Seine, though

[1] The American objection was largely a personal objection to Montgomery, who
did not conceal his opinion of their deficiencies. They would probably have
accepted Alexander, as they had done in North Africa and Italy. But Churchill
needed Alexander's prestige in order to keep the Italian theatre going, and so
refused to release him.
[2] This was the only strategic point submitted to the war cabinet in the last two
years of the war. It had been told vaguely of Anzio, but not of the date.
[3] Ten thousand instead of forty thousand.

nearer, was more heavily fortified and offered no great port as a prize. West of the Seine involved a longer sea voyage, but it was just within range of fighter-cover; it was less fortified, and victory there would bring control of Cherbourg. It was decided on. At the same time, elaborate plans were developed to deceive the Germans. A non-existent army was built up in south-east England, and dummy craft assembled to move it to the Pas de Calais. Wireless messages were poured out in the eastern Channel. More bombs were dropped on the Pas de Calais than in Normandy. This was a game well suited to British ingenuity. The Germans were almost completely deceived—only Hitler guessed right, and he hesitated to back his hunch. The larger part of the German forces was kept east of the Seine, and even after D-day the Germans believed that the real attack was still to come. Their mistake was increased by ignorance. Their reconnaissance aeroplanes were shepherded to eastern England where they saw what they were intended to. All diplomatic correspondence leaving England was censored—an unprecedented act applied even to de Gaulle, much to his annoyance.

The plan of battle was to Montgomery's taste. The British forces would land on the eastern sector of the chosen coast and push towards Caen. The Americans would land at the base of the Cotentin peninsula further west. They would secure Cherbourg and build up their forces for a break-out, while the British wore the Germans down in a slogging match round Caen. This was Alamein over again on a larger scale, and it worked, though not without setbacks. D-day was fixed for 5 June. The weather proved stormy. Eisenhower postponed invasion for twenty-four hours. He was promised better weather for 6 June and, at 4 a.m. on 5 June, said: 'O.K. let's go.' The great operation started twenty-four hours later. Nearly 200,000 men were engaged that day in naval operations (two thirds of them British); 14,000 air sorties were flown. Neither the U-boats[1] nor the German air force were able to interfere. By the evening of 6 June 156,000 men had been put ashore.[2] Three days later the bridgeheads had been safely consolidated.

---

[1] Only five ships were sunk by U-boats throughout the campaign.
[2] Two men did not land in France that day: Churchill and King George VI. Churchill had proposed to accompany the landing forces, and was deterred only when the king declared that, in that case, he would go too. This was perhaps the only occasion when Churchill was overruled by the monarch whom he served.

Not everything went well. The British failed to carry Caen in the first onslaught. Both armies were delayed by a storm, the worst for forty years, which blew from 19 to 22 June. Montgomery was undismayed as long as he was wearing down German strength. He did not always make his intentions clear to his superiors. When he launched an offensive against the Germans on 18 July, he implied that this would bring large territorial gains and even a breakthrough to the Seine. It did not do so, and criticism then began that Montgomery was too slow and methodical. Tedder, who was impatient for more airfields, urged Eisenhower to dismiss Montgomery and put an American commander in his place. Eisenhower, though also dissatisfied, held his hand. Montgomery's offensive served his purpose. The German armour was pinned down on the eastern sector of the front. On 25 July the Americans broke through in the west and began a vast sweep through France.

Hitler completed the German defeat by ordering a counter-attack towards Avranches in an attempt to cut the American line of communications. The German forces were checked and finally encircled at Falaise. Their resistance collapsed in mid-August; 50,000 were taken prisoner. Many escaped, and Montgomery was again criticized for moving slowly on the northern flank of the Falaise pocket. At any rate the Allied forces stormed forward—over the Seine, over the Somme. Paris was liberated on 25 August. De Gaulle defiantly arrived there and established his authority before either the Americans or the Communists could forestall him. By now there were over two million Allied soldiers in France—three fifths of them American. The Americans had at last become preponderant on land. On 1 September Eisenhower took command of the land forces. Montgomery reverted to command of the British army group and was made a field marshal the same day.

Complete victory seemed near. On 15 August Allied forces, mostly American, landed in the south of France also—a belated triumph for American views of strategy. The landing had been planned in order to distract German strength from the north. Postponement destroyed its purpose,[1] and the Americans insisted on it only from obstinacy. They were determined not to be tricked by Churchill into any further Mediterranean

---

[1] It was now the landing in the north which distracted the Germans from the south.

adventures.[1] The Allied armies were now advancing in France on a wide front. Not, however, without disagreements. Montgomery was by this time convinced that he could run a campaign better than Eisenhower and did not conceal this belief from the British chiefs of staff or from Eisenhower himself. Montgomery wanted a single great drive north against the Germans—of course under his command. Eisenhower, with American generals to consider, spread out the resources more evenly.

The dispute was probably overdone both then and still more subsequently. Montgomery's armies received as much as the supply lines would carry, and the real failure, if any, was his: the failure, when Antwerp was captured, to open the Schelde between it and the sea. Even so, Montgomery was given resources and encouragement for a daring venture to outflank the Siegfried line. Parachutists were sent forward to seize bridges over the Rhine on 17 September. Much of their enterprise was successful. At Arnhem, their most northern target, they failed, and land forces could not reach them. There was an echo of old faults: a parachute-commander too concerned about a 'neat drop' and not concerned enough about seizing the bridge; land commanders without a sense of urgency. Maybe Montgomery went against his nature when he laid on a dashing improvised plan. At any rate the German defences were stabilized by the end of September.

D-day and its sequel brought alleviation of spirit to English people. Many had been doubtful of total victory despite their outward calm. Now unconditional surrender promised to become an early reality. The end of the second war was less abrupt and surprising than that of the first. By July 1944 most English people decided, whether rightly or not, that the war was as good as won. Holidaymakers again enjoyed the beaches from which they had been excluded for five years—a most practical symbol of victory. The inspiration was fortunate. People needed it in order to surmount their last trial. On 13 June the first flying bomb fell on London. There was a new evacuation—nearly one and a half million people left London before the end of July. These pilotless aeroplanes were unnerving. They came at all hours of day and night, and their characteristic drone could be heard until silence preluded the fall of the

[1] Even at this late hour, Churchill again pressed the alternative of landing at the head of the Adriatic or even at Bordeaux. Perhaps he, too, was being obstinate.

bomb. 6,184 people were killed, nearly all in London. Effective measures of defence were found. The aircraft after all moved no faster than an ordinary aeroplane. The anti-aircraft guns were moved to the coast, and fighters were left free to operate inland. By August 80 per cent. of the flying bombs which came over were being destroyed.[1] On 7 September Duncan Sandys, who had been in charge of the defensive plans, announced: 'The Battle of London is over.'

He was right only in regard to flying bombs.[2] On 8 September, the day after Sandys' boast, the first rockets reached London. These were a greater danger than the flying bombs, though less alarming psychologically—they fell without warning. They caused more destruction, and no defence was found against them. Plans were laid to abandon London, and indeed London survived only because the rockets were few and late. They were expensive to produce,[3] and the advance of the Allied armies overran most of their launching sites soon after the attack began.[4] Eleven hundred and fifteen rockets killed 2,754 people —a costly procedure, but hard enough on the inhabitants of London. The rockets, though unavailing, were a portent: they were the writing on the wall for Great Britain that she had lost her island-security and that any future war would bring obliteration.

Even the more immediate future posed terrible problems. Until D-day British policy had been concerned only with victory, and any other thought had been subordinated to this. Now the European war was likely to end some time in 1945, if not in 1944. The great questions which had been in eclipse began to demand answers. What was to be the shape of the world after the war? What was to happen to Germany? How was Great Britain to maintain her position as a Great Power? How, indeed, immediately after the war, was she to keep alive? What lay in store for the British Empire? The other great Allies, Soviet Russia and the United States, though also looking

---

[1] 10,000 flying bombs were launched; one quarter went astray; 7,400 were observed; 1,846 of these were destroyed by fighters and 1,878 by gunfire.

[2] A few still came over. The last fell on London on 28 Feb. 1945; the last to explode on Datchworth on 1 Mar.

[3] A rocket was twenty times as expensive to produce as a flying bomb and six times as expensive as a bomber, which had in any case a longer life. Hence Cherwell argued that they would not be used. His reasoning was right; his conclusion wrong.

[4] The last rocket fell at Orpington on 27 Mar. 1945.

towards the future, were driven less hard by apprehension. American strength, economic as well as military, had increased prodigiously during the war, and most American statesmen approached the problems of peace in a spirit of detached idealism. Roosevelt remained confident that he could improvise solutions as the problems turned up. Soviet Russia, though catastrophically ravaged, had also increased her strength greatly in the military field. After the war she would, it appeared, be the only continental Power, in both Europe and Asia, with an army of any size. Her people would have to face many years of hardship and misery, but Stalin was confident that' he could maintain his dictatorship, indeed probably believed that he could maintain it more easily over an impoverished people. At any rate, he had little doubt that Soviet Russia would remain a Great Power.

Great Britain was at the end of the road: her production of munitions past its peak, her armed forces quivering at their summit, her currency reserves run down, two thirds of her export trade lost. She needed a better world for her own sake, and not only for that of others. The partnerships of war had to be continued into peacetime. Most English people took this for granted. They turned in on themselves and thought mainly of social security, housing, and full employment, not of foreign affairs. They assumed, almost without question, that American generosity would continue indefinitely; most of them assumed also that the Soviet rulers had become indistinguishable from social democrats. Churchill alone faced the problems of the future and found no easy answers. To some extent, he was handicapped by his own past. Unlike Lloyd George, he could not tear up his existing outlook and start afresh. He counted too much on American friendship, particularly on his friendship with Roosevelt. He remembered too clearly the old peril of bolshevism. This is a dark subject. Some writers of high authority held, and still hold, that Stalin wished to establish communism throughout Europe, and this seemed, at the very least, a plausible suspicion in view of the chaotic conditions which were expected to follow the war. On the other hand, Stalin, to judge from his acts, seems to have been concerned only for the security of Soviet Russia and her frontiers, and to have asked nothing from Europe except to be left alone. No clear answer can be given until the distant day when the obscurity, overhanging Soviet policy and history, is dispelled. In any case, Churchill had to invent the Bolshevik peril, whether it existed or not. Common danger from Germany had drawn Great Britain and the United States together. Common danger from Soviet Russia was needed to keep them together once Germany was defeated.

There was another, though more temporary, way of prolonging the Anglo-American alliance. The war in the Far East had still to be fought and won. The Japanese, though checked, were far from being defeated. The Americans thought that they could do this on their own. The British wanted to be done with war, yet insisted on pushing into the Far Eastern war in order to show that they were still useful to the Americans. Of course, the British had also interests of their own in the Far East. They wanted to establish the security of India and to recover the lost imperial territories. They were already within sight of accomplishing these aims. In March 1944 the Japanese undertook a belated advance into Assam, assisted by the so-called Indian National army, a force of no great size. They were defeated at Imphal after three months of fighting. The way was clear for a British invasion of Burma and beyond that for the recovery of Singapore. This private war did not interest the Americans. Their concern was with the Pacific.

Churchill took an initiative. He met Roosevelt at Quebec from 11 to 16 September, and declared that the British navy was ready to join the Pacific war. Roosevelt, himself anxious to cement Anglo-American relations, accepted the offer over protests from the American navy. From this moment 'Stage II' —the period when Germany had been defeated and Japan had not—became a central point of British policy. It solved many difficulties. War industry could be gently run down; demobilization cautiously begun. Lend-lease would go on, ostensibly against Japan, actually to help the transition from war to peace. It was in British interests that Stage I—the defeat of Germany—should be over as soon as possible, Stage II prolonged as long as possible, and this is what good judges expected to happen. Germany would be defeated early in 1945. After that the Far Eastern war would last at least another eighteen months. Many British misfortunes stemmed from the fact that it lasted only three.

European questions were also discussed at Quebec, though

the war not much. The main campaign against Germany had
passed from the combined chiefs of staff to Eisenhower. The
only step taken at Quebec was to release the strategic air forces
from his control. Churchill pleaded for reinforcements to the
Italian front. The Americans alone had reserves in hand, and
refused. The Italian front, they insisted, was to pin down
German forces, not to launch a second invasion of Germany.
The future of Germany came up in a curious way. Morgenthau,
the American secretary of the treasury, was at Quebec to discuss lend-lease. He offered $3,500 million for the British during
Stage II, and a credit of $3,000 million for non-military pur-
poses. He had also a plan for destroying all German industry
and turning Germany into 'a country primarily agricultural
and pastoral in character'. Cherwell persuaded Churchill that
the ending of German competition would provide a wonderful
opening for British exports. Churchill swallowed the bait.
Roosevelt approved also, without much thought. Back in
Washington, he repented and forbade all speculation about the
future of Germany. Churchill had already been harassed with
criticism from Eden and from the war cabinet. He was relieved
to acquiesce in Roosevelt's ban. Other plans proved less controversial. There were plans for a world security organization
at Dumbarton Oaks; plans for world finance at Bretton Woods
which barred any future 'autarky'—another British misfortune;
plans in detail for further lend-lease, which suffered from the
old defect: the American negotiators made promises which the
British took as firm agreements, and Congress later did not
fulfil them.

The greatest question was not discussed at Quebec. Roosevelt
refused to be drawn on the question of relations with Soviet
Russia. He always put off questions until they became actual.
He believed, since the meeting at Teheran, that he was on
intimate terms with Stalin, while, on the other side, he suspected
that Churchill's anti-bolshevism was a cloak for imperialist
designs. Churchill had declared: 'I did not become His Majesty's
First Minister in order to preside over the dissolution of the
British Empire.' Roosevelt could have added, under his breath,
that he was not fighting the war in order to preserve it. Roosevelt's attitude made it impossible for Churchill to play the anti-
bolshevik card; Stage II, in any case, made it unnecessary.
Besides it is by no means clear when Churchill's anti-bolshevism

came to the surface even in his own mind. With him one emotion easily eclipsed another, and affection for his 'wartime comrade' Stalin was still strong. Soviet historians have accused Churchill of pursuing an anti-Bolshevik policy as early as the autumn of 1942, and some western writers have praised him for the same reason. This seems to be wisdom, or the lack of it, after the event. When Churchill went to Moscow from 9 to 17 October 1944, he was still in search of agreement and hoped to get it.

His hope was largely fulfilled. Churchill and Stalin shared out the political control of eastern Europe with odd statistical precision: Rumania 90 per cent. Russian; Greece 90 per cent. British; Hungary and Yugoslavia 50–50. Poland presented more difficulty. Great Britain was in the war because of her alliance with Poland. Many thousands of Poles were fighting gallantly on the British side. On the other hand, the Anglo-Polish alliance specifically did not apply against Russia. Most English people, including Churchill, acknowledged the injustice of the prewar Soviet–Polish frontier, established by the treaty of Riga in 1921, and were prepared to recognize the frontier drawn by Soviet Russia in 1939, which was also more or less the Curzon line of 1919. The exiled Polish government in London were adamant against any surrender of territory. Churchill pressed them hard and had already almost reached the point of breaking with them. Anglo-Soviet agreement would have been easy if frontiers alone had been in question. There was a larger obstacle. Stalin wanted a Poland friendly to Soviet Russia after the war. Here, too, Churchill agreed. The two were, however, far from agreeing over means. Churchill wanted free elections in Poland as elsewhere. Stalin had confidence only in Polish Communists, and not much in them. Later there were mutual accusations of bad faith. The accusations were too sharp. Churchill's wishes for Poland and Stalin's wishes both made sense. They could not be reconciled. Free elections in Poland immediately after the war, even if possible, would not have produced a government friendly to Soviet Russia. This was a problem without solution.

In October 1944 there was still hope for a compromise. Churchill returned home full of confidence. He told the house of commons on 27 October: 'Our relations with Soviet Russia were never more close, intimate and cordial than they are at the present time.' Stalin's good faith was soon demonstrated in action. The Germans withdrew from Greece during the early autumn. The resistance forces there were mostly Communist or under Communist control. The British government backed the king of Greece in the name of democracy, though the king's past record was far from democratic. Sixty thousand British troops were sent to Greece and defeated the resistance after considerable fighting. Stalin sent no aid to the Communists and made no protest. In England criticism was not so easily silenced. It was voiced by nearly all the newspapers, including *The Times* and the *Manchester Guardian*.[1] There was a motion of censure in the house of commons (7–8 December) and, though it was defeated by 281 votes to 32, only 23 Labour members supported the government—24 voted against, and the rest abstained. Churchill held on his course. He went to Greece with Eden on Christmas Day, and imposed a provisional government under Archbishop Damaskinos, whom he described, with a private chuckle, as 'a scheming medieval prelate'. Churchill's opposition to communism was confirmed, and no doubt Stalin's belief that he had a free hand in his own zone was confirmed also.

Anglo-American, not Anglo-Soviet, relations were strained during the winter. The Allied forces in the west were strung out from Antwerp to the Swiss frontier. It did not occur to anyone that the Germans might attack. The line was particularly thin in the Ardennes, scene of the French disaster in 1940. Hitler resolved to repeat his success there. On 16 December the Germans began a powerful offensive. In three days they advanced 45 miles and dreamt of reaching Antwerp. Then the drive flagged. The Americans were strong in resistance. Eisenhower gave Montgomery temporary command of all forces, British and American, on the northern flank; and Montgomery, in his usual patient way, waited until the Germans had outrun their strength. By Christmas Day the German onset had been stayed. Ten days later they were pushed back. The battle left a bitter taste. Montgomery implied to newspapermen that he had saved the Americans from disaster. He made matters worse by a prolonged wrangle with Eisenhower over future strategy. Montgomery still wanted a single offensive in northern

---

[1] The *Manchester Guardian* took a high democratic line. *The Times* followed its usual principle of being strong upon the stronger side. It had been pro-German before the war and was now pro-Russian and pro-Communist for the same reason.

Germany under his command. Eisenhower insisted on a general advance. The British chiefs of staff were called in to support Montgomery. The Americans backed Eisenhower and got their way. Behind the dispute lay a greater shadow. Victory in the west seemed to be receding. The war might not be over until the end of the year or at best be won mainly by the Russians.[1]

It was in the gloom of this shadow that Churchill and Roosevelt met Stalin at Yalta from 4 to 11 February 1945. Roosevelt wanted to get the war over as soon as possible both in Europe and the Far East. Soviet Russia had much aid to offer, Great Britain comparatively little, and Roosevelt, opportunistic as ever, subordinated every other aim to that of securing Russian aid. He succeeded: Stalin gave a promise of further Russian offensives against Hitler and, even more important, a solid promise that Russia would enter the war against Japan three months after the end of the European war. As well, he accepted American plans for the United Nations Organization—Roosevelt's pet child. Understandably, Roosevelt was satisfied. In the more immediate questions he stood aside, acting as mediator between Stalin and Churchill, and finally proposing that the problems should be left for further brooding.

Churchill tried to resist over the amount of German reparations; over the extent of German territory to be given to Poland as compensation for her losses in the east; and over the government of Poland. He was arguing from weakness: British power was declining, and Roosevelt gave little support. Churchill would have forfeited American sympathy still more if he had sounded the anti-Bolshevik alarm. He had to profess faith in Stalin's good will and, as often happens when men have to do something, was largely sincere in his profession. In any case, the later criticisms of Roosevelt were misplaced. Soviet armies controlled most of eastern Europe, and the Western Allies had no resource other than Stalin's good will, unless they fell back belatedly on alliance with Hitler—a course which no one contemplated. The conference at Yalta ended in a blaze of friendship. The Western Powers yielded really only over one point: the Soviet nominees were recognized as the provisional government

[1] On 12 Jan. 1945 the war cabinet contemplated that the war would not be over before 31 Dec. 1945. On 22 Jan. the chiefs of staff reported: 'Because of the new Russian offensive, the position has been transformed', and they expected the war to be over in mid-April, mid-June, or at the worst early November. Ehrman, *Grand Strategy*, vi. 380.

of Poland 'with the inclusion of democratic leaders from Poland itself and from Poles abroad'. This was too much for some English Conservatives. The men of Munich began to re-form. Twenty-five M.P.s voted against the motion to approve Yalta on 27 February, and a junior minister resigned.[1] This was a troublesome portent for Churchill's future as Conservative leader.

The immediate anxiety was over the course of the war, and this was soon dispelled. The Germans had used their last resources in the battle of the Ardennes. As well, the strategic air offensive belatedly achieved decisive results. This was mainly the work of the Americans. Once released from Eisenhower's control, their strategic air force returned to the precision bombing of Germany's oil supplies and brought her armies almost to a standstill. The aim of bomber command was less sure. Portal, chief of the air staff, was converted to the attack on oil. Tedder, the deputy supreme commander, still asked for attacks on communications. Harris remained unrepentant and dismissed these plans as 'panaceas'. He defied the clearest orders from his nominal superior and in January 1945 challenged Portal to dismiss him. Portal dared not do so. Harris enjoyed great prestige with the public and still more with the crews of bomber command. He was the only British commander of the second World war who could serenely go his own way. A face-saving device was found. The attack on German morale was revived in a new form. One further devastating onslaught, or 'Thunderclap', might cause this morale to collapse, when it was already crumbling under the Russian offensive. If the attack also aided the Russians, so much the better.

Harris found no difficulty this time in conforming. Berlin was the first target chosen. Then it was decided to attack a town which had been virtually untouched before, and Dresden was chosen instead. On the night of 14 February it was devastated. The Germans alleged that up to a quarter of a million people had been killed.[2] The attack on Dresden was no different in character

---

[1] The junior minister was Henry Strauss, parliamentary secretary to the ministry of town and country planning. Of the other rebels, one, Lord Dunglass (later Sir Alec Douglas-Home), subsequently became Conservative prime minister and another, Peter Thorneycroft, Conservative chancellor of the exchequer and minister of defence.

[2] The correct figure is now known to have been 25,000. In all 593,000 German civilians were killed by bombing. H. Rumpf, *The Bombing of Germany* (1963), 164.

from previous attacks on other towns, though greater in effect, and the policy underlying it had been repeatedly approved—by Churchill himself, by Eden, by Sinclair, the secretary for air, and collectively by the war cabinet. But ministers had never been as frank with the public as they had been among themselves. They had always pretended that the bomber offensive was being conducted against strategic targets and that German civilians were being killed only by a regrettable accident. Only in this way, Sinclair explained, 'could he satisfy the inquiries of the Archbishop of Canterbury, the Moderator of the Church of Scotland and other significant religious leaders whose moral condemnation of the bombing offensive might disturb the morale of Bomber Command crews'.[1] Now the politicians, led by Churchill, rounded on Harris and saddled him with sole responsibility for the strategy of indiscriminate destruction. They launched a myth which has endured to the present day. The strategic air offensive was formally ended on 16 April. Thereafter bomber command received no acknowledgement. Churchill did not mention it in his victory broadcast on 13 May. No campaign medal was struck for it. Harris was not allowed to issue his final dispatch. Alone among successful British war-leaders, he was not elevated to the house of lords.[2]

The bombing of Dresden came when the Allied armies were still stuck west of the Rhine. It was their new advance in March which made it seem unnecessary or immoral. On 7 March American forces crossed the Rhine at Remagen. On 23 March Montgomery's armies crossed the Rhine further north and penetrated into the Ruhr. In early April Alexander's armies broke into the valley of the Po. Final victory was not won without final dissensions. The British still complained against

[1] Sinclair to Portal, 28 Oct. 1943. Webster and Frankland, *Strategic Air Offensive*, iii. 1943. Further to sustain morale, Anglican chaplains were maintained on the strength of all air-stations.
[2] Though nearly all chief commanders received peerages, none received a grant of money, as most had done after the first World war. This was an interesting change of social attitude. In 1919 England was still trying to live in the past, and it was assumed that generals and admirals should be admitted into the aristocracy with suitable endowments, as Marlborough, Wellington, and many lesser figures had been before them. By 1945 people felt that commanders, other ranks, and for that matter civilians had all been doing their duty and that money rewards would be invidious. Perhaps, too, it was expected that the war-leaders would do well enough on the profits of their memoirs or by becoming directors of limited companies.

Eisenhower's strategy of the broad advance. Churchill wanted to take Berlin—more, it seems, from the effect on the Germans than to forestall the Russians. Stalin complained that Alexander was secretly negotiating with German emissaries. Division among the Allies was indeed Germany's last hope. The hope was strengthened when Roosevelt died on 12 April.[1] Hitler believed that this had saved him as the death of the tsarina Elizabeth saved Frederick the Great in 1762. He was wrong about himself, though right maybe in a longer run about Germany. Truman, the new president, had none of Roosevelt's vision as international leader and wanted to turn his back on the rest of the world as soon as possible. He did not intend to prop up Great Britain. On the other hand, he was quick to take offence at Soviet complaints or opposition. Now and not before, Churchill was free to sound the anti-Bolshevik alarm and had to do so. It was the only way of securing American assistance for Great Britain and of maintaining American participation in world affairs. It was also perhaps more justified by changing events great and small, from Russia's victory over the Germans to the harassments of Tito, the Yugoslav dictator, at Trieste.

Allied unity lasted long enough to achieve total victory, and not much longer. On 28 April Mussolini and his mistress were shot by Communist partisans, and their bodies hung upside down in Milan. On 29 April the German forces in Italy surrendered unconditionally to Alexander. On 30 April Hitler killed himself and his mistress whom he had married on the previous day. Their bodies were burnt in the yard outside his bunker. The remains were found by the Russians and subsequently destroyed. On 4 May the German forces in northwestern Germany surrendered unconditionally to Montgomery. Admiral Doenitz, whom Hitler had nominated as his successor, attempted to end the war in the west, while continuing to fight against the Russians. His proposal was rejected, and at 2.41 a.m. on 7 May the Germans signed an instrument of unconditional surrender on all fronts at Eisenhower's headquarters.[2] To please the Russians the instrument was ratified at Zhukov's

[1] Marshall had been doing most of the work for him during the previous weeks. On the other hand, observers announced their discovery of Roosevelt's failing powers at Yalta only after his death.

[2] Montgomery received the Germans himself, and his chief of staff was not present. Eisenhower did not meet the Germans and left them to his staff officers. A characteristic difference.

headquarters in Berlin at 11.30 p.m. on 8 May. In a final stroke of muddle the Western Allies celebrated VE-day (Victory in Europe) on 8 May, the Russians on 9 May.[1] Churchill announced victory in the house of commons on the afternoon of 8 May, and the two houses of parliament proceeded to St. Margaret's, Westminster, where they gave thanks for victory. The church bells were rung, floodlights took the place of the blackout. Crowds once more danced in the streets, as they had done on armistice day, 1918. The king attended a service of thanksgiving in St. Paul's and received addresses of congratulation from both houses of parliament.

The rejoicing, though even more justified, was this time more temperate. Few Englishmen now imagined that victory was itself a solution, an end of all problems and difficulties. The problems seemed greater, and people were more aware of them. Some of the problems proved less grave than had been feared. There were no great plagues in Europe. The United Nations Relief and Rehabilitation Administration, set up in November 1943, saved Europeans from starvation. Civil order was restored with comparative ease. Communism did not come within sight of success in any European country except where it was sustained by Soviet arms. On the other hand, relations between the Western Powers and Soviet Russia turned sour. Any chance of permanent friendship was lost when President Truman forgot about the reconstruction loan to Soviet Russia which Roosevelt had contemplated. The Allied leaders held their last meeting at Potsdam from 17 July to 2 August. They reached agreement of a kind over the reparations which each of the occupying Powers could exact from its zone of Germany. The Russians annexed Königsberg, and the Poles were authorized to administer German territory as far as the Oder and the Western Neisse until the conclusion of a peace treaty with Germany— a treaty never in fact concluded. There was deadlock over every other subject, particularly over the political systems in the countries which the Soviet armies had liberated. The meeting at Potsdam marked indeed the beginning of 'the cold war' and therefore of postwar history.

There was one curious episode at Potsdam which must have

---

[1] Eisenhower's headquarters meant to keep the news of the German surrender secret until after the ratification in Berlin. An American reporter broke the ban, and the British and American governments had to admit that the war was over.

surprised the impregnable Soviet dictator. Churchill appeared in glory at the first session as British representative. He was absent from the second. A new prime minister, Attlee, took his place. This was a clear symbol that the British people had abandoned their absorption in world affairs. The end of the German war created an awkward political situation at home. Parliament was in its tenth year, and Churchill had declared as early as 31 October 1944 that it would be wrong to continue the existing house of commons after the Germans had been defeated.[1] Many of the Labour party, though not all its leaders, were eager to resume independence and to conduct an aggressive campaign against the Conservatives for social welfare. On the other hand, the Japanese war was still to be won—a task which, it was thought, would take a further eighteen months. Churchill was also anxious to carry the government's plans for reconstruction as an agreed programme—no doubt in the hope of moderating them.

On 18 May therefore he proposed to the Labour and Liberal parties that the coalition should continue until the end of the Japanese war.[2] Sinclair, the Liberal leader, hesitated. Attlee, the Labour leader, at first hesitated also, having, it seems, little confidence in a Labour victory. Bevin supported the continuation of coalition more openly. They were pulled back into line by the annual party conference, then in session at Blackpool. On 21 May Attlee replied to Churchill, offering only to continue the coalition until October, when there should be a general election. Churchill rejected this offer and insisted that if there were to be a general election it should take place at once, in early July. This was a sensible decision: it would have been intolerable for the coalition to go on with a general election hanging over it. There was also no doubt some calculation of party advantage. The Conservatives wanted a general election while they could exploit Churchill's national prestige and before economic difficulties accumulated.[3]

On 23 May Churchill resigned, thus bringing the National

---

[1] Churchill, *Second World War*, vi. 510.

[2] Churchill proposed to overcome his previous promise of a general election by a referendum, seeking permission for parliament to continue. It would have been awkward if the permission had been refused, and the two other leaders did not look kindly on the idea.

[3] Churchill took a straw vote among Conservative ministers. All favoured an immediate election. Churchill, *Second World War*, vi. 511.

government to an end.[1] He then formed a 'caretaker' government, predominantly of Conservatives, with such National Liberals and so-called Independents as were prepared to stay with them. On 28 May he entertained the leading members of the former government at 10 Downing Street and said, 'The light of history will shine on all your helmets', after which the parties resumed their strife as though coalition had never existed. The Conservatives relied chiefly on the glory of Churchill's name, and he, egged on by Beaverbrook, zestfully turned against Labour the talent for political vituperation which he had previously reserved for Hitler. His greatest card was to discover in Professor Harold Laski, then chairman of the Labour party, the sinister head of a future British Gestapo. This card proved ineffective. The electors cheered Churchill and voted against him. They displayed no interest in foreign affairs or imperial might. They were not stirred by any cry to Hang the Kaiser or to extract reparations from Germany.[2] They cared only for their own future: first housing, and then full employment and social security. Here Labour offered a convincing programme. The Conservatives, though offering much the same programme, managed to give the impression that they did not believe in it. Folk memory counted for much. Many electors remembered the unemployment of the thirties. Some remembered how they had been cheated, or supposed that they had been cheated, after the general election of 1918. Lloyd George brought ruin to Churchill from the grave.

[1] The war cabinet was also automatically dissolved. In the caretaker government, Churchill set up a cabinet of the ordinary peacetime type—including, that is, all the principal ministers. Attlee followed Churchill's example in this as in many other matters, and the cabinet has remained at about twenty members, despite occasional talk of reducing it.

[2] Englishmen had been taught by Keynes that a claim for reparations brought general misfortune. In fact considerable reparations were successfully exacted from Germany. The trial of war criminals was agreed policy between the parties and among the great Allies. On 8 Aug. 1945 the British, American, and Soviet governments, subsequently joined by the French, agreed to set up an international tribunal for these trials at Nuremberg. Many German leaders were tried, and most of them convicted. Some of the convictions were for true war crimes—mass murder and the killing of prisoners of war. The tribunal also devised the crime of preparing or waging aggressive war, which meant in practice war against one or more of the Allies. Yet the leaders of the Allied countries were often criticized for not preparing war against Germany effectively or for failing to wage a 'preventive' (that is, an aggressive) war themselves. The German leaders, especially the generals, could assert that they were really convicted for the crime of having lost, and the moral effect of the Nuremberg trials was, at best, questionable.

Voting took place on 5 July. There were only three uncontested elections,[1] against forty in 1935. Both Labour and Conservative ran more than 600 candidates; the Liberals ran 306. The results were announced on 26 July, to allow time for the services to vote. It is thought that they voted overwhelmingly for Labour. At all events, the result was a striking Labour victory: 393 Labour M.P.s against 213 Conservatives and their allies, 12 Liberals, and 22 Independents.[2] As usual, the electoral system favoured the winning party. Labour obtained only 47·8 per cent. of the votes despite its great majority, and many Labour men sat for constituencies with comparatively few voters. Labour had now much more the appearance of being a national party. Less than half the Labour M.P.s were classified as 'workers' (against no Conservatives), and forty-six had been to Oxford or Cambridge (against 101 Conservatives), formerly the universities of the privileged.

Churchill resigned in the late afternoon of 26 July and advised the king to send for Attlee. Within half an hour Attlee was prime minister, thus thwarting any projects there may have been to put Morrison or Bevin in his place as leader. The new cabinet ministers were more experienced than their predecessors in earlier Labour governments. Five of them had sat in the war cabinet at one time or another; all the rest had held some ministerial office, except for Aneurin Bevan, the minister of health. Attlee had intended to make Dalton foreign secretary and Bevin chancellor of the exchequer. At the last minute he changed them round—perhaps prodded by the king, perhaps not.[3] The new parliament met on 1 August. The king's speech on 16 August announced an ambitious programme: nationalization of the coal industry and of the bank of England; social security; a national health service. Hugh Dalton wrote: 'After the long storm of war . . . we saw the sunrise.'[4]

There was a different, unexpected sunrise and a new sort of storm. Great Britain's economic position in the world depended

---

[1] At Armagh, West Rhondda, and the Scotland division of Liverpool.

[2] This was the largest number of Independents returned in modern times—evidence no doubt how the party system had been weakened during the war.

[3] The king suggested the change when he saw Attlee on 26 July. Wheeler-Bennett, *George VI*, 638. On the morning of 27 July, however, Attlee told Dalton: 'almost certainly the Foreign Office', and informed him of the change only at 4 p.m. Dalton, *The Fateful Years*, 468–9. Either, therefore, Attlee was not influenced by the king or his mind worked slowly.

[4] Ibid. 483.

on the continuation of lend-lease, and that seemed safe for a long time in view of the Japanese war. British forces had entered Rangoon on 3 May and were now preparing to go further. The Americans had other ideas and called the tune. They intended a direct invasion of Japan. The British had no choice but to acquiesce. British and Commonwealth forces were placed under American orders.[1] The great operation was, however, never launched. By the end of March 1945 the American scientists were confident that they would have atomic bombs ready for use by the late summer. President Truman decided that the bombs should be used against Japan.[2] By an agreement made at Quebec in August 1943, atomic weapons could not be used without British consent. Despite this, the consent had not been sought. The British authorities[3] hastily gave their consent on 2 July without hearing the arguments for using the bombs or inquiring how they were to be used.

This was a sad gesture. The British issued a blank cheque which they could not refuse, and the Americans accepted the cheque without attaching any value to it. They seem indeed to have forgotten that they needed British consent. Two bombs were dropped: the first on Hiroshima on 6 August, the second on Nagasaki on 9 August. On 14 August the Japanese government resolved to accept terms nominally of unconditional surrender, which in fact preserved the authority of the emperor. On 2 September General MacArthur received the formal capitulation of all Japanese forces in Tokio bay. Mountbatten was allowed to receive the Japanese surrender in South-east Asia at Singapore on 12 September, only after MacArthur had given his permission. The Anglo-American relationship had become that of patron and client. The atomic bombs were a sterner portent. Though they ended the war against Japan, they also foreshadowed the coming of Doomsday.

Victory over Japan was officially celebrated on 2 September. This marked the end of the war and the beginning of Great

---

[1] This last campaign was controlled solely by the American joint chiefs of staff, not by the combined chiefs of staff. The British thought themselves lucky to be kept informed.

[2] See Note A, p. 601.

[3] The British chiefs of staff were not informed or consulted about atomic weapons, nor was the war cabinet. The affair was confined to Churchill, Sir John Anderson, and Field Marshal Wilson, head of the British joint staff mission in Washington. The decision to consent was made solely by Churchill, without consulting the cabinet.

Britain's postwar troubles. On 14 August the optimistic plans of the Labour government were interrupted by a warning from the treasury that the country faced 'a financial Dunkirk'; without substantial American aid, it would be 'virtually bankrupt and the economic basis for the hopes of the public nonexistent'.[1] Three days later, on 17 August, American aid was cut off. President Truman directed that lend-lease should end on VJ-day. The legacy of the war seemed almost beyond bearing. Great Britain had drawn on the rest of the world to the extent of £4,198 million. £1,118 million of this had been raised by the sale of overseas investments and other capital assets. British 'invisible' income from overseas had been halved —from £248 million in 1938 to £120 million in 1946. £2,879 million was uncovered external debt, mostly in the form of sterling balances. The British mercantile marine was 30 per cent. smaller in June 1945 than it had been at the beginning of the war. Exports were little more than 40 per cent. of the prewar figure. On top of this, government expenditure abroad—partly for relief, mainly for the armed forces—remained five times as great as prewar. In 1946, it was calculated, Great Britain would spend abroad £750 million more than she earned.[2]

Great Britain would have to export far more than she had done before the war and seemed less equipped to do it. Something like 10 per cent. of the prewar national wealth at home had been destroyed—say £1,700 million—some by physical destruction, the rest by running down capital assets. The coal industry had lost over 80,000 workers; textiles had lost 300,000. Nor could industrial resources be directed exclusively into the export trades. English people expected and deserved immediate improvements in their living conditions after the hardships of the war. At the very lowest, new houses and new clothes could not be delayed. All this seemed to impose impossible tasks.

Yet there were great assets, less visible, on the other side. Despite nearly 400,000 killed in the war,[3] the employed population was three million greater than in 1939, partly from an increase in the labour force, partly from the virtual elimination

[1] The treasury paper was written by Keynes. Hancock and Gowing, *British War Economy*, 546.

[2] This estimate was excessive, as often happened with Keynes. The actual unfavourable balance turned out to be £295 million.

[3] 300,000 members of the armed forces; 60,000 civilians; 35,000 members of the merchant navy.

of unemployment. Moreover, the second war, unlike the first, stimulated or created new industries which could hold their own in peacetime. During the second World war, and not before, Great Britain took the decisive jump industrially from the nineteenth into the twentieth century. Before the war Great Britain was still trying to revive the old staples. After it, she relied on new developing industries. Electricity, motor cars, iron and steel, machine tools, nylons, and chemicals were all set for expansion, and in all of them output per head was steadily increasing. The very spirit of the nation had changed. No one in 1945 wanted to go back to 1939. The majority were determined to go forward and were confident that they could do so.

In the second World war the British people came of age. This was a people's war. Not only were their needs considered. They themselves wanted to win. Future historians may see the war as a last struggle for the European balance of power or for the maintenance of Empire. This was not how it appeared to those who lived through it. The British people had set out to destroy Hitler and National Socialism—'Victory at all costs'. They succeeded. No English soldier who rode with the tanks into liberated Belgium or saw the German murder camps at Dachau or Buchenwald could doubt that the war had been a noble crusade. The British were the only people who went through both world wars from beginning to end.[1] Yet they remained a peaceful and civilized people, tolerant, patient, and generous. Traditional values lost much of their force. Other values took their place. Imperial greatness was on the way out; the welfare state was on the way in. The British empire declined; the condition of the people improved. Few now sang 'Land of Hope and Glory'. Few even sang 'England Arise'. England had risen all the same.

---

[1] 'British' here means, perhaps for the last time, the peoples of the Dominions and of the Empire as well as of the United Kingdom. Strictly, the British were a few days late entering the first war, compared to the continental Powers, and two days late entering the second, compared to Poland and Germany. But their overall participation in the two wars was longer than that of any other country, enemy or Allied.

NOTES

NOTE A. *The decision to use the atomic bombs.* This decision, being purely American, is not of direct concern in British history. It was, however, a fateful act of terrifying importance. The arguments seem to have been almost entirely practical and strategic. It was believed by most, though not by all, American authorities that blockade and non-nuclear bombing would not force the Japanese to surrender unconditionally and that invasion would be costly and prolonged. Though the Japanese government had put out feelers to end the war, they had not accepted unconditional surrender, and the atomic bombs were used to reinforce the peace party in Japan, as indeed they did. It could even be argued that they caused less Japanese loss of life than the continuation of ordinary warfare would have done. There were more general considerations, though they carried less weight. Soviet Russia was due to enter the war against Japan at the beginning of August. The American chiefs of staff, however, expected this intervention to be effective only on the Chinese mainland and not in the home islands. The President and the state department in the prevailing atmosphere of Soviet–American friction would have liked to get through without Soviet assistance at all. This is, however, far from saying, as some ingenious speculators have done, that the atomic bombs were dropped mainly as a demonstration against Soviet Russia.

There was no doubt a vaguer hope that the display of atomic power would act as a general deterrent against future wars. There was also a more pressing and immediate impulse in the minds of the scientists and others who had been involved in the project. They wished to demonstrate to Congress that the money spent had not been wasted. Many also were actuated by scientific curiosity: having prepared an experiment, they wished to see the results. The discussion showed strange blank spots. Few foresaw the enormous increase in potential nuclear destruction which would follow within a few years. Practically no one imagined that any country except the United States would be able to develop atomic bombs in the near future. Practically no one reflected on the contaminated fallout which would follow a nuclear explosion. War suspends morality. In wartime men are deliberately killed and maimed, and from this it was an easy step to killing and maiming future generations. Nuclear weapons were 'just another big bomb'. When Truman heard the news from Hiroshima, he was excited and said: 'This is the greatest thing in history.'[1]

[1] The decision to use the atomic bomb is analysed in J. Ehrman, *Grand Strategy*, vi. 275–309.

BIBLIOGRAPHY

HISTORY gets thicker as it approaches recent times: more people, more events, and more books written about them. More evidence is preserved, though by no means all is yet available. Decay and destruction have hardly begun to work. The student of recent English history has some alleviations. Nearly all the books are in English, except for those relating to foreign affairs. Most of them were published in England and are therefore certain to be found in the copyright libraries (the British Museum, the Bodleian, and the Cambridge University library).[1] The more important books published in the United States are also likely to be in some English library. All, by definition, were published since 1914. There is therefore no need to consult older lists and catalogues.

A third advantage is more equivocal. The period has, as yet, to be studied almost entirely in printed sources. The text of this book was completed in July 1964, that is, exactly fifty years after the first events which it records, and was thus entirely within the compass of the fifty-year rule. There is much confusion about this rule, not least in high places. Strictly speaking, it applies only to the official papers of government departments. Since the Crown never dies, Crown copyright is theoretically eternal, and it was an edict of emancipation when the government laid down, first by rule of thumb and in 1958 by statute, that public records should be opened after fifty years (the period when ordinary copyright expires), with certain reasonable exceptions to protect individuals, such as tax returns and criminal proceedings. The period of closure is, of course, much too long and rests on no basis of sense except the analogy with private copyright. Secrets have lost their contemporary value long before their fifty years is up. It is often said that civil servants should be protected from publicity during their life time. Why? The official military histories name generals, who are equally public servants, and distribute to them blame or even occasionally praise. Civil servants deserve the same treatment. The rule is in fact an unworthy survival from the time when

---

[1] This is not true of pamphlets which are often difficult to trace and many of which have vanished altogether.

government was a 'misterie', reserved for the Crown and its servants. Such rigmarole has no place in a community which claims to be democratic.

The rule has had other unfortunate consequences. Ministers assume, unjustifiably, that, since everything must be revealed after fifty years, nothing may be revealed before then. Hence, for instance, their obstinate refusal to allow any study of the first World war. Still worse, the rule has been extended far beyond its original field of official papers and has been used to enforce cabinet secrecy. This was a doctrine, not a rule, and rested only on convention. It no doubt made sense that the proceedings of an existing cabinet should not be revealed in detail, though they sometimes were. What happened after a cabinet's fall was a matter of individual discretion and good manners, and a former prime minister was in no position to control his colleagues. The creation of a cabinet secretariat in 1916 changed this situation. The cabinet office demanded the return of cabinet papers from a minister on his resignation and even invoked the Official Secrets Act against any who refused,[1] though the house of commons had been assured that the act would be used only against junior clerks. Moreover, it extended its claim to any papers, however private, which related to cabinet affairs or even to politics in general, and many owners of private papers have been led to believe that they, too, were bound by the fifty-year rule. Some enlightened owners have placed their papers in a public library so that they should be available to researchers and have then had the papers barred against themselves or against persons authorized by them. This happened with the Balfour papers when they were placed in the British Museum.[2]

This ban rests on bluff. Private papers are private property. Their owners can use them when and as they like. There is no obligation to reveal private papers after fifty years. There is also no obligation to keep them secret for a single day, and some

[1] Lloyd George was an early sinner. He compelled Austen Chamberlain and Arthur Henderson to return their cabinet papers when they resigned in 1917 (Repington, *First World War*, ii. 278). On the other hand, he made a pact with Lansbury in 1933 to defy any such demand. He kept his side of the pact. Lansbury's biographer, however, succumbed during the tense atmosphere of the second World war and was deprived not only of the official papers, but of most of his personal correspondence as well.

[2] The Museum has now relented, and private papers are opened with the owner's consent.

owners have behaved generously, though not without anxiety and harassment. In any case, there is much selective publication, by individuals and by the government also. Privileged authors, such as Churchill, have been allowed to publish their official records to the general benefit. At least one, Eden (now Lord Avon), has been even more privileged and has been allowed to comb the archives. As well, there have been official histories of both World wars (military for the first, military and civil for the second), all drawing extensively on public records, and a large publication from the archives of the foreign office between the wars. All these volumes rest on a contradiction. If, as their authors and editors claim, they reveal everything essential, nothing remains to conceal, and the archives could be opened without harm to all. If, on the other hand, there are still secrets, the authors and editors have not kept their promise to the public. The unofficial historian can only register his protest and repeat with Charles A. Beard: 'Official archives must be open to all citizens on equal terms, with special privileges for none.'[1]

GUIDES AND SOURCES

At any rate, we have to make do mainly with printed sources. As an initial guide, there is *British History since 1926* (1960), a select bibliography by C. L. Mowat. The Historical Association publishes an *Annual Bulletin of Historical Literature*, which has a brief section on history since 1914. The *Author Catalogue of the London Library* covers books to the end of 1950, the *Subject Catalogue* those to the end of 1953. The *British Museum Catalogue of Printed Books* and *Subject Index* are, of course, even fuller. A new edition of the *General Catalogue* is now being published. It gives a photographic reproduction of the set in the Reading Room with its handwritten corrections. The *British National Bibliography* is an annual list of books published since 1950. Beyond this, the simplest course is to consult a librarian or to wander round the shelves. Three specialist libraries are particularly useful: that of the Royal Institute of International Affairs at Chatham House; the British Library of Political and Economic Science at the London School of Economics; and the collection of books on both World wars at the Imperial War

---

[1] The period of secrecy has now been reduced to 30 years.

Museum. This museum produces cyclostyled quarterly lists of accessions and also detailed bibliographies, ranging from women's work in the second World war to T. E. Lawrence.

P. and G. Ford have performed a great service to students in their *Guide to Parliamentary Papers* (1956) and *A Breviate of Parliamentary Papers 1900–16* (1957); *1917–39* (1951); *1940–54* (1961). The 1917–39 volume has a general introduction, explaining the compilers' methods and how to use the volumes. They exclude statistical returns, foreign and Dominions affairs, ecclesiastical and military and naval matters. They include 'economic, social, constitutional questions, and matters of legal administration' (i.e. matters which have been, or might have been, the subject of legislation or have dealt with 'public policy'). R. Vogel, *A Breviate of British diplomatic blue books 1919–1939* (1963), partly fills a gap left by the Fords. *The Guide to the Contents of the Public Record Office*, vol. 2, lists the state papers and departmental records deposited there; most, of course, are not yet available.

Non-parliamentary papers greatly increased in number during this period as a measure of economy.[1] They are an uncharted sea, and it adds to the confusion that some of them, promised in parliamentary papers, did not come out. There are two introductory guides: *Government Information and the Research Worker* (1952) and *Published by H.M.S.O.* (1960). Then one has to struggle with the annual *Catalogue of Government Publications*, now called *Official Indexes, Lists, Guides, Catalogues*.

To discover what happened and exactly when, *The Times*, with its annual *Index*, is the most immediate resource and nearly always reliable for its news, though not, of course, for its interpretation. No other newspaper produces an index. *Keesing's Contemporary Archives* have given a summary of the news since 1931. The *Annual Register* is still more summary. Its editor, M. Epstein (named as such on the title-page from 1921 to 1945), was a man of strong views: favourable, for instance, to MacDonald, hostile to Baldwin and to appeasement. As he was also editor of *The Statesman's Yearbook* for most of the period, a statement is not made truer by appearing in both volumes. Nor was the information in *The Statesman's Yearbook* always kept up to date: the figures of religious allegiance remained unchanged for twenty years and, like other figures, are reliable only for the first year of their appearance. The *Survey of International Affairs*,

[1] It was not necessary to give free copies to all members of parliament.

published annually since 1925, was also stamped with the personality of its editor, A. J. Toynbee and, in its later years particularly, is an historical document rather than an objective record. The *Dictionary of National Biography*, covering 1912–21 and then a volume for each decade, together with the *Concise Dictionary*, *1901–1950*, is an invaluable work of reference, not wholly free from the editorial outlook of Oxford academics. To take two names at random, it does not include E. D. Morel or Ronald Firbank. Yet Morel had great influence on British foreign policy, and Firbank's books are still read, which is more than can be said for many writers included in the Dictionary. Some of the entries are glorified obituaries; some are studies of high value and contain original information. *Who's Who*, published annually, and *Who Was Who* (four volumes covering 1897 to 1950) are also a matter of editorial choice. The entries were provided by the individuals included and are therefore not always accurate. Sometimes there are mistakes, sometimes—as with previous marriages—deliberate omissions.

Other works of reference are *The Statesman's Year-Book* and the *Constitutional Year Book* (until 1939). Most professions published annual lists, as did many government departments. These can be found on the reference shelves of all public libraries, as can *Dod's Parliamentary Companion*. *The Times* has produced a guide to the house of commons after every general election, except between 1922 and 1924. Proceedings in parliament (commonly known as *Hansard*) have been officially reported since 1908. The reports, though still relying on the antiquated method of individual shorthand, are in general extremely accurate. Few members try to tamper with their speeches afterwards and, when they do, rarely with success. There are two limitations on *Hansard*'s accuracy. The reporters did not include casual cries, unless these contributed to the progress of debate; hence, for instance, they omitted Amery's famous call to Greenwood on 2 September 1939. Nor was any record kept of the secret sessions held in both World wars—unlike the French Chamber, which kept a secret record, published later. It would also be a convenience if *Hansard* abandoned the pretence that the house of commons was composed of some 600 independents and gave the party allegiance of members.

Government statistics are a primary source of great importance. They must be used with caution. They were compiled for the practical use of the department concerned and for no other. The returns of the unemployed, for example, issued by the ministry of labour since 1922, record the registered unemployed, not all those unemployed, and when some 200,000 names were removed from the register, as happened between 1931 and 1933, this did not necessarily mean that the number of unemployed went down. Processed statistics are even more dangerous. Like other processed products, these reduce coarse bits and pieces to a smooth, plausible substance, which is then given a flavour by the manufacturer. Moreover, the terms of reference and the details included were constantly changing, so that comparative statistics over a period of years are often little more precise than the generalizations of a literary historian. An extreme example was the cost-of-living index in the second World war, which was based on estimates of need forty years before[1] and could there- fore be rigged to push up the real cost of living without com- plaint from the trade unions. It is unlikely that we shall ever get statistics of perfect accuracy or completeness. We are on safe ground only when we talk of tendencies. Still, it is better to flounder among the statistics than not to get wet at all.

The leading source is the *Statistical Abstract of the United King- dom* (annually to 1939–40) and the *Annual Abstract of Statistics* (since 1946). Most departments produce their own annual returns. Here another word of caution is necessary. Some re- turns (including the census) relate to England and Wales; some to Great Britain; some to the United Kingdom (i.e. including all Ireland until 1922 and Northern Ireland thereafter). It is very easy to be caught out on this.[2] The most useful are the Census *Reports* and *Tables*, covering each decennial census from 1911 to 1951 (there was no census in 1941), the registrar generals' *Annual Report* (to 1920) and *Statistical Review* (thereafter); the *Census of Production* (1924, 1930, and 1935 only); the *Abstract of Labour Statistics* (to 1936) and the *Labour Gazette*; *Agricultural Statistics for England and Wales*; *Annual Report of the Department of Mines* (1920–38) and *Ministry of Fuel and Power, Statistical Digest* (1944–56); *Annual Statement of Trade*; *Report of the Commissioners of Custom and Excise* and of the *Commissioners for Inland Revenue*;

[1] It included a generous allowance for 'red flannel'.
[2] One important work of reference gives British empire casualties for the first World war and United Kingdom casualties for the second without noticing the difference.

National Income and Expenditure (since 1941); *Local Taxation Returns*; *Ministry* (formerly *Board*) *of Education, Annual Reports.*

The official histories of both World wars and the series of documents on foreign policy between the wars are also, in large part, original sources, which I have put under their subject-headings as a matter of convenience.

Two compilations do the work for all but the most devoted student. *Abstract of British Historical Statistics* by B. R. Mitchell, with the collaboration of Phyllis Deane (1962), gives economic tables of almost everything from the eighteenth century to 1938 and sometimes later.[1] *British Political Facts 1900–1960* by David Butler and Jennie Freeman (1963) gives ministers, elections, parties, much other information, and a few statistics.

There is no large-scale general treatment of this period, nothing like Halévy's books, for example. The only complete account from 1900 to 1961 is *Twentieth-Century Britain* by Alfred F. Havighurst (1962), which is admirably wide and well informed. By far the best book on the interwar years is *Britain between the Wars, 1918–1940*, by C. L. Mowat (1955), rich in bibliographical references and particularly strong on social and economic themes. I have found myself constantly relying on it despite a struggle for independence. *Britain's Locust Years 1918–1940* by William McElwee (1962) is slighter and also, as its title suggests, rather tendentious in an enlightened, conservative way. I doubt whether older books, such as *The Reign of George V* by D. C. Somervell (1935), have now much value except as showing how events appeared to contemporaries. Two books covering a longer period are useful for their concluding chapters. They are *The Common People, 1746–1946* by G. D. H. Cole and R. W. Postgate (rev. ed. 1946), and *Great Britain since 1688* by K. B. Smellie (1962).

Much of the evidence and still more of the interpretation must be sought in periodicals. The articles are too many to be listed in this bibliography, especially as some of the most important appeared in periodicals not specifically historical—political, economic, administrative, or general. Of historical periodicals, *History Today* and *The Journal of Modern History* are particularly

---

[1] Where Mitchell and Deane stop at 1938, the later figures, so far as they are known, can be found in *Annual Abstract of Statistics*, no. 85, which covers 1937–47. There is also a useful publication by the U.S. Economic Cooperation Mission to the United Kingdom, including statistics and graphs, entitled *Economic Development in the United Kingdom 1850–1950*.

useful for recent history. The *English Historical Review* gives a list
of periodical articles each year in its July number, and there is
more than one large-scale annual index of periodicals, which
can be consulted in any good library.

NON-LITERARY SOURCES

Until recently our knowledge of the past was mostly second-
hand: records by one man of what he and others said and did.
Every human witness is fallible, particularly when he writes
about himself, and the more evidence we have, the more
questioning we often become. Now we have recording instruments for both sight and sound, and they preserve the past for
us in a new, more direct way, though, of course, they are still
ultimately operated by a fallible human being. Photographs,
both still and moving, are composed by the cameraman and
change in style almost as much as paintings did. Even the sound-
engineer shapes, to some extent, the voice of the speaker. Still,
historians should use these records much more than they have
done so far. A time will come when every history faculty will
possess gramophone-cubicles and film-theatres, which will be as
much used as libraries or lecture-rooms—maybe more. Most of
the records, when preserved at all, are still in commercial hands.
I give only preliminary indications of where they can be found.

Photographs

These are the oldest form of mechanical record, beginning
with Fenton's magnificent pictures of the Crimean war. The
largest collection in England is the Radio Times Hulton Picture
Library, owned by the British Broadcasting Corporation, a
commercial library with no facilities for research students. It is
particularly rich after 1938, when *Picture Post*, which started the
collection, was founded. Most newspapers and press agencies
have collections, especially British International Photographic
Press Agencies. The Imperial War Museum has more than $3\frac{1}{2}$
million prints and negatives, covering both World wars, though
inadequately until 1916. Selections are often displayed. The
National Portrait Gallery has a large rather haphazard collection, which can be consulted by arrangement, and, more
systematically, the National Portrait Record, which contains
every prominent figure (including even Fellows of the British

Academy), starting in 1917. The Victoria and Albert Museum has just acquired an exhibition, covering the first fifty years of press photography.

The outstanding periodical is the *Illustrated London News*. There are also many illustrated books, often with a general text. Among them are Cecil Beaton, *Time Exposure* (1941); Richard Bennett, *A Picture of the Twenties* (1961); James Laver, *Between The Wars* (1961); L. Fritz Gruber, *Famous Portraits of Famous People . . .* (1960); Y. Karsh, *Faces of Destiny* (1947) and *Portraits of Greatness* (1959); R. H. Poole, *The Picture History of Fifty Years, 1900–1951* (n.d.); Alan Ross, *The Forties: a Period Piece* (1950); Paul Tabori, *Twenty Tremendous Years: World War II and after* (1961); *The Times, Britain 1921–1951* (1951). For the two World wars: *The Times History of the War (1914–1918)*, 22 vols. (1914–19); H. W. Wilson and J. A. Hammerton (ed.), *The Great War*, 13 vols. (1914–19); A. J. P. Taylor, *The First World War: an Illustrated History* (1963); and Walter Hutchinson (ed.), *Pictorial History of the War*, 15 vols. (1939–45).

Of course the older forms of visual record—painting and sculpture—have continued. There are many striking busts by Jacob Epstein. The paintings range from Orpen's portraits of statesmen and generals of the first World war to Graham Sutherland's of Churchill and Beaverbrook. Many of these works are still in private hands; others are in galleries here and overseas. Official artists were employed in both World wars, starting in 1916 with Muirhead Bone and swelling to over 250 artists in the second. The Imperial War Museum owns most of these paintings, though a good many are always out on loan. The articles in the *Dictionary of National Biography* give references to portraits of their subjects.

Sound Recordings

Here again we are mainly dependent on the B.B.C. Its Sound Archives are a private collection, not open to the public, and consist mainly of B.B.C. broadcasts from about 1932 onwards. They include speeches, commentaries, interviews, war reports. A few appear in commercial catalogues. Some have been acquired by the British Institute of Recorded Sound, which also happens to possess 5,000 records made in Nazi Germany. Churchill's war speeches are the only historical records which still appear in the long-playing catalogues, though the companies have others (including the Christmas addresses of George V) which are available at special request.

Films

The National Film Library has a printed catalogue of *Silent News Films 1895–1933* (2nd edition 1964); it contains 2,272 items. *Sound News Films to 1945* are listed on cards. The Imperial War Museum has 5,000 miles of film, covering the two World wars, including over 800 titles for the first war and many more for the second, when official cameramen often went into the front line. As well as direct newsreels, there are composed films, such as *The Battle of the Somme* in the first war, and *Desert Victory* (the battle of Alamein) in the second; these derive, of course, from authentic material. On the other hand, commercial companies have been producing war-films for a long time, starting with *All Quiet on the Western Front* or even *Shoulder Arms*, and it is easy to mistake studio-sets for the real thing. Many people, for instance, imagine that Eisenstein's *Ten Days That Shook the World* is a genuine record of the Bolshevik revolution, not a reconstruction of John Reed's book. Of course, such films are often illuminating in the way an historical novel is. For that matter, many films, not strictly historical, are extremely interesting as records of contemporary life. The subject is not yet explored, and even a preliminary catalogue is beyond me.

BIOGRAPHIES

There is an enormous stock of political memoirs in this period, most of which contain original material. I list the more general in this section and refer to others under various subject-headings, no doubt an imperfect arrangement. It is said that many autobiographies in this period by prominent figures were 'ghosted'— that is, written by someone other than the ostensible author. This is sometimes avowed on the title-page, where the book is described as written in collaboration with a professional author. It is more often not avowed. Reference to a research assistant or thanks for literary aid may give an indication. Normally we must presume that an author accepts responsibility for what appears under his name.

Monarchs

King George the Fifth: His Life and Reign by Sir Harold Nicolson

(1952) is an almost impeccable work of political biography, urbanely tactful in its revelations. *George V* by John Gore (1941) and *Queen Mary* by James Pope-Hennessy (1959) are purely personal. *A King's Story* by the duke of Windsor (1951) and *The Heart has its Reasons* by the duchess (1956) are useful only for Edward VIII's abdication. *King George VI* by Sir J. W. Wheeler-Bennett (1958) is long and rather courtly. Access to the royal archives is given generously—a loophole in the fifty-year rule, which perhaps magnifies the role of monarchs.

Prime Ministers

Memories and Reflections, vol. ii, by H. H. Asquith (1928), has some information, particularly Lord Crewe's account of the fall of the first Coalition. *The Life of Lord Oxford and Asquith* by J. A. Spender and Cyril Asquith (1932) has more; its approach is aggressively 'squiffite'. Tom Jones gave a brief portrait and some personal impressions in *Lloyd George* (1951). Frank Owen used the Lloyd George papers, unsatisfactorily, in *Tempestuous Journey* (1954). There is an official biography by G. M. Thomson (1948). Others are best passed over in silence. *The Unknown Prime Minister* by Robert Blake (1955) has much new information on Law, though rather dull even about a dull man. *Stanley Baldwin* is treated slightly and slightingly by G. M. Young (1951). *My Father* by A. W. Baldwin (1955) is a son's defence. There is nothing on MacDonald except Elton's *Life* (1939), which goes only to 1919. *Neville Chamberlain* by Keith Feiling (1946) is extremely useful, though few noticed this at the time. The more recent life by Iain Macleod (1961) adds nothing to it. Churchill has written his own memoir-histories of both world wars, but there is as yet no good biography. C. R. Attlee, prime minister at the very end of the period, wrote *As It Happened* (1954), certainly a funny thing, and Francis Williams recorded for him, *A Prime Minister Remembers* (1961), which shows how much a prime minister can forget.

Other Ministers, sorted according to party allegiance:

CONSERVATIVE. *Arthur James Balfour* by Kenneth Young (1963), though an improvement on the earlier life by Mrs. Dugdale, runs rather thin for his later years: there is a certain amount on foreign policy during the first World war, little of interest thereafter. *Lansdowne* by Lord Newton (1929) has material on his peace letter. Sir Charles Petrie has dealt with the two Unionist rivals: *Walter Long* (1936), which is mainly party stuff, and *Austen Chamberlain*, vol. ii (1940), which is important for the first World war and for foreign policy later. Chamberlain's own *Down The Years* (1935) adds a little. *Lord Derby* by Randolph Churchill (1959) is packed with raw material: it is particularly useful for the conflict between Lloyd George and the generals and for the return to party government in 1922. *Birkenhead* by his son, 2 vols. (1933–5), and revised one-volume edition (1959), has comparatively little. *My Political Life*, vols. ii and iii, by L. S. Amery (1953) covers the entire period, drawing richly on his contemporary diaries. Viscount (Lord Robert) Cecil wrote in vindication of the League of Nations, *A Great Experiment* (1941), and also a volume of autobiography, *All The Way* (1949). There is not much in *Carson* by Ian Colvin (1933), nor in *Jix* by H. A. Taylor (1933).

Some Memories by Lord Eustace Percy (Lord Percy of Newcastle) (1958) is good on Baldwin and MacDonald and informative on education. *I Remember* by Lord Swinton (1948) is also useful for the National governments. *Old Men Forget* by Duff Cooper (Lord Norwich) (1953) is more accomplished than most political autobiographies; it helps to explain why many men found Duff Cooper attractive and also why he was not a great success as a minister. *Fullness of Days* by Lord Halifax (originally Edward Wood, then Lord Irwin) (1957) is aloof, urbane, and uninformative particularly on foreign affairs. *Nine Troubled Years* by Lord Templewood (Sir Samuel Hoare) (1954) combines autobiography and advocacy; it is the most telling, though also the rashest, defence of appeasement. Templewood's *Empire of the Air* (1957) is another mixture of the same sort, important for the R.A.F. F. Lindemann (Lord Cherwell) presumably counts as a Conservative, though he came into politics by the back door: *The Prof* by R. F. Harrod (1959) is mainly personal; *The Prof in Two Worlds* by Lord Birkenhead (1961) is the official life. Two civil servants ended as Conservatives after prolonged havering. *Prejudice and Judgment* by P. J. Grigg (1948) deals mainly with his time in the civil service. *Sir John Anderson* (Lord Waverley) by Sir J. W. Wheeler-Bennett (1962) is a marmoreal monument, important for Ireland, India, and the civil side of the second World war. *Memoirs* by Lord Woolton (1959) is the autobiography of another Conservative war-recruit. J. A. Salter (Lord Salter) perhaps comes into the same class: *Personality in Politics* (1947) and *Memoirs of a Public Servant* (1961) reveal his equivocal position.

LIBERALS. *Twenty Five Years* by Sir Edward Grey, vol. ii (1925), though mainly on foreign affairs, has a certain amount on general politics until the fall of the first Coalition. *Memoirs* by Lord (Sir Herbert) Samuel (1945), though slight, is important for the outbreak of the first World war, the general strike, and the National government. *Retrospect* by Lord (Sir John) Simon (1952) reveals only what was known already. *An Unfinished Autobiography* by H. A. L. Fisher (1940) is a rare voice from the Coalition Liberals. *Reginald McKenna* by Stephen McKenna (1948) has a little on the first Coalition and on the first postwar Conservative governments. *The Private Papers of Hore-Belisha* by R. J. Minney (1960) represents the National Liberals; it is important for events just before and just after the outbreak of the second World war. *Viscount Addison*, also by R. J. Minney (1959), can count either as Liberal or Labour; either way, his biography reveals little. *Haldane* by Sir F. Maurice, vol. ii (1929), was another Liberal who went over to Labour; there is some interesting material on constitutional questions and on the first Labour government.

LABOUR. Most Labour memoirs are distinguished, even in this drab field, by their pedestrian quality and are best avoided. *Memoirs* by J. R. Clynes, 2 vols. (1937–8), are hardly an exception, but necessary for the first World war and the two Labour governments. The *Autobiography* by Philip Snowden, 2 vols. (1934), is redeemed by malice, especially on the end of the second Labour government. *Arthur Henderson* by Mary A. Hamilton (1938), though based solely on published material, is an attractive portrait of Labour's anchorman. *George Lansbury* by Raymond Postgate (1951), on the other hand, does not bring out the unique quality of the most prominent figure on the Left. *Ernest Bevin* by Alan Bullock, vol. i (1960), is important for his work as a union leader and in the Labour party, but stops short when he took office; for the later period and also for a few anecdotes, we still have to use the life by F. Williams (1952). *Herbert Morrison: an Autobiography* (1960) is often revealing, despite its cautious tone. *My Story* by J. H. Thomas (1937) is interesting only because of the circumstances which produced it. The *Memories* of Thomas Johnston (1952) are mainly about Scotland; they have something on the second Labour government. Josiah Wedgwood would no doubt prefer to be remembered as *The Last of the Radicals* by C. V. Wedgwood (1951) rather than as a Labour cabinet minister. The *Memoirs* of Hugh Dalton—vol. i, *Call Back Yesterday* (1953) and vol. ii, *The Fateful Years* (1957)—run, politically, from 1924 to 1945; based largely on his diaries, they are a rich source of anecdote, some of it reliable. *Stafford Cripps* by Colin Cooke (1957) shows little appreciation of Cripps as a socialist, but is useful for the years of the second World war.

NON-PARTY. A few ministers come genuinely under this heading. Smuts is an obvious example. *Smuts, the Sanguine Years* by W. K. Hancock (1962) covers his time in the war cabinet without openly using any papers still cloaked by the fifty-year rule; nevertheless, it is important, though often evasive, for the war and the peace conference. Kitchener can perhaps claim a similar position. His *Life* by Sir George Arthur, vol. iii (1920), has some original material. *Kitchener* by Philip Magnus (1958) has a little more and gives a good, though unsympathetic, picture. Some men, not ministers, merit inclusion here because of their great influence on policy. Such are *Lord Norman* (Montagu Norman) by Henry Clay (1957)—financial policy particularly in the twenties; *Lord Lothian* (Philip Kerr) by J. R. M. Butler (1960)—appeasement and relations with the United States early in the second World war; and *John Maynard Keynes* (Lord Keynes) by R. F. Harrod (1951)—economic and financial policy throughout the interwar and second war periods.

Other biographies

This section starts with backbenchers and goes on to men distinguished by their work outside parliament. *Sailors, Statesmen and Others* by J. M. Kenworthy (Lord Strabolgi) (1932) has value for the first World war and for Labour politics in the twenties. *I Fight to Live* by Robert (Lord) Boothby (1947) is the work of a Conservative who entered parliament in 1924 and supported Churchill against appeasement. *Eleanor Rathbone* by Mary Stocks (1949) is the life of an Independent woman M.P., who was the leading advocate of family allowances. *So Far . . .* by W. J. Brown (1943) is important for the second Labour government; otherwise it is mainly concerned with trade union affairs in the civil service. *After All* by Norman Angell (1951) also concerns the second Labour government, but is mostly about his work as an advocate of the League of Nations. *My Life of Revolt* by David Kirkwood (1935) and *Conflict without Malice* by E. Shinwell (1955) are the memoirs of Clydesiders, neither of them very important. *C. F. G. Masterman* by Lucy Masterman (1939) has a certain amount on the Liberals after the first World war. *Horatio Bottomley* by Julian Symons (1955) brilliantly handles the greatest demagogue of the age. *Remembering My Good Friends* by Mary A. Hamilton (1944) is an attractive volume of Labour reminiscences. *Inside The Left* by A. Fenner Brockway (1942) is important for the I.L.P. So also is his life of F. W. Jowett—*Socialism over Sixty Years* (1946). William Gallacher was the only Communist M.P. to write memoirs. They are very poor stuff: *Revolt on the Clyde* (1936) and *The Rolling of the Thunder* (1947). *Aneurin Bevan* by Michael Foot, vol. i (1962), is primarily a work of polemics, forcefully written.

The *Memoirs* of Sir Almeric Fitzroy, clerk to the privy council, vol. ii (1925), contain some information and impressions. *Seebohm Rowntree* by Asa Briggs (1961) is important for welfare policy and Lloyd George. *Salvidge of Liverpool* by Stanley Salvidge (1934) is useful for Unionist affairs in Law's time. *Men and Work* by Lord (Sir Walter) Citrine (1964) has much valuable material, especially during the general strike, when it perhaps exaggerates the friendliness of Baldwin and other Conservative leaders. *The Diaries 1912–1924* (1952) and *1924–1932* (1956) of Beatrice Webb, edited by M. I. Cole, present Labour affairs in a condescending light. *Harold Laski* by Kingsley Martin (1953) has some value for the Left in the thirties. *Diary with Letters* by Thomas Jones (1954), formerly assistant secretary to the cabinet, is incomparably the best source for the appeasers. *Clifford Allen* by A. Marwick (1964) shows how a prominent member of the I.L.P. became an upper-class appeaser. The memoirs of Communists usually provide little illumination, as can be seen from *Serving My Time* by Harry Pollitt (1940), leader of the party for most of the period. *New Horizons* by J. T. Murphy (1942) is the work of a Communist who lapsed. The best picture comes in the two books by Claud Cockburn, *In*

Time of Trouble (1956) and *Crossing the Line* (1958)—brilliant records by one who ceased to be a Communist without becoming an anti-Communist.

Other autobiographies and memoirs are listed under the two World wars; the press; Ireland; and foreign policy; and a few under social and literary history.

THE FIRST WORLD WAR

The official histories are a primary source. Facts in *Principal Events* (1922); figures in *Statistics of the Military Effort of the British Empire* (1922). The histories, though produced under the authority of the cabinet office, were closely controlled by the service departments concerned. This is particularly true of the naval and air histories. *Naval Operations* by Sir Julian Corbett and Sir Henry Newbolt, 5 vols. (1920–31), for instance, fails to give a detached account of Jutland or of anti-submarine war. Similarly, *The War in the Air*, by Sir Walter Raleigh and H. A. Jones, 6 vols. (1922–37), is sustained advocacy for an independent air force. The army historians had a freer run. In particular *Gallipoli* by C. F. Aspinall-Oglander, 2 vols. (1929–32), is a most accomplished and independent work, from which all later accounts of the campaign largely derive. *France and Belgium* by Sir James Edmonds and others, 14 vols. (1922–48), is also, in its way, a remarkable achievement, though with some defects. Edmonds, an engineer-officer, at first regarded most British generals with a sceptical eye. Later he was drawn into polemics against Churchill and Lloyd George, and his attempts to revise the figures of German casualties upwards became something of an obsession.[1] The other military histories are *East Africa* by C. Hordern, vol. i only (1941); *Egypt and Palestine* by Sir G. Macmunn and C. Falls, 2 vols. (1928–30); *Italy* by Sir James Edmonds and others (1949); *Macedonia* by Cyril Falls, 2 vols. (1933–5); *Mesopotamia* by F. Moberley, 4 vols. (1923–7); and *Togoland and the Cameroons* by F. Moberley (1931). Nearly all the volumes have maps in separate volumes of cases. The strategical direction of the war escaped the attention of the official historian with two exceptions: Aspinall-Oglander made full use

[1] In each volume, as it came out, Edmonds included corrections, usually small, of its predecessors. The volumes are therefore incomplete, unless a conscientious librarian has pasted the sheets of errata in their appropriate place. Only Edmonds's first volume came out in a revised edition (1933).

of the reports by the Dardanelles commission, and Edmonds discussed strategy, though solely in terms of the western front. Other official histories are *Transportation on the Western Front* by A. M. Henniker (1937); *The Merchant Navy* by Sir A. Hurd, 3 vols. (1921–9); and *Seaborne Trade* by C. A. Fayle, 3 vols. (1920–4). All the official histories, incidentally, are out of print.

The medical histories of both World wars hardly concern the ordinary student. Some histories were kept secret. *A History of the Blockade* by H. W. C. Davis (1920) was generally released in 1959; *The Blockade of the Central Powers 1914–1918* by A. C. Bell (1937) in 1961. *The History of the Ministry of Munitions*, 12 vols. (1920–4), though never put on sale, was distributed to some public and university libraries, where it can now be seen. Apart from this, no civil department seems to have compiled a history of its doings during the first World war,[1] and we have to fall back on the series produced by the Carnegie Endowment. These volumes, though written independently, have something of an official character. Most of the authors had served in the department concerned, and the others had been, at any rate, closely associated with one.

The series includes two introductory guides: *British War Administration* by J. A. Fairlie (1919) and *Dictionary of Official War-Time Organization* by N. B. Dearle (1928), who also produced a volume of statistics, *The Labour Cost of the Great War to Great Britain* (1940). The most important and stimulating of the others are *British Food Control* by W. H. Beveridge (1928); *Trade Unions and Munitions* and *Workshop Organization* by G. D. H. Cole (both 1923); *The War and the Shipping Industry* by C. E. Fayle (1927); *Experiments in State Control* by E. M. H. Lloyd (1924)—particularly wide-ranging; *Food Production in War* by T. H. Middleton (1923); J. Stamp, *Taxation during the War* (1932); J. A. Salter, *Allied Shipping Control* (1921); *The Cotton Control Board* by H. D. Henderson (1922); *Labour Supply and Regulation* by Humbert Wolfe (1923); *Labour in the Coal-Mining Industry* by G. D. H. Cole (1923). The editor, F. W. Hirst, wrote a general volume, *The Consequences of the War to Great*

---

[1] The Food volume in the official history of the second World war refers to a secret history of the ministry of food in the first, which was preserved in the board of trade. Perhaps this was an enlarged version of Beveridge's volume in the Carnegie series.

Britain (1934). As Hirst was a radical anti-war individualist, he did not regard either the war or its consequences with a favourable eye. The Carnegie series projected a volume on the central direction of the war, but this was never written, and the war-cabinet thus escaped the historian—as it did also in the second war. We have to make do with the two *Reports of the War Cabinet* (1917 and 1918) and with Hankey's lecture, *Government Control in War* (1945). Outside the Carnegie series, though similar in treatment, are *British Railways and the Great War*, by E. A. Pratt, 2 vols. (1921); and the *British Coal Mining Industry during the War* by R. A. S. Redmayne (1923).

War Books by Cyril Falls (1930) gives an annotated guide on the most important books published up to 1930; the comments are not without personal prejudice. There is, strangely enough, no general account of politics during the first World war, other than the British chapters in *The War Behind the War* by F. P. Chambers (1939) and A. J. P. Taylor, *Politics in Wartime* (1964). There is, however, one excellent account on the civil and economic side: *State Intervention in Great Britain (1914–1919)* by S. J. Hurwitz (1949). Churchill was early in the field with *The World Crisis*, 5 vols. (1923–9), a mixture of history and auto-biography. Lloyd George produced *War Memoirs*, 6 vols. (1933–6), continued as *The Truth about the Peace Treaties*, 2 vols. (1938). These contain some autobiography, much polemic, and many passages from the proceedings of the war cabinet. Memoirs, predominantly political, include: *Apologia of an Imperialist*, by W. A. S. Hewins, vol. ii (1929)—Unionist backbencher; *Politics from Within*, 2 vols. (1924) and *Four and a Half Years*, 2 vols. (1934) by Christopher Addison—Lloyd George's principal adherent among the Liberals; *War Diary* and *Intimate Diary of the Peace Conference and After* by Lord Riddell—press lord and intimate of Lloyd George's; *From Day to Day 1914–21* by Lord Sandhurst, 2 vols (1928–9)—lord chamberlain until 1921; *The First World War* by C. à. C. Repington, 2 vols. (1920)—military correspondent of *The Times* and later of the *Morning Post*; *In London during the Great War* by M. MacDonagh (1935)—a *Times* reporter; *The Prime Minister's Secretariat* by Joseph Davies (1951) —one of Lloyd George's private secretaries; *Journals and Letters* by Lord Esher, vol. iv (1938)—a power behind the scenes. *The Supreme Command 1914–1918* by Lord (Sir Maurice) Hankey, 2 vols. (1961), is a mixture of contemporary record and later comment by the secretary to the cabinet, which manages to reveal little at great length. It is continued, more drably, in *The Supreme Control* (1963), which summarizes the organization of the peace conference. *Proconsul in Politics* by A. M. Gollin (1964) is a new and important account of Milner's part in the war. High above all these ranks *Politicians and the War* by Lord Beaverbrook, 2 vols. (1928–n.d.), a most remarkable account of political warfare, combining inside knowledge and understanding. *Men and Power 1917–1918* (1956) is still richer in original material; maybe it exaggerates the intensity of the struggle between Lloyd George and the generals, still more that between Lloyd George and the king. However, Beaverbrook's version has permanently stamped the history of the time. Perhaps the best picture of Lloyd George at the height of his power is in a work of fiction: *Lord Raingo* by Arnold Bennett (1926).[1] *Conscription and Conscience* by J. W. Graham (1922) deals with the conscientious objectors.

The military history of the war has also not been written specifically as a British experience and we must use the general histories. *A History of the Great War* by C. R. M. F. Cruttwell (1936) is probably still the best of these. Later books include *A Short History of World War I* by Sir James Edmonds (1951)— a distillation from his official histories—and *The First World War* by Cyril Falls (1960), who also worked on the official histories. More stimulating and more controversial are the various works by B. H. Liddell Hart, especially *The Real War* (1930) and *The War in Outline* (1936). Of the commanders, Sir John French (earl of Ypres) was first in the field with *1914* (1919); he was rebuked by the king for writing it. *Haig* is well served in the biography by Duff Cooper, 2 vols. (1936). *The Private Papers of Douglas Haig*, edited by Robert Blake (1953), presents him in a less favourable light. *Haig, the Educated Soldier* by John Terraine (1963) is an essay in vindication; educated courtier would be a more appropriate title. Sir William Robertson wrote powerfully in his own defence, *Soldiers and Statesmen*, 2 vols. (1926). *Soldier True* by Victor Bonham-Carter (1963) reinforces this defence with further letters. *Sir Henry Wilson, Life and Diaries* by C. E. Callwell, 2 vols. (1927), is highly revealing for

[1] The account of Lord Raingo's first appearance in the house of lords was given to Bennett by Beaverbrook and reproduces his own experience. Raingo's private life is also based on that of a war-minister (neither Lloyd George nor Beaverbrook).

both military and political affairs. Sir Ian Hamilton showed his generous character in *Gallipoli Diary*, 2 vols. (1920). Gough also defended himself in *The Fifth Army* (1931). There is a life of *Jellicoe* by Sir Reginald Bacon (1936) and of *Beatty* by W. S. Chalmers (1953). *Trenchard* by Andrew Boyle (1962) has great value not only for the rise of an independent air force, but for Trenchard's unique influence as chief of the air staff between 1919 and 1929. The biographies and memoirs of many other generals and admirals are too numerous to list.

E. L. Spears wrote two brilliant books, *Liaison 1914* (1930), an account of the first months in France, and *Prelude to Victory* (1939), dealing with Nivelle's short-lived command. Spears and Churchill are the only men who have produced books of high literary and historical merit about both wars. *From Chauffeur to Brigadier* by C. D. Baker-Carr (1930) recounts the troubles of a tank officer. *Marshal Foch* by J. P. Du Cane (1920) is the personal narrative with documents, little known, of the British liaison officer at supreme headquarters. There is a certain amount, rather wild, in *Fisher's Correspondence*, edited by A. J. Marder, vol. iii (1959). Lord Ironside tells the story of a forgotten campaign in *Archangel 1918–1919* (1953). *Lessons of Allied Co-operation 1914–1918* by Sir Frederick Maurice (1942) briefly sheds light on a neglected subject. Popular works on the various battles and campaigns come out all the time and must be omitted. I make exceptions only for Trumbull Higgins, *Churchill and the Dardanelles* (1964), which discovers regretfully that Churchill was not alone responsible; *The Battle of the Somme* by A. H. Farrar-Hockley (1964); and *In Flanders Fields* by Leon Wolff (1959), a very good, fair account of the 1917 campaign.

Life in England during the war is described in *While I Remember* by Stephen McKenna (1922); *How we Lived Then* by Mrs. C. S. Peel (1929); *The Home Front* by Sylvia Pankhurst (1932); *Society at War* and *Britain Holds On* by C. E. Playne (1931–3). There is a curious anthology of private letters, *Everyman at War*, edited by C. B. Purdom (1930). One contemporary novel is a valuable historical document: *Mr. Britling Sees It Through* by H. G. Wells (1916). The war poems were also, for the most part, contemporary and therefore rank high as evidence. The most important for the historian are those by Rupert Brooke, Charles Sorley, Siegfried Sassoon, Isaac Rosenberg, Robert Graves, and Wilfred Owen. The memoirs and novels, being written later, are less first-hand. I select a few largely for their influence when they came out: *Disenchantment* by C. E. Montague (1922) despite its mannered style; *Undertones of War* by Edmund Blunden (1928); *Goodbye to All That* by Robert Graves (1929); *Memoirs of an Infantry Officer* by Siegfried Sassoon (1930); *Death of a Hero* by Richard Aldington (1930); *Her Privates We* by Private 19022 (Frederic Manning) (1930)—the unexpurgated edition in 2 vols. is entitled *The Middle Parts of Fortune*; *The Spanish Farm Trilogy* by R. H. Mottram (1927); *Some Do Not* (1924), *No More Parades* (1925), *A Man Could Stand Up* (1926), and *Last Post* (1928) by Ford Madox Ford; *Journey's End* by R. C. Sherriff (1928), a play; *Old Soldiers Never Die* by Frank Richards (1933); and *In Parenthesis* by David Jones (1937), a prose rhapsody. *Seven Pillars of Wisdom* by T. E. Lawrence (1926) is ostensibly about the Arab revolt. No doubt this is a random, unfair selection.

POLITICAL

General

There are many books on how public affairs worked, constitutional history as it used to be called. Most of them are by authorities on Politics in the academic sense, and the approach is therefore rather different from that of the historian who is more interested in people than in institutions. The older works are listed in earlier volumes of this history. *A Hundred Years of English Government* by K. B. Smellie (2nd edition 1950) now comes up to 1945, with stress on administrative development. *Cabinet Government* (3rd edition 1959) and *Parliament* (2nd edition 1957) by W. Ivor Jennings combine history and description. The most recent work is *The British Cabinet* by J. P. Mackintosh (1962); nearly half is on the years after 1914. Two working politicians have expressed general opinions: *Thoughts on the Constitution* by L. S. Amery (1947), and *Government and Parliament* by Herbert Morrison (1954). *British Government since 1918*, edited by Sir Gilbert Campion (1950), is a collection of valuable essays. *The Organization of British Central Government 1914–1956*, edited by D. N. Chester and written by F. M. G. Willson (1956), is an indispensable survey, based on much inside knowledge. It contains a chronological table, showing when departments were created and the changes of function between them. *Defence by*

Committee by F. A. Johnson (1960) presents the committee of imperial defence in a flattering light. There is some gossipy information in *The Powers behind the Prime Ministers* by Sir Charles Petrie (1959). *Cabinet Government and War 1890–1940* by John Ehrman (1958) is a useful set of lectures.

The Electoral System 1918–1962, by D. E. Butler (1963) summarizes electoral law and each general election. *Parliamentary Representation* by J. F. S. Ross (2nd edition 1948) analyses age, occupation, &c., of M.P.s and also advocates proportional representation. There is a somewhat favourable picture of *The House of Lords and Contemporary Politics, 1911–1957* by P. A. Bromhead (1958). *British Political Parties* by R. T. McKenzie (2nd edition, 1963) is a little too confident in its judgements. Neither the Conservative nor the Liberal party has received serious historical treatment. The Labour party is better off. *Labour Party Annual Conference Reports* are the basic source. *A History of the Labour Party from 1914* by G. D. H. Cole (1948) is the fullest treatment, with some reserved autobiographical touches. *Short History of the Labour Party* by H. Pelling (1961) is slighter and more recent. Among lesser parties, *The Communist Party* by H. Pelling (1958) is competent, though summary; *The Fascists in Britain* by Colin Cross (1961) is a good popular account. *Growth of Public Employment in Great Britain* by Moses Abramovitz and Vera Eliasberg (1957) gives much statistical information. *Higher Civil Servants* in Britain by R. K. Kelsall (1955) discusses their educational and class background. K. B. Smellie has written a useful *History of Local Government* (3rd edition, 1958).

There are few secondary works of detail devoted to general politics. Lord Beaverbrook, in his last book, manages to make *The Decline and Fall of Lloyd George* (1963) as dramatic as the rise. It contains much original material and shows little decline in literary power. *The First Labour Government 1924* by R. W. Lyman (1957) is a useful account. *The General Strike* by Julian Symons (1957) is a lively, recent narrative, with information from some who participated in it. An older book, *The General Strike* by W. H. Crook (1931), still has value, and there is important information in *General Strikes and Road Transport* by George Glasgow (1926). *Nineteen Thirty-One: Political Crisis* by R. Bassett (1958) is an exhaustively detailed analysis which corrects earlier versions. Bassett himself was a Labour candidate who went with MacDonald. *The Mutiny at Invergordon* is by a participant, K. Edwards (1937). The disputes over economic and fiscal policy, which occupied much of the early thirties, I have put, perhaps illogically, under economic history. *The British General Election of 1945* by R. B. McCallum and A. Readman (1946) began this fashion in instant history.

The Irish Question

I have treated this solely as it concerned English history, though most of the books, of course, do not. *John Redmond's Last Years* by Stephen Gwynn (1919) draws on the records which Redmond carefully kept and deals particularly with the negotiations of 1916 and 1917. *Redmond* by D. Gwynn (1932) adds further details. *Recollections of the Irish War* by Darrell Figgis (1927) is useful, though not altogether reliable. *Ireland for Ever* by F. P. Crozier (1932) is the work of a British officer who turned against repression. R. Bennett has given a not very adequate account of *The Black and Tans* (1959). Among biographies are *Michael Collins* by P. Beasley, 2 vols. (1926); *Craigavon* by St. John Ervine (1949)—Ulster Unionist; *Records and Reactions 1856–1939* by Lord Midleton (1939)—Southern Unionist; and *Annals of an Active Life* by N. Macready (1924)—the British general commanding in Ireland. *The History of Partition* by D. Gwynn (1950) tells the story from a moderate point of view; *The Indivisible Island* by F. Gallagher (1960) from a republican. *The Irish Republic* by D. Macardle (1937) is favourable to de Valera. *Peace by Ordeal* by Frank Pakenham (1935) describes brilliantly the final negotiations, with much information derived from de Valera. *Protest in Arms* by Edgar Holt (1960) is the best recent general narrative. More academic discussion is in *Ulster and the British Empire* (1937) and *Ireland and the British Empire* (1939) by Henry Harrison, last of the Parnellites; and in *The Irish Free State* by N. Mansergh (1934). Finally, a novel, *The Informer* by Liam O'Flaherty (1929), and a play, *The Plough and the Stars* by Sean O'Casey (1926).

The Dominions, India, and Africa

These, too, I include only as they concern English history. *War Government in the Dominions* by A. B. Keith (1921) has a certain amount on the imperial war cabinet and conference. *The Development of Dominion Status* by R. M. Dawson (1936) covers a wider period. K. C. Wheare explains the constitutional position in *The Statute of Westminster and Dominion Status* (1938). *The Survey of British Commonwealth Affairs* by W. K. Hancock discusses in vol. i (1937) problems of nationality, in vol. ii (i) (1940) problems of economic policy. Vol. ii (ii) by N. Mansergh (1952) discusses problems of external policy. It is continued in *Problems of Wartime Cooperation and Post-War Change* by N. Mansergh (1958). Background for India is in *The Reconstruction of India* by E. Thompson (1931). R. Coupland describes the constitutional arguments, as seen from the British side: *The Indian Problem 1833–1935* (1942); *Indian Politics, 1936–42* (1943); *The Cripps Mission* (1942); and *India: a Restatement* (1945). *The Transfer of Power in India* by E. P. Menon (1947) gives the Indian side. The most recent account is *The Last Years of British India* by M. Edwardes (1963).

I have said little about Africa in the text, though developments were taking place which became important later. *African Survey* by Lord Hailey (1938) is a monumental book. *Nigeria: a Critique of British Colonial Administration* by W. R. Crocker (1936) and *Kenya from Within: a short political history* by W. McGregor Ross (1927) are useful for particular colonies.

FOREIGN POLICY

A complete bibliography would need a list of all the works on international affairs and on general history during the period. There are short lists for the first World war in A. J. P. Taylor, *The Struggle for Mastery In Europe* (1954), and for the interwar years in A. J. P. Taylor, *The Origins of the Second World War* (1961). Here I keep to British sources and to books on predominantly British themes, with some inevitable exceptions. It cannot be said, for example, that the *Diaries 1914–1918* of Lord Bertie of Thame, 2 vols. (1924), provide much information on foreign policy, even though the author was British ambassador at Paris. On the other hand, the American ambassador in London has much to tell about Grey: *Life and Letters of W. H. Page* by B. J. Hendrick, vol. 3 (1925). The records left by President Wilson's confidential agent are even richer: *Intimate papers of E. M. House*, edited by C. Seymour, 4 vols. (1926).

There are few scholarly studies of foreign policy during the first World war other than the thorough, distinguished work on

The Balfour Declaration by L. Stein (1961). *Great Britain and Austria-Hungary* by H. Hanak (1962) is mainly about public opinion and the attempts to shape it. So, in a different way, is *The League of Nations Movement in Great Britain 1914–1919* by H. R. Winkler (1952), a novel and most useful book. The minority view of foreign policy is given in *Builders of Peace* by Mrs. H. M. Swanwick (1924), an inadequate history of the U.D.C.; *Peace without Victory* by L. W. Martin (1958), an account of President Wilson's relations with the English Radicals; and the fifth lecture in A. J. P. Taylor, *The Troublemakers* (1957). The story of the Stockholm conference and related topics is in A. Van der Slice, *International labor, diplomacy and peace, 1914–1919* (1941). Relations with the Bolsheviks are well treated in *Memoirs of a British Agent* by R. H. Bruce Lockhart (1932); *Anglo-Soviet Relations 1917–1921*, vol. i, *Intervention and the War* by R. H. Ullman (1961), with important material from Milner's papers; and *British Labour and the Russian Revolution* by S. R. Graubard (1956).

The peace conference of 1919 is badly served from the British side. Even the proceedings of the Council of Four are theoretically under the fifty-year ban, though in fact the full official record has been published in the American *Papers Relating to the Foreign Relations of the United States. 1919*, 2 vols. (1942–3). P. Mantoux, the interpreter, has also published his notes: *Les Délibérations du Conseil des Quatre*, 2 vols. (1955). *The History of the Peace Conference*, edited by H. W. V. Temperley, 6 vols. (1920–4) gives a formal record. *Peacemaking 1919* by Harold Nicolson (1933) combines the contemporary diary and later comments of a junior official who became disillusioned. *The Economic Consequences of the Peace* by J. M. Keynes (1919) was a book of almost unparalleled influence. Its arguments are controverted in *The Carthaginian Peace* by E. Mantoux (1946). *Public Opinion and the Last Peace* by R. B. McCallum (1944) is interesting, though impressionistic.

The main source for the interwar period is *Documents on British Foreign Policy, 1919–1939*, edited by E. L. Woodward, Rohan Butler, and J. P. T. Bury, the volumes of which have been coming out since 1946. Only the third series, covering 1938–9, is complete. The documents are drawn almost entirely from the archives of the foreign office and therefore fail to give a complete picture for a period when foreign policy was often decided elsewhere. Moreover, unlike the pre-1914 volumes edited by Gooch and Temperley, this series gives very few private letters and even fewer minutes. The effect is unduly official. A number of ambassadors wrote memoirs, some of which have historical value. *An Ambassador of Peace* by Lord d'Abernon, 3 vols. (1929–31), is important for relations with Germany during the Locarno period. *Lessons of My Life* (1943) and *The Mist Procession* (1955) by Lord (Sir Robert) Vansittart stir sympathy for whose who had to deduce policy from Vansittart's elusive prose. *Home and Abroad* by Lord Strang (1956) rests on the secondary works more than it provides material for them. *The Inner Circle* by Sir Ivone Kirkpatrick (1959) presents its author in an unduly favourable light. *Failure of a Mission* by Sir Nevile Henderson (1940) is a straightforward, honest account of his time at Berlin.

Curzon: The Last Phase by H. Nicolson (1934) is an exciting, rather over-dramatized, account of the making of the treaty of Lausanne. Eden (Lord Avon) gave his prewar memoirs in *Facing The Dictators* (1962). The book has many new passages from the foreign office archives. They were chosen, of course, to vindicate the author, and similar research, conducted, say, on behalf of Neville Chamberlain, might well produce a different effect. In any case, Eden did not face the dictators; he pulled faces at them. There is a curious account of the attempts to marshal respectable opinion against Chamberlain in *Focus* by E. Spier (1963). *It Might Happen Again* by Lord Chatfield (1947) complains of the failure to rearm. *The Defence of Britain* by B. H. Liddell Hart (1939) shows the limitations even of an enlightened critic. The books which K. Zilliacus wrote under the name of 'Vigilantes' were of great contemporary significance; his outlook is revealed also in *Mirror of the Past* (1944).

There are brief general accounts in *British Foreign Policy since Versailles* by W. N. Medlicott (1940) and in *British Foreign Policy in the Interwar Years* by P. A. Reynolds (1954). European questions are discussed in *Britain and France between Two Wars* by A. Wolfers (1940) and *Great Britain, France and the German Problem 1919–1939* by W. M. Jordan (1943). *A History of the League of Nations* by F. P. Walters, 2 vols. (1958) has a good deal on British policy. Most of the books on the nineteen-thirties still grope in the twilight of contemporary judgements. Almost the only one which shows a ruthlessly historical attitude is

Democracy and Foreign Policy by R. Bassett (1952), an examination of the Manchurian affair which destroys many myths. *The Spanish Civil War* by Hugh Thomas (1961) is a sound general account. *Britain Divided* by K. W. Watkins (1963) discusses British opinion on the Spanish civil war in a rather pedestrian way. *Munich and the Dictators* and *From Munich to Danzig* by R. W. Seton-Watson (both 1939) and *Munich* by J. W. Wheeler-Bennett (1948) are now useful only as reflections of contemporary opinion. A more recent book, *Munich* by K. Eubank (1958), does not add much.

The standard work on the outbreak of war, now seriously dated, is *Diplomatic Prelude* by L. B. Namier (1947). Volumes ii and iii of the *Survey of International Affairs* for 1938 (1951 and 1953) and the two volumes for 1939—*The World in March 1939* (1952) and *The Eve of War 1939* (1958)—were compiled after the war and are therefore in part historical studies. *The Appeasers* by M. Gilbert and R. Gott (1962) plays the old tunes with a few enrichments. Two American books are indispensable: *The Challenge to Isolation* by W. L. Langer and S. E. Gleason (1952), with many quotations from the diplomatic correspondence, and *Germany's Economic Preparations for War* by B. Klein (1959), which distinguishes clearly between myth and reality.

Foreign policy during the second World war remains an obscure subject. Most of the information derives from Churchill and is necessarily one-sided. *British Foreign Policy in the Second World War* by E. L. Woodward (1962) is an official history, summarizing the foreign office papers; as the foreign office played only a marginal part, the book provides little enlightenment. There is much material from the American side up to Pearl Harbour in *The Undeclared War* by W. L. Langer and S. E. Gleason (1953), and even more in the record of Roosevelt's confidential adviser: *The White House Papers of Harry L. Hopkins*, edited by R. E. Sherwood, 2 vols. (1948-9). *Stalin's Correspondence with Churchill, Attlee, Roosevelt, and Truman* (1958) is a source of great importance. The wartime volumes of the *Survey of International Affairs* are occasionally useful as works of reference. One of them, *America, Britain and Russia, Their Co-operation and Conflict 1941-46* by W. H. McNeill (1953), is a book of outstanding scholarship and understanding.

ECONOMIC

In recent times the state has played a much greater part in economic affairs, and economics inevitably stray over into politics. There are two good general histories. *An Economic History of England 1870–1939* by W. Ashworth (1960) is a brilliant book, though its later part, dealing with our period, is rather slight. The author is inclined to hurry events along the way he wants them to go, and I have not escaped his influence. *The Development of the British Economy 1914–1950* by S. Pollard (1962) is rather pedestrian, but encyclopaedic in its range. *The British Economy 1920–1957* by A. J. Youngson (1960) is a collection of essays on independent themes. *The Decline and Fall of British Capitalism* by K. Hutchison (1951) is an accomplished literary picture, rather overdrawn. *Economic Survey 1919–1939* by W. A. Lewis (1949) ranges effectively over the world in small compass.

There are many books on shorter periods. *Some Economic Consequences of the War* by A. L. Bowley (1931) gives a brief, stimulating summary. *Aspects of British Economic History 1918–1925* by A. C. Pigou (1947) is a most illuminating book, which combines profound grasp and inside information. *The Great Depression* by L. Robbins (1934) gives a *laissez faire* interpretation, staggeringly old fashioned even at the time. Its views are sharply controverted in *The Inter-War Years and other Papers* by Sir Hubert Henderson (1955). Other useful summaries are in *Slump and Recovery* by H. V. Hodson (1938), and in two books promoted by the British Association: *Britain in Depression* (1935) and *Britain in Recovery* (1938).

Comparative statistics on overseas trade are amply displayed in *British Overseas Trade from 1700 to the 1930's* by W. Schlöte (1952); *Growth and Stagnation in the European Economy* by I. Svennilson (1954); and *Great Britain in the World Economy* by A. E. Kahn (1946). Figures of national income, not always agreeing, are to be found in *Studies in the National Income 1924–1938* by A. L. Bowley (1942) and in three books by Colin Clark: *National Income 1924–1931* (1932); *National Income and Outlay* (1937); and *The Conditions of Economic Progress* (1957 edition).

Fiscal

The raw material is in *British Budgets 1913–1920* (1929) and *1921–1933* (1933) by B. Mallet and C. O. George. Very clear exposition in *The Finances of British Government, 1920–1936* (1938) and *British Public Finances. Their Structure and Development 1880–1952* (1954), both by Ursula K. Hicks. *Studies in British Financial Policy 1914–1925* by E. V. Morgan (1952) is original and enlightening. Useful, though less original, is *British Finance 1930–1940* by W. A. Morton (1943). A. T. Peacock and J. Wiseman trace *The Growth of Public Expenditure in the United Kingdom* (1961). The history of Protection is given in *A History of British Tariffs 1913–1942* by D. Abel (1945) and in *Tariff Problems in Great Britain 1918–1933* by R. K. Snyder (1944). The results of Protection are in *Great Britain under Protection* by F. C. Benham (1941) and *'National' Capitalism* by E. Davies (1939). *Britain's Economic Strategy* by E. V. Francis (1939) discusses general policy.

Particular Industries

The reports of the Sankey commission (S.P. 1919, xi and xii) and of the Samuel commission (S.P. 1926, xiv, with minutes of evidence, &c., as non-parliamentary papers) are important for the coal industry. General survey in *The Coal-Mining Industry* by J. H. Jones and others (1939). The other side in *The Miners: Years of Struggle 1910–1930* by R. P. Arnot (1953). The most important surveys by the Balfour Committee on Industry and Trade are on *Overseas Markets* (1925), *Industrial Relations* (1926), *The Metal Industries* (1928), and *The Textile Industries* (1928). Steel is well treated in *The Economic History of Steelmaking* by D. L. Burn (1940); agriculture in *History of English Farming* by C. S. Orwin (1949). A. Plummer catalogues *New British Industries* (1937). There are many studies of individual firms, such as *The History of Unilever* by Charles Wilson, 2 vols. (1954).

Work and Wages

Post-War History of the British Working Class by G. A. Hutt (1937) is less economic than the title suggests. Raw material in *Prices and Wages in the United Kingdom 1914–1920* by A. L. Bowley (1921), and in *Wages and Salaries in the United Kingdom 1920–1938* by A. L. Chapman and R. Knight (1953). On the unemployed, *British Unemployment policy since 1930* by R. C. Davison (1938) and *Unemployment Insurance in Great Britain 1911–1948* by F. Tillyard and F. N. Ball (1949). Wal Hannington, the Communist organizer, describes *Unemployed Struggles 1919–1936* (1936).

The best account is in a novel, *Love on the Dole* by W. Greenwood (1933).

SOCIAL

The Condition of the British People 1911–1945 by M. Abrams (1945) is a brief statistical survey. More detailed and fundamental are the successive surveys by A. M. Carr Saunders and D. Caradog Jones, *Social Structure of England and Wales* (1st edition 1927; 2nd edition 1937), and, with C. A. Moser, *Survey of Social Conditions in England and Wales* (1952). *The Condition of Britain* by G. D. H. Cole and M. I. Cole (1937) presents a more critical picture. *The Changing Social Structure of England and Wales 1871–1951* by D. C. Marsh (1958) is also enlightening. *Rich Man, Poor Man* by John Hilton (1944) breaks new ground in short space. *Poverty and Progress* by B. S. Rowntree (1941) is a record of advance. *Housing and the State 1919–1944* by M. Bowley (1945) is of exhaustive importance. *The Social Services* by W. H. Wickwar (1936) is also useful. More literary accounts are in *England After War* by C. F. G. Masterman (1922), and *English Journey* by J. B. Priestley (1934). More general still are *The Long Week-End* by R. Graves and A. Hodge (1940), not very reliable; *Our Times 1912–1952* by V. Ogilvie (1953); *The Twenties* by J. Montgomery (1957); *Life's Enchanted Cup* by Mrs. C. S. Peel (1933); and *The Thirties* by M. Muggeridge (1940), a very entertaining book. *English Women's Clothing in the Present Century* by C. W. Cunnington (1952) presumably comes in here.

Education

The many books on this subject treat education as a lump. They recount the increase in the number of those taught with little discussion of what was taught. This is much like ordering food in a restaurant without specifying the dishes. The most useful are *Short History of English Education* by H. C. Barnard (1947); *The Silent Social Revolution* by G. A. N. Lowndes (1937); *Education in Britain since 1900* by S. J. Curtis (1952); *Policy and Progress in Secondary Education* by J. Graves (1943); and *Education in Transition* by H. C. Dent (1944). *Red Brick University* by B. Truscott (E. A. Peers) (1943) was epoch-making. Before it, civic universities did not know that they were inferior. After it, academic snobbery never looked back.

The Press and Broadcasting

The only general account is *Dangerous Estate* by F. Williams (1957); it is popular and inadequate. The report of the Royal Commission on the Press (Cmd. 7700, 1949) has the most detailed information. *The History of The Times, Volume IV*, 2 vols. (1954), tells a great deal about the struggle for ownership and the paper's dealings with foreign affairs, little about how the paper was run. *Geoffrey Dawson and Our Times* by E. Wrench (1955) is more informative. G. Lansbury told the early history of the *Daily Herald* in *The Miracle of Fleet Street* (1923). Hugh Cudlipp has written a lively account of the *Daily Mirror* in *Publish and Be Damned* (1953)—Bartholomew's guiding principle. E. Hyams has written a history of the *New Statesman* (1963), which achieves the remarkable feat of discovering a consistent attitude towards foreign affairs in the paper during the nineteen-thirties. *Northcliffe* by R. Pound and G. Harmsworth (1959), though very long, fails to bring out his great and unique qualities as a newsman. Northcliffe is also the central figure in *Struggle* by Evelyn Wrench (1935) and in two books by Sir Campbell Stuart—*Secrets of Crewe House* (1920) and *Opportunity Knocks Once* (1952). Tom Clarke, another Northcliffe man, wrote *My Northcliffe Diary* (1931) and also *My Lloyd George Diary* (1933).

Beaverbrook by Tom Driberg (1954) is a not very satisfactory biography. *Headlines All My Life* by A. Christiansen (1961) is the autobiography of a Beaverbrook editor who excelled in presentation. *Politicians and the Press* by Lord Beaverbrook (1926) has a certain amount on his beginnings as a newspaper proprietor and is also a first essay for the political histories which he wrote later. Some of the information in it is of great importance. *Lord Southwood* (Elias of Odhams) by R. J. Minney (1955) is all the subject deserves. Two other editors have biographies. *C. P. Scott* (of the *Manchester Guardian*) by J. L. Hammond (1934) tells little about the paper or, indeed, about anything else. *Robert Donald* (of the *Daily Chronicle*) by H. A. Taylor (1934) is of considerable importance for the first World war. This period is also covered in *The Press in War Time* by E. T. Cook (1920) and *The Press and the General Staff* by N. Lytton (1921). David Low, the most influential cartoonist of the age, collected his works in *Years of Wrath* (1946). His *Autobiography* (1956) is less effective.

Asa Briggs is writing *The History of Broadcasting in the United Kingdom.* Two out of four volumes have appeared (1961–5). The solemn tone is suited to the subject. *British Broadcasting: A Study in Monopoly* by R. H. Coase (1950) cuts deeper. *Into The Wind,* the autobiography of Lord (J. C. W.) Reith (1949), is more revealing still.

The Arts and Literature

The best course is to study the works rather than to read books about them. Thus the volumes which N. Pevsner is bringing out, county by county, on *The Buildings of England* draw attention to most modern buildings of importance. The volumes also contain much useful information on the changing characters of towns. *London except the Cities of London and Westminster* (1952) in particular, gives illuminating details of the retreat from centre to suburbs. Pictures have to be looked at wherever they can be found. The Tate Gallery is the principal collection of modern British art. John Rothenstein has two volumes on *Modern English Painting—From Sickert to Smith* (1950) and *From Lewis to Moore* (1956).

The principal works of Delius, Vaughan Williams, Walton, and Holst are in the current record catalogues. Concert programmes, particularly of the Hallé orchestra and the Royal Philharmonic Society, are a guide to contemporary taste. I am not competent to discuss jazz music, though it was a serious and influential art. Both jazz and light music, for instance by Ivor Novello, are likely to survive the more solemn strains of Dame Ethel Smythe and Sir Arnold Bax.

Films of the interwar period are revived fairly often, particularly at the National Film Theatre. Not many are of English origin. Hitchcock's thrillers are virtually the only ones. Chaplin should perhaps count as English and certainly became more English in spirit as he grew older. Others, such as Greta Garbo or the Marx brothers, though American, have some importance, in that most English people saw them.

Sport ranks as a form of art and deserves a more extended treatment than I have given it. There are reminiscences by many cricketers and tennis-players. Football can be adequately treated only when some historian makes a detailed study, based on the records of the individual clubs.

In drama, Shaw's plays are still performed, though their

main interest is now as period pieces. *Heartbreak House* (1920) attempted to say something significant about the first World war. *Back to Methusaleh* (1921) contains, in its second part, tolerably funny caricatures of Asquith and Lloyd George. Maugham's plays, though largely written in the twenties, are Edwardian. The plays of Noel Coward and J. B. Priestley are more contemporary in their different ways. Galsworthy and Drinkwater seem to have sunk below the horizon.

There are two staid introductions to literature: *Fifty Years of English Literature* by R. A. Scott-James (1951) and *Twentieth Century Literature* by A. C. Ward (1956). The concluding volume in the Oxford History of Literature—*Eight Modern Writers* by J. I. M. Stewart (1963)—is of use to the historian only for its chronological table, which gives the principal works published between 1880 and 1941. Most novels are really set twenty or thirty years back, whether avowedly or not. Thus Galsworthy, Joyce, and even, I think, D. H. Lawrence are purely prewar in spirit. H. G. Wells attempted to keep up with the times, as in *The World of William Clissold* (1928) and *Experiment in Autobiography* (1934). Arnold Bennett also prided himself on being up to date, as may be seen from his *Journals 1911–28* (1933). The novels of Evelyn Waugh are sometimes regarded as accurate pictures of their age. If so, it is an age transformed by farce and fantasy, and not far removed from the world of P. G. Wodehouse. *Mr. Norris Changes Trains* by C. Isherwood (1935) is, however, uniquely representative of the thirties. The poets of that decade have considerable historical interest, due to their political commitment. They are surveyed in *The Thirties: A Dream Revolved* by Julian Symons (1960), which is partly autobiographical. More direct autobiographies are *The Whispering Gallery* and *I am My Brother* by John Lehmann (1955 and 1960); *The Buried Day* by C. Day Lewis (1960); and *World within World* by S. Spender (1951). The poems of Auden and MacNeice need no autobiographical accompaniment. An influential work of the early thirties was *The Coming Struggle for Power* by J. Strachey (1932), which is more literary than its title suggests. A full list of books published by the Left Book Club would be useful. *Guilty Men* by Cato (M. Foot, F. Owen, and P. Howard) (1940) is a political pamphlet which may rank as literature.

THE SECOND WORLD WAR

We are blessed again with official histories, civil this time as well as military. Most of the authors took part in the campaigns or departments which they describe, many of them specifically as historians. Next time, no doubt, they will write the histories beforehand. The volumes derive largely from official sources and are thus of great value. Unfortunately they give no references to unpublished sources.[1] It is therefore not possible to tell when an author is relying on evidence and when he is dogmatizing. The civil histories apply anonymity to both ministers and civil servants. This breaks down with Churchill and so creates the perhaps misleading impression that he ran the war all on his own.

The raw material is once more in *Statistical Digest of the War* (1951). The chronological tables, however, have to be chased through the successive volumes of *Grand Strategy*. Four of the projected six volumes have appeared: *II*—September 1939 to June 1941—by J. R. M. Butler (1957); *III*—June 1941 to August 1942—by J. M. A. Gwyer and J. R. M. Butler (1964); *V*—August 1943 to September 1944—and *VI*—October 1944 to August 1945—by John Ehrman (1956). The essential material in the volumes lies in the exchanges between Churchill and the chiefs of staff's committee. It is almost impossible to discover what part, if any, was played by the war cabinet. The tone is complacent and uncritical except in the two last volumes.

There are detailed accounts of each campaign. *The Campaign in Norway* by T. K. Derry (1952) is remarkably frank. *France and Flanders 1939-1940* by L. F. Ellis (1953) is also fairly outspoken. *Victory in the West*, vol. i, also by L. F. Ellis (1962) leans over in favour of Montgomery. The accounts of the campaigns outside Europe are longer and more pedestrian. Of *The Mediterranean and the Middle East* by I. S. O. Playfair, three out of the projected six volumes have been published (1954-60); of *The War against Japan* by S. W. Kirby, three out of five (1957-62). *The War at Sea* by S. W. Roskill, 3 vols. (1954-61) is extremely clear and competent, though naturally inclined to see events from the navy's point of view. The two air histories are in a class by themselves. *The Defence of the United Kingdom* by Basil

[1] Volumes with full references have been placed in the respective departments and will presumably be released in the distant future.

Collier (1957) does justice to Dowding. *The Strategic Air Offensive against Germany* by C. Webster and N. Frankland, 4 vols. (1961), is the most ruthlessly impartial of all official histories. These volumes supersede the earlier official series of popular military histories.

The civil histories also manage to dodge the war cabinet. The introductory survey on *British War Economy* by W. K. Hancock and M. M. Gowing (1949), though gracefully composed, suffers from having to anticipate the detailed volumes. *British War Production* by M. M. Postan (1952) is more precise. *Problems of Social Policy* by R. M. Titmuss (1950) is a remarkable exercise in creative understanding. Other general volumes (not in order of merit) are *Agriculture* by K. A. H. Murray (1955); *Civil Defence* by T. H. O'Brien (1955); *Civil Industry and Trade* by E. L. Hargreaves and M. M. Gowing (1952); *Coal* by W. H. B. Court (1951); *The Economic Blockade* by W. N. Medlicott, 2 vols. (1952–9); *Financial Policy* by R. S. Sayers (1956); *Food* by R. J. Hammond, 3 vols. (1951–6); *Inland Transport* by C. I. Savage (1957); *Manpower* by H. M. D. Parker (1957); and *Merchant Shipping and the Demands of War* by C. B. A. Behrens (1955). *Oil* and *Education* seem to have fallen by the wayside. The War Production series is more technical, but the ordinary historian needs *The Control of Raw Materials* by J. Hurstfield (1953) and *North American Supply* by H. D. Hall (1955). An official history of *Britain and Atomic Energy 1939–45* by M. M. Gowing (1964) has just appeared. Two unofficial histories deserve a mention: *The Theatre at War* by Basil Dean (1956) and *Women in Green: the Story of the W.V.S.* by C. Graves (1948).

The Second World War by Winston Churchill, 6 vols. (1948–54)—each volume with an individual title—is a mixture of official history, based on contemporary records, and personal memories. The work is, of course, slanted in the author's favour, sometimes deliberately, often not. It demands a critical examination which it has not yet received, and Churchill's version of the second World war is likely to dominate the writing of its history for many years to come. Churchill's *Speeches* have been collected into a number of volumes (1938 et seq.). They also rank as a primary source. Apart from Churchill, there are few civilian or political memoirs devoted specifically to the war years, and it is difficult to break into the political history. E. L. Spears, being an M.P., is perhaps an exception, though his brilliant book, *Assignment to Catastrophe*, 2 vols. (1954), is mainly about the fall of France.

The military leaders, however, have had a field day. Hardly one has not written his memoirs or had them written for him. Beginning at the top, Ironside, C.I.G.S. at the beginning of the war, has published *Diaries* (1962), full of ineffective complaints against the civilian ministers. Dill left nothing. Brooke (Lord Alanbrooke) empowered Sir Arthur Bryant to turn his diaries and later memories into connected narrative: *The Turn of the Tide* (1957) and *Triumph in the West* (1959). The result, a mixture of arrogance and pettishness, was unfair to Brooke and to others. Cunningham, commander-in-chief in the Mediterranean and later first sea lord, wrote *A Sailor's Odyssey* (1951)— attractive, harmless, and not very important. Ismay's *Memoirs* (1962) show unquestioning loyalty to Churchill, his old master. Two staff officers lower down are less singleminded: *War at The Top* by C. Hollis (and J. Leasor) (1959), and *The Business of War* by J. Kennedy (1959). The curious will observe that German staff officers had similar grievances against Hitler.

Of the field commanders, *Bomber Offensive* by A. T. Harris (1947) is appropriately aggressive. *The Central Blue* by J. Slessor (1957) also strikes a confident tone. John Connell has written a biography of *Auchinleck* (1959), derived largely from private papers; the tone is honourable and rather sad. The *Memoirs* of Lord Alexander of Tunis (1962) are singularly conventional; they mean no offence and give none. The *Memoirs* of Lord Montgomery of Alamein (1958) are also much in character; they effervesce with a self-confidence which others may have found irritating. *Operation Victory* by F. de Guingand (1948), Montgomery's chief of staff, reinforces the impression. *Overture to Overlord* by F. Morgan (1950) is a useful and lively account by Cossac. There is much evidence in American sources, too many to list here.

Secondary Works

These are surprisingly few except at a very popular level. *The Second World War 1939–1945* by J. F. C. Fuller (1949) demonstrates that the author should have been entrusted with the conduct of the war. A more recent account is *The War: A Concise History 1939–1945* by L. L. Snyder (1962), though it is naturally weighted on the American side. I select a few books on detail which are either informative or stimulating. *The Phoney War on the Home Front* by E. S. Turner (1961) is as entertaining as its title suggests. *War Begins at Home* by Tom Harrisson and Charles Madge (1940) is an essay in mass-observation. *Challenge of Conscience* by D. Hayes (1949) tells the story of the conscientious objectors. *Operation Sea Lion* by R. Wheatley (1958) is the best account of Hitler's projects for invasion. *The Battle of Britain* by Basil Collier (1962) is an effective popular version of his official history. *The Bombing of Germany* by Hans Rumpf (1963), drawing on German sources, makes a fair assessment of the British air offensive. *The Battle of the Atlantic* and *The Battle for the Mediterranean* both by D. Macintyre (1961 and 1964) are good narratives, perhaps a little too favourable to the navy. *Main Fleet to Singapore* by R. Grenfell (1951) is a sustained attack on British strategy in the Far East before the outbreak of war there. *Dieppe; The Shame and the Glory* by T. Robertson (1962) uses Canadian sources both for the background and for the actual raid; its account is a great improvement on the treatment in the official histories.

Winston Churchill and the Second Front 1940–43 by T. Higgins (1957) is an ingenious, and not unjustified, polemic against Churchill, though it overlooks the practical obstacles in the way of a second front, as American generals tended to do at the time. *The Desert Generals* by C. Barnett (1960) is also a polemical work —in favour of Wavell and Auchinleck, against Churchill and Montgomery. Montgomery can be better assessed by detailed examination of his battles, especially *El Alamein* by M. Carver (1962), a most efficient volume. There are good accounts of two daring projects which failed in *Anzio* by W. Vaughan-Thomas (1961) and *Arnhem* by C. Hibbert (1962). *The Struggle for Europe* by Chester Wilmot (1952) is primarily a first-hand account by a radio commentator of the campaign in northern France. It is important also for launching two myths: one that Eisenhower prevented Montgomery from winning the war in 1944, the other that there was a great lost opportunity in the Balkans. *Islands in Danger* by A. and M. Wood (1955) deals with the Channel Islands under German occupation.

Works of literature are fewer and less enlightening about the second World war than about the first. Though the second war affected people's lives even more than the first had done, it was not a profound spiritual experience. There was no doubt or disenchantment. Despite Churchill's rhetoric, the war was fought in prose, even prosaically. Some young poets, particularly Alun Lewis and Sidney Keyes, continued to write poems when they joined the forces, but they were not war-poets in the old sense. A few poems by Dylan Thomas and Edith Sitwell come nearer to the war's spirit. There are many individual reminiscences—particularly about occupied Europe, the Burma campaign, and escapes from prison camps. They are adventure stories, not specifically war books.

The best approach is to go through the files of *Horizon*, the periodical which Cyril Connolly edited throughout the war and for a short time afterwards. This contains many contemporary impressions—and also many excellent short stories. Some novels are set in the war. Until recently none illuminated it. Now, if future generations want to know what the second World war was like, they can safely be referred to the trilogy by Evelyn Waugh: *Men at Arms* (1952); *Officers and Gentlemen* (1955); and *Unconditional Surrender* (1961).

LATE NEWS (*April 1965*)

Asquith by Roy Jenkins (1964) has some new material, including innocuous passages from his letters to Venetia Stanley. *Gallipoli* by R. R. James (1965) gives at last a full study of the military and political muddle. It is deplorable that a work of such distinction provides no references. *The Deluge* by A. Marwick (1965) is a valuable account of economics and social life during the first World war. *Vansittart in Office* by Ian Colvin (1965) has some fragments, more about the author than the subject. *The Reckoning* by Lord Avon (Anthony Eden) (1965) is the second volume of the Eden Memoirs. It runs from February 1938 to the end of the second World war, and its handsome pages provide a great deal of uninteresting information. *Wavell* to June 1941 by John Connell (1964) is useful for the Desert war and for Wavell's conflicts with Churchill. *Tobruk* by M. Carver (1964) is of high technical competence. The scientific side of war is variously illuminated in *Design and Development of Weapons* by M. M. Postan, D. Hay, and J. D. Scott (1964)—a volume in the official civil history; *Tizard* by R. Clark (1965)—the biography of a leading intermediary between scientists and the services; and *The Mare's Nest* by D. Irving (1964)—the guesses, true and false, about the German rockets.

SUPPLEMENTARY BIBLIOGRAPHY

(AUGUST 1969)

THE period of secrecy imposed on official records has been reduced from fifty to thirty years. Scholars will soon be able to explore the entire period covered by this book, and much no doubt will have to be revised. But scholars work slowly, and we are not likely to reap the harvest of freedom for another ten or fifteen years. Meanwhile I add some titles which have appeared since this book was written. The arrangement is that of the original bibliography.

The work of reference by David Butler and Jennie Freeman has been revised and extended. It is now *British Political Facts 1900–1967* (1968). There are now two general treatments, each covering a longer period than this book. *Contemporary England 1914–1964* (1967) by W. N. Medlicott is particularly strong on foreign affairs. In *Britain in the Century of Total War: Peace and Social Change, 1900–1967* (1968), Arthur Marwick develops the theme which he first propounded in *The Deluge*, that war brings advance as well as destruction.

Lady Lloyd-George, Lloyd George's unofficial wife for thirty years and his official wife for two, describes their life together in *The Years that are Past* (1967). The biography of Winston Churchill, begun by Randolph Churchill and to be completed by Martin Gilbert, has not yet reached the period covered by this book. Lord Moran gives a somewhat clinical account of the later years in *Churchill* (1966). *Churchill and Beaverbrook* by Kenneth Young (1966) offers an interesting study in friendship and politics, mainly important for the second World war. *Former Naval Person* by Sir Peter Gretton (1968) gives a highly skilful survey of Churchill's influence on the Royal Navy and naval policy.

There have been a few political biographies. *Lord Reading* by Montgomery Hyde (1967) is a success story. *Walter Monckton* by Lord Birkenhead (1969) has a little on the abdication of Edward VIII. The second volume of *Ernest Bevin* by Alan Bullock (1967) covers the years of the second World war in suitably ponderous fashion. Harold Macmillan published two volumes of political autobiography during this period: *Winds of Change* (1966) and *The Blast of War 1939–45* (1967). Sir Oswald Mosley in *My Life* (1968) is informative for his years in the Labour movement and tails off when he comes to Fascism. *Smuts: the Fields of Force* (1968) by W. K. Hancock deals primarily with South African affairs.

Unofficial figures provide more interesting material. Andrew Boyle presents *Montagu Norman* (1967) as an advocate of financial stability who was himself far from stable. Walter (later Lord) Citrine kept a diary and prints much of it in *Men and Work* (1966). B. H. Liddell Hart has written two volumes of *Memoirs* (1965), describing his attempts to modernize the British army. *Beatrice Webb* by Kitty Muggeridge and Ruth Adam (1968) is mainly a personal portrait. *Editor* by Kingsley Martin (1968) gives a characteristically gay and chaotic account of his life on the *New Statesman* between 1931 and 1945. There are some outstanding diaries by political observers. *Chips: the Diary of Sir Henry Channon*, edited by Robert Rhodes James (1967), is a rich compound of snobbery and folly. The *Diaries 1930–39* (1966) and *1939–45* (1967) of Harold Nicolson present a winning personality who gradually turned querulous. *Whitehall Diaries 1916–25*—with more to come—by Thomas Jones (1969) are records, cautiously indiscreet, by the deputy secretary to the cabinet. It would be rash to take Tom Jones at his own valuation. *The Years of the Week* by Patricia Cockburn (1968) supplements the autobiographical works by her husband.

The outstanding work on the first World war is *From the Dreadnought to Scapa Flow* by A. J. Marder. Volume ii deals with *The War Years: to the Eve of Jutland 1914–1916* (1965) and volume iii with *Jutland and After* (*May 1916–December 1916*) (1966), and there are two more volumes to come. It is not often that a book can be described as the final word on its subject. This is one of the rare cases. *Great Britain and the War of 1914–1918* by E. L. Woodward (1967) is a large-scale survey, not altogether in touch with the latest researches. *Men Who March Away* by I. M. Parsons (1965) is an anthology of first World war poetry. *The Long Trail* by John Brophy and Eric Partridge (1965) assembles the soldiers' songs and slang of the first World war, unfortunately bowdlerized. Perhaps the student would do better with the gramophone record of *Oh! What a Lovely War* (1963)—the stage-show, not the film. *British Strategy and Politics*

(1965) by P. Guinn will probably need some modification as the archives are examined.

In political affairs there is still an excessive interest in the Left. *The Revolutionary Movement in Britain 1900–21* (1967) by W. Kendall puts the blame for failure on Moscow. *The British Communist Party* by L. J. Macfarlane (1966) is a routine study, and *The Clydesiders* by R. H. Middlemas (1965) is much the same. *Left in the Centre* by R. E. Dowse (1966) does rather better with the I.L.P. *The Downfall of the Liberal Party* by Trevor Wilson (1966) seems to have started with the view that it was all the fault of Lloyd George and to have changed course midway.

On particular themes, D. E. Moggridge has analysed the arguments preceding *The Return to Gold 1925* (1969). S. W. Roskill is treating *British Naval Policy between the Wars*. The first volume (1968) runs from 1919 to 1929. R. Skidelsky provides a background to the crisis of 1931 in *Politicians and the Slump: The Labour Government of 1929–31* (1967). I was delighted to find my amateur guesses confirmed by an economist in *Economic Recovery in Britain* by H. W. Richardson (1967). Brian Inglis has made a detailed survey of *The Abdication* (1966). Lord Beaverbrook left a more personal narrative of *The Abdication of King Edward VIII*, which I edited (1966). On Irish affairs, there is only the life of *John Dillon* by F. S. L. Lyons (1968). The fiftieth anniversary of the Easter rising was disappointingly unproductive.

On foreign policy, R. H. Ullman has produced a second volume, as good as the first, of his *Anglo-Soviet Relations 1917–1921*. It is called *Britain and the Russian Civil War* (1968). Roger Louis analyses British imperialist policy in *Great Britain and Germany's Lost Colonies* (1967). *The Chanak Affair* by David Walder (1969) is one of the first books to benefit from the opening of the official records. J. F. Naylor presents a favourable picture of *Labour's International Policy* (1969). Moderate 'revisionism' is shown in *The Roots of Appeasement* by Martin Gilbert (1966); slightly more persistent revisionism in *Munich 1938* by Keith Robbins (1968).

The official military histories of the second World war advance with a deliberation more appropriate to the first. There is a second volume of *Victory in the West* (1969); a fourth volume of *The Mediterranean and the Middle East* (1966); and a fourth volume of *The War against Japan* (1965). The military leaders continue to attract attention and to seek it. The memoirs of

Sholto Douglas are called *Years of Command* (1966), those of Arthur Tedder, *With Prejudice* (1966)—not much news in either. John Connell devoted two volumes to *Wavell* (1964 and 1969).

Of secondary works, *Three Days to Catastrophe* by Douglas Clark (1966) describes the abortive plans to aid Finland. *The Breaking Wave* by Telford Taylor (1967) at last discriminates between the invasion plans of the German army and of the *Luftwaffe*. Laurence Thompson disturbs some complacent versions in *1940* (1966). G. M. Thomson goes gingerly round the political alarms of 1942 in *Vote of Censure* (1968). Trumbull Higgins continues his one-man campaign in *The Soft Underbelly* (1969). The same subject is discussed with more detachment by Michael Howard in *The Mediterranean Strategy in the second World war* (1968). This is a foretaste of his volume iv on *Grand Strategy*, which will complete the official series. Ian Hamilton has compiled an anthology of *The Poetry of War 1939–45* (1965), which provides an interesting comparison with the poetry of the first World war. Evelyn Waugh transformed his trilogy into a single volume, entitled *Sword of Honour* (1965). The impact is even more powerful than before. Its admirers will be interested to know that Trimmer married a Johannesburg Jewess and is greatly scared about his safety and fortune.

LIST OF CABINETS, 1914–45

1. ASQUITH'S LIBERAL CABINET

(*from 5 August 1914*)

Prime minister:[1] H. H. Asquith.
Lord chancellor: Viscount Haldane.
Lord president: Earl Beauchamp.
Lord privy seal
Secretary for India } Marquis of Crewe.
Chancellor of the exchequer: D. Lloyd George.
Home secretary: R. McKenna.
Foreign secretary: Sir E. Grey.
Colonial secretary: L. Harcourt.
Secretary for war: Earl Kitchener.
Secretary for Scotland: T. M'Kinnon Wood.
Chief secretary for Ireland: A. Birrell.
First lord of the admiralty: W. Churchill.
Chancellor of the duchy of Lancaster: C. Masterman.
President of the board of trade: W. Runciman.
President of the local government board: H. Samuel.
President of the board of agriculture: Lord Lucas.
President of the board of education: J. Pease.
Postmaster general: C. Hobhouse.
First commissioner of works: Lord Emmott.
Attorney general: Sir J. Simon.

Change

February 1915: Masterman, having failed to find a seat in the house of commons, resigned and was succeeded as chancellor of the duchy of Lancaster by E. Montagu.

2. ASQUITH'S COALITION CABINET

(*formed May 1915*)

Prime minister: H. H. Asquith.
Lord chancellor: Lord Buckmaster.
Lord president: Marquis of Crewe.
Lord privy seal: Earl Curzon.
Chancellor of the exchequer: R. McKenna.
Home secretary: Sir J. Simon.
Foreign secretary: Sir E. Grey.

---

[1] Every prime minister throughout the period was strictly first lord of the treasury, but the more popular title was now established.

Colonial secretary: A. Bonar Law.
Secretary for war: Earl Kitchener.
Secretary for India: A. Chamberlain.
Secretary for Scotland: T. M'Kinnon Wood.
Chief secretary for Ireland: A. Birrell.
First lord of the admiralty: A. Balfour.
Chancellor of the duchy of Lancaster: W. Churchill.
President of the board of trade: W. Runciman.
President of the local government board: W. Long.
President of the board of agriculture: Earl of Selborne.
President of the board of education: A. Henderson.
First commissioner of works: L. Harcourt (cr. Viscount 1916).
Minister of munitions: D. Lloyd George.
Minister without portfolio: Marquis of Lansdowne.
Attorney general: Sir E. Carson.

Changes

July 1915: Lord R. Cecil, parliamentary foreign under-secretary, entered
the cabinet. *November 1915*: Carson resigned and was succeeded as attorney
general by Sir F. E. Smith; Sir H. Samuel succeeded Churchill, resigned,
as chancellor of the duchy of Lancaster. *January 1916*: Samuel succeeded
Simon, resigned, as home secretary and was succeeded as chancellor of the
duchy of Lancaster by E. Montagu, who remained also financial secretary
to the treasury. Lord R. Cecil became minister of blockade, while remaining
parliamentary under-secretary to the foreign office. *July 1916*: Lloyd George
succeeded Kitchener (deceased) as secretary for war and was himself succeeded as minister of munitions by E. Montagu; T. M'Kinnon Wood succeeded Montagu as chancellor of the duchy of Lancaster, becoming also
financial secretary to the treasury, and was himself succeeded as secretary
for Scotland by H. Tennant; Selborne resigned and was succeeded as president of the board of agriculture by the Earl of Crawford; Birrell resigned
and was succeeded as chief secretary for Ireland by H. Duke. *August 1916*:
Henderson became paymaster general with a seat in the cabinet and was succeeded as president of the board of education by the marquis of Crewe.

3. LLOYD GEORGE'S WAR CABINET

(formed December 1916)

Prime minister: D. Lloyd George.
Lord president: Earl Curzon.
Chancellor of the exchequer: A. Bonar Law.
Ministers without portfolio: Arthur Henderson.
                               Viscount Milner.

Changes
(all of ministers without portfolio except where otherwise stated)

May–August 1917: G. N. Barnes, minister of pensions, acted as a member of
the war cabinet during Henderson's absence in Russia.[1] *June 1917*: J. Smuts[2]

---

[1] Barnes continued to attend the war cabinet during the short period between
Henderson's return and resignation. Curson protested in vain against this irregularity.   [2] A member of the South African parliament.

joined the war cabinet; Sir E. Carson, previously first lord of the admiralty, joined the war cabinet. *August 1917*: Henderson resigned, and G. N. Barnes, resigning as minister of pensions, took his place in the war cabinet. *January 1918*: Carson resigned. *April 1918*: Milner left the war cabinet, becoming secretary for war; A. Chamberlain joined the war cabinet. *January 1919*: Law became lord privy seal and was succeeded as chancellor of the exchequer by A. Chamberlain, both remaining members of the war cabinet; Smuts left the war cabinet; Sir E. Geddes, previously first lord of the admiralty, joined the war cabinet.

LLOYD GEORGE'S COALITION CABINET

(formed November 1919)

Prime minister: D. Lloyd George.
Lord Chancellor: Lord Birkenhead (cr. Viscount 1921, Earl 1922).
Lord president: A. J. Balfour (cr. Earl 1922).
Lord privy seal: A. Bonar Law.
Chancellor of the exchequer: A. Chamberlain.
Home secretary: E. Shortt.
Foreign secretary: Earl Curzon (cr. Marquis 1921).
Colonial secretary: Viscount Milner.
Secretary for war (combined with air): W. Churchill.
Secretary for India: E. Montagu.
Chief secretary for Ireland: I. Macpherson.
Irish viceroy[1]: Viscount French.
First lord of the admiralty: W. Long (cr. Viscount 1921).
President of the board of trade: Sir A. Geddes.
Minister of health: C. Addison.
Minister of agriculture: Lord Lee of Fareham.
President of the board of education: H. A. L. Fisher.
Minister of munitions: Lord Inverforth.
Minister of labour: Sir R. Horne.
Minister of transport: Sir. E. Geddes.
Minister without portfolio: G. Barnes.

Changes

January 1920: Barnes resigned. *March 1920*: Sir A. Geddes resigned. Horne succeeded him as president of the board of trade and was himself succeeded as minister of labour by T. Macnamara. *April 1920*: Sir H. Greenwood succeeded Macpherson as chief secretary for Ireland: Sir L. Worthington-Evans became minister without portfolio. *February 1921*: Churchill became colonial secretary and was succeeded as secretary for war by Worthington-Evans,[2] Lord Lee succeeded Long as first lord of the admiralty and was succeeded as minister of agriculture by Sir A. Griffith-Boscawen. *March 1921*: The ministry of munitions was abolished, and Inverforth left the cabinet. Law retired and was succeeded as lord privy seal by A. Chamberlain. *April 1921*: Horne succeeded Chamberlain as chancellor of the exchequer and was himself succeeded as president of the board of trade by S. Baldwin. Addison became minister without portfolio and was succeeded as minister of health by Sir A. Mond. Viscount Fitzalan succeeded French as Irish viceroy. *July 1921*: Addison resigned. *November 1921*: Sir G. Hewart, attorney general, entered the cabinet. Sir E. Geddes resigned; his successor as minister of transport was not in the cabinet. *March 1922*: Hewart resigned (becoming lord chief justice); his successor as attorney general was not in the cabinet. Montagu resigned and was succeeded as secretary for India by Viscount Peel. *April 1922*: the earl of Crawford, first commissioner of works, entered the cabinet.

LAW'S CONSERVATIVE CABINET

(formed October 1922)

Prime minister: A. Bonar Law.
Lord chancellor: Viscount Cave.
Lord president
Chancellor of the duchy of Lancaster } Marquis of Salisbury.
Chancellor of the exchequer: S. Baldwin.
Home secretary: W. C. Bridgeman.
Foreign secretary: Marquis Curzon.
Colonial secretary: Duke of Devonshire.
Secretary for war: Earl of Derby.
Secretary for India: Viscount Peel.
Secretary for Scotland: Viscount Novar.
First lord of the admiralty: L. S. Amery.
President of the board of trade: Sir P. Lloyd-Greame.
Minister of agriculture: Sir R. Sanders.
President of the board of education: E. F. L. Wood.
Minister of labour: Sir A. Montague-Barlow.
Minister of health: Sir A. Griffith-Boscawen.

Change

March 1923. N. Chamberlain succeeded Griffith-Boscawen, resigned, as minister of health.

BALDWIN'S FIRST CONSERVATIVE CABINET

(formed May 1923)

This was the same as Law's cabinet with the following change and additions:

Prime minister
Chancellor of the exchequer } S. Baldwin
Lord privy seal: Lord R. Cecil.

Financial secretary to the treasury: Sir W. Joynson-Hicks.
Secretary for air: Sir S. Hoare.
Postmaster general: Sir L. Worthington-Evans.

The marquis of Salisbury resigned as chancellor of the duchy of Lancaster, and his successor in this office was not in the cabinet.

Changes

August 1923: Baldwin resigned as chancellor of the exchequer and was succeeded by N. Chamberlain, who was himself succeeded as minister of health by Joynson-Hicks. Joynson-Hicks's successor as financial secretary to the treasury was not in the cabinet.

MACDONALD'S FIRST LABOUR CABINET

(formed January 1924)

Prime minister
Foreign secretary } J. R. MacDonald.
Lord chancellor: Viscount Haldane.
Lord president: Lord Parmoor.
Lord privy seal: J. R. Clynes.
Chancellor of the exchequer: P. Snowden.
Home secretary: A. Henderson.
Colonial secretary: J. H. Thomas.
Secretary for war: S. Walsh.
Secretary for India: Lord Olivier.
Secretary for Scotland: W. Adamson.
Secretary for air: Lord Thomson.
First lord of the admiralty: Viscount Chelmsford.
Chancellor of the duchy of Lancaster: J. Wedgwood.
President of the board of trade: S. Webb.
Minister of agriculture: N. Buxton.
President of the board of education: C. P. Trevelyan.
Postmaster general: V. Hartshorn.
First commissioner of works: F. W. Jowett.
Minister of labour: T. Shaw.
Minister of health: J. Wheatley.

BALDWIN'S SECOND CONSERVATIVE CABINET

(formed November 1924)

Prime minister: S. Baldwin.
Lord chancellor: Viscount Cave.
Lord president: Marquis Curzon.
Lord privy seal: Marquis of Salisbury.
Chancellor of the exchequer: W. S. Churchill.
Home secretary: Sir W. Joynson-Hicks.
Foreign secretary: A. Chamberlain.
Colonial secretary: L. S. Amery.

Secretary for war: Sir L. Worthington-Evans.
Secretary for India: Earl of Birkenhead.
Secretary for air: Sir S. Hoare.
Secretary for Scotland: Sir J. Gilmour.
First lord of the admiralty: W. Bridgeman.
Chancellor of the duchy of Lancaster: Viscount Cecil.
President of the board of trade: Sir P. Cunliffe-Lister.[1]
Minister of agriculture: E. F. L. Wood.
President of the board of education: Lord E. Percy.
First commissioner of works: Viscount Peel.
Minister of labour: Sir A. Steel-Maitland.
Minister of health: N. Chamberlain.
Attorney general: Sir D. Hogg.

Changes

April 1925: The Earl of Balfour succeeded Curzon as lord president. *June 1925*: Amery became also Dominions secretary. *November 1925*: W. Guinness succeeded Wood as minister of agriculture. *October 1927*: Lord Cushendun succeeded Cecil as chancellor of the duchy of Lancaster. *March 1928*: Hogg was created Viscount Hailsham and succeeded Cave as lord chancellor. Hogg's successor as attorney general was not in the cabinet. *October 1928*: Peel succeeded Birkenhead as secretary for India and was himself succeeded as first commissioner of works by the Marquis of Londonderry.

MACDONALD'S SECOND LABOUR CABINET

(*formed June 1929*)

Prime minister: J. R. MacDonald.
Lord chancellor: Lord Sankey.
Lord president: Lord Parmoor.
Lord privy seal: J. H. Thomas.
Chancellor of the exchequer: P. Snowden.
Home secretary: J. R. Clynes.
Foreign secretary: A. Henderson.
Colonial and Dominions secretary: Lord Passfield.
Secretary for war: T. Shaw.
Secretary for India: W. Wedgwood Benn.
Secretary for air: Lord Thomson.
Secretary for Scotland: W. Adamson.
First lord of the admiralty: A. V. Alexander.
President of the board of trade: W. Graham.
Minister of agriculture: N. Buxton.
President of the board of education: Sir C. P. Trevelyan.
Minister of labour: Margaret Bondfield.
Minister of health: A. Greenwood.
First commissioner of works: G. Lansbury.

[1] Formerly Lloyd-Greame.

Changes

June 1930: Hartshorn succeeded Thomas as lord privy seal. Thomas became dominions secretary, Passfield retaining the colonial office. C. Addison succeeded Buxton as minister of agriculture. *October 1930*: Lord Amulree succeeded Thomson (deceased) as secretary for air. *March 1931*: H. B. Lees-Smith succeeded Trevelyan, resigned, as president of the board of education; H. Morrison, minister of transport, entered the cabinet; T. Johnston succeeded Hartshorn as lord privy seal.

MACDONALD'S FIRST NATIONAL CABINET

(*formed August 1931*)

Prime minister: J. R. MacDonald.
Lord chancellor: Lord Sankey.
Lord president: S. Baldwin.
Chancellor of the exchequer: P. Snowden.
Home secretary: Sir H. Samuel.
Foreign secretary: Marquis of Reading.
Secretary for India: Sir S. Hoare.
Dominions secretary: J. H. Thomas.
President of the board of trade: Sir P. Cunliffe-Lister.
Minister of health: N. Chamberlain.

MACDONALD'S SECOND NATIONAL CABINET

(*formed November 1931*)

Prime minister: J. R. MacDonald.
Lord chancellor: Lord Sankey (cr. Viscount 1932).
Lord president: S. Baldwin.
Lord privy seal: Lord Snowden.
Chancellor of the exchequer: N. Chamberlain.
Home secretary: Sir H. Samuel.
Foreign secretary: Sir J. Simon.
Colonial secretary: Sir P. Cunliffe-Lister.
Dominions secretary: J. H. Thomas.
Secretary for war: Viscount Hailsham.
Secretary for India: Sir S. Hoare.
Secretary for air: Marquis of Londonderry.
Secretary for Scotland: Sir A. Sinclair.
First lord of the admiralty: Sir B. Eyres-Monsell.
President of the board of trade: W. Runciman.
Minister of agriculture: Sir J. Gilmour.
President of the board of education: Sir D. Maclean.
Minister of labour: Sir H. Betterton.
Minister of health: Sir E. Hilton Young.
First commissioner of works: W. Ormsby-Gore.

Changes

July 1932: Lord Irwin succeeded Maclean (deceased) as president of the board of education. *September 1932*: Baldwin succeeded Snowden as lord privy seal, while remaining lord president; Gilmour succeeded Samuel as home secretary and was himself succeeded as minister of agriculture by W. Elliot; Sir G. Collins succeeded Sinclair as secretary for Scotland. *December 1933*: Baldwin resigned as lord privy seal, and his successor in that office was not in the cabinet; Sir K. Wood, postmaster general, entered the cabinet. *June 1934*: O. Stanley succeeded Betterton as minister of labour.

BALDWIN'S NATIONAL CABINET

(*formed June 1935*)

Prime minister: S. Baldwin.
Lord chancellor: Viscount Hailsham.
Lord president: J. R. Macdonald.
Lord privy seal: Marquis of Londonderry.
Chancellor of the exchequer: N. Chamberlain.
Home secretary: Sir J. Simon.
Foreign secretary: Sir S. Hoare.
Colonial secretary: M. MacDonald.
Dominions secretary: J. H. Thomas.
Secretary for war: Viscount Halifax.
Secretary for India: Marquis of Zetland.
Secretary for air: Sir P. Cunliffe-Lister (cr. Viscount Swinton).
Secretary for Scotland: Sir G. Collins.
First lord of the admiralty: Sir B. Eyres-Monsell (cr. Viscount Monsell).
President of the board of trade: W. Runciman.
Minister of agriculture: W. Elliot.
President of the board of education: O. Stanley.
Minister of labour: E. Brown.
Minister of health: Sir K. Wood.
First commissioner of works: W. Ormsby-Gore.
Minister without portfolio for League of Nations Affairs: A. Eden.
Minister without portfolio: Lord E. Percy.

Changes

November 1935: Halifax succeeded Londonderry as lord privy seal and was himself succeeded as secretary for war by A. Duff Cooper; Thomas and M. MacDonald exchanged offices. *December 1935*: Eden succeeded Hoare as foreign secretary. *March 1936*: Sir T. Inskip joined the cabinet as minister for the coordination of defence; Percy resigned. *May 1936*: Ormsby-Gore succeeded Thomas, resigned, as colonial secretary, and was himself succeeded as first commissioner of works by Earl Stanhope. *June 1936*: Hoare succeeded Monsell as first lord of the admiralty. *October 1936*: Elliot succeeded Collins as secretary for Scotland and was himself succeeded as minister of agriculture by W. S. Morrison; L. Hore-Belisha, minister of transport, entered the cabinet.

CHAMBERLAIN'S NATIONAL CABINET
(*formed May 1937*)

Prime minister: N. Chamberlain.
Lord chancellor: Viscount Hailsham.
Lord president: Viscount Halifax.
Lord privy seal: Earl de la Warr.
Chancellor of the exchequer: Sir J. Simon.
Home secretary: Sir S. Hoare.
Foreign secretary: A. Eden.
Colonial secretary: W. Ormsby-Gore.
Dominions secretary: M. MacDonald.
Secretary for war: L. Hore-Belisha.
Secretary for India and Burma: Marquis of Zetland.
Secretary for air: Viscount Swinton.
Secretary for Scotland: W. Elliot.
First lord of the admiralty: A. Duff Cooper.
President of the board of trade: O. Stanley.
Minister of agriculture: W. S. Morrison.
President of the board of education: Earl Stanhope.
Minister of labour: E. Brown.
Minister of health: Sir K. Wood.
Minister for the coordination of defence: Sir T. Inskip.
Minister of transport: L. Burgin.

Changes

February 1938: Halifax succeeded Eden as foreign secretary and was succeeded as lord president by Hailsham, who was himself succeeded as lord
chancellor by Lord Maugham. *March 1938*: Earl Winterton, chancellor of
the duchy of Lancaster, entered the cabinet. *May 1938*: MacDonald succeeded Ormsby-Gore as colonial secretary and was himself succeeded as
dominions secretary by Lord Stanley; Kingsley Wood succeeded Swinton
as secretary for air and was succeeded as minister of health by Elliot, who
was himself succeeded as secretary for Scotland by D. J. Colville. *October
1938*: Stanhope succeeded Duff Cooper as first lord of the admiralty and
was succeeded as president of the board of education by De La Warr, who
was himself succeeded as lord privy seal by Sir J. Anderson; MacDonald
succeeded Stanley (deceased) as dominions secretary, while retaining
the colonial office. *January 1939*: W. S. Morrison succeeded Winterton
as chancellor of the duchy of Lancaster and was succeeded as minister of
agriculture by Sir R. H. Dorman-Smith; Inskip became dominions secretary
in place of MacDonald and was succeeded as minister for the coordination
of defence by Lord Chatfield. *April 1939*: Burgin became minister without
portfolio and was succeeded as minister of transport by E. Wallace. *July
1939*: Burgin became minister of supply.

CHAMBERLAIN'S WAR CABINET
(*formed September 1939*)

Prime minister: N. Chamberlain.
Lord privy seal: Sir S. Hoare.

Chancellor of the exchequer: Sir J. Simon.
Foreign secretary: Viscount Halifax.
Secretary for war: L. Hore-Belisha.
Secretary for air: Sir Kingsley Wood.
First lord of the admiralty: W. S. Churchill.
Minister for the coordination of defence: Lord Chatfield.
Minister without portfolio: Lord Hankey.

Changes

January 1940: O. Stanley succeeded Hore-Belisha, resigned, as secretary for war. *April 1940*: Hoare and Wood exchanged offices; the ministry for the coordination of defence was abolished, and Chatfield left the war cabinet.

CHURCHILL'S WAR CABINET

(*formed May 1940*)

Prime minister }
Minister of defence } W. S. Churchill.
Lord president: N. Chamberlain.
Lord privy seal: C. R. Attlee.
Foreign secretary: Viscount Halifax.
Minister without portfolio: A. Greenwood.

Changes

August 1940: Lord Beaverbrook, minister of aircraft production, joined the war cabinet. *October 1940*: Sir J. Anderson succeeded Chamberlain, resigned, as lord president; Sir K. Wood, chancellor of the exchequer, and E. Bevin, minister of labour, entered the war cabinet. *December 1940*: Halifax became ambassador to the United States, while remaining a member of the war cabinet, and was succeeded as foreign secretary by A. Eden, who entered the war cabinet. *May 1941*: Beaverbrook became minister of state, remaining in the war cabinet; his successor as minister of aircraft production was not in the war cabinet. *June 1941*: Beaverbrook became minister of supply, remaining in the war cabinet; O. Lyttelton became minister of state in the Middle East and a member of the war cabinet. *4 February 1942*: Beaverbrook became minister of war production, remaining in the war cabinet; his successor as minister of supply was not in the war cabinet. *19 February 1942*: Beaverbrook resigned as minister of war production and left the war cabinet; Sir S. Cripps became a member of the war cabinet and succeeded Attlee as lord privy seal; Attlee became deputy prime minister and dominions secretary, remaining in the war cabinet; Wood left the war cabinet, while remaining chancellor of the exchequer. *22 February 1942*: Greenwood resigned and left the war cabinet. *March 1942*: Lyttelton became minister of production and remained in the war cabinet; he was succeeded as minister resident in the Middle East by R. Casey,[1] who became a member of the war cabinet. *October 1942*: Cripps resigned as lord privy seal and left the war cabinet; his successor as lord privy seal was not in the war cabinet;

---

[1] A member of the Australian parliament.

H. Morrison, home secretary, entered the war cabinet. *September 1943*: Anderson succeeded Wood (deceased) as chancellor of the exchequer, while remaining in the war cabinet, and was succeeded as lord president by Attlee, whose successor as dominions secretary was not in the war cabinet. *November 1943*: Lord Woolton, minister for reconstruction, entered the war cabinet.

CHURCHILL'S CARETAKER CABINET

(*formed May 1945*)

Prime minister ⎫
Minister of defence ⎬ W. S. Churchill.

Lord president: Lord Woolton.
Lord privy seal: Lord Beaverbrook.
Chancellor of the exchequer: Sir J. Anderson.
Home secretary: Sir D. Somervell.
Foreign secretary: A. Eden.
Colonial secretary: O. Stanley.
Dominions secretary: Viscount Cranborne.
Secretary for India and Burma: L. S. Amery.
Secretary for war: Sir J. Grigg.
Secretary for air: H. Macmillan.
First lord of the admiralty: B. Bracken.
President of the board of trade ⎫
Minister of production ⎬ O. Lyttelton.
Secretary for Scotland: Earl of Rosebery.
Minister of agriculture: R. S. Hudson.
Minister of labour: R. A. Butler.

ATTLEE'S LABOUR CABINET

(*formed July 1945*)

Prime minister ⎫
Minister of defence ⎬ C. R. Attlee.

Lord chancellor: Viscount Jowitt.
Lord president: H. Morrison.
Lord privy seal: A. Greenwood.
Chancellor of the exchequer: H. Dalton.
Home secretary: C. Ede.
Foreign secretary: E. Bevin.
Colonial secretary: G. Hall.
Secretary for India and Burma: Lord Pethick-Lawrence.
Dominions secretary: Viscount Addison.
Secretary for Scotland: J. Westwood.
President of the board of trade: Sir S. Cripps.
Minister of agriculture: T. Williams.
Minister of education: Ellen Wilkinson.
Minister of labour: G. Isaacs.
Minister of health: A. Bevan.
Minister of fuel and power: E. Shinwell.

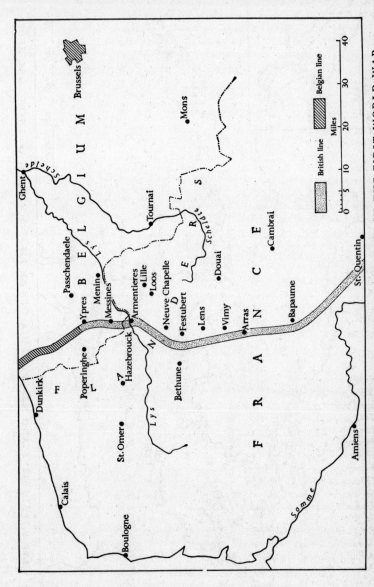

MAP I. THE WESTERN FRONT, BRITISH SECTOR, IN THE FIRST WORLD WAR

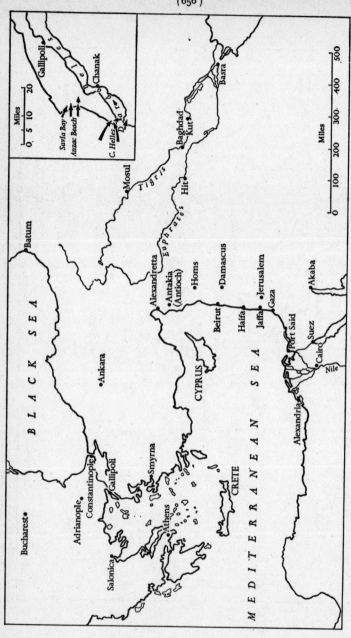

MAP 2. PALESTINE AND MESOPOTAMIA IN THE FIRST WORLD WAR. INSET: GALLIPOLI

MAP 3. THE PARTITION OF IRELAND

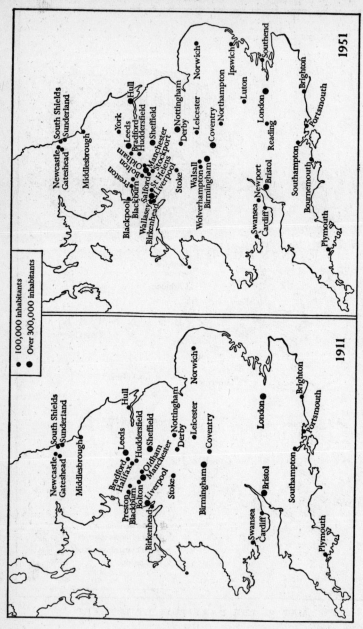

MAP 4. URBAN ENGLAND, 1911 AND 1951

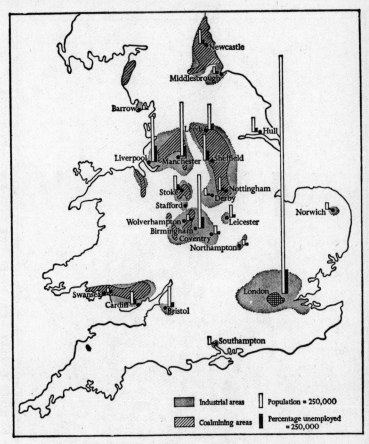

MAP 5. INDUSTRIAL ENGLAND, 1931

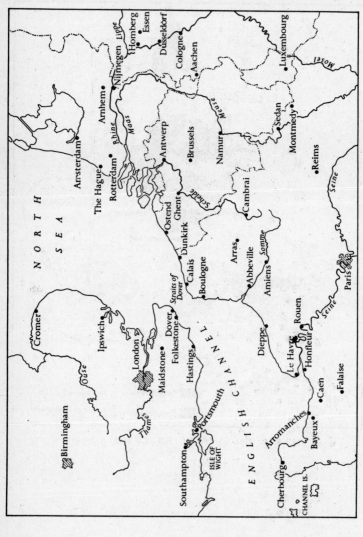

MAP 6. NORTH-WEST EUROPE IN THE SECOND WORLD WAR

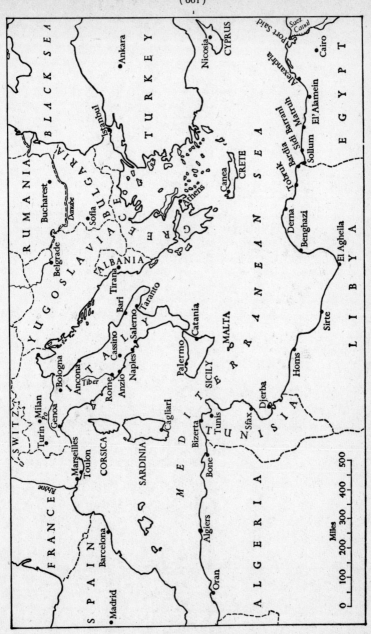

MAP 7. THE MEDITERRANEAN IN THE SECOND WORLD WAR

INDEX

77 & n.; makes admiralty responsible for shipbuilding, 79; increases transports to France, 101.

Maclean, Sir D., 127 n.

Macmahon, Sir H., 71.

Macmillan, H., 120 n., 354.

Macmillan, Lord, committee on finance and industry, 287.

McNeill, John, 21, 56.

Macpherson, Sir Ian, 117.

Mademoiselle from Armentières, 549.

Madrid, 393, 478.

Maginot line, 415, 460, 484.

Malaya, 531, 540–1, 542, 546.

Maleme, air field at, 527.

Malta, no first-class base east of, 230; Gort governor of, 486 n.; naval force at, 520; attacks from, on enemy convoys, 523, 559; in danger, 531; weakness of, 541; out of action, 554; Italian fleet surrenders at, 573.

Malvern, 179.

Man of Property, The, 178.

Manchester, representation of, 116; population of, 167; newspapers printed in, 234 n.; change from trams to buses in, 303; prosperous, 304; Lib–Lab alliance in, 266 n.; has no repertory theatre, 314; Popular Front meeting at, 397.

Manchester Guardian, during first World war, 27; supports Lloyd George, 28 n., 66 n., 252; contributions to, 61, 167, depends on Scott family, 194; becomes a national newspaper, 234; points logic of Covenant, 300; opposes intervention in Greece, 590 & n.

Manchester Town Hall, Lloyd George at, 112.

Manchester university, 347 n.

Manchuria, Japanese invade, 298 n., 299, 363, 380; League and, 370–2, 384; affair discredits Simon, 378.

Mandates, invented, 133.

Manning, F., 549 n.

Manpower budget, 512, 564–5.

Marconi scandal, 74 n.

Margesson, D. R., 473 & n., 474.

Markiewicz, countess, 128 n.

Marlborough, 1st duke of, 48 n., 592 n.; Churchill's life of, 356, 480.

Marlowe, T., 244 & n.

Marne, battle of (1914), 10, 32–33, 108, 109; Germans cross (1918), 102.

Married Love, 165.

Marshall, G., wants direct attack on Germany, 553, 555; and North Africa, 560; wants to shift to Pacific, 562; goes to Algiers, 564; Churchill wrangles with, 573; does not become supreme commander, 575 n.

Martin, Kingsley, 310–11.

Marx, K., 260.

Mary, Queen, on George VI, 402; goes to Badminton, 457.

Masaryk, T., 107, 439 n.

Massingham, H. W., and *Nation*, 27, 252 n., 311.

Master agreement, 533.

Matapan, battle of, 526.

Maubeuge, B.E.F. at, 7.

Maurice, Sir F., charges of, against Lloyd George, 104–5, 117–18; debate on charges, 74 n., 105, 126, 219.

Maxton, J., and Campbell case, 225; great orator, 235 n.; extremist, 347; supports Popular Front, 397; blesses Chamberlain's mission, 429.

Maxwell, Sir J., 56.

May, Sir G., economy committee of, 287, 288, 291; and tariff committee, 330.

Means test, 352–3, 367, 393.

Mediterranean, shipping losses in, during first World war, 85; British claim mastery in, 384; fleet in, 400, 486; campaign in, 515, 520–2; Italian convoys in, 523; Hitler does not take seriously, 524; British losses in, 530–1; ABC–1 agreement and, 536; British there because they were there, 546; shipping in, 555; and second front, 558; further campaign in, 560, 563; Americans divert landing craft from, 572; Churchill wishes to persist in, 573–4; British command in, 575 n.; loses significance, 576.

Meerut, trial at, 255.

Megiddo, battle of, 110.

Meighen, A., 261.

Mein Kampf, 95.

Melba, N., 232.

Mellor, W., 142, 381.

Memoirs of an Infantry Officer, 361 n.

Mensdorff, count, Smuts negotiates with, 115–16.

Meredith, G., 178.

Mers-el-Kebir, 494.

Mersey tunnel, 338 n.

Mesopotamia, campaign in, 49, 98; Anglo-French agreement on, 50, 70; inquiry on campaign, 58; malaria in, 126. *See also* Irak.

Metropolitan water board, 257.

Metternich, C., 177.

Metz, 109.

Mexico, 84 n.

Middle East, new British empire in, 152; conflicts with France in, 215; R.A.F. dominate, 231; Wavell commands in, 460; Hitler has no plans in, 522, 524; expansion of command